PSYCHOPATHOLOGY

Modern Applications of Psychology
under the editorship of
Joseph D. Matarazzo

Psychopathology

—The Science of Understanding Deviance

James D. Page | Temple University

Aldine • Atherton | Chicago • New York

First published 1971 by
Aldine·Atherton, Inc.
529 South Wabash Avenue
Chicago, Illinois 60605

Library of Congress Catalog Card Number 75–140012
ISBN 202-26014-3
Printed in the United States of America

Second Printing 1971

Third Printing 1972

To Dorothy, Margot, and Bruce

Preface

A basic premise of this book is that the symptoms of psychopathology represent extreme variations of normal behavior. The principles and processes involved in perception, thinking, emotions, and problem-solving are the same in normal and disturbed persons. The quality of the end products varies, but this too is relative. The difference between abnormal behavior and normal behavior is one of degree rather than kind: abnormal behavior is less appropriate, less effective, less adaptive, and more distressing than normal behavior, but it is not essentially distinct in form or manifestation. The determinants of abnormal behavior are as complex and varied as the determinants of normal behavior. In both instances, personality structure and behavior are the products of the cumulative interaction of the individual's particular genetic inheritance, physical and social environments, and personal life experiences. Behavior change comes as a result of significant modification in these pertinent variables. Change for better or for worse may occur at any time during the life of the individual.

I have retained the traditional classification and nomenclature systems. Since the literature of psychopathology is based on the officially recognized diagnostic categories, no other choice is available. But I have discarded the assumption of separate disorders and other features of the medical model of disease, and I use the familiar diagnostic terms simply as convenient descriptive labels to identify the major ways in which human beings characteristically react when overwhelmed by the stresses of life. I regard abnormal behavior as continuous with normal behavior. Maladaptive reaction patterns are extreme and persistent variations of the behavior patterns of normal individuals under stress, and variations in symptom patterns or diagnoses correspond to variations noted in the responses of normal persons to stress situations. The interpretation of symptoms as reactions to stress provides an explanation for the occurrence of similar forms of behavior disturbances in all cultures.

Increased acceptance of the idea that mental disorders represent problems in living rather than diseases has had the dual effect of broadening the field of psychopathology and of stimulating interest in new approaches. One of the aims of this book is to examine these new developments, with particular attention to the multidisciplinary approach to deviant behavior. At the same time I have attempted to differentiate the classical subject matter of psychopathology, as represented by the concept of mental disorders, from other forms of deviant behavior. I suggest that the designation of mental disorder be restricted to involuntary disturbances in behavior marked by varying degrees of impairment in higher order psychosocial functioning. In making this suggestion my intent is not to exclude voluntary, nonincapacitating forms of deviance from the field of psychopathology, but simply to avoid confusing every form of deviant behavior with mental disorder. The enlarged field of psychopathology should include the scientific study of criminal behavior, civil disobedience, social protest, and sexual deviation.

I should like to express my indebtedness to past and present colleagues whose theories and research constitute the substance of this book. In the selection and organization of material I have relied heavily on student reaction. Dr. Joseph D. Matarazzo read the entire manuscript and made many constructive suggestions. Best of all, he was a constant source of encouragement. Mrs. Barbara Salazar did an excellent job of editing. Robert Hernan and Ginger Rooks were a great help in library research. Angela Provitera provided valuable assistance with various phases of the manuscript preparation. Special thanks are due to my competent secretary, Linda Gattinella, who cheerfully typed numerous drafts. By finally refusing to type any further revisions, she precipitated the long postponed delivery of the manuscript.

Contents

CHAPTER ONE

The Nature of
Abnormal Behavior

Psychopathology shares with other behavioral sciences a basic interest in understanding human behavior. It differs from related disciplines in that the emphasis is on investigating the nature and causes of abnormal rather than normal reactions. More specifically, psychopathology is concerned with the study of undesirable, maladaptive, and disruptive forms of abnormal behavior. It focuses on persons with psychosocial deficits, who in varying degrees experience difficulty in coping effectively with the problems of daily life, who are personally unhappy, and whose reactions are often a source of concern or distress to their families and associates. The objectives of psychopathologists include the utilization of clinical and research findings in the early detection, effective treatment, and prevention of psychosocial disorders. The scientific study of psychopathology is a recent development, but its subject matter has bewildered, fascinated, and disturbed man throughout his history. Some of the more familiar terms used by ancient, primitive, and modern societies to identify abnormal behavior include madness, demonic possession, insanity, lunacy, running amok, going berserk, mental disease, and personality disorders. Two more specific contemporary labels are neurosis and psychosis.

The Universality of Disordered Behavior

There is a dual significance in the fact that every known language includes at least one word that specifically refers to irrational, disordered behavior. First, it establishes the universality and timelessness of aberrant human reactions. Second, the invention and use of special terms to denote abnormal behavior indicate that people everywhere have long been aware of certain distinctive features of psychopathology that differentiate it from crime, immoral conduct, and other types of deviance from group norms. The familiarity of the general public with the distinguishing characteristics of psychopathology is evidenced by the fact that the diagnosis of madness, however it may be labeled, is initially made by the victim himself or by his family and close associates. The specific characteristics differentiating psychopathological behavior from other forms of deviant behavior and from normal behavior will be considered in greater detail later on. At this point we shall note only that a common feature of most of the changing names applied to psychologically disturbed individuals in diverse cultures is the implication that these persons have relatively little voluntary control over their behavior in at least some areas of life in which the vast majority of people react quite differently. In former centuries it was assumed that evil spirits or lunar influences were responsible for the unpredictable reactions of "possessed" victims. More recently abnormal behavior has been interpreted as the involuntary by-product of a disease process, the expression of unconscious impulses, or faulty habit patterns. In any case, the relatively uncontrolled nature of pathological behavior has been repeatedly and consistently observed; it is mainly the explanations for it that have changed. The various aliases of madness also agree in conveying the idea that the behavior they designate is defective, unexpected, irrational, inappropriate, disruptive, and detrimental. An added implication is that persons who exhibit this sort of behavior are troubled and troublesome.

A distinction must be made between basic features of pathological behavior that are essentially constant in all societies and incidental, culture-dependent aspects that are variable. Basically, psychosocial disorders in all societies are characterized by disturbances in volition, thinking, feeling, communication, and conduct that interfere with effective and satisfying personal and social adjustment. A person with significant defects in these critical psychosocial functions would in all probability be considered abnormal in any society. But the outward form or surface symptoms of such disturbances and the interpretations provided for them vary from culture to culture. In much the same way that people acquire the expressive styles and beliefs and superstitions of their respective societies, they also learn the cultural models of the way possessed or mentally disturbed persons are expected to behave. Thus a depressed, suicidal person in a primitive society may imagine he has a moth sickness that compels him to jump into the community campfire. A similarly afflicted person in a highly moralistic society may seek death through drowning, in order to be cleansed of his sins. In an unusual manifestation of madness in ancient times, known as lycanthropy, the afflicted person imagined himself to be a wild beast, usually a wolf, in human form, and acted accordingly. The underlying condition is still with us under the new label of *depersonalization*. Since it is no longer fashionable to believe that people can transform themselves into animals, the expressed symptoms have changed. Today, a person suffering from depersonalization is more apt to report a hazy sense of loss of identity or a distortion of body image. The body may seem altered in some way, may be felt to be changing into something undesirable, or may be experienced as if it belonged to another person.

Other seemingly exotic examples of psychopathology noted in former times and in primitive societies also turn out, on closer examination, to be essentially equivalent to the more "rational" symptoms observed in present-day mental patients (Yap, 1951; Arieti and Meth, 1959). There is obviously no basic difference between the illiterate person who claims his thoughts are being read and controlled by the "evil eye" and his more sophisticated contemporary who claims his mind is controlled by an electronic computer. Nor is there any real difference between the African tribesman who believes he is being watched and followed by a giant leopard and the deluded New Yorker who imagines he is being watched and followed by the FBI. The mentally disturbed person in our own society who senses that he is losing self-control and asks to be hospitalized before he commits some horrible crime is exhibiting essentially the same behavior as the Ojibwa Indian who believes he is possessed by a cannibalistic monster called *windigo,* and in terror either commits suicide or asks to be killed before he starts eating his family and friends, whom he perceives as beginning to resemble edible animals (Wallace, 1966). The more dramatically expressed *koro* and *shook yong* reactions of the illiterate natives of the Far East (Linton, 1956) correspond to the widespread male dread of impotence. The modern housewife who in a moment of desperate confusion impulsively kills her children to punish her husband or to protect them from future misfortunes is a psychological cousin of Medea of the Greek myth.

An example of the universality of the basic characteristics of psychopathology is provided by the great Japanese classic *The Story of Genji*. This eleventh-century novel by Murasaki Shikibu contains a description of what appears to be a psychotic reaction in a lady of the court (Page, 1962). At the time of her entrance into the story, she is in her thirties. Her illness started several years before, and her behavior has been getting progres-

sively more peculiar, uncontrolled, and unpredictable. In keeping with the
high standards of neatness and cleanliness of the court ladies, she has previously been tidy and well groomed. Now her hair is in a hopeless tangle.
Although there are many servants in the household, she allows no one to
come near her, and her room has become filthy and disordered. Periodically she behaves violently. At other times she weeps quietly by herself,
imagining (without cause) that her husband is speaking ill of her father.
For days she lies motionless on her bed in a state of complete exhaustion.
At times she seemed barely conscious of what is going on around her. In accord with the modern concept of ambivalence, she is described as perverse:
her frenzy drives her to play the most unaccountable and offensive tricks
on the very people she most wishes to please. For some time she has refused to permit her husband to make love to her, and has been unable to
manage the household. The husband concludes that her illness is perma-
ment, and going from bad to worse. He therefore feels justified in bringing
a younger woman into the home as mistress and homemaker. On one occasion, finding his wife lucid for a moment, the husband takes advantage of
the opportunity to explain to her in a calm, reassuring manner that her illness has made it necessary to have another woman in the house, but that
he will always provide for her, look after her, and treat her kindly. The
wife seems to understand and accept the situation, as a good Japanese wife
should. That evening, when the husband dresses for his visit with the other
woman, she helps him with his coat. But as he is about to put on his riding
cloak, she suddenly leaps up, seizes a large charcoal brazier, and empties
it over his head. The servants who witness this scene are terrified that the
husband will "not understand"; if he thinks she is in possession of her senses
and has deliberately covered him with burning coals, he may leave her.
The husband, however, realizes that she cannot be held responsible,
though he is angered by the look of complete unconcern with which she
surveys the havoc she has just created. But he controls himself and, acting
much as a contemporary husband would do in a similar situation, sends for
professional help. Priests are called in to exorcise the madwoman, who by
this time is cursing and raving. After being pulled about and cudgeled by
the priests for some time, she becomes somewhat quieter; but the next day
she is still distracted and resumes her raving. Fearful that she may again
attempt to disfigure him, the husband stays out of her way for the next several days. Reflecting the popular belief of that period, the author of *Genji*
casually mentions that the woman is "possessed." But two more plausible
explanations are also offered. The husband, "who knew her as she ought to
be, could realize that her present savagery and malice were merely the result of her illness, but a stranger would be terrified and disgusted." And anticipating by some eight hundred years Freud's (1949) comparison of psy-

chosis with the acting out of a dream with all its absurdities, delusions, and illusions, the author has the husband explain to his wife that her distorted mental state is due to the fact that she has abandoned herself unresistingly to wild dreams and imaginings.

Changing Concepts of Abnormal Behavior

SUPERNATURAL EXPLANATIONS

Up until the eighteenth century, aberrant reactions, with rare exceptions, were attributed to some form of supernatural intervention. Most proposed explanations assumed that the affected individual was an innocent victim of evil spirits, sorcery, soul loss, astrological influences, or some other accidental occurrence. At times it was believed that madness was an expression of divine punishment inflicted on sinners, violators of taboos, and wicked persons who had voluntarily made a pact with the devil. Although short on scientific validity, the supernatural interpretations of ancient, primitive, and preliterate man were based on actual observations of disordered behavior. As such, they provide significant insights into the universal characteristics of abnormal behavior.

THE CONCEPT OF MENTAL DISEASE

The idea that behavioral disturbances are due to some underlying brain or biochemical defect was initially introduced about 400 B.C. by the comparatively enlightened Hippocratic physicians of ancient Greece, who disagreed with the then popular belief that madness was caused by divine or demonic intervention. Largely as a result of the influence of Greek physicians who migrated to other countries, the mental disease concept was for a time accepted in Rome and other Mediterranean countries. Following the decline of Greco-Roman civilization, however, physical explanations of abnormal behavior were again replaced by supernatural beliefs. Advances in medicine during the nineteenth century rekindled interest in the extension of the medical model to include "diseases" of the mind as well as of the body. The concept of mental illness was first applied to those severely disturbed or psychotic patients who were characterized by confusion, disorientation, profound apathy, hallucinations, hyperactivity, acute excitement, rigidity of posture, and stumporous depressive states. Since these "symptoms" superficially resembled the delirious reactions of physically ill patients with high fevers and the behavior of intoxicated or drugged persons, it seemed reasonable to assume that psychotic patients were suffering from some as yet undetermined lesions of the brain, metabolic disturbances, or other organic defects. From this premise it followed that research efforts should be directed toward the identification of the specific physical causes and the development of medical cures. An early biochemical formulation of the basic hypotheses of the mental disease concept was reported by Thudichum in 1884:

> Many forms of insanity are unquestionably the external manifestations of the effects upon the brain substance of poisons fermented within the body, just as mental aberrations accompanying chronic alcoholic intoxication are the accumulated effects of a relatively simple poison fermented out of the body. These poisons we shall, I have no doubt, be able to isolate after we know the normal chemistry to its uttermost detail. And then will come in their turn the crowning discoveries of the antidotes to the poisons and to the fermenting causes and processes which produce them.

During the late nineteenth and early twentieth centuries, Emil Kraepelin, a German psychiatrist, gained strong support for the mental illness concept by developing a widely accepted nomenclature and classification system based on the medical model of separate diseases. According to Kraepelin (1907), mental disorders were disease entities analogous to physical diseases. More specifically, he held that the diseases of the mind, like the diseases of the body, could be subdivided into separate types, each of which had its specific organic cause, was distinguished by a disease-specific pattern of symptoms, and followed a characteristic course with a predictable outcome. Since the disease was considered the critical factor, Kraepelin's approach stressed the importance of isolating and identifying the symptoms that were associated with each disease. Precise diagnosis and detailed classification were considered the first critical steps in determining the specific organic cause for each disorder. In accordance with the traditional medical model of infectious diseases, it was assumed that once the underlying neurological or biochemical cause had been discovered and corrected, the disease-specific symptoms would disappear. Little attention was given to possible psychosocial determinants, personal frustrations and conflicts, or the psychological meaning of symptoms. This narrowly defined disease model was especially favored by psychiatrists working with hospitalized psychotic patients.

The concept of illness was gradually extended to include neuroses, antisocial behavior, alcoholism, childhood maladjustments, marital problems, and other mild forms of deviant behavior. For these more benign disorders, some psychological pathogenic agent—intrapsychic conflict, sexual repression, fixation, emotional trauma, unresolved guilt—was usually considered the basic underlying cause. The overall rationale, however, remained the same. It was presumed that these milder disturbances in behavior represented surface manifestations of some specific, internal source of "psychic infection," which had to be identified and eliminated. The conversion of mental disorders to the medical model was facilitated by the use of such familiar terms as patient, diagnosis, therapy, cure, and mental hospital. The mental illness concept reached its peak of popularity and acceptance during the early decades of the present century. In more recent years the premises and implications of the sickness model have been challenged and severely attacked by psychiatrists, psychologists, and sociologists. Szasz (1961), a psychiatrist, has referred to the mental illness concept as a myth that has outlived its usefulness.

Criticisms of the mental illness concept. A major practical criticism centers about the sterility of the disease model. A half century of intensive research has failed to substantiate the basic assumption that disturbances in behavior are directly caused by some neurophysiological pathogenic agent. The disease approach has only been successful in certain disorders, marked by gross neurological or physical defects, which were formerly mistakenly diagnosed as mental disorders because of the concomitant presence of impairment in psychological functioning. An outstanding example is general paresis, a neurological disorder associated with mental disturbances, which has been found to be due to diffuse brain damage caused by syphilis. The search for specific psychological defects responsible for particular forms of mild mental disorders has also been unproductive. It is now generally recognized that the causes of severe and mild disturbances in behavior are multiple and varied.

A second major criticism of the mental disease concept is that it has promoted a pessimistic attitude regarding treatment and prognosis. Acceptance of the premise that there was little purpose in therapy until the underlying causes were first determined dampened interest in experimentation. This negative attitude was reinforced by the disappointing results obtained when drastic empirical procedures, including brain surgery and shock techniques, were periodically tried. The development of modern psychoactive drugs has greatly facilitated the care and management of patients, but no claim is made that these drugs are specific cures. The role of tranquilizing and energizing drugs is comparable to that of aspirin in providing a temporary relief of symptoms. And the use of psychological techniques aimed at uncovering the unconscious source of the patient's difficulties, or at helping him to gain insight into the nature and source of his problems, has proved no more effective in treating mental disorders than no formal treatment at all.

A third general criticism has to do with the impact of the mental illness model on the patient's perception of himself, the image conveyed to the public, and the attending consequences. At the time it was initially introduced, the concept of mental illness served the useful purpose of encouraging public acceptance of the idea that the psychologically disturbed were

sick individuals in need of treatment rather than witches, sinners, or malin-
gerers. The extension of the medical umbrella to cover mental disorders,
however, has been only partially effective in transferring to the mentally
ill the sympathetic attitudes traditionally expressed toward the physically
ill. The prefix "mental" has led to a number of unfavorable inferences and
practices. As Sarbin has noted (1969), classifying a person as "mentally ill"
has come to serve as justification for subjecting him to isolation, segre-
gation, involuntary incarceration, brain surgery, and various unpleasant
forms of physical and psychological treatment. Persons labeled "mentally
ill" tend to be feared, avoided, rejected, sometimes pitied, but nearly always degraded. The process that converts a person into a mental patient
carries with it the potentiality for self-devaluation. To be labeled and considered a mental patient or even a former mental patient does little to boost
one's self-esteem or social acceptance (Phillips, 1963). According to Scheff
(1966a), the social deviant's acceptance of the label "mental patient" may
lead to his acting out the culturally defined role of mental patient. Questions asked by doctors when the patient is being examined often provide
useful cues as to how he is expected to behave. The patient who learns and
plays his designated role well, as defined by the cultural stereotype, is rewarded by receiving special sickness benefits. Those who deviate from the
expected role may be denied these benefits. Those who protest too vigorously against being considered sick or confined to a hospital are often considered to have proved themselves to be acutely disturbed, and are isolated
or sedated until they learn to conform. Scheff maintains that once a person
has been publicly labeled a mental patient, he may find himself discriminated against when he attempts to reestablish himself within the community following his recovery. A kind of vicious circle is established: the more
the social deviant enters into the role of the mentally ill, the more he is defined by others as mentally ill, and the more he is defined by others as mentally ill, the more he enters into the role, and so on. An important feature
of Scheff's hypothesis is that deviant behavior is often transitory. The labeling of such behavior as mental illness by society and the acceptance of this
verdict by the patient have the effect of stabilizing and fixating the
deviance.

EMERGING NEW CONCEPTS

Loss of confidence in the validity and utility of the mental disease concept
has led to a critical rethinking of the nature of abnormal behavior. Issues
involving causation and treatment in particular are being viewed from a
broader perspective. The current trend is to deemphasize medical terms
and approaches and to attach greater importance to psychological, sociological, educational, and legal concepts. The use of the term "mental dis-

ease" has to a large extent been dropped. Agreement has not yet been reached on the selection of a new term. Some widely used interim designations include mental disturbances, behavior disorders, and psychosocial problems. Szasz (1961) has proposed that mental disorders should be redefined as *problems in living,* which involve deviations from accepted moral, social, ethical, and legal norms. Scheff (1966*b*) and others favor the concept of *residual deviance* or *residual rule breaking.* According to this viewpoint, mental disorders are more appropriately defined as residual forms of rule breaking for which society has no explicit label. Residual deviance (mental disorder) is what is left after all other forms of norm violation, such as crime, immorality, perversion, drunkenness, and bad manners, have been excluded. Erikson (1968) has contributed the concept of *identity crisis* to describe mental disturbances occurring mainly in young persons. Sarbin (1969) has suggested that the mentally disturbed should be viewed as persons who have failed to establish acceptable social identities or roles.

Multiple interacting causes. Studies of specific biological, psychological, and sociocultural factors are still being conducted. However, the current objective is limited to an assessment of the relative importance of specific factors as co-contributory agents. The hope of someday discovering a single cause for each disorder has been abandoned. Most authorities today agree that while the determinants of abnormal behavior may differ in kind and in quality from the determinants of normal behavior, they are no less complex and varied. Standard textbooks on theories of normal personality development (Hall and Lindzey, 1957; Wepman and Heine, 1963) and on theories of psychopathology (Millon, 1967) cover basically the same material. The broad generalization that the personality and behavior of the normal individual reflect his total life history, as shaped by the cumulative interaction of his genetic inheritance, his physical and social environments, and his personal experiences, is equally applicable to the personality and behavior of persons described as mentally disturbed.

The key words are "individual," "cumulative interaction," and "total life history." As the product of a distinctive combination of interactive determinants, every individual—and this includes identical twins—differs in certain respects from every other person. The uniqueness of each individual is responsible for the infinite variations in personality traits and reaction patterns noted in normal and abnormal persons. However, no one is completely unique. As Kluckhohn and Murray (1961) have noted, every man is in certain respects like all other men, and in certain respects every man is more like some other men than others. Similarities observed among individuals are presumably due to the presence of common or equivalent determinants. With regard to *cumulative interaction,* students of behavior agree that the effects of nature and nurture are so tightly meshed and interdependent as to be practically inseparable. Biological factors influence the individual's selection of his environment and the use he makes of it. Environmental factors influence the development of the individual's genetic potentialities, so that some are realized and others are not. Because of inherent differences in mental capacities and temperament, children reared in the same home will differ markedly in learning, exploratory activities, acquired attitudes, and reaction to shared traumatic experiences. Given a particular set of genes, an infant may develop one of several potential personalities depending on the culture in which he is reared, his socioeconomic opportunities, the personalities of his parents, their style of child rearing, and his personal life experiences. The interaction of multiple determinants limits, but does not rule out, the importance of specific variables. Other factors being constant, the odds in favor of normal behavior are greatly increased if a child inherits sound genes rather than defective ones; is reared in a stable home by loving parents rather than in a disrupted home by rejecting parents; or is rarely rather than frequently subjected to extreme stresses. "Other factors," however, are seldom constant in real life. Depending on the interactive significance of other variables, the potential contribution of specific "good" or "bad" determinants may be accentuated, suppressed, distorted, or even reversed. The promises of heredity can be canceled by the environment and vice versa.

The major purpose of emphasizing the terms *cumulative interaction* and *total life history* is to correct two popular misconceptions regarding the etiology of mental disorders. Among the general public there is a common tendency to make the error of attributing the cause of mental illness to some recent traumatic experience such as a disappointing love affair, a death in the family, adverse business affairs, or whatever. Current traumatic situations that are followed by the onset of overt symptoms are more appropriately interpreted as precipitating factors that release or trigger symptomatic reactions in predisposed individuals whose adaptive resources have been progressively depleted over a period of many years. The second misconception, encouraged by many theories of psychopathology, is that early childhood experiences are of crucial significance in the development of behavior disorders. It is true that the roots of behavior pathology are often established during the early formative years. But whether the final outcome is a healthy or twisted personality is determined in great measure by the presence of favorable or unfavorable modifying influences during adolescence and adulthood. Attempts to relate specific early child-rearing practices to adult personality have been unsuccessful (Orlansky, 1949; Sewell, 1952). There is no evidence that any isolated childhood experience, such as strictness of toilet training, is the cause of mental disorder during adulthood. A more valid explanation is that the method of toilet training and other specific childhood events reflect the pattern of mothering and the family climate to which the child is exposed day after day and year after year until he finally marries and leaves home (Schaefer and Bayley, 1960). And even then, through his choice of a marital partner, the child with a history of adverse childhood training may re-create in his own family the same pathogenic environment he has supposedly left behind. There is also the possibility that in revolting against the way he was reared, the individual may go to the opposite extreme and create a different but equally pathogenic environment in his own home. Another factor that contributes to the belief in the importance of the early formative years is the continuing influence of genetic defects. Genetic defects that cause faulty personality development during childhood continue to exert their harmful effect throughout the life of the individual. However, once more it should be noted that personality development is a continuous process, ever responsive to current and future influences. At any point during adolescence and adulthood, significant experiences may modify or even drastically alter personality organization and functioning for better or for worse. No one is destined to become a mental patient because of his heredity or childhood experiences. Conversely, a good genetic endowment or a favorable childhood may increase one's resistance to adverse influences in later life, but it does not give him a guaranteed immunity against the development of a mental disorder.

Normal-abnormal continuum. In contrast to earlier approaches that accentuated differences between normal and abnormal behavior, the present trend is to restore the psychologically disturbed to the human fold by accentuating the unbroken continuity of normal and abnormal behavior. The personality traits and reactions of mental patients may thus be viewed as more extreme, more inappropriate, and more maladaptive manifestations of similar traits and reactions noted in normal persons. What distinguishes the individual who exhibits a problem in living is a set of personality attributes, as shaped by his total psychobiosocial developmental history, which are not adequate or flexible enough to enable him to cope effectively with the pressures and problems of human life. The adaptive resources of some individuals are so limited that they "break" under the ordinary difficulties of everyday life. For other individuals, an extremely severe stress may be required to precipitate impaired functioning. More often than not it is difficult to pinpoint the precipitating factor. Some seemingly minor or incidental experience may serve as the last straw for a person already overburdened with an accumulation of problems or faulty habits of adjustment, resulting in his psychological collapse.

The continuum concept provides a simpler and far more cogent explanation for "symptoms" than the indefensible hypothesis that symptoms represent the surface expression of some assumed underlying disease. In addition, the conclusion that abnormal behavior is an extreme manifestation of characteristic human behavior accounts for the occurrence of essentially similar patterns of maladaptive reactions in all societies and in the same culture over time. More specifically, most so-called mental symptoms represent extreme variations of the ways in which human beings characteristically behave when overwhelmed by the stresses, frustrations, and disappointments of life. Typical human reactions to stress, which under certain conditions are referred to as symptoms, include confusion and indecision; impairment in learning, memory, thinking, and judgment; incoherent communication; emotional overreaction with concomitant somatic symptoms; self-blame and self-attack; hostile-aggressive behavior directed against others; and withdrawal-surrender-escape reactions. Another common reaction to stress that is shared by normal and disturbed persons is the unconscious utilization of one or more of the defense mechanisms described in Table 1.1. Both groups find these defenses useful in preserving self-esteem, averting further disorganization, or restoring some sort of order or equilibrium. The main differences between normal stress reactions and "abnormal symptoms" is that the latter are more persistent, less appropriate in relation to the person's known recent experiences, less controlled, more severe, more incapacitating, and more disturbing to the individual and/or his society.

Table 1.1.   Common defense mechanisms

Defense mechanism	Characteristics
Repression	Spontaneous or nondeliberate exclusion from consciousness of memories, impulses, and ideas that would constitute sources of anxiety, fear, guilt, shame, or humiliation if the individual were aware of them. Repressed desires and thoughts are not permanently lost or forgotten. They are pushed back to the outer, darker fringes of consciousness, where their continued but unacknowledged presence may contribute to vague feelings of anxiety and be revealed in dreams and other situations when vigilance is reduced.
Compensation	Exaggerated efforts to attain success or distinction in one's area of inferiority or in some other field. A common defense against feelings of inadequacy, failure, or personal defects, either real or imagined.
Rationalization	Invention of "good" reasons to discount failures or to justify engaging in experiences that might otherwise be perceived as damaging to one's self-esteem. Thus disappointments may be softened by "sour grape" rationalization; personal defects and misfortunes may be converted into blessings in disguise ("sweet lemon" rationalization).

Table 1.1.   (continued)

Defense mechanism	Characteristics
Projection	The attributing of blame for one's weaknesses, mistakes, and misdeeds to others as means of safeguarding self-esteem and avoiding self-censure.
Reaction formation	A self-deceptive ruse whereby the individual defends himself against undesired personal qualities or temptations by sincerely believing and acting as if he did not have the qualities or were repelled by what actually tempts him. Thus a mother who unconsciously rejects her child may be overly affectionate and protective; extreme modesty may constitute a protective reaction against repressed erotic desires.
Denial	An unconscious, selective (not deliberate) perceptual blindness to unpleasant facts which protects the individual from the necessity of facing intolerable thoughts, wishes, deeds, and situations.
Regression	A retreat from current difficulties distinguished by reversion to immature or infantile modes of gratification and behavior.
Displacement	Transference of emotional feelings from one person or object to another, "safer" person or object. Thus hostile feelings aroused by a spouse may be redirected and discharged against a family pet.
Identification	Related to imitation and role copying but more thoroughgoing than either, since the individual who identifies with significant others adopts their attitudes, values, and behavior as his own. Usually the individual identifies with the desirable attributes of others, but he may also identify with their undesirable characteristics—aggressiveness, for example. An important factor in personality development.
Introjection	A special form of identification in which the attitudes, values, and behavior of another person are internalized. Feelings associated with this other person are now directed toward the self.

New therapy concepts. The ineffectiveness of older techniques designed to locate and resolve intrapsychic conflicts dating back to early childhood has led to a shift in strategy. Newer forms of psychotherapy focus on the here-and-now problems confronting the individual. Particular attention is given to identifying current personal, interpersonal, and environmental factors that support and maintain maladaptive behavior. The goals have been scaled down. Psychoanalysis is no longer regarded as a magic tool for creating happy, successful personalities. The more realistic objective of modern therapy is to modify those aspects of behavior that interfere with reasonable standards of appropriate, adequate, and satisfying functioning. The attainment of this objective may involve the elimination of specific symptoms, a change of attitudes, the development of increased self-direction and responsibility, the acquisition of social skills, and so on. In other words, the present thrust is toward extending the individual's control of his behavior and his environment by increasing the scope and range of his behavior and the choices available to him. An important feature of the new approach is the increased demands that are made on the patient to be an active partner in the therapeutic process. Psychotherapy is viewed as a learning or problem-solving experience in which therapist and patient, working together in an atmosphere of understanding and trust, objectively examine the patient's current difficulties and "mistakes," and consider alternative solutions or improvements that are consistent with the potentialities of the patient and the realities of his situation. As friend and mentor the therapist may influence the patient's choice of action and provide whatever assistance he can while the patient is trying out new approaches. Final decisions, however, rest with the patient, who sooner or later must assume responsibility for living his own life.

Professional personnel. As long as mental disorders were considered a kind of sickness, a strong case could be made for the need for physicians to exercise major control over the treatment of patients in office practice, psychiatric clinics, and mental hospitals. The medical specialty of psychiatry still remains the dominant profession in the mental health field. The emergence of psychological and sociological concepts as substitutes for the medical model, however, has markedly increased the involvement of other disciplines and professions. (See Supplementary Report 1.) Clinical psychology especially has made giant strides in recent years toward attaining an independent status equal to that of psychiatry. Albee (1969) and others have suggested that the time has come for psychology to divorce itself from medicine and develop its own concepts, treatment centers, and techniques. As replacements for the traditional clinics and hospitals, he favors the establishment of special schools and social centers where educational and training procedures would be employed to build up the individual's strengths and assets. An advantage claimed by Albee for such centers is that they would relieve the shortage of professional personnel in the mental health field. The new centers could be staffed by college graduates who had received special training. In defense of the medical point of view, Grinker (1969) has pointed out that there is considerable advantage in retaining the traditional diagnostic categories, since so much information is available on their etiology, prognosis, therapies, and so on. He regards much of the current controversy as a problem in semantics. He believes that a closer collaborative effort between medicine and other disciplines is preferable to the parceling out of territories to various professional groups. Psychology, with its emphasis on learning principles, has made and can continue to make an important contribution within the present medical framework. He disagrees with Albee's suggestion that psychologists withdraw from psychiatric institutions and establish their own therapy centers, their own language, their own therapeutic techniques. If this were to happen, psychology would isolate itself from the mainstream of psychiatry.

But the controversy over models, concepts, and terminology is not an exercise in semantics. The familiar rhyme "Sticks and stones may break my bones but names will never hurt me" is not true. The derogatory names usually applied to psychologically disturbed individuals can and do hurt, and should be changed. Popular misconceptions regarding the extreme dangerousness and incurability of mental patients should be corrected. If behavior disturbances were regarded as problems in living, as indeed they are, they would assume a more optimistic image in the public mind, and this improved image itself would have therapeutic value. On the other hand, care should be taken not to throw out the baby along with the bath water. Disordered behavior, however it is called, is a reality that at one time or another afflicts a substantial portion of the population. As a rule, the impairment in functioning, if properly handled, is transitory, and recovery is good. But during the period of disordered functioning behavior tends to be unpredictable, uncontrolled, ineffectual, detrimental, and disruptive. A small percentage of cases show homicidal or suicidal tendencies. The sickness model has lost credibility and the treatments suggested by this model have proved relatively ineffective. Until the emerging new concepts and approaches are more firmly established, however, reliance will continue to be placed mainly on the traditional techniques for the care and management of psychologically disturbed persons. The future calls for bold innovations and increased involvement of all the behavioral and social sciences, medicine included, in furthering our understanding of problems in living and in developing more effective therapeutic and preventive measures.

Summary

The scope of abnormal behavior, as defined in this book, is restricted to psychopathological deviations that at various times have been referred to as madness, demonic possession, mental disease, and psychosocial problems. The outward expression of disordered behavior and the explanations offered for it vary from culture to culture, but their basic features are timeless and much the same the world over. The essential sameness of mental disorders in all cultures is due to the fact that "mental symptoms" represent extreme variations of the ways in which human beings characteristically behave when they are overwhelmed by the stresses and disappointments of life. Symptoms differ from "normal" stress reactions in being more persistent, less appropriate, more severe, less controlled, and more disturbing to the individual and/or his society. Abnormal and normal behavior represent different positions along a common continuum. The determinants of abnormal behavior differ qualitatively from the determinants of normal behavior but are no less complex and varied.

Up until the eighteenth century madness was generally attributed to supernatural influences. The disease concept of mental disorders was popular during the late nineteenth and early twentieth centuries. The numerous criticisms of this medical approach have stimulated interest in broader concepts that view mental disorders as psychosocial problems in living or special examples of norm violation. Recent interpretations have been accompanied by a radical shift in therapeutic approaches. Modern psychotherapy focuses on reeducation and social rehabilitation rather than on uncovering and resolving intrapsychic conflicts. Learning principles are utilized in the alleviation of current personality problems and the strengthening of assets.

Supplementary Report 1. Principal Professions Active in Mental Health

Practically all of the social and biological sciences, as well as the humanities, are involved with one or another of the multiple facets of psychopathology (Page, 1966). Pastoral counseling is an important activity of the clergy of all faiths. The legal profession is directly concerned with laws regulating the admission of patients to mental hospitals, the determination of mental incompetence, and the establishment of criteria for a defense of insanity. The medical sciences are directly involved in the neurological aspects of deviant behavior, psychopharmacology, and genetic research. In a 1969 survey conducted by the National Institute of Mental Health, it was noted that 29 percent of sociologists and 15 percent of anthropologists in institutions of higher education reported mental health as their professional specialty. The closest ties of psychopathology are with the professions of psychiatry, psychoanalysis, clinical psychology, and psychiatric social work.

Psychiatry is the medical specialty devoted to the diagnosis, treatment, and study of mental disorders. To qualify as a psychiatrist, a person must complete the usual requirements for an M.D. degree and then take postgraduate training in psychiatry. In the treatment of mental patients, psychiatrists rely mainly on therapeutic interview techniques. As licensed physicians they may administer drugs and apply various biophysical therapies.

Psychoanalysis is a particular school of thought and a special form of therapy. Psychoanalysts accept the Freudian or neo-Freudian interpretation of mental disorders and adhere to certain formal treatment procedures that stress the recall and interpretation of significant early childhood experiences with emphasis on repressed, unconscious material. Specific psychoanalytic procedures include the establishment of a transference relationship between patient and analyst, free association, and dream analysis. Any professionally qualified person in the field of mental health who has undergone psychoanalysis himself and who is a graduate of a recognized psychoanalytic training institute may call himself a psychoanalyst. However, most psychoanalytic training institutes in this country accept only physicians as trainees. As a result, psychoanalysis is essentially a subdivision of psychiatry. About 10 percent of all psychiatrists in the United States describe themselves as psychoanalysts. Most of them are located in large cities.

Clinical psychology is a specialty within the general field of psychology, devoted to the diagnosis, treatment, and study of personality disorders. Qualifying training includes the completion of a doctoral degree in psychology and one or more years of internship. Clinical psychologists may use any psychological treatment procedures they are qualified by training to administer. A currently favored approach is the application of learning theory principles to behavior modification.

Most *psychiatric social workers* have graduate degrees in social work. Their duties include interviewing of patients and relatives, follow-up home visits, and supervision in the community of patients discharged from mental institutions. In recent years psychiatric social workers have become increasingly involved in psychotherapy.

Members of all four professions work in mental hospitals, community clinics, universities, and related social agencies. All may engage in private practice, but a much higher proportion of psychoanalysts and psychiatrists devote full time to office practice. Particularly in hospital and clinic settings psychiatrists, clinical psychologists, and psychiatric social workers may function as a team, with each contributing the special skills of his profession. Traditionally the psychiatrist has assumed major responsibility for treatment, the clinical psychologist has assumed major responsibility for psychodiagnosis and research, and the psychiatric social worker has assumed major responsibility for the taking of case histories and the counseling of relatives of patients. The more recent trend has been in the direction of overlapping roles. Clinical psychologists and psychiatric social workers are becoming more active in therapy and psychiatrists are becoming more involved in research.

The extent to which the four professions are active in the mental health field varies in different parts of the country. In a survey of the total population of professional personnel working in a Chicago metropolitan community, Spray (1968) found that 25 percent were psychiatrists, 16 percent were psychoanalysts, 33 percent were clinical psychologists, and 26 percent were psychiatric social workers. Considerable variation was noted with respect to the major activities of the four groups. Eighty-five percent of the psychoanalysts listed therapy as their major activity as compared to 70 percent of the psychiatrists, 21 percent of the clinical psychologists, and 20 percent of the psychiatric social workers. Twenty-two percent of clinical psychologists listed teaching and research as their major activities as compared to 11 percent of psychiatric social workers, 9 percent of psychiatrists, and 5 percent of psychoanalysts. The balance of the time was spent in counseling, casework, diagnosis, administration, and supervision.

References

ALBEE, G. W. "Emerging Concepts of Mental Illness and Models of Treatment: The Psychological Point of View." *American Journal of Psychiatry* 125 (1969): 870–76.

ARIETI, S., and METH, J. M. "Rare, Unclassifiable, Exotic Psychotic Syndromes." In *American Handbook of Psychiatry,* ed. S. Arieti, vol. 1, pp. 546–63. New York: Basic Books, 1959.

ERIKSON, E. H. *Identity: Youth and Crisis.* New York: Norton, 1968.

FREUD, S. *An Outline of Psychoanalysis.* New York: Norton, 1949.

GRINKER, R. R. "Emerging Concepts of Mental Illness and Models of Treatment: The Medical Point of View." *American Journal of Psychiatry* 125 (1969): 865–69.

HALL, C. S., and LINDZEY, G. *Theories of Personality.* New York: Wiley, 1957.

KLUCKHOHN, C., and MURRAY, H. A. "Personality Formation: The Determinants." In *Personality in Nature, Society, and Culture,* ed. Kluckhohn and Murray, pp. 53–67. New York: Knopf, 1961.

KRAEPELIN, E. *Clinical Psychiatry.* New York: Macmillan, 1907.

LINTON, R. *Culture and Mental Disorders.* Springfield, Ill.: Charles C. Thomas, 1956.

MILLON, T. *Theories of Psychopathology.* Philadelphia: Saunders, 1967.

NATIONAL INSTITUTE OF MENTAL HEALTH. *Sociologists and Anthropologists.* Public Health Service publication no. 1884. Washington, D.C.: U.S. Government Printing Office, 1969.

ORLANSKY, H. "Infant Care and Personality." *Psychological Bulletin* 46 (1949): 1–48.

PAGE, J. D. "Description of a Psychotic Reaction in Eleventh-Century Japan." *American Journal of Psychiatry* 119 (1962): 271–72.

———. *Approaches to Psychopathology.* New York: Columbia University Press, 1966.

PHILLIPS, D. L. "Rejection as a Consequence of Seeking Help for Mental Disorders." *American Sociological Review* 28 (1963): 963–72.

SARBIN, T. R. "The Scientific Status of the Mental Illness Metaphor." In *Changing Perspectives in Mental Illness,* ed. S. C. Plog and R. B. Edgarton. New York: Holt, Rinehart & Winston, 1969.

SCHAEFER, E. R., and BAYLEY, N. "Consistency of Maternal Behavior from Infancy to Preadolescence." *Journal of Abnormal Psychology* 61 (1960): 1–6.

SCHEFF, T. J. *Being Mentally Ill.* Chicago: Aldine, 1966(*a*).

———. "A Sociological Theory of Mental Disorders." In *Approaches to Psychopathology,* ed. J. Page. New York: Columbia University Press, 1966(*b*).

SEWELL, W. H. "Infant Training and the Personality of the Child." *American Journal of Sociology* 58 (1952): 150–57.

SHIKIBU, M. *The Tale of Genji*, trans. Arthur Waley. New York: Random House, 1960.

SPRAY, S. L. "Mental Health Professions and the Division of Labor in a Metropolitan Community." *Psychiatry* 31 (1968): 51–60.

SZASZ, T. S. *The Myth of Mental Illness*. New York: Harper & Row, 1961.

THUDICHUM, J. W. L. *A Treatise on the Chemical Constitution of the Brain.* London: Balliere, Tindall & Cox, 1884.

WALLACE, F. C. "Anthropology and Psychopathology." In *Approaches to Psychopathology,* ed. J. Page, pp. 30–59. New York: Columbia University Press, 1966.

WEPMAN, J. W., and HEINE, R. W. *Concepts of Personality*. Chicago: Aldine, 1963.

YAP, P. M. "Mental Diseases Peculiar to Certain Cultures." *Journal of Mental Science* 97 (1951): 313–27.

CHAPTER TWO

Classification of
Psychosocial Problems

The influence of the disease concept on the classification of abnormal behavior is apparent in the choice of diagnostic labels, such as schizophrenia, neurasthenia, involutional melancholia, and hypochondriasis. The idea of grouping mental disorders in categories and subtypes cannot be entirely blamed on the adoption of the medical model, however. Man is an inveterate classifier. Confronted by the confusing differences among individuals, human beings commonly seek to simplify the situation by arranging them in neat but obviously artificial categories: good and bad, tall, medium, and short, bright, average, and stupid. The myriad manifestations of abnormal behavior are similarly placed in arbitrary categories: simpleminded, crazy, nervous, or simply peculiar or queer. The more sophisticated prefer to use such terms as retarded, psychotic, neurotic, and disturbed. The utility of these terms is limited by the fact that they are too broad and ambiguous to be meaningful when they are applied to specific individuals.

One of the earliest attempts at classifying mental disorders is reported in the writings of Hippocrates. Hippocrates recognized three principal mental diseases: mania (uncontrolled excitement), melancholia (varied forms of psychoses), and phrenesis, or frenzy. The latter apparently referred to acute delirium reactions marked by fever and excitement. He also described cases that would now be classified as phobias, hypochondriasis, and obsessive-compulsive reactions. In the intervening twenty-three centuries, hundreds of other diagnostic labels have been coined. The naming game has not been limited to Western societies. Primitive people have also

20

invented multiple descriptive terms to differentiate various types of madness. The Iban people of Sarawak recognize nineteen different forms (Schmidt, 1964).

Modern psychiatry still favors the classification of mental disorders in major categories and related subcategories. This model goes back to the work of Kraepelin (1856–1929), a German psychiatrist, who is credited with establishing the first widely used psychiatric classification. Kraepelin's original contribution consisted of the concepts of dementia praecox (later renamed schizophrenia) and manic-depressive psychosis. His detailed descriptions of the symptom patterns associated with these two major psychoses and their subtypes still constitute the nucleus of current psychiatric classification. The wide acceptance and continued use of Kraepelin's model have had the advantage of promoting a uniform nomenclature—at the high cost of perpetuating outdated terms and concepts. Periodically, makeshift attempts have been made to improve the classifications. To a large extent the psychopathologists of each country have gone their own ways in making additions and revisions. As a consequence, the classification systems in current use vary from country to country, and in some countries from hospital to hospital (Stengel, 1959). The diagnosis applied to a particular patient thus depends more on his place of residence than on his mental condition. The official French classification for example, includes several diagnostic labels that are not used elsewhere: acute confused state, chronic systematized delirium, mental disequilibrium. Technically there are no schizophrenic patients in France, since the official classification system does not include schizophrenia as a diagnostic category. In countries where the same labels are used, they are often interpreted differently. In the United States the diagnosis of schizophrenia is broadly applied to a wide variety of mental patients, many of whom would be classified in England as suffering from a psychotic depressive reaction. The results of a cross-national study reported by Kramer (1969) indicate that one-third of all persons admitted to mental hospitals in England and Wales are diagnosed as suffering from some type of affective psychosis, as compared with 11 percent in the United States. Conversely, about twice as many patients are classified as schizophrenics in the United States as in England.

Comprehensive reviews of the purposes, advantages, and shortcomings of psychiatric classification has been reported by Katz, Cole, and Barton (1965) and Zubin (1967). Menninger (1963) has contributed an excellent historical perspective. Some repeatedly noted but as yet unresolved problems are these:

1. Who should be classified as a mental patient and why? A commonly used operational definition is that a person is a mental patient if he seeks or is referred for treatment for some disturbance or impairment in behavior

that is considered a source of distress, disability, discomfort, or concern by the individual or his society. The objection to this definition is that it is too broad. To be meaningful and valid, a classification system should have some rational, unifying base. The reasons for psychiatric referral are too varied to justify including all of them under the common heading of mental disorders. Frequently reported complaints by self-referred patients include feelings of depression, loss of control of thoughts, suicidal impulses, sexual problems, loneliness, courtship and marital problems, and failure to achieve what the patient feels he should. A person may be referred for treatment by a member of his family, a friend, or some public official on the grounds that he is a danger to himself or others, is unable to care for himself, or is unwilling or unable to conform to expected social standards. More specifically, symptoms may include threats, excessive belligerence, conduct embarrassing or irritating to family or friends, excessive drinking, refusal to speak or eat, underachievement, immaturity of behavior, and social incompetence. Law-enforcement agents may refer lawbreakers for treatment when it is suspected that they are not criminally responsible for their actions or are unable to assist in their own defense because of mental disorders (Gruenberg, 1965).

2. How many categories of abnormal behavior should there be, and which should be included? The need for classifying the diverse manifestations of abnormal behavior in some orderly way is universally acknowledged. Disagreement exists as to choice of method, number of classes and subtypes, and the criteria that should be used for their selection. The root of controversies associated with these issues is that the "symptoms" of mental patients do not fit neatly into clearly defined, discrete categories. Each patient to some extent exhibits a unique combination of traits and reactions. Any classification restricted to a manageable number of categories is of necessity artificial. The variations in symptom constellation noted among mental patients merge and overlap to such an extent that decisions as to the number and kinds of diagnostic categories selected are necessarily arbitrary and subject to constant revision. The traditional and still most widely accepted procedure has been to rely on insights derived from clinical observations in identifying recurring combinations of symptoms that appear to occur together as a cluster or syndrome. The classification systems in current use in various countries consist of about eight to twelve major categories. Most categories include subdivisions that provide for more specific diagnosis. Thus a particular patient's behavior may be classified as psychotic and diagnosed more precisely as a schizophrenic, manic, or depressive reaction. This traditional approach to classification has been consistently used by the American Psychiatric Association, whose members have been mainly responsible for the development of a uniform nomencla-

ture system in the United States. The 1968 revision, which is described in the following section, is the most recent of a long series of essentially similar revisions dating back to 1917. General acceptance of the APA nomenclature system for diagnosis, preparation of statistical reports, and teaching purposes has given it official status in this country. The APA system and similar models adopted in other countries have served the important function of providing a convenient and reasonably effective method for organizing and recording the data of psychopathology. When applied and interpreted in a consistent fashion, the standard diagnostic labels constitute a useful language system for communicating technical information, though they have a number of shortcomings: (*a*) the recognized categories and subtypes have ill-defined, overlapping boundaries; (*b*) the inference that the separate categories constitute separate kinds of disorders is highly questionable; (*c*) the built-in rule of one diagnosis per patient ignores the wide range of significant differences among similarly diagnosed persons; and (*d*) the exclusive preoccupation with "symptoms" fails to take account of the patient's assets and strengths, which are as important to the total clinical picture as his defects.

1968 APA Classification

Recognizing the essential sameness of psychological disturbances in all countries, the World Health Organization has for some time been promoting a standard international nomenclature for diagnosis and classification. In 1968 the American Psychiatric Association officially adopted, with minor modifications, the Eighth Revision of the International Classification of Diseases. The ten major categories and the principal subtypes are listed and briefly described in Table 2.1. The APA classification adheres closely to the medical model of disease. The first six categories (mental retardation, organic brain syndrome, psychosis, neurosis, psychophysiological disorders, and personality disorders) are considered to represent separate forms of mental illness. It is acknowledged that the remaining four categories may be interpreted as isolated reactions or situational maladjustments rather than clearly defined disorders. But the emphasis remains on the presence of symptoms. In principle, the symptoms constitute the main basis for choice of diagnosis. The diagnostic process consists in comparing the individual patient's behavior (as determined by clinical examination, psychological tests, and case-history data) with the symptom descriptions accompanying the categories. In actual practice, however, subjective considerations and the examiner's training background influence the choice of diagnosis. Interexaminer agreement is fostered through consensual acceptance of certain rules. When a patient exhibits a variety of symptoms that cut across two or more categories, the rule is to assign the diagnostic label that is associated with the more severe disorder. Thus a depressed or phobic patient who also shows impairment in reality testing (as indicated by the presence of hallucinations and delusions) is diagnosed as psychotic rather than neurotic. Another rule is that the diagnosis of organic brain syn-

Table 2.1. 1968 APA classification of mental disorders

Classification	Symptoms	Subcategories
Mental retardation	Subnormal intellectual functioning, originating at birth or during early childhood; impairment of learning ability and/or social adjustment or maturation	Various, from borderline to profound; also differentiated with reference to associated physical condition

Organic brain syndrome (resulting from impairment of brain tissue function from whatever cause)	Impairment of orientation, memory, judgment, comprehension, learning ability, etc.; instability and shallowness of affect	Nonpsychotic organic brain syndrome
		Organic brain syndrome accompanied by psychotic symptoms:
		  senile dementia
		  alcoholic psychosis
		  cerebral arteriosclerosis
		  general paresis

Psychosis	Gross impairment of psychological functioning resulting in inability to meet ordinary demands of life; severe perceptual distortions (hallucinations, delusions); profound alterations in mood; marked impairment of language ability and/or memory	Schizophrenia (disturbances in thinking, social withdrawal, bizarre behavior) Affective psychosis (extreme depression or elation that so dominates the mental life of the patient that he loses contact with his environment in either small or great degree) Paranoid states (delusions, usually persecutory or grandiose)

Neurosis	Anxiety, either directly felt and expressed or controlled by conversion, displacement, or other psychological mechanism; no gross distortion ·or misrepresentation of external reality; no gross personality disorganization	Various, including:
		  anxiety neurosis
		  phobias
		  hysteria
		  obsessive-compulsive neurosis
		  depressive neurosis
		  neurasthenia
		  depersonalization
		  hypochondria

Classification	Symptoms	Subcategories
Psychophysiological (psychosomatic) disorders	Various physical symptoms caused by emotional factors; usually limited to symptoms involving a single organ system that is under control of autonomic nervous system	Mainly skin, musculoskeletal, respiratory, cardiovascular, gastrointestinal, and genitourinary disorders of psychogenic origin
Personality disorders	Deeply ingrained behavior patterns related to patient's basic personality structure; generally recognizable by time of adolescence or earlier	Various, including: personality disorders sexual deviations alcoholism drug addiction or dependence
Special symptoms	Usually limited to a single specific symptom, which varies from patient to patient	Various, including: speech disorders specific learning problems tics and other psychomotor disorders sleep disorders feeding disorders eneuresis encopresis cephalalgia
Transient situational disturbances	Acute but temporary reactions to overwhelming environmental stress, with no apparent underlying mental disorder; symptoms vary in severity	Many, classified according to patient's developmental stage (adjustment reactions of infancy, childhood, adolescence, adult life, old age)
Behavior disorders of childhood and adolescence	Behavior disorders more transient and fluid than psychoses, neuroses, and personality disorders, but more stable, internalized, and resistant to treatment than transient situational disturbances	Various, including: hyperkinetic reaction withdrawing reaction overanxious reaction runaway reaction unsocialized aggressive reaction group delinquent reaction
Conditions without manifest psychiatric disorder and non-specific conditions	Problems of sufficient severity to warrant examination and treatment although patients are psychiatrically normal	Various, including: social maladjustment marital maladjustment occupational maladjustment dyssocial behavior

drome takes precedence over other possible diagnoses if there is any evidence of brain damage. The age of the patient is an important determining factor. A special category is reserved for children. Alcoholism in young people or incipient alcoholism at any age is classified as a personality disorder; chronic alcoholism in persons past middle age is usually categorized as chronic brain syndrome. The diagnosis of schizophrenia is preferred to affective disorder for a psychosis occurring during adolescence. The choice of diagnostic category is also influenced by the duration of symptoms. Severe as well as mild reactions to known stressful experiences are classified as transient situational disturbances if they terminate in a few hours or days. If prolonged, the same reactions are assigned some other diagnostic label that seems to fit the persisting symptoms.

EVALUATION

A serious limitation of the APA classification is that it fails to define a mental disorder or to spell out criteria for assigning a person to any particular category. After it has been decided that a person is suffering from some mental disorder, the symptom descriptions of various disorders included in the APA's manual provide a frame of reference for arriving at a specific diagnosis; but the manual is silent on the critical questions of how and on what basis the initial decision is made. The presence of symptoms may be a dependable indicator of certain physical diseases, since some physical symptoms, such as the presence of cancer cells or blood in the urine, are noted only in sick persons, but there are no absolute or fixed symptoms of mental disorders. Any and all of the traits or reactions identified as symptoms in the APA classification are also present in the general population. Whether a particular trait or reaction is considered normal or abnormal is determined by its attending consequences and society's evaluation of it. For example, if two fully clothed persons jump off a high bridge into ice-cold water within seconds of each other, the first may be described as suicidally depressed and the second as a hero.

Some so-called mental symptoms differ mainly in degree from similar personality traits commonly noted in the general population. Among alleged symptoms that actually represent intensified "normal" personality traits are extreme suspiciousness, heightened irritability, excessive dependency, and emotional instability. As previously indicated, other so-called mental symptoms differ from "normal" reactions to overwhelming stress situations mainly in severity, duration, and appropriateness. A strong case could be made for an interpretation of the "disorders" included in the APA classification as merely various ways in which human beings often react to stress. This explanation is readily applicable to manic excitement, depressive-surrender reactions, alcoholism, hyperkinetic or runaway behavior in children, and the emotional overresponsiveness of neurotics. In addition, schizophrenia could be considered a massive social withdrawal reaction and paranoia a form of projection marked by heightened defensiveness and belligerence, all of which are exhibited at one time or another by just about everyone.

A second major criticism is the misleading implication that the ten listed categories constitute separate and distinct disorders. The clearly defined symptomatic distinctions made between categories in manuals and textbooks do not hold up when applied to actual patients. Symptoms that are considered key characteristics of a particular disorder are often absent in patients diagnosed as suffering from that disorder, but may be present in patients placed in some other category. This overlapping of symptoms across categories is a clinical commonplace and has been documented in a statistical study conducted by Zigler and Phillips (1961). Some representative findings are summarized in Table 2.2. The investigators concluded that "although some relationships exist between symptoms and diagnoses, the magnitude of these relationships is generally so small that membership in a particular diagnostic group conveys only minimal information about the symptomatology of the patient."

For classification purposes, it may be expedient to include in the same diagnostic category individuals who share certain traits or behavior styles; but it is a mistake to assume that persons assigned to a particular category

Table 2.2. Percentage of individuals in total sample and in each diagnostic category manifesting each symptom

Symptom	Total sample (N = 793)	Manic-depressive behavior (N = 75)	Psycho-neurotic behavior (N = 152)	Character disorder (N = 279)	Schizo-phrenic behavior (N = 287)
Depression	38%	64%	58%	31%	28%
Suspiciousness	35	25	16	17	65
Hallucinations	19	11	4	12	35
Suicidal ideas	15	29	23	15	8
Withdrawal	14	4	12	7	25
Assaultiveness	12	5	6	18	5
Self-depreciation	12	16	16	8	13
Maniacal outburst	9	11	6	7	12
Bizarre ideas	9	11	1	2	20
Apathy	8	8	8	4	11
Euphoria	5	17	2	2	5
Mood swings	5	9	5	4	4

Adapted from E. Zigler and L. Phillips, "Psychiatric Diagnoses and Symptomatology," *Journal of Abnormal and Social Psychology*, 63 (1961): 69–75.

constitute a homogeneous group. Similarly diagnosed persons are known to differ markedly in their personality assets and liabilities, the constellation and severity of their symptoms, their prospects for recovery, and their responsiveness to specific therapies. Nor is it safe to assume that patients who exhibit similar symptoms share similar developmental histories. Similar symptom syndromes may result from varied combinations of causes. Failure to take account of the heterogeneity of patients to whom the same diagnostic label has been applied has been a major obstacle in research efforts aimed at identifying the causes of particular disorders and devising specific treatments for them.

Finally, the APA classification lacks cohesiveness. There is no consistent, unifying rationale. Mental deficiency, for example, is totally unrelated to the other disorders. Some disorders are differentiated on the basis of etiological considerations, others on the basis of the age of the patient or the social setting associated with the disturbance in behavior.

The most cogent argument for the continued use of the traditional diagnostic categories included in the 1968 APA classification is that some orderly medium for the systematic organization of the data of psychopathology is essential for teaching and administrative purposes and for meaningful communication among professional workers. Alternative proposals, which we shall consider later, are still being explored. Until some better system is devised, tested, and widely accepted, there is no real choice. On the plus side, retention of the traditional nomenclature of the APA classification has the following advantages:

1. Official acceptance of the 1968 revision by the American Psychiatric Association guarantees that, barring some dramatic change, it will continue for several years to be the nationally accepted reference for the preparation of local, state, and national statistical reports on mental disorders in the United States.
2. The 1968 revision is very similar to the recommended international classification, and its use therefore facilitates cross-cultural comparative studies.
3. The research literature of past and current studies is based on the use of the traditional APA nomenclature. Much of this material could be discarded without any great loss, but some is highly informative and valuable.
4. The traditional diagnostic labels have considerable empirical usefulness in identifying the nature and extent of psychosocial malfunctioning and in differentiating severe, moderate, mild, and transient disturbances. For example, a diagnosis of paranoid state conveys a great deal of information about the patient's behavior.

In view of these advantages, we are justified in using the 1968 APA revision. On the other hand, there is no need to accept the APA classification uncritically and in toto. By the simple expedient of redefining concepts and terms it is possible to correct some of the more obvious errors of the APA classification. In line with this compromise solution, the term "mental disorder" is used in this book to refer to defects in psychosocial functioning that differ mainly in degree and duration from similar disturbances in functioning that are commonly noted in normal individuals. The traditional diagnostic terms will be used simply as convenient labels for describing certain kinds of reaction patterns or clusters of traits that tend to occur together. In other words, only the symptom information customarily associated with the traditional diagnostic categories will be retained. Thus the designation "schizophrenia" merely indicates the general behavior pattern exhibited by a patient. This is quite different from referring to an individual as a schizophrenic, or implying that he is the victim of a specific disorder called schizophrenia. When I designate a person as schizophrenic, I mean that he is out of touch with and seemingly indifferent to his social environment, is more or less exclusively absorbed with his inner private world, and exhibits any of a variety of related symptoms. With these stated reservations and modifications in mind, we can now proceed to a general description of the traditional diagnostic categories as listed in the 1968 APA classification.

Traditional Diagnostic Categories

MENTAL RETARDATION

Older labels for the condition we now call mental retardation include mental deficiency and feeblemindedness. Diagnosis is based on intelligence test findings and social history data that indicate subnormal intellectual functioning from infancy or early childhood with impairment of either learning or social maturation or both. The degree of retardation may be indicated by such terms as borderline, mild, moderate, severe, and profound. In addition, patients may be classified with respect to associated or known cause. The main clinical subcategories include retardation following infection, intoxication, trauma, or some physical agent, and retardation associated with disorders of metabolism, gross brain disease, diseases and conditions due to unknown prenatal influence, chromosomal abnormality, premature birth, or psychosocial or environmental deprivation. Mental retardation has strong historical ties with clinical psychology and psychiatry, but in recent years medicine and education have become increasingly involved in this field.

ORGANIC BRAIN SYNDROME

Organic brain syndrome is a broad category that includes all mental disorders, exclusive of mental retardation, that are caused by or associated with diffuse impairment of brain tissue function from any cause. The basic common syndrome consists of mild to severe impairment of orientation, memory, comprehension, learning ability, and judgment, plus instability and shallowness of affect. This core syndrome is directly attributable to impairment of brain tissue functioning. In addition to the core syndrome, patients with brain disorders may also exhibit a variety of psychotic, neurotic, or other behavioral symptoms. These associated or superimposed symptoms may be precipitated by the organic brain disorder, but they are more directly related to the patient's inherent personality, emotional conflicts, home situation, and other psychosocial factors. A distinction is made between acute and chronic brain disorders and between psychotic and nonpsychotic disorders. The term "acute" is applied to reversible or temporary disorders, such as the symptoms associated with alcoholic intoxication. When the brain has been permanently damaged, the condition is referred to as chronic. Patients with acute or chronic brain damage are classified as psychotic if their psychosocial functioning is so grossly impaired that they are unable to meet the ordinary demands of life. The principal psychoses associated with organic brain syndrome are senile dementia, psychosis with cerebral arteriosclerosis, alcoholic psychosis, general paresis, and psychosis with epilepsy. The diagnosis of nonpsychotic organic brain syndrome is applied to brain-damaged patients exhibiting only the core syndrome, or the core syndrome plus other relatively mild behavioral disturbances.

PSYCHOSIS

The label of "psychosis" is essentially restricted to the most severe behavior disorders that occur in adults and children. A differentiation has historically been made between organic psychoses, associated with observable or presumed brain damage, and functional psychoses, in which there is no clear evidence of gross organic pathology. Organic psychoses are classified as organic brain syndrome. When no specific mention is made of organic involvement, the term "psychosis" refers to so-called functional disorders. The general assumption is that functional disorders are mainly due to the interaction of predisposing genetic defects and adverse life experiences. The specific symptoms associated with psychotic behavior vary considerably from patient to patient and may overlap with similar symptoms observed in patients assigned to other diagnostic categories. A significant distinctive feature of psychotic behavior is that it is relatively independent of voluntary control or external reality. The psychotic individual may be troubled by unwanted thoughts or emotions that are seemingly inappropriate to his current life experiences, or he may report sensations and perceptions that either have no factual external basis or which represent a gross misinterpretation of actual events. A second distinctive feature consists of varying degrees of personality disintegration with consequent significant impairment in personal and social functioning. As a rule, the behavior of psychotic individuals is so defective and disorganized that they require care or supervision. Most psychotic patients are unable to relate effectively to other persons, to support themselves, or to manage their affairs with reasonable competence. When the patient's behavior endangers his life or constitutes an intolerable threat or distress to the community, voluntary or compulsory commitment to a mental hospital is usually recommended. Otherwise, treatment in the home, a general hospital, or an outpatient clinic is currently favored.

The psychotic person finds it difficult or impossible to differentiate between fantasies and actual experiences. Wishes tend to be confused with facts; imagined dangers, slights, and misdeeds are accepted as real, and real ones are grossly exaggerated or misinterpreted. Whereas normal people attempt to adapt their behavior to the expectations and demands of the physical and social environment, the psychotic's reactions are more or less exclusively dominated by inner dictates. In the context of his private, inner orientations, a psychotic individual's overt behavior may be meaningful and logical; but to an outsider, unaware of what is going on in the patient's mind, the ideas, feelings, and actions he expresses may well seem strange, irrational, and somewhat frightening in their apparent lack of control and in their unpredictability. It is difficult even for a close friend to understand why a formerly quiet, polite student should one day stand up in class, accuse the professor of reading his mind and stealing his ideas, and later barricade himself in his room and threaten to kill anyone who tries to enter.

The personality disintegration and reality distortion characteristic of psychoses are strikingly apparent in delusions and hallucinations. Delusions are persistent false beliefs, out of keeping with the individual's cultural background, which are uncritically accepted as true. Thus a patient may mistakenly but firmly believe that people are talking about him and spreading lies about him, that he has unusual powers, that his body has been changed in some mysterious way, or that he has committed some unmentionable sin. Hallucinations consist of sensory perceptions experienced while awake in the absence of pertinent external stimuli. In contrast to an illusion, which represents an erroneous perception of a real sensory impression—mistaking a twisted branch for a snake, for instance—

a hallucination is a cerebral or mental phenomenon that is produced independently of the sense organs. In the words of Esquirol, who initially described the psychological nature of hallucinations in 1817: "A person is said to labor under a hallucination . . . who has a thorough conviction of the perception of a sensation, when no external object, suited to excite this sensation, has impressed the senses." Most hallucinations are auditory: the patient "hears" voices. Second in order of frequency are visions. Gustatory, olfactory, and kinesthetic hallucinations are relatively uncommon and difficult to differentiate from illusions.

Patient reaction to hallucinations is variable. When the content of the experience is pleasant or is interpreted as a favorable message from God, the patient may be amused or elated. As a rule, however, hallucinations are perceived as warnings, threats, and accusations that evoke alarm, protest, rage, and terror. The voices may be fought against or automatically obeyed. Hallucinations are independent of the sense organ's ability to function as well as of external stimuli. Blind patients may "see" visions and deaf patients may "hear" voices if at some time in the past their vision or hearing has been normal. The "voices" are widely interpreted as representing the externalized projection of the patient's own thoughts. In effect, the patient is covertly talking to himself. McGuigen (1966) has demonstrated that the onset of auditory hallucinations is preceded by an increase in covert oral behavior as measured by a recording instrument attached to the larynx. Delusions and hallucinations are not exclusively limited to psychotic persons. Other types of mental patients, and normal persons as well, may also hold onto false beliefs and experience hallucinations. What distinguishes psychotic behavior is not the presence or absence of delusions and hallucinations per se, but rather the extent to which they pervade, dominate, and distort the person's perceptions, feelings, decisions, and actions.

Psychotic reactions are subdivided into three major categories: *schizophrenia, affective disorders,* and *paranoid states.* Schizophrenia is distinguished by disturbances in thinking and social withdrawal. The affective psychoses include extreme mood swings that usually terminate in good recovery after a few weeks or months. During the acute phase patients may be excited, elated, and hyperactive or depressed, sad, and underactive. In contrast to other psychotic reactions that are accompanied by a general disorganization of personality and gross impairment in general functioning, paranoia and paranoid states consist mainly of a capsulated persecutory or grandiose delusional system in an otherwise relatively intact personality. The patient's functioning is unaffected in areas outside of his delusional system.

NEUROSIS

The terms "psychoneurosis" and "neurosis" are used interchangeably. Neurotic behavior is distinguished from psychotic behavior by the relative absence of significant personality disorganization and the absence of gross impairment in reality testing and social functioning. Persons described as neurotic may repress or attempt to ignore unpleasant facts, but they do not distort or falsify external reality to the extent of experiencing delusions and hallucinations. Neurotic reactions are a source of acute personal distress and they frequently interfere with the individual's capacity for enjoyment and achievement, but they do not interfere unduly with his ability to carry on his work and other routine activities. Treatment, if any, is usually conducted in outpatient clinics and therapists' offices. As a rule, the neurotic takes the initiative in seeking therapy. The chief characteristic of neurosis is anxiety, which is often mixed with guilt feelings. A favored theory is that neurotic anxiety is an expression of unconscious inner conflicts. The anxiety may be directly expressed in the form of an overwhelming feeling of apprehension with concomitant rapid heartbeat, difficulty in breathing, and related physical symptoms associated with acute emotional disturbances. Other neurotic reactions include amnesia, irrational fears, dual personality, chronic fatigue, obsessive thoughts, compulsive rituals, depressed feelings, and hysterical conversion symptoms. These varied reactions are thought to represent indirect manifestations of or defenses against basic anxiety. Some of the main criteria utilized for differentiating neuroses from psychoses are summarized in Table 2.3.

PSYCHOPHYSIOLOGICAL DISORDERS

Psychophysiological disorders, more popularly called psychosomatic disorders, are caused by emotional factors and are characterized by physical symptoms involving a single organ system, usually one that is under the control of the autonomic nervous system, such as the respiratory, cardiovascular, and gastrointestinal systems. Emotional factors appear to be especially significant in such disorders as hypertension, peptic ulcer, asthma, anorexia, dysmenorrhea, migraine, and dermatitis. Since these disorders may also have physical causes, it is important to rule out any possible physical cause before assuming psychological origin.

PERSONALITY DISORDERS

Personality disorders include a variety of deeply ingrained maladaptive patterns of behavior that appear to be directly related to the basic personality makeup of the individual. Subjective anxiety is minimal. The

Table 2.3. Comparison of psychoses and neuroses

Psychoses	Neuroses
Marked loss of voluntary control over thoughts, emotions, and impulses. A psychosis may be compared to the automatic turning on of a master switch that takes over and regulates the individual's perceptions, feelings, and actions.	Some impairment of volition, but the individual is aware of the threatened loss of self-control. With effort, he can usually moderate the loss or resume control.
Impaired capacity for differentiating between reality and subjective experiences. Fantasies are accepted as events. Reality may be altered by the substitution of subjective experiences (delusions and hallucinations).	The individual can discriminate between reality and subjective experiences, but personal factors may unduly influence the selective perception or distortion of external stimuli and events. The individual may try to ignore reality, but he doesn't substitute subjective experiences for reality.
The patient accepts his condition. He may not realize or may deny there is anything wrong with him or his behavior. He lives his psychosis.	The neurotic is aware of the presence of symptoms, and in most instances tries to control them and/or seeks outside help.
Marked personality disorganization. Capacity for effective and appropriate social functioning is particularly impaired. Hospitalization or supervised home care is usually required.	Functioning capacity may be lowered but personality remains relatively intact, so that the individual may continue to function relatively effectively with respect to his regular occupational, home, social, and community affairs. Interpersonal relations may be disturbing but are not destroyed.

category designation is somewhat confusing, since all psychological disturbances may be described as personality disorders. An alternate label that is often applied is *character disorders*. A further source of possible confusion is the fact that one of the four subtypes listed in the APA classification is also referred to as personality disorders. This subcategory consists mainly of individuals who in personality structure resemble psychotics or neurotics—people with paranoid personalities, explosive personalities, hysterical personalities, and passive-aggressive personalities—but are not now either psychotic or neurotic. The three other subcategories are sexual deviations, alcoholism, and drug dependence.

SPECIAL SYMPTOMS

The category of special symptoms is restricted to patients whose psychopathology is manifested by a single specific symptom, such as reading disability, insomnia, stuttering, and anorexia nervosa. Common fear reactions present in otherwise normal persons—fear of dogs, snakes, spiders, riding in airplanes, and so on—are more appropriately included in this category than regarded as neurotic phobias.

TRANSIENT SITUATIONAL DISTURBANCES

Acute temporary reactions to overwhelming environmental stress that occur in presumably normal individuals may be mild or very severe, but they are usually of short duration. If symptoms persist for a long period after the stress is removed, another diagnosis may be more appropriate. Examples include panic reactions to dangerous situations, depression associated with school failure, and temper outbursts due to frustrations.

BEHAVIOR DISORDERS OF CHILDHOOD AND ADOLESCENCE

Here are included disturbances in behavior in children and adolescents, not associated with brain damage, that are not serious enough to be classified as psychoses, neuroses, or personality disorders. They are more stable, internalized, and resistant to treatment than transient situational disturbances and involve a larger segment of the personality than the disorders classified as special symptoms. Characteristic manifestations include overaggressiveness, excessive and unrealistic fears, timidity, and antisocial behavior.

CONDITIONS WITHOUT MANIFEST PSYCHIATRIC DISORDER

Psychiatrically normal persons may have marital, occupational, or social problems of varying severity that are more appropriately described as maladjustments than as mental disorders. This category is designed to cover such problems.

Prevalence of Psychological Disorders

Statistics on the occurrence of mental disorders are usually expressed in terms of expectancy, prevalence, and incidence rates. Expectancy figures represent actuarial predictions of the probability that a person may be expected to develop a mental disorder at some time during his life. Prevalence rates indicate the total number of mentally disturbed persons per unit of population as of a particular day. Incidence rates indicate the number of new cases occurring during the year per 100,000 of the general population. With the exception of field studies, which usually include both treated and untreated cases, most statistical reports are limited to treated cases. The magnitude of expectancy, prevalence, and incidence rates is a function of the criteria employed (Dohrenwend and Dohrenwend, 1965). If only grossly incapacitating or definitely harmful reactions that persist for several months were counted, about 10 percent of the population might be expected to develop a severe mental disorder, exclusive of senile deterioration, sometime during their lives. The number of seriously disturbed patients in the total population on a particular date (prevalence rate) is about 1 to 2 percent; and the incidence rate of new cases per year is about 1 per 400 general population. If mild and transient cases were included, however, the lifetime expectancy, current prevalence, and annual incidence rates would have to be multiplied by at least four.

Data on the relative prevalence of specific disorders are essentially limited to patients in treatment. As Table 2.4 indicates, the disorders of 80 to 90 percent of persons over fifteen years of age seeking treatment for the first time are diagnosed as either organic brain disorders, psychoses, neuroses, or personality disorders. The distribution of the diagnoses varies somewhat with the type of treatment facility. Neuroses and personality disorders account for more than 60 percent of patients seen in clinics and private practice. Organic brain disorders, psychoses, and personality disorders account for 75 percent of admissions to public mental hospitals, with each disorder being equally represented. The most prevalent psychosocial disorders noted among admissions to general hospitals are psychoses and neuroses. Each accounts for about 30 percent of admissions. The ratio of psychoses to neuroses among patients treated in clinics and private practice is about 1 to 3, whereas in public mental hospitals psychoses outnumber neuroses 2 to 1. The distribution by diagnosis of first admissions to private mental hospitals is practically identical with that reported for general hospitals. The resident population of public mental hospitals, which consists mainly of patients requiring long-term care, is dominated by schizophrenics, who account for 50 percent of the daily census. Second in relative frequency are patients with chronic brain syndrome. Psychoneurosis and personality disorder each accounts for 2 to 3 percent of the resident population of public mental hospitals.

Reliability of Diagnosis

The usual procedure in evaluating the reliability of diagnosis is to ascertain the degree of agreement between two or more clinicians classifying the same patients. Most of the older studies stressed the low reliability of psychiatric diagnosis. However, Beck (1962) and others have noted that these earlier investigations were poorly controlled. Methodological errors in earlier studies included: small numbers of cases, the selection of nonrepresentative patient populations, marked differences in experience and training among judges, lack of uniform patient information, and long time intervals between first and second diagnoses. When attempts have been

Classification of Psychosocial Problems

Table 2.4. Diagnostic distribution of mental patients by type of treatment facility

	Percent of admissions		
Diagnosis	Public mental hospitals, first admission[a] (N = 135,476)	General hospitals, all discharged alive[a] (N = 305,743)	Clinics and private practice, new cases[b] (N = 3,957)
Organic brain syndrome	26%	15%	4%
Psychosis	24	31	12
Personality disorders	25	15	27
Neurosis	11	29	35
Transient situational disturbances	4	3	9
Psychophysiological disorders	1	3	1
Other disorders	9	4	12
TOTAL	100%	100%	100%

[a] Based on patients in mental institutions and general hospitals with psychiatric service in United States in 1965 (U.S. Department of Health, Education, and Welfare, Public Health Service publication no. 1597, pts. 2 and 3 [Washington, D.C.: U.S. Government Printing Office, 1966]).

[b] All patients over fifteen years of age treated in clinics and private office practice in Monroe County, New York, in 1961 and 1962; patients with prior histories of inpatient care or recent prior outpatient contact excluded. Adapted from E. A. Gardner, "The Role of the Classification System in Outpatient Psychiatry," in Classification in Psychiatry and Psychopathology, ed. M. M. Katz, J. O. Cole, and N. E. Barton, U.S. Public Health Service publication no. 1584 (Washington, D.C.: U.S. Government Printing Office, 1968).

made to correct for these pertinent variables, reliability figures have been more encouraging. Summary findings based on studies reported by Schmidt and Fonda (1956), Norris (1959), Kreitman et al. (1961), and Sandifer et al. (1964) indicate 80–90 percent interjudge agreement for organic brain syndrome, 75–85 percent agreement for psychoses, and 55–70 percent agreement for neuroses. For all mental patients reported on two separate occasions to a central psychiatric register, Babigan (1965) noted 79 percent agreement between initial and subsequent diagnoses by different examiners. These reliability figures for the major categories are quite impressive, particularly when the vagueness of the categories, the subjectivity of the evaluative process, and the contaminating effect of examiner bias are taken into account (Matarazzo, 1965). With respect to more specific diagnosis, interexaminer agreement of about 70 percent has been reported in several studies of schizophrenia. Reliability studies indicate low diagnostic consistency for other specific types of psychoses and neuroses. The process by which different examiners arrive at the same diagnosis is not clearly understood. Clinicians typically explain their diagnostic agreement by noting that diagnosis is made on the basis of the symptomatic picture presented by the patient. This explanation is not very convincing, since experienced clinicians are well aware that many symptoms are associated with more than one diagnosis. A more cogent explanation is that examiners tend to make unconscious interpretations of the social significance of particular symptoms or combinations of symptoms. When symptoms are associated with or result in serious impairment in functioning, a diagnosis of psychosis is made. Patients with similar symptoms who exhibit mild impairment in functioning are assigned some more benign diagnosis, such as neurosis or personality disorder. Experimental evidence relating psychiatric diagnosis to level of social competence has been reported by Phillips, Broverman, and Zigler (1966).

Since psychiatric diagnoses influence the clinical conception of the nature of the disorder, the choice of treatment, and the prognosis, it is reassuring to know that the labels assigned to patients have some measure of reliability. Positive findings of diagnostic consistency among examiners, however, should not be regarded as proof of the existence of separate major categories. Interjudge agreement in diagnosis is contingent on the judges' learning and adhering to a predetermined set of differentiating criteria. By accepting and following a standard set of guidelines, a number of examiners can easily agree 80 or more percent of the time when they place people in discrete categories on the basis of traits that are obviously not discrete at all, but largely arbitrary points on a continuum—tall, medium, short, for example, or bright, average, dull.

Alternative Approaches to Classification

UNITARY CONCEPT

Karl Menninger (1963), an American psychoanalyst, has been an outspoken critic of the concept of separate and distinct psychiatric categories. He advocates a unitary concept in which health and disease are viewed as opposite ends of a single continuum. The normal end of the continuum is represented by health, happiness, success, and achievement. At the disease end, there is misery, failure, and delirium. Mental health is not static; it fluctuates along the scale in accordance with the stresses the individual experiences and his adaptive resources. Successive stages can be marked off along the continuum to indicate the relative severity of mental illness as reflected in degree of disorganization, lack of control, personal discomfort, and social maladjustment. Menninger interprets symptoms as emergency devices that the individual uses to help restore his equilibrium when it is threatened. At first, relatively mild devices are employed. If these succeed, they may continue for as long as they are needed and then disappear. If these mild regulatory devices fail, however, the individual may be forced to resort to more drastic devices at an increased cost in impaired functioning and inner suffering. The progressive stages or levels of dysfunction described by Menninger are summarized in Figure 2.1. Normal coping devices that usually are of short duration or have negligible adverse effects include crying, boasting, daydreaming, retreat in sleep, and moderate use of alcohol. If the stress persists and the individual is unable to work out a better solution, first-level dysfunction symptoms may appear—worry, somatic complaints, impotence, and so on. Depending on his adaptive resources and life circumstances, the individual may move upward toward health or step down further. Symptoms at the second level of dysfunction represent more desperate emergency reactions, and the devices employed to cope with them are those traditionally labeled neurosis or character disorder. Movement from this level may also be up or down. If it's down, the next step is a breakdown of control and the emergence of aggressive-hostile behavior. The fourth level of dysfunction represents an admission of defeat that is associated with futile protests, inward withdrawal, despondency, confusion, and general disorganization. The "psychotic" level may be transitory, a temporary retreat from life. There is still a good possibility that treatment and/or the natural recuperative processes of the organism will restore equilibrium and put the patient

Mental health

Normal coping devices: crying, working, sleeping, boasting, use of alcoholic beverages, daydreaming.

First level of dysfunction: worry, instability, inhibition, minor somatic symptoms, mild sexual dysfunction.

Second level of dysfunction: fainting, phobias, intoxication, compulsions, self-mutilation, perverse sexual modalities, inadequate personalities, use of addictive drugs.

Third level of dysfunction: breakdown in control of aggressive impulses leading to chronic or episodic acts of violence.

Fourth level of dysfunction: pervasive feelings of despondency and hopelessness; erratic disorganized excitement; bizarre behavior, mutism, posturing, incoherent speech; paranoid delusional themes; confused delirious states.

Fifth level of dysfunction: gross deterioration, suicide, continuous wild excitement leading to death from exhaustion.

Mental illness

Figure 2.1. Menninger's unitary concept of mental disorders

back on the road to health. The fifth stage is the end of the line, and there is little hope of return.

It is apparent that Menninger has no quarrel with the concept of mental illness. He accepts the occurrence of the traditional, clinically observed syndromes. His main contention is that these syndromes, along with other symptom manifestations, should be regarded as qualitative and quantitative variations in levels or degrees of dysfunction rather than as separate disorders. The underlying premise that the same individual may at various times exhibit "neurotic" or "psychotic" symptoms has significant implications. For example, it might be argued that if the various reaction patterns of mentally disordered persons represent changing makeshift adjustments of varying quality to life problems, there can be no sound justification for research directed toward the discovery of disorder-specific causes and disorder-specific therapies. Instead, research efforts might more profitably be concentrated on general causes applicable to all types of abnormal behavior and broad-spectrum therapies. But the issue isn't that simple. There remains the troublesome problem of explaining why some patients stop at the first or second level of dysfunction while others drop down to level four or five. And why do some patients show good recovery while others remain at the same levels for long periods or progressively decline? One possible explanation is that differences in genetic endowment and life experiences contribute to individual differences in adaptive resources. In other words, the causes, and possibly the required treatment, for higher level (psychotic) dysfunctions differ from those for lower level dysfunctions. The hypothesis that the determinants of psychotic behavior differ from the determinants of neurotic behavior is strongly supported by genetic studies and military data. A consistent finding of twin studies is that hereditary factors play a far more significant role in the etiology of psychoses than of neuroses. Military data indicate that the severity of external stress has a direct effect on the incidence of neurotic behavior but no demonstrable effect on the incidence of psychotic behavior (Glass, 1957). The incidence of neurotic behavior in the armed forces is higher in wartime than during peace. It rises when combat stress is high and drops when battle stress is reduced. Victorious units have a lower incidence of neurotic reactions than defeated or demoralized units. On the other hand, the incidence rate of psychotic behavior among members of the armed forces is about the same year after year. It is unaffected by war, peace, severity of combat stress, defeats, or victories. Data on civilian populations also indicate that severe stresses increase the incidence of neurotic behavior but have no significant effect on the relative occurrence of psychotic behavior (Reid, 1961). These findings clearly imply that psychotic reactions are mainly determined by constitutional factors but neurotic reactions are more influenced by current stress situations. Consistent with these noted differences in etiology, the traditional approach has been to favor drugs, shock techniques, and other biological forms of therapy for psychosis, and psychotherapy for neurosis. However, the etiological differences are mainly differences in degree. Psychogenic, biogenic, and sociogenic variables are involved to some extent in all mental disorders, so that the use of a certain treatment procedure with patients exhibiting varied types of disorders is not necessarily contraindicated.

STATISTICALLY IDENTIFIED SYNDROMES

Starting in 1933 with the pioneer studies of T. V. Moore, researchers have attempted to develop more objective and precise classification systems based on statistical evidence rather than clinical impressions. The procedure is known as the factorial approach. The first step consists in collecting pertinent observational, interview, or test information on a large, heterogeneous population of mental patients. These data are then analyzed with the aid of appropriate statistical techniques to locate intercorrelated traits or factors that tend to occur together as a cluster and which are relatively independent of other symptom clusters or syndromes. The factorial approach has been employed in distinguishing the main syndromes noted in behavior problems in children (Dreger et al., 1964), neuroses (O'Connor, 1953), and psychoses (Wittenborn, 1964). The series of studies on the syndromes of psychoses reported by Lorr, Klett, and McNair (1963) provides a good example of the method. These investigators have developed a special scale (Inpatient Multidimensional Psychiatric Scale) consisting of seventy-five behavioral items. Using the scale as a guide, the examiner interviews the patient and then rates or checks all items. Findings are converted to standard scores that indicate the patient's relative standing with respect to each of the basic syndromes identified. The ten major syndromes defined by Lorr and his associates are listed and described in Table 2.5. These syndromes were initially established by studies of patients in the United States. Similar psychotic syndromes have been reported in studies of hospitalized patients in Japan and five European countries (Lorr and Klett, 1969).

As is apparent from Table 2.5, the syndromes isolated by statistical techniques correspond fairly well with recognized clinical syndromes. The agreement is not surprising, since the traditional diagnostic categories are based on the noted recurrence of certain symptom clusters. There are, however, some critical differences. In contrast to the traditional reliance on subjective clinical impressions, the factorial approach involves the recording and measurement of certain designated traits. The greater objectivity of the latter procedure makes for greater interexaminer reliability. The

Table 2.5.   Ten major syndromes of psychosis

Syndrome	Characteristics
Excitement	Lack of restraint, excessive speed in speech and action, elevated mood, overactivity, dominance over others
Hostile belligerence	Irritability, suspiciousness, bitterness, contempt and criticism of others
Paranoid projection	Patient believes that people talk about, conspire against, and persecute him; feels controlled by external forces
Grandiose expansiveness	Attitude of superiority; patient hears voices praising him, believes he has unusual powers
Perceptual distortion	Patient hears voices, sees visions, believes familiar things have changed
Anxious intropunitiveness	Patient is critical of himself, apprehensive, depressed, suicidal; expresses feelings of guilt and sinfulness
Retardation and apathy	Slowed speech and movements, lack of goals; patient is uncommunicative, forgetful
Disorientation	Patient does not know where he is, how old he is, the season of the year
Motor disturbances	Patient assumes peculiar postures, talks to himself, grins or giggles inappropriately
Conceptual disorganization	Patient gives irrelevant or incoherent answers to questions, repeats words or fixed phrases, drifts away from the subject under discussion

Adapted from M. Lorr, C. J. Klett, and D. M. McNair, *The Syndromes of Psychosis* (New York: Macmillan, 1963).

traditional classification system requires the examiner to assign a patient to a single diagnostic category; either he's schizophrenic or he isn't. No provision is made for obvious qualitative or quantitative differences noted among patients assigned to the same diagnostic category. The factorial approach assumes that each syndrome represents a dimension of personality and that every individual exhibits all of the syndromes in varying degrees.

In a more recent study, Lorr, Klett, and Cave (1967) have noted that the ten psychotic syndromes listed in Table 2.5 are reducible to five higher order constructs. These are hypothesized to represent disorganized hyperactivity, schizophrenic disorganization, paranoid process, hostile paranoia, and anxious depression. A major criticism of the statistical approach is that the specific syndrome identified is a function of the input data. When investigators study similar populations but ask different questions of their subjects, the reported syndromes vary in number and in kind. For example, Phillips and Ravinovitch (1958) have reported three major syndromes that could be interpreted as avoidance of others, self-depreciation and turning against the self, and self-indulgence and turning against others. On the basis of patient response to a structured clinical interview, Burdock and Hardesty (1968) have identified ten basic trait clusters that differ somewhat from the Lorr list: (1) anger-hostility, (2) conceptual dysfunction, (3) fear-worry, (4) incongruous behavior, (5) incongruous ideation, (6) lethargy-dejection, (7) perceptual dysfunction, (8) physical complaints, (9) self-depreciation, and (10) sexual problems. So far the factorial approach has been limited to research studies. Further work is needed to determine which and how many factors are most relevant for classification purposes.

An important advantage of the factorial approach is that it avoids futile controversy as to whether a neurosis is a mild form of a psychosis or whether a person in developing a psychosis first goes through an intermediate neurotic stage. If we accept Eysenck's (1961) findings, which indicate that neuroticism and psychoticism are independent factors, the diagnostic issue is not whether a person is neurotic or psychotic but whether he scores higher on the neuroticism dimension than on the psychoticism dimension. If a person shows a relative predominance of neurotic reactions and later his neurosis becomes more severe, he will still be classified as neurotic. On the other hand, a marked increase in psychotic behavior with a diminution of neurotic behavior would necessitate a change of diagnosis from a neurosis to a psychosis. Theoretically, a person may show an equal amount of neuroticism and psychoticism. In such cases there is a tendency to favor the diagnosis of psychosis.

INDIVIDUAL CASE STUDY

The third alternative is to recognize the uniqueness of each individual and to concentrate on the study of single cases. The rationale is that more can be learned about the nature, causes, treatment, and prevention of personality disturbances through the intensive study of individual patients than through the study of groups, since the heterogeneity of groups tends to confuse and blanket observations. Adolf Meyer (1866–1950), founder of the psychobiological school of psychiatry, was an early advocate of this approach. Meyer viewed psychological disturbances as maladaptive habit patterns acquired by the individual as the natural result of his particular physical, social, and psychological life history (Lief, 1939; Muncie, 1959). In the past the individual approach has been mainly utilized in case studies and autobiographical reports by former patients. More recently, well-controlled experimental studies have been conducted on single cases (Krasner and Ullmann, 1965; Davidson and Costello, 1969). The utility of the method is best illustrated by the contributions of Freud. Most of his theories represent generalizations derived from insights gained through the comprehensive study of individual patients. The single-case method has been found particularly effective in developing and demonstrating procedures for behavior modification (Ullmann and Krasner, 1965). Procedures worked out in individual cases have been shown to be readily applicable to other patients with similar problems.

Schreber's autobiographical memoirs of his nervous illness provides an excellent illustration of the potentialities of the single-case method. This classical case study, which was originally reported in 1911, provided the basis for Freud's views on the role of latent homosexuality in paranoia. The Schreber case also offers strong support for the continuity or unitary concept. Schreber served for many years as a judge of the county court in Leipzig. At the time of his initial admission to a psychiatric clinic, at the age of forty-two, his outstanding symptom was severe hypochondriasis. He was discharged after six months and resumed his judicial duties. Then at the age of fifty-one he had a relapse and was hospitalized for nine years, during which time he wrote his memoirs. The second illness started off as an anxiety neurosis. This was followed by hypochondriacal delusions and suicidal depression. Later he exhibited catatonic stupor, maniacal excitement, compulsive bellowing, negativism, obsessive-compulsive behavior, and massive delusions. He believed that he was gradually being transformed into a female. At various times he could have been diagnosed on the basis of his changing symptoms as suffering from schizophrenia, chronic mania, involutional melancholia, paranoia, obsessional neurosis, and transvestism. Despite his severe symptoms, his capacity for clear and logical reasoning remained unimpaired. His superior intelligence enabled him to examine his madness and offer reasonable explanations for his strange behavior.

Summary

The actual existence of the various types of mental disorders included in official classification systems is highly questionable. The chief merit of the concept of separate and distinct psychiatric disorders is that it serves as a useful fiction in imposing a semblance of order on the confusing data of psychopathology. When the rules for identifying particular "disorders" are clearly defined and uniformly interpreted, examiners show a reasonable level of agreement in the diagnosis and differentiation of mental deficiency, organic brain syndrome, psychosis, and neurosis. For specific subtypes and milder reactions, interexaminer reliability is low. There is some factual basis for the claim that the traditional diagnostic labels constitute a convenient kind of shorthand for communicating useful information with respect to the nature of the impairment in psychosocial functioning, the relative severity of personality disorganization, and the probable prognosis. However, the artificiality of the arbitrarily defined categories, plus the fact that persons assigned the same diagnosis often have little in common, limits the accuracy of the information communicated. Clinical inferences associated with a particular disorder frequently do not apply to individual cases.

What have been traditionally referred to as separate disorders represent extreme, maladaptive, and disturbing expressions of recurring patterns of traits and reactions commonly noted in normal individuals under stress. The major varieties of syndrome patterns observed in mental patients are more appropriately regarded as examples of recurring personality types or behavior styles than as discrete forms of mental disorder. The statistical method of factor analysis provides a more objective technique for identifying these recurring syndromes than the traditional diagnostic procedure based on clinical impression. The factor approach sidesteps the "disorder" controversy and in addition provides a more comprehensive profile description of the individual on the basis of his relative rating on each syndrome. The unitary concept of behavior disturbances, advocated by Menninger, has particular significance for the continuity vs. discontinuity issue.

References

AMERICAN PSYCHIATRIC ASSOCIATION. *Diagnostic and Statistical Manual of Mental Disorders.* Washington, D.C., 1968.

BABIGAN, H. W. "Diagnostic Consistency and Change in a Follow-up Study of 1,215 Patients." *American Journal of Psychiatry* 121 (1965): 895–901.

BECK, A. T. "Reliability of Psychiatric Diagnoses: 1. A Critique of Systematic Studies." *American Journal of Psychiatry* 119 (1962): 210–16.

BURDOCK, E. I., and HARDESTY, A. S. "Psychological Test for Psychopathology." *Journal of Abnormal Psychology* 73, no. 1 (1968): 62–69.

DAVIDSON, P. O., and COSTELLO, C. G. *Experimental Studies of Single Cases.* New York: Van Nostrand Reinhold, 1969.

DOHRENWEND, B. P., and DOHRENWEND, B. S. "The Problem of Validity in Field Studies of Psychological Disorder." *Journal of Abnormal Psychology* 70 (1965): 52–69.

DREGER, R. M., et al. "Behavioral Classification Project." *Journal of Consulting Psychology* 28 (1964): 1–13.

ESQUIROL, J. E. D. *Mental Maladies: A Treatise on Insanity,* trans. E. K. Hunt. Philadelphia: Lee & Blanchard, 1845.

EYSENCK, J. J. "Classification and the Problems of Diagnosis." In *Handbook of Abnormal Psychology,* ed. H. J. Eysenck. New York: Basic Books, 1961.

GARDNER, E. A. "The Role of the Classification System in Outpatient Psychiatry." In *Classification in Psychiatry and Psychopathology,* ed. M. M. Katz, J. O. Cole, and W. E. Barton, Public Health Service publication no. 1584. Washington, D.C.: U.S. Government Printing Office, 1968.

GLASS, A. J. "Observations upon the Epidemiology of Mental Illness in Troops During Warfare." In *Symposium on Preventive and Social Psychiatry*, sponsored by Walter Reed Army Institute of Research and National Research Council. Washington, D.C.: U.S. Government Printing Office, 1957.

GRUENBERG, E. M. "Epidemiology and Medical Care." In *Classification in Psychiatry and Psychopathology*, ed. Katz, Cole, and Barton, pp. 76–98.

KATZ, M. M.; COLE, J. O.; and BARTON, W. E., eds. *Classification in Psychiatry and Psychopathology*, Public Health Service publication no. 1584. Washington, D.C.: U.S. Government Printing Office, 1965.

KRAMER, M. "Cross-National Study of Diagnosis of the Mental Disorders: Origin of the Problem." *American Journal of Psychiatry* (supplement) 125, no. 10 (1969): 1–11.

KRASNER, L., and ULLMANN, L. P. *Research in Behavior Modification*. New York: Holt, Rinehart & Winston, 1965.

KREITMAN, N.; SAINSBURY, P.; MORRISSEY, J.; TOWERS, J.; and SCRIVENER, J. "The Reliability of Psychiatric Assessment: An Analysis." *Journal of Mental Science* 107 (1961): 887–908.

LIEF, A., ed. *The Common-Sense Psychiatry of Adolf Meyer*. New York: McGraw-Hill, 1948.

LORR, M., and KLETT, C. J. "Cross-Cultural Comparison of Psychotic Syndromes." *Journal of Abnormal Psychology* 74, no. 4 (1969): 531–43.

——, ——, and CAVE, R. "Higher-Level Psychotic Syndromes." *Journal of Abnormal Psychology* 72, no. 1 (1967): 74–77.

——, ——, and MCNAIR, D. M. *The Syndromes of Psychosis*. New York: Macmillan, 1963.

MCGUIGEN, F. J. "Covert Oral Behavior and Auditory Hallucinations." *Psychophysiology* 3 (1966): 73–80.

MATARAZZO, J. D. "The Interview." In *Handbook of Clinical Psychology*, ed. B. B. Wolman, pp. 403–50. New York: McGraw-Hill, 1965.

MENNINGER, K.; MAYMAN, M.; and PRUYSER, P. *The Vital Balance*. New York: Viking Press, 1963.

MOORE, T. V. "The Essential Psychoses and Their Fundamental Syndromes." *Studies in Psychology and Psychiatry* 3 (1933): 1–128.

MUNCIE, W. "The Psychobiological Approach." In *American Handbook of Psychiatry*, ed. S. Arieti, pp. 1317–32. New York: Basic Books, 1959.

NORRIS, V. *Mental Illness in London*. London: Chapman & Hall, 1959.

O'CONNOR, J. P. "A Statistical Test of Psychoneurotic Syndromes." *Journal of Abnormal and Social Psychology* 48 (1953): 581–84.

PHILLIPS, L.; BROVERMAN, I. K.; and ZIGLER, E. "Social Competence and Psychiatric Diagnosis." *Journal of Abnormal Psychology* 71 (1966): 209–14.

—— and RABINOVITCH, M. S. "Social Role and Patterns of Symptomatic Behaviors." *Journal of Abnormal and Social Psychology* 57 (1958): 181–86.

REID, D. D. "Precipitating Proximal Factors in the Occurrence of Mental Disorder: Epidemiological Evidence." *Milbank Memorial Fund Quarterly* 2 (1961): 229–45.

SANDIFER, M. G., JR.; PETTUS, C.; and QUADE, D. "A Study of Psychiatric Diagnosis." *Journal of Nervous and Mental Disease* 139 (1964): 350–56.

SCHMIDT, H. O., and FONDA, C. P. "The Reliability of Psychiatric Diagnosis." *Journal of Abnormal and Social Psychology* 52 (1956): 262–67.

SCHMIDT, K. E. "Folk Psychiatry in Sarawak." In *Magic, Faith, and Healing*, ed. A. Kiev. New York: Free Press, Macmillan, 1964.

SCHREBER, D. P. *Memoirs of My Nervous Illness* (1902), ed. and trans. J. Macalpine and R. A. Hunter. London: Dawson & Sons, 1955.

STENGEL, E. "Classification of Mental Disorders." *Bulletin of the World Health Organization* 21 (1959): 601–63.

ULLMANN, L. P., and KRASNER, L. *Case Studies in Behavior Modification.* New York: Holt, Rinehart & Winston, 1965.

WITTENBORN, J. R. "Psychotic Dimensions in Male and Female Hospital Patients: Principal Components Analysis." *Journal of Nervous and Mental Disease* 138 (1964): 460–67.

ZIGLER, E., and PHILLIPS, L. "Psychiatric Diagnoses and Symptomatology." *Journal of Abnormal and Social Psychology* 63 (1961): 69–75.

ZUBIN, J. "Classification of the Behavior Disorders." *Annual Review of Psychology* 18 (1967): 378–406.

CHAPTER THREE

Criteria of
Psychopathology

In daily life, evaluations and decisions are constantly being made, and with reasonable accuracy, as to the relative normality or abnormality of our own behavior and others'. On what basis are these decisions made? Is it possible to isolate and identify the key criteria? Do the rules vary from culture to culture, or are they universal? The complexity of the problem precludes simple or final answers. Psychopathological behavior is more easily recognized than defined. In ordinary life the recognition of disordered functioning is greatly simplified by the fact that the evaluation is a global and continuous process that takes into consideration the previous personality of the individual, the relative appropriateness of his behavior in the total situational context, and the net effect of the behavior on the individual and others. These important modifying factors are not readily incorporated in specifically defined criteria. The more precisely the criteria are defined, the more exceptions there are likely to be. On the other hand, the more broadly the criteria are defined, the less usful they are.

Any criteria that are proposed must take account of certain known facts. Since the onset of behavior indicative of psychopathology is usually detected initially by the individual himself and/or his family and associates, one basic requirement is that the signs be readily observable by the average person. Secondly, the continuity of normal-abnormal behavior requires that the criteria be applicable to all degrees of disordered functioning, from slips of the tongue and "freezing" on examinations, which are periodically noted in normal persons, to the most severe forms of psychotic disturbances. Finally, the criteria must be culture-free. As we saw earlier, the outward forms of abnormal behavior are in great measure shaped by the models and learning experiences of the cultures in which they occur, but the essential features remain the same in all cultures. The incidental nature of cultural differences in surface symptomatology has been highlighted in studies reported by Tooth (1950), Carothers (1953), and others, which show that the Westernization of non-Western cultures is accompanied by a corresponding shift in symptomatology. As preliterate people become more sophisticated, the supernatural content of their delusions is gradually replaced by more "modern" symptoms, such as complaints of control by electricity, hypochondriacal reactions, and paranoid trends (Lambo, 1955). With respect to cross-cultural criteria, a distinction must be made between the recognition of abnormality and the tolerance of it. Some societies may be more tolerant of certain forms of disruptive, maladaptive behavior than others. Cultures may differ markedly in their interpretations of the causes of abnormal behavior, and in their attitudes, treatment, and management of people in whom it occurs. However, a person classified as mentally disturbed in one society would in all probability be regarded as abnormal in all societies. Even when a person's delusions parallel the cultural beliefs of his own society or another, the disorganized quality of other facets of his life establish his abnormality. A concise summary of the cross-cultural aspects of abnormality has been presented by Linton (1956, p. 62):

> All societies provide examples of psychotics, neurotics, and hysterics, who are recognized as such by members of that society. The symptomatologies associated with these abnormal states differ from society to society in ways which strongly suggest that they are shaped by cultural influences. The methods employed by different societies in dealing with individuals of these different types, including the social utilization of certain forms of psychotic abnormality, also differ. However, it seems certain that abnormality of this sort is absolute . . . . Individuals having the constitutional defects responsible for such abnormalities would be abnormal in any society. At most, particular cultural factors may lead to the manifestations or suppression of symptoms at various levels of defect intensity.

Some Broad General Criteria

PRESENCE OF SYMPTOMS

As we noted earlier, the existence of a mental disorder cannot be defined or inferred from the presence of symptoms. There are no fixed, absolute symptoms of mental disorder. Any and all of the ideas, feelings, and reactions noted in mental patients are also observed in more moderate, better controlled, and more socially acceptable form in normal individuals and in cured mental patients. It is only after a trait or reaction has been critically examined and evaluated as abnormal that it can be considered a symptom. Under different circumstances and in different settings, the same reaction would be regarded as normal. Anxiety, suspiciousness, depressed moods, feelings of hostility, and guilt reactions are experienced by the mentally sound as well as the unsound. The same may be said for more favorable traits—affection, altruism, joy, friendliness. Normal people as well as mentally disturbed persons distort reality to suit their needs, cling to obviously false beliefs, and are troubled by conflicts. The more bizarre feelings and actions of the psychotic are experienced by normal individuals in their dreams and fantasies. Anyone who has had difficulty shaking off the effects of a terrifying nightmare or who has drifted off into a hazy, confused, dreamlike state while running a high fever has a pretty good idea of what it means to be psychotic. The prejudices of normal people resemble the delusions of the mentally disturbed in that they are irrational and false subjective beliefs that cannot be readily corrected by factual evidence or appeals to reason. Almost any symptom may be a normal or even laudable act if it is adequate and appropriate in duration, time, place, and manner of expression, and if its effects are beneficial to the individual and his society. Apprehension is a normal reaction to danger, grief is a normal reaction to a tragic personal experience, and anger is a normal reaction to injustice. For a person to kill a stranger when "ordered" to do so by an imaginary voice is certainly a sign of abnormality, but there are many situations (self-defense, soldiers in combat) in which society sanctions the killing of strangers. For a layman to claim communication with God is suggestive of psychopathology, but some degree of literal or figurative communication with God is expected of religious leaders in most societies. Instead of being symptomatic of a neurosis, guilt is an asset when it serves as motivation for good moral conduct. Fear may also have positive value. In studies made of persons exposed to stress situations, it has been found that anticipatory fear acts as a safeguard against more pathological reactions (Janis, 1966). The defensive function of anticipatory fear has been substantiated in animal studies. In comparing the incidence of behavior derangements induced in emotional and nonemotional strains of rats through air-blast stimulation, Martin and Hall (1941) noted that fearful rats were less affected than fearless rats. The overt expression of fear served to dissipate emotional tension and thereby acted as a safety valve. In the case of the fearless, nonemotional rats, the accumulated strain of exposure to auditory stress eventually led to explosive reactions marked by gross behavior disorganization and convulsive seizures. The importance of evaluating the appropriateness and consequences of specific traits also applies to seemingly normal behavior. Orderliness for the sake of order approaches symptomatic compulsive behavior. The mother who lives for her children may be suspected of neurotic manipulation rather than nobility of character, if the objective of her self-sacrifice is a permanent enslavement of her children.

NORM DEVIATION

The vague criterion of norm deviation poses two problems: defining the norm and distinguishing between favorable and unfavorable deviations. A popular but not very enlightening interpretation of the norm is based on the *statistical model,* which arbitrarily defines as normal the usual, most commonly noted, or typical reactions of the great majority of the population. All unusual or atypical reactions, whether good, bad, or indifferent, are considered abnormal. The statistical criterion has the merit of including most people within the normal fold and of recognizing the relativity of normality and abnormality. However, the exclusive dependence on the frequency of occurrence of any form of behavior, independent of its value, is a major limitation. On the basis of the statistical criterion, the essence of normality would be mediocre, common behavior. Behavior that was better than average would paradoxically have to be described as abnormal. As a rule, the reactions of the majority satisfy minimal standards of sound behavior; but on occasion the majority may panic, participate in mob violence, or be misled into sanctioning concentration camps and other atrocities. Another important drawback of the statistical criterion is that it is culture-bound. With respect to mental health, it does not matter much whether behavior that is common in one culture is rare in another or seldom observed in the same culture in a later generation. What is important, from the point of view of mental health, is the relative effectiveness of behavior in satisfying basic human needs and in contributing to the psychobiosocial well-being and enhancement of the individual and his society. As far as these objectives are concerned, the statistical criterion is useful in delimiting *average normal* behavior—the way most of the people in a society behave most of the time. Normal functioning that is better than average is more appropriately designated as *ideal normal* than as abnormal behavior. The term "abnormal" is best restricted to defective, disordered functioning.

Defining deviation from the norm on the basis of the *relative unexpectedness* of behavior represents a refinement of the statistical model. The reactions of the mentally disturbed are admittedly more unexpected, puzzling, and unpredictable than those of normal individuals. On the other hand, many unexpected reactions either have no bearing on mental health or are more indicative of ideal normal than of abnormal behavior. Outstanding acts of kindness or flashes of brilliance in average students may be unexpected, but they are perfectly normal. Furthermore, not all unexpected detrimental reactions are abnormal in the sense of being pathological. As we saw in Chapter 1, in our discussion of Scheff's (1966) concept of residual deviance, the field of behavior pathology is restricted to residual norm violations for which society provides no explicit label. Undesirable deviations from the norm, whether expected or not, are not usually included under the heading of mental disorders if some more specific designation such as criminal behavior, sexual perversion, or sinfulness is pertinent.

The *social conformity* criterion of normality is subject to the general criticism that carbon-copy behavior is a poor measure of normality. Conversely, originality and individuality are not defensible criteria of abnormality. Most societies encourage their members to acquire and accept their prevailing behavior patterns, customs, and value systems. Among other reasons, conformity is desired because it contributes to the identity and solidarity of the group, promotes harmony in interpersonal relations, and provides stability and continuity to the culture. On the other hand, most societies allow for individual variations and periodic changes. It is realized that extreme or rigid conformity is neither satisfying to individual self-esteem nor beneficial to society. To be just like everyone else is to be a nonentity, a ditto mark, a nameless face in the crowd. Conformity is an adaptive device, not a goal. It is essentially instrumental behavior, helpful in satisfying affiliation needs (Walker and Heyns, 1962). A person may conform to a group's behavior patterns in order to gain or retain membership in the group; but the real goal is to be accepted, approved, and liked as a distinct person. The usual solution is a compromise. The individual conforms sufficiently to maintain membership in the group while simultaneously developing and preserving a separate personal identity. Society is acceptive of the conformist, but it recognizes and rewards the individual whose favorable distinctive actions set him apart from and ahead of the common herd. In short, leaders are more honored than followers. Experimental studies have shown that outstanding leaders are characterized by independence of thought and action and steadfast adherence to their own convictions, perceptions, and opinions despite apparent disagreement with the group (Crutchfield, 1955).

With respect to mental health, the reason for conformity or nonconformity is more significant than the degree. The mentally disturbed do not indulge in nonconforming behavior because they reject the cultural model or wish to be different. Many desperately want to be more like other people; but because of their faulty perception of the social norm and their relative inability to control their thoughts and actions, they are unable to do so. Nonconforming behavior among normal persons is usually a matter of voluntary choice. The nonconforming behavior of hippies differs from that of mentally disturbed and normal individuals in its deliberate flaunting of conventionally accepted behavior. The high degree of social conformity observed in some mentally disturbed persons is often a defense against insecurity. In addition to enabling one to avoid the stresses of decision-making, conformity reduces personal responsibility for one's actions. For the timid and ill at ease, conformity provides a protective camouflage.

Some Specific Criteria

A number of attempts have been made to identify more precisely the salient characteristics of abnormal and normal behavior. While differing in their choices of critical factors, authorities agree in favoring multiple criteria, each conceived as a continuum ranging from normal behavior at one end through borderline reactions to abnormal behavior at the other end. A second point of agreement, particularly represented by the contributions of Jahoda, Shoben, Kluckhohn, and Linton, has been the selection of traits applicable to various cultures. According to Jahoda (1958), the mentally disturbed differ from normal persons in being relatively deficient in these key characteristics: (1) awareness, acceptance, and correctness of self-concept; (2) continued growth and self-actualization; (3) integration and unity of personality; (4) autonomy and self-reliance; (5) perception of reality and social sensitivity; and (6) mastery of the environment and adequacy in meeting the demands of life. Deficiencies in these traits are assumed to be indicative of abnormality. Shoben (1957) maintains that behavior is normal to the extent that it reflects man's unique capacity for symbolization and social involvement. Among the distinctive human potentialities correlated with normal behavior, Shoben lists aptitude for capitalizing on past experience, self-control, ability to envision ideals, social reliability, and capacity to act independently in relation to others and at the same time to acknowledge one's need for others. Kluckhohn's position, as reported by Leighton, Clausen, and Wilson (1957), is that all cultures define as mentally ill those persons who are inaccessible to communication, whose behavior is drastically at variance with cultural norms, and who do not have adequate control over their aggressive impulses. The inability of the mentally disturbed person to transmit, receive, and decode messages involving thoughts and feelings has also been noted by Ruesch and Bateson (1951). For Linton (1956, p. 63), "the tests of absolute normalcy are the individual's ability to apprehend reality as understood by his society, to act in terms of this reality, and to be effectively shaped by his society during his developmental period."

Normal behavior includes, then, (1) effective psychological functioning (competence in self-evaluation, reality-testing, learning, meeting demands of life), (2) appropriate social functioning (social sensitivity, dependability, actions in accord with cultural norms), and (3) self-control and integration of personality. The effect of normal and abnormal functioning on the individual and his society adds two additional differentiating criteria. Normal behavior is (4) personally satisfying and (5) socially acceptable, whereas abnormal behavior is a source of discomfort or distress to the individual and/or his family and associates.

Proposed Criteria

Although the extensive theoretical, clinical, and experimental literature on psychopathology is primarily concerned with the etiology, interpretation, diagnosis, and treatment of mental disorders, it is also a rich source of information on the distinguishing characteristics of mental patients. The main conclusion that may be derived from this heterogeneous material is that some criteria are more valid than others; but all five of the following key criteria, as well as other, less well-defined ones, are involved in evaluating mental health. To complicate matters, a person may be rated as normal with respect to one or more of the criteria listed on Figure 3.1 and abnormal in regard to others. The final decision entails a balancing of positive and negative components. This is an ever present problem, since all mental patients retain areas of normal functioning in varying degrees. A final qualifying point is that the criteria for mental disorders are more stringent than those for abnormal behavior. Momentary, infrequent abnormal acts that have no significant detrimental effects on the person or his society are usually not considered signs of mental disorder. This differentiation is consistent with the continuum concept, which holds that mental disorders represent extreme or serious manifestations of abnormal reactions that are also noted in normal individuals.

DEFECTIVE PSYCHOLOGICAL FUNCTIONING

Clinical and experimental data confirm that the severity of psychological deficit and psychopathology are positively related. The mental functions most impaired tend to be the more distinctively human abilities: attention, perception, reasoning, reality-testing, judgment, learning, memory, communication, and creativity. In brain-damaged persons there is often a permanent loss of these capacities. In psychologically disturbed persons the capacity is retained but its use is impaired or distorted. Thus a person may have the capacity to think, but not to think logically. The functioning impairment may often be reduced by increasing the patient's motivation.

Psycho- pathology	Average- normal	Ideal- normal

Proficiency of psychological functions

Inadequate		Superior
Impaired		Effective
Disordered		Integrated

Quality of social functioning

Inadequate		Superior
Egocentric		Social interest
Discordant		Harmonious

Degree of voluntary control

Uncontrolled		Controlled
Unconscious		Conscious
Rigid		Flexible
Inhibited		Spontaneous

Society's evaluation

Unacceptable		Laudable
Liability		Asset
Disruptive		Satisfying
Threatening		Beneficial

Individual's evaluation

Unacceptable		Gratifying
Liability		Asset
Distressing		Satisfying
Threatening		Comforting

*Figure 3.1. Five basic criteria for evaluating degree of normality-abnor-
mality.*

Experimental studies summarized by Lang and Buss (1965) indicate that the defective functioning often appears to be due to the disruptive effects of intrusive stimuli. This condition, referred to as *overinclusion,* is marked by apparent inability to screen out or exclude task-irrelevant mental acts, emotions, impulses, ideas, and external stimuli that interfere with performance. Overinclusion has been attributed to a lowering of vigilance or to impairment in the voluntary control of behavior. The latter explanation has the advantage of also accounting for the overexclusion of associations and stimuli noted in depressed patients.

DEFECTIVE SOCIAL FUNCTIONING

The essentials of this criterion, as suggested by Scheff, Kluckhohn, and Linton, consist of the relative inability of the individual (1) to apprehend and be effectively shaped by the cultural model and (2) to refrain from engaging in actions that are drastically at variance with the cultural norm. The term "inability" serves to exclude criminal, immoral, and other presumably voluntary forms of social deviation. The focus on local culture serves to discount intercultural variations in customs, values, and interpersonal relationships. In effect, the acknowledgment of the culture as the frame of reference is a restatement of the principle that the relative normality or abnormality of a specific behavior can be evaluated only in terms of its situational effectiveness and appropriateness. In cultures similar to ours, which emphasize the importance of harmonious social relationships and individual responsibility, the major signs of defective social functioning include inadequate control of aggressive impulses, excessive distrust and suspicion of others, incoherent communication, irresponsibility, self-destructive tendencies, and psychological incapacity for self-care and autonomous behavior.

A more pervasive defect is related to what Adler (1939) has referred to as a lack of social interest. In developing his basic theory, that much of human behavior may be explained on the basis of striving for superiority to compensate for universal feelings of inferiority, Adler was confronted with the problem of differentiating between the compensatory style of life of neurotics and that of normal individuals. He concluded that normal individuals' strivings for superiority are tempered by a genuine interest in the feelings and welfare of others. The life style of the neurotic, on the other hand, is egocentric. His goal is to achieve a personal sense of superiority, whether real or imaginary, without regard to the feelings of associates or the interests of society. The egocentrism of the disturbed person is not like that of the show-off. In most instances the disturbed individual is reserved and avoids attracting attention to himself. His egocentrism is more precisely described as a narrowing of interest to himself. This self-centeredness may include other members of the family who are perceived as extensions of himself. Although the disturbed person may be aware of and interact with his social environment, he is usually so preoccupied with his circumscribed world that he has little interest in other people, except insofar as their behavior has some direct personal significance to him. A dramatic example of this self-centeredness has been reported by Wilmer (1958, p. 4). A hospitalized psychiatric patient witnessed the sudden and rather violent death of a fellow inmate. "It's been a long day for John Allen," he remarked to the attending physician as they both looked upon the body. "Is that his name?" inquired the doctor. "No," replied the patient. "I'm John Allen." The marked lack of social feeling that is characteristic of autistic children practically from birth suggests that the inability to establish close emotional ties with others may be at least partly biological in origin. In most adult patients, however, limited emotional involvement with others and repeated preoccupation with themselves appear to be acquired defenses against repeated disappointments encountered in earlier social experiences.

LOSS OF SELF-CONTROL

Impairment of conscious self-control is the most critical single criterion of psychopathology. The unexpectedness, inappropriateness, irrationality, and defective quality of abnormal behavior is due to the fact that it is uncontrolled. Public awareness of the loss of control accompanying mental disorders is reflected in such popular descriptive terms as "out of one's mind," "running amok," "going berserk," and "nervous breakdown." The most convincing evidence is provided by the disturbed person himself. Try as he will, the neurotic cannot rid himself of his fears, worries, and compulsions, even when he realizes they are senseless. A major source of the psychotic's anguish is the realization that he has no control over his feelings and impulses and is powerless to turn off the threatening voices and disturbing thoughts that assail him. The invention of enemies, who for some unknown reason are controlling his sensations and actions by electronic devices, represents a closure attempt to make sense of the inexplicable. As precautions against the threat of loss of control, the psychotic person may drastically curtail his activities, strengthen his inhibitions, and become extremely rigid in thought and action. These defensive measures involve a renunciation of functions and of control. The overcontrolled person has little freedom of choice; his actions are prescribed as well as circumscribed. Loss of self-control is particularly evident in serious mental disorders, but it is also characteristic of minor disturbances in adults and children: temper tantrums, enuresis, poor concentration, restlessness, impulsivity, and stammering.

All theories of psychopathology since ancient times have in one way or another acknowledged the obvious impairment of voluntary control accompanying mental disorders. One of the earliest tests of madness, reported by Homer, was based on this observation. When the members of the conscription committee for the Trojan wars called on Ulysses, they found the reluctant warrior plowing the beach and sowing it with salt. To find out whether Ulysses was really mad or only feigning madness, they placed his son Telemachus in the path of the plow. To avoid killing his infant son, Ulysses changed the direction of the plow, and in so doing demonstrated that he was in command of his faculties and his actions, and hence was only pretending to be mad.

The theory of demonology recognized the helplessness of the disturbed person by assigning responsibility for his disordered behavior to evil spirits and demons who somehow had gained possession of him. The concepts of bewitchment and lunacy similarly attributed control of behavior to external sources. With the rejection of supernatural explanations, the origin of disordered behavior has been localized within the individual; but the relative loss of voluntary control in mental disorders has continued to be recognized. A significant corollary of the disease concept of psychopathology was the assumption that the mentally ill person had no more control over his disordered behavior than the physically ill patient had over his physical symptoms. The nonresponsibility of the mentally disturbed person for his behavior is the keystone of legal tests of insanity. Criminal culpability is based on the premise that the individual is capable of rational choice, and of his own free will chooses to engage in offenses he knows are wrong.

The tension theory developed by Pierre Janet (1943), a French psychiatrist, provides an ingenious explanation for the observed losses of functions noted in neuroses. Janet's basic premise was that a certain level of psychic energy is essential for the unification and integration of various parts of the mind. If the tension level is reduced below a critical point, certain functions become dissociated from the mainstream of consciousness. These emancipated functions, which are no longer subject to volition, may be temporarily lost or may continue to operate independently. As a rule, a relatively small segment of the mind becomes dissociated, and the symptomatic manifestation consists mainly of amnesia, inability to speak or to move some part of the body, irrational fear, a recurring tic or spasm, or some other relatively specific dysfunction. Occasionally a massive dissociation, amounting to a division of the personality, occurs. In this case the two separated personalities may alternate, so that the individual may have access only to memories and functions that are part of the personality in charge at the time. Janet held that energy level is mainly determined by heredity. Contributory factors that may deplete and reduce the energy supply include debilitating physical diseases, excessive fatigue, and emotional shocks. The significance of loss of control in schizophrenics was emphasized by Bleuler (1950), who maintained that the primary symptoms in this group of disorders consisted of a looseness of the associative links in thinking, ambivalence, and the dominance of behavior by fantasies.

The issue of conscious control of behavior pervades psychoanalytic theory and treatment. According to Freud (1949), mental disorders occur when the ego or conscious portion of the personality, which is charged with the triple responsiblity of holding in check repressed id impulses, heeding the prohibitons of the superego, and adapting to the demands of reality, loses mastery of the situation. Mental symptoms represent the involuntary acting out of unconscious impulses and emergency defenses against a more serious breakdown in functioning. The essence of neurotic behavior, as defined by Kubie (1958), is that it is rigidly channeled by forces that predetermine the automatic repetition of certain acts, irrespective of their appropriateness or any other consideration. One of the major aims of psychoanalytic therapy is to restore and extend ego control by uncovering the unconscious and thereby increasing the conscious portion of the personality that is more accessible to voluntary control.

The restricted flexibility of neurotic behavior, emphasized by Horney, calls attention to another facet of the impairment of self-control. For Horney (1945), the core of neurosis is a conflict born of incompatible and irreconcilable attitudes toward other persons. The basic conflict interferes with adaptive, appropriate behavior by imposing a rigid one-track response set. The origin of the conflict is traced to adverse parent-child relationships that make the child feel helpless, insecure, and anxious. Adverse factors may include parental inconsistencies, overdomination, indifference, lack of reliable warmth, unkept promises, and so on. In attempting to cope with a social world that is perceived as unpredictable and potentially hostile, the child has a choice of three main strategies. He may (*a*) move toward people and attempt to obtain a feeling of security and belonging by being submissive and dependent; (*b*) move against people and fight his way through life; or (*c*) move away from people and build a world of his own, in which books, nature, and dreams take the place of social interaction. If early childhood experiences are not too destructive or if the damage produced is offset by more favorable interpersonal experiences during adolescence, the child learns to combine and integrate all three approaches so that they complement one another. The normal individual is thus free to move toward, against, or away from people, and can alter his reaction to fit the situation. The neurotic, on the other hand, has no choice. He is a prisoner of the particular response set established during early childhood. Whether this response is appropriate or not, there is only one move he can make. In all situations, he can either comply, fight, or remain aloof. If he tries to step outside of the rigid mold, he is overwhelmed by anxiety. Illustrative of the neurotic's dilemma is the person who needs and wants friends, but who is unable to relate to others or can relate to them only in an aggressive or hostile manner.

The concept of man as a self-knowing and self-regulating organism responding to stimuli and making decisions on the basis of rational, deliberate choice is more idealistic than real. However, it is precisely because it is an ideal, a model of the way men wish to behave, that conscious voluntary control is a sound criteria of optimal normal behavior. Control of one's thoughts, feelings, impulses, and behavior is a prerequisite for peace of mind, personal confidence, and spontaneity of reactions. Problem-solving and successful adaptation depend in great measure on one's capacity to shift deliberately from one course of action to another, to experiment, and to alter his objectives at will. Unless a person has command of himself, he cannot afford the exhilarating but risky experience of letting himself go, exploring the unknown, and reaching for the stars. Disciplined self-direction is required for responsiblity, dependability, and accountability in meeting one's social obligations. Without self-control, no one could postpone the immediate gratification of desires for more satisfying delayed rewards.

SOCIETY'S EVALUATION

The presence and severity of defective, uncontrolled psychosocial functioning may be noted or inferred from direct observation of the individual's behavior, self-report data, interview information, and case-history material. With the aid of standardized tests such as the Wechsler Adult Intelligence Scale, the Rorschach Inkblot Test, the Thematic Apperception Test, and the Minnesota Multiphasic Personality Inventory, the amount of impairment or deviation of specific functions from the norm may be expressed in quantitative terms. These and other sources of data provide the raw material for evaluating behavior, but the actual decision as to the presence of psychopathology is made by the individual and by the society of which he is a member. The evaluative process centers about three basic questions: Do the available data indicate an impairment or disorder of psychosocial functioning? Is the dysfunction so severe that it significantly disrupts the individual's social and/or personal adjustment? Can the disturbance in behavior be accounted for on the basis of some "natural" explanation, such as physical illness, ignorance, intoxication, or some recent traumatic experience? A clear verdict of psychopathology requires affirmative answers to the first two questions and a negative answer to the third. When differences of opinion exist between society and the individual, greater weight is given to society's evaluation if the behavior is considered likely to endanger or have a detrimental effect on the group; but if the behavior has a greater effect on personal adjustment than on the welfare of the group, greater importance is attached to the individual's own evaluation.

The role of society as the arbiter of normal and abnormal behavior is shared by three groups: (a) the family and close friends of the individual; (b) neighbors, associates, and other persons having direct contact with him; and (c) professionally trained persons recognized by the society as experts or authorized evaluators. In our society formal diagnosis is chiefly the responsibility of psychiatrists and clinical psychologists. Other specialists who may be involved in diagnosis include psychiatric social workers and counseling psychologists. Although court officials are not directly concerned with diagnosis, they are charged with the task of interpreting and enforcing laws pertaining to criminal responsibility, compulsory hospitalization when it is in the public interest, and the safeguarding of the person and property of the mentally incompetent.

Relatives, friends, and professional experts may differ in the relative emphasis placed on various criteria. Certain criteria may be more heavily weighted in some cultures than in others. In general, however, there appears to be substantial agreement within and between cultures with respect to two main points. Behavior is evaluated as pathological (1) if psychosocial functioning is so impaired and disordered that the individual is unable to cope with the ordinary problems of human life and (2) if aggressive impulses are uncontrolled and uncontrollable.

In extreme instances, behavior disorder may be so marked that the individual is incapable of caring for himself or of maintaining even minimal contact with his social environment. Milder degrees of impairment may be characterized by undue dependency, ineffectualness, substandard productivity, and social inadequacy. In interpreting these deficiencies, the critical factor is the relative *inability* of the individual to care for himself because of involuntary psychosocial defects. Deliberate substandard performance and behavior disorders due to physical disease, drugs, or age are excluded.

Uncontrolled aggression is not tolerated in any society, since unprovoked and unpredictable attack reactions endanger the welfare and safety of the group. To a lesser degree, society is also intolerant of persons whose erratic and impulsive behavior is a source of undue annoyance or apprehension.

To these two basic criteria may be added a third that has special significance for the family group. This has to do with the acute emotional distress exhibited by most patients. Other members of the family may deny or overlook disordered functioning in a loved one, but their compassion for the all too apparent suffering of the bewildered, tormented, depressed, or suicidal person may convince them that he is mentally ill and in urgent need of treatment. Therapists also attach considerable significance to the severity of the inner distress of the individual in their evaluation of abnormal behavior.

At the family and community level, there is often a reluctance to interpret deviant behavior as evidence of mental disorder. A person who by professional psychiatric standards would be classified as mentally disturbed may be described by his peer group as "strange," "odd," "high-strung," or "different." Unless he engages in some drastic actions, the unequivocal decision that he is in fact mentally ill may be evaded for months or even years. Mild deviations are often discounted by associates on the grounds that "everyone has some peculiarities" or "there are all kinds of people in the world" (Cummings and Cummings, 1957). Sporadic disturbances in functioning and mood changes may be attributed to the fact that the person was upset, tired, or not feeling well. Consistent with the concept of residual deviance, serious or persistent maladaptive reactions may be explained as due to poor health, overwork, loss of sleep, drinking, or a change of life (Yarrow et al., 1955). Whenever possible, an attempt is made to account for disorganized behavior as a natural, normal reaction to a specific situation or traumatic experience. Only as a last resort is the label of mental disorder applied to disorganized, uncontrolled, inexplicable behavior that is perceived by the peer group as irrational and inappropriate.

In evaluating normal behavior, there is essential agreement by family, community, and specialist that to satisfy minimum requirements of mental health the individual should be about as able as other members of his peer group to take care of himself, to cope with everyday problems, and to get along with his social group. If the individual is an asset to his community, a comfort and joy to his family, and a social benefactor, so much the better.

THE PERSONAL DISTRESS FACTOR

A final indispensable criterion for evaluating the relative normality of behavior is the subjective feeling of the individual. Particularly in mild disorders, when no obvious psychological deficits are discernible and social adjustment is adequate, inner torment may be the main indicator of psychopathology. The anguish of the mentally disturbed is often a blend of anxiety, dread, guilt, dejection, rage, and hate. The ind'vidual may be bewildered, seething with resentment, or full of self-pity. The net effect is that he is miserably and hopelessly unhappy—so much so that relief may be sought in death. Emotional distress and unhappiness are, of course, also noted in normal individuals. What distinguishes the mentally disturbed person is the seeming inappropriateness of his anguish. Relatives, friends, and even the person himself are unable to offer any reasonable explanation to account for the presence, duration, or severity of the emotional disturbance. The normal person who has good cause to be frightened, worried, depressed or angry may be no less disturbed and unhappy; but the appropriateness of his reaction, which usually gains him the understanding, sympathy, and support of associates, somehow makes his distress more bearable.

The mental patient's emotional reaction is incongruous because, like everyone else, he adjusts his behavior to fit his personal standards, but his standards differ in degree or in kind from the standards of society. Because of their subjective and egocentric basis, his self-expectations may be unreasonable for one of his capabilities or life situation, or his standards may have been acquired at so early an age that in his adult years he is hardly aware of what they are. Behavior may conform to personally acceptable adult standards but violate "forgotten" or "rejected" childhood values. A simple example of discrepancy between social and personal standards is the student with high academic aspirations who is unhappy and plagued with feelings of inferiority whenever he receives a B grade. His roommate may be delighted with C grades but regard himself as a total failure if he is not elected president of the class. Unrealistic moral values acquired during childhood may result in acute guilt feelings for transgressions that society overlooks or forgives, and which the individual may intellectually realize are trivial or long past. His nervous system is less accommodating, however; it neither forgets nor forgives. The imbalance between behavior and self-concept in persons with mental disorders has been confirmed in several experimental studies (Wylie, 1961), in which it has been noted that neurotics report a greater discrepancy than normal individuals between their actual selves and their ideal selves. These findings have suggested the possibility that a narrowing of the gap between the patient's descriptions of his actual self and his ideal self may be a good indication of the effectiveness of therapy: the smaller the discrepancy following therapy, the greater the improvement (Rogers, 1951).

Criteria in Summary

As is apparent from our discussion of specific criteria, the normality-abnormality concept is closely associated with basic human values. This relationship has been explored in a series of articles compiled by Nunokawa (1965). With the universality of psychopathology in mind, I have focused on those criteria that reflect more or less universally accepted human values. Thus it is reasonable to assume that all societies prefer their members to be capable of self-control rather than uncontrolled, to be psychologically competent rather than incompetent, to be rational rather than irrational, to be assets rather than liabilities or threats to the community, and to be contented rather than miserably unhappy. With respect to the psychopathological implications of these values, three modifying factors must be considered. The first is related to the familiar concept of residual deviance. As a rule, deviation from accepted cultural standards is not regarded as a sign of psychopathology if some other explanation can be made for it: physical illness, a natural reaction following a traumatic experience, intoxication, fatigue, sinfulness, criminality, bad temper, stupidity. Secondly, an allowance has to be made for minor local variations in the spelling out of common values. Societies may agree in principle that behavior is abnormal if it constitutes an intolerable threat to the well-being of the group but differ somewhat in evaluating the kinds of behavior that are regarded as threats and in specifying what represents an intolerable threat. Similarly, standards of adequate psychosocial functioning may be higher in one society than in another. The third factor is the relativity of abnormality and normality. If we generalize from the pattern of individual differences usually observed in regard to more readily measured physical traits among the general population, we may reasonably infer that if accurate objective scales were available for measuring the five criterion variables we have discussed, the distribution of scores for a large randomly selected sample of the population would be continuous and would conform to the familiar bell-shaped curve. As Figure 3.1 indicates, a relatively small proportion of the total population would have composite scores that would place them at either the extreme left (pathological) or at the extreme right (ideal-normal) end of the distribution curve. The great majority of the population, with scores in the middle ranges of the distribution, might be described as "average-normal." The unbroken continuity of scores has a direct bearing on the meaningfulness of estimates regarding the prevalence of mental disorders. Depending on the arbitrarily selected cutoff point that differentiates psychopathological from average-normal behavior, the proportion of the total population classified as mentally disturbed may range from less than 1 percent to 25 percent. The use of different procedures and standards in establishing cutoff points provides the simplest explanation for the wide discrepancies reported in field studies on the relative prevalence of psychological disorders in various communities and countries (Dohrenwend and Dohrenwend, 1965).

Subject to these modifying factors, behavior may be defined as abnormal to the extent that it is not subject to voluntary control, is characterized by inadequate, inappropriate, and maladaptive psychosocial functioning, and is evaluated by the individual and/or his society as an undue liability or a source of intolerable distress or threat. Conversely, behavior may be defined as normal (average through ideal) to the degree that it is subject to voluntary control, represents the optimal development and expression of higher order psychosocial functions, and is considered to contribute to the satisfaction and enhancement of the individual and the society to which he belongs.

Motivation Pattern and Psychopathology

Although it is not directly concerned with criteria for differentiating normal from abnormal behavior, a significant difference between normal and abnormal persons is their approach to life. By and large, normal individuals have a positive orientation. Even if they have not been too successful up to the present time, they retain hope for the future. Frustrations and conflicts are regarded as problems to be resolved and challenges to be met. Normal individuals are task-oriented. They strive toward achievement, rewards, and happiness. The motivational pattern of the disturbed person, on the other hand, is often essentially negative. His main concern is to defend and protect himself against possible failure, anxiety, guilt, and rejection. Frustrations and conflicts are perceived as crises, leading to despair, resignation, and further defensive measures. Basic needs for achievement and recognition are expressed in unrealistic, grandiose goals. These may serve as compensations for low self-esteem, but the disturbed person makes no real or sustained effort to translate his ambitions into achievements. Constantly preoccupied with protecting himself from possible failures and disappointments, he faces a gloomy, unrewarding future.

Psychopathology and Cultural Relativism

Wide individual variations in personality and behavior characterize the members of all societies. The culturalization process, however, may accentuate or inhibit the overt manifestation of certain latent human potentialities and thereby impart a somewhat distinctive quality to the behavior of the group. Differences in cultural indoctrination account for tribal and national characteristics and for the "strange" ways of foreigners. An interesting contribution of anthropological research has been the observation that in primitive and relatively isolated societies the socialization process occasionally encourages the development and casual acceptance of behavior patterns that resemble reactions considered symptomatic of mental disorder in other societies. This observation was for a time erroneously interpreted as supporting the doctrine of *cultural relativism;* that is, the idea that behavior regarded as pathological in one society may be normal in another. Although the writings of Ruth Benedict (1934) are frequently quoted as the principal source of evidence supporting the concept of cultural relativism, it should be noted that Dr. Benedict repudiated this interpretation of her data in a private communication to Wegrocki (1939). Far from wishing to prove the cultural relativism of psychopathology, she was actually seeking to demonstrate how cultural influences selectively promote or inhibit the development and overt expression of latent human potentialities. Through describing personally adjusted primitive people who exhibited behavior patterns that superficially resembled what would be considered mental symptoms in our society, she wanted to show that "interculturally adequate functioning and fixed symptoms could not be equated." It is now generally recognized that the concept of relativism was based on the illogical premise that if A resembles B, then A must be the same as B. There is a world of difference between the disordered, inappropriate, and detrimental reactions of mentally disturbed persons in this country and the seemingly similar but adequately controlled and socially approved reactions noted in some primitive societies. The senseless mutilation of victims by a demented person in our culture cannot be equated with the headhunting or scalping practices of primitive societies. The taking of a head or scalp in cultures that formerly sanctioned such activities was incidental to the basic objective, which in most instances was to kill a recognized enemy of one's tribe who would have done the same thing if he could. The anatomical souvenir was both proof and a memento of the warrior's skill and bravery in combat, a gory equivalent of the souvenirs of battle brought home by soldiers everywhere. A headhunter in New Guinea who started collecting the heads of members of his own village (an act that would be comparable to homicidal behavior in our society) would be promptly executed by his fellow tribesmen as irresponsible and dangerous.

An American housewife who believed that any neighbor who entered her kitchen did so for the sole purpose of poisoning her food would qualify as a pathologically suspicious person; but a Dobuan housewife who thought the same thing would be considered prudent and normal, and for a good reason. From infancy the Dobuans are taught to believe that anyone who has not shared the milk of the same mother is a potential enemy and, given a chance, will do them harm (Fortune, 1932). This is not a delusion; it is a fact of Dobuan life that must be faced. Neighbors and even husbands and wives do try their hand at casting spells and practicing black magic on one another. To be unaware of or to ignore this reality would suggest some impairment in perception and judgment. But even here the rule of appropriateness holds. A Dobuan may covet his neighbor's yams, but the only "normal" way he may get them is to use black magic on them, so that they will tunnel their way underground and pop up in his garden.

The trance states of a shaman or medicine man in a primitive society may superficially resemble the trance states of mentally disordered persons in our society, but there is the important difference of voluntary control. The trance state of the disturbed person is involuntary and independent of self-control. The trance state of the shaman, like the trance state of a spiritualistic medium in our society, is part of his professional act. The shaman decides when he will go into a trance and when he will come out of it. A hysterical type of personality may be a prerequisite for going into a genuine trance state, but the ability to do so on demand and only on appropriate occasions is indicative of normal functioning. The shaman's purpose in going into a trance is to communicate with the spirit world. Fraud would be suspected if he didn't make a convincing show of sending his spirit out of his body. No words of wisdom or guidance are expected from the deranged person. The shaman, if he wishes to keep his job and prestige, is expected to bring back messages that will satisfy his clients, whose requests are usually concerned with the prediction of future events and the curing of illness. To do this with seemingly reasonable efficacy, the shaman must have his wits about him. Far from being out of touch with his environment, confused and dazed—as is true of the distrubed person subject to trance states—the shaman must be astute, alert, and a step or two ahead of his clients. From her analysis of field studies of shamanism among the Alaskan Eskimos on St. Lawrence Island, Murphy (1964, p. 77) concluded:

> For a shaman to become a successful healer he had often to display an exceptional ability in emotional control and in taking responsibility. Despite the frenzy reached in a seance and the seizures of possession, the performance as a whole is a highly styled drama, the impact of which is largely related to its control by the key director—the shaman. In addition, the full-fledged shaman who is capable of dealing with the crises of illness and death and of offering psychological support to groups of individuals taken into his spiritual custody displays qualities that can hardly be separated from those of leadership, responsibility, and power.

The necessity of evaluating the nature and consequences of an act before passing judgment on its psychiatric significance is well illustrated by the former potlatch custom of the Kwakiutl Indians on Vancouver Island. According to Benedict, the behavior of the host at these affairs, if accepted at face value, would resemble the ravings of megalomaniac paranoid persons in our society. Actually, the potlatch was an institution that conformed to all the listed criteria of normality. In brief, the potlatch consisted of a meeting of chiefs of neighboring tribes. On these occasions the host made grandiose claims for his tribe, insulted his invited guests, and tried his best to humiliate them by giving away and destroying blankets, canoes, oil, incised copper tablets, and other valuable objects. The guests' honor required them to reciprocate even more lavishly later. On the surface, the boasting, the insulting behavior, and the destruction of property might appear pathological; but it was all a planned, prearranged show in which each participant acted out his role according to recognized rules. The designated role of the host was to build up the prestige of his tribe by belittling rivals through the conspicuous destruction of wealth. The prescribed role of the guests was to suffer through the ordeal in silence and await their turn to play the part of the bragging, insulting, property-destroying host. The boasts and taunts were limited to previously agreed-upon areas and were conventional and stereotyped. Whatever detriment there was in the way of hurt feelings and destruction of property was more than compensated for by the fact that the potlatch was the Kwakiutls' substitute for war (Codere, 1950). Verbal insults took the place of arrows, and goods were destroyed instead of human beings. The tribe whose chief disposed of the greatest amount of property was the winner. But this would have been a Pyrrhic victory if the winner were impoverished. To avoid this calamity, which would have had psychopathological overtones, the chief was permitted to give away and destroy only property the tribe had collected over a period of many months and put aside for this specific purpose. In other words, an expendable portion of the wealth of the tribe was budgeted for a spectacular advertising program designed to gain prestige. In many respects, the potlatch was similar to the war of words that is being fought today in the United Nations and reinforced by the competition among rival nations to see which can launch the biggest and most expensive satellites. (The dangers were also similar, for in spite of the rules, it was not unknown for a chief to bankrupt himself, with consequences that can only be described as dire.)

The normality of the potlatch is further illustrated by the rules that governed similar activities within the tribe. A commoner who wished to gain or maintain prestige could call in his friends and neighbors and build up his ego by a great show of giving away his belongings. However, the friends were honor-bound to repay the host by returning twice as much as they had received from him within a year or suffer loss of face. Meanwhile, someone else was likely to make him the not entirely willing recipient of similar gifts, which he in turn was required to return with 100 percent interest. The situation could become very complicated and very expensive, but if a man could manage to exercise sufficient control over the gift-giving, he could achieve enormous prestige. Somewhat analogous practices of self-aggrandizement through conspicuous consumption and conspicuous waste in our society have been described by Veblen (1934). "Keeping ahead of the Joneses" is a more subtle variant of the potlatch.

How a person classified as deranged in one society would fare in another depends on many things. One important factor is the relative tolerance of the second culture toward the particular form of disorder. It is quite possible that some cultures would be more accepting of the behavior than others, but no culture would regard the person as normal. The essence of psychopathology, as Linton noted (1956), lies in the person's inability to function adequately and appropriately in the context of reality as reality is defined and understood by his society. Since the ways in which reality can be defined are limited, this defect would accompany the patient and be apparent anywhere. A paranoid person who went to a primitive society where suspiciousness was an accepted trait would be quickly spotted as "peculiar" because he would be suspicious about the wrong things at the wrong times in the wrong way. In other words, he would be unable to follow the ancient rule, "When in Rome, do as the Romans do."

In discussing the attitudes of primitive peoples toward the mentally disturbed, Linton acknowledges that disturbed persons are sometimes regarded with awe and treated well. But the relatively favorable status of the psychotic is due more to fear than to anything else. The superstitious belief that the psychotic is possessed by evil spirits tends to make primitive people wary of incurring the hostility and wrath of these spirits. There is no society where the genuine psychotic is liked, admired, or given high social status. In order to gain prestige and acquire power, a leader must be capable of appraising situations in realistic terms and of exploiting situations to his advantage. This is an ability the psychotic does not have. When the patient is violent, so that the nuisance of caring for him is greater than the fear of evil spirits, it is not uncommon for primitive societies to kill him and seek comfort in the rationalization that his "soul" had already gone away, and it was only the body that was making trouble.

Legal Criteria of Mental Disorders, Insanity, and Incompetence

Legal standards of abnormal behavior are influenced by but independent of other criteria. The law is specifically concerned with establishing rules and procedures for (1) the hospitalization of the mentally deranged, (2) the determination of insanity in criminal cases, and (3) defining and determining mental incompetence.

VOLUNTARY AND INVOLUNTARY HOSPITALIZATION

The law distinguishes between involuntary and voluntary admission to mental hospitals. In the United States, each state has its own statutory criteria for hospital admission. Most other countries have national regulations. Involuntary hospitalization, which deprives the patient of his freedom against his will, is based on the police power of government to take any action that it considers necessary to safeguard the public welfare. Most of the older statutes specifically limited the state's power to the commitment to hospitals of persons who were dangerous to themselves or others. More recent legislation permits the involuntary hospitalization of anyone who needs care or treatment but lacks sufficient capacity to make a responsible decision. Thus a person may be hospitalized without his consent to prevent harm to other persons or to property, to relieve his family of responsibility for his care, and to provide asylum for social misfits. Involuntary hospitalization has two main objectives: to protect the individual and society and to provide treatment. Since compulsorily committed patients are deprived of their freedom, the courts and legislatures in the United States have recently become sensitive to issues concerned with the civil liberties of the mentally ill. Some important decisions have recently been handed down by courts. In the case of *Lake* v. *Cameron*, a federal circuit court ruled that before an indigent person can involuntarily be committed to a mental hospital, the state must explore alternatives less drastic than full-time hospitalization. In the case of *Rouse* v. *Cameron*, the court ruled that a mental patient must either be given adequate treatment or be released. In 1969 California adopted the Canterman-Petris-Short Act, which distinguishes three classes of persons who may be involuntarily hospitalized: those who are gravely disordered and whose care can be entrusted to a conservator, those who are imminently suicidal, and those who are imminently dangerous to others. The imminently suicidal person can be confined for two successive fourteen-day periods. At the end of that time, he must be released even if he is still suicidal. A person considered imminently dangerous by virtue of the fact that he has actually inflicted physical harm on another can be confined against his will, after a hearing, for ninety days. If during the initial ninety-day confinement he has threatened, attempted to harm, or actually inflicted physical harm on another, he may be confined for an additional ninety days. The actual procedure for involuntary hospitalization varies from state to state and from country to country. In most instances, the first step is taken by some member of the family, who arranges for a psychiatric examination of the patient. If the physician's examination indicates sufficient grounds for hospitalization, a formal application is filed with the proper authorities. The next steps are likely to include the serving of the patient with a legal notice, a prehearing examination, and court commitment. Most states make provision for trial by jury to determine cause for hospitalization, but this procedure is usually waived in uncontested civil cases. Involuntary hospitalization is usually for an indeterminate period. The time of the patient's release is usually left to the discretion of hospital authorities. All states recognize the right of the patient to correspond with attorneys and pertinent public officials and to seek a writ of habeas corpus as a means of securing his discharge.

Alternatively, patients may apply directly for hospital treatment. The procedures are essentially similar to those for admission to a general hospital for a physical disorder. In many European countries over 70 percent of hospitalized patients have sought admission voluntarily. The major advantage of voluntary admission is that the patient may secure his release on short notice by written application. If the voluntarily admitted patient poses a definite threat to himself or others, however, the hospital may arrange for his involuntary detention.

INSANITY

Insanity is a legal concept that has no medical or psychological counterpart. Strictly defined, the term "insanity" refers only to such gross mental impairment that a person cannot distinguish right from wrong, and therefore cannot be held responsible for his acts. The concept of insanity has been introduced into law to cover exceptions to the basic rationale of criminal law, which assumes that all adult persons are capable of free and rational choice. It follows that if a person willfully engages in illegal offenses with criminal intent, he is responsible for his actions and liable to punishment. The law further assumes that punishment is warranted as a means of deterring the individual and others from committing crimes. The applicability of these legal premises to the mentally deranged has long been questioned. For many centuries madness was regarded as an extenuating factor in criminal cases. It was not until 1843, however, that a definite set of criteria for evaluating insanity, known as the M'Naghten rules, was established. These rules and other "tests" of insanity are summarized in Supplementary Report 2. The determination of insanity is a judicial function. Psychiatrists and psychologists may be called as expert witnesses to state their opinions regarding the mental status of the defendant, but the decision rests with the court. When a defendant is adjudged criminally irresponsible on the grounds of insanity, he may be committed to a mental hospital, referred for treatment, or discharged; he is not imprisoned. The mitigating features of insanity are applicable only in those cases to which the criteria apply. The fact that a criminal is clearly suffering from a mental illness does not exonerate him from criminal responsibility. With respect to the M'Naghten rules, for example, a mentally ill person is considered legally responsible if at the time of committing a crime he knew the nature and the quality of his offense and knew that what he was doing was wrong. The position of the law in such cases is that the presence of a mental disorder that began after the commission of the crime is irrelevant. The purpose of the M'Naghten rules is to exclude from criminal culpability only those people who, because of mental illness, are incapable of distinguishing right from wrong.

MENTAL INCOMPETENCE

The legal concept of incompetence comes under civil law. Here the problem is not to determine criminal responsibility, but simply to protect the person and property of the mentally incompetent and at the same time safeguard the interests of his relatives and society. Incompetence is not dependent on the presence or absence of a mental disorder or hospitalization. A person requiring hospitalization for a mental disorder can still be considered legally competent to handle his affairs. Conversely, a person adjudged incompetent by a court may or may not be diagnosed as suffering from some mental disorder. The legal criterion of incompetence is directly concerned with the individual's inability to manage his person and property with ordinary prudence. The inability may be due to mental or physical disability, senility, or spendthrift tendencies. A person adjudged incompetent is deprived of his civil rights and has a legal status comparable to that of a minor. In the case of mental patients, incompetence proceedings may be merged with hospitalization or treated separately. As a rule, incompetence proceedings are initiated by a relative or friend, who files a petition with the appropriate court. This is followed by a court hearing. Several states provide for a jury trial. If the court finds the defendant incompetent, a guardian is usually appointed to look after him and his property. Contracts and public transactions entered into by a person adjudged incompetent are invalid. Incompetence is often a critical feature of litigation over the validity of wills.

Psychopathology and Criminal Behavior

Strictly defined, a crime consists of the violation, by an act of commission or omission, and with criminal intent, of recognized laws of society for which punishment is prescribed by law. This restriction automatically excludes all manifestations of psychopathology that do not involve specified legal offenses. The total crime rate for mentally deranged persons is no higher than that for the general population (Rappeport and Lassen, 1965, 1966). When the deranged do commit criminal acts, a distinction is made between culpable offenses and crimes for which the individual is not held criminally responsible by reason of insanity.

The criteria established for defining abnormal behavior provide a convenient set of guidelines for differentiating criminal behavior from antisocial forms of psychopathology. A person is considered criminal rather than insane if he commits an offense punishable by law and shows no significant impairment in higher order psychological functioning or in his ability to exercise voluntary control over his actions. Society usually considers such behavior criminal if the evidence suggests that the offender was in possession of his mental faculties and willfully engaged in some antisocial act for personal gain. As might be expected, it is sometimes difficult to make a clear distinction between criminal and psychopathological behavior. There is often an element of doubt in cases involving impulsive antisocial acts, "purposeless" crimes, and crimes that are so clumsily performed as to invite apprehension. The boundary lines are particularly hazy when offenses represent violations of the moral rather than the legal code. These doubtful cases, along with other ill-defined antisocial acts, are included under the heading of *sociopathy*. This is admittedly a category of expediency, but it has the merit of recognizing and identifying borderline reactions.

Summary

No act, feeling, or thought is, of itself, normal or abnormal. Behavior that deviates from the usual, the expected, or the conventional may be abnormal, superior, or qualitatively equivalent to the norm. Before a meaningful decision can be made as to the relative normality or abnormality of a specific trait or reaction, it is essential to consider the appropriateness of the behavior, to assess the degree of impairment in functioning, and to evaluate the effect or consequences of the behavior on the individual and his society. To take account of infinite variations in appropriateness, effectiveness, and value, we may regard extreme abnormal and "ideal" normal behavior as opposite ends of multiple continua. In most instances, specific behavior would be rated in the middle ranges and designated "average normal." The five criteria selected for differentiating abnormal from normal behavior have to do with (1) the relative proficiency of higher order psychological functioning, (2) the relative appropriateness of social behavior, (3) the degree of voluntary control, (4) the degree to which the behavior is perceived and evaluated by society as desirable and beneficial or as unacceptable and detrimental, and (5) the degree to which the behavior is perceived by the individual as satisfying or distressing. Each criterion is considered a separate continuum. The decision as to the relative normality or abnormality of behavior depends on a composite evaluation. In principle, the proposed criteria are applicable in all societies. Some cultures may be more tolerant than others of specific forms of deviant behavior, but no society would regard as normal a person whose behavior was so impaired, disordered, and uncontrolled that he constituted a liability, a threat, or a source of undue distress to himself and/or his social group. Since there are no fixed or absolute mental symptoms, no psychiatric significance should be attached to the observation that certain patterns associated with mental disorders in one culture are casually accepted in another. On the surface, the insulting of guests and the destruction of property at the potlatch of the Kwakiutls may seem aberrant, but the fact that the potlatch serves as a substitute for war establishes the normality of the behavior.

Criminal behavior is any act for which punishment is prescribed by law and which is committed with criminal intent. Since most forms of abnormal behavior do not involve legal violations, a clear distinction can usually be made between psychopathological and criminal behavior. In doubtful cases, the criteria described for differentiating normal from abnormal behavior are also helpful in differentiating abnormal from criminal behavior. Unless there is evidence of some significant impairment in self-control or higher order mental functioning, the commission of an illegal offense is considered a criminal act. The legal concept of insanity is focused on the issue of criminal responsibility. However, the proposed rules of insanity are quite similar to the criteria described for defining abnormal behavior. For example, the M'Naghten rules are mainly concerned with impairment in higher order psychological functions. The key point is whether the defendant was aware of the nature and quality of his act and could distinguish right from wrong at the time of committing the crime. The "irresistible impulse," New Hampshire, and Durham rules all imply a loss of voluntary control.

Supplementary Report 2. Legal Tests of Insanity

M'Naghten rules. The M'Naghten rules were formulated in England following the trial and acquittal of Daniel M'Naghten in 1843 on a charge of murder. M'Naghten, who believed that he was being persecuted by the Tory party, had intended to kill the prime minister, Sir Robert Pell. In error he shot and killed the prime minister's private secretary. He was found not guilty on grounds of insanity. Stimulated by interest in this case, the House of Lords asked the judges of England a series of questions related to the law of insanity and crime. Their answers to two of these questions, which were specifically concerned with what jurors should be told when insanity is offered as a defense by a person charged with the commission of a crime, have come to be known as the M'Naghten rules (Whitlock, 1963, p. 20). In part the judges stated:

> Jurors ought to be told in all cases that every man is to be presumed to be sane, and to possess a sufficient degree of reason to be responsible for his crimes, until the contrary be proven to their satisfaction; and that to establish a defense on the ground of insanity, it must be clearly proved that, at the time of committing the act, the party accused was labouring under such a defect of reason, from disease of the mind, as not to know the nature and quality of the act he was doing or, if he did know it, that he did not know he was doing what was wrong.

Alone or in combination with other tests of criminal responsibility, the M'Naghten rules are applied in most states in this country. In essence the critical issue is whether the defendant had the capacity to know right from wrong with respect to the specific act with which he is charged. The principal limitation is that the rules pertain only to impairment of cognitive or intellectual functions, whereas insanity affects the will, the emotions, and the whole personality of the patient. Because of a mental disease a person may commit a crime even though he knows the act is wrong and forbidden by law. The law's answer to this objection is that the purpose of the rules is not to exclude all mentally disabled persons from criminal culpability, but only those who are incapable of making rational choices, for whom punishment would serve no useful purpose. Other criticisms and sources of controversy involve the ambiguity of such terms as "wrong" and "know." Do the rules apply to moral or legal wrongs, or both? Should knowledge of the nature and quality of one's act be limited to intellectual awareness, or should it include what clinicians refer to as emotional insight?

Irresistible impulse test. The purpose of the irresistible impulse test is to exclude from criminal responsibilty persons who know the difference between right and wrong but who are driven to commit a criminal act by an irresistible impulse resulting from a mental condition. An obvious difficulty is the problem of distinguishing between irresistible and unresisted impulses. A second source of possible disagreement is the status of impulsive criminal acts committed during moments of rage, jealousy, or some other overriding passion. The irresistible impulse criterion has the advantage of acknowledging the impaired self-control of the mental patient. When used in conjunction with the M'Naghten rules, it allows for defects in volitional as well as cognitive abilities. The irresistible impulse test has been accepted in about fifteen states, but it is nowhere relied on as the sole criterion. Where it is accepted, it is always used in combination with the M'Naghten rules or some other criterion of criminal responsibility.

New Hampshire and Durham test. As early as 1871 the New Hampshire Supreme Court rejected the M'Naghten rules and offered a new rule: that a defendant is not guilty if the crime of which he is accused is the product or result of a mental disease. Eighty-three years later the "product rule" of New Hampshire was accepted with minor modifications by the United States Court of Appeals for the District of Columbia. In the case of *Durham* v. *United States* the court held that "an accused is not criminally responsible if his unlawful act was the product of mental disease or mental defect." A later amplification of the ruling includes a statement to the effect that an act is the product of a disease if it would not have occurred except for the disease or defect. From the point of view of the psychiatrist or clinical psychologist, the advantage of the Durham rule is that it permits him to report his findings in his own language rather than in the cramped expressions of legal terminology (Watson, 1959). Specifically, the psychiatrist is asked to supply psychiatric data and his opinions on three questions: (1) Has the defendant a mental illness? (2) Is the alleged criminal act a product of the mental illness? (3) How did the mental illness cause the defendant to commit the alleged crime? Questions of guilt and of the actual presence of a mental disease or defect are for the judge and jury to decide. Critics of the Durham test have commented on the ambiguity of the key terms "mental disease" and "product." The former is a relative and changing concept. It is more reasonable to consider the commission of a crime as an integral component than as an isolated product of a mental disorder. Roche (1958) has suggested that the "product" question is a legal rather than a psychiatric issue, and should be answered by the jury.

The model penal code. As enacted in Vermont, this test (Lindman and McIntyre, 1961, p. 334) provides that "a person is not responsible for criminal conduct if at the time of such conduct as a result of mental illness or defect he lacks adequate capacity either to appreciate the criminality of his conduct or to conform to the requirements of the law." In principle, the code, which has been accepted only in Vermont, combines the M'Naghten and irresistible impulse tests, but the insertion of the key word "adequate" allows for degrees of impairment of cognitive and volitional capacity. A second provision of the code, which has not been cited, is designed to exclude as a qualifying mental disease the antisocial conduct of sociopaths.

References

ADLER, A. *Social Interest*. New York: Putnam, 1939.

BENEDICT, R. *Patterns of Culture*. Boston: Houghton Mifflin, 1934.

BLEULER, E. *Dementia Praecox or the Group of Schizophrenics*. New York: International University Press, 1950.

CAROTHERS, J. C. *The African Mind in Health and Disease,* monograph 17. Geneva: World Health Organization, 1953.

CODERE, H. *Fighting with Property,* American Ethnological Society monograph 18. New York: J. J. Augustin, 1950.

CRUTCHFIELD, R. S. "Conformity and Character." *American Psychologist* 10 (1955): 191–98.

CUMMINGS, E., and CUMMINGS, J. *Closed Ranks: An Experiment in Mental Health Education*. Cambridge: Harvard University Press, 1957.

DOHRENWEND, B. P., and DOHRENWEND, B. S. "The Problem of Validity in Field Studies of Psychological Disorder." *Journal of Abnormal Psychology* 70 (1965): 52–69.

FORTUNE, R. F. *Sorcerers of Dobu*. New York: Sutton, 1932.

FREUD, S. *An Outline of Psychoanalysis*. New York: Norton, 1949.

HORNEY, K. *Our Inner Conflicts*. New York: Norton, 1945.

JAHODA, M. *Current Concepts of Positive Mental Health*. New York: Basic Books, 1958.

JANET, P. *The Major Symptoms of Hysteria*. New York: Macmillan, 1943.

JANIS, I. L. *Contours of Fear: Psychological Studies of War, Disaster, Illness, and Experimentally Induced Stress*. New York: Wiley, 1966.

KUBIE, L. S. "Neurotic Process as a Focus of Physiological and Psychoanalytic Research." *Journal of Mental Science* 104 (1958): 518–34.

LAMBO, T. A. "The Role of Cultural Factors in Paranoid Psychosis Among Yomeba Tribe." *Journal of Mental Science* 101 (1955): 239–66.

LANG, P. J., and Buss, A. H. "Psychological Deficit in Schizophrenia: 11. Interference and Activation." *Journal of Abnormal Psychology* 10 (1965): 77–106.

LEIGHTON, A. H.; CLAUSSEN, J. A.; and WILSON, R. N. "Some Issues Reexamined." In *Explorations in Social Psychiatry*, ed. A. H. Leighton et al., p. 104. New York: Basic Books, 1957.

LINDMAN, F. T., and MCINTYRE, D. M., JR. "The Mentally Disabled and the Law." *Reports of the American Bar Foundation on the Rights of the Mentally Ill*. Chicago: University of Chicago Press, 1961.

LINTON, R. *Culture and Mental Disorders*. Springfield, Ill.: Charles C. Thomas, 1956.

MARTIN, R. F., and HALL, C. S. "Emotional Behavior in the Rat. V. The Incidence of Behavior Derangements Resulting from Air-Blast Stimulation in Emotional and Non-Emotional Strains of Rats." *Journal of Comparative Psychology* 32 (1941): 191–204.

MURPHY, J. M. "Social Change and Mental Health." In *Causes of Mental Disorder: A Review of Epidemiological Knowledge*, pp. 280–340. New York: Milbank Memorial Fund, 1959.

———. "Cross-Cultural Studies in the Prevalence of Psychiatric Disorders." *World Mental Health* 14 (1962):53–65.

———. "Psychotherapeutic Aspects of Shamanism on St. Lawrence Island, Alaska." In *Magic, Faith, and Healing*, ed. A. Kiev, pp. 53–83. New York: Free Press, Macmillan, 1964.

NUNOKAWA, W. D. *Human Values and Abnormal Behavior*. Chicago: Scott, Foresman, 1965.

RAPPEPORT, J. R., and LASSEN, G. "Dangerousness: Arrest Rate Comparisons of Discharged Patients and the General Population." *American Journal of Psychiatry* 121 (1965): 776–83.

——— and ———. "The Dangerousness of Female Patients: A Comparison of the Discharge Rate of Discharged Psychiatric Patients and the General Population." *American Journal of Psychiatry* 123 (1966): 413–19.

ROCHE, P. Q. *The Criminal Mind*. New York: Farrar, Straus & Cudahy, 1958.

ROGERS, C. R. *Client-Centered Therapy*. Boston: Houghton Mifflin, 1951.

RUESCH, J., and BATESON, G. *Communication: The Social Matrix of Psychiatry*. New York: Norton, 1951.

SCHEFF, T. J. "A Sociological Theory of Mental Disorders." In *Approaches to Psychopathology*, ed. J. Page. New York: Columbia University Press, 1966.

SHOBEN, E. J. "Toward a Concept of the Normal Personality." *American Psychologist* 12 (1957): 183–89.

TOOTH, G. C. *Studies in Mental Illness in the Gold Coast*. London: Her Majesty's Stationery Office, 1950.

VEBLEN, T. *The Theory of the Leisure Class*. New York: Modern Library, 1934.

WALKER, E. L., and HEYNS, R. W. *An Anatomy for Conformity*. Englewood Cliffs, N. J.: Prentice-Hall, 1962.

WATSON, A. S. "Durham Plus Five Years: Development of the Law of Criminal Responsibility in the District of Columbia." *American Journal of Psychiatry* 116 (1959): 289–97.

WEGROCKI, H. J. "A Critique of Cultural and Statistical Concepts of Abnormality." *Journal of Abnormal and Social Psychology* 34 (1939): 166–78.

WHITLOCK, F. A. *Criminal Responsibility and Mental Illness.* London: Butterworth, 1963.

WILMER, H. A. *Social Psychiatry in Action: A Therapeutic Community.* Springfield, Ill.: Charles C. Thomas, 1958.

WYLIE, R. C. *The Self Concept.* Lincoln: University of Nebraska Press, 1961.

YAP, P. M. "Mental Diseases Peculiar to Certain Cultures: A Survey of Comparative Psychiatry." *Journal of Mental Science* 97 (1951): 313–27.

YARROW, M. R.; SCHWARTZ, C. G.; MURPHY, H. S.; and DEASY, L. C. "The Psychological Meaning of Mental Illness in the Family." *Journal of Social Issues* 11 (1955): 12–24.

CHAPTER FOUR

Abnormal Behavior in
Historical Perspective

From prehistoric times large and small groups of people living together as social units have been confronted with the omnipresent problem of what to do with deviant members whose disorganized, relatively uncontrolled behavior constitutes an undue liability, a threat, or a source of intolerable distress to the rest. The words used to describe these troubled and troublesome individuals, the interpretations proposed to explain their strange behavior, and the actions taken in behalf of or against these social misfits make a fascinating chapter in man's endless struggle against superstitious beliefs and inhumane practices. The usual zigzag pattern of human progress is clearly evident in the history of psychopathology. Periods of advance have been followed by periods of stagnation and regression. Time and again similar concepts have emerged, faded, and been rediscovered. Some of the recurring ideas are best dismissed as repeated errors. Others represent significant, enduring insights into behavior pathology.

Abnormal Behavior in Primitive and Ancient Societies

SPIRIT POSSESSION

The invention of a spirit world provided prehistoric, primitive, and non-literate man with a simple explanation for all unusual or perplexing phenomena. Realizing his relative powerlessness, early man attributed favorable events to the actions of good spirits and unfavorable occurrences to intervention by evil spirits. This universally applicable concept of causation was ideally suited to explain hallucinations, delusions, and other irrational and seemingly uncontrollable reactions associated with madness. The obvious explanation was that a spirit had somehow entered the body of the victim and gained possession of his senses, speech, and actions. In various places at various times over thousands of years spirits have been identified as demons, furies, imps, incubi, and devils. The discovery of partially healed pierced skulls dating back to the Stone Age has led to the intriguing speculation that Paleolithic man not only accepted the prevalent belief in spirit possession but worked out an ingenious cure: the chipping of a hole in the head of "possessed" persons to facilitate the departure of the evil spirits (Selling, 1943). Toward the end of the first half of the twentieth century, modern man also briefly experimented with drilling holes in the skills of mental patients. The later-day rationale, however, was that the cutting of the neural pathways connecting prefrontal lobes with the older centers of the brain that regulate emotions might help alleviate the emotional distress of mental patients. Modern man no longer believes in spirit possession, but old superstitions fade slowly. When a friend ceases to be his familiar self and starts to act strangely, we still ask, "What's gotten into him?"

PRIMITIVE SOCIETIES

Five main theories of disease causation have been noted among primitive people (Clements, 1932). In addition to possession by spirits, disease was thought to be caused by loss of soul, breach of taboo, sorcery, and object intrusion. The soul-loss theory is based on the assumption that a person's soul wanders about at night while he is asleep, and may leave the body when he sneezes or is suddenly frightened. The capture of the detached soul by the ever present evil spirits causes illness. This theory may be related to the clinical observation that many mental patients are confused, out of touch with their environment, or complain of loss of identity. Murphy (1964) has described two forms of treatment that are practiced by the shamans of an Eskimo village on St. Lawrence Island. The shaman first sends out his spirit-familiar to search for and release the captured soul. If this fails, the shaman may conduct a ceremony to change the name of the patient, thus giving him a new soul. Moth sickness among the Navajo Indians provides an interesting example of taboo violation as the reputed cause of disordered behavior (Kaplan and Johnson, 1964). If a man violates the incest taboo with his sister, it is thought that a moth will thereupon crawl inside his head and exert pressure between his eyes, which will cause him to be attracted to flames, like the moth, until finally he is driven to jump into the fire. Disease sorcery assumes that disease results from the enmity of other persons, who work their evil will by means of witchcraft, black magic, voodoo, and the evil eye. Treatment consists of magical countermeasures: secret rituals, potions, effigies, and so on. Finally, disease has been thought to be caused by foreign objects in the patient's body. To cure the disease, the medicine man had to remove the objects by sucking them out or administering emetics.

The theories and therapies of primitive people are less scientific than modern ones, but there are basic similarities between them. The theory of taboo violation is related to current views on the role of guilt. The suspiciousness, distrust, and hostility often observed in mental patients fits in nicely with belief in sorcery. Spirit possession and lost-soul theories seem curiously applicable to the pervasive anxiety and feelings of helplessness commonly noted in mental patients. The object-intrusion hypothesis is analogous to the theory of organic pathology. The clinical observations that treatment is more successful when patient and therapist agree on the causes of illness and when both have confidence in the effectiveness of the therapeutic procedures employed are equally applicable in primitive and Western societies. The common practice among primitive people of extending treatment to the entire family has recently been adopted by modern psychiatry. Extended group therapy is helpful in reducing the lonely isolation and rejection of the patient and in facilitating his reacceptance by his group. Other points of similarity include the use of suggestion, persuasion, and confession. The prestige of the shaman is in some respects greater than that of his modern counterpart. In primitive societies the medicine man may function as physician, priest, magician, moral arbiter, and judge. These varied roles are illustrated in the following account, reported by Field (1955, p. 820), of psychotherapeutic practices in rural Ghana. Witchcraft is here accepted as the basic cause of the disturbance. Bewitched patients, most of whom would be classified as neurotic or depressed in our society, attend special shrines set aside in the forest.

The practitioner conducts the first hearing of any case ceremonially before his shrine. The accompanying ritual need not concern us here, except in its function of enhancing prestige, strengthening suggestion, and fortifying reassurance. He then most thoroughly investigates the family history and the stresses to which the suppliant is subjected. He ferrets out the envies, spites, rivalries, marital troubles, kinship disputes, and temperamental clashes. Ruthlessly he lays bare everyone's secrets. Astonishing tales of guilt and misdemeanor often emerge. Then he sums up the situation as he sees it and as the suppliants have now to see it. He announces who should confess and apologize to whom. He admonishes, he advises, he knocks hands together. He cleans, he reassures. Sometimes he keeps a suppliant for a long stay of treatment in his forest compound, giving food and a change of scenery. Between him and the suppliant springs up a striking transference which he handles with masterly skills, referring his own influence over the suppliant to the deity of the shrine, to whose permanent protection he is now commended.

ANCIENT TIMES

The popular belief in ancient Egypt, Israel, Greece, and Rome was that madness was caused by spirits sent by some god or goddess. A distinction was made between persons whose benign behavior suggested possession by good spirits and those who were violent and destructive, who were believed to be possessed by evil spirits. The early books of the Bible stressed the idea that madness was a divine punishment: "The Lord shall smite thee with madness." Two of the four kinds of madness described by Plato (429–347 B.C.) in *Phaedrus* implied possession by good spirits. These were prophetic madness, as illustrated by the ecstatic state of Apollo's oracle at Delphi, and poetic madness, in which muses provided inspiration for creativity. The other two types were erotic madness and ritual madness, induced by orgiastic religious rites. The assumption of divine causation had the advantage of reducing or eliminating personal responsibility. Plato recommended that if a mad person engaged in antisocial behavior, he should not be punished, but should undergo purification rites. His family should pay damages and assume responsibility for keeping him from wandering about the city. Plato's views on the etiology of mental disorders were clouded with mysticism. He recognized the contribution of psychological and intrapsychic factors to irrational behavior, but at the same time he accepted supernatural explanations.

The more enlightened Hippocratic physicians of ancient Greece rejected the popular belief in spirit possession (Chadwick and Mann, 1950). Hippocrates (460–357 B.C.) maintained that an unhealthy brain was the "seat of madness and delirium, of the fears and frights that assail us, often by night, sometimes even by day: there lies the cause of insomnia and sleepwalking, of thoughts that will not come, forgotten duties and eccentricities." The unhealthy state of the brain was thought to be related to an imbalance in the body "humors," probably hereditary. The recognized bodily fluids or humors consisted of blood, yellow bile, phlegm, and black bile. An excess of blood was considered a favorable factor, leading to a "sanguine" temperament—a cheerful, hopeful attitude. A predominance of yellow bile was assumed to be associated with choleric or irascible behavior. Too much phlegm resulted in sluggishness and apathy. Melancholy was thought to be caused by an excess of black bile. A favored treatment for mental disorders was the administration of hellebore, a plant with purgative properties that is related to the buttercup family. The Hippocratic concept of humors, and particularly the belief that melancholia resulted from an excess of black bile, persisted for many centuries. The specific treatment, logical enough if one accepts the premise, consisted in bleeding the patient as a means of eliminating the excess bile. The darkness of the blood provided a measure and proof of the presence of black bile. Bloodletting was approved and practiced by recognized medical authorities well into the nineteenth century. The readily demonstrated effectiveness of profuse bleeding in quieting disturbed patients undoubtedly contributed to the continued use of the method.

Hippocrates considered hysteria a physical disorder limited to women. The classical symptoms of this disorder—paralysis of an arm or a leg or loss of voice—were assumed to be due to the lodging of the uterus in various parts of the body during the course of its restless wanderings. The recommended remedy of marriage and pregnancy suggests that the ancient Greeks associated the illness with sexual frustrations. Two thousand years later, Freud suggested a similar interpretation. Since "hysteria" is derived from the Greek word for uterus, this diagnosis was applied only to female patients. This practice continued up until the late nineteenth century, despite repeated clinical observations that typical hysterical symptoms also occurred in men.

The rational approach to mental illness, seeded in Greece, was transplanted to ancient Rome by Greek physicians. One of the more enlightened psychiatrists in Rome during the first century B.C. was Asclepiades. A former resident of Asia Minor, he differentiated chronic from acute diseases and related mental disorders to emotional disturbances. He objected to bloodletting and mechanical restraints and advocated the use of baths, music therapy, and occupational therapy. Cicero (106–43 B.C.) also stressed the significance of emotional disturbances. Interestingly, the strongest of the four passions or perturbations described by Cicero was *libido,* or violent desire. He maintained that in cases of "furor" the breakdown in intellectual capacity makes the person legally irresponsible for his actions. Under Roman law, the mentally ill were deprived of their freedom of action, and guardians were appointed to look after their personal business affairs. Case descriptions of mental patients reported by Plutarch and Aretaeus during the first century A.D. leave no doubt that the major psychological forms of human afflictions were the same then as they are now. Anticipating later discoveries, Aretaeus noted that mania and melancholia were different phases of the same disorder and that certain mental diseases appeared to be extreme manifestations of the preexisting personality makeup of the patient. Galen (130–200 A.D.), the last of the great Roman physicians, attributed mental disorders to disharmony between the rational, irrational, and lustful parts of the soul; that is, faulty personality integration. His major contribution consisted in collecting and coordinating the medical knowledge of his time. This information was forgotten during the succeeding Dark Ages and subsequently rediscovered (Zilboorg and Henry, 1941; Mora, 1967).

Abnormal Behavior in the Middle Ages

The concept of mental disorder as a result of natural causes and the humane treatment introduced by the ancient Greeks and Romans were for a time preserved in the Arab world. The first asylums and mental hospitals were built in Baghdad, Damascus, and other Near Eastern cities as early as the eighth or ninth century. Medieval Europe slipped back to belief in demonic possession. Since demonology fell within the province of the church, the clergy assumed responsibility for treatment. Up until about the thirteenth century, the official position of the church was that the insane were innocent victims of the devil. During this period many of the mentally disturbed found refuge in convents and monasteries. Some of the milder techniques used by the priests for driving out demons included prayer, exorcism, sprinkling with holy water, and visits to shrines. If these methods failed, a deranged person might be fed vile concoctions or flogged in the expectation that the devils within would tire of so unsatisfactory a host and move out.

WITCHCRAFT

Never far removed from the concept of possession by demons was the suspicion that possessed persons were actually witches in league with the devil. Many alleged witches were in fact heretics who continued to worship pagan deities and engage in pagan rites. Beginning about the fourteenth century, demonology, witchcraft, and mental disease were linked together. It was mainly women who were accused of witchcraft, since it was commonly believed that the insatiable lust of women led them to invite possession by the devil and to do his bidding, to the harm of man (Robbins, 1959). Church and state united in a campaign against witches. Inquisitors were appointed to hunt down and bring to justice the traitorous witches, who, forsaking their allegiance to God, had joined the forces of Satan. This tragic decision may have been partly dictated by the need for scapegoats to blame for the uncertainties and tensions of a society plagued by epidemics and torn by the political, religious, and social dissensions that marked the disintegration of the feudal system. In 1487 two monks, Sprenger and Krämer, published the *Malleus maleficarum* ("A Hammer for Witches"), which served as a handbook for the detection, indictment, trial, and punishment of witches (Summers, 1951). The mentally deranged, and especially those who claimed special powers or whose feelings of guilt led them to confess freely to all sorts of wrongdoing, were natural targets. During this reign of horror, which lasted for two centuries and briefly touched this country (the Salem witch trials), thousands of confused, disturbed, or merely disliked persons were convicted of witchcraft and burned (Lea, 1939). In Massachusetts there were no burnings; all the witches of Salem were hanged, except one (a man), who was pressed to death by stones. About fifty times as many women as men were condemned as witches. During the sixteenth century Johann Weyer, a German physician, and Reginald Scot, an English justice of the peace, attempted to expose the fallacy of confusing mental illness with witchcraft. It was not until 1738, however, that England repealed the Witchcraft Acts, and 1782 that the last European witch was decapitated in Switzerland. A witch was killed in Mexico as recently as the nineteenth century, and in many parts of the world belief in witches has still not completely died out.

MASS HYSTERIA

The episodes of so-called mass hysteria that swept through Europe from the thirteenth to the eighteenth centuries are more appropriately described as examples of mass suggestibility or group contagion than as manifestations of individual mental illness. These events were usually set off when one person started to sing, dance, bark, or throw a fit, and others followed suit. As people copied and reinforced one another's behavior, the process could be kept up for several hours or even days, or it could be quickly terminated by the simple expedient of separating the participants. Hunter and Macalpine (1963) cite an interesting example of an "epidemic of hysterics" that occurred in 1787 in a cotton "manufactory." A girl put a mouse inside the blouse of another girl who had a great dread of mice. The second girl immediately started to have a fit, which continued for twenty-four hours. On the following day three more girls were seized in the same manner, on the third day six more, and on the fourth day another fourteen—twenty-four in all. It was thought that a particular disease had been introduced by a bag of cotton. Symptoms included anxiety, strangulation, tearing of hair, and dashing the head against the walls. A doctor was called. He promptly cured all patients by administering electric shocks from a portable electric machine. No new cases occurred after the community was assured that the complaint was merely nervous and easily cured. More recent examples of mass hysteria include the widespread panic reactions of listeners to Orson Welles's radio dramatization of H. G. Wells's *The War of the Worlds* in 1938 (Cantril, 1947) and the episode of the phantom anesthetist of Mattoon (Johnson, 1949). In the town of Mattoon, Illinois, a woman reported to the police that a prowler had crept up to her open window and sprayed her and her daughter with a sweet-smelling gas, causing nausea and partial paralysis of the legs. The local newspaper published the story, and a large number of people then developed similar symptoms.

The Sixteenth to Eighteenth Centuries

The gradual decline in belief in demons and witchcraft reopened the age-old questions of the causes of aberrant behavior and the ways in which the mentally ill should be treated. During this period there was a revival of interest in theories of humoral imbalance, for which the prescribed treatment was bloodletting. Increased attention was also given to two other beliefs with a long history: the therapeutic use of shock and the effect of the stars and moon on behavior. Popular interest in astrology was exploited by Mesmer in his development of a new therapeutic technique, which today is recognized as hypnosis. The attitude of the public toward the mentally deranged continued to be extremely unfavorable. Although no longer burned as witches, the psychologically disturbed were neglected, feared, abused, and rejected. The presence of an "insane" person in the family was regarded as a disgrace and was kept a closely guarded secret. The more fortunate of these disturbed persons were kept at home, where more often than not they were locked up in attics, barns, and cellars. The homeless, if harmless, were treated as pariahs. Ill fed, poorly clad, ridiculed, and driven from place to place, they led the lives of unwanted dogs. If they seemed to pose a threat to others, they were jailed or shut up in lunatic asylums.

SHOCK THERAPY

The history of psychiatry is spotted with the periodic discovery of the use of shock as a homeopathic medium for restoring sanity (Zilboorg and Henry, 1941). Under the guise of therapy, mental patients in the past have been lowered into snake pits, tossed from high cliffs into the sea, beaten over the head or had hot irons applied to their heads to straighten out their thinking, and spun in special whirling contraptions until they lost consciousness. During the seventeenth century Van Helmont of the Netherlands advocated extinguishing madness by ducking the patient's head first under water until his "upper parts" were drowned, after which he was, if possible, revived. The famous English neurologist Thomas Willis (1621–1677) treated a "furious" maid by ordering that she be carried out of the house in the middle of the night and put in a boat. There her clothes were to be pulled off and she was to be tied with a rope and dunked in the river to the brink of death (Hunter and Macalpine, 1963). In the 1930s more "scientific" shock therapies were reintroduced. Insulin was used to produce a deep coma; drugs and electric shock were used to produce convulsions. No valid scientific explanation for these primitive measures has ever been offered. The temporary improvement occasionally noted following shock treatment may have been due to the mobilization of resources against a real threat to existence, just as stuporous patients may be temporarily re-stored to normal functioning by forcing them to breathe an asphyxiating gas mixture containing an excess of carbon dioxide for a few moments. When psychotic persons acquire some acute physical illness, their mental symptoms are often temporarily improved. A threat to life apparently takes precedence over psychological problems.

LUNACY

The popular term "lunacy" is a legacy of the superstitious belief that the moon was somehow associated with madness. For a time, institutions for the mentally disturbed were officially called lunatic asylums. The support-ing evidence for the lunacy theory was the repeatedly confirmed observa-tion that mental disturbances tended to be intensified on nights when the moon was full. Two down-to-earth explanations for this lunar effect are that (1) mental patients may have acted out their expected role and (2) the increased illumination on full-moon nights kept the patients awake and active.

MESMERISM AND HYPNOSIS

Although his theories and practices bordered on quackery, Franz A. Mesmer (1734–1815) may be credited with stimulating scientific interest in the importance of psychological factors in the etiology and treatment of mental disorders. A student of theology, astrology, and medicine, this Austrian physician mixed his learning to develop a dramatic technique that became known as mesmerism His basic theory was that an invisible mag-netic fluid emanating from the stars influenced the health of human beings. An imbalance of this fluid in the body caused illness. The imbalance could be corrected by the touch of a magnetic wand. Later Mesmer became convinced that his hands had healing power because the magic fluid also flowed from his own body in the form of "animal magnetism." Following some initial success in Vienna, he was accused of being a charlatan by his medical colleagues and forced to leave the city. In 1778 he went to Paris, where his showmanship won him a brilliant but short career. In the words of Zilboorg and Henry (1941, p. 343), "He magnetized people in private and in public, singly and en masse, bringing them into what was called a *crisis*, that is to say a variety of singular attacks of laughing, crying, con-vulsive contortions, unconsciousness, and clairvoyance." People flocked to his treatment salon, where they gathered around a *baquet,* a troughlike structure from which protruded iron rods that could be applied to various parts of the body. At the critical moment Mesmer, dressed in flowing robes and with magic wand in hand, would appear and direct the treatment. The impressive ritual, the touching and stroking of the patient's body to reestablish the balance of the magnetic influence, and the confidence of the patient in the efficacy of the treatment were undoubtedly effective in temporarily curing or improving many neurotic symptoms. But the spectacular, theatrical aspects of mesmerism also made it a passing fad. In 1784 a comedy that poked fun at Mesmer was successfully presented in Paris. That same year a committee of distinguished scientists appointed by the Academy of Science to investigate magnetism turned in an unfavorable report. The committee concluded that the key to the phenomenon was imagination. The claimed effects of magnetism could be produced by imagination alone; magnetism without the critical ingredients of faith and imagination produced nothing. The committee further reported that the repeated excitement of the imagination to induce crisis was harmful and that the spectacle of public magnetic treatments might lead observers to imitate the crisis behavior noted in others. Mesmer's flourishing practice dwindled and he retired to private life.

There is some doubt whether Mesmer was an outright impostor and fraud who attempted to exploit the gullible, or a sincere person who accidentally stumbled on a powerful therpeutic technique that was too complex for him to grasp. His idea of animal magnetism is similar to the present-day concept of rapport and the intangible effect of the personality of the therapist on the patient. Mesmerism, which was renamed hypnosis by James Braid in 1843, has turned out to be the phoenix of medicine and psychopathology. Repeatedly buried by criticisms, it keeps on rising again. From about 1840 to 1850 mesmerism was used to induce an anesthetic trance state for the performance of painless surgical operations by Elliotson in England and Esdaille in India. The opposition of more conservative physicians, together with the development of gases for inducing anesthesia, soon discouraged this practice; but the anesthetic effects of hypnosis are currently being utilized in dentistry and obstetrics.

The use of hypnosis as a curative agent of neuroses, earlier recognized by Elliotson and others, was richly documented by A. A. Liébault (1823–1904) and H. Bernheim (1837–1919) in France. Known as the leaders of the Nancy school, Liébault and Bernheim established that the curative effect of hypnosis was based on the power of suggestions given to the patient while he was in a sleeplike state. After World War I another French doctor, Émile Coué (1924), discovered the curative effects of conscious autosuggestion. Treatment consisted of the repetition twenty times each morning and night of the magic formula: "Day by day in every way I am getting better and better."

In addition to demonstrating the effectiveness of suggestion in the removal of symptoms, the early studies of hypnosis provided strong support for the theory that psychological factors were responsible for the physical symptoms of hysteria. A significant late-nineteenth-century observation made at Jean Charcot's famous neurological clinic at the Salpêtrière was that the whole range of bodily symptoms associated with hysteria (paralysis, deafness, anesthesia, fits) could be readily produced and eliminated by the simple expedient of verbal suggestions given to the hypnotized subject. The ease with which the symptoms could be manipulated by the examiner ruled out neurophysiological explanations. One of Charcot's more significant discoveries was that when a hysterical patient reported a paralysis or anesthesia of the hand or leg, the extent of the loss of function was defined by the part of the hand covered by a glove or the part of the leg extending from the knee downward. In short, the symptoms were demarcated by the popularly recognized limits of the body rather than by the anatomical distribution of nerves. However, Charcot (1825–1893) erred in concluding that hypnosis is related to hysteria and that only persons with hysterical tendencies are hypnotizable. The alternative view of the Nancy school, that hypnosis is simply a condition of increased suggestibility and that most willing and cooperative persons can be hypnotized, has prevailed.

CUSTODIAL ASYLUMS

Special institutions for the custody of mental patients were established in several countries before the fifteenth century. However, Spain is credited with building the first hospital in Europe for the care of the mentally ill, in 1409 in Valencia. Spanish priests also built the first mental hospital on the American continent in Mexico in 1556. In 1547 Henry VIII gave the Hospital of St. Mary of Bethlehem to the city of London to serve as an asylum for lunatics. Bethlehem, popularly pronounced Bedlam, soon deteriorated from a hospital to a zoo where the insane were brutally treated and exposed to the public for a fee. The term "bedlam" is derived from the wild, confused scenes associated with Bethlehem Hospital. It was a favorite amusement in old London to visit the place and watch the antics of the lunatics. This practice was not abolished until the late eighteenth century.

   In other European countries, where custodial institutions for the insane began to appear during the seventeenth and eighteenth centuries, the mentally ill fared no better. The incarceration of lunatics was essentially a police action designed to protect society. The welfare and treatment of the inmates was of no importance. The attitude of the keepers of the early public asylums was that the insane were senseless, dangerous brutes who could be kept under control only by chains and the generous application of whips. Treatment was anchored in the use of force and the curative value of discipline and fear. Royalty was not exempted. When King George III had one of his recurring attacks of mania, his attendants had no compunction about knocking him down and tying him up. In colonial America conditions were possibly worse (Deutsch, 1946). In 1751 Benjamin Franklin drew up a petition recommending that a hospital be built to care for the increasing number of "persons distempered in mind and deprived of their rational faculties: who were a source of terror to their neighbors, wasted their substance to the injury of themselves and their families, and were exploited by the wicked." A few years later some rooms were reserved for mental patients in the cellar of the Pennsylvania Hospital. It was not until 1773 that the first mental hospital in this country was constructed, in Williamsburg, Virginia. As in Europe, the mentally ill in colonial America were chained to their cell walls, bled, purged, beaten, blistered, and whirled.

Humane Reforms

Toward the end of the eighteenth century, enlightened leaders, including A. Muller in Germany and V. Chiarugi in Italy, protested against brutal restraints and demanded more humane care for the deranged. In France the champion of humane reforms was Philippe Pinel (1745–1826). Although he is best known as the man who freed the insane from their chains, Pinel can justifiably be given the higher title of father of modern psychiatry. His *Treatise on Insanity*, published in 1801, established Pinel as one of the great pioneers in the field of psychopathology. His contributions included:

1. Introduction of the concept that a mental hospital should be a place for treatment rather than custodial care. Pinel held that most forms of mental disease were transitory. Under favorable conditions they ran their course and were self-corrective. While recognizing that the passage of time was the main healing agent, he believed that recovery could be facilitated through good physical care, an adequate diet, and the establishment of a therapeutic hospital environment marked by humaneness, kindliness, and optimal liberty for each patient consistent with safety.

2. Rejection of the then popular practices of bloodletting, excessive administration of drugs, and reliance on the use of punitive measures. He wrote: "To detain maniacs in constant seclusion, and load them with chains, to leave them defenseless to the brutality of underlings, on the pretense of danger to be dreaded from their extravagances: in a word, to rule them with a rod of iron, is a system of superintendence more distinguished for its convenience than for its humanity or its success."

3. Introduction of a scientific approach to the study of mental dis-

orders. He maintained that a detailed case record should be kept on each patient. The record should include the historical development of the disorder from its onset, the registering of new facts and changes as they occurred, and a follow-up of the eventual outcome. The numerous case histories reported in his book illustrate the unchanging nature of behavior pathology. His detailed case records led him to conclude that there was no direct connection between the specific character of the symptoms and the nature of the presumed cause. Consistent with his scientific approach, Pinel maintained that before any claim could be made for the effectiveness of any treatment procedure, one should first know the outcome of the disorder when left to the unassisted efforts of nature; that is, spontaneous recovery, no change, or deterioration.

4. Development of a simple classification system consisting of five major forms of mental disorders: melancholia, mania without delusions, mania with delusions, dementia or the loss of the thinking faculty, and idiocy.

5. Recognition of the importance of emotional and psychogenic factors in the etiology of most mental disorders. He thought that attacks of mania were generally no more than irascible emotions prolonged beyond their ordinary limits.

The reform movement in England was spearheaded by the Quakers, who, under the leadership of William Tuke, opened the York Retreat in 1796 to provide a mild system of treatment based on understanding, affection, liberty, and comfort. Progress was slow, however, particularly in large public asylums. The use of chains was gradually discouraged, but patients were still restrained by leather straps and straitjackets. In 1840 R. G. Hill reported a three-year experiment in total nonrestraint in a small English asylum. The results were spectacular. All recent cases were discharged as recovered; inmates were orderly, quiet, and clean in their personal habits; and no suicides or serious accidents occurred. However, opposition against the system, particularly by the attendants, was so great that Hill was forced to resign his appointment. It remained for John Conolly (1784–1866) to demonstrate that Hill's concept of total abolition of mechanical restraint could be successfully applied in a large public asylum. The elimination of all restraint was only one part of Conolly's system. His chief concern was to create what in recent years has been called a *therapeutic community* conducive to the prompt recovery of the patient. This included the selection and training of kind, cheerful, and conscientious attendants, individualized treatment, and the replacement of fear with hope.

Although the humane, nonrestrictive movement of the mid-nineteenth century was limited to a few hospitals, it was highly effective. For all admissions to selected hospitals in England and Massachusetts during the period 1830–1850, the recovery or improvement rate at discharge was about 60 percent (Hunter and Macalpine, 1963; Bockoven, 1956). For patients admitted within a year of onset of illness, the recovery or improvement rate was 70 percent. Even more impressive, most recovered or improved patients remained well the rest of their lives. In a follow-up study conducted by Park on over a thousand patients hospitalized between 1833 and 1846, information gathered thirty-six to sixty years after hospitalization showed that 54 percent had remained well or were in reasonably good mental health when they died (Bockoven, 1956). These results compare very favorably with those of the best mental health programs of today. These early optimistic figures were apparently influenced by favorable patient response to the personal interest in their welfare shown by the hospital staff and to the spirit of enthusiasm and confidence with which the new techniques were used.

The effectiveness of these intangible, subjective factors in relieving symptoms and modifying behavior is now well recognized. Medicine provides numerous similar examples of the direct relationship of the therapeutic effectiveness of new drugs and the physician's confidence in the treatment, which somehow is communicated to the patient. Commenting on this phenomenon, Sir William Osler facetiously advised that new drugs should be used when they first come out, before they cease to be effective. The high recovery rate reported by mid-nineteenth-century hospital administrators who were deeply concerned with the welfare of their patients may be attributed to what has been recently described as the *Hawthorne effect*. While investigating the effects of physical changes in the environment of factory workers at the Hawthorne plant of the Western Electric Company, a group of industrial psychologists discovered that the production of workers was influenced mainly by management's interest in trying to improve working conditions (Roethlisberger, 1941). The critical factor was not the nature of the physical change but the more complex issue of worker morale. Innovations such as increasing the amount of illumination, lengthening rest periods, and serving special lunches were found to increase the production of experimental groups. At the same time, control groups who were aware of the ongoing experiment but whose own work conditions were not changed showed an almost equal improvement in production.

The favorable results attained in the few model hospitals of the mid-nineteenth century were neither typical of the period nor predictive of the immediate future. As more and bigger mental hospitals were built during the late nineteenth and early twentieth centuries, treatment became more impersonal and less effective. The earlier spirit of optimism was gradually replaced by a pessimistic attitude toward the curability of psychoses. The popular view of the late nineteenth and early twentieth centuries, that psychoses were diseases analogous to physical disorders for which no medical cure had yet been discovered, discouraged therapeutic efforts and held discharges to a minimum. A more hopeful attitude toward the treatment of severe mental disorders did not appear again until several years after the close of World War II.

The Mental Disease Era: 1850–1950

CUSTODIAL HOSPITALS

During the century when psychoses were viewed as diseases, Western society regarded the wholesale commitment of mental patients to locked institutions located in rural areas as an ideal solution that protected society and at the same time was in the patient's best interests. The medical concept of disease cannot be blamed for the dismal conditions of the custodial mental hospitals of the late nineteenth century and the first half of the twentieth century; but the implied erroneous assumption that treatment of psychoses was futile until the underlying physical causes were discovered did not help much. As late as 1950 most mental hospitals were crowded and often unhygienic. As a rule, food was inadequate, monotonous, and unappetizing. Dietary deficiencies were common. There were little or no provisions for stimulating the patients' interests or occupying their time. As long as patients remained docile and sat quietly week after week, doing absolutely nothing, they were in turn left alone. But if they became restless and obstreperous, they were immediately sedated, immobilized in straitjackets, or isolated in padded cells. A common technique for quieting disturbed patients consisted of wrapping them in wet sheets till they resembled Egyptian mummies. Too often the medical staff consisted of underpaid physicians who were untrained in psychiatry and were responsible for so many patients that their activities were limited to treating incidental physical illnesses and keeping up with administrative details. The prevailing attitude toward the patients was one of wary apprehension. Patients were confined in locked wards with barred windows. When let out for an occasional airing or a trip to the auditorium to see a movie, they were herded under guard. Fear of what patients might do was carried to such extremes that they were denied the use of forks and knives, so that all meals had to be eaten with spoons. It was considered too risky to trust a patient with matches, pens, lighters, or belts. In short, patients were perceived as dangerous and "crazy," and they acted accordingly.

During the first half of the twentieth century, the hospital regime was based on the sincerely believed but untested premise that mental patients were totally incompetent. Attendants supervised every move; patients were told when to go to bed, what clothes to wear, and when and where to smoke. Attendants were selected for their size and strength. Their job was to maintain order and discipline, prevent assaultive, destructive, or suicidal behavior, and enforce security measures. They were not expected to have any understanding of behavior disorders, to accept patients as fellow human beings in distress, or to be interested in them as individuals. Care of a sort was provided, but no one actually cared much for the individual patient. This impersonal atmosphere tended to create a silent society in which no one communicated with anyone else, the names of doctors, nurses, and attendants were often unknown to those in their charge, meals were eaten in silence, and patients who shared the same ward month after month remained total strangers to one another. This approach had limited therapeutic value. However well meaning, the dull, repressive, dependency-encouraging program tended to fixate and accentuate mental disorders and make them in fact incurable. The good patient was the robot who passively adapted to the program without protest and did what he was told with no show of initiative or independence. A patient who reacted against the forced confinement, arbitrary rules, and tedious idleness was labeled as troublesome and assigned to a "disturbed" ward. If such transfers upset the patient even more, as they usually did, he was subjected to massive sedation, physical restraint, and the "quiet room." Docile patients characterized by social withdrawal were given every opportunity to retreat completely into a hazy dream world, to become slovenly in their personal habits, to spend their days staring blankly into space, and to regress to a simple vegetative state. The social apathy encouraged by this type of regime was strikingly illustrated during World War II by the reaction to air raids of chronic patients in English mental hospitals (Hemphill, 1941). The blaring of sirens, the continuous gunfire, and the explosion of bombs in the vicinity of mental hospitals had no more impact on the patients than watching a motion picture. Having left the world of reality, they had no interest or feeling for what was happening on the outside.

Several writers have suggested that the bleak impersonal environment of custodial hospitals may be mainly responsible for converting acute transitory reactions to chronic incurable conditions (Goffman, 1961; Kantor and Gelineau, 1965; Ullmann, 1967). The term *social breakdown syndrome* has been applied by Gruenberg (1967) and others to the dependency, apathy, withdrawal, and lack of responsibility fostered by institutionalization. The development of social breakdown appears to be directly related to the duration of hospital stay (Honigfeld and Gillis, 1967). Once chronicity has been established, the possibility of rehabilitation and release to the community is very slim. Studies summarized by Paul (1969) indicate that after two years of continued hospitalization in a traditional mental institution, the probability of release and prolonged stay in the community runs about 6 percent.

DRASTIC PHYSICAL TREATMENT

The discouraging state of mental hospitals during the first half of the present century is largely past history. The better mental hospitals of today more closely resemble general hospitals. The emphasis is on intensive treatment, social rehabilitation, and early discharge. A major reason for dwelling on past conditions is that only by seeing clearly how desperate the situation really was can we understand the wide acceptance of insulin shock therapy, electroconvulsive therapy, and brain surgery during the 1930s and 1940s. In retrospect, these drastic measures may seem reminiscent of the punitive "curative" methods resorted to in bygone centuries; but in their day, they were widely used and highly regarded (Kolinowsky and Hoch, 1952; Freedman et al., 1967). The first of the treatments by biological ordeal, introduced by Sakel in 1933, consisted of massive injections of insulin. By reducing the sugar content of the blood and thereby interfering with the normal metabolic processes in the brain, insulin therapy produced a deep coma marked by diffuse motor, sensory, and autonomic disturbances. The severity of the neurobiochemical changes brought considerable risk to the life of the patient, so that the method required good hospital facilities and excellent medical and nursing staffs. No sound rationale for the method was ever presented. The treatment rested on the hope that the massive neurobiochemical upheaval might miraculously straighten out whatever was wrong with the patient. Although some success was reported with certain types of schizophrenic patients, most of the recoveries turned out to be temporary (Staudt and Zubin, 1957). The final verdict appears to be that insulin shock was moderately helpful in shortening the hospital stay of selected patients who would eventually have been discharged as improved even if they had received no treatment.

In 1934 Meduna advanced the theory that a biological antagonism existed between schizophrenia and convulsions, and that there therefore were therapeutic possibilities in subjecting schizophrenic patients to a series of convulsions. As a means of inducing convulsions, he recommended injecting patients with metrazol. One technical objection to the method was that it was difficult to control the severity of the convulsion. If too little of the drug was given, there was no convulsion; if too much, the violence of the patient's movements caused fractures and other injuries. A second disadvantage was that the patients objected strenuously to the treatment because of the acute fear they experienced in the brief interval between the injection and the loss of consciousness that accompanied the onset of the convulsion. The use of metrazol was therefore discontinued after Cerletti and Bini demonstrated in 1938 that better controlled convulsions, marked by immediate loss of consciousness, could be more conveniently induced by passing an electric current of 100 volts or so for a fraction of a second across electrodes placed on the sides of the forehead. Electroshock sharply reduces the amount of oxygen in the brain, as insulin therapy does, but for a different reason. Insulin reduces the amount of glucose available for oxidation; the high brain activity during electroshock depletes the available supply of oxygen and glucose. Contrary to Meduna's original hypothesis, electroconvulsive shock therapy has been found to be ineffective with schizophrenics but useful in the treatment of the depressive reactions. However, the procedure creates understandable resistance in patients. Unfavorable complications associated with electroshock include transient memory impairment and a low but real risk of fractures of the vertebrae, dislocation of the jaw, and respiratory arrest. A variety of psychological, psychoanalytic, and neurological theories have been advanced, but no convincing rationale for the use of electroconvulsive therapy (ECT) has yet emerged (Miller, 1967).

The most drastic of the extreme physical therapies, initiated by pioneer studies reported by Moniz in 1936 and Freeman and Watts in 1942, consisted of various surgical procedures designed to slice, puncture, mash, or remove certain areas of the prefrontal lobes of the brain. As a rule, this radical surgical approach was restricted to severely disturbed, agitated, and unmanageable patients who had failed to respond to insulin or electroshock therapy. The underlying theory was that severing the nerve fibers connecting the frontal lobe with the dorsomedial nucleus of the thalamus (considered to be the control center of the emotions) would help relieve emotional unrest. In some instances, the operation did have the effect of transforming restless, tense, and destructive patients into relaxed, carefree, and easily managed ones. But all treated patients were left with permanent brain damage. Most received no benefit from the operation, and some were reduced to lethargic, insensitive, deteriorated shells of human beings. Psychosurgery has been discontinued for mental patients, but serendipity saved it from being a total loss: the procedure has been found effective in reducing intractable pain in cases of incurable cancer.

Mental Hospitals Today and Tomorrow

Mental hospitals today serve two quite distinct purposes. One is to provide intensive short-term care and treatment for acute or new cases. The other is to provide care for chronic cases.

NEW ADMISSIONS

Modern mental hospitals are endeavoring with considerable success to create a therapeutic environment for recently admitted patients. Extensive use is made of psychoactive drugs, individual and group therapy, and social activities, both to restore normal functioning and to prevent withdrawal, dependency, and the social breakdown syndrome. Patients are treated as responsible human beings and are given considerable freedom. Admission wards are open and comfortably furnished. Voluntary admission, a procedure similar to admission to general medical hospitals, is encouraged. In many European countries, as we have already noted, from 70 to 80 percent of admissions are voluntary. The figure is considerably lower in the United States, but it is rising. Voluntary admission has several advantages. It avoids the traumatic experience associated with compulsory commitment and the resentment often aroused when a person is "put away" against his will. The duration of hospital stay of legally committed patients is essentially at the discretion of hospital authorities. The voluntarily admitted patient may request his release whenever he wishes. Requests for release are honored except in those comparatively few instances when there is good reason to believe that release might unduly endanger the welfare of the patient or of society. The aim of modern mental hospitals is to discharge patients as soon as possible. It is not uncommon for hospitals today to discharge 75 percent of new cases within a year of admission. Many are released within a few weeks or months. Some patients relapse and are readmitted, but the great majority can and do remain in the community when adequate provisions are made for continued treatment in outpatient clinics, day-care centers, and other community facilities.

The treatment of new cases by mental hospitals is increasingly being shared with general medical hospitals. In 1965 the number of mental patients admitted to psychiatric wards of general hospitals was twice as large as the total number of first admissions to all public and private mental hospitals in the United States. In addition, many patients who in former years would have been admitted to mental hospitals are now being treated in private practice and in community clinics. Since 1955 the total resident population of public mental hospitals has been slowly decreasing. This is mainly the result of more liberal discharge rates. The number of total admissions to public mental hospitals continues to show a slight annual increase, despite the greater use being made of general hospitals and community facilities. The increase in number of new admissions to treatment centers is partly due to the yearly increase in general population and partly attributable to increased willingness on the part of disturbed persons to seek treatment.

CHRONIC PATIENTS

Chronic patients constitute approximately two-thirds of the resident hospital population. Most of these are long-term residents who have been continuously hospitalized for five or more years. Some have spent the major portion of their lives in mental hospitals. Heroic attempts to rehabilitate these "hard core" chronic cases have so far had meager success. *Vocational retraining* has been found to be moderately successful in improving work skills, but experimental groups do not differ from nontrained control groups with respect to rehospitalization or personal and social adjustment (Paul, 1969). *Milieu therapy,* which is characterized by increased social interaction, encouragement of informal communication between staff and patients, and group activities directed toward "normal" functioning, has been shown to be effective in decreasing bizarre behavior and improving social reactions. Several studies (Ellsworth, 1964; Sanders et al., 1967) have reported high discharge rates for chronic patients exposed to milieu or intensive resocialization programs. Most discharged patients, however, fail to adjust in the community and have to be rehospitalized. When correction is made for rehospitalization, the net release figures are only slightly higher for experimental than control groups, if they differ at all (Paul, 1969).

A promising new approach is the establishment of what Ayllon has called "token economy wards" for chronic hospitalized patients. The procedure involves the application of basic principles of social learning and motivation in a rigidly controlled environment. The principle of positive reinforcement is utilized to increase the frequency of desired behavior. Aides, nurses, and other ward personnel are instructed to maintain close observation of patients. Whenever a patient makes a "good" response (making his bed, interacting well with others, being on time for meals), a staff member immediately reinforces the favorable action by giving the patient one or more tokens—special cards or poker chips that serve as money on the ward. Each day the patient must earn enough tokens to pay for his meals, bed, and extras such as the privilege of living in better quarters, special snacks, reading material, and choice of clothing. The reinforcement program is tailored to the individual so that all may earn enough tokens to provide for the essentials with little effort. Improvement in behavior results in a higher rate of reinforcement. If the patient makes no favorable responses or fights the system and thus fails to earn the required tokens, he may have to skip a meal or sleep on a cot rather than a comfortable bed. Apart from some periodic mild deprivation, the use of coercive or preventive measures to eliminate eccentric or symptomatic behavior is avoided on ethical and moral grounds. It is assumed that simply ignoring or not reinforcing undesirable behavior will result in the decrease of such behavior and its eventual elimination. In view of the extent of control exercised by the environment in token economy programs, special attention is paid to safeguarding patients' rights. Patients are given the opportunity to transfer to another ward whenever they wish (Ayllon and Azrin, 1968). Token economy programs have been found to be highly effective in furthering self-maintenance, increasing social responsiveness, and decreasing bizarre behavior. So far the major goal of token economy programs has been to improve personal and social behavior within the hospital. There are some indications that the programs may contribute to increased discharge rates. However, the continued application of reinforcement principles in the community may be necessary to preserve and extend improvements begun within the hospital. One way this can be done is to establish special halfway houses in the community, where patients live and work together in a controlled environment.

FAMILY AND COMMUNITY ROLE

The weak link in hospital treatment is failure to provide adequate followup care and treatment for discharged patients. Chronic patients in particular need continued community support to prevent relapses and rehospitalization. Prerelease training programs designed to help families to cope effectively with discharged patients is one possible solution. Supplementary measures include day centers, outpatient clinics, and sheltered workshops. For patients who have no families to go to, an alternate possiblity is the establishment of special homes in the community where small groups of patients may create a mutually supportive "family group" of their own.

PROGNOSIS FOR HOSPITALIZED PATIENTS

Paul (1969) has reviewed the extensive literature on prognostic studies relating individual patient characteristics to outcome. The most consistently noted findings are: (1) the longer a person remains in a mental hospital, the poorer are his chances of release; (2) the prognosis is poor for patients whose chief means of adjustment before hospitalization was withdrawal from social interaction; (3) the discharge rate is higher for married patients than for single, divorced, or widowed patients; and (4) educational level and socioeconomic status are positively correlated with favorable prognosis. Outcome figures following mental hospitalization vary with the patient population studied, intensity of treatment, discharge criteria, and length of follow-up measures. Data reported by Bockoven and Soloman (1954) are representative of results obtainable by maximum treatment. The population studied consisted of one hundred acutely psychotic patients admitted to the Boston Psychiatric Hospital. The average length of hospital stay was seventy-five days. By the end of this period, 70 percent were returned to the community and the remainder were transferred to other mental hospitals for continued care. One year after discharge, 72 percent were in the community and 20 percent were in other mental hospitals. The remainder had either died or moved out of the state. At the end of five years, seventy-six of the original hundred patients were living in the community, twelve were in mental hospitals, and twelve had either died or left the state. Those in the community were not necessarily completely cured, but their level of social functioning was adequate to permit them to get along in the community.

A New Look at Hospitalization and the Chronic Patient

While critical of the rationale and therapeutic effectiveness of mental hospitals, Braginsky, Braginsky, and Ring (1969) question whether hospital practices are entirely to blame for "creating" chronic patients. Their view is that many patients choose continued hospitalization as a career. Braginsky and his associates do not deny or minimize the fact that hospitalized patients have genuine problems. What they object to is the prevalent belief that chronic patients suffer from some disintegrative disease that results in the profound impairment of virtually all psychological functions. Particularly for chronic patients whose mental condition is sufficiently benign to permit them to live in open wards, hospitalization provides a perpetual vacation from the cares and responsibilities of the outside world. The accommodations at a public mental hospital are not so luxurious as at a first-class resort, but the advantages, facilities, and mode of living are similar. The permanent resident in a good modern mental hospital literally has it made. Food, shelter, clothing, medical and dental care, and other necessities are provided without charge. The patient has unlimited leisure to do as he pleases. Furthermore, he is encouraged as part of his treatment to listen to music, watch movies and television, read, swim, bowl, shoot pool, take long walks, cultivate hobbies, attend classes in arts and crafts, go to parties within the institution and so on. All that is expected of him in return is that he accept the label of mental patient and act the part well enough to avoid being discharged. By learning and playing the hospital game well, patients may in great measure control their length of hospitalization, the extent of their privileges, and the time and conditions of their discharge (if they wish to be discharged) and readmission.

Braginsky and his associates may have exaggerated the situation a bit in viewing the patient-hospital relationship "as a function of a hedonistic calculus where the hospital is seen as a potential pleasure dome and the patient as an architect of his own personal Shangri-La" (p. 132), but they have bolstered their hypothesis with a series of confirmatory studies. According to their findings, chronic patients are by no means as disoriented, helpless, and ineffectual as they are usually considered. When it serves their purposes, they are capable of pursuing and attaining rational goals. Observational and experimental data indicate that chronic patients on open wards are manipulative and resourceful individuals who are able to satisfy their primary motivations with surprising frequency and ease. When taking tests or being interviewed, schizophrenics, who have been traditionally described as out of touch with reality and devoid of insight, can and do regulate the impression they make on the hospital staff so that the staff will act in accordance with their goals. Patients who want to leave the hospital present self-descriptions that play down their psychopathology. On the other hand, those who prefer to remain in the hospital skillfully describe themselves as "too sick" to be discharged, but not so disturbed that they should be exiled to the closed back wards.

The particular motivations of patients determine the kinds of information they learn about the hospital's facilities and personnel. If their primary objective is to enjoy a long hospital stay, they systematically go about structuring their activities to permit maximum freedom within the institution while making sure they will not be considered eligible for release. Possible threats to their preferred style of life are averted by ingratiating behavior or the selective avoidance of those staff members who might limit the patient's actions. Some patients are masters of the art of being invisible. Patients who plan a long stay in the hospital soon arrange matters so that they can lead the kind of life that they formerly were able to enjoy only on weekends or on vacation. In short, madness has its methods. Many chronic patients realize they have a good thing going and take full advantage of it. The exploitation of mental hospitals by some patients is, of course, not restricted to American ingenuity. I remember a conversation I had some years ago with an administrator of the mental hospital program in France, who was concerned with the possible abuse of recently enacted laws that liberalized hospital admission procedures. It seems there was quite an astonishing increase in the number of Parisians who applied for voluntary, short-term admission to mental hospitals located near coastal resort areas during the vacation season.

Whether one believes that hospitals create chronic patients or that patients elect to remain long-term hospital guests, the results are the same. Chronic patients accumulate in mental hospitals, and the longer they stay, the poorer is their chance of return to the community. Braginsky and his associates acknowledge that mental hospitals serve a useful purpose in providing a temporary refuge from intolerable life problems. However, they believe that the hypocrisy and degradation associated with acceptance of the patient role is too high a price to pay for some relief from societal pressures. As an alternative, they advocate the establishment of retreat communities, somewhat analogous to the monasteries and convents of the Middle Ages, where troubled persons could go to enjoy a respite from daily life and find renewal. The retreats would consist of publicly supported small communities. Facilities would be similar to those available at vacation resorts. There would be no necessity to have or maintain symptoms to satisfy residence requirements. Length of stay would be determined by the needs and wishes of the individual and the availability of space. It is assumed that most would want to return home after a brief stay. Persons who decided to remain as permanent residents could participate in the running of the establishment.

Braginsky and his associates have deliberately overstated their case for emphasis. It is true that all large mental hospitals have a substantial number of fairly well-adjusted patients for whom the hospital provides a convenient and relatively comfortable retreat. In most instances the staff tacitly goes along with the wishes of the patients, because the patients serve useful functions as assistants to attendants and ward workers. Other "recovered" patients are kept on because previous release has resulted in their prompt readmission. For most patients, however, hospitalization offers little reward. Recently admitted acutely disturbed patients are obviously unhappy. Their goals are relief from their symptoms and early discharge. The chronic patients in the locked back wards, who constitute the great majority of the resident population, derive little pleasure from their drab, restricted environment. For these long-term cases, small nursing homes may provide a better solution than hospitalization. A simple safeguard against encouraging newly admitted persons to become chronic patients might be the limitation of any patient's stay in a mental hospital to three months. If at the end of this period a patient still required psychiatric attention, some alternative form of community care could be provided. The proved effectiveness of modern drugs in moderating symptoms has virtually eliminated the need for prolonged hospitalization.

Psychopharmaceutical Drugs

The development, starting about 1952, of tranquilizing and antidepressant drugs has been a major influence in revolutionizing the care of mental patients. Psychoactive drugs have no curative power, but they are highly effective in relieving symptoms. Chemotherapy is particularly useful with psychotics, since it helps the patient maintain contact with the social environment, reduces emotional tensions, and decreases bizarre behavior. As a result, patients on medication can be allowed greater freedom and self-direction in mental hospitals than was possible before, can be discharged as soon as symptoms are brought under control, and can be treated in general hospitals and other community facilities. Whether a discharged patient succeeds in living in the community or has to be rehospitalized often depends on whether he continues to take his medication.

Tranquilizing drugs are also known as neuroleptics. They produce marked sedation without inducing sleep. Chlorpromazine, the first tranquilizer to be developed, is still the one most widely used with psychotic patients. Along with a long list of other related drugs, chlorpromazine is effective in relieving tension and anxiety; reducing hyperactivity, impulsiveness, and aggressiveness; and controlling hallucinations, delusions, and destructive behavior. There are wide individual differences in reactions to tranquilizing drugs. Choice of drug and dosage level must be adapted to the individual patient. After the optimum dosage has been determined, the usual policy is to experiment with lower dosages, since tranquilizing drugs may have toxic side effects: muscular rigidity, tremors, respiratory difficulties, skin rashes, jaundice. In the treatment of neuroses, personality disorders, and psychosomatic disorders, milder tranquilizers are preferred, such as Librium or Miltown. Side effects associated with these milder drugs include drowsiness, apathy, giddiness, hypotension, nausea, and syncope.

Three classes of drugs are used in the treatment of depressions. These are technically known as Impramine-type drugs, monoamine oxidase inhibitors, and psychomotor stimulants. The side effects of these antidepressants include drowsiness, dizziness, dry mouth, jaundice, profuse sweating, nausea, and palpitations. The *Comprehensive Textbook of Psychiatry,* edited by Freedman, Kaplan, and Kaplan (1967), provides a convenient source of information on drug therapy.

Summary

The various theories of psychopathology proposed by primitive, ancient, and modern man represent attempts to explain dysfunctions in accordance with prevalent beliefs and knowledge. Early hypotheses were about evenly divided between theories of external causation (spirit intervention, disease, sorcery, demonic possession, lunacy, bewitchment) and theories of internal or personal causation (loss of soul, breach of taboo, object intrusion, brain disease). In general, treatment procedures were related to the assumed cause. Another variable in treatment has been the periodic confusion of madness with badness. When possession by spirits was considered an accident over which the victim had no control, treatment was sympathetic and gentle. When collusion with evil spirits or witchcraft was inferred, harsher measures were used. Human suggestibility provides the simplest explanation for the periodic outbreaks of mass hysteria. Suggestion was also largely responsible for the dramatic effects and cures produced by Mesmer during the latter part of the eighteenth century.

Special institutions for the care of the mentally ill were established in Arabic countries as early as 800 A.D. A few small hospitals were started in several European countries during the fifteenth and sixteenth centuries. These early hospitals usually provided no more than custodial care. During the seventeenth and eighteenth centuries, when the mentally ill were degraded to the status of wild animals, mistreatment was the rule. Humane reforms were introduced toward the end of the eighteenth century. The revival of interest in the Hippocratic idea that mental disorders were the products of organic pathology helped reduce the stigma associated with mental illness. The application of the medical model of disease to behavior disorders influenced the rapid expansion of mental hospital facilities in this country during the first half of the twentieth century. Acceptance of the disease model favored experimentation with drastic shock techniques during the 1930s and 1940s, but an important contributory factor was the desperate need to provide some type of active treatment.

The present trend is to avoid admitting patients to special mental institutions whenever possible, and to treat them instead in general hospitals and other community facilities. A major criticism of the former practice of encouraging patients to enter mental hospitals is that the isolation of patients from the community and the dull, rigid hospital routine tend to encourage chronicity and the development of the social breakdown syndrome. At the same time, some chronic patients use mental hospitals as comfortable retirement centers. Modern mental hospitals emphasize intensive treatment and early discharge. Current methods of rehabilitating chronic hospitalized patients include milieu therapy and token economy programs. Both techniques have been found to be effective in improving the "normal" functioning of patients within the hospital. The present weak link in the therapeutic chain is the frequent relapse of patients after they return to the community. The rate of rehospitalization could be reduced through the development of more effective aftercare community programs. The discovery of tranquilizing and antidepressant drugs has been a major factor in revolutionizing the care and management of mental patients.

References

AYLLON, T., and AZRIN, N. *The Token Economy: A Motivational System for Therapy and Rehabilitation.* New York: Appleton-Century-Crofts, 1968.
BOCKOVEN, J. S. "Moral Treatment in American Psychiatry." *Journal of Nervous and Mental Disease* 124 (1956): 167–94, 292–321.

—— and SOLOMAN, H. C. "Five-Year Follow-up Study of One Hundred Patients Committed to the Boston Psychiatric Hospital." *New England Journal of Medicine* 251 (1954): 81–87.

BRAGINSKY, B. M.; BRAGINSKY, D. D.; and RING, K. *Methods of Madness: The Mental Hospital as a Last Resort*. New York: Holt, Rinehart & Winston, 1969.

CANTRIL, H. *The Invasion from Mars*. Princeton, N.J.: Princeton University Press, 1947.

CHADWICK, J., and MANN, W. N. *The Medical Works of Hippocrates*, pp. 190–91. Oxford: Blackwell Scientific Publications, 1950.

CLEMENTS, F. E. "Primitive Concepts of Disease." *University of California Publications in American Archeology and Ethnology* 32, no. 2 (1932): 185–252.

COUÉ, E., and ORTON, J. L. *Conscious Autosuggestion*. New York: Appleton-Century-Crofts, 1924.

DEUTSCH, A. *The Mentally Ill in America*. New York: Columbia University Press, 1946.

ELLSWORTH, R. B. "The Psychiatric Aide as Rehabilitation Therapist." *Rehabilitation Counseling Bulletin* 7 (1964): 81–86.

FIELD, M. J. "Witchcraft as a Primitive Interpretation of Mental Disorders." *Journal of Mental Science* 101 (1955): 826–33.

FREEDMAN, A. M.; KAPLAN, H. I.; and KAPLAN, H. S., eds. *Comprehensive Textbook of Psychiatry*, pp. 1251–95. Baltimore, Md.: Williams & Wilkins, 1967.

FREEMAN, W., and WATTS, J. W. *Psychosurgery*. Springfield, Ill.: Charles C. Thomas, 1942.

GOFFMAN, E. *Asylums*. Garden City, N.Y.: Doubleday, 1961.

GRUENBERG, E. M. "The Social Breakdown Syndrome: Some Origins." *American Journal of Psychiatry* 123 (1967): 12–20.

HEMPHILL, R. D. "The Influence of War on Mental Disease." *Journal of Mental Science* 87 (1941):170–82.

HONIGFELD, G., and GILLIS, R. "The Role of Institutionalization in the Natural History of Schizophrenia." *Diseases of the Nervous System* 28 (1967): 660–63.

HUNTER, R., and MACALPINE, I. *Three Hundred Years of Psychiatry, 1535–1860*. London: Oxford University Press, 1963.

JOHNSON, D. M. "The Phantom Anesthetist of Mattoon: A Field Study of Mass Hysteria." *Journal of Abnormal and Social Psychology* 40 (1945): 175–86.

KANTOR, D., and GELINEAU, V. "Social Processes in Support of Chronic Deviance." *International Journal of Social Psychiatry* 11 (1965): 280–89.

KAPLAN, B., and JOHNSON, D. "The Social Meaning of Navaho Psychopathology and Psychotherapy." In *Magic, Faith and Healing*, ed. A. Kiev. New York: Free Press, Macmillan, 1964.

KOLINOWSKY, L. B., and HOCH, P. *Shock Treatments, Psychosurgery, and Other Somatic Therapies in Psychiatry*. New York: Grune & Stratton, 1952.

LEA, H. C. *Materials Toward a History of Witchcraft*, ed. A. C. Howland, 3 vols. Philadelphia: University of Pennsylvania Press, 1939.

MILLER, E. "Psychological Theories of ECT: A Review." *British Journal of Psychiatry* 113 (1967): 301–11.

MORA, G. "History of Psychiatry." In *Comprehensive Textbook of Psychiatry,* ed. A. M. Freedman and H. I. Kaplan, pp. 2–34. Baltimore: Williams & Wilkins, 1967.

MURPHY, J. M. "Psychotherapeutic Aspect of Shamanism on St. Lawrence Island, Alaska." In *Magic, Faith, and Healing,* ed. A. Kiev, pp. 53–83. New York: Free Press, Macmillan, 1964.

PAUL, G. L. "Chronic Mental Patients: Current Status—Future Directions." *Psychological Bulletin* 71 (1969):81–94.

PINEL, P. *A Treatise on Insanity* (1801). New York: Hafner, 1962.

ROBBINS, R. H. *The Encyclopedia of Witchcraft and Demonology.* New York: Crown, 1959.

ROETHLISBERGER, F. J. *Management and Morale.* Cambridge: Harvard University Press, 1941.

SANDERS, R.; SMITH, R. S.; and WEINMAN, B. S. *Chronic Psychosis and Recovery.* San Francisco: Jossey-Bass, 1967.

SELLING, L. S. *Men Against Madness.* New York: Garden City Books, 1943.

STAUDT, V., and ZUBIN, J. "A Biometric Evaluation of the Somatotherapies in Schizophrenia." *Psychological Bulletin* 54 (1957):171–96.

SUMMERS, M. *Malleus maleficarum.* London: Pushkin Press, 1951.

ULLMANN, L. P. *Institution and Outcome: A Comparative Study of Psychiatric Hospitals.* New York: Pergamon Press, 1967.

ZILBOORG, G., and HENRY, G. W. *A History of Medical Psychology.* New York: Norton, 1941.

CHAPTER FIVE

Psychogenic Theories

Although valid in principle, our earlier statement that abnormal behavior, like normal behavior, is the product of the cumulative interaction of biological, sociocultural, and psychological factors is too broad to satisfy scientific requirements. We need to know more precisely which of the multiple psychobiosocial codeterminants of personality and behavior are of particular significance. If we assume that the significant codeterminants of normal behavior are the same as those of abnormal behavior, there still remains the problem of differentiating qualitative and quantitative variations that influence differences in outcomes. Considerable progress has been made in both theory and research in identifying what appear to be the key determinants of personality and behavior. These include the stability and intactness of the nervous system, general physical health, innate temperament, the nature of parent-child and peer interactions, the shaping influences of the culture and subculture, and the scope and quality of personal life experiences. Some limited success has been attained in identifying variations in these key determinants that contribute to abnormal behavior. Much of this information is still at the theoretical level, and therefore must be considered tentative. The more difficult and perhaps most critical task of examining and evaluating the effects of the interaction of significant codeterminants has barely been begun.

The Role of Theories

Theories are tentative principles offered to explain observed phenomena. A theory is, by definition, speculative and expendable. A theory does not have to be true to be useful. Negative findings that discount the importance of some suggested explanation serve the useful function of narrowing the field of inquiry to more promising alternatives. What is required of a theory is that it be relevant to facts and capable of generating testable hypotheses. A theory should be more than a wild guess, but even good theories that are based on empirical observations are merely promising ideas in need of more supportive evidence. A common practice in scientific research is to develop a series of alternative theories that may be tested one after the other to determine which, if any, have some factual basis. The more substantiated theories are then reexamined so that the researcher may determine which one provides the simplest and most economical explanation for the observed phenomenon. Until more definite information is gathered on the relative merits of the large number of suspected determinants of abnormal behavior, partisan commitment to particular theories has the advantage of focusing attention on specific variables and encouraging their detailed study. Care must be exercised in accepting and defending as gospel what ought to be regarded as expendable hypotheses, however.

An excellent illustration of the role, value, and tentativeness of theories is provided by the contributions of Sigmund Freud, the founder of psychoanalysis. Freud's claim to fame rests on his genius as a creator of provocative theories. The originality of his insights opened new perspectives and stimulated extensive research on the interpretation of dreams, human psychosexual development, the role of the unconscious, the significance of early parent-child relations in the etiology of neuroses, psychotherapy, and a host of related topics. Freud was strongly biased in favor of his theories and reserved to himself alone the right to add to them and revise them. As a scientist, however, he recognized the speculative nature of his ideas. In discussing his theory of human drives he stated (1922, p. 76): "I might be asked whether I am myself convinced of the views here set forth, and if so how far. My answer would be that I am neither convinced myself, nor am I seeking to arouse conviction in others. More accurately, I do not know how far I believe them." On another occasion he wrote (1935, p. 144): "Looking back, then, over the patchwork of my life's labors, I can say that I have made many beginnings and thrown out many suggestions. Something will come of them in the future. But I cannot tell myself whether it will be much or little."

Psychoanalysis

Freud was initially interested in understanding and explaining behavior and in developing new methods of treatment. Gradually he incorporated his views on psychopathology within a more general framework that encompassed normal as well as abnormal behavior. In this broader context, neuroses were regarded as an extreme variation of normal personality development and functioning. Freud consistently acknowledged the importance of genetic and constitutional factors. A biological foundation was ascribed to many of his key concepts. His major contributions, which collectively constitute the substance of psychoanalysis, consisted of several loosely interrelated theoretical constructs on the determinism of behavior, the role of the unconscious, the libido hypothesis, the structure of personality, and human psychosexual development. These are best described in his own lucid writings (Freud, 1933, 1956). Other good references are the books of Hendrick (1939) and Holzman (1970).

THE DETERMINATION HYPOTHESIS

A fundamental tenet of psychoanalysis is that behavior is motivated. There are underlying antecedent causes and psychological explanations for the ways people behave. Freud saw meaning and purpose even in such seemingly accidental occurrences as slips of the tongue, the forgetting of the name of a friend, the misplacing of objects, and the content of dreams. To Freud, dreams represented attempts at wish fulfillment. The concept of determinism was also applied to mental symptoms. Among other possible explanations, neurotic symptoms might represent indirect forms of wish fulfillment, defenses against anxiety, and compromise solutions to conflicts.

Freud recognized two basic life drives. The first, which was by far the strongest, consisted of sexual or libido impulses, which were broadly interpreted to include a number of pleasurable activities. The second consisted of ego drive, which served the organic needs of nutrition and self-preservation. In his later years (1922) Freud added the controversial concept of a death drive to explain aggressive, destructive, and suicidal behavior. This motivational system was supplemented by certain guiding principles. The behavior of children, sociopaths, and many neurotics was thought to be mainly dominated by the *pleasure principle*. This principle, which is the controlling factor in the sex drive, is characterized by the avoidance of pain and the seeking of pleasure through the immediate gratification of emotional needs, regardless of future consequences. In older and more mature persons, the pleasure principle comes under the control of the *reality principle*, which encourages the temporary denial of immediate pleasure in the interest of longer term gain. The reality principle is closely associated with the ego drives. Its purpose is to regulate the behavior of the individual so that his actions conform to the moral, social, and physical requirements of the external world. The death drive is guided by the *nirvana principle*. In his use of the term, Freud retained some of the Buddhist connotation of final release from disturbing desires and life problems through death.

THE ROLE OF THE UNCONSCIOUS

Freud believed that much behavior was motivated by unconscious forces. He distinguished three levels of consciousness: the conscious, the preconscious, and the unconscious. The conscious consists of events, memories, and impulses of which the individual is clearly aware at the moment. The preconscious is the storehouse of surface memories and desires of which one is not conscious at the moment, but which are readily recallable. The unconscious is a convenient abstraction for identifying thoughts, emotions, memories, and impulses that are not readily assessible to voluntary control. Their presence is indicated by the fact that they influence behavior even though the individual is not aware of their existence or nature. The unconscious includes primitive sexual and aggressive impulses that are part of man's biological heritage. The second major source of unconscious material consists of thoughts, memories, and wishes that were once conscious but which have been repressed because they were too shocking, painful, or shameful to tolerate. Unconscious material is denied direct access to awareness because it would be disturbing to the individual. Unconsious impulses are not dormant, however. They are constantly seeking expression. Often they may slip past the censor in the disguised form of fantasies and dreams. Much of the strange behavior of the mentally disturbed is attributed to the acting out of unconscious wishes and conflcts. In contrast to the contents of consciousness, which are internally consistent and related to current events, the contents of the unconscious are timeless, independent of logic, and unconcerned with the demands of reality or the rules of society.

THE LIBIDO HYPOTHESIS

The term *libido* is a Latin word that originally connoted sexual passion. Freud used the word in two ways: to indicate the aim and the energy strength of the sex drive. The libido hypothesis assumed that most of the energy generated by the metabolic processes of the body was transformed into sexual energy, and that the discharge of this energy followed a predetermined course. During early childhood, libido energy is mainly concentrated and discharged in the oral and anal regions. Later on, the major flow is to the genital region, with sex activity as the main outlet. If the appropriate outlet is blocked, some suitable substitute object or channel of expression may be sought. Thus sex energy that ideally should be directed toward a heterosexual object may be displaced on a person of the same sex, resulting in homosexual urges, or displaced on an object that serves as a fetish.

PERSONALITY STRUCTURE

As an aid in describing the inner dynamics of behavior, Freud arbitrarily arranged the varied and often antagonistic drives, needs, values, attributes, and functions of the personality into three categories. Each was conceived as a separate component of the total personality. The fictional separation was personified by the now familar names of id, superego, and ego. The id is the agent of the unconscious. It is dedicated to the immediate gratification of sexual and aggressive impulses and the uninhibited pursuit of pleasure. It is unconcerned with the demands of reality, with morals, social values, or logic. Contradictory impulses may coexist side by side, neither influencing the other. The superego is partly conscious but mainly unconscious. It is the component of the personality that is charged with the responsibility of enforcing the morals, values, and ethics the child acquires through introjection from his parents and society. It also includes moral inclinations acquired through biological evolution. The superego serves as both conscience and ego ideal. The ego is mainly conscious but it maintains contact with the unconscious. The ego corresponds to the "I" that is concerned with the mundane functions of perceiving, learning, remembering, and thinking. Freud thought of the ego as an extension of the id which had been modified through interaction with the external world to serve the needs of the id and self-preservation.

Hartmann (1939) has upgraded the autonomy and functions of the ego. He has proposed that the newborn child possesses innate ego functions that permit him to adapt to an average expectable environment. When necessary for survival and optimal adaptation, the ego may take on the added function of modifying the environment. The position of the ego in relation to the id and the superego is that of administrative officer. Its main duties are to (1) satisfy the self-preservation and adaptation needs of the individual, (2) modulate the primitive wishes of the id so that they may be expressed in a manner consistent with the requirements of the outer world, (3) enforce repression, and (4) reconcile the antagonistic strivings of the id and superego. In the discharge of its many duties, the ego often becomes the battleground for conflicts between the demands of the id and the restrictions of society and between the strivings of the id and the prohibitions of the superego. Failure on the part of the ego to perform its diverse functions adequately leads to anxiety and the emergence of neurotic defenses. As Greenson has noted (1959, p. 1402), all neurotic phenomena "are the result of an insufficiency of the ego's normal function of control. . . . Symptoms are either manifestations of involuntary discharges or rigidities which indicate inappropriate and unrealistic controls." The conflict in neurosis is usually between the ego and the id, but the superego may also participate.

When allied with the id against the ego, the superego may contribute to depressions, obsessive-compulsive reactions, and some forms of masochism. According to psychoanalytic doctrine, a psychosis represents a complete breakdown of ego control and defenses and the free and direct expression of id impulses and unconscious material.

THE PSYCHODYNAMIC HYPOTHESIS

Psychoanalytic explanations of behavior tend to have a historical bias. It is assumed that the experiences of the past shape and influence later behavior. To understand present behavior it is often necessary to find its antecedents. For example, a typical Freudian explanation of impotence in adult life is that the patient had an unresolved attachment to his mother when he was a child, and is still equating all women with her.

PSYCHOSEXUAL DEVELOPMENT

According to psychoanalytic theory, human psychosexual development follows a biologically predetermined sequence. The area of concentration of libido energy and its appropriate form of expression shift with successive stages. Each stage is marked by certain personality traits. The main phases are:

Oral stage. From birth to about eighteen months, sex energy is concentrated in the mouth region. This is the period of dependency, receiving, and oral incorporation. Later on, biting or oral aggressive behavior becomes dominant. Some residual manifestations of the oral phase in adults are smoking, drinking, and kissing. Oral character traits include optimism or pessimism, trust or distrust, and placidness or aggressiveness. Fixation at and subsequent regression to the oral phase are associated with the psychoses and certain forms of alcoholism.

Anal stage. From about eighteen months to three years, the erogenous zones consist of the anus, rectum, and bladder. Expulsion and retention are the main sources of pleasure. During this period the child who is not toilet-trained may come into conflict with his parents. Anal character traits include orderliness, punctuality, stubbornness, irresponsibility, overgenerosity, stinginess, and submissiveness. Fixation and regression at this level are associated with obsessive-compulsive reactions and certain types of character disorders.

Phallic stage. Between the ages of three to six years, the sex organs become the erogenous zones. Pleasurable sensations obtained from touching and feeling may lead to masturbation. The object of the libido is now shifted from the bodily self to the parent of the opposite sex. The boy's desire for the mother and feelings of hostile rivalry toward the father are referred to as the Oedipus complex. The girl's desire for the father and feelings of hostile rivalry toward the mother are called the Electra complex. Fixation and regression at this level are associated with the neuroses.

Latency stage. From about six to twelve years, interest in sex is secondary to interest in intellectual and physical activities. This is also a period of increased aggressiveness, represented by fighting, particularly in boys. The child spends an increasing amount of time outside the home with friends of the same sex. Codes of behavior become more structured. Fixation and regression at this level are associated with certain character disorders.

Genital stage. With the onset of puberty at about the age of twelve, interest in sex is revived. During puberty it is mainly expressed in a return of earlier phases. The intensification of both sex and aggressive drives during adolescence leads to romantic infatuations, radical idealism, rebelliousness against authority, and the search for personal identity. Heterosexual maturity, the final stage of psychosexual development, is usually not attained until early adulthood.

Normal, healthy individuals proceed smoothly from one phase to the next. As adults they have stable, satisfying heterosexual interests and attachments. The person potentially subject to a mental disorder remains fixated or arrested at a childhood level of development. Fixation may be due to either inadequate or excessive gratification. It is assumed that adjustment difficulties in adult life lead to regression to the individual's point of fixation. The earlier the fixation and subsequent level of regression, the more severe the disorder. The fixation constitutes the nucleus of the difficulty, and the adult disorder is built around this core.

ERIKSON'S MODIFICATION

Freud's theory of psychosexual development has been criticized on the grounds that it places undue emphasis on the early childhood period, is too narrowly confined to the biological aspects of sex, and fails to take adequate account of the psychosocial aspects of human development. Erikson (1963), an American psychoanalyst, has attempted to improve the Freudian model by outlining a broader eight-stage sequence of psychosocial development. Each of the stages, described in Table 5.1, is assumed to be distinguished by a specific conflict and associated with specific traits. Succeeding stages are dependent on the solution and integration of earlier ones. The two contributions of Erikson that have gained widest acceptance are his concept of basic trust during infancy and his analysis of identity crises during adolescence. Optimum identity is marked by a sense of psychosocial well-being, a feeling of being at home in one's body, a sense of

*Table 5.1.   Erikson's eight stages of psychosocial
development*

Stages	Basic conflict	Associated basic virtues
Oral-sensory	Basic trust vs. mistrust	Hope
Muscular-anal	Autonomy vs. doubt	Will power
Locomotor-genital	Initiative vs. guilt	Purpose
Latency	Industry vs. inferiority	Competence
Puberty and		
adolescence	Identity vs. role confusion	Fidelity
Young adulthood	Intimacy vs. isolation	Love
Adulthood	Generativity vs. stagnation	Care
Maturity	Ego integrity vs. despair	Wisdom

Adapted from Erik Erikson, *Childhood and Society* (New York: Norton, 1963).

knowing where one is going, and inner confidence of anticipated recognition from significant others (Erikson, 1968). The neurotic is confused and uncertain about these things.

PSYCHOANALYTIC TREATMENT

Analytic therapy is intensive, long-term, and expensive. Four to five treatment sessions per week for a period of two or more years are required for a complete analysis. Somewhat oversimplified, analytic treatment has two intermediate objectives. One is to retrace the patient's psychosexual development with the aim of locating the source of the problem and freeing him from early childhood fixations and distortions. The second is to help the patient uncover, understand, and come to terms with troublesome unconscious material so that repression is no longer necessary. Utilizing insights thus gained, the analyst then works toward the reconstruction of a sounder personality, one that is capable of coping more effectively with life problems and of deriving satisfaction from normal heterosexual activities. In other words, the goal is to strengthen the ego at the expense of the id by making the unconscious conscious. Psychoanalysts maintain that if current symptoms are eliminated by direct or short-term techniques that fail to penetrate to the underlying causes, they will soon be followed by other substitute symptoms.

The four main analytic techniques are *free association, dream analysis, interpretation,* and *transference.* Free association and dream analysis are used to tap the unconscious. In free association the patient reclines on a couch and reports whatever words, thoughts, or feelings happen to come to mind, no matter how trivial or personal they may seem. This procedure facilitates the expression of repressed memories and impulses, which are constantly seeking discharge. Freud referred to dreams as "the royal road to the unconscious." During sleep, when ego vigilance is reduced, repressed ideas and impulses are expressed in slightly disguised form in dreams. Free associations elicited by the manifest content of a dream lead to its latent content or real meaning. These procedures are not as simple as they may seem. The patient resists the recall of painful or guilt-laden memories. Helping the patient to overcome his resistance is an important part of the analyst's task.

The role of the analyst has been described as one of compassionate neutrality. He listens, occasionally suggests a possible interpretation, is understanding and considerate. At the same time he takes care not to permit his own personality to intrude upon the patient. One of his main functions is to serve as a transference object. Transference is a special relationship that develops between the patient and his analyst. In expressing and reliving his past, the patient transfers to the analyst the affection, resentment, hostility, and guilt he formerly felt toward his parents and other significant figures. Transference brings the neurosis into the open, where it can be examined and analyzed. The displaced, inappropriate, and often intense reactions of the patient toward his analyst are referred to as a transference neurosis. The interpretation of the transference neurosis helps the patient gain insight into his problems and to realize that these childhood feelings and reactions are no longer appropriate or rational in the context of his present adult life. The resolution of the transference neurosis is an important part of the cure. Freed of childhood fixations and the necessity of expending large amounts of energy to maintain repression, the patient can move on to normal interrelationships and more productive activities.

AN EVALUATION OF CLASSICAL PSYCHOANALYSIS

The theories of classical psychoanalysis have been repeatedly attacked, not only by outsiders but by dissenters within the psychoanalytic group. The main targets of critics have been Freud's view on sex, the unconscious, and the critical importance of early childhood experiences in determining behavior. Sex, even when broadly interpreted to encompass affection and love, is only one of several basic human needs. The appropriateness of assigning sexual significance to the early stages of infantile development has been frequently challenged. Cross-cultural studies have failed to confirm the universality of the Oedipus complex. Studies designed to test psychoanalytically derived hypotheses regarding early parent-child relations have resulted in inconclusive findings (Medinnus, 1967). In a sense, these findings do not contradict psychoanalytic theory, since Freud hedged his bets to provide for opposite effects. However, his heads-I-win-tails-you-lose strategem is a major weakness, since it makes his theories untestable. The major criticism of psychoanalysis as a form of treatment is that it is less effective than shorter, more economical, and less esoteric procedures that are more widely applicable (Eysenck, 1965). The classical techniques of free association, dream analysis, and transference require that the patient be relatively healthy, highly motivated, and adept in expressing and interpreting his thoughts and feelings. Despite these criticisms, classical psychoanalysis remains the favored approach of many psychiatrists and clinical psychologists. Most psychoanalysts who question the validity of some Freudian theories nevertheless continue to use the classical method of treatment.

Interpersonal Theories

The interpersonal theory of psychopathology is mainly identified with Harry Stack Sullivan. However, the central idea that the individual is the product and at times the victim of intrafamilial, social, and cultural experiences has also been proposed by Alder, Horney, Fromm, Scheff, and others.

Alfred Alder (1870–1937) was associated with Freud for a brief period, but he soon made a complete break with psychoanalysis and founded his own school, which he called *individual psychology.* Adler (1929, 1939) maintained that the principal human motive was the striving for superiority or power. He interpreted this paramount striving as a compensatory reaction to underlying feelings of inferiority. He assumed that feelings of inferiority were universal and acquired early in life. The helpless infant, who is completely dependent on the whims and actions of adults, learns the meaning of inferiority while still in the crib. Feelings of inadequacy are further nurtured, according to Adler, by the presence of organ defects, parental overindulgence or rejection, and the child's ordinal position in the family. The pampered, overindulged child is literally spoiled. He is of little value to himself or others once he leaves the protective hothouse atmosphere of his home. Unable to compete on equal terms with the outside world, he is susceptible to neurotic subterfuges. Or he may expect and demand the good things of life without any effort or sacrifice on his part. If he is denied, he feels justified in engaging in antisocial or criminal behavior to get what he imagines life owes him. The rejected child learns from daily home experiences that he is an inferior, unworthy person. The only child usually has the same home experiences and shares the same difficulties as the spoiled child, unless the reason he is an only child is that his parents dislike caring for a child and take good care not to have another; in that case he is not only rejected, but lonely as well. The eldest child is in a favored position, but much is expected of him. His lead is constantly being threatened by younger siblings who are trying to catch up with and pass him. As the baby of the family, the youngest child may be pampered, ignored, or pushed around by the rest. Children of famous parents are particularly susceptible to inferiority feelings, since they may feel that more is expected of them than they can possibly deliver.

By the age of five, each child creates for himself what Adler referred to as a *style of life*. This is a relatively enduring pattern of behavior that is tailored to overcome the individual's inferiority complexes. The life style influences the person's approach to the three fundamental challenges of life: adjustment to society, vocation, and love. The normal individual develops a style of life and related goals that lead to realistic, effective, and socially useful solutions. He has real interest in other people, which makes him a cooperative and helpful friend, a responsible worker, and a considerate partner in love. The neurotic individual is deficient in social feeling, and his life style is egocentric and parasitic. Fearful of failure, he avoids competition and selects lofty or unrealistic goals that he cannot be expected to attain or that lead to hollow triumphs. Neurotic symptoms are unintentionally exploited to excuse failure, to gain the attention and services of others, or to exaggerate meager achievements. Since the neurotic does not dare to engage in any activity that may result in failure, he adopts a cautious yes-but attitude toward all life challenges. "I would like to go to college, but . . ."

Adlerian treatment is direct and short-term. It is aimed at helping the patient to gain insight into his style of life and fictional goals, to build up his self-confidence, and to encourage him to acquire more effective behavior patterns that will enable him to achieve realistic, socially useful goals. The conversational method is used. No attempt is made to uncover the unconscious. Transference is discouraged. The therapist adopts the role of an understanding but objective friend. The major criticism of individual psychology is that it is too simple. All conflicts and disorders are reduced to the single formula of striving for superiority and egocentric goals to compensate for inferiority feelings. The chief merit of Adlerian concepts and practices is that they provide a rational common-sense approach to certain types of problems in children and adults for which counseling and guidance are often useful.

HARRY STACK SULLIVAN

Harry Stack Sullivan (1892–1949) was particularly interested in understanding schizophrenia, which he considered a grave disorder in living rather than a disease entity. He believed that the disorder occurred chiefly in persons "fixed" at the early adolescent level of personality, where sexual problems of intimacy with others are pressing issues (Mullahy, 1967). In his concern with schizophrenia, Sullivan differed from most psychoanalytic theorists, whose hypotheses were derived mainly from the study of neurotic patients. Sullivan (1953) recognized two basic motives: the satisfying of the biological needs of the organism for food, water, sleep, and sex, and the pursuit of the psychological need for security. The latter includes the need for status recognition and the need for intimacy with others. The satisfaction of these needs requires interaction with others from birth to death. During the early years, the child is mainly dependent on the mother for his survival. The good mother, who responds to the infant's signs of need tensions with tenderness, promotes the development of a feeling of confidence in interpersonal situations and a sense of security. The mother who responds to the child's need signals with anxiety communicates her emotional disturbance to the infant. The repeated occurrence of anxiety in interpersonal contacts inside and outside the home favors a self-system or personality marked by feelings of insecurity. If the individual is reasonably successful in fulfilling his biological and psychological needs with a minimum of anxiety, his confidence in himself is increased along with his self-esteem. Excessive anxiety, combined with low self-esteem and a feeling of insecurity in interpersonal situations, leads to personality disintegration and mental illness.

Attitudes toward the self, which constitute the core of the self-system, mainly reflect the appraisals made of the individual by his parents, peers, teachers, and associates. A distinction is made between the "good me," the "bad me," and the "not me." Those aspects of personality that elicit approval from significant others are considered part of the "good me"; those that lead to disapproval and anxiety are part of the "bad me"; and those that evoke rejection, shame, and loathing may become part of the "not me." Since the overt manifestation of "not me" and "bad me" behavior patterns would result in massive anxiety and loss of self-esteem, they tend to be repressed or dissociated. These self-system referents are learned and subject to modification as the individual matures and progresses through what Sullivan described as the stages of infancy, childhood, juvenile era, preadolescence, and adolescence. The first two stages cover the first five years of life, when the child's conception of himself is essentially determined by the pattern of mothering and intrafamilial experiences he encounters. During the juvenile period, from age five to eight, the child's range of experiences is extended to include interactions with peers and teachers. These new learning experiences may reinforce or alter the child's previously acquired perception of himself and his behavior patterns. The preadolescent period, covering the years from eight to twelve, is marked by the need for a close relationship with one or more peers of the same sex. A major change at this age is a transition from egocentrism to collaboration and nonsexual love. The establishment of a close relationship with one or more peers, plus the sharing of interests and feelings, helps the preadolescent to see the world as others see it. Self-appraisals may be clarified or modified. The period of adolescence is marked by a gradual shift from dependence to independence. Decisions involving vocational choice and moral standards may be associated with significant changes in the self-system and self-esteem. With the development of the gonads, interpersonal relations become complicated by the sex urge. The need for intimacy with a person of the opposite sex may conflict with the need for security if attempts to establish a heterosexual relationship meet with rejection or disdain.

Mental disorders, according to Sullivan, result from distorted perceptions of the self and others, which in turn are associated with the repressed or dissociated "not me." If the anxiety resulting from a threatened loss of control is checked by substitutive techniques, such as obsessive-compulsive rituals, the outcome is a neurosis. If substitutive techniques fail and the dissociated impulses emerge into conscious awareness, the outcome is panic and the emergence of psychotic symptoms. The focus of therapy is on the self-system of the individual and the defenses he has developed to cope with his insecurities. The role of the therapist is that of a participant observer. A major objective of therapy is to correct the individual's distorted perception of himself and others in the direction of greater "consensual validation." Personality reconstruction is considered desirable but not essential. A more limited but still acceptable goal is for the patient to recognize the sources of his anxiety and to learn more adaptive patterns of personal interaction. Sullivan was more interested in therapy than in developing a systematic theory. The strength of his approach was also its weakness: he confined himself to a limited range of observable data. The dynamics of intrapsychic processes were largely neglected.

KAREN HORNEY

Karen Horney's position represents a moderate modification of classical psychoanalysis. She rejected Freud's biologically oriented view that the basic conflict in psychoneuroses is between man's inherent sexual and aggressive drives and the repressing forces of society. According to Horney (1939, 1945), psychoneuroses are generated by disturbances in human relationships and influenced by cultural factors. Although acknowledging the prime significance of early childhood experiences in molding the neurotic personality, she also recognized the importance of conflicts in later life. The child early acquires feelings of isolation and insecurity as a result of exposure to such adverse environmental influences as absence of affection, parental domination, and overprotection. He develops a basic anxiety that causes him to dread the environment as a whole, and he builds up defenses to protect himself from his anxiety. In attempting to get along in a potentially hostile world, the child represses his own hostile impulses and may (*a*) move toward people and obtain security and a sense of belonging by being submissive and dependent, (*b*) move against people and aggressively fight his way in the world, or (*c*) move away from people and live in an isolated private world. Normal people combine and integrate these three attitudes and thus achieve a balanced, unified personality. For reasons Horney does not explain, the neurotic has a rigid personality and is unable to achieve this unity, with the consequence that these contradictory attitudes remain irreconcilable. Horney maintains that it is this conflict between contradictory and incompatible attitudes that constitutes the basic core of neuroses. The important point is not the presence of a conflict but the nature of the conflict. Normal people frequently have conflicts, but these are concerned with an actual and voluntary choice between two desirable possibilities; for example, whether to marry or to go to graduate school. The neurotic is driven by equally compelling forces in opposite directions, and he has no choice in the matter. Thus a student may be torn between a desire for friends and a dislike of people. The neurotic is also characterized by a discrepancy between his potentialities and his accomplishments. The aim of therapy is to resolve inner conflicts by changing those conditions within the personality which have brought them into being. The standard psychoanalytic techniques are used to help the patient become aware of his conflicts and their effect on his personality.

ERICH FROMM

Erich Fromm has been mainly concerned with the impact of modern society on personality development and psychopathology. Acting through the agency of the family, society imposes a "social character" on the individual. Fromm describes five basic character types: receptive, exploitive, hoarding, marketing, and productive. Each of these occurs in all societies, but in various periods of history the social climate may favor the development of one or another of these character types. Modern society, according to Fromm, tends to produce a standard, uniform personality that can be readily sold and exchanged in the marketplace. Typical traits associated with the marketing character are opportunism, inconsistency, suppression of individual qualities, and lack of genuineness in human relationships. The need to think, act, and feel like everyone else thwarts man's need for individual identity and expression and interferes with meaningful relationships with other persons and with nature. Neuroses and antisocial behavior represent attempts to escape from a "sick" conformity-imposing society that alienates man's basic needs and creates overwhelming feelings of loneliness. With respect to treatment, Fromm relies on the usual psychoanalytic techniques. His writings have attracted more popular than scientific interest. His vision of utopia is a communitarian humanistic society made up of productive, creative individuals.

The Family as an Etiological Factor

Practically all psychogenic theories imply or specifically state that much of psychopathology is acquired through faulty family interaction. The unique aspect of family theories is that the emphasis is shifted from the individual to the family as a whole (Beels and Ferber, 1969). This point of view arose out of clinical observations that the effectiveness of individual therapy was largely influenced and frequently undone by the action of the family. Often clinical improvement in one member of the family was followed by the appearance of overt symptoms in some other member. In other words, the presence of symptoms in a particular member of the family represented a homeostatic and shifting expression of family pathology. The conception of the patient as the scapegoat of the underlying family pathology represents a sharp departure from the traditional view, which assumes that intrapsychic disturbances centered in the patient are the major determinants of disordered functioning. If it is assumed that the family is the major source of pathology, the obvious corrective procedure is to treat the family.

Family therapy is an approach rather than a technique. It involves the simultaneous treatment of two or more persons. Some family therapists like to work with a small number of relatives. Others insist on the attendance of all members of the family, including children and babies. The particular procedures used vary with individual therapists. Some work alone; others prefer to have a colleague, preferably one of the opposite sex, present at meetings. Some therapists follow essentially the psychoanalytic model, encouraging the participants to talk over their feelings, grievances, and conflicts (Boszormenyi-Nagy and Framo, 1965). The premise is that the family has for a long time been covering up secrets, perpetuating myths, and presenting distorted images of one another. The confrontation of the family with the truth is thought to have therapeutic value. Among other functions, the role of the therapist is to promote free communication, note inconsistencies and contradictions, expose hypocrisy and projection, cut off endless bickering over irrelevant issues, facilitate mutual understanding, and enlist cooperative effort that will result in improved family relationships. Other family therapists have little interest in uncovering the underlying causes of family friction or of helping the members to gain insight into their problems (Haley and Hoffman, 1967). They see their role as that of experts providing guidance and instruction in ways in which the family members can communicate and relate more effectively. The goal is to improve the interaction of the family members so that each will have increased independence and sense of personal worth. The straightening out of lines of communication among family members and the moderation of the family power struggle is considered the main objective of family meetings. All family therapists share the common goal of aiding the family to function better as a group. The aim is not to increase the cohesiveness of the family, however. On the contrary, the intent is to promote the growth and differentiation of individual members through improving the functioning of the family as a unit. As Bowen has said (1966), the purpose of family therapy is to separate the individual from the undifferentiated family ego mass.

Family therapy differs from group therapy in many respects. In group therapy, the members meet as strangers and outside of therapy sessions have no close contact with one another. There is no particular interest in the mental health of the group as a unit. The group is simply a device for facilitating the improvement of the individual members. In family therapy the members have a close past, present, and future association with one another. The concern is with the well-being of the total family. Family therapy may be combined with individual therapy for certain members. An important difference between individual and family therapy is that in individual therapy considerable emphasis is placed on the confidentiality of private communication. In family therapy, secrets and feelings are openly shared. A unique feature of family therapy is that it provides a valuable source of nonverbal data. The postures, facial expressions, gestures, and preferred seating arrangements of the participants are often more meaningful than what is said.

Family therapy was initially tried out with schizophrenic patients and their families. Therapeutic success of the method with this population has been modest, but the procedure did expose prevalent misconceptions regarding the nature of schizophrenia. When patients who gave every indication of being apathetic, withdrawn, and out of touch with their environment in a hospital ward were placed in a family therapy setting, they surprisingly behaved much like the "normal" members of the family. As soon as they returned to the ward, they reverted to their schizophrenic role.

Family therapy is currently extensively used in the treatment of marital problems, family crises, parent-child conflicts, neuroses, and other personality and behavior disturbances in children and adults. Research data on the effectiveness of the procedure are meager, in part because the usual criteria for evaluating outcome in individual patients are not applicable. As we noted earlier, family therapists are not particularily interested in the removal of symptoms in individual patients. Their goal is to improve the total system of family communication and interaction; if this is achieved, an improvement in the effectiveness and adjustment of each member of the family is supposed to come as a by-product. According to Ackerman (1966), the procedure is contraindicated when there is evidence of an irreversible trend toward the breakup of the family or when one parent is afflicted with a progressive paranoid condition or manifests deeply rooted and intractable sociopathic traits.

The family therapy approach has shown a steady gain in converts since its inception in the early 1950s. However, the great majority of therapists still prefer the more traditional method of treating patients on an individual basis.

EVALUATION OF THE FAMILY ROLE

While differing on specifics, virtually all therapists agree that adverse intrafamilial factors are a major contributory cause of psychopathology. The evidence for this viewpoint consists essentially of clinical observations. Especially if one starts with the premise that family factors have causal significance, confirmatory data can be readily found. It is a rare patient whose family history does not include one or more of the following unfavorable items: broken home, early death of one or both parents, actual or emotional divorce of parents, overprotective or overcontrolling parents, rejecting parents, sibling rivalry, marital or family discord, deviant behavior in some member of the family, overstrict or overlax standards, inconsistent or severe discipline, overly close family ties, unrealistic parental expectations. However, these "pathogenic" signs are also frequently noted in the family backgrounds of normal individuals.

A first step in evaluating the role of the family in psychopathology is to compare the frequency of unfavorable family factors in pertinently matched groups of mental patients and normal persons. The few studies in which this has been done indicate that the family backgrounds of mental patients do not differ significantly from those of normal persons (Frank, 1965). A second, more rigorous test consists of determining whether certain kinds of family pathology are associated with specific forms of abnormal behavior. From his review of the extensive literature on this point, Frank concluded that the same patterns of adverse parent-child relationships have been noted in schizophrenics, neurotics, and delinquents.

More refined and better controlled studies may eventually reveal differences between the home backgrounds of mental patients and normal persons. But there would still remain the problem of explaining why and how some children are adversely affected by family pathology while most of their brothers and sisters escape with minor defects or are indistinguishable from the normal population. Differential outcome in siblings may be due to family changes over time and to variations in the ways in which the same parents rear and relate to their children. An alternate and more cogent explanation is that the unique genetic endowment of each child influences the differential impact of the family environment and in some measure also influences the types of responses the child elicits from his parents. The role of the family is further modified by experiences outside the home during childhood and later years. In summary, the family is important, but it is only one of several contributory and interactive factors that collectively shape personality development and behavior.

Phenomenology

Phenomenology is a concept borrowed from philosophy that stresses the individual's subjective perception of himself and the outer world as the critical determinant of behavior. Maslow (1962), Allport (1961), and other advocates of this approach tend to agree that the basic human motive is the maximum development of inherent potentialities in a manner expressive of and consistent with one's self-concept. Little attention is given to conflicts or unconscious impulses. The occurrence of anxiety and maladjustment are related to the thwarting of self-fulfillment needs and/or threats to the self-structure.

CARL ROGERS

The best known of the phenomenological theories is the client-centered model developed by Carl Rogers (1959, 1961). Reality is defined in terms of the individual's perception and awareness of his experiences. Experiences that are perceived by the infant as favorable to the actualization of his inherent potentialities are evaluated positively and elicit approach responses. Those perceived as negating this objective are evaluated negatively and avoided. As the child develops, selected experiences related to awareness of being and functioning become organized and identified with the concept of self. As awareness of self emerges, the child soon learns that to be favorably regarded by parents and others is satisfying and rewarding. The internalization of this need for positive regard leads to the more important need of positive self-regard. If a person receives unconditional acceptance and approval from others, he acquires a sense of unconditional positive self-regard and personal worth. This fortunate experience leads to the development of an ideal or fully functioning person, one in whom there is no incongruence between self and potentialities, who has no defenses because he needs none, who is open to experience, spontaneous, self-reliant, and creative. On the other hand, if the individual receives conditional positive regard—if he receives approval only occasionally and inconsistently—the outcome is less favorable. Disapproved experiences that are incongruent with the self-structure are either denied or distorted in such a way as to seem congruent with the self. Defenses are erected against these denied or distorted experiences. If these defenses prove unsuccessful, the resulting threat to the self-structure leads to anxiety and disorganized behavior. Associated symptomatic manifestations may reflect emergency adjustments or the overt, direct expression of experiences hitherto distorted or denied.

Treatment involves a reversing of the defense process. Previously threatening experiences must be accurately symbolized in awareness and integrated into the self-concept. The client-centered therapist attempts to build up the patient's self-regard by genuinely offering unconditional positive regard in a context of empathic understanding. He tries to see the world from the patient's point of view, to sense and reflect his perceptions, distortions, strivings, feelings, and experiences. The premise is that sincere acceptance and understanding of the patient as he is reduces his need for defenses. The main criticisms of this approach center about its incompleteness. Rogers does not spell out the innate potentialities of man in general or of the specific individual. His description of the development of the self-structure is sketchy. The role of emotions, and particularly of aggression, is relatively neglected. The preoccupation with subjective constructs excludes other relevant, objective data. On the plus side, Rogers has initiated and stimulated numerous research studies that have contributed to an understanding of psychopathology and the therapeutic process.

Existentialism

Persons taking the existentialist approach have been more interested in formulating a point of view or describing how man ought to be than in developing a personality theory. Existentialism represents a phenomenologically embedded attempt on the part of theologians, philosophers, psychologists, and psychiatrists to emphasize the uniqueness and freedom of the individual and the critical significance of meaning and values. Stress is placed on a person's right to be himself, to be guided by his own experiences and decisions, and to accept responsibility for his choices. Most of the major contributions have been made by Kierkegaard, Nietzsche, Heidegger, Jaspers, Sartre, Binswanger, Frankl, and other European writers. Leading exponents in this country include Rollo May (1961), Paul Tillich (1952), and Adrian Van Kamp (1967).

The existentialists posit a basic confrontation between being and nonbeing. To be authentic, a person must make a commitment to life and be willing to accept risks in expressing his freedom and actualizing his full potentialities. To do otherwise is to suffer loss of meaning and a reduction or alienation of self, which are considered to constitute the basis for mental disorders. No specific therapeutic techniques are proposed. The role of the therapist, as Van Kamp describes it, is to foster an atmosphere that will enable the patient to realize the unique meaning of his existence within his particular life situation, to face his personal responsibility, and to accept both the joys and the unavoidable pain and suffering of human life.

Learning Theories

Learning is a difficult term to define. The occurrence of learning is inferred from the presence of some new activity, a change in behavior, or the increased probability that a given stimulus will elicit a particular response. However, as Hilgard and Bower note (1966, p. 2), learning is only one of several possible explanations for behavior change. "Learning is the process by which an activity originates or is changed through reacting to an encountered situation, provided that the characteristics of the change in activity cannot be explained on the basis of native response tendencies, maturation, or temporary states of the organism (e.g., fatigue, drugs, etc.)." In addition, the prevalent assumption that learning is mainly concerned with the manipulation of stimuli and responses tends to disregard the fact that learning is a function of the total organism. How a person will react to current stimuli and what he will learn from exposure to certain experiences will depend on his genetic potentialities, his prior developmental history, the state of the organism at the time, and a host of other modifying variables. Commenting on the latter point, Mowrer writes (1965, p. 245): "Stimuli never produce or cause behavioral responses in the manner implied by S-R connectionism or reflexology. A stimulus S may suggest a particular response R. But the fact that S is present does not at all mean that the subject is obliged or 'forced' to make a particular R—or, indeed, any R at all."

CLASSICAL CONDITIONING

Classical conditioning is also known as Pavlovian conditioning, after its discoverer, I. P. Pavlov. In his early work Pavlov (1927) demonstrated how irrational behavior (a dog salivating at the sound of a bell, for example) can be learned. Pavlov trained a dog to stand in a loose harness in a quiet room where there was a minimum of distracting stimuli. A bell was sounded, and a few seconds later food was presented to the animal. On the early trials, the sounding of the bell did not elicit salivation, but the food did. After a number of trials in which the sounding of the bell was paired with the presentation of food, the sound of the bell alone elicited salivation. When the bell was repeatedly sounded without being immediately followed by the presentation of food, salivation gradually decreased and finally stopped. This process is called *experimental extinction*.

In Pavlov's experiments the food presented to the dog constituted an *unconditioned stimulus;* the sound of the bell was a *conditioned stimulus.* Salivation associated with the presentation of food was an *unconditioned response.* Salivation in response to the conditioned stimulus of the bell was a *conditioned response.* Once a conditioned stimulus has been established, similar but different stimuli, as for example a sound other than that produced by the bell, may elicit the conditioned response. This phenomenon is referred to as *stimulus generalization.* Selective *discrimination* of and response to a particular signal is established by pairing the unconditioned stimulus (food) only with the specific signal. Discrimination training leads to the extinction of the response to generalized but inappropriate stimuli.

Classical conditioning offers a possible explanation for the acquisition of irrational fears and other disruptive emotional responses. In 1920 Watson and Rayner experimentally demonstrated the conditioning of a fear reaction in an eleven-month-old child named Albert. Previous observations had shown that Albert had no fear of a white rat but was readily frightened by unexpected loud noises. The white rat (conditioned stimulus) was presented to Albert, and just as his hand touched the animal, a steel bar was struck with a hammer behind Albert's head (unconditioned stimulus). Albert reacted to the sound with a violent startle, fell forward, and buried his face in the mattress. A repetition of the paired stimulii elicited a similar reaction with whimpering. A week later the white rat was presented without any accompanying sound. Albert started to reach for the rat, but when the rat nosed his hand, Albert quickly jerked his hand away. Albert was then exposed to five more paired presentations of the rat with the noise. When the rat was next presented, Albert started to cry and crawl away as rapidly as he could. At the following and final session, it was observed that Albert's conditioned fear had spread or become generalized to include a variety of furry objects: a rabbit, a dog, a fur coat, and a Santa Claus mask.

OPERANT CONDITIONING

Operant conditioning is most closely associated with the contributions of B. F. Skinner (1938, 1957). Ferster and Perrot (1968) have provided a convenient summary of its basic principles and technical terms. One important difference between classical and operant conditioning is that the order of the response is reversed. In classical conditioning the subject is presented with a stimulus, which elicits a response. In operant conditioning, the experimenter waits until the subject makes some desired response or some approximation of it, and then reinforces the behavior by some suitable "reward." For example, if the experimenter wants to get a noncommunicative mental patient to talk, he may sit with him and speak casually or engage in some sort of activity that will encourage conversation. Whenever the patient says something, the experimenter shows interest and responds in a friendly manner, thus reinforcing the act of speaking in the patient with the aim of increasing the frequency of his speech. If the patient says nothing, the experimenter may initially reinforce any mouth movement by offering the patient a cigarette or some chewing gum. After mouth movements have been reinforced until they are readily elicited, the patient may be required to make a vocal sound before his behavior is rewarded. During later trials, intelligible speech may be required before the patient is given the selected reinforcer. This step-by-step process is referred to as *successive approximation* or *shaping*. The rate of learning is usually improved if reinforcement is intermittent rather than continuous.

Operant conditioning may be used in the acquisition or modification of almost any behavior that is within the repertoire and capabilities of the organism. This gives it an important advantage over classical conditioning, which is largely limited to simple reflex or emotional behavior. Operant conditioning may also be used to decrease the frequency of undesired behavior. Undesired behavior may be decreased or eliminated by the omission of reinforcement, or *negative reinforcement*. Negative reinforcement may consist of the denial of some desired or expected object or response, or the administration of shock or some other aversive stimulus. A standard technique for decreasing the occurrence of temper tantrums in children is to ignore the child completely when he engages in such behavior. Ayllon (1963) has described an interesting example of the use of food deprivation as a negative reinforcement for food stealing by an obese mental patient. Whenever the woman approached a table other than the one reserved for her alone or took an excessive amount of food from the dining-room counter, nurses immediately removed her from the room and she missed the meal. In two weeks she stopped stealing food.

A somewhat paradoxical learning technique that may be considered a special form of negative reinforcement is called *satiation*. The procedure has long been used by owners of candy stores, who have learned from experience that if they encourage new employees to eat all the candy they want, most employees soon become literally "fed up" with candy and rarely want any. Resnick (1968) has demonstrated that the satiation technique can be effective in helping people to stop smoking. Subjects were required to double or triple their former consumption of cigarettes for a week. A follow-up inquiry conducted four months later showed that the satiated subjects had reduced the number of cigarettes smoked per day more than 50 percent. Twenty-five of the forty satiated subjects, or about 60 percent, had stopped smoking. In contrast, the smoking rate for most members of a control group remained unchanged, and only four of the twenty control subjects had stopped smoking by the end of the four-month follow-up period.

Two other techniques closely related to satiation are *negative practice* and *implosive therapy*. Negative practice consists in deliberately repeating over and over again some undesirable motor habit (Dunlap, 1932; Yates, 1958). The technique has been found fairly effective in eliminating tics, spasms, stammering, and other motor habits. One possible explanation is that the repeated voluntary performance of a habit brings it under voluntary control. In operant terms, the endless repetition may be considered aversive training. Implosive therapy has been described by Stampfl and Levis (1967), who recommend its use in the treatment of a wide variety of psychopathological problems. It is based on the hypothesis that past conditioning causes certain objects and situations to elicit anxiety. Patients are asked to imagine or verbalize these anxiety-producing stimuli, to dwell on them at length and repeatedly. By reinstating or symbolically reproducing the anxiety-eliciting stimuli in the therapeutic situation where the usual reinforcement does not occur, the anxiety response is extinguished. As in all operant procedures, it is irrelevant whether the patient understands or accepts the significance of the cues. All that is necessary to eliminate the anxiety is to re-present the conditioned cues in the absence of primary reinforcement. In effect, the therapist forces the patient to be flooded with anxiety-provoking cues that he would normally attempt to avoid in daily life. The repeated nonreinforced exposure leads to the extinction of the anxiety.

MODELING BEHAVIOR

Bandura (1962, 1969) has emphasized the use of modeling procedures in the acquisition of new performances and the modification of established behaviors. Modeling behavior consists of imitating the behavior of another person, and thus is essentially a form of social learning. For modeling behavior to occur, the individual must have the necessary skills to imitate the behavior of the model and be motivated to do so. When backed up by positive reinforcement, imitation is an efficient technique for learning the social roles that are expected of a person in various situations. The social value of acquired performances and roles will, of course, depend on the model. Thus, a child exposed to undesirable models may learn to be aggressive, fearful, suspicious, hypochondriacal, exploitive, or antisocial. In the absence of appropriate models, the individual may fail to acquire the varied skills and roles required for effective functioning. The absence of competence in varied roles may contribute to the rigidity and nonadaptiveness that is characteristic of psychopathological behavior.

LEARNING THEORY AND BEHAVIOR DISORDERS

The idea that behavior disorders consist primarily of maladaptive attitudes and reaction patterns resulting from errors or deficiencies in learning is not new. Watson rejected the then prevalent disease model of mental disorders as early as 1924. He maintained that faulty habits constituted the basis of personality disturbances and that the cure consisted in retraining. Personality disturbances arise

> from habit distortion—distortion carried to the point where compensatory factors (serviceable habits) are not sufficient to carry the individual along in society. . . . The proof that personality disturbances are due to long-continued behavior complications and not to organic disturbances appears from the fact that, in many cases, under new and suitable environments, the old reactions can be broken down and new ones entrained. . . . The retraining ("cure"), although more difficult, is neither more nor less mysterious and wonderful than teaching the infant to reach for candy and to withdraw his hand from a candle flame [1924, p. 449].

What is new is that learning theory today has gained wide acceptance both as an explanation of the ways in which abnormal behavior is acquired and as a rationale for treatment. There is now an extensive and rapidly growing body of literature on the effectiveness of the application of learning principles to the treatment of all types of behavior disorders (Kanfer and Phillips (1970). The difficulty of conducting longitudinal studies on human subjects has limited research efforts to document the premise that behavior disorders are caused by deficits and errors in learning and maintained by current reinforcement procedures that perpetuate established behaviors. Animal studies strongly support the hypothesis that abnormal behavior is learned in the same way that normal behavior is learned, although there is some question whether experimentally induced behavior disturbances in animals are valid analogues of human psychopathology. Learning theory, however, does pose two puzzling questions. At some time or other everyone is exposed to dramatic situations and makes undesirable responses that are reinforced. Why, then, doesn't everyone acquire fears, guilt feelings, and faulty habit patterns? Secondly, learning theory holds that "wrong" responses that lead to negative reinforcement are supposed to "extinguish," or die out. Why do the maladaptive and distressing symptoms of the neurotic persist? One answer, suggested by Hollingworth (1930, p. 95), is that there is more to a neurosis than the establishment of a faulty habit. "To be neurotic is above all to be the kind of person who is always forming such unserviceable or unsagacious habits even under circumstances or in a world where other prople form useful ones." And perhaps to be neurotic is to cling to maladaptive habits that normal people outgrow or learn to discard. Genetic factors may predispose some people to acquire and retain maladaptive reaction patterns. After all, people exhibit wide individual differences in innate capacity for learning most skills and behaviors. There is no reason why aptitude for learning how to cope effectively with problems in living should be an exception to the rule.

Summary

The various psychogenic theories are best considered as complementary rather than discrete. Each adds to and merges with the others to form an increasingly accurate description of man. The stark Freudian image of human behavior as dominated by primitive sexual and aggressive impulses and unconscious strivings is moderated by Adler's concept of social interest and brightened by the existentialists' addition of authenticity, self-fulfillment, and values. The emphasis of psychoanalysis on intrapsychic conflicts is balanced by the importance attached by Sullivan and others to interpersonal relationships and the stress placed by modern behavior theorists on the role of learning. The direct frontal attack on current symptoms favored by learning theorists offsets the analysts' preoccupation with the search of the past for insights that will explain present behavior. All of these theories have one thing in common: none of them makes a sharp distinction between the determinants of normal and abnormal behavior. The basic processes underlying personality development and behavior are the same. Because of the complexity of the ingredients and the total operation, the end products differ. The more extreme variations that have unfavorable effects on the individual and his society are labeled abnormal.

References

ACKERMAN, N. *Treating the Troubled Family.* New York: Basic Books, 1966.
ADLER, A. *The Practice and Theory of Individual Psychology.* New York: Harcourt, 1929.
———. *Social Interest.* New York: Putnam, 1939.
ALLPORT, G. W. *Pattern and Growth in Personality.* New York: Holt, Rinehart & Winston, 1961.
ANSBACKER, H., and ANSBACKER, R. *The Individual Psychology of Alfred Adler.* New York: Basic Books, 1956.
AYLLON, T. "Intensive Treatment of Psychotic Behavior by Stimulus Satiation and Food Reinforcement." *Behavior Research and Therapy* 1 (1963): 53–61.

BANDURA, A. "Social Learning Through Imitation." *Nebraska Symposium on Motivation,* ed. M. R. Jones, pp. 211–69. Lincoln: University of Nebraska Press, 1962.

———. *Principles of Behavior Modification.* New York: Holt, Rinehart & Winston, 1969.

BEELS, C. C., and FERBER, A. "Family Therapy: A View." *Family Process* 8, no. 2 (1969): 280–318.

BOSZORMENYI-NAGY, I., and FRAMO, J., eds. *Intensive Family Therapy.* New York: Harper & Row, 1965.

BOWEN, M. "The Use of Family Theory in Clinical Practice." *Comparative Psychiatry* 7 (1966): 345–74.

DUNLAP, K. *Habits: Their Making and Unmaking.* New York: Liveright, 1932.

ERIKSON, E. *Childhood and Society.* New York: Norton, 1963.

———. *Identity, Youth, and Crisis.* New York: Norton, 1968.

EYSENCK, H. J. "The Effects of Psychotherapy." *International Journal of Psychiatry* 1 (1965): 99–142.

FERSTER, C. B., and PERROT, M. C. *Behavior Principles.* New York: Appleton-Century-Crofts, 1968.

FRANK, G. H. "The Role of the Family in the Development of Psychopathology." *Psychological Bulletin* 64 (1965): 191–205.

FREUD, S. *Beyond the Pleasure Principle.* London: International Psychoanalytic Press, 1922.

———. *New Introductory Lectures on Psychoanalysis,* trans. J. H. Sprott. New York: Norton, 1933.

———. *Autobiography.* New York: Norton, 1953.

———. *The Standard Edition of the Complete Psychological Works of Sigmund Freud.* London: Hogarth Press, 1956.

FROMM, E. *Man for Himself.* New York: Holt, 1947.

———. *The Sane Society.* New York: Holt, 1955.

GREENSON, R. R. "The Classical Psychoanalytic Approach." In *American Textbook of Psychiatry,* ed. S. Arieti, vol. 2, pp. 1399–1416. New York: Basic Books, 1959.

HALEY, J., and HOFFMAN, L. *Techniques of Family Therapy.* New York: Basic Books, 1967.

HARTMANN, H. *Ego Psychology and the Problem of Adaptation,* trans. David Rapaport. New York: International Universities Press, 1958 (1939).

HENDRICK, I. *Facts and Theories of Psychoanalysis.* New York: Knopf, 1939.

HILGARD, E. R., and BOWER, G. H. *Theories of Learning.* New York: Appleton-Century-Crofts, 1966.

HOLLINGWORTH, H. L. *Abnormal Psychology.* New York: Ronald Press, 1930.

HOLZMAN, P. S. *Psychoanalysis and Psychopathology.* New York: McGraw-Hill, 1970.

HORNEY, K. *New Ways in Psychoanalysis.* New York: Norton, 1939.

———. *Our Inner Conflicts.* New York: Norton, 1945.

KANFER, F. H., and PHILLIPS, J. S. *Learning Foundations of Behavior Therapy.* New York: Wiley, 1970.

MASLOW, A. H. *Toward a Psychology of Being.* Princeton, N.J.: Van Nostrand, 1962.

MAY, R. *Existential Psychology.* New York: Random House, 1961.

MEDINNUS, G. R., ed. *Readings in the Psychology of Parent-Child Relations.* New York: Wiley, 1967.

MOWRER, O. H. "Learning Theory and Behavior Therapy." in *Handbook of Clinical Psychology,* ed. B. B. Wolman, pp. 243–73. New York: McGraw-Hill, 1965.

MULLAHY, P. "Harry Stack Sullivan's Theory of Schizophrenia." *International Journal of Psychiatry* 4 (1967): 492–521.

PAVLOV, I. P. *Lectures on Conditioned Reflexes,* trans. G. V. Anrep. London: Oxford University Press, 1927.

RESNICK, J. H. "Effects of Stimulus Satiation on the Overlearned Maladaptive Response of Cigarette Smoking." *Journal of Consulting and Clinical Psychology* 32, no. 5 (1968): 501–5.

ROGERS, C. R. "A Theory of Therapy, Personality, and Interpersonal Relationships, as Developed in the Client-Centered Framework." In *Psychology: A Study of a Science,* ed. S. Koch, vol. 3, pp. 184–256. New York: McGraw-Hill, 1959.

————. *On Becoming a Person.* Boston: Houghton Mifflin, 1961.

SKINNER, B. F. *The Behavior of Organisms.* New York: Appleton-Century-Crofts, 1938.

————. *Verbal Behavior.* New York: Appleton-Century-Crofts, 1957.

STAMPFL, T. G., and LEVIS, D. J ."Essentials of Implosive Therapy: A Learning-Theory-Based Psychodynamic Behavioral Therapy." *Journal of Abnormal Psychology* 72, no. 6 (1967): 496–503.

SULLIVAN, H. S. *Interpersonal Theory of Psychiatry.* New York: Norton, 1953.

TILLICH, P. *The Courage to Be.* New Haven: Yale University Press, 1952.

VAN KAMP, A. "The Goals of Psychotherapy from the Existential Point of View." In *The Goals of Psychotherapy,* ed. A. R. Mahrer. New York: Appleton-Century-Crofts, 1967.

WATSON, J. B. *Psychology from the Standpoint of a Behaviorist.* Philadelphia: Lippincott, 1924.

———— and RAYNER, R. "Conditioned Emotional Responses." *Journal of Psychology* 3 (1920): 1–14.

YATES, A. J. "The Application of Learning Theory to the Treatment of Tics." *Journal of Abnormal and Social Psychology* 56 (1958): 175–82.

CHAPTER SIX

Biological Factors

Biological factors are involved in practically all facets of human behavior. They influence particularly the range and level of the organism's learning aptitudes, physiological drives, basic temperament, stress tolerance, adaptive resources, and response capabilities. Individual differences in these and other functions are partly due to individual variations in neurophysiological and biochemical traits. The major cause of biological individuality is the unique genetic endowment of each child. Other sources of biological individuality that have special psychiatric significance include brain damage incurred during the process of birth; nutritional deficiencies, particularly during infancy and early childhood; toxic substances produced within or taken into the body; and debilitating physical diseases.

In comparison with the elusiveness of the variables associated with psychogenic theories of psychopathology, the biological variables that are thought to have pathogenic significance are more tangible and more readily accessible to experimental study. For example, the role of genetic factors may be investigated by ascertaining whether the incidence of behavior disorders among the parents, children, and siblings of mental patients is significantly higher than chance expectancy. The importance of heredity may be further evaluated by comparing the relative incidence of specific types of maladaptive behavior among close versus distant relatives and for monozygotic versus dizygotic twins. Hypotheses regarding other biological variables may be conveniently tested by comparing the relative prevalence of psychopathology in persons with histories of birth injury, brain damage, or nutritional deficiencies with matched groups of normal control subjects. The statistical findings of such studies are important in differentiating significant variables from incidental ones. But proof of a causal relationship between biological factors and psychopathology calls for more than sup- portive statistical evidence. What is needed is more specific information on (1) the ways in which genetic and other biological factors contribute to the development of abnormal behavior and (2) the reasons the effects of these variables differ so much from individual to individual. Variations in behav- ior commonly noted in identical twins and in persons with similar biologi- cal defects confirm the basic premise regarding the multiple interactive determinants of behavior.

Genes and Abnormal Behavior

The child-to-be receives in full his genetic inheritance at the moment of conception, when the sperm cell contributed by the father penetrates and unites with the ovum provided by the mother to form a single fertilized cell or zygote. Along with the gift of live, each parent passes on, via the repro- ductive cells, one of each of his or her twenty-three pairs of chromosomes. When the twenty-three randomly assorted chromosomes received from the father are paired with the twenty-three received from the mother, the zygote has the normal human complement of forty-six chromosomes. As the zygote develops through cell division, each cell of the body receives a dup- licate set of the original twenty-three pairs of chromosomes. Twenty-two of the paired chromosomes are referred to as autosomes. The remaining pair, identified by the symbols XX in females and XY in males, consists of the sex chromosomes. Since all children born to the same parents receive a random assortment of the parental chromosomes, the chances of two sib- lings' receiving exactly the same set of chromosomes are considerably less than one in a billion. It is equally rare for siblings to have no chromosomes in common. The physical similarities noted among siblings are due to shared chromosomes.

Under suitable conditions, chromosomes may be seen with the aid of a high-powered microscope. Each of the paired autosomes has a somewhat distinctive rodlike appearance. The Y sex chromosome is considerably smaller than the X. By enlarging photographs taken of the microscopic field and cutting out each chromosome, it is possible to match paired chromo- somes and arrange the pairs in some systematic fashion on the basis of their size and shape. Taking advantage of variations in the appearance of chro- mosomes, geneticists have developed a standardized numbering system, ranging from 1 through 23, to identify specific chromosome pairs. The sex chromosome pair, for example, is numbered 23. Anomalies occasionally oc- cur, so that a person has one less or one more than the standard forty-six chromosomes. Irregularities in the number and intactness of chromosomes are usually, but not always, accompanied by physical defects and/or mental retardation. Down's syndrome is a well-known example of mental deficiency associated with the presence of forty-seven chromosomes. The condition is described in Supplementary Report 3.

GENES

The chromosomes contain the genetic substance responsible for the transmission of inherited traits. Paired chromosomes have paired genes that serve similar functions. Both paired genes may be recessive or both may be dominant, or one may be recessive and the other dominant. The number of human genes is unknown but it is assumed that there are many, all of them capable of exact self-duplication. Recent discoveries have shown that the chemical composition of genes consists mainly of deoxyribonucleic acid, or DNA. In other words, genes are nucleic acid segments. The structure of the DNA molecule resembles a double spiral staircase twisted in the form of a helix. The spirals are made up of alternating sugar and phosphate units. The steps connecting the two spirals are formed by varied combinations of adenine, guinine, thymine, and cytosine. The various arrangements of these chemical substances in a nucleic acid segment or gene provides a kind of molecular Morse Code. Chemical messages from the DNA are transferred to other molecules referred to as RNA, because of their ribonucleic acid composition. The RNA molecules move out into the cytoplasm of the cell and initiate reactions that lead to the synthesis of particular enzymes, as directed by the DNA code messages. These enzymes in turn influence chemical interactions that affect the structure and metabolic processes of the body. To the extent that the resulting bodily structures and metabolic processes influence behavior, genes may be credited with indirectly contributing to behavior.

GENOTYPE AND PHENOTYPE

As we have seen, genes act as predisposing or contributory agents rather than as causal agents. It is a fundamental tenet of genetic theory that the action of any specific gene is influenced by its interaction with other genes and with the internal and external environment. This tenet is expressed in the concepts of genotype and phenotype. The *genotype* is the particular combination of genes possessed by the individual. The *phenotype* consists of the observable physical and behavioral characteristics that arise from the interaction of the genotype and its environment. In different environments, one genotype may result in a variety of phenotypes. The extent of the limitation varies with the trait. For certain physical traits that are mainly dependent on the interaction of genes—eye color is one—the phenotypic variation is extremely restricted under usual environmental conditions. Consequently, the outcome is highly predictable in accordance with

Mendelian principles. For physical traits that are more dependent on the external environment, the range and variety of the overt expression of innate predisposition are much greater. For example, a person's genotype sets limits on the range of his possible physical height. Within this potential range, the person's actual maximum height (his phenotype) is greatly influenced by diet, physical illness, and influential socioeconomic factors. Similarly, biological inheritance may impose a range limit on intellectual potentialities, but the individual's actual functioning abilities may be markedly influenced by environmental factors. Phenylketonuria, described in Supplementary Report 3, serves as a good illustration of a genetically determined form of mental deficiency in which the actual phenotypic outcome may be drastically modified by diet. This supplementary report also includes a description of Huntington's chorea. The neurological defect associated with this disorder is inherited; the associated psychological reactions have a more complex origin.

GENES AND TEMPERAMENT

Genetic factors are largely responsible for individual variations in the raw materials from which all personalities are fashioned. The characteristics and properties of the biological building blocks set limits on the general design, complexity, and stability of the personality structures that may be built with them. The limits are broad and flexible, however, particularly among human beings. The particular personality actually developed by a child with a given genotype is greatly influenced by the molding pressures of his culture and his learning experiences within and outside the home. Because of the complex interaction of nature and nurture, it is often difficult to isolate their respective contributions. In general, however, heredity appears to be the more dominant factor in the determination of temperament traits, whereas the environment appears to be mainly responsible for attitudes, values, and social behavior. As Gordon Allport says (1961, p. 34):

> Temperament refers to the characteristic phenomena of an individual's emotional nature, including his susceptibility to emotional stimulation, his customary strength and speed of response, the quality of his prevailing mood, and all peculiarities of fluctuation and intensity in mood, these phenomena being regarded as dependent upon constitutional make-up, and therefore largely hereditary in origin.

From the moment of birth infants exhibit wide individual differences in activity, intensity of reaction, adaptability, distractability, quality of mood, and other temperament qualities (Escalona, 1968; Thomas et al., 1968). Freud (1950, p. 316) recognized that "each individual ego is endowed from the beginning with its own peculiar dispositions and tendencies." Experimental data indicate that the early social behavior of infants is to a great extent controlled by innate predispositions. Monozygotic twins, who have the same genotype, show much greater intrapair resemblance than dizgotic twin pairs with respect to the development of smiling, social orientation, and fear of strangers (Freedman, 1963). Individual differences in temperament noted during infancy tend to persist, in modified form, through childhood to adulthood. The consistency of temperament traits from infancy to later years has been amply demonstrated (Gesell et al., 1939; MacKinnon, 1942; Neilon, 1948; Schaefer and Bayley, 1963). One of the most dramatic findings has been that behaviors exhibited during early childhood are moderately good predictors of analogous behaviors during early adulthood (Kagan and Moss, 1962).

TWIN STUDIES

The search for factual evidence to support the hypothesis that genetic factors contribute to temperament and personality disorders has relied mainly on the study of twins. The particular significance of twins for genetic studies rests on the fact that there are two kinds of twins: monozygotic (MZ) and dizygotic (DZ) pairs. MZ twin pairs have exactly the same genotype; DZ pairs differ in genotype. This biological distinction provides the rationale for the interpretation of twin data. Findings are interpreted as favoring heredity when intrapair resemblances for MZ twins are significantly greater than for DZ twins. Conversely, the role of the environment is given greater weight when the degree of intrapair resemblance is about the same for MZ and DZ twins. Monozygotic or identical twins are the products of a single fertilized cell produced by the union of one sperm and one ovum. At an early stage in its development the single zygote divides, with the eventual birth of two separate infants. MZ twins have exactly the same set of genes, are always of the same sex, and usually look very much alike. Disygotic or fraternal twins, on the other hand, are the products of the fertilization of two separate ova by two separate sperm cells. The degree of genetic similarity of DZ twin pairs is the same as for ordinary siblings. The main biological difference is that DZ twins are of the same age. DZ twins may or may not be of the same sex, and they may resemble or differ from one another as much or as little as ordinary siblings. About 1 in every 90 pregnancies terminates in the birth of twins. One-third of all twin births are of the MZ variety and two-thirds are of the DZ variety. Half of the latter are of the same sex. Blood grouping procedures are currently favored for determining whether twins of the same sex are identical or fraternal. Criteria used in earlier studies included fingerprint ridge count, similarity of eye color, and similarities and differences in other physical traits.

Most twin studies focused on the genetics of temperament have been conducted with normal subjects. The usual procedure has been to compare MZ and DZ twins for intrapair resemblances in scores attained on standarized temperament-personality tests. The twin method may be modified by the addition of a sibling group. The inclusion of sibling pairs provides a further check on the role of the environment. If the environment is the major determinant, the degree of intrapair resemblance should be about the same for MZ and DZ pairs, and DZ pairs should be more alike than siblings who differ in age. As a rule, degrees of intrapair agreement on test scores have been expressed in terms of correlation coefficients. High positive correlations indicate close intrapair agreement; low correlations indicate that the scores attained by one twin are unrelated to the scores attained by the other. High negative correlations indicate an inverse relationship. Since temperament and personality traits cannot be precisely measured, correlation coefficients of over .50 are generally regarded as high.

The results of a comparative study of twins and siblings that I conducted are summarized in Table 6.1. As is apparent, findings differ for specific traits. For the three traits most closely related to temperament, *general activity, restraint,* and *masculinity-femininity,* the intrapair correlation for MZ twins was significantly higher than that for DZ pairs. No significant

Table 6.1.   Product-moment correlations for same-sexed pairs of MZ and DZ twins and siblings less than two years apart on the Guilford-Zimmerman Temperament Survey

	Correlation coefficient[a]		
Traits	MZ (N = 25)	DZ (N = 26)	Sibs (N = 25)
General activity	.52	−.22	−.14
Restraint	.59	.16	.18
Masculinity-femininity	.51	.27	.33
Ascendance	.69	.39	.14
Thoughtfulness	.61	.43	.11
Personal relations	.58	.42	.14
Objectivity	.43	.41	.22
Emotional stability	.31	.33	−.19
Friendliness	−.22	.27	.28
Sociability	.57	.27	.46

[a]*R* of .38 and .49 are significant at the .05 and .01 levels respectively.

differences were noted between the correlations for DZ pairs and siblings. For both groups the correlations were low. These findings suggest that heredity is the main determinant for general activity, restraint, and masculinity-femininity. The findings with respect to *ascendance, thoughtfulness,* and *personal relations* may best be interpreted as reflecting the combined effect of nature and nurture. For these traits, correlations were higher for MZ pairs than for DZ pairs, and higher for DZ pairs than for siblings. The correlation patterns for the remaining four traits favor the interpretation that they are determined principally by environmental factors. Age-related environmental factors appear to be relatively more important for *objectivity* and *emotional stability* than for *friendliness* and *sociability.* For the former two traits, the correlations for MZ and DZ twins were of the same magnitude; those for siblings were lower. No consistent differences were noted for the three groups with respect to friendliness and sociability.

The starting point in twin research involving behavior disorders is to locate an otherwise unselected series of patients, each of whom has the disorder being investigated and has a living twin. A study is then made of the co-twins of these index cases to determine the proportion of instances in which both members of a pair have the same disorder. It is generally assumed that the importance of heredity is confirmed if the concordance rate for a disorder (both co-twins similarly affected) is significantly greater for MZ than for DZ twin pairs of the same sex. A comprehensive summary of twin findings on a variety of disorders is reported in Table 6.2. For all disorders listed, the concordance rates for MZ twins are definitely higher than for same-sexed DZ twins. The greatest contrast between the two types of twins is found in cases of epilepsy. This finding is not surprising, since

Table 6.2.   Concordance of mental disorder in MZ and same-sexed DZ twin samples

Type of Disorder	Percent of Concordance		Number of twin pairs		Number of studies
	MZ	DZ	MZ	DZ	
Schizophrenia	68%	13%	280	448	5
Affective psychoses	70	28	87	97	6
Epilepsy	54	7	95	119	7
Criminality	66	32	131	130	6
Neuroses	43	23	47	56	5
Senile psychosis	44	27	41	15	3

Adapted from E. Essen-Moller, "Twin Research and Psychiatry," *Acta Psychiatrica et Neurologica,* 39 (1963): 65–77; reprinted in *International Journal of Psychiatry,* 1 (1965): 466–75.

a large proportion of convulsive disorders is associated with innate brain defects. When there is no history of organic or toxic pathology from birth onward, subtle cerebral defects, which show up as atypical brain waves on electroencephalographic tests, are noted in an unusually high percentage of the parents and relatives of convulsive-prone patients. The second greatest contrast between concordance rates for MZ and DZ twins is found in cases of schizophrenia. For each of the other disorders the concordance rate for MZ twins is about twice as high as that for DZ pairs.

The fact that the concordance rates for MZ pairs falls considerably short of 100 percent limits the importance of heredity but does not rule it out. As we noted earlier, a basic tenet of genetic theory is that the phenotype or overt expression of an innate predisposition is dependent upon the interactive effect of environmental factors. A person who has inherited a genotype associated with a particular disorder has a greater than chance expectancy of developing that disorder. Whether he actually exhibits overt symptoms depends on the presence or absence of other significant modifying factors. Thus an individual may have an "abnormal" genotype but a "normal" phenotype. A person genetically predisposed to schizophrenia has a relatively high probability of developing behavior traits associated with the disorder, but he will actually develop them only if he is exposed to relevant adverse environmental experiences. Under more favorable environmental circumstances, he may never exhibit overt symptoms, even though he retains the gene defect and transmits it unaltered to his offspring in accordance with genetic principles.

Criticism of twin data. A valid criticism of the figures reported in Table 6.2 is that they were based on institutionalized patients, most of whom were severe, chronic cases. Since 1965 investigators have deliberately attempted to study twins drawn from more representative populations by including nonhospitalized twins as well as hospitalized cases and selecting cases on the basis of consecutive admissions to treatment centers of all types. As a result of these and other refinements in sampling procedures, the magnitude of the concordance rates has been substantially reduced for both types of twins, but the relative differences in rates for MZ and DZ twins have remained the same. (More recent twin figures for schizophrenia are reported in Chapter 9.) A second, more elusive criticism is that MZ twins, by virtue of being identical, tend to share a common social environment to a greater extent that DZ twins, and hence the higher concordance rates noted for MZ pairs may be due to environmental rather than genetic factors.

The latter criticism is debatable. The argument that MZ twins share a common social environment to a greater degree than DZ pairs has been substantiated in several studies (Smith, 1965). However, no evidence has yet been presented to support the claim that these environmental differences, which for the most part are minor, are the pertinent variables responsible for the higher concordance rates of MZ twins. A strong counter-argument in favor of genetics is that research data on schizophrenia and manic-depressive psychoses, reported in Table 6.3, indicate that the concordance rate for DZ pairs is about the same as for ordinary siblings. If the degree of environmental similarity were the deciding factor, the con-

Table 6.3. Expectancy rates for DZ co-twins and siblings of psychotic patients

	Expectancy rates	
Psychosis	*DZ twins*	*Siblings*
Schizophrenia	15%	12%
Manic-depressive psychosis	26	23

Adapted from F. J. Kallman, "The Genetics of Mental Illness," in *American Handbook of Psychiatry,* ed. S. Arieti (New York: Basic Books, 1959), vol. 1, pp. 175–96.

cordance rates for DZ twins should be considerably higher than for siblings who differ in age. This obviously is not the case—at least for psychoses. The greater importance of genetic factors in the etiology of schizophrenia is further confirmed by studies of separated twins and of children of schizophrenic mothers reared in foster homes. (Research data with respect to these two special groups are discussed in Chapter 9.)

Genetic Predispositions: A Closer Look

TEMPERAMENT

If we assume that susceptibility to impaired psychosocial functioning is partly determined by heredity, the next step is to identify the nature of the innate predisposing factors. The most promising of the various proposed theories is that temperament attributes constitute the genetic component that often contributes most directly to vulnerability or resistance to psychopathology. This hypothesis has the advantage of including abnormal behavior within the general framework of normal behavior; it avoids the dubious practice of inventing a separate set of causes and explanations for deviant behavior. The temperament characteristics of prospective patients may be viewed as simply differing in degree from similar traits present in the general population. Temperament qualities associated with specific disorders include:

Neurosis: high anxiety level, rigidity, emotional overresponsiveness.

Schizophrenia: introvertive tendencies, low energy level, relative absence of spontaneity, relative incapacity for experiencing and expressing joy.

Manic-depressive psychosis: marked mood swings from elation to depression, low frustration tolerance, dependence.

Antisocial behavior: impulsivity, aggressiveness, restlessness, relative lack of social sensitivity, inadequate inhibitory controls.

Temperament deviations, however extreme, neither produce nor constitute behavior disorders. The main role of temperament is to create an emotional climate that influences the ways in which the individual acts toward others and others react to him. A timid, apathetic, inhibited child is apt to elicit a minimum of positive responses from parents, peers, and associates. In turn, the relative absence of social reinforcements will tend to discourage the child's subsequent efforts to relate to and become involved with others. Repeated encounters of indifference, frustration, and rejection in interpersonal situations will tend to accentuate introvertive tendencies and lead to avoidance and distrust of other people. Since one's self-image is influenced by the ways in which one is perceived and treated by significant others, the self-concept of the ignored, rejected child may remain relatively underdeveloped and be distorted by feelings of unworthiness and hopelessness. In extreme cases the individual may turn his back on the cold, unfriendly world and seek refuge in a private schizophrenic world of his own. Conversely, a sociable, outgoing, energetic, responsive child who elicits favorable responses from his family and peers is likely, as the result of repeated successful experiences, to acquire a favorable self-image, an optimistic outlook, and confidence in coping with daily problems. Temperament and environment work hand in hand to reinforce and stabilize innate predispositions.

The hypothesis that temperament is a major contributory cause of psychopathology has the merit of being subject to experimental testing. Thomas and his associates (1968) are currently conducting a comprehensive longitudinal study that is designed to investigate the relation of temperament characteristics observed in children during infancy to their subsequent personality development and susceptibility to behavior disorders. By the age of ten, 42 of the 136 children being studied had exhibited clinical signs of behavior disturbances. Most of the disturbed children had been described as "difficult" babies. During infancy they were distinguished by irregularity in biological function, predominance of withdrawal response or intense reactions to new stimuli, low adaptability, and frequent expression of negative moods. Behavior problems were rarely noted in children who had been "easy" babies. As infants these problem-resistant children were characterized by biological regularity, predominantly positive moods, rapid adaptability, and low to mild intensity of reactions. The authors are careful to note that no particular pattern of temperament per se results in or provides immunity against a behavior disturbance. Recognizing the multiple determinents of behavior, they conclude (1968, p. 182) that deviant as well as normal development is the result of the interaction between given characteristics of temperament and significant features of the child's intrafamilial and extrafamilial environments.

In another longitudinal study (Fish et al, 1965), predictions were made as to possible schizophrenic outcome in a group of infants. Three out of a total of sixteen infants examined were judged to be vulnerable to schizophrenia on the basis of marked behavioral irregularities noted when they were a month old. All sixteen children were examined again when they were nine or ten. At that time all three of the "vulnerable" children exhibited behavior disturbances. The child who had shown the most severe impairment in infancy had developed an overt psychosis. The other two "vulnerable" children had developed less severe disorders. A third longitudinal study, involving older children, is being conducted by S. A. Mednick. Since his research has special significance for schizophrenia, his findings will be reported in Chapter 9, which is devoted to that disorder.

NEUROBIOCHEMICAL DEFECTS

During the period when it was thought that mental disorders were analogous to physical disorders, serious attention was given to the theory that the genetic component of psychoses might consist of some neurophysiological, biochemical, or metabolic anomaly. The theory was kept alive by periodic positive findings. Unfortunately, on more careful reexamination these encouraging discoveries have invariably turned out to be accidental and nonreplicable or due to dietary deficiences and other extraneous factors associated with a chronic institutionalized population. The search for specific neurobiochemical pathogenic agents has been all but abandoned. Current biological research is more concerned with the interaction between biochemical events and other pertinent behavioral variables that are involved in the organism's adjustment to its environment. Under normal circumstances, inborn metabolic variations and other biochemical predisposing factors are not sufficiently variant to produce significant disturbances in behavior, but they might do so under conditions of stress and other adverse environmental circumstances that induce more extreme biochemical changes (Russell, 1965).

DEFECTS IN GENETIC PROGRAMMING

In contrast to neurobiochemical theories, which are essentially based on the engine model, programming theories favor the more sophisticated computer model. Taking into consideration the basic concept of nature-nurture interaction, it is possible that impaired psychosocial functioning may result from:

1. Defects in genetic coding that lead to:
   (a) An absence of built-in programs for initiating certain critical actions or for appropriately handling certain kinds of input data.
   (b) Errors in programming that result in faulty analysis of input data.
2. Environmental errors, represented by:
   (a) A lack of a response suitable to elicit programmed data, which interferes with or distorts the sequential pattern.
   (b) Faulty input data that fail to trigger available programs, set off "wrong" built-in programs, or lead to other erroneous responses.

Other possible sources of disordered functioning include the inherent incapacity of the organism to assimilate or cope with certain experiences, breakdown resulting from the overloading of the system, neural short-circuiting, feedback interference, absence of inhibitory controls, and defects in the biological filtering system that screens and regulates sensory input, associations, and responses.

A good illustration of genetic programming is the spontaneous occurrence of specific behaviors at certain stages in development. These critical-period behaviors—species-specific patterns of courtship, mating, nesting behavior, infant care, and seasonal migration—are more evident in lower organisms than in man. The successful mating of animals requires males and females to adhere to a genetically determined, species-specific sequence of courting behavior. Slight variations in the courtship patterns of related species interfere with the step-by-step sequence, stop the process, and thereby inhibit cross-breeding. The presence of inherent programs in human beings is indicated by the spontaneous occurrence at certain age levels of speech sounds, smiling, negativism, acceptance of strangers, heterosexual impulses, and so on. Irregularities in the expression of these critical-stage responses or the failure of appropriate reinforcement may have unfavorable developmental consequences. A child whose smiles are never reinforced by the responding smiles of others soon stops smiling. Irregularities or deficiencies in the expression or reinforcement of heterosexual impulses may interfere with normal sexual development.

The adverse consequence of an environment that fails to nurture and reinforce innate behavior tendencies is most clearly apparent in neglected infants brought up in orphanages that provide nothing but custodial care. The effects vary, but most children reared from birth under such conditions, with a minimum of stimulation, fondling, and attention, show marked retardation in intelligence and language development (Yarrow, 1961). Frequently noted personality disturbances include social apathy, excessive crying, sporadic outbursts of rage, rigid posturing, stereotyped motor responses, and difficulty in establishing normal interpersonal relationships.

A somewhat related hypothesis is that human beings have an intrinsic need for a minimum level of sensory stimulation. Deprivation of or lack of variety in external sensory input may result in a compensatory intensification of internal mental activity—increased reverie, rehearsal of memories, and an upsurge of normally suppressed impulses with their accompanying affects. Thus the psychotic's break with outer reality may result in increased absorption with inner fantasies and impulses and an increased sensitivity to bodily sensations. The shift to internal stimulation may account for transient disturbances in psychological functioning frequently noted in laboratory experiments in which human subjects have been isolated and exposed for several hours or a few days to conditions of either monotonous or markedly reduced sensory stimulation. The effects vary from subject to subject and are influenced by the instructions they receive and other factors, but perceptual errors, difficulty in thinking, disorientation, and confusion are commonly observed, and transient delusions and hallucinations occur occasionally (Solomon, 1961). Similar disturbances have been reported by seamen sailing alone on extended voyages, explorers, truck drivers on all-night trips, stratosphere pilots, and persons in solitary confinement.

There is a possibility that psychological disturbances may be directly or indirectly related to inherent defects in the inhibitory mechanisms of the organism (Diamond et al., 1963). Under usual circumstances, the organism is bombarded by a wide variety of stimuli. Some protective filter or inhibition of response is essential for concentration of attention, selective perception, logical thinking, and coherent speech. All choice behavior involves the inhibition of alternatives. Defects in the filter or inhibitory mechanism may contribute to the hyperactivity and distractability of the manic patient and to the word-salad speech and overinclusive thought processes of the schizophrenic. Massive inhibition, resulting in stimulus underload, may be related to the loss of feelings and the paralysis of thought and action characteristic of the depressed patient.

Some deficiency in genetic programming is highly probable in autistic children. These children are characterized from birth by a pathological absence of interest in and responsiveness to other human beings. Unlike normal children, who reach out for human contact and affection, autistic children experience outer reality as a source of intolerable irritation (Mahler, 1952). When social cues are forced on them, they either overreact or make no response at all. Autistic children do not welcome cuddling like normal babies, form no attachment to their mothers, are more interested in inanimate than animate objects, and treat people as if they were objects. Speech either never develops or is severely limited. In a somewhat different context Bowlby (1960) has suggested that there is a critical stage for primary attachment to the maternal figure. If this does not take place within a certain developmental period, the capacity is lost or impaired.

Animal Research

Most of the experimental work on the genetics of behavior and disordered functioning has been carried out with animals. Our review would be incomplete without some mention of the findings of these studies. Animal research has demonstrated the presence and location of specific brain mechanisms that when stimulated produce sensations of pleasure or pain, induce feeding in satiated animals, initiate mating behavior, and evoke or inhibit rage reactions (Magoun, 1965). Lorenz' observations on the imprinting of following behavior in ducks, which have been more systematically studied by Hess (1959), have an important bearing on related human phenomena associated with critical developmental periods and irrational childhood fixations. Ducks are genetically programmed to follow a moving model. This program is effective for only a few hours after birth. Usually the mother is the only moving object around during this critical period, so the duckling follows her, and the action of following the mother becomes imprinted on the duckling. But if a person takes the place of the mother, the duckling follows him instead, and thereafter ignores its mother and other ducks as well. Other contributions of animal studies have consisted mainly of the confirmation, under better controlled experimental conditions, of observations and hypotheses initially derived from human data.

Harlow's (1962) famous study of monkeys deprived of normal mother-infant and infant-infant tactile interactions illustrates the relation of genotype to phenotype. More significantly, it identifies some of the environmental variables that, at least in monkeys, can transform a "normal" genotype into an "abnormal" phenotype. Monkeys separated at birth from the mother and reared during the first year in wire cages that prevent any physical contact with other monkeys develop a variety of abnormal behavior patterns. In some respects their reactions resemble those of autistic children. They are mute, stare fixedly into space, rock back and forth, and exhibit sporadic, violent frenzies of rage. At the age of three, monkeys reared in isolation show infantile sexual behavior, absence of grooming, exaggerated aggression, and absence of affectional interaction with other monkeys. When physically mature, socially deprived monkeys resist hetero-sexual approaches or are clumsy and inept in mating behavior. Unmoth-ered females that eventually submit to patient, experienced breeding males turn out to be terrible mothers. As Harlow describes them, they are help-less, heartless mothers, practically devoid of maternal feelings. The neglect and rejection experienced by the infants of these mothers have adverse effects on their phenotypic development. In comparison with infants who receive normal mothering, the infants of motherless mothers are deficient in social play and sexual behavior and are hyperaggressive in peer inter-action (Arling and Harlow, 1967).

Laboratory studies conducted with a variety of animals have consistently confirmed the importance of genetic factors in determining behavior traits in animals (Hall, 1941; Scott and Fuller, 1965). Starting with a hetero-geneous population of a particular species, the experimenter finds it relatively simple, by selective breeding over two or more generations, to produce strains of animals that are predominantly fearful, stable, active, inactive, timid, or aggressive. These variations in temperament are cor-related with differences in autonomic response patterns. The environment seems to have relatively little effect in modifying the innate temperament of animals. Beagle puppies reared from birth with terrier litter mates grow up to be quiet, inhibited, shy, typical beagles; terrier puppies reared with beagles show the characteristic terrier traits of liveliness and excitability (James, 1951).

Dykman, Murphree, and Ackerman (1966) have reported a series of studies comparing the behavior patterns of the offspring of nervous and stable pointer dogs. Initially the parent population was rated for emotional stability on the basis of the presence or absence of such traits as excessive startle response to noises, avoidance of humans, and timidity. Behavior tests conducted on first- and second-generation offspring of stable and nervous parents indicated marked differences in the two lines of dogs with respect to exploratory behavior, reaction to noise, change in heartbeat at being petted by a human, and field behavior. Generalizing from differences in conditioned cardiac responses noted in stable and nervous dogs, Dyk-man and his associates concluded that the conditioned reflex is dependent upon innate patterns of reactivity. Second-generation puppies taken from their mothers at birth and reared by humans did not differ on behavior tests from siblings that had been reared by their mothers. In a subsequent study (Murphree, Peters, and Dykman, 1967), pointer dogs selectively bred for emotional stability showed an increase in heart rate when petted by a human. Unstable dogs showed no change in cardiac response to hu-man stimulation. The behavior of crossbred dogs (one parent stable, one parent nervous) resembled that of the stable parent in the natural home environment and that of the unstable parent in laboratory test situations.

Another important contribution of animal studies has been the finding that genetic factors influence the impact of environmental stresses. The effects of the stimulation of infant rats on their subsequent emotionality as adults varies considerably with the genetic strain of the animals (Levine and Broadhurst, 1963). In his pioneer studies on experimentally induced neuroses in dogs, Pavlov (1927, 1941) noted that the inherent temperament of the dog appeared to be a critical factor in determining relative vulnerability to neurotic behavior. Under Pavlov's experimental design, the dog was restrained in a loose harness and subjected to a difficult discrimination problem that exceeded his capacity. In one variation, a conflict was produced between cortical excitatory and inhibitory responses. A circle of light was flashed on a screen and food was presented almost simultaneously, so that the circle became a signal for food and the dog was conditioned to salivate whenever he saw it. After this positive conditioned response had been established, an ellipse of light was substituted for the circle; but each time the ellipse was thrown on the screen, food was withheld. In effect, the dog was conditioned not to salivate at the ellipse. The dog readily learned to discriminate between the circle and the ellipse. The experimenter then proceeded to make discrimination more difficult by using a series of ellipses that more and more approached a circle. The dog succeeded in making the proper discrimination as long as the axes of the ellipse were as 7 to 8. When the axes were as 8 to 9, the discrimination proved too fine for the dog and he broke down. All earlier established discriminations—even the easiest ones—were now lost. The dog salivated indiscriminately at the ellipse, the circle, the experimenter, and the laboratory apparatus. In addition, he was extremely upset and excited. He tore at the restraining harness, barked, whimpered, rejected food, and was generally unmanageable. Attempts to continue with the experiment on subsequent days were unsuccessful. Merely preparing the animal for experimentation reinstated the intense emotional excitement.

Whether experimentally induced neuroses in animals are strictly analogous to neurotic behavior in humans is a moot question (Hunt, 1964). It has been argued that conditioned emotional reactions represent "normal" responses to unsolvable and inescapable problems. What is significant for our purpose is the marked variation in response made by a number of animals. The emotional disturbance may be mild or severe, transient or permanent. Some animals become extremely agitated, others pass into a trance state marked by rigidity and negativism. Pavlov related response variation to the innate temperament of the dogs. Highly excitable (choleric) and inhibited (melancholic) dogs were considered to be highly susceptible to neuroses. Cheerful (sanguine) and calm (phlegmatic) dogs were regarded as being constitutionally resistant to neuroses. Without necessarily subscribing to Pavlov's views on temperament, subsequent workers (Masserman, 1943; Liddell, 1944) have confirmed the fact that some animals are highly susceptible to experimental neuroses while others are highly resistant to them. Gantt (1944) has reported a detailed study of a dog named Nick who exhibited a lifelong neurosis following his exposure to a conflict situation, though other dogs exposed to the same conflict situation showed only mild agitation, from which they soon recovered.

The case for heredity as a critical factor in psychopathology would be greatly strengthened if it could be shown that a substantial proportion of animals reared in their natural habitats spontaneously developed atypical, maladaptive behavior patterns that set them apart from the pack, herd, or flock. But this type of evidence is difficult to come by. Wild animals that are handicapped by behavior peculiarities and deficits soon die or are killed. The same fate awaits disturbed house pets and farm animals. Evidence for the spontaneous occurrence of psychopathology in animals is limited to a small number of cases reported by alert observers in animal research laboratories. Hebb (1947) has described two examples of neuroses occurring spontaneously in chimpanzees. One exhibited a phobic reaction; the other was subject to periods of depression. Since the known life experiences of the affected animals did not differ from those of their cagemates, Hebb concluded that the underlying causes must have been some constitutional defects. Newton and Gantt (1968) have reported a detailed case history of a psychotic male French poodle. The dog was born in the laboratory. From an early age he was extremely timid, avoided contact with humans, and was easily intimidated by other dogs. His characteristic response to the presence of a person was a catatonic-like reaction marked by posturing, immobility, and cerea flexibilitas. Other peculiarities included homosexual tendencies and an atypical reaction to alcohol. The effect of alcohol on most dogs is to inhibit sexual activity; the catatonic dog reacted to alcohol with increased sexual activity, though in moderate doses alcohol improved the catatonic dog's behavior so that he appeared almost normal. Newton and Gantt attributed the dog's abnormal behavior to inborn constitutional defects.

Summary

Each organism's unique genetic endowment is a major determinant of its biological and behavioral individuality. The chemical codes contained in the genes initiate and in large measure regulate the complex biological processes associated with human growth and development. At every stage, however, the actual or phenotypic expression of genetic potentiality is subject to modification by environmental influences. The interactive contributions of the culture, the family, and personal learning experiences have marked effects on the style and content of psychosocial reactions. As far as deviant behavior is concerned, the main contribution of genetic endowment appears to be in the area of temperament. The inherent temperament of the individual, as reflected in activity level, prevailing mood, adaptability, and intensity of reactions, does far more than influence his own reactions. The effect his behavior has on parents and other significant persons in large measure determines how others react to him. In other words, the individual tends to create his own social and emotional environment. The self-reinforcing interaction of the child and his environment may have a desirable consequence to his development if his innate temperament traits are positive. But if his innate traits are negative, their reinforcement by unfavorable interactions with others may result in extreme deviations. These extremely deviant temperament characteristics, when combined with defensive symptomatic reactions, may be considered the main substance of maladaptive behavior patterns that are referred to as mental disorders. Although subject to other interpretations, the findings of longitudinal studies of children, twin data, and animal research are consistent with the hypothesis that innate temperament plays the stellar role in the etiology of behavior disturbances. Other possible biological contributions to psychopathology include various irregularities in genetic programming which lead to behavior deficiencies or the faulty handling of input data. Here also heredity is a contributory rather than an exclusive agent. Genes may set potential limits and favor certain reactions, but the actual resulting behavior is always the product of the interaction of nature and nurture.

Supplementary Report 3. Genetic Physical Disorders with Associated Behavior Deficits

Down's syndrome is a more recent name for a type of mental deficiency that was formerly called mongolism. The term mongolism was initially applied by Langdon-Down in 1866 to describe a type of mental deficiency characterized by a fold of skin continuing from the upper eyelid over the inner angle, among other physical features. The effect of this extra fold is a superficial Oriental appearance. The condition has nothing to do with the Mongoloid race. Earlier studies indicated that the disorder (1) was not present in the parents, (2) occurred with about equal frequency at all socioeconomic levels, (3) invariably affected both or neither of monozygotic twins, (4) rarely affected both members of dizygotic twin pairs, and (5) occurred more frequently in children born to older women but was unrelated to the age of the father. These data suggested that the disorder had some connection with the mother, had a genetic origin, but was not inherited in the usual sense that defective genes present in the parents are passed on to the child. The etiological picture remained confused until 1959, when Lejeune, in France, discovered that children with Down's syndrome had forty-seven chromosomes instead of the standard forty-six. In terms of the identifying numbers assigned to human chromosomes, the anomaly usually consists of an extra chromosome 21 (three in place of the usual two). The explanation for the extra chromosome, which is contained in the ovum, is attributed to the nondisjunction of a parent cell during meiotic division. Following the reduction process, one germ cell has twenty-four chromosomes and the other only twenty-two. The former, when fertilized by a germ cell having a normal complement of twenty-three chromosomes, results in a total of forty-seven in the offspring. The reason for the nondisjunction is not clearly understood. For mothers over forty-five, the risk of having a child with Down's syndrome is about 1 in 50. Tests have been developed that make it possible to detect the presence of the gene defect in the fetus early in pregnancy. The birth of these handicapped children may now be prevented by medical intervention.

Phenylketonuria, or PKU, is an inherited metabolic disorder that accounts for about 1 percent of the population of institutions for mental defectives. The specific cause consists of the presence of a recessive autosomal gene that interferes with the normal production of an enzyme called phenylalanine hydroxylase. This enzyme is essential for oxidizing phenylalanine to tyrosine. Phenylalanine is an amino acid present in all proteins. Its faulty metabolism leads to the accumulation of phenylalanine in the blood and the excretion of phenylpyruvic acid in the urine. The metabolic disturbance somehow interferes with normal brain development during the crucial period of infancy. In addition to mental retardation, the disorder is marked by convulsions, temper outbursts, and rough skin. A simple blood test, which is required in many states, has been developed for detecting elevated phenylalanine levels in newborn infants. By placing affected infants on a special diet low in phenylalanine for several years, it is possible to prevent mental retardation from this cause and related symptoms. Although phenotypically normal with respect to intelligence, treated children retain their original genotype and pass on to their offspring the gene defect they acquired from their parents. Because of the recessive nature of the defective gene, the risk of mental deficiency may be reduced if persons known to be genetically susceptible to phenlyketonuria marry into families free of the gene defect. Heterozygotic carriers are free of overt symptoms but have a reduced enzyme level, which can be detected by a test for tolerance of phenylalanine. The success attained in the prevention of this disorder shows that the common belief that hereditary disorders are incurable is not necessarily so. Far from being cause for pessimism, the establishment of a biochemical basis for a disorder may provide the key for its effective treatment and prevention.

Huntington's chorea is a progressive degenerative disease of the central nervous system that is marked by diffuse brain atrophy. A single dominant autosomal gene is responsible for the disorder. Case history data indicate that 50 percent of the children of affected parents will also develop the disorder if they live long enough. Unaffected children are free of the dominant genes, so that their children are unaffected. The onset of overt neurological symptoms is usually delayed until the victim is between thirty and forty years old. The symptom picture is the same today as it was when it was originally described by Huntington in 1872. Physical symptoms consist of irregular, involuntary, and uncontrollable movements of the face, neck, and extremities: facial grimaces, poorly articulated speech, shuffling gait, and jerky circular movements of the hands. The appearance of choreiform symptoms may be preceded or accompanied by changes in personality and behavior. Common psychological symptoms include moodiness, irritability, apathy, obstinacy, irascibility, and paranoid trends. As the disorder progresses, there is a general mental deterioration. Suicide is not uncommon (Kolb, 1968). There is no known treatment.

References

ALLPORT, G. W. *Pattern and Growth in Personality*. New York: Holt, Rinehart & Winston, 1961.

ARLING, G. L.; and HARLOW, H. F. "Effects of Social Deprivation on Maternal Behavior of Rhesus Monkeys." *Journal of Comparative and Physiological Psychology* 64 (1967): 371–77.

BOWLBY, J. "Separation Anxiety." *International Journal of Psychoanalysis* 41 (1960): 1–25.

DIAMOND, S.; BALVIN, R.; and DIAMOND, F. *Inhibition and Choice*. New York: Harper & Row, 1963.

DYKMAN, R. A.; MURPHREE, O. D.; and ACKERMAN, P. T. "Litter Patterns in the Offspring of Nervous and Stable Dogs: II. Autonomic and Motor Conditioning." *Journal of Nervous and Mental Disease* 141, no. 4 (1966): 419–31.

ESCALONA, S. *The Roots of Individuality*. Chicago: Aldine, 1968.

ESSEN-MOLLER, E. "Twin Research and Psychiatry." *Acta Psychiatrica et Neurologica* 39 (1963): 65–77. Reprinted in *International Journal of Psychiatry* 1 (1965): 466–75.

FISH, B.; SHAPIRO, T.; HALPERN, F.; and WILE, R. "The Prediction of Schizophrenia in Infancy: III. A Ten-Year Follow-up Report of Neurological and Psychological Development." *American Journal of Psychiatry* 121 (1965): 768–75.

FREEDMAN, D. "Heredity Control of Early Social Behavior." In *Determinants of Infant Behavior,* ed. B. M. Foss, vol. 3, pp. 149–53. New York: Wiley, 1963.

FREUD, S. "Analysis, Terminable and Interminable." In *Collected Papers,* vol. 5, p. 316. London: Hogarth Press, 1950.

GANTT, W. H. *Experimental Basis for Neurotic Behavior*. New York: Hoeber 1944.

GESELL, A., et al. *Biographies of Child Development*. New York: Harper, 1939.

HALL, C. S. "Temperament: A Survey of Animal Studies." *Psychological Bulletin* 38 (1941): 909–43.

HARLOW, H. F. "The Heterosexual Affectional System in Monkeys." *American Psychologist* 17 (1962): 1–9.

HEBB, D. O. "Spontaneous Neuroses in Chimpanzees: Theoretical Relations with Clinical and Experimental Phenomena." *Psychosomatic Medicine* 9 (1947): 3–16.

HESS, E. H. "Imprinting." *Science* 130 (1959): 133–41.
HUNT, H. F. "Problems in the Interpretation of 'Experimental Neurosis.'"
    Psychological Reports 15 (1964): 27–35.
JAMES, W. J. "Social Organization Among Dogs of Different Temperaments:
    Terriers and Beagles Reared Together." *Journal of Comparative and Physio-
    logical Psychology* 44 (1951): 71–77.
KAGAN, J., and MOSS, H. A. *Birth to Maturity: A Study in Psychological De-
    velopment.* New York: Wiley, 1962.
KALLMAN, F. J. "The Genetics of Mental Illness." In *American Handbook of
    Psychiatry,* ed. S. Arieti, pp. 175–234. New York: Basic Books, 1959.
KOLB, L. *Noyes' Modern Clinical Psychiatry,* 7th ed. Philadelphia: Saunders,
    1968.
LEVINE, S., and BROADHURST, P. L. "Genetic and Ontogenetic Determinants of
    Adult Behavior in the Rat." *Journal of Comparative and Physiological Psy-
    chology* 56 (1963): 423–28.
LIDDELL, H. S. "Conditioned Reflex Method and Experimental Neurosis." In
    Personality and Behavior Disorders, ed. J. McV. Hunt, vol. 1, pp. 389–412.
    New York: Ronald Press, 1944.
MACKINNON, K. M. *Consistency and Change in Behavior Manifestation.* Society
    for Research in Child Development Monographs, no. 30 (1942).
MAGOUN, H. W. "Brain Mechanisms for Innate and Emotional Behavior." In
    Handbook of Clinical Psychology, ed. B. B. Wolman, pp. 181–96. New York:
    McGraw-Hill, 1965.
MAHLER, M. S. "On Child Psychosis and Schizophrenia: Autistic and Symbiotic
    Infantile Psychosis." *Psychoanalytical Study of the Child,* vol. 7. New York:
    International Universities Press, 1952.
MASSERMAN, J. H. *Behavior and Neurosis.* Chicago: University of Chicago
    Press, 1943.
MURPHREE, O. D.; PETERS, J. E.; and DYKMAN, R. A. "Effect of Person on
    Nervous, Stable, and Crossbred Pointer Dogs." *Conditional Reflex* 2, no. 4
    (1967): 273–76.
NEILON, P. "Shirley's Babies After Fifteen Years: A Personality Study." *Journal
    of Genetic Psychology* 73 (1948): 175–86.
NEWTON, J. E. O., and GANTT, W. H. "The History of a Catatonic Dog." *Con-
    ditional Reflex* 3 (1968): 45–61.
PAVLOV, I. P. *Lectures on Conditioned Reflexes,* trans. G. V. Anrep. London:
    Oxford University Press, 1927.
———. *Conditioned Reflexes and Psychiatry,* trans. W. W. Gantt. New York:
    International Publishers, 1941.
RUSSELL, R. W. "Biochemical Factors in Mental Disorders." In *Handbook of
    Clinical Psychology,* ed. B. B. Wolman, pp. 197–215. New York: McGraw-
    Hill, 1965.
SCHAEFER, E. R., and BAYLEY, N. *Maternal Behavior, Child Behavior, and Their
    Intercorrelations from Infancy Through Adolescence.* Society for Research in
    Child Development Monographs, vol. 28, no. 3 (1963).
SCOTT, J. P., and FULLER, J. L. *Genetics and the Social Behavior of the Dog.*
    Chicago: University of Chicago Press, 1965.
SMITH, R. T. "A Comparison of Socioenvironmental Factors in Monozygotic
    and Dizygotic Twins, Testing an Assumption." In *Methods and Goals in Be-

havior Genetics, ed. S. G. Vandenburg, pp. 45–61. New York: Academic Press, 1965.

SOLOMON, P., ed. *Sensory Deprivation.* Cambridge: Harvard University Press, 1961.

THOMAS, A.; CHESS, S.; and BIRCH, H. *Temperament and Behavioral Disorders in Children.* New York: New York University Press, 1968.

YARROW, L. J. "Maternal Deprivation: Toward an Empirical and Conceptual Re-evaluation." *Psychological Bulletin* 58 (1961): 459–90.

CHAPTER SEVEN

Sociocultural Theories

Most sociocultural theories either are of a global nature or deal with some specific factor such as the relation of psychopathology to economic status, social disorganization, and social change. A notable exception is the sociological theory of mental disorders outlined by Scheff (1966). As we saw in Chapter 1, Scheff prefers the term *residual deviant behavior* to mental illness. Residual deviant behavior consists of violations of certain social norms for which society has no precise name. He recognizes that the underlying causes of residual deviance may include a variety of biogenic, psychogenic, and sociogenic factors, but he maintains that most residual deviance is either denied or transitory. The most important single factor in the structuring and stabilization of mental illness is the reaction of society. In the crisis that occurs when a deviant is publicly labeled as a mental patient, the confused, disturbed person is highly suggestible and may see no alternative to the proffered role of mental patient. More specifically, Scheff suggests that in many instances deviant behavior represents a normal reaction to a stress situation, and if it were only regarded in this light it would be transitory.

The labeling of such behavior as symptomatic of psychopathology and the pressure exerted on the disturbed person to seek treatment serve to accentuate and fixate the disturbance. The medical tradition of playing it safe by diagnosing illness in cases of doubt contributes to this error. The questions asked and the answers expected during the psychiatric examination provide clues as to the way in which the person should behave to qualify as a mental patient. The culturally defined stereotypes of mental illness are further clarified and reaffirmed in interaction with members of the family and associates. The labeled deviant, whose behavior confirms the medical and societal diagnosis, may be rewarded and receive benefits for conforming to the conventionally accepted stereotype. Once the label of mental patient has been publicly applied, the individual usually finds himself discriminated against when he seeks to return to normal status. He is treated with suspicion, distrust, and apprehension by his family, employer, and associates. If he accepts the role of deviant and thinks of himself as a "mental case," his ability to control and modify his own behavior may be impaired. His acceptance of therapy confirms his role as a mental patient. The longer the course of recommended therapy, the more the patient may perceive himself as a sick person in need of treatment. Thus psychotherapy, as Frank has noted (1961, p. 7) in a slightly different context, may to some extent create the illness it treats.

Sociocultural Factors

CULTURE AND PERSONALITY

Culture is the total way of life of a people or social group. It may be thought of as a highly flexible mold. The shaping influences of a society contribute to intragroup similarities in personality, but they do not negate the role of biological and experiential factors that make for individual uniqueness. The range and variety of personality types is about the same in all cultures. At times the culture may actually reinforce biological individuality by identifying at an early age persons who show promise of developing distinctive traits required for special roles—the self-induced trance state of shamans, for example—and nurturing the maximum growth of these distinctive traits in these selected individuals. The main thrust of culture, however, is aimed at furthering the homogeneity of the group by promoting uniformity in personality and behavior. Cultural anthropologists accept the genotype-phenotype model of biology with respect to the plasticity of personality development. A basic tenet of cultural anthropology is that each infant is born with potentialities for developing a variety of behavior characteristics. The molding influences of the culture into which an infant is born determines in great measure which of his inherent potentialities are realized and which are suppressed.

Benedict (1934), an early advocate of the plasticity of human personality, has contributed an interesting account of the role of culture in shaping personality differences noted in the past between the savage Plains Indians and the quiet, restrained Pueblo Indians of North America. Historically the Plains Indians were buffalo hunters. The pattern of their culture encouraged dangerous living, emotional excesses, and violence. Mothers deliberately provoked their children to have temper tantrums to "make them strong." The toughening training of boys included exposure to hunger, thirst, and pain. Tribal ceremonies included orgiastic dances and the use of intoxicating drugs. The ideal man among the Plains Indians was brave, reckless, and cruel, and most Sioux and Crow warriors acquired these traits. In contrast, the Pueblo Indians of the Southwest, as represented by the Pueblos, Hopis, and Zunis, cultivated the gentler traits of moderation, restraint, and mildness. Children were taught to be cooperative, flexible, and easygoing. They were treated with kindness and understanding and seldom scolded or punished. An orderly, even-tempered life, free of excesses, excitement, and violence, constituted the cultural ideal. Stimulating drugs had no part in their rituals, and their dances consisted of the slow, monotonous thumping of the feet. Individualism, competition, greed, and aggressiveness were systematically discouraged and suppressed. Little importance was attached to possessions or success. The most valuable objects were the sacred things used in ceremonials. These were privately owned, but any qualified person was free to borrow them. If a man acquired more worldly goods than his neighbors, he was expected to redistribute his wealth during the great winter festivals. Selfish strivings for power and authority were disparaged. A person who sought to be a leader was scorned and censured. Persistently ambitious individuals were hung by their thumbs until they were cured of this folly. If a man consistently won at running races, he was disbarred from competition in order to give others a chance to win. When high offices had to be filled, the group selected the best qualified man and forced him to accept. The selected person was expected to try to avoid the honor.

Another well-known example of the role of culture in shaping personality is the contrast reported by Margaret Mead (1935) between the gentle, cooperative Mountain Arapesh of New Guinea and the aggressive, distrustful Mundugumor. The two groups lived within a hundred miles of each other, but in culture and personality they were poles apart. The Arapesh culture in many respects resembled that of the Pueblo Indians. The Arapesh believed that the security of the individual and the group depended on mutual goodwill, cooperativeness, and interpersonal dependency. Their culture fostered personal warmth, kindliness, congeniality, and responsiveness to the requests of others. Social acceptance, rather than personal achievement, was the dominant motive. From infancy the child was trained to regard the outside world as friendly and helpful. Babies were wanted and pampered. They were breast-fed for years, and the breast was always available to comfort the older child when he was in pain or frightened. Children received no training in initiative or competition. There were no races, no games with opposing sides, no rewards for personal enterprise. Fighting between youngsters was not permitted. The Arapesh solution to courtship and marriage was early trial "marriage" arranged by the parents. By the age of six or seven, all girls were betrothed and went to live in the households of their future husbands. The marriage was not consummated until the children grew up, but this arrangement provided a test of compatibility. If the betrothed children did not get along with one another, the girl went back to her family while there was still time to arrange for a more suitable trial marriage. Fathers avoided the potential conflict between the old and new generations by retiring from active life as soon as their eldest sons reached adolescence.

The Mundugumor culture, on the other hand, encouraged feelings of hostility, mutual distrust, and violence. Every man, woman, and child was expected to look out for his own best interests. Babies were unwanted. Antipregnancy magic was practiced, and if pregnancy occurred anyway, each parent blamed the other. Mundugumor mothers suckled their children while standing up. The moment the infant stopped nursing, he was dropped into an uncomfortable basket. The child soon learned to fight for every drop of milk. He held on tightly to the nipple and sucked as rapidly as possible. As a result he frequently choked from trying to swallow too fast, much to the exasperation of both mother and child. The fact that babies were unwanted was a result of local marriage customs. A man was permitted to have several wives, and the principal way of acquiring a new wife was to exchange one's daughter for the daughter of another man. The mother feared pregnancy because she might give birth to a daughter who could be used by her husband to acquire a new wife. The father feared pregnancy because if the child turned out to be a boy, he had fathered a potential rival. The principal way the son could acquire a wife was to trade his sister for the sister of another young man. The father tried to make home life as difficult as possible for his sons in the hope that they would run away at an early age and leave his daughters at his sole disposal. The mother sided with her sons against the father. The threat that a boy might grab off all the sisters and exchange them for wives for himself turned brother against brother. Daughters resented being marriage pawns and often expressed their hatred of mother, father, and brothers by eloping.

Some of the findings and implications of the extensive literature on culture and personality that have special significance for psychopathology are these:

1. The role of culture in shaping personality (and in producing personality types especially vulnerable to particular mental disorders) does not exclude the significance of genetic factors. Particularly in small, isolated, inbred societies, the emergence of a modal or basic personality type may be partly due to selective breeding. When a culture favors particular personality characteristics, individuals genetically endowed with potentialities for the desired traits will be preferred as mates. Over several generations,

this selective marital factor, which in turn influences the number of children born with the favored potentialities, will result in a relatively homogeneous genetic population. Deviants will still occur, but their relative number will be gradually dimished. The effectiveness of selective breeding in creating desired behavior attributes has been repeatedly demonstrated in animal studies.

2. As we can see by the examples we have examined and the study of the Hutterites summarized in Supplementary Report 4, the molding influence of the culture is pervasive, consistent, and continuous throughout the life of the individual. The significance, if any, of a particular infantile experience depends on the extent to which it is an integral part of the total indoctrination and training program.

3. The success of culture (or heredity) in creating uniform or standard human personalities is limited. Under favorable circumstances, culture and heredity working together may produce similar personality traits in a substantial proportion of a tribe or social group. A closer examination, however, indicates the highly individual character of each member (DuBois, 1944). Even the most rigid cultures produce an infinite variety of personalities. Furthermore, the personality types "typical" of certain cultures are found in all societies.

4. The fact that certain cultures, such as the Mundugumor, accepted as normal some attitudes and traits that would be suggestive of psychopathology in our culture again points to the unreliability of "symptoms" as cross-cultural indicators of psychopathology. Whether a person is distrustful or friendly, hated or loved by his family, in itself has nothing to do with his mental health. As long as he retains enough voluntary control over his impulses, emotions, and mental faculties to behave reasonably well and appropriately in accordance with the demands and expectations of his culture, he is a normal person from a psychiatric point of view and is so regarded by his society.

CULTURE AND PSYCHOPATHOLOGY

The extensive literature on the role of culture in the development of mental disorders (reviewed by Linton, 1956; Leighton and Hughes, 1961; Wallace, 1967; and others) indicates that (1) no culture is free of mental disorders, (2) the major patterns of clinical syndromes are found in all large heterogeneous societies, and (3) the overt form or content of symptoms is mainly learned and hence culture-bound. The universality of mental disorders may be attributed to the presence of pathogenic influences in all cultures and to the inevitable pressures, frustrations, and conflicts of human life.

With respect to this general summary, the occurrence of the major clinical syndromes in all advanced countries of the world has long been recognized. In the past, the labels have varied. More recently, most countries have accepted, with minor modifications, the eighth revision of the International Nomenclature and Classification System proposed by the World Health Organization of the United Nations. Wherever hospitals or clinics staffed by Western personnel have been established in primitive or nonliterate countries, all of the major clinical syndromes have been observed in the native population. Earlier studies of primitive societies, based on casual field observations, emphasized the more dramatic and visible forms of psychopathology. The better controlled, more recent investigations have confirmed the occurrence of all of the major forms of mental disorders in primitive societies (Field, 1960; Toker, 1966; Elsarrag, 1968). The simplest explanation for the presence of similar clinical syndromes in various cultures is that the major varieties of mental disorders represent characteristic human forms of maladaptive reactions to intolerable stress situations. Human beings characteristically react to the inevitable problems of life with the anxiety and rigidity associated with neurosis, the conversion symptoms of hysterics, the inner retreat of schizophrenics, the hopeless despair of the depressed, and the disorganized hyperactivity of manics. There is some evidence that in most Western countries the same criteria are used in deciding the kinds of patients who are hospitalized. The five countries listed in Table 7.1 differ markedly in the number of available hospital beds and admission regulations, but in all of them the two major symptoms cited as reasons for hospitalization are delusions and hostile, belligerent behavior. One or both of these socially disturbing reactions are present in 82 to 90 percent of representative samples of consecutive male admissions be-

Table 7.1. Incidence of specific symptoms noted at time of hospitalization among male patients consecutively admitted to public mental hospitals in five countries[a]

	Percent of admissions					
Symptom	United States	France	Italy	Spain	Portugal	Range
Delusions	60%	56%	66%	52%	54%	52–66%
Hallucinations	36	32	30	36	28	28–36
Hostile belligerence	72	52	60	58	66	52–72
Delusions and/or hostile belligerence	86	88	90	82	90	82–90
Suicide attempts	2	4	4	4	2	2– 4

Adapted from J. D. Page, "Cultural-National Differences in Symptomatology in Hospitalized Psychotic Patients." *Yearbook of the American Philosophical Society* (1965): 343–44.
[a]Data are based on fifty consecutive male admissions, aged twenty-five to fifty, for each country, exclusive of persons diagnosed as mentally defective, acutely alcoholic, or brain damaged.

tween the ages of twenty-five and fifty, exclusive of alcoholics and patients with brain disorders.

The effect of culture on the outward form of psychopathology is most apparent in the content of symptoms. Whether a patient believes his thoughts and actions are being controlled by an evil spirit, a sorcerer, or an electronic computer depends on his social background. The contrast in patterns of fantasy and mobility observed in Irish and Italian schizophrenics in this country (Opler and Singer, 1956) illustrates how variations in contemporary subcultures may influence overt symptoms. A study of Japanese and Filippino male paranoid patients in Hawaii (Enright and Jaeckle, 1963) indicated that the Japanese were more restrained and inhibited than the Filippinos. At a broader level, culture may be thought to influence the relative incidence of specific types of mental disorders. The incidence of toxic and brain disorders in a culture may be directly related to the prevalence of drug usage, dietary deficiencies, syphilis, or other exogenous pathogenic factors. Alcoholism, for example, is rare in Islamic countries. The comparatively high recorded rate of schizophrenics in West Africa may be due in part to the prevalence of trypanosomiasis, a form of sleeping sickness that is transmitted by the bite of an infected tsetse fly. This disease is associated with schizophrenic-like symptoms (Tooth, 1950).

There is some evidence that in cultures described by anthropologists as shame-oriented, psychiatric disorders are likely to take the form of antisocial, aggressive, acting-out behavior that is more disturbing to society than to the individual. In guilt-oriented cultures such as the Hutterite, on the other hand, there is a higher occurrence of depressive reactions. In Reisman's (1950) terminology, shame cultures are "other-directed," since society at large controls and enforces moral conduct, whereas guilt cultures are "inner-directed," since the individual is expected to be responsible for his own conduct and to assume blame for his misdeeds.

The role of culture in shaping symptoms may be seen especially clearly in unusual reactions observed in specific localities: *amok* and *latah* in Malaysia, *koro* in China, *windigo* among the Objibwa Indians, and *piblokto* among the Arctic Eskimos (Leighton and Hughes, 1961). *Amok* was a culture-bound type of rage reaction in which the disturbed individual would suddenly grasp his dagger and run about in a frenzy, madly slashing at anyone in his way. *Latah,* a condition mainly noted in women, has been described as an intense fear reaction marked by shuddering and the involuntary imitation of the actions and words of others. *Koro* was a form of sexual anxiety formerly noted among Chinese men; those who fell victim to it were convinced that their sex organs were shrinking and disappearing into their abdomens, and that when this happened they would die. *Piblokto* also appears to have been a dramatic fear reaction. The deranged Eskimo would run out naked in subzero temperatures and mimic the sounds of Arctic birds and animals. These exotic disorders may at one time have been common in certain cultures, but they are now rare. Other, less dramatic cultural differences in surface symptoms are also disappearing. As rural, backward, tribal populations enter urban areas and become exposed to Western influences, the clinical manifestations of mental disorders approximate those of the European white settlers (Wittkower and Fried, 1959).

CULTURE AND INCIDENCE RATES

Whether certain cultures have a higher incidence of mental disorders than others is difficult to determine. A major obstacle is the absence of valid criteria for deciding how "sick" a person must be before he is counted as deranged. The extreme variations in the prevalence rates of psychological disorders noted in epidemiological studies conducted in various parts of the world are mainly due to variations in the conception of mental disorder (Dohrenwend and Dohrenwend, 1965). The variability in cultural standards applies mainly to mild disorders. Most authorities agree that the incidence of severe disorders (psychoses) is about the same in all cultures, primitive as well as Western (Kiev, 1964). On the basis of a survey of mental disorders among the natives of the South Pacific, Berne (1960) concluded that the same proportion of every large population, whether Anglo-Saxon, Polynesian, or Melanesian, develops a psychosis each year. Differences in the recorded number of patients in various cultures are related to such incidental factors as the availability of doctors and hospital facilities and the societies' relative tolerance of various forms of deviant behavior. In support of this hypothesis, Berne noted that the incidence rates of first admissions to mental hospitals in New Zealand were the same for people of European stock and for Maoris. This finding is consistent with earlier reports. Some years ago Winston (1934) noted that mental disease was as prevalent in Samoa as in rural areas of the United States. Lin (1953) observed that the incidence of psychosis among the natives of Formosa was on a par with that of central Germany.

In determining whether the incidence of mental disorders is increasing, we must make a distinction between severe and mild disorders. As for admissions to mental hospitals, which are limited to the more severe disorders, there is conclusive evidence that the hospital admission rate per 100,000 population for ages under fifty is about the same today as it was in 1840 (Goldhamer and Marshall, 1949; Page and Landis, 1943; Dunham, 1966). In other words, the transition from the horse-and-buggy era to the jet age has not resulted in any noticeable increase in admissions to mental hospitals. It is reasonable to assume that the proportion of unhospitalized psychotic patients has also remained about the same over the past century.

The available data thus refute the popular belief that the pressures and strains of modern life have resulted in an increase in severe mental disorders. It is quite possible that cases of neuroses and other mild disorders have increased, but in the absence of valid long-range comparative data, the issue remains unproved.

SOCIAL FACTORS

Socioeconomic status, social disorganization, and social change are also thought to be related to mental disorders. Occasionally, as in times of war, economic depression, and transition from tribal to city living in developing countries, it is possible to evaluate the significance of these variables separately. As a rule, however, they are closely interrelated. For example, low-income areas tend to be more disorganized, to have a higher population turnover, and to include a higher proportion of migrant and immigrant residents than high-income areas. A rough measure of the relation of socioeconomic status to diagnosis is provided by a comparison of first admissions to high-cost private hospitals with first admissions to publicly supported state hospitals. First admissions to public mental institutions in the United States outnumber first admissions to private mental hospitals about 4 to 1. A higher proportion of first admissions to public hospitals than private hospitals are diagnosed as senile, psychotic with arteriosclerosis, drunk or alcoholic, and drug addicts. The proportions of persons with schizophrenic reactions and personality disorders other than alcoholism to total admissions are about the same in public and private institutions. The percentage of first admissions diagnosed as psychoneurotic is three times as great in private mental hospitals as in public institutions. Manic-depressive and psychotic depressive reactions also constitute a higher proportion of admissions to private mental institutions.

The interpretation of these and related findings noted in field studies is not easy. The possibility that socioeconomic background either has a direct effect on the relative incidence of specific disorders or is influential in favoring the development of certain symptom patterns cannot be ruled out. On the other hand, reported class differences in the relative distribution of specific disorders may be a result of (1) examiner bias (the doctor may tend to assign more "favorable" labels to better educated and wealthier patients), (2) class differences in defining and recognizing a psychiatric problem, or (3) differences between classes in available or preferred procedures for handling certain types of deviant behavior. The higher proportion of disturbed elderly persons admitted to public than to private mental hospitals, for example, may be related to the greater prevalence of biological defects among the more poorly educated and less economically successful members of society, the harder life of the culturally disadvantaged, the higher incidence of nutritional deficiencies that contribute to impaired mental functioning in the indigent aged, or the inability of the less affluent to care for incompetent aged parents or relatives at home or to place them in nursing homes. Examiner bias has long been recognized. In 1932 P. Janet, a French psychiatrist, wrote:

> If the patient is poor he is committed to a public hospital as psychotic; if he can afford the luxury of a private sanitarium he is put there with a diagnosis of neurasthenia; if he is wealthy enough to be isolated in his own home under constant watch of nurses and physicians he is simply an indisposed eccentric.

A major limitation of hospital admission data is that they are based on restricted samples. Even in countries that provide adequate facilities, the number of unhospitalized persons exhibiting neurotic and psychotic behavior is as great as or greater than the number of hospitalized mental patients. More comprehensive data are provided by field studies, which attempt to count or estimate the total number of treated and untreated cases for a whole population in a specified geographical area. But this approach introduces other problems. There is no objective, valid test that can be routinely administered to a large population to differentiate between disturbed and normal persons. The criteria used have been loose, and investigators often include doubtful cases that more stringent screening would exclude. Another limitation is that almost all field studies have been concerned with the prevalence rather than the incidence of mental disorders. *Incidence rates* include only new cases that have developed during a designated period of time (usually a year). *Prevalence rates,* which run much higher than incidence figures, are determined by counting all mental patients in the population on a particular day or year and dividing this number by the total population. Prevalence rates are loaded in favor of chronic, long-term cases. Prevalence rates are actually better measures of the effects of socioeconomic status on the duration of mental illness than of its occurrence.

In fourteen out of eighteen field studies on the relation of prevalence rate to socioeconomic status (Dohrenwend and Dohrenwend, 1965), maximum rates were found at the lowest social stratum; maximum rates were reported in three studies for the middle and in one study for the highest social stratum. Minimum rates were reported for the lowest social stratum in three studies, in the middle social group in five studies, and in the highest stratum in ten studies. The inverse relationship noted between social class and prevalence of mental disorder applies to all psychological disorders combined. When investigators focus on specific disorders, field studies indicate that the total prevalence of neurosis and psychosis, both treated and untreated, is not related to social class. Maximum and minimum rates have been reported for these two classes of disorder about as often in the lowest socioeconomic group as in some other class (Dohrenwend and Dohrenwend, 1967). Psychosis in children has also been found to be unrelated to social class (McDermott et al., 1967). The higher prevalence rate for all disorders combined at the lowest social stratum is partly due to the disproportionate number of alcoholics, asocial personalities, and persons with other character disorders reported at this socioeconomic level. In ten of the thirteen field studies reviewed by the Dohrenwends (1967), the highest rates of character disorders were found in the lowest social class.

SOCIAL DISORGANIZATION AND CHANGE

Earlier studies indicated that the incidence of schizophrenia was higher in deprived neighborhoods than in middle-class urban areas. However, more recent reports, in which corrections were made for the greater mobility or population turnover in the deprived areas, reduce the difference to a statistically insignificant point. The only disorder that does appear to have a higher corrected incidence in disorganized communities is sociopathy (Dunham, 1966). Social changes, in particular the changes accompanying migration, the transition from war to peace and from peace to war, and the increased urbanization of developing nations, do not in themselves appear to constitute hazards to mental health (Murphy, 1961). Most studies report no increase in rates of admission to mental hospitals in the civilian population during wartime and no increase in the incidence of psychoses among military personnel. There is a decrease in the rate of mental disorders among prisoners of war. Repeated air raids may lead to an increase in neurotic and psychosomatic complaints in civilian populations, however, and combat soldiers and pilots, exposed to prolonged stress, also tend to show an increase in neuroses and psychosomatic reactions (Reid, 1961).

ANOMIE AND MENTAL DISORDERS

Kleiner and Parker (1966) have investigated the relationship between mental illness, social mobility, and Dirkheim's four characteristics of anomie: lack of integration with significant reference groups, inability to perceive realistic barriers to achievement, high status aspirations, and low self-esteem. Their findings, based on the results of a study of almost three thousand members of an urban Negro population, are in partial conflict with Durkheim's theory of an invariant relationship between social mobility, anomie, and deviant behavior. Kleiner and Parker found that mobility and mental illness are correlated at some strata in the social hierarchy, but not at others. Their data show that rates of mental disorder are higher among downwardly mobile individuals in low-status occupations and upwardly mobile individuals in high-status positions than among their nonmobile status peers. In addition, both upwardly mobile and downwardly mobile individuals exhibit the characteristics of anomie.

SOCIAL CLASS AND THERAPY

A number of studies (Hollingshead and Redlich, 1958; Reissman et al., 1964) indicate a definite relationship between social class and source of referral for treatment, type of treatment offered and accepted, and duration of treatment. The majority of psychotic patients in the highest socioeconomic groups were self-referred or referred by family and friends. Most middle-class patients were referred by physicians; and most psychotic patients in the lowest socioeconomic class were referred by the police, the courts, or social agencies. Upper-class and upper-middle-class neurotics attending outpatient clinics are more often assigned to senior staff members and receive intensive "depth" treatment, whereas lower-middle-class and lower-class neurotics are more often assigned to junior staff members and tend to receive "directive" supportive therapy or medication. Lower-class psychotic patients stay in hospitals longer than upper-class patients, but neurotic lower-class patients tend to discontinue outpatient or private office treatment much sooner than do patients from higher classes. Apart from the cost factor, the early withdrawal from treatment of the lower-class neurotics appears to be due to their dissatisfaction with the traditional "talking out" forms of psychotherapy, which stress self-understanding and personality reconstruction. Most of them want the doctor to tell them what to do or to give them something that will make them well. Many uneducated neurotic patients believe they are physically ill and expect pills and needles, along with the sympathy usually given the sick. Freud (1950, p. 401) foresaw the special therapeutic problems that might be posed by the poor and suggested a possible remedy:

> We shall probably discover that the poor are even less ready to part with their neuroses than the rich because the hard life that awaits them when they recover has no attraction, and illness in them gives them more claim to the help of others. Possibly, we may often be able to achieve something if we combine aid to the mind with material support.

Demographic Data

AGE

Since the development of a mental disorder is a gradual process, precise information on age of onset is difficult to obtain. Comprehensive data, however, are available on the age distribution of patients at the time of first admission to a mental hospital. On the basis of this criterion, the incidence

rate of mental disorders, as illustrated in Figure 7.1, is lowest for ages under fifteen, rises sharply between the ages of fifteen and thirty-four, shows
a slight but consistent drop between the ages of thirty-five and sixty-four,
rises slightly between sixty-five and seventy-four, and is highest for those
seventy-five and older. The decline for the age period thirty-five to sixty-
four is a relatively new development that is mainly due to the sharp decrease
in recent years of patients suffering from general paresis and manic-depressive psychosis admitted to mental hospitals. Older studies showed a relatively constant admission rate for ages twenty-five to sixty-five.

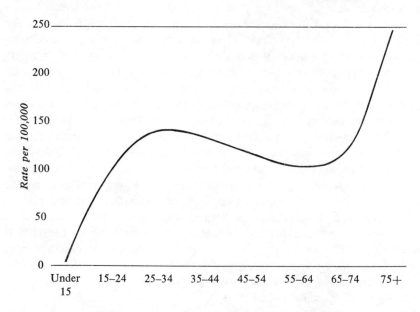

*Figure 7.1. Incidence rate of mental disorder by age at first admission
to a public or private mental hospital in the United States in
1965*

The combining of all disorders blankets certain other significant aspects
of age. A comparison of the age distributions of first admissions by specific
disorders indicates that each disorder mainly occurs during a particular
age period and that the distribution pattern for most disorders tends to be
bell-shaped. The modal age period for transient situational disturbances is
between fifteen and twenty-four, for schizophrenia from fifteen to forty-
four, for psychoneuroses from twenty-four to forty-four, for affective psychoses from forty-five to fifty-five, and for organic brain disorders between
sixty-five and eighty-four. The age boundaries of specific diagnoses are

more supportive of the discrete than the continuity concept of mental disorders. The fact that each disorder appears to have a critical age of occurrence may be related to underlying biological defects that "mature" or are expressed at different times. But the age correlation may also be accounted for on the basis of psychosocial factors.

SEX

Learning and behavior disorders in children occur at least three times more often in boys than in girls (Kessler, 1966). The greater incidence of reading and other learning problems in boys may be related to their slower rate of maturation (Bentzen, 1963). The greater aggressiveness of boys and their tendency to "act out" emotional difficulties may account for sex differences noted in the incidence of behavior disorders during the preadolescent years. There are some indications that emotional problems of a neurotic nature are more prevalent among adolescent girls than adolescent boys.

At the adult level, field studies reviewed by the Dohrenwends (1965, 1967) report (1) no consistent sex differences in the prevalence of total psychological disorder, psychoses, or schizophrenia; (2) a tendency for affective disorders to occur more often in women than in men; (3) consistently higher rates of neurosis for women; and (4) consistently higher rates of character disorders for men. These findings suggest that males and females are equally vulnerable to psychological disorders and equally susceptible to gross schizophrenic disorganization. In the case of milder disorders, however, the two sexes tend to react differently to life problems. Females more often react by becoming depressed, nervous, or emotional. Males more often turn to alcohol or engage in aggressive or some other form of socially unacceptable behavior.

MARITAL STATUS

Among patients admitted to state mental hospitals, the incidence of mental disorders is lowest for married people and highest for the divorced and separated. The admission rates for the single and widowed fall about midway between those for the married and divorced (Landis and Page, 1938; Thomas and Locke, 1963). One possible explanation for these findings is that marriage contributes to the prevention of mental disorders. An alternative explanation is that marriage acts as a selective factor. Unstable individuals are less successful in finding marriage partners; if they do marry, they tend to be divorced fairly soon (Loeb, 1966). Another explanation is that marital status is unrelated to real incidence rate. The lower hospital admission rate for married individuals may be simply due to the fact that if a disturbed person is married, he has a far greater chance of being cared for at home than someone who has no one to care for him. This advantage, to a lesser degree, would be shared by widowed and single individuals living with their families.

Summary

Sociocultural theories are concerned with a variety of related but independent issues. One theory that has virtually gained the status of fact holds that society acts as the arbiter in deciding what types of norm violations indicate behavior disorders. Scheff (1966) suggests that the main criterion is residual deviance. The label of "neurotic" or "psychotic" is applied to persons exhibiting disturbing, socially unacceptable behavior that does not fit other culturally recognized categories of deviance. Thus a person is not usually considered mentally disordered if his deviant behavior can be described as drunkenness, sex perversion, criminality, stupidity, prejudice, or bad manners. Labeling a person as neurotic or psychotic has two major consequences. First, he is expected to conform to local stereotypes of mental illness. If he does so, thus permitting his symptoms to become fixed, he is granted the privileges and benefits associated with the "sick" role. If he fails to do so, society washes its hands of any responsibility for his care. He is dismissed as a troublesome person. Second, he is isolated and treated as a social outcast. Long after he has recovered, he is still regarded by associates with apprehension and distrust.

Research data on the hypothesis that sociocultural factors may directly cause mental disorders have been essentially negative. The best guess is that the total incidence of psychopathology is about the same in all cultures. Culture mainly influences symptom content, the attitude of the group toward mental deviants, and treatment procedures. This does not preclude the possibility that certain clinical forms of psychopathology are more prevalent in some cultures than in others. Field studies on socioeconomic factors suggest that the total prevalence of psychopathology may be higher at the lowest social stratum than among other classes. This finding appears to be due mainly to the disproportionate number of alcoholics, antisocial personalities, and other types of deviants found at the lowest socioeconomic level. The source of referral and type of treatment given a mental patient is related to his socioeconomic status.

Demographic data indicate that the total prevalence of psychopathology is about the same for males and females. Females tend to have higher prevalence rates for neurosis and affective psychosis, whereas men have higher rates for character disorders. These findings suggest sex differences in ways of reacting to problems. Under stress women more often become nervous, depressed, and emotionally upset, while men more often resort to alcohol, become aggressive, and engage in other forms of acting-out behavior. The incidence of admissions to mental hospitals is lowest for the married population and highest for divorced and separated persons.

Supplementary Report 4. Mental Illness Among the Hutterites

A good test case of the theory that mental disorders are the products of the stresses, pressures, and fast tempo of modern life is provided by the Hutterites, a cohesive religious sect of German origin dating back to the early sixteenth century. About 1875 101 married couples and their children migrated to this country and established culturally isolated settlements in the Dakotas, Montana, and the prairie provinces of Canada. Apart from adopting a highly mechanized form of agriculture, the Hutterites have preserved their original customs with minimal interaction with the outside world. All of the present population are descendants of the original immigrant group.

The Hutterites are farmers dedicated to simple communal living. They do not believe in education beyond grammar school. Radios, movies, television, jewelry, and other luxury items are taboo. Their homes consist only of bedrooms, all of which are furnished alike. Property is owned by the group rather than the individual, meals are served in common dining rooms, and elected group leaders assign the work. Every member is provided with a high level of social and economic security from womb to tomb.

The group takes such good care of its own that it was for a long time thought that the great security of their system resulted in a complete absence of mental illness. This was supported by the conspicuous absence of Hutterites in mental hospitals. However, a research team that gained the cooperation of the group and made a field study of the Hutterites in 1951 found that well over 2 percent of the group either had active symptoms of mental disorder or had recovered from some such disorder (Eaton and Weil, 1955). In attempting to account for the presence of so many disturbed persons, the investigators suggested that there may be genetic, organic, or constitutional predispositions that will cause mental illness in any society, no matter how protective and stable it may be. In most societies schizophrenia is far more prevalent than manic-depressive psychosis, but the reverse is true among the Hutterites. Since there is a definite tendency for manic-depressive psychosis to run in families, a possible explanation for this atypical finding is that some of the original immigrants had a genetic predisposition to manic-depressive psychosis that has been inherited by their inbred descendants. An alternate, but not necessarily contradictory, explanation is that the cultural pattern may favor depressive reactions. The indoctrination system of the Hutterites teaches its members to look for blame and guilt within themselves rather than in others. By precept and example, the members are taught to repress aggressive impulses. The effectivenss of this training is shown by the fact that murder, arson, severe physical assault, sex crimes, and other forms of violence are extremely rare. Self-blaming starts at an early age. Melancholy moods are regarded by teachers as the primary emotional problem of Hutterite schoolchildren. When a person develops signs of mental disorder, the closely knit social group provides a highly therapeutic atmosphere by demonstrating strong support, guidance, tolerance, and love for him.

The predominance of depressive reactions fits in with the austere and puritanical customs of the sect. Security and stability are achieved through insistence on strict conformity to a predetermined and extremely narrow way of life. But, as the investigators noted, the rigid cultural mold has not resulted in stereotyped personalities. Despite uniformity in the externals of living, there are great variations in personality among the members of the sect. On projective personality tests, the Hutterites show strong antisocial and aggressive impulses, even though they effectively repress these feelings in daily life.

References

BENEDICT, R. *Patterns of Culture*. Boston: Houghton Mifflin, 1934.

BENTZEN, F. "Sex Ratios in Learning and Behavior Disorders." *American Journal of Orthopsychiatry* 33 (1963): 92–98.

BERNE, E. "A Psychiatric Census of the South Pacific." *American Journal of Psychiatry* 117 (1960): 44–47.

DOHRENWEND, B. P., and DOHRENWEND, B. S. "The Problem of Validity in Field Studies of Psychological Disorder." *Journal of Abnormal Psychology* 70 (1965): 52–69.

DOHRENWEND, B. P., and DOHRENWEND, B. S. "Field Studies of Social Factors in Relation to Three Types of Psychological Disorders." *Journal of Abnormal Psychology* 72 (1967): 369–78.

DuBois, C. *The People of Alor*. Minneapolis: University of Minnesota Press, 1944.

DUNHAM, H. W. "Epidemiology of Psychiatric Disorders as a Contribution to Medical Ecology." *Archives of General Psychiatry* 14 (1966): 1–19.

EATON, J. W., and WEIL, R. J. *Culture and Mental Disorders: A Comparative Study of the Hutterites and Other Populations*. Glencoe, Ill.: Free Press, 1955.

ELSARRAG, M. E. "Psychiatry in the Northern Sudan: A Study in Comparative Psychiatry." *British Journal of Psychiatry* 114 (1968): 945–48.

ENRIGHT, J. B., and JAECKLE, W. R. "Psychiatric Symptoms and Diagnosis in Two Sub-cultures." *International Journal of Social Psychiatry* 2 (1963): 12–17.

FIELD, M. J. *The Search for Security*. Evanston, Ill.: Northwestern University Press, 1960.

FRANK, J. D. *Persuasion and Healing*. Baltimore: John Hopkins Press, 1961.

FREUD, S. *Collected Papers*, vol. 2, pp. 401–2. London: Hogarth Press, 1950.

GOLDHAMER, H., and MARSHALL, A. *Psychoses and Civilization*. Glencoe, Ill.: Free Press, 1949.

HOLLINGSHEAD, A. B., and REDLICH, F. C. *Social Class and Mental Illness*. New York: Wiley, 1958.

JANET, P. *La force et la faiblesse psychologiques*. Paris: Moloine, 1932. Quoted in K. Menninger et al., *The Vital Balance,* p. 29. New York: Viking Press, 1963.

KESSLER, J. W. *Psychopathology of Childhood.* Englewood Cliffs, N.J.: Prentice-Hall, 1966.

KIEV, A., ed. *Magic, Faith, and Healing.* New York: Free Press, Macmillan, 1964.

KLEINER, R. J., and PARKER, S. *Mental Health in an Urban Negro Community.* New York: Free Press, Macmillan, 1966.

LANDIS, C., and PAGE, J. D. *Modern Society and Mental Disease.* New York: Rinehart, 1938.

LEIGHTON, A. H., and HUGHES, J. M. "Cultures as a Causative of Mental Disorder." *Milbank Memorial Fund Quarterly* 39, no. 3 (1961): 446–88.

LIN, T. "A Study of the Incidence of Mental Disorder in Chinese and Other Cultures." *Psychiatry* 16 (1953): 313.

LINTON, R. *Culture and Mental Disorders.* Springfield, Ill.: Charles C. Thomas, 1956.

LOEB, J. "The Personality Factor in Divorce." *Journal of Consulting Psychology* 30 (1966): 562.

MCDERMOTT, J. F., JR., et al. "Social Class and Mental Illness in Children: The Question of Childhood Psychosis." *American Journal of Orthopsychiatry* 37 (1967): 548–57.

MEAD, M. *Sex and Temperament in Primitive Cultures.* New York: Morrow, 1935.

MURPHY, H. B. M. "Social Change and Mental Health." *Milbank Memorial Fund Quarterly* 3 (1961): 385–445.

OPLER, M., and SINGER, J. L. "Contrasting Patterns of Fantasy and Mobility in Irish and Italian Schizophrenics." *Journal of Abnormal and Social Psychology* 53 (1956): 42–47.

PAGE, J., and LANDIS, C. "Trends in Mental Disease." *Journal of Abnormal and Social Psychology* 38 (1943): 518–24.

REID, D. D. "Precipitating Proximal Factors in the Occurrence of Mental Disorder: Epidemiological Evidence." *Milbank Memorial Fund Quarterly* 2 (1961): 229–45.

REISMAN, D. *The Lonely Crowd: A Study of Changing American Character.* New Haven: Yale University Press, 1950.

REISSMAN, F.; COHEN, J.; and PEARL, A., eds. *Mental Health of the Poor.* New York: Free Press, Macmillan, 1964.

SCHEFF, T. J. "A Sociological Theory of Mental Disorders." In *Approaches to Psychopathology,* ed. J. D. Page, pp. 250–68. New York: Columbia University Press, 1966.

THOMAS, D. S., and LOCKE, B. Z. "Marital Status, Education, and Occupational Differentials in Mental Illness." *Milbank Memorial Fund Quarterly* 41, no. 2 (1963): 145–60.

TOKER, E. "Mental Illness in the White and Bantu Population of the Republic of South Africa." *American Journal of Psychiatry* 123 (1966): 55–65.

TOOTH, G. *Studies of Mental Illness in the Gold Coast.* London: H. M. Stationery Office, 1950.

WALLACE, F. C. "Anthropolgy and Psychiatry." In *Comprehensive Textbook of Psychiatry,* ed. A. M. Freedman, H. I. Kaplan, and H. S. Kaplan, pp. 195–201. Baltimore: Williams & Wilkins, 1967.

WINSTON, E. "The Alleged Lack of Mental Disease Among Primitive Groups." *American Anthropologist* 36 (1934): 234–38.
WITTKOWER, E. D., and FRIED, J. "Cross-cultural Approach to Mental Health Problems." *American Journal of Psychiatry* 116 (1959): 423–28.

CHAPTER EIGHT

Schizophrenic Reactions

If the concept of schizophrenia did not exist, it would be necessary to invent an equivalent diagnosis to provide a broad-range label for the most severe and most perplexing forms of disorganized human behavior. Periodic attempts have been made to delineate schizophrenic reactions on the basis of gross disturbances of association, impaired thinking, delusions and hallucinations, and profound breakdown in interpersonal relations. In practice, however, schizophrenia has been and remains a catch-all diagnosis for diverse psychotic reactions exclusive of the more clearly defined manic-depressive states.

Table 8.1 includes a partial listing of the bewildering array of dysfunctions presumed to be symptomatic of schizophrenia. The concurrent presence of several of these symptoms is usually required to establish a diagnosis of schizophrenia. Another critical but necessarily delayed diagnostic sign is limited improvement or response to treatment. Sooner or later the label of schizophrenia is assigned to most chronic mental patients who are free of obvious brain pathology. In the United States the concept of schizophrenia is broadly interpreted to include several borderline categories as well as the more conventional ones. These borderline reactions consist of a combination of schizophrenic features and symptoms associated with some other disorder. For example, a schizo-affective reaction, which is one of the clinical types recognized in the 1968 APA classification, is a combination of schizophrenic symptoms and pronounced depression or elation. American psychologists also use diagnoses such as ambulatory schizophrenia and psychoneurotic schizophrenia, which are not included in the APA classification system. Patients so designated usually present a mixture of neurotic and schizophrenic symptoms. This broad interpretation affords

175

Table 8.1   Clinical signs considered indicative of schizophrenic behavior

Clinical signs	Characteristics
Anhedonia	Impaired ability to experience or integrate feeling of pleasure
Ambivalence	Concurrent love-hate feelings for the same person or object
Attention interference	Impaired capacity for maintaining a mental set of readiness; difficulty in focusing attention on a specific topic; inability to exclude irrelevant material
Autism	Thinking and behavior dominated by wishes, fears, and fantasies; marked subjectivity of interpretations
Chaotic sexuality	Confusion as to gender; strange sexual fantasies
Cognitive slippage	Disorganized, overinclusive, or underinclusive association of ideas
Disturbances in affect	Inappropriate moods; apathy; intense anxiety; blunting of affect
Disturbances in volition	Blocking, inhibition, negativism, indecision
Hypersensitivity	Oversensitivity and overresponsiveness to others; easily hurt feelings
Interpersonal difficulties	Lack of skills or capacity for relating to others; emotional distance; distrust of others
Lack of insight	Inability to realize or denial that one's behavior is abnormal
Loss of ego boundaries	Identity confusion; blurring of boundaries between self and external world; belief that others can invade and control one's inner life
Loss of voluntary control	Spontaneous and unpredictable appearance and expression of thoughts, sensations, impulses, and reactions, independently of voluntary decision and choice
Motor disturbances	Motionlessness; rigidity; waxy flexibility; echopraxia; stereotyped movements; grimaces; stupor
Perceptual disturbances	Hallucinations; illusions; errors in estimating size, time intervals, etc.
Progressive deterioration	Increase in intensity and frequency of symptoms; a critical sign, but cannot be considered significant until one or more years after onset of symptoms
Reality-testing impairment	Difficulty in distinguishing fantasies from real life experiences; misperception and misinterpretation of external events; ideas of reference
Social withdrawal	Isolation and insulation from social environment; turtle-like retreat into one's shell; preoccupation with self
Speech disturbances	Incoherent, rambling speech; muteness; stilted speech; "word salad": neologisms, echolalia, private language
Thinking disturbances	Bizarre delusions; irrational thought; shift from abstract to concrete thinking

a more optimistic outlook with respect to prognosis. In addition, it tends to accentuate the importance of psychosocial factors in the etiology of schizophrenia. Many European psychiatrists favor a more constricted concept, placing greater emphasis on the etiological significance of organic pathology and genetic defects. This narrower concept acknowledges the variability of outcome. Some patients go on to become chronic deteriorated cases; the symptoms of others are arrested at some mild stage or show good clinical improvement following a severe psychotic episode. However, it is thought that complete recovery, with full restitution of functions, is rare, and that the disorder almost invariably has residual effects. A good clinical description of this more restricted concept has been provided by Slater (1968, p. 15):

> Schizophrenia is an illness affecting the mind and the personality of the patient in a way which is seldom completely resolved; after an attack of illness there is nearly always some degree of permanent change of personality, and if there are several attacks this change will become more and more marked. This change is one that de-individualizes and dehumanizes the patient, and leaves him, above all, with impaired capacities for normal affective responses. While an attack of illness is proceeding there will be one or more of a series of distinctive symptoms: hallucination in a clear state of consciousness, passivity feelings, primary delusional experiences, and rather typical forms of thought disorder. After recovery, often only partial, some of these symptoms may persist; but principal disabilities will be in the form of various psychological defects.

Aberrant reactions that correspond closely to modern descriptions of schizophrenia have been noted in ancient civilizations and all known primitive societies. Epidemiological data indicate that the rate of occurrence of schizophrenia has been relatively stable for the past hundred years. The expectancy rate is about the same in all countries. With minor allowances made for variations in the strictness of the criteria used, the findings of studies conducted in the United States, several European countries, and Japan agree that about 1 percent of the general population may be expected to develop the disorder during their lifetimes (Slater, 1968). The number of new cases that develop each year, whether hospitalized or not, runs about 150 per 100,000 general population.

The onset of schizophrenic behavior usually occurs during late adolescence and early adulthood. In a substantial number of cases the disorder persists for many years. The resulting accumulation of patients in hospitals and in the community shoots up the prevalence rate. At any point in time, the combined rate for chronic and recent cases is at least 300 per 100,000 population (Mishler and Scotch, 1963; Crocetti and Lemkau, 1967). In the United States about 20 percent of first admissions to public mental hospitals and over 50 percent of the resident populations of these hospitals are classified as schizophrenic. Close to 75 percent of all annual first admissions diagnosed as schizophrenic are from fifteen to forty years old. The peak incidence rate occurs between the ages of twenty-five and thirty-five. Since several years may intervene between the occurrence of the disorder and initial hospitalization, the actual age of onset is somewhat earlier than these figures indicate. No significant sex differences have been noted in the incidence or prevalence of schizophrenia. For hospitalized patients the median age at time of initial admission is slightly lower for males than for females; however, this finding is probably due to a greater delay in hospitalizing female patients than to real sex differences in age of onset of symptoms. In our culture, many of the early signs of schizophrenia (social withdrawal, passivity, and preoccupation with fantasies) are more tolerated in adolescent girls than in boys, and in any case parents are inclined to postpone for a longer period the hospitalization of psychologically disturbed daughters than sons.

Origins of the Concept of Schizophrenia

The symptom patterns of schizophrenia have been described for thousands of years. Up to the end of the eighteenth century, however, all psychoses were either grouped together under the general heading of madness or separated into two categories, melancholia and mania. Depressed patients were considered to be suffering from melancholia and all others were classified as maniacs. In 1801 Pinel added the category of *dementia,* which he identified as a disorder in thinking. His description of dementia corresponds very closely with contemporary descriptions of schizophrenia. Among other symptoms he noted impaired thinking, defective judgment, insulated ideas that followed one another without connection, broken sentences, diminished sensibility to external impressions, disparity between emotions and ideas, withdrawal, and inattentiveness.

In 1849 John Conolly described a condition mainly present in young persons, in which "the intellect, the affections, the passions, all seem inactive and deadened, and the patients become utterly apathetic" (Noyes and Kolb, 1963, p. 326). The term *dementia praecox* (literally, premature dementia) was first used by Morel in 1860. He applied this diagnosis to a fourteen-year-old boy who had formerly been bright and cheerful, and for no apparent reason had become withdrawn, sullen, morose, forgetful, and extremely hostile toward his father. In 1871 Hecker used the term *hebephrenia* to designate a mental disease of puberty and adolescence that quickly terminates in mental deterioration. In 1874 Kahlbaum contributed the term *catatonia* to describe a condition in which the patient is mute, motionless, stares fixedly into space, shows no reaction to sensory impressions, and sometimes exhibits a waxy flexibility of the body. At about the same time, several other investigators independently described a *paranoid* form of mental illness, marked by delusions of persecution. In 1896 Kraepelin brought together under the general heading of *dementia praecox* the disorders of catatonia, hebephrenia (a disorder marked by silliness, delusions, and hallucinations) and some of the paranoid psychoses. He maintained that these three reactions represented different manifestations of the same disease. Later on he added a fourth subtype, *simple schizophrenia,* which had been originally described by Diem in 1903. Kraepelin maintained that these four seemingly unrelated disorders were all caused by some as yet unspecified metabolic disease of early adolescence that led to progressive mental deterioration.

In 1911 Bleuler suggested that the term *schizophrenia* be substituted for dementia praecox. Bleuler considered the term dementia praecox misleading, since the condition was not limited to young persons and did not always lead to progressive deterioration. His observations, as well as Kraepelin's own data, indicated that many patients showed marked clinical improvement. His choice of a new label was intended to call attention to what he regarded as the key feature of the group of schizophrenias: a splitting of the psychic functions. What he meant by this was not the polarization of two different personalities, as occurs in neurosis, but a disunity of personality functioning: fragmentation of ideas, incongruence between ideas and emotions, rapid shift and change of ideas, mental blocking, and other signs of intrapsychic disharmony and contradictory tendencies. Bleuler shared Pinel's view that schizophrenia essentially represented a disturbance in thinking. He distinguished between primary and secondary symptoms. Primary symptoms included a loosening of associations, autistic thinking, disturbances of affect, and ambivalence. Primary symptoms were related to a possible underlying morbid somatic process. The secondary symptoms, which included hallucinations and delusions, were considered to represent psychological attempts at adaptation to the primary disturbance. In later revisions of his basic textbook, Bleuler distinguished between "process" and "reactive" forms of schizophrenia. By "process schizophrenia" he meant an endogenous progressive disease. The term "reactive" implied that the schizophrenia was reversible and induced by situational factors. This distinction has been refined and extensively studied by subsequent investigators.

Another important early contributor to the concept of schizophrenia was Adolf Meyer. As early as 1906 he criticized the concept of dementia praecox as a disease entity. He believed that the clinical picture of schizophrenia was more logically seen as a set of maladaptive reactions to the patient's life experiences and he advocated the study of the patient's total life history as a means of learning the origin and accumulation of faulty reaction habits. Following the lead of Sullivan (1953), many contemporary psychologists and psychiatrists agree that much schizophrenic behavior consists of ineffective and socially unacceptable patterns of interpersonal reaction.

Traditional Clinical Types of Schizophrenia

SIMPLE SCHIZOPHRENIC REACTION

The typical development of simple schizophrenic reaction consists of an insidious pattern of gradual social withdrawal, reduction of interest in external events, and indifference to the usual social amenities. The fundamental wish of people exhibiting this reaction is apparently to be left alone to do nothing. Personal hygiene is neglected. Patients rarely bathe, and they are untidy in appearance and dress. Motor responses are slow. Speech is more or less restricted to grunts and monosyllables. The disorder is usually stationary and chronic. Delusions and hallucinations do not occur. If left alone and permitted to do as they please, these patients cause relatively little trouble; but if thwarted or pushed into action, they may be irritable and nasty.

One such young man, until committed to a mental hospital at the age of twenty-one, had impressed his neighbors and teachers as being a quiet, well-behaved, calm youngster. In fact, he was considered a model child. A careful scrutiny, however, revealed a long history of maladjustment. All his life the patient had chewed his bedsheets in his sleep. He wet the bed until the age of fourteen. As a child he rarely played with other children, and he never had any close friends. During his high school years he would periodically lock himself in his room for several hours at a time and refuse to come out even for meals. During adolescence he avoided girls. He was a good student until about the tenth grade, but after that his work began to decline. His high school teachers complained that he spent too much time daydreaming. He attended college for one semester but went to classes infrequently and rarely handed in assignments. After dropping out of college, he bummed around the country for a few months and then returned home. At the insistence of his mother, he sought employment, but was fired from three jobs in the space of a month. He then stopped looking for work and stayed in his room. Most of his time was spent lying in bed or staring vacantly out of a window. He rarely spoke to members of the family. He ate by himself and refused to shave or take baths. Whenever his mother tried to get him to change his clothes or take a walk—anything at all except lie in bed staring out of the window—he would call her obscene names until she left him alone. On one occasion he became so enraged that he struck her to "shut her up." This led to his being committed to a mental hospital.

HEBEPHRENIC SCHIZOPHRENIC REACTION

Hebephrenic reactions represent one of the more extreme chronic forms of personality disorganization. Characteristic symptoms include impaired thinking, disconnected speech, shallow and inappropriate affect, inappropriate giggling, facial grimaces, and stereotyped mannerisms. Delusions and hallucinations, if present, are bizarre and disorganized. When hebephrenic patients are not under medication, they contentedly spend hours talking and smiling to themselves or conversing with imaginary persons.

An unmarried woman of thirty who had always been considered somewhat odd gradually became clumsy in her housework and erratic in her behavior. As time went on she started to listen to imaginary voices. Periodically she would laugh and giggle to herself for no apparent reason. She would frequently go about the house half undressed. On one occasion she attempted to seduce a much younger brother. She was hospitalized shortly after she took to walking naked in the garden at night under the impression that the man in the moon was her secret lover. When interviewed on admission to the hospital she stated that through her sexual union with the moon, heaven and earth had been united.

CATATONIC SCHIZOPHRENIC REACTION

Catatonic reaction is marked by either stupor or extreme excitement. The onset of acute symptoms may be abrupt, but there is usually a long history of poor social adaptation. In the stuporous or withdrawn state, the patient is uncommunicative and unresponsive. Some assume peculiar postures and maintain them for long periods. They may sit or stand rigidly without seemingly moving a muscle for hours at a time. In an extreme case the withdrawn catatonic may be mute, inaccessible, and literally helpless. Some patients show extreme rigidity of the body and others manifest a waxy flexibility of the limbs. Catatonic excitement is characterized by diffuse excitement and hyperactivity, but the patient usually remains rooted in one spot. Speech is inconsistent, incoherent, and repetitive. There appears to be a serious disturbance in volition. Some patients are extremely passive and robot-like in their responses to commands, while others are extremely negativistic and contrary. Particularly if a patient is bedridden and rigid, he may seem dead to the world, but later he may give a good account of everything that went on around him. Impulsive suicidal attempts are occasionally noted, but as a rule the intent is not so much to die as to be reborn.

One young woman, recently married, was rushed to the hospital by her husband after she had made a pseudo attempt at suicide by inflicting superficial cuts on the *outside* of her wrists. She was somewhat excited when admitted to the hospital, so she was given a sedative and put to bed. During the night she became very disturbed, threw objects around, and banged her head savagely against the wall. She was then transferred to a mental hospital, where she soon lapsed into a catatonic stupor. In going through her bureau, the husband came across a note written by his wife entitled "The Perfect Suicide." The plan outlined was a disappearance act rather than a suicide. The would-be suicide was supposed to leave her home in the middle of the night and travel by train to a distant town. She was to take nothing with her. After arriving at a large city, she was to buy a complete new wardrobe. Her traveling clothes were to be destroyed, since they might be identified and traced. The next step was to dye her hair, change her features through plastic surgery, and develop a new personality.

PARANOID SCHIZOPHRENIC REACTION

Paranoid reactions are marked by poorly organized delusions of persecution or grandeur, hallucinations, and ideas of reference (the assumption that the words and actions of other people refer to oneself). Patients tend to be suspicious, aloof, sensitive, and egocentric. The prevailing theme is that people are against them and in diffuse ways are maltreating or plotting against them. The delusions of persecution may be reinforced by hallucinations. Hallucinations are usually auditory; patients hear their enemies call them bad names, talk about them, and threaten them. Other common hallucinations include staring faces, unusual body sensations that patients attribute to the actions of their enemies, and peculiar odors. Their grandiose ideas are extravagant, as in the case of a veteran attending college who wrote several lengthy letters to the college president. The letters were rambling and incoherent, but the general idea seemed to be that the student was the human depository for the A-bomb formula. He blamed enemy agents for his frequent absences from classes. He stated that several of his alleged classmates were actually enemy agents who had been assigned to get him drunk so that they could obtain the A-bomb secret from him. His psychology professor was accused of reading his mind and forcing him to do things against his will. Here and there the letters contained veiled threats. The school authorities got in touch with the student's father, who took his son home. After a few days the family decided that they were unable to take care of him at home and arranged for his admission to a veterans' hospital.

Paranoids are in much better contact wtih their environment and are more responsive to it then nonparanoid schizophrenics (Silverman, 1964).

Sensory input is augmented by extensive scanning behavior. In contrast, nonparanoid schizophrenics tend to be indifferent to novel stimuli and inattentive to the environment. They show limited scanning and have a more restricted sensory input.

OTHER SCHIZOPHRENIC REACTIONS

The APA classification includes a condition referred to as *acute schizophrenic episode*. This reaction is often associated with confusion, perplexity, ideas of reference, emotional turmoil, dreamlike dissociation, and generalized excitement. Many patients recover within a few weeks. Sometimes the disorganization is progressive and takes on the characteristics of catatonic, hebephrenic, or paranoid schizophrenia. A more internationally accepted category is *schizo-affective reaction*. This diagnosis is applied to patients showing a mixture of schizophrenic symptoms and pronounced elation or depression. In Scandinavian countries, the distinguishing label of *schizophreniform psychosis* is often used to describe schizophrenic reactions characterized by acute onset, clear-cut precipitating factors, and a relatively good prognosis. Psychoses occurring in children are sometimes referred to as *childhood schizophrenia*. There is considerable doubt, however, whether these reactions should be considered schizophrenic at all. The symptoms associated with psychosis in infants and young children differ from those seen in adults. Furthermore, genetic studies indicate that it is rare for so-called childhood schizophrenic reactions to occur in the children of schizophrenic parents. Severe personality and behavior disturbances occurring during childhood are more appropriately referred to as infantile autism when they occur in infants and child psychosis in older children.

The Process-Reactive Continuum

The traditional subdivision of the group schizophrenias into simple, hebephrenic, catatonic, and paranoid types rests on observed differences in clinical symptoms. An alternate approach is to divide schizophrenics into two main subgroups on the basis of poor or good prognosis. This approach is best represented by the widely accepted concept of *process* and *reactive* schizophrenia. Other dichotomous terms that at one time or another have been suggested to differentiate patients with poor chances for recovery from those with good chances for recovery include nuclear and peripheral schizophrenia, chronic and episodic or acute schizophrenia, true schizophrenia and schizophreniform psychosis, and dementia praecox and schizophrenia. These pairs of terms are similar to but not necessarily synonymous with the process-reactive concept.

Although specifically concerned with poor versus good outcome, the process-reactive dichotomy also implies a differential course of development. By definition, the term "process" refers to a gradual step-by-step development. The typical process patient has a long premorbid history of maladjustment going back to early childhood. The appearance of frank psychotic symptoms during adolescence is only a continuation of preexisting behavior patterns. In reactive schizophrenia, on the other hand, the early personality development is, on the surface at least, reasonably normal. The onset of symptoms is sudden and often precipitated by some current traumatic experience or conflict. Kantor and Herron (1966) have suggested that process schizophrenia is associated with a failure to develop a structured self-image during early childhood. The self-image remains unformed or is very primitive. In reactive schizophrenia an adequate self-image is formed, but some specific stress precipitates a breakdown in later years.

The greater severity, longer premorbid history of maladjustment, and poorer outcome of process schizophrenia suggest the possibility that genetic factors are relatively more important in its etiology than in that of reactive schizophrenia. Some support for this inference is provided by schizophrenic twin studies, but the evidence is far from conclusive. Kringlen (1968) noted a high degree of intrapair agreement in type of psychosis developed by monozygotic twins. When both of a pair of MZ twins exhibited clinical signs of either process or reactive schizophrenia, the type of disorder was the same for both. If one displayed signs of typical (process) schizophrenia, so did the other; if one was diagnosed as having a schizophreniform (reactive) psychosis, so was the other. On the other hand, the concordance rate for typical schizophrenia was no greater than the concordance rate for schizophreniform psychosis: in all cases in which one monozygotic twin displayed signs of either type of schizophrenic reaction, about 30 percent of the co-twins showed the same signs and the remaining 70 percent were apparently unaffected. One interpretation that may be made of Kringlen's findings is that different genes are involved in the two types of schizophrenia, but the genetic loadings are of the same magnitude. Gottesman's findings (1968), however, suggest that heredity may indeed play a greater role in process schizophrenia. He noted a much higher concordance rate in cases of severe disorder with poor prognosis than in cases of a mild schizophrenic reaction with good outcome.

PROCESS-REACTIVE SCALES

A number of rating scales and self-report questionnaires for measuring the process-reactive dimension have been developed. Four of the better known instruments are the Elgin or Wittman, Kantor et al., Phillips, and

Ullmann-Giovannoni Scales. These are described in Supplementary Report 5. The scales have good interrater reliability. Despite differences in kinds of behavior sampled, scores on the four tests show high intercorrelations. In addition, it has been found that all four measures are correlated with marital status. For patients over twenty-five, marital status alone is about as good a predictor of favorable outcome as any of the scales (Ullmann, 1967; Meichenbaum, 1969). A cogent explanation for the agreement of the various scales is that they all measure what Zigler and Phillips (1962) have referred to as general social competence. Experimental studies indicate that the performance level of process schizophrenics on varied tasks is inferior to that of reactive schizophrenics. This finding is hardly surprising, since the relative adequacy of behavior constitutes the main criterion for initially differentiating the two groups.

The extensive literature on the process-reactive continuum and the related issue of good versus poor prognosis in schizophrenia (Garmezy, 1965; Offord and Cross, 1969) points to the conclusion that process and reactive types do not constitute two discrete, dichotomous groups. All tests and measures indicate that schizophrenic reaction is a continuous dimension. The "typical" process schizophrenic is at one end of the continuum and the "typical" reactive schizophrenic is at the opposite end of the same continuum. Most schizophrenics are located somewhere between these two extremes. The main advantage of the process-reactive concept is that it enables investigators, by selecting patients at either end of the continuum, to obtain comparatively homogeneous groupings. This advantage is an important consideration in research studies.

CHARACTERISTICS OF PROCESS SCHIZOPHRENIA

Clinical features:

1. Insidious, gradual development as contrasted with acute onset.
2. Early age of first hospitalization.
3. Absence of any relevant external precipitant.
4. Mild neurological signs suggestive of minimal brain damage.
5. Presence of marked disturbances in thinking.
6. Flat affect, absence of tension, confusion, anxiety, neurotic symptoms.
7. Turning against others rather than self-depreciatory or depressive trends.
8. More severe psychopathology than the average hospital admission.

Social and personal history factors:

1. Poor schoolwork.
2. Difficulties in peer-group adjustment starting in early childhood.

3. Introverted rather than extroverted personality.
4. Slight if any dating behavior during early adolescence.
5. Absence of any satisfying love attachment.
6. Failure to marry.
7. Poor employment record.
8. History of schizophrenia in the family.

Research Findings and Related Theories

Two points should be kept in mind in evaluating the extensive clinical and experimental literature on schizophrenia. The first is that no specific finding holds for all schizophrenics. Deficits noted in some patients are absent in others. Actually, it is a rare symptom or trait that occurs in even a bare majority of schizophrenics. Only about a third of schizophrenics, for example, report hallucinations. Second, behavior deviations associated with schizophrenia are not limited to schizophrenics. Similar disturbances in psychosocial functioning are noted in more moderate and better controlled form in normal individuals. Furthermore, reactions like those of schizophrenia occur in a wide variety of other conditions. Several infectious diseases are accompanied by behavior disturbances that mimic schizophrenic reactions. Disturbances in association and thinking, hallucinations, delusions, distortions in body image, perceptual aberrations, and other typical schizophrenic behavior may result from the taking of LSD and other drugs, sensory deprivation, prolonged loss of sleep, and oxygen deprivation (Chapman, 1969). There is, however, an important difference. As soon as a person recovers from an infectious disorder or the immediate effects of drugs, loss of sleep, or sensory deprivation, his schizophrenic-like reactions disappear. In schizophrenia, the disturbances in functioning are the disorder.

SENSORY AND INTELLECTUAL FUNCTIONS

Schizophrenics show no impairment in hearing, vision, and other sensory functions, and their intellectual capacity is comparable to that of the general population. Reported lowered performance on intelligence tests prior to and following the onset of the psychosis may be accounted for on the basis of population selection factors (Lane and Albee, 1968) and disturbances in motivation, attention, affect, and spontaneity (De Luca, 1967). Under proper conditions, the preservation of intellectual functions can be demonstrated even in chronic cases (Bleuler, 1950; Hamlin, 1969).

SOCIAL WITHDRAWAL

Process schizophrenia, particularly in chronic cases, is characterized by extreme social withdrawal. These patients are frequently described as shut in, introverted, detached, and apathetic. Therapists find it difficult to establish contact with them and to gain their confidence. The usual psychoanalytic procedure is not applicable, since these patients fail to develop the essential transference relationship. Schizophrenics are particularly sensitive to social stimulation. They appear fearful of emotional involvement with others. The withdrawal and social aversion of schizophrenics is usually attributed to a series of experiences, beginning in childhood, that has convinced them that the social world is hostile. People are never to be trusted, only feared, fought, or ignored. The basic distrust may be related to parental rejection, inconsistent discipline, ridicule, unreasonable demands, violation of confidences, overdomination, and so on. Withdrawal provides a defense against further hurts and threats. Hartog's colorful description (1966, p. 336) of withdrawal behavior in a fear situation is applicable to schizophrenic withdrawal:

> I stood there petrified with wordless, incomprehensible fear. . . . I felt all initiative, all desire to resist slowly drain out of me, and I began to be overcome by a drowsy indolence, a fatalistic resignation, a dreamy feeling of unreality. I seemed to withdraw, slowly, into a small secret hiding place within myself, a warm, secure, utterly intimate contentment that grew into somnolence as I slowly drifted out of reach of reality and all its threats and horrors. I could be attacked, brutalized, tortured, shot; I knew that as long as I managed to stay hidden in that secret place inside myself, so snug and safe and yet with such feeling of space and solitude about it that it seemed as large as the world, I would feel no pain, no terror, no despair, nothing, just this inexpressible sense of well-being and remoteness.

UNPREDICTABILITY OF BEHAVIOR

A general characteristic of schizophrenics is a high rate of unpredictable reactions in daily life and in clinical and experimental situations. When we speak of the unpredictability of schizophrenic behavior we are referring not to any qualities of individuality or originality of the patient's behavior, but simply to the fact that it is erratic and inappropriate. Schizophrenics as a group have a tendency to overrespond to small stimuli and not to respond strongly enough to strong stimuli. They may react to incidental stimuli and ignore significant stimuli, or they may fail to differentiate between irrelevent and relevant stimuli. The same kind of stimuli in totally different contexts may elicit the same perseverative response. Old familiar situations may be reacted to as if they were new and new situations as if they were old. Shakow (1967, p. 63) has attempted to explain this as the result of some defect in an assumed central control system that interferes with the integration of stimuli and the maintenance of a regulating mental set:

> In schizophrenia there is a distinct weakening of the control center that serves the integrating and organizing function of the interrelated cognitive, affective

and cognitive processes and makes possible the establishment of "generalized" or major sets. Accompanying this weakening is a tendency for "segmented" patterns to come to the fore and become inordinately important.

MOTIVATION

The schizophrenic's poor performance on complex experimental tasks is frequently attributed to his low motivation. It would be more accurate to say that schizophrenics as a group are less responsive than normal people to social types of incentives, but are fully as responsive to reinforcing agents that directly affect their physical well-being and personal interests. In a survey of the literature, Buss (1966) concluded that verbal praise and urging have relatively little effect on the test performance of schizophrenics. This finding is consistent with Cameron's early observation (1938) that schizophrenics are little concerned with other persons' reactions to them. However, when the experimental situation is structured so that a "correct" response leads to the elimination of electric shock, white noise, or other noxious stimuli, the performance of schizophrenics shows as much improvement as that of normal persons, or even greater improvement. Fontana and Kline (1968) found that the patient's speed of response on a simple reaction-time test was greatly influenced by his perception of the outcome of his performance: if he thought a good performance would facilitate the attainment of his current goals within the hospital, he responded much more quickly than he did if he thought his personal goals would be hindered by a good performance.

SPEECH DISTURBANCES

The majority of schizophrenics are uncommunicative. They rarely initiate conversation. If asked a direct question, they may give a brief answer, remain silent, or make some cryptic and seemingly irrelevant response. Since speech is a medium of interpersonal communication, the sparse or mystifying speech of the schizophrenic may reflect his alienation or disinterest in his social environment. Deluded patients may refrain from speaking because they are afraid to express inner thoughts or are ordered by voices to keep silent. In contrast with their limited social speech, some schizophrenics do a lot of talking to themselves. Sometimes private talking is inaudible; at other times it is loud and clear. The outpouring of words is more likely to be reflexive than deliberate, a disorganized monologue rather than a medium of communication (Matarazzo, 1962). The ideas expressed in schizophrenic speech appear to consist of free associations and the spontaneous verbalization of fleeting inner thoughts. The net result is a kind of word salad that is as confusing to other schizophrenics as it is to normal individuals. The following example illustrates the incoherence, disconnectedness, and seeming irrelevance of schizophrenic speech:

Maybe I will sacrifice . . . The old test will start over again. In fact, it's glor-
ifying. Wait a minute, will you please? I don't like this, it kind of chokes me;
will you please undo it, Daddy? I like nature. If you get cold nothing can
affect it, it won't rust. Hair, it might be robin redbreast. I like my conscience,
though. They have tried in every generation. I love you. Ivory complexions.
Whiskey, darling—that wasn't whiskey that calmed me, but the milk; that
was the only thing that saved me. Summer is passing, so far we have gone.
If God said I want to make the world perfect then they will have to do it
themselves. There isn't a hole in my head. Joan of Arc, was she your daughter
too? I like gingerbread but I like milk too. You hurt that nerve, didn't you?
Oxygen, will you please give me that? I'm going to stop your heart with it.
Chop the arteries off and your heart stops. A snake can't swallow but it can
climb up the family tree if they have the trees they want.

The word salad of schizophrenics may occasionally be quite poetic or
suggestive of some profound but elusive meaning. One schizophrenic spoke
of "a bonfire of delight" and "the attainment of ethereal bliss through poly-
technical science and soul exploration."

The tendency of some schizophrenics to create new words or neologisms
is not, of itself, strange. Many normal individuals enjoy coining new words.
The difference is that "normal" neologisms can be readily deciphered. They
are usually produced by condensing two familiar words into one. Often the
intent is to create a new term that adds a humorous twist: "reminusances,"
"brunch," "sinema." The origin of schizophrenic neologisms is usually ob-
scure. The coined terms appear to be private words whose meaning is
known only to the patient.

Schizophrenic neologisms	*Patient interpretation of word*
bedrudgers	persecutors
iava	supper
gruesor	gruesome and sorrowful
poive	pleasant saying

Some schizophrenic monologues consist almost exclusively of such neologisms and are completely incomprehensible to anyone who has not pains-
takingly learned the patient's private language—which the schizophrenic
is not likely to permit.

THOUGHT DISTURBANCES

Disturbances in association and thinking are generally regarded as the
most outstanding characteristics of schizophrenic behavior. Diagnosis usually rests on the presence of delusions or the patient's tendency to give unusual, irrelevant, illogical, or peculiar responses to questions (Hunt and
Arnhoff, 1955). Interestingly, most patients show no significant impairment

in their ability to generate ideas, to use abstract concepts, or to solve problems. Particularly in the early stages, schizophrenics often complain of too many thoughts running through their heads at the same time (McGhie and Chapman, 1961). Schizophrenics may exhibit a high degree of ingenuity or idiosyncrasy in interpreting proverbs, sorting out objects, and evolving concepts.

What distinguishes schizophrenics is the seeming irrationality and bizarreness of their thoughts. An outstanding feature of schizophrenic thinking, which Cameron (1938) has called overinclusiveness, consists of failure to stay within the boundaries of an assigned task and to exclude irrelevant or inappropriate material. Research findings reported by Payne and his associates (1966) indicate that overinclusive thinking is present in about 50 percent of acutely schizophrenic patients. Among chronic patients the frequency of occurrence is about the same as for the general population.

When a young female patient was asked to report her associations to the word "day," she answered, "Night, April fifteenth, immaculate conception." To the question "Are you married?" she responded, "Yes. There are many bad women in the world who should be punished. The Lord is the father of my child." If one knows the patient's case history, it is sometimes possible to follow the train of thought. In this case, the strange responses were probably due to the intrusion of inner ideas. About a year before she was admitted to the hospital the patient had had a brief love affair with a young man. They had had only one sex experience, but she had become pregnant. Shortly afterward the young man had married another girl.

Sometimes the derailment of associations appears to be related to the patient's responding to the dominant meaning of a word instead of its contextual meaning (Chapman, Chapman, and Miller, 1964). A classical example has been reported by Bleuler (1950). The patient had been asked if there was something weighing heavily on his mind. The response was: "Yes. Iron is heavy." Sometimes the omission of significant connections results in the appearance of fragmentary or unduly concrete thought. Thus a patient may define a donkey as "big ears." Under further questioning, however, the answer can usually be improved to "a horselike animal with big ears." When asked to sort objects into categories—any sort of groupings that may occur to them—schizophrenics can and do utilize the conventional categories of color, size, shape, and function, but in addition they frequently make other, private sortings: objects they like and objects they don't like, or objects that have some personal significance to them and others that have no special meaning (McGaughren and Moran, 1956).

A variety of theories has been proposed to account for the disordered cognitive processes of schizophrenics. Since reactions similar to schizophrenic disturbances in association and thinking are commonly noted in normal persons under stress, no unique interpretation may be required. The disordered mental functioning of schizophrenics may be attributed to their highly aroused state, their preoccupation with or avoidance of inner problems, and their unconcern with whether their reactions make "sense" to others. However, the eccentricity of schizophrenic thinking and the persistence of the disturbance have led workers in the field to favor more elaborate theories. These have been reviewed by Boren (1968). Most theories presume the presence of some developmental, psychological, or neurophysiological defect that results in difficulties in the processing of complex stimuli, response interference, a loss of inhibitory control, or regression to childhood styles of thinking. Meehl (1962) has suggested that some neural integrative defect of genetic origin may be responsible for the "cognitive slippage" of schizophrenics. Fisk (1961) has proposed that overactivity of the reticular activating system might account for the distractability of schizophrenics.

Several investigators (Payne, 1966; Yates, 1966) have attributed disturbances in association and thinking to defects in a postulated filter system. The filter system hypothesis was originally introduced by Broadbent (1958) to explain the selectivity of attention and perception in normal individuals. Some selective mechanism is necessitated by the fact that the nervous system can process only a very small part of the total stimuli bombarding the organism from within and without at any one moment. When functioning properly, the filter system limits sensory input to a manageable number of messages that are pertinent to the organism in its current state. The irrelevant associations and overinclusive thinking of schizophrenics, then, could be related to filter defects that result in the indiscriminate passage of an excessive number of stimuli. Conversely, the paucity of ideas and constricted thinking noted in some patients might be due to a clogged or closed filter system that excludes stimuli. Family studies of schizophrenics (Lidz et al., 1965; Singer and Wynne, 1965) indicate that in comparison with the parents of normal controls, the parents of schizophrenics have greater difficulties in conceptual thinking and have more blurred and fragmented styles of thinking and communication. These data may be interpreted as supporting a learning theory or a genetic theory or both. Wynne (1968) and Singer explicitly state that both gene-determined and intrafamilial factors may contribute to the development of disordered thinking in schizophrenics. They also note that deviant responses on various psychological tests, which indicate disturbances in association and thinking, are not restricted to the families of schizophrenics. The same type of responses also occur in nonschizophrenic families, but less frequently.

AFFECTIVE DISTURBANCES

Schizophrenics exhibit the full gamut of human emotions. They may be tender, brutal, loving, cold, hostile, elated, depressed, sensitive, callous, excited, or apathetic. In general, however, they differ from the normal population in three principal ways: (1) their emotional reactions are inappropriate to known external events, (2) they appear to be relatively deficient in their capacity to experience joy and pleasure, and (3) they are unduly anxious. As far as outsiders can judge, the silly giggling of hebephrenics, the hostile belligerence of paranoids, the extreme excitement or panic reactions of the acutely disturbed, and the detached indifference of simple and chronic schizophrenics bear no relationship to external reality. Ambivalence of feelings—the simultaneous expression of love and hate—are more commonly noted in schizophrenics than in normal persons.

Rado (1956, 1962) believes that a diminished capacity for experiencing pleasure, which is partly genetic in origin, is a major differentiating characteristic of persons who develop schizophrenia. The deficiency is referred to as *anhedonia*. The schizophrenic's relative incapacity for enjoyment makes for an empty, meaningless existence. He derives little satisfaction from his accomplishments or talents. Unable to enter and share the emotional life of others, and with diminished capacity to express warmth and affection, he is left out in the cold. He responds to his outsider status with fear and rage. Having so few sources of pleasure, the potential schizophrenic cannot afford any loss. The suffering caused by the death of a parent, the loss of a friend, or a broken love affair, which an emotionally richer person can overcome, may be a catastrophic experience for a schizophrenic. Rado favors a modified psychoanalytic treatment in which emphasis is placed on emotional reeducation. On an experimental basis, Heath (1964) has investigated the possibility of providing the schizophrenic with increased pleasurable sensations by means of electrical stimulation of the pleasure center of the brain. The technique, modeled after experiments conducted with animals, consists in implanting an electrode in the pertinent area of the brain. The patient can activate the electrode at will and give himself a shot of pleasure by pressing a button. The procedure works temporarily, but it is not considered a definitive cure for schizophrenia.

The high anxiety level of schizophrenics is inferred from their emotional hyperresponsiveness. Obvious signs of intense emotional arousal are frequently noted during the early, acute stages. The anxiety of chronic, nondeluded patients is less apparent; most of them, on the surface at least, appear to be unresponsive, listless, and apathetic. But beneath the surface there is tension. Studies of the psychophysiological reactions of these patients to experimentally induced stress situations indicate a higher than normal degree of cortical and autonomic arousal (Venables, 1966). Perhaps the surface apathy of chronic schizophrenics serves as an inhibitory defense against overstimulation. Differences of opinion exist as to whether the extreme anxiety of schizophrenics is a learned reaction or an expression of innate temperament. There is, however, considerable clinical and experimental evidence that schizophrenia-prone individuals have long histories of emotional instability dating from early childhood.

Mednick (1958) has utilized the anxiety of the preschizophrenic as the cornerstone of his theory of schizophrenia. In essence, the theory holds that the disturbances in association and thinking that distinguish schizophrenia represent learned stratagems for avoiding anxiety. Starting in childhood, the hyperresponsive preschizophrenic learns to avoid arousal stimuli by switching his attention to some neutral or distant association or thought. The substituted thought enables him momentarily to avoid the arousal stimulus. The maneuver results in a reduction in arousal level, which serves to reinforce the association between the arousal stimulus and the avoidant thought. The reduction in arousal resulting from pairing arousal stimuli with avoidant thoughts increases the probability that the individual will resort to avoidant thoughts on subsequent occasions when he is confronted with arousal stimuli. After many such reinforced learning trials, the individual acquires a repertoire of conditioned avoidance responses (irrelevant thoughts) that help him to control his autonomic hyperresponsivity. When these responses become so spontaneous that they interfere with sustained thought processes and dominate the individual's thinking, he may be classified as schizophrenic. Mednick and Schulsinger (1968) have reported experimental data that indicate that high-risk children of schizophrenic mothers show greater autonomic hyperresponsiveness and quicker rates of recovery from autonomic imbalance than control subjects. The hypothesis of conditioned avoidance responses is difficult to test and remains unconfirmed.

SELF-CONCEPT

The clinical impression that schizophrenics have a somewhat fragmented and unstable concept of self has received some experimental confirmation. Guller (1966) has shown that the schizophrenic's self-concept is more readily disrupted by experiences of failure than the normal person's. There is some evidence that schizophrenics show greater deviation in sex-role patterns than the general population. McClelland and Watt (1968) noted that female schizophrenics tend to react assertively and aggressively, in a manner usually thought of as masculine, whereas schizophrenic males tend to be sensitive, quiet, and withdrawn, as the "typical" female is thought to be. A number of male schizophrenics report delusions of undergoing a change of sex, or being a woman or neuter (Gittleson and Levine, 1966). A small percentage of schizophrenics experience a distortion in body image, either overestimating or underestimating the size of body parts and sensations of body change. Similar disturbances in body image occasionally occur in normal subjects undergoing unusual stress (Fisher, 1964).

Contributory Etiological Factors

The causes of schizophrenic behavior are multiple, cumulative, and interactive. The unraveling and isolating of specific contributory factors and the analysis of their interaction remain a challenge for the future. Considerable progress has been made in identifying some of the major components, however. Current data support the following general conclusions:

1. The relative probability that a person will manifest overt schizophrenic behavior is directly correlated with the closeness of his genetic kinship with a known schizophrenic. The highest risk is shared by a monozygotic co-twin of a schizophrenic and a child whose mother and father are both schizophrenics. The morbidity risk is about the same for dizygotic co-twins, siblings, parents, and children with one schizophrenic parent. The expectancy rate is considerably lower for half-siblings, uncles, nieces, cousins, and other distant relatives.

2. It is probable that the hereditary component in schizophrenia consists of two or more genes (polygenes) rather than a single gene.

3. The phenotypic or overt expression of a schizophrenic genotype is quite variable. About 40 percent of the monozygotic co-twins of schizophrenics also develop schizophrenia. Another 30 to 40 percent of the co-twins exhibit schizophreniform reactions, character disturbances, or neurotic symptoms; the remainder are symptom-free or essentially normal. When both co-twins develop schizophrenia, intrapair differences are often noted with respect to specific symptoms and prognosis. In short, the overt outcome of a genetic predisposition is greatly influenced by the facilitating, modifying, or inhibitory interacting influence of nongenetic variables.

4. What specifically is transmitted by the gene defect is unknown. The general presumption is that coding errors embedded in the chemistry of one or more genes lead to the development of some neurobiochemical condition that in turn influences the individual's relative predisposition to schizophrenic behavior. The presence of the gene defect is considered a necessary prerequisite for schizophrenia, but the nature of the disturbance in functioning that actually occurs, if any, depends on the interactive effects of other adverse psychosocial and/or biological factors. The search for neurological or metabolic anomalies uniquely present in schizophrenia has so far been unsuccessful. One consistent finding that may have some etiological significance is that the great majority of persons who in later life develop schizophrenia are characterized from early childhood by certain seemingly inborn temperament traits. Specifically, potential schizophrenics appear to be constitutionally more passive, introverted, and emotionally hypersensitive than the normal population.

5. Family pathology is considered the main environmental agent in the etiology of schizophrenia. Earlier studies emphasized the role of the

mother. The hypothesis was that possessive, overcontrolling, domineering mothers contributed to the development of schizophrenic offspring by preventing the growth of their children as independent, autonomous persons. But research findings have brought this concept into question. Similar patterns af restrictive mothering have been observed in studies of physically ill and mentally retarded children. It would appear, then, that preschizophrenic children, along with other handicapped and problem children, require and elicit maternal protectiveness and control. Thus the inadequacies and dependency needs of preschizophrenic children may be the cause rather than the result of their mothers' attitudes.

A more general hypothesis is that marital conflicts, family disorganization, and confused communication between parents and children may contribute to the development of schizophrenic behavior. Pathogenic styles of perception and contradictory modes of communication within families, for example may lead to the acquisition of behavior patterns associated with schizophrenia. It is also possible that the children may model their behavior after that of disturbed parents, share their delusions and distortions, or serve as scapegoats for the displacement of family pathology. The significance of these familial factors has recently been challenged by studies of adopted children. Children of schizophrenic mothers who have been reared from birth in foster homes by normal adoptive parents show about the same incidence rate for schizophrenia as children reared by their own schizophrenic mothers.

6. Psychodynamic theories stress the etiological significance of early unfavorable parent-child experiences that burden the preschizophrenic with feelings of insecurity, distrust, hostility, and despair. The child's prospects of adjustment are further weakened by a vaguely defined and essentially negative self-concept. He perceives himself as inadequate, unworthy, unappreciated, and unlovable.

7. Attempts to demonstrate a causal relationship between socioeconomic status and vulnerability to schizophrenia have been unsuccessful. Schizophrenia appears to be randomly distributed at all socioeconomic levels, with one notable exception: in large industrialized cities a disproportionately large number of schizophrenics are found in the lowest socioeconomic group. The available evidence suggests that this finding is due to the downward social drift of schizophrenics.

8. Data on the relative incidence of schizophrenia in different cultures are fragmentary and inconclusive. The alienation of the schizophrenic from his culture may be interpreted as a symptom, a result, or a cause of his disordered behavior.

9. A number of theories have been proposed linking schizophrenia with a variety of neurological, biochemical, and metabolic factors (Hamwich et al., 1967; Zubin and Shagass, 1969). Further research may eventually in-

dicate that some specific neurobiological defect is associated with certain selected patients. So far, however, the findings of experimental studies have been more suggestive than conclusive.

Treatment and Outcome

The availability of drugs that control acute symptoms plus changing public attitudes toward mental patients have encouraged increased use of general hospitals, community organizations, and home care in the treatment of schizophrenics. Approximately 75 percent of schizophrenics admitted to mental hospitals are returned to the community within a few months and another 10 percent may be discharged after a longer stay. Many are readmitted once or twice, and a small percentage become permanent residents.

The most commonly used drug in the treatment of schizophrenic symptoms is chlorpromazine. A large number of other drugs are available for patients who show undesirable side effects or are unresponsive to chlorpromazine. In many cases, however, and particularly in process-reactive cases, when patients have long histories of progressive impairment in psychological functioning and social behavior, it is difficult to say exactly what constitutes improvement or recovery. When patients have been admitted to mental hospitals, their hospital records are often used as rough criteria of outcome. The findings of a three-year follow-up study of 588 patients admitted to veterans' hospitals conducted by Sherman et al. (1964) are representative of prognosis in hospitalized schizophrenics. The treatment process was considered an unqualified success in 23 percent of the cases: they left the hospital after a short stay and were not readmitted to a VA hospital. Ten percent remained continuously hospitalized over the three-year period and hence were considered clear theraputic failures. At one time or another 90 percent of the initial group left the hospital. At the end of the three-year period 66 percent of the total group were out of the hospital and 34 percent were in the hospital. Again married patients showed a better prognosis than those who remained single. A paradoxical but understandable observation noted by Carstairs (1967) is that discharged patients who go to live with strangers, where emotional involvement is minimal, have a better outcome than those who return to their own families.

CLIENT-CENTERED THERAPY

A comprehensive research study on the application of client-centered therapy to schizophrenics has been reported by Rogers and his associates (1967). As far as overall outcome was concerned, the results were about the same for the intensively treated patients and the matched control group, which had been exposed only to the general hospital program. There was some evidence that the nature of the therapeutic relationship had some effect on outcome. Those patients who perceived a high degree of harmony with their therapists were independently rated as showing the greatest positive change. Therapist-client relationships rated high in empathy ranked second in degree of personality change. The control group followed next. Patients whose relationships with their therapists were marked by little or no agreement or empathy showed no change or even regressive change.

GOOD AND POOR THERAPISTS

Betz and Whitehorn (Whitehorn and Betz, 1960; Betz, 1967) have demonstrated that some therapists are far more effective than others in achieving immediate results with schizophrenics. Good or *A* therapists had a 75 percent improvement rate, as contrasted with poor or *B* therapists, who had a 27 percent improvement rate. The more successful *A* doctors differed from their B colleagues in more frequently (1) grasping the personal meaning and motivation of the patient's behavior, (2) interacting more freely and actively with the patient, and (3) setting limits on the kind and degree of obnoxious behavior they would permit, but not seeking to interpret or instruct. *B* doctors were either passively permissive or pointed out the patient's mistakes and misunderstanding in an instructional style. On the Strong Vocational Interest Inventory, the *A* physicians had interest patterns similar to those of lawyers and certified public accountants, while *B* therapists had interest patterns similar to those of printers and teachers of mathematics and the physical sciences. The difference in interest patterns suggests that *A* therapists had a more problem-solving and less mechanical approach than *B* doctors. An interesting footnote is that eventually time, the great healer, almost evened the score. Follow-up data collected five or more years after discharge indicated that 65 percent of the patients treated by *B* doctors were improved, as compared with 77 percent of the patients of *A* doctors.

OPERANT CONDITIONING

Response-contingent reinforcement techniques have been found to be highly effective in modifying or eliminating specific symptoms of schizophrenic patients (Ullmann and Krasner, 1969). The usual procedure in such experiments is first to determine the base rate of some frequently emitted specific symptom. Subsequent responses that are in the direction of the desired change are then selectively reinforced. For example, if the target objective is to decrease bizarre verbalizations, the experimenter will smile and make some encouraging comment whenever the patient makes a coherent or sensible remark. As a rule, incoherent or "sick" talk is ignored, but shock or some other negative reinforcement may be used to decrease the frequency of bizarre speech. Success is measured by the amount of decrease in the frequency of the symptom response and increase in the frequency of desired behavior.

Operant conditioning principles have been found to be particularly helpful in modifying the ward behavior of chronic patients. Many hospitals have established token economy wards where the environment is carefully controlled so that patients receive systematic reinforcement for appropriate behavior. Members of the staff promptly hand out tokens to patients whenever they exhibit any desired behavior. Since tokens are required to "pay" for the necessities as well as the luxuries of hospital life, patients are motivated to learn to conform to the rules of the game. The rules are modified somewhat from patient to patient so that the earning of tokens is kept within each patient's capability. In essence, patients are paid for assuming responsibility for self-care and "normal" behavior. Although operant conditioning and token economy programs have demonstrated their effectiveness in improving the ward behavior of schizophrenics, it should be added that the procedures have negligible curative value. The stability of induced behavior changes is dependent on the continuation of reinforcement. When reinforcement is discontinued, there is a relapse and a return of symptoms.

COMMUNITY CARE

The effectiveness of home care for schizophrenics has been experimentally explored by Pasamanick and his associates (1967). The study involved an eighteen-month follow-up of outcome in three comparable groups of schizophrenic patients: a group treated at home with drugs, a group given placebos while being cared for at home, and a hospital-treated control group. The drug and placebo groups were visited regularly in their homes by public health nurses. The home visits by the nurses and the drug medication were the principal ingredients in the treatment program. Only the project director knew whether the home-care patients were receiving drugs or placebos. An evaluation made at the end of the project showed that 77 percent of the drug-treated group were able to remain continuously at home as compared with 34 percent of those receiving placebos. Over the total follow-up period, the drug-treated patients were home 90 percent of the time, the placebo cases 80 percent, and the hospital control group 75 percent. Failures in the home-care program usually occurred within six months. When patients treated at home had to be removed to a hospital, it was usually because they exhibited bizarre or dangerous behavior or because the responsible relatives could no longer cope with the patient and his needs. In general, patients cared for at home showed greater improvement in mental status, psychological test performance, domestic functioning, and social participation than those who received routine hospital care. Most of the improvement in performance occurred during the first six months of the study. Improvement was limited to a return of functioning to the prepsychotic level.

Summary and an Attempted Synthesis

Schizophrenia is a broad descriptive label applied to persons marked by gross personality disorganization and severe impairment in psychosocial functioning. About 1 percent of the general population in all countries exhibit psychosocial deficits associated with the disorder at some time during their lives. The onset of overt symptoms usually occurs between the ages of fifteen and forty. The heterogeneity of reactions and of persons included within the vaguely defined boundaries of schizophrenia has long been recognized. No satisfactory rationale or set of criteria has yet been formulated for what Bleuler has referred to as the group of schizophrenias. There is little evidence that the traditional clinical subtypes (simple, hebephrenic, catatonic, and paranoid) have any basis in reality as separate disorders or that they represent different manifestations of a single disease entity. About all that patients assigned to the same subcategory have in common is some similarity in surface symptoms. The process-reactive concept has some value in differentiating persons with a relatively favorable prior history of social interaction, who tend to have a relatively favorable prospect for recovery, from patients with a prior history of social inadequacy, for whom the prognosis is poor. It seems, however, that the symptoms of the patients in these two groupings differ more in degree than in kind. Process schizophrenia and reactive schizophrenia represent end positions of a single continuum rather than discrete disorders.

The more basic issue of what constitutes or distinguishes schizophrenic behavior remains unresolved. A tentative hypothesis is that the crucial element is social withdrawal. The multiple determinants of social withdrawal as a mode of adustment or life style will be considered in the following chapter, which is concerned with the origins of schizophrenic behavior. Our present interest is in seeing how many pieces of the puzzle of schizophrenia can be put together if the following premises are accepted as valid: (1) from early childhood the preschizophrenic has experienced difficulty in relating to others and in establishing satisfying interpersonal relationships; (2) with each succeeding year the gulf separating him from other human beings is widened; (3) alone and friendless, he withdraws more and more within himself; (4) a point is finally reached where in despair or protest he gives up the seemingly hopeless task of being understood and accepted by others, and shuts the door on the outer world and retreats into a private inner world. The transition is neither planned nor deliberate. Some persons experience acute panic as they sense that they are losing control of their ability to move freely from one world to the other and are no longer able to distinguish outer-world experiences from inner-world fantasies; others have feelings of profound relief when they at last give up the unequal struggle to cope with reality and shut it all away from them. By the time the patient is diagnosed as a schizophrenic, the priority of the inner world has been established. Safe within the fortress of the self, the schizophrenic may look out at the outer world, but his interest is limited to those external events that have personal significance for him.

Under these conditions, the behavior of the schizophrenic, when evaluated in accordance with the expectations and standards of his society, is erratic and unpredictable, apathetic, undermotivated, and unresponsive. No longer interested in keeping up appearances to impress others, the schizophrenic may become careless in his grooming and manners and indifferent to the social amenities. Coherent speech and logical thinking require both concentrated attention and interest in effective social communication. The schizophrenic who is preoccupied with his inner world couldn't care less if others find his speech incomprehensible and his thoughts confusing. His disorganized speech and thoughts may actually serve as a protective barrier against intrusion. Since the self-concept is to a great extent a product of the reflected opinions and evaluations of significant others, the limited interpersonal involvement of the preschizophrenic accounts in large part for his fragmented self-concept. Social withdrawal involves more than making no demands on others that might lead to rebuffs. The individual must maintain a constant state of alertness to protect himself against possible threats from the external alien world. Interpersonal and new situations, in particular, provoke anxiety in him. But social withdrawal does not solve all of his problems. He is still left with his frustrated sexual urges, his social needs, his unfulfilled aspirations, and his painful memories of real or imagined wrongs. These still pressing problems are expressed in wild fantasies, delusions, and hallucinations. If in acting out or reacting to his delusions and hallucinations the individual inadvertently breaks the rules of society, his behavior may be perceived by others as bizarre, annoying, and occasionally dangerous.

Although the schizophrenic prefers to have as little as possible to do with the outside world, he is aware of external events. His functioning capacity is not significantly impaired. When it serves his purpose, he can effectively perform tasks that result in the elimination of painful stimuli. He can learn to modify his symptoms and "normalize" his behavior to earn tokens that can be exchanged for desired objects. This adaptability, however, does not extend to placing trust in a therapist or readily confiding his secrets. Psychotherapy is difficult and often unrewarding to both patient and therapist. Sensitive therapists with extraordinary understanding, empathy, and patience may slowly effect positive changes. Those who lack these gifts may do more harm than good.

Unless a schizophrenic is a real source of danger to himself or others, commitment to a mental hospital is best avoided. The patient perceives his "incarceration" as one more proof of his rejection by society. After he gets over his initial resentment, he may realize that permanent hospitalization ideally serves his objective of social withdrawal and resignation from life. The development of drugs that are highly effective in reducing inner turmoil and alleviating overt symptoms has made it possible to care for patients at home and in the community. Neighborhood day-care centers where schizophrenics can be taught social skills in a friendly, acceptive, clublike atmosphere may be more effective than talking-out or confrontation forms of therapy.

Supplementary Report 5. Scales for
Assessing Process and Reactive Schizophrenia

The four measures most commonly used to assess process and reactive schizophrenia are the Elgin or Wittman Prognostic Scale, the Kantor-Wallner-Winder List of Criteria, the Phillips Scale, and the Ullmann-Giovannoni Self-Report Scale. All four scales yield continuous distributions of scores. Most schizophrenic patients cluster in the middle range of scores. Extreme scores on one end are considered indicative of process schizophrenia, and extreme scores on the other end are considered indicative of reactive schizophrenia.

The Elgin Prognostic Scale. The Elgin scale was devised by Wittman in 1941, and subsequently revised by Becker and Steffy (Becker, 1956; Steffy and Becker, 1961.) Items on the Elgin scale consist mainly of factors thought to have prognostic significance. Information for scoring is obtained from case-history data. The Becker revision provides for scaled ratings on (1) defect of interests versus definite display of interests, (2) insidious versus acute onset, (3) degree of difficulty in social adjustment during childhood, (4) extent of heterosexual contact, (5) careless indifference versus worry and self-consciousness, (6) duration of psychosis, (7) extent of hebephrenic symptoms, and (8) presence or absence of precipitating conditions. The major difficulty with this scale is that the wording of the descriptive labels is imprecise. Much of the information needed for scoring the numerous items are not available in the typical case history. Factor analytic studies indicate that the test mainly measures withdrawal behavior and reality distortion. Interrater reliability is quite high, but the test has low predictive significance regarding outcome (Garmezy, 1965). Watson and Logue (1969) have reported intercorrelations of .45 and .70 between the Elgin scale and the Ullmann-Giovannoni and Phillips scales respectively. Soloman and Zlotowski (1964) have reported an overall correlation of .87 between the Elgin and Phillips scales.

The Kantor-Wallner-Winder List of Criteria. Kantor and his associates have reported a developmental scale based on the presence or absence of certain designated forms of maladjustment or pathological signs in the case history of the patient. Indicators of process schizophrenia during childhood include early psychological trauma and prolonged physical illness. Process indicators for the period from the fifth year to adolescence include difficulties in school, introverted behavior, sudden changes in behavior, and an overprotective or rejecting mother. Process indicators during the adolescent period are failure to develop heterosexual interests, insidious onset of psychosis, and poor response to treatment. Adult characteristics associated with process schizophrenia include massive paranoia, low tolerance for alcohol, somatic delusions, loss of normal inhibitions ("indecent" behavior), and absence of depressive features. This scale has not been used much, and available data on its reliability and validity are limited.

The Phillips Scale. The scale developed by Phillips (1953) has been the most widely used. Originally it had three subsections dealing with premorbid history, possible precipitating factors, and clinical signs of disorder. More recently the abbreviated Phillips Scale, limited to premorbid history, has been used. The items included on this scale deal mainly with social factors: past and present sexual adjustment, friendships or the lack of them, leadership qualities, and general interpersonal adjustment. Information required for scoring items is usually readily obtainable from case-history data and interviews with the patient and his parents. Data summarized by Garmezy (1965) indicate that the scale is a highly reliable instrument. Interrater correlations of .90 have been reported in several studies. The scale has been found to be valid in differentiating patients with good prospects for recovery from those for whom the prognosis is poor. As might be expected from the content of items, scores on the premorbid scale are highly correlated with marital status. High intercorrelations with other proccess-reactive measures have usually been noted.

The Ullmann-Giovannoni Scale. Ullmann and Giovannoni (1964) have prepared a simple self-report measure of the process-reactive continuum. The inventory consists of a list of twenty-four questions that are asked directly of the patient. The test is essentially a measure of social competence. Specific items deal with marital status, level of education, duration of employment, the ability to make and keep friends during the teen years, social interactions, duration of hospital stay, and so forth. Watson and Logue (1969) have reported correlations of .45 between the Ullmann-Giovannoni and Elgin scales and .60 between the Ullmann-Giovannoni and Phillips scales.

References

BECKER, W. C. "A Genetic Approach to the Interpretation and Evaluation of the Process-Reactive Distinction in Schizophrenia." *Journal of Abnormal and Social Psychology* 53 (1956): 229–36.

BETZ, B. J. "Studies of the Therapist's Role in the Treatment of the Schizophrenic Patient." *American Journal of Psychiatry* 123 (1967): 963–71.

BLEULER, E. P. *Dementia Praecox or the Group of Schizophrenias* (1911). New York: International Universities Press, 1950.

BOREN, W. E. *Schizophrenia Research and Theory*. New York: Academic Press, 1968.

BROADBENT, D. E. *Perception and Communication*. London: Pergamon Press, 1958.

BUSS, A. H. *Psychopathology*. New York: Wiley, 1966.

CAMERON, N. "Reasoning, Regression, and Communication in Schizophrenics." *Psychological Monographs* 50, no. 1 (1938).

CARSTAIRS, G. M. "Social Factors Influencing the Genesis and Outcome of Schizophrenia." In *The Origins of Schizophrenia*, ed J. Romano, pp. 270–75. New York: Excerpta Medica Foundation, 1967.

CHAPMAN, L. J. "Schizomimetic Conditions and Schizophrenia." *Journal of Consulting and Clinical Psychology* 33 (1969): 646–50.

————, CHAPMAN, J. P., and MILLER, G. A. "A Theory of Verbal Behavior in Schizophrenia." In *Progress in Experimental Personality Research*, ed. B. A. Maher, pp. 49–77. New York: Academic Press, 1964.

CROCETTI, G. M., and LEMKAU, P. V. "Schizophrenia, 11: Epidemiology." In *Comprehensive Textbook of Psychiatry*, ed. A. M. Freedman, H. I. Kaplan, pp. 599–603. Baltimore: Williams & Wilkins, 1967.

DE LUCA, J. M. "Direct Measurement of Differential Cognitive Deficit in Acute Schizophrenia." *Journal of Abnormal Psychology* 72, no. 2 (1967): 143–46.

FISHER, S. "Body Image and Psychopathology." *Archives of General Psychiatry* 10 (1964): 5–29.

FISK, F. A. "A Neurophysiological Theory of Schizophrenia." *Journal of Mental Science* 107 (1961): 828–38.

FONTANA, A. F., and KLINE, E. B. "Self-preservation and the Schizophrenic 'Deficit.'" *Journal of Clinical and Consulting Psychology* 32 (1968): 250–56.

GARMEZY, N. "Process and Reactive Schizophrenia: Some Conceptions and Issues." In *Classification in Psychiatry and Psychopathology*, ed. M. M. Katz, J. O. Cole, and W. E. Barton, pp. 419–66. Washington, D.C.: U.S. Government Printing Office, 1965.

GITTLESON, N. L., and LEVINE, S. "Subjective Ideas of Sexual Change in Male Schizophrenics." *British Journal of Psychiatry* 112 (1966): 779–82.

GOTTESMAN, I. I. "Severity/Concordance and Diagnostic Refinement in the Maudsley-Bethlem Schizophrenic Twin Study." In *The Transmission of Schizophrenia*, ed. D. Rosenthal and S. S. Kety, pp. 37–48. New York: Pergamon Press, 1968.

GULLER, I. "Stability of Self-concept in Schizophrenia." *Journal of Abnormal Psychology* 71 (1966): 275–79.

HAMLIN, R. M. "The Stability of Intellectual Function in Chronic Schizophrenia." *Journal of Nervous and Mental Disease* 149 (1969): 496–503.

HAMWICH, H. E.; KETY, S. S.; and SMYTHIES, J. R. *Amines and Schizophrenia*. London: Pergamon Press, 1967.

HARTOG, J. D. *The Captain*. New York: Antheneum, 1966.

HEATH, R. G. "Pleasure Response of Human Subjects to Direct Stimulation of the Brain: Physiologic and Psychodynamic Considerations." In *The Role of*

Pleasure in Behavior, ed. R. G. Heath, pp. 219–43. New York: Harper & Row, 1964.

HIGGINS, J., and PETERSON, J. C. "Concept of Process-Reactive Schizophrenia: A Critique." *Psychological Bulletin* 66 (1966): 201–6.

HUNT, W. A., and ARNHOFF, F. N. "Some Standardized Scales for Disorganization in Schizophrenic Thinking." *Journal of Consulting Psychology* 19 (1955): 171–74.

KANTOR, R. E., and HERRON, W. G. *Reactive and Process Schizophrenia.* Palo Alto, Calif.: Science and Behavior Books, 1966.

————, WALNER, J. M., and WINDER, C. L. "Process and Reactive Schizophrenia." *Journal of Consulting Psychology* 17 (1953): 157–62.

KRINGLEN, E. "An Epidemiological-Clinical Twin Study on Schizophrenia." In *The Transmission of Schizophrenia,* ed. D. Rosenthal and S. S. Kety, pp. 49–63. New York: Pergamon Press, 1968.

LANE, E. A., and ALBEE, G. W. "On Childhood Intellectual Decline of Adult Schizophrenics: A Reassessment of an Earlier Study." *Journal of Abnormal Psychology* 73 (1968): 174–77.

LIDZ, T.; FLECK, S.; and CORNELISON, A. R. *Schizophrenia and the Family.* New York: International Universities Press, 1965.

McCLELLAND, D. C., and WATT; N. F. "Sex-Role Alienation in Schizophrenia." *Journal of Abnormal Psychology* 73, no. 3 (1968): 226–39.

McGAUGHREN, L. S., and MORAN, L. J. " 'Conceptual Levels' versus 'Conceptual Area' Analyses of Object-Sorting Behavior of Schizophrenic and Neuropsychiatric Groups." *Journal of Abnormal and Social Psychology* 52 (1956): 43–50.

McGHIE, A., and CHAPMAN, J. "Disorders of Attention and Perception in Early Schizophrenia." *British Journal of Medical Psychology* 34 (1961): 103–16.

MATARAZZO, J. D. "Prescribed Behavior Therapy: Suggestions from Interview Research." In *Experimental Foundations of Clinical Psychology,* ed. A. J. Bachrach. New York: Basic Books, 1962.

MEDNICK, S. A. "A Learning Theory Approach to Research in Schizophrenia." *Psychological Bulletin* 55 (1958): 316–27.

———— and SCHULSINGER, F. "Some Premorbid Characteristics Related to Breakdown in Children with Schizophrenic Mothers." In *The Transmission of Schizophrenia,* ed. D. Rosenthal and S. S. Kety, pp. 267–91. New York: Pergamon Press, 1968.

MEEHL, P. E. "Schizotaxia, Schizotypy, Schizophrenia." *American Psychologist* 17 (1962): 827–38.

MEICHENBAUM, D. H. "Validation Study of Marital Status and the Self-report Scale for Process-Reactive Schizophrenia." *Journal of Consulting and Clinical Psychology* 33 (1969): 351–56.

MISHLER, E. G., and SCOTCH, N. A. "Sociocultural Factors in the Epidemiology of Schizophrenia." *Psychiatry* 26 (1963): 315–51.

NOYES, A. P., and KOLB, L. C. *Modern Clinical Psychiatry.* Philadelphia: Saunders, 1963.

OFFORD, D. R., and CROSS, L. A. "Behavioral Antecedents of Adult Schizophrenia: A Review." *Archives of General Psychiatry* 21 (1969): 267–83.

PASAMANICK, B.; SCARPETTI, F. R.; and DINETY, S. *Schizophrenics in the Community: An Experimental Study in the Prevention of Hospitalization.* New York: Appleton-Century-Crofts, 1967.

PAYNE, R. W. "The Measurement and Significance of Overinclusive Thinking and Retardation in Schizophrenic Patients." In *Psychopathology of Schizophrenia,* ed. P. H. Hoch and J. Zubin, pp. 77–97. New York: Grune & Stratton, 1966.

PHILLIPS, L. "Case History Data and Prognosis in Schizophrenia." *Journal of Nervous and Mental Disease* 117 (1953): 515–25.

PINEL, P. *A Treatise on Insanity* (1801). New York: Hafner, 1962.

RADO, S. *Psychonanalysis of Behavior,* 2 vols. New York: Grune & Stratton, 1956, 1962.

ROGERS, C. R., ed., with GEUDLIN, E. T., KIESLER, D. J.; and TRUAX, C. B. *The Therapeutic Relationship and Its Impact: A Study of Psychotherapy with Schizophrenics.* Madison: University of Wisconsin Press, 1967.

SHAKOW, D. "Some Psychophysiological Aspects of Schizophrenia." In *The Origins of Schizophrenia,* ed. J. Romano, pp. 15–26. New York: Excerpta Medica Foundation, 1967.

SHERMAN, L. J.; MOSLEY, E. C.; GING, R.; and BOOKBINDER, L. J. "Prognosis in Schizophrenia: A Follow-up Study of 588 Patients." *Archives of General Psychiatry* 10 (1964): 123–30.

SILVERMAN, J. "Scanning Control Mechanism and 'Cognitive Filtering' in Paranoid and Nonparanoid Schizophrenia." *Journal of Consulting Psychology* 28 (1964): 385–93.

SINGER, M. T., and WYNNE, L. C. "Thought Disorder and Family Relations of Schizophrenics: IV. Results and Implications." *Archives of General Psychiatry* 12 (1965): 201–12.

SLATER, E. "A Review of Earlier Evidence on Genetic Factors in Schizophrenia." In *The Transmission of Schizophrenia,* ed. D. Rosenthal and S. S. Kety. New York: Pergamon Press, 1968.

SOLOMON, L., and ZLOTOWSKI, M. "The Relationship Between the Elgin and the Phillips Measures of Process-Reactive Schizophrenia." *Journal of Nervous and Mental Disease* 138 (1964): 32–37.

STEFFY, R. A., and BECKER, W. C. "Measurement of the Severity of Disorder in Schizophrenia by Means of the Holtzman Inkblot Test." *Journal of Consulting Psychology* 25 (1961): 555.

STEPHENS, J. H.; ASTRUP, C.; and MANGRUM, J. C. "Prognosis in Schizophrenia." *Archives of General Psychiatry* 16 (1967): 693–98.

SULLIVAN, H. S. *Conceptions of Modern Psychiatry.* New York: Norton, 1953.

ULLMANN, L. P. *Institution and Outcome: A Comparative Study of Psychiatric Hospitals.* New York: Pergamon Press, 1967.

——— and GIOVANNONI, J. M. "The Development of a Self-report Measure of the Process-Reactive Continuum." *Journal of Nervous and Mental Disease* 138 (1964): 38–42.

——— and KRASNER, L. *A Psychological Approach to Abnormal Behavior.* Englewood Cliffs, N.J.: Prentice-Hall, 1969.

VENABLES, P. "Psychophysiological Aspects of Schizophrenia." *British Journal of Medical Psychology* 39 (1966): 289–97.

WATSON, C. G., and LOGUE, P. E. "Interrelationships of Several Process-Reactive Measures." *Journal of Consulting and Clinical Psychology* 33, no. 1 (1969): 120–22.

WHITEORN, J. C., and BETZ, B. J. "Further Studies of the Doctor as a Crucial Variable in the Outcome of Treatment with Schizophrenic Patients." *American Journal of Psychiatry* 117 (1960): 215–23.

WITTMAN, P. "A Scale for Measuring Prognosis in Schizophrenic Patients."
  Elgin State Hospital Papers 4 (1941): 20–33.
WYNNE, L. C. "Methodological and Conceptual Issues in the Study of Schizo-
  phrenics and Their Families." In *The Transmission of Schizophrenia*, ed.
  D. Rosenthal and S. S. Kety, pp. 185–99. New York: Pergamon Press, 1968.
YATES, A. J. "Psychological Deficit." In *Annual Review of Psychology*, ed.
  P. R. Farnsworth, 1966, pp. 111–44.
ZIGLER, E., and PHILLIPS, L. "Social Competence and the Process-Reactive Dis-
  tinction in Psychopathology." *Journal of Abnormal and Social Psychology*
  65 (1962): 215–22.
ZUBIN, J., and SHAGASS, C., eds. *Neurobiological Aspects of Psychopathology*.
  New York: Grune & Stratton, 1969.

CHAPTER NINE

Origins of
Schizophrenic Behavior

Schizophrenic behavior is the end product of the interaction of biological, experiential, and sociocultural factors. The role of any specific factor can be evaluated only in the context of its interaction with other significant variables. The relative importance of particular pathogenic agents may vary considerably from patient to patient, but in no case is any single factor the sole determinant.

The Genetics of Schizophrenia

The principal research methods used to investigate the genetic component of schizophrenia are the family method, the twin method, longitudinal studies of high-risk children, and comparative studies of children reared in their biological families and in adoptive homes. Studies of families, twins, and high-risk children indicate the importance of genetic factors by demonstrating the degree to which the incidence rate for schizophrenia is directly correlated with degree of consanguinity. Findings may be considered to support the genetic hypothesis if schizophrenia occurs more frequently among closely related people than among distant relatives. This interpretation has been challenged by the observation that people who are closely related are more likely to share a common environment than those more distantly related. Twin data, most of which indicate significantly higher concordance rates (both twins schizophrenic) for monozygotic than dizygotic pairs, provide good support for the genetic hypothesis, although the

207

fact that both types of twins are reared together in the same family does not completely rule out the possible importance of environmental factors. As we noted earlier, in addition to having an identical set of genes, monozygotic twins tend to have more similar life experiences than dizygotic twins. The occurrence of schizophrenia in both twins of MZ pairs reared apart constitutes dramatic evidence in favor of heredity, but only a small number of such cases have been reported. The most conclusive genetic data have come from the study of children of schizophrenic parents reared in foster or adoptive homes.

FAMILY STUDIES

Family studies begin with the selection of a representative group of patients whose clinical history and behavior meet predetermined criteria warranting a diagnosis of schizophrenia. These individuals are referred to as *index cases.* Investigators then conduct careful individual studies of close and distant relatives of the index cases to determine the presence or absence of schizophrenic behavior and/or other forms of pathology. An age correction is usually made in calculating expectancy rates for young persons, presently free of overt symptoms, who have not yet attained the age when the onset of symptoms usually occurs.

Overall findings of the extensive literature on family studies have been reviewed by Slater (1968). A concise summary is presented in Table 9.1. The figures listed refer to definite schizophrenics. If doubtful or borderline cases of schizophrenia were added, the reported percentages would be increased about 25 percent. A further correction would have to be made to include other forms of pathology. As far as definite schizophrenics are concerned, the data clearly indicate that the morbidity risk is directly correlated with the closeness of blood ties. As compared with a chance expectancy rate of 1 percent for the general population, the average expectancy rates among the relatives of schizophrenics range from about 2–3 percent for nephews, cousins, and grandchildren to 37 percent for children of two schizophrenic parents. These findings are consistent with genetic principles, but they cannot be regarded as conclusive evidence that schizophrenia has a solely genetic origin, since behavioral similarities in relatives may be due to the influence of nurture rather than nature, or of a combination of the two. The most objective conclusion is that the data reflect the interactive effect of both nature and nurture. However, a slight weighting in favor of genetic influence might be inferred from the fact that the expectancy rate for a child with one schizophrenic parent is the same whether the father or the mother is schizophrenic. From a genetic point of view, the child's risk should be the same. At the same time, it is difficult to reconcile this finding with environmental theories that emphasize the greater role of the mother in child rearing and home management. Another finding that may be interpreted as somewhat more partial to the genetic than the environmental position is that the expectancy rate for siblings is three times greater than for half-siblings. The close agreement of expectancy rates for parents, children, and siblings (11 to 14 percent) is consistent with the fact that these three groups have the same degree of genetic overlap.

Table 9.1.   Expectation of schizophrenia for relatives of schizophrenics

Relationship	Percentage of expectation
Parents	11%
Children	
Both parents schizophrenic	37
Mother schizophrenic	14
Father schizophrenic	14
Siblings	
Neither parent schizophrenic	9
One parent schizophrenic	12
Half-sibs	3
Grandchildren	3
First cousins	3
Nephews and nieces	2

Adapted from E. Slater, "A Review of Earlier Evidence on Genetic Factors in Schizophrenia," in *The Transmission of Schizophrenia,* ed. D. Rosenthal and S. S. Kety (New York: Pergamon Press, 1968), pp. 15–26.

The observation that the children of two schizophrenics have a 37 percent risk of developing the disorder requires some elaboration. This figure does not accurately reflect the combined effect of nature and nurture. Only 22 percent of these children remained in continuous residence at home with one or both parents up to the age of fifteen. The remainder were reared by relatives or placed in foster homes or under agency care for varying periods of time (Erlenmeyer-Kimling, 1968). A large proportion of the nonschizophrenic children developed other disorders. Only about a third succeeded in making a reasonably normal adjustment (Rosenthal, 1967).

TWIN STUDIES

The twin approach requires (1) the selection of a number of known schizophrenic patients (index cases) who have living twins, (2) tracing the cotwins and examining them for the presence or absence of schizophrenia or some other disorder, and (3) determining by blood tests or other criteria whether the twins are of the monozygotic or dizygotic variety. In earlier twin studies the index cases were chosen mainly from the resident populations of mental hospitals, and therefore included an unduly large number of severe chronic cases. More recent investigators have attempted to correct for this error by gathering data on total populations or on consecutive admissions to clinics and hospitals. The findings of older and more recent studies agree that the concordance rate for monozygotic twins is about four to five times higher than for dizygotic twins. As Table 9.2 indicates, however, the absolute magnitude of concordance rates for both types of twins was considerably higher in the older studies than in the more recent ones. In data gathered prior to 1962, the mean concordance rate for identical twins was 64 percent, as compared with 14 percent for dizygotic twins. The comparable figures for more recent studies, exclusive of those reported by Tienari, show concordance rates of 36 percent for monozygotic and 8 percent for dizgotic twins. The contrast in concordance rates for the two types of twins confirms the importance of genetic factors in the development of schizophrenic behavior. Most investigators agree that several genes, rather than one dominant one, are involved. Interestingly, the concordance rate for monozygotic twins noted in recent studies is practically identical with the incidence rate for the children of two schizophrenic parents.

Table 9.2.   Concordance rates for MZ and same-sexed DZ twins

Investigator	Country	Number of pairs		Percentage of concordance	
		MZ	DZ	MZ	DZ
Earlier reports:[a]					
Rosanoff (1934)	U.S.A.	41	53	61%	13%
Essen-Moller (1941)	Sweden	11	27	64	15
Kallmann (1946)	U.S.A.	174	296	69	11
Slater (1953)	U.K.	37	58	65	14
Inouye (1961)	Japan	55	11	60	18
Recent studies:					
Harvald and Hauge (1965)[a]	Denmark	7	31	29	6
Gottesman and Shields (1966)[a]	U.K.	24	33	42	9
Tienari (1968)[b]	Finland	17	–	6–36	–
Kringlen (1968)[c]	Norway	55	90	38	10

[a]Reported by I. I. Gottesman and J. Shields, "Contributions of Twin Studies to Perspectives on Schizophrenia," in *Progress in Experimental Personality Research,* ed. B. A. Maher (New York: Academic Press, 1966), vol. 3, pp. 1–84.
[b]P. Tienari, "Schizophrenia in Monozygotic Male Twins," in *The Transmission of Schizophrenia,* ed. D. Rosenthal and S. S. Kety (New York: Pergamon Press, 1968), pp. 27–36.
[c]E. Kringlen, "An Epidemiological-Clinical Twin Study on Schizophrenia," in *ibid.,* pp. 49–63.

The findings that only about one-third of monozygotic pairs are concordant for schizophrenia have sometimes been misinterpreted as minimizing the significance of heredity. Proponents of heredity as the decisive factor are not particularly concerned with this criticism, since genetic theory assumes that the overt expression of a genetic predisposition is greatly influenced by other factors. In this connection it may be added that another 40 percent of monozygotic co-twins of schizophrenics develop other disorders. That still leaves a substantial number who are "normal" from a psychiatric standpoint (Kringlen, 1968).

Twins discordant for schizophrenia provide a valuable source of material for investigators studying the significance of other factors in the modification of genetic predispositions. Some of the earlier studies suggested that the concordance rate for female pairs was higher than that for male pairs. Better controlled recent investigations, which report the same concordance rates for male and female twins, have ruled out the possible significance of sex in concordance or discordance (Shields, 1968). Kringlen noted that co-twins of schizophrenics who later became schizophrenic themselves often had difficult relationships with their fathers and were overprotected by their mothers in childhood. Pollin and Stabenau (1968) have reported a

Table 9.3. Early characteristics of 100 pairs of MZ twins discordant for schizophrenia

	Outcome of co-twins	
Characteristic	*Schizo-phrenic*	*Nonschizo-phrenic*
‚Neurotic as child	16	1
Submissive	37	4
Sensitive	38	5
Serious; worrier	22	4
Illness of central nervous system as child	17	4
Birth complication (any)	24	6
Asphyxia at birth	12	3
Dependent	12	3
Quiet, shy	25	8
Stubborn	20	7
Weaker than co-twin	27	11
Dominant	14	30
Outgoing, lively	13	35
Spokesman for pair	7	22
Better at school than co-twin	8	29
More intelligent than co-twin	–	16

Adapted from W. Pollin and J. R. Stabenau, "Biological, Psychological, and Historical Differences in a Series of Monozygotic Twins Discordant for Schizophrenia," in *The Transmission of Schizophrenia*, ed. D. Rosenthal and S. S. Kety (New York: Pergamon Press, 1968), pp. 317–32.

comprehensive review of findings on the early childhood characteristics of monozygotic twins discordant for schizophrenia. Some of the more significant findings are reported in Table 9.3. In comparison with nonaffected co-twins, a higher proportion of the twins who later became schizophrenic had histories of birth complications and diseases of the central nervous system. As children the schizophrenic twins were described as more neurotic, submissive, sensitive, and dependent. A co-twin who did not become schizophrenic was more likely to have been the leader and spokesman for the pair during childhood, more outgoing, and more intelligent.

Twins reared apart. A total of sixteen cases have been reported in which schizophrenia occurred in monozygotic twins reared apart (Slater, 1968). Fourteen of the twin pairs were separated soon after birth or during infancy. The other two pairs were separated at the ages of three and seven. Ten of the sixteen cases, or 63 percent, were concordant for schizophrenia. In the remaining six cases only one of the twins of each pair developed the disorder. These figures are in complete agreement with those obtained in earlier comparable studies for monozygotic twins brought up together. The fact that the concordance rates are the same for twin pairs reared together and apart suggests that genetic factors are largely responsible for the development of schizophrenia.

LONGITUDINAL STUDIES

Practically all information available on schizophrenia is based on studies of patients *after* the onset of the disorder. These data have two major drawbacks: (1) when distinctive psychological or biological characterists are noted, it is difficult to decide whether these represent causal factors or incidental by-products of the disorder; (2) attempts to assess the etiological significance of childhood experiences are vulnerable to the unreliability of memories of events that happened twenty years ago or more. Ideally, information should be gathered on patients prior to the onset of the disorder. There is, of course, no sure way of predicting who will develop a mental disorder, but the odds can be improved somewhat by studying the offspring of schizophrenic parents. As a group, children with one schizophrenic parent have about a 15 percent risk of developing the disorder. This approach is being utilized by Mednick (1967) in his longitudinal study of high-risk and low-risk children. In selecting high-risk children, Mednick chose only those whose mothers had definite histories of process schizophrenia, as confirmed by prolonged hospitalization. Children whose mothers had no psychiatric history were chosen for the low-risk group. The low-risk and high-risk children were matched on other pertinent variables. In 1962, when the study was started, the children had an average age of fifteen years. Mednick plans to follow up these children for twenty years. The investigation is being conducted in Denmark, where a central national register is kept on every psychiatric hospitalization. The population being studied consists of 207 high-risk children and 104 low-risk children or normal controls. Each of the high-risk children is paired with another high-risk child. The assumption is that, at the most, only one of each pair will actually become schizophrenic. It will therefore be possible to compare high-risk children who become schizophrenic with high-risk children who do not become schizophrenic. Each low-risk child is matched with a pair of high-risk children to form a triad. The expectation is that about 15 percent of the high-risk children and about 1 percent of the low-risk children will become schizophrenic.

Preliminary results indicate that as a group the high-risk children differ in many aspects from low-risk children. On all measures, however, the two groups show considerable overlap. A substantial proportion of high-risk children do not exhibit traits and reactions identified with their group. Table 9.4 lists significant findings noted between the two groups with respect to school behavior. During the school years, high-risk children tend to be withdrawn, sensitive, easily upset, and passive. They are loners who

Table 9.4. School behavior of high-risk and low-risk children as reported by teachers without knowledge of children's group membership

Items on which groups differed at .05 level	Percent "yes"	
	High-risk	Low-risk
Was pupil left back?	10%	3%
Was pupil seen by psychologist?	13	1
Is pupil passive, taking no initiative?	52	36
Is pupil a loner, avoiding his classmates' activities?	33	21
Is pupil rejected by his classmates?	18	8
Does pupil get upset for almost no reason?	23	12
Does pupil become withdrawn when excited?	22	8
Is pupil abnormally active?	63	80
Is pupil abnormally subdued?	24	15
Is pupil abnormally sensitive?	22	18
Is pupil nervous?	37	14
Do you think the pupil will have a serious psychiatric illness in the future?	19	4
Did pupil attend any special classes (for retarded, for poor readers, etc.)?	24	12

Adapted from S. A. Mednick, "The Children of Schizophrenics," in *The Origins of Schizophrenia*, ed. J. Romano (New York: Excerpta Medica Foundation, 1967), pp. 179–200.

are avoided or rejected by their classmates. The descriptive picture derived from school behavior agrees well with other available data. The findings suggest that observations by teachers can be conveniently used in the early identification of children who have a high risk of becoming schizophrenic in later years. Mednick and Schulsinger (1968) have also reported some other interesting preliminary findings:

1. There is a general trend for the births of high-risk subjects to have been attended with difficulties.

2. The high-risk group consistently shows a shorter period of latency of galvanic skin response (GSR) to stress stimuli than low-risk children. This shorter latency suggests that the high-risk group is characterized by a volatile autonomic nervous system that is easily and quickly aroused by mild stress. The high-risk group also shows faster autonomic recovery from the effects of stress stimuli.

3. Disorders of association, which are characteristically associated with schizophrenia, to some extent also are characteristic of high-risk children. As a group they tend to give more idiosyncratic and fragmented responses on single-word association tests.

4. In general, the home lives of the high-risk children are characterized by frequent parental quarrels. The mother is seen as the dominant parent. The children tend to see her as scolding, unreliable, and not to be trusted with their confidences. (But it must be remembered that the high-risk group was chosen from among children whose mothers, not fathers, were schizophrenic. It is reasonable to assume that this finding would be reversed if it were the fathers that were schizophrenic.)

5. During adolescence, high-risk children show some early signs of functioning impairment. Their performance on intelligence tests is slightly below the performance of low-risk children. Tests that require concentration and effort show particular impairment. The high-risk child tends to have a restricted social life. These findings suggest the beginning of a pattern of withdrawal under stress.

Five years after the onset of the study, when the children had an average age of twenty, follow-up data indicated that twenty of the high-risk children, or close to 10 percent, had manifested severely abnormal behavior. Of these disturbed children, thirteen had been admitted to psychiatric facilities or placed under psychiatric care. The remaining seven manifested bizarre symptomatic behavior or were described as schizoid, delinquent, or alcoholic. Although these findings are limited to a few cases, preliminary data indicate that the high-risk disturbed children differ in several respects from matched high-risk children who so far have behaved normally. In comparison with the normal group, the disturbed children were separated from their mothers earlier because the mothers required hospitalization for psychiatric treatment. Perhaps the most significant finding to date is that the high-risk children who have already developed schizophrenia or some other psychiatric abnormality had a much higher incidence of complications during gestation or birth. Seventy percent of the disturbed high-risk group had histories of anoxia, prematurity, prolonged labor, umbilical cord complication, mother's illness during pregnancy, breech presentation, etc. Only 15 percent of the normal high-risk group had experienced complications during gestation or birth. Although the hypothesis is highly tentative, Mednick (1970) has suggested that brain damage during pregnancy and birth, in combination with genetic and environmental factors, may be responsible for the development of some forms of schizophrenic behavior. Twin data (Table 9.3) provide significant confirmation of this hypothesis. When only one member of a pair of MZ twins develops schizophrenia, the affected twin more often has a history of asphyxia following delivery, birth complications, or central nervous system illness during early childhood. The implication that brain damage associated with pregnancy and birth complications may be a contributory factor raises the interesting possibility that the incidence of schizophrenia might be significantly reduced through improved prenatal and delivery care.

INTRAFAMILIAL INTERACTIONS

Adverse parent-child relationships, marital discord, confused communication, and other signs of intrafamilial disturbances have been repeatedly noted in studies of schizophrenics. The interpretation of these findings is another matter. Before serious consideration can be given to the idea that family pathology is the cause of schizophrenic behavior, it must be demonstrated that (1) the incidence of pathology is significantly higher in schizophrenic that in nonschizophrenic families, (2) the observed pathology is not the result of or a reaction to special problems created by the presence of one or more disordered members within the family, and (3) removal of a child from the assumed pathogenic influences of a schizophrenic family would decrease the risk of his developing the disorder. The issue is still not fully resolved. It is generally recognized that the family environment is an important contributory factor in the personality structure and the general adjustment level of any individual. However, research data offer little support for the specific hypothesis that a pathological parental attitude or family disorganization is the direct cause of schizophrenic behavior. The basic contribution of the family to schizophrenia appears to be the transmission of defective genes from maladjusted parents to their vulnerable offspring.

Parental attitudes. The popular stereotype of the domineering schizophrenic mother and the weak, ineffectual father is admittedly an oversimplification. The father is often the dominant parent (Fontana, 1966).

The range of individual differences in the feelings and reactions of parents toward their preschizophrenic children and in their styles of child rearing is probably as great as among the general population. Fleck (1963) has suggested that the parent-child relationship varies with the sex of the patient. The mothers of schizophrenic sons tend to be dominant, intrusive, and engulfing, while the fathers are passive and ineffectual. In the case of schizophrenic daughters, the mothers are uninvolved and emotionally distant while the fathers are often paranoid and narcissistic. They are disparaging of the opposite sex, but at the same time they may behave seductively toward their daughters. In other words, the same-sexed parent fails to provide an attractive model for identification, and the model presented by the parent of the opposite sex arouses distrust and hostility. The net effect is that identification with either parent is precluded (Caputo, 1963).

The variability of parent-child interactions in schizophrenic families makes it difficult to attach great causal significance to any particular interaction pattern. On the other hand, too many studies have described the mothers of chronic schizophrenics as possessive, overcontrolling, restrictive, and intrusive to allow us to dismiss the stereotype casually. Even if this description were found to fit only a relatively small percentage of schizophrenics, it would still be significant if these traits were more characteris ic of the mothers of schizophrenics then of other mothers. But the evidence on this point is negative. In studies in which an attempt has been made to control for the possibility that the presence of a "problem" child may influence the mother's behavior, the results have been consistent and unequivocal: no significant differences in maternal overprotection, overcontrol, and related attitudes have been found between the mothers of schizophrenics and the mothers of brain-injured, retarded, or delinquent children and of psychologically normal children who are diabetic or physically handicapped. In his review of these studies, Mednick (1967) suggests that the family discord associated with schizophrenia, as well as the pathological attitudes of the mother, are the result rather than the cause of the disorder.

Marital discord. Although marital discord is by no means unknown in "normal" families, schism between husband and wife is especially characteristic of schizophrenic families (Lidz et al., 1965). In marriages that exist in a chronic state of disequilibrium and discord there is little or no sharing of problems and satisfactions. Each spouse is caught up in his or her own difficulties and in pursuing egocentric objectives. The disregard of the needs of the partner leads to increasing ill will, recurring threats of separation, and mistrust. Communication consists primarily of coercive efforts and defiance. Husband and wife compete in undercutting each other in the eyes of their children. This may be done to gain the children's sympathy and loyalty or simply to hurt and spite the marital partner. In this struggle the wife usually has an advantage of sorts. She spends more time with the children than the husband does, and the husband's common assumption that she and the children alike are naturally subordinate to him tends to arouse in her a resentment that the children find it easy to share. Human beings who are defined as inferior show a strong tendency to resent those who define themselves as superior, and to form a united front against them. The more the husband reduces his wife to the instrumental role of household servant, the more he is himself reduced to the instrumental role of provider of financial support. This is a game in which there can be no winners, only losers—not least the children of this sorry pair.

The term "marital skew" has been used to describe another mutually destructive pattern, in which the psychopathology of the dominant partner is accepted and supported by the healthier spouse. This arrangement appears to satisfy the dependency or masochistic needs of the weaker partner. The accord presented by the parents leaves the children little choice but to go along with the *folie en famille*. The maintenance of the illusion that abnormality is normal requires adroitness in evading too close examination of certain issues. A double set of standards may be required, one for home life and another for adjustment outside the home.

The double bind. The double-bind hypothesis has been advanced by Bateson and his associates (1956). The basic premise is that much of the irrational and disorganized behavior of schizophrenics is the result of their prolonged exposure during the formative years to a confusing pattern of contradictory messages. The prospective schizophrenic is required to make some response, but since the messages he is receiving are contradictory, whatever he says or does is bound to be "wrong"—an impossible situation. A child may be asked to come and sit on his mother's lap, for example, but her tone makes it clear that she hopes he won't. It is usually assumed that the child is the victim and the mother the creator of the bind. However, children also are adept at putting their parents in situations in which they can't win no matter what they do.

The double bind consists essentially of three orders or injunctions. The primary message is usually verbally expressed and consists of an order to do or not to do something. This primary message is accompanied by a secondary contradictory communication that is usually expressed indirectly by posture, gesture, or tone of voice. The third message is an injunction, usually unexpressed but nevertheless quite clearly communicated, prohibiting the victim from escaping from the field. Since the messages are contradictory, no appropriate reaction is possible. The individual may have difficulty in recognizing that the messages are contradictory because one communication is verbal and the others are nonverbal and hence not clearly defined. If the child does understand that the messages are contradictory, and says so, he is simply told that he is mistaken. Bateson tells of a young schizophrenic who had made a fairly good recovery when he was visited in the hospital by his mother. He welcomed her by impulsively putting his arms around her shoulders, whereupon she stiffened. When the young man, sensing her hostile reaction, withdrew his arms, she asked, "Don't you love me anymore?" The son blushed, and the mother said, "Dear, you must not be so easily embarrassed and afraid of your feelings." When he returned to the ward, the patient promptly assaulted an aide.

Haley (1960) has suggested a modification of the double bind that has the same result, confused communication. According to this concept, the members of the schizophrenic's family are constantly qualifying and disqualifying their own statements and the statements of the others. They say one thing and do another. Letters of mothers of schizophrenics contain interesting examples of this incongruence (Weakland and Fry, 1962). In writing to her hospitalized schizophrenic son, a mother may caution him against the dangers of smoking, and then add in a postscript that she is mailing him a carton of cigarettes.

The child as victim. The family theory of schizophrenia requires some modification to take account of the fact that only about 15 percent of the children and siblings of schizophrenics manifest overt signs of the disorder. One possibility is that the deleterious effects of family pathology are restricted to those members of the family who are genetically predisposed to mental disorder. Those favoring an environmental point of view have argued that the differential outcome in children of the same family may be due to the fact that the parents have a closer relationship with the schizophrenic child than with the others. The standard explanation, offered by Lu (1961, 1962), Wynne and Singer (1963), and others is that from infancy the child who later becomes schizophrenic is more deeply involved in the family's emotional life than his nonschizophrenic siblings. The potential schizophrenic submits to the mother's domination, while the normal sibling rebels. The vulnerable child is confined to the constricted, pathological atmosphere of the home; the normal sibling enjoys greater freedom and becomes more involved with the outside world. To a greater degree than his siblings, the preschizophrenic child accepts the contradictory parental expectations that he be dependent and at the same time strive for perfection and high achievement.

The child "selected" as a victim may be the most docile one, the biologically weakest, or the child who happens to be born during a period of maximal marital conflict or family crisis (Stabenau and Pollin, 1968). On the basis of their retrospective study, Prout and White (1956) conclude that the preschizophrenic child has been more sensitive, more dependent, and less outgoing than his healthier sibling from infancy. His greater need for attention and support may have invited maternal overprotection.

Family therapists have suggested that the dynamics and needs of the family system may require different children to play different roles. Thus one child may be selected to serve as the "sick" or "bad one," another the "healthy one," and a third the "conscience of the family." Lidz and his co-workers (1965) question whether many of the children of schizophrenic families are actually unaffected. They agree that only about 15 percent of the siblings are clinically schizophrenic, but claim that a large additional number suffer from a variety of other mild or borderline conditions.

The assumption of a family etiology of schizophrenia has certain treatment implications. According to Lidz (1967), a basic aim is to free the individual of his symbiotic ties with his parents and to help him become a person in his own right, with his own separate identity. Distortions in behavior are interpreted not as personal defenses but rather as learned distortions that have been imposed upon him by his parents as they attempted to work out their own problems. An important function of the therapist is to encourage the patient to accept and trust his own feelings and ideas, and to question the ideas and feelings he has acquired from his parents.

ADOPTION STUDIES

The strongest evidence against the importance of family environment as the cause of schizophrenia comes from studies of children of schizophrenic mothers who have been reared from infancy in foster or adoptive homes. Heston (1966) reported the pioneer investigation in this area. A more detailed analysis of findings has been presented by Heston and Denney (1968). The experimental subjects were forty-seven children born to hospitalized schizophrenic mothers. Fifty control subjects were selected from the records of the same foundling homes that received the experimental subjects. The mothers of the control children had no history of psychiatric disorder. All of the children in both groups were considered physically normal at birth. The two groups were matched individually for sex, length of time in child-care institutions, and type of eventual placement (adoptive home, foster home, or institution). The psychiatric outcome was determined when the children in the two groups had reached a mean age of thirty-six years. The results strongly supported a genetic etiology for schizophrenia. Five of the forty-seven children of schizophrenic mothers, or 11 percent, also became schizophrenic. None of the control group of adopted children of normal parents developed schizophrenia. Another 44 percent of the experimental group had histories of other forms of psychopathology, including neurosis, sociopathic personality, and criminal behavior. Only 18 percent of the control group had histories of some type of psychiatric or social disability other than schizophrenia. The divorce rate was the same for the two groups. One other interesting finding was that the experimental group had more colorful life histories. As adults, the normal children of schizophrenic mothers were more spontaneous, had more imaginative hobbies, and were engaged in more creative work than the normal children of normal mothers.

Heston's main conclusion, that children of schizophrenic mothers reared in adoptive homes have about the same expectancy of becoming schizophrenic as children reared by their biological mothers, has been confirmed by Karlson (1966) and Rosenthal and his associates (1968). Karlson studied outcome among the siblings of schizophrenics who had been adopted before the age of one and reared apart from their biological parents. He found that six out of twenty-nine siblings of schizophrenics who had been reared in adoptive homes also became schizophrenic. This represents a total of 21 percent, which is slightly higher than the figure usually found for siblings of schizophrenics reared in their parental homes. None of the foster siblings reared in the same homes as the adopted children became schizophrenic. Rosenthal and his associates compared the adopted children of schizophrenic parents with the adopted children of nonschizophrenic parents, and found that out of a total of thirty-nine adopted children of schizophrenic parents, three were eventually diagnosed as schizophrenic and another six were considered borderline schizophrenics. Out of a total of forty-seven children of nonschizophrenic parents, none were diagnosed as schizophrenic and only one was considered a borderline case.

Psychodynamic Theories

Recent psychodynamic approaches are represented in the writings of Arieti and Laing. Arieti (1967) has outlined four stages in the development of schizophrenia. The first stage of early childhood is the seeding period. The future patient is raised in a home environment that offers him a modicum of security and trust. Early interpersonal relations with parents are characterized by intense anxiety and devastating hostility. The child is forced to sustain the impact of intense negative emotions, of tension, fear, and anxiety. He tends to participate as little as possible in the unpleasant external reality, and escapes into an overdeveloped fantasy world. For a longer period than the average child, he interprets the world, life, and himself on the basis of images, symbols, magical wish fulfillment, and other primary processes. Ideas of causality are confused. He believes that whatever occurs is brought about by unpleasant clusters of images that represent his parents, and especially his mother. With the development of language, he tends to interpret the world paleologically. Similarity is confused with identity. Certain characteristics of his mother or his ways of dealing with her are unconsciously generalized to all women. His self-identity is very shaky.

Despite the emotional turmoil of this period, most of these children go on to the second stage, in which behavior is more realistic and appropriate. The child becomes aware that the family does not constitute the whole world, and he begins to build up hope for his own future. Although he may still harbor serious doubts about his personal worth, he is able to construct a more stable self-image. In the majority of cases the process of disorder stops at this stage, so that a psychosis never develops. The individual more or less succeeds in adjusting to life.

If the defenses acquired during the second stage are effective, the child proceeds to the third stage, which has its onset around the time of puberty. Sexual maturity, with its implications of broader life problems with which the individual will be expected to cope, may be the precipitating factor. Handicapped by defects in his early development, the young person may come to believe not only that his family is unwilling to accept his inadequacy, but that the world at large finds him wanting. Adolescents who later become schizophrenic tend to select concepts and categories that have a gloomy emotional tone. They see these concepts as final; they permit no exceptions. The future patient acquires a negative self-image. Particularly in the sexual realm he sees himself as inadequate, as having no definite sexual identity, as a homosexual or undesirable as a sexual partner. The future patient perceives his future as bleak and hopeless. As long as he lives he will be unacceptable to others. He does not fit; he is alone. His self-image is so unfavorable that he may become unacceptable to himself. It is at this point that *preschizophrenic panic* occurs. There is an upsurge of repressed early experiences of the first stage. The individual sees himself as totally defeated, worthless, and with no possibility of redemption.

Unless this inner demoralization is arrested, the individual goes on to the fourth or psychotic stage. The psychosis represents a defense against his terrifying and devastating self-image. The paranoid process frees him from the need for self-accusation. "Other people" now call him names, accuse him, and ridicule him. The "external" persecution causes fear and anxiety, but this is more bearable than self-blame. One can defend oneself against external danger, deny external accusations, fight back against persecutors, but there is no defense or escape from self-accusation. During the period of panic, everything "inside" the patient appears in a state of turbulent change. This too is externalized during the psychotic stage, when the outside world appears difficult and strange.

Laing (1965) has presented an existential-phenomenological interpretation of schizophrenia. His main point is that the schizophrenic has failed to develop a firm cohesive sense of personal identity. His insecurity concerning his existence as a real person is traced to early childhood, when he felt unloved, unnoticed, or rejected. Because of his tenuous concept of self, the schizophrenic cannot cope effectively as an autonomous person with the problems of life. The psychosis represents an attempt to preserve the self. The bizarreness and obscurity of behavior often noted in schizophrenics is their way of protecting themselves from intrusion. The schizoid person feels exposed and vulnerable to others, different, lonely, isolated, and filled with despair. He is frightened of the world, afraid that any contact with others will be penetrative, fragmenting, and engulfing. His self-concept is so limited that he believes that if he shares anything of himself with others, he will be depleted and sucked dry. Despite his longing to be loved for his real self, the schizophrenic is extremely afraid of being loved. Any form of understanding by others is a threat to his defensive system, which is distorted and subjective. The schizophrenic suffers from a divided self. One part consists of a secret self that is characterized by an inner withholding of compliance and passive defiance of the outer world. The other part is a false outer self that represents the patient's surface compliance with the expectations of significant others in his life. The false self serves to maintain the appearance of normality. When a psychosis is fully developed, the veil of the false self is removed and we see the secret true self.

Schizotaxia, Schizotype, and Schizophrenia

Meehl (1962) has outlined a comprehensive theory of schizophrenia that takes account of the interaction of genetic and environmental factors. For Meehl, the significant diagnostic indicators of schizophrenia are (1) disturbances in thinking or "cognitive slippage"; (2) interpersonal aversiveness—the patient's distrust of social involvement because of fear of rejection; (3) anhedonia, or defect in the capacity to experience pleasure; and (4) ambivalence or affect confusion, characterized by simultaneous feelings of love and hate.

Meehl starts with the assumption that the genetic predisposition to schizophrenia consists of some defect in neural integration. This inherited neural defect, which he christened *schizotaxia,* is the essential prerequisite. Persons lacking this genetic neural defect have little or no risk of developing schizophrenia, but all schizotaxic individuals develop *schizotypic* personalities regardless of the favorableness of their social learning histories. Schizotypic personalities exhibit in varying degrees the four core behavior traits listed above. Whether the process stops at this level or goes on to an actual psychosis depends on several additional factors. Schizotypic persons who have the good fortune to inherit little readiness for anxiety, physical vigor, and strong resistance to stress, and whose interpersonal learning experiences are favorable, become well-compensated "normal" schizotypes. The minority of schizotypics, who inherit great readiness for anxiety, little physical vigor, and low resistance to stress, and who are subjected to an ambivalent regime imposed by a domineering, possessive, "cold" parent, go on to develop the clinical signs of schizophrenia.

Social and Cultural Factors

SOCIAL CLASS

In 1939 Faris and Dunham reported an inverse relationship between social class and incidence rates of schizophrenia as reflected in first admissions to mental hospitals serving the Chicago area. Subsequent investigations have consistently reported an excessive rate of schizophrenia in the lowest (Class V) social group for large industrialized urban communities (Mishler and Scotch, 1963). However, this finding has been limited to the lowest class. For Classes I through IV (professional to semiskilled workers), the occurrence of schizophrenia is about the same (Dunham, 1964). It has also been found that the concentration of schizophrenia in the lowest social class does not occur in small towns and in rural communities (Kohn, 1968).

Two theories have been suggested to account for the unusually high rate of schizophrenia in the lowest socioeconomic strata of large urban communities. The first is that schizophrenia is produced by the conditions of poverty, mobility, and social isolation that prevail in disorganized slum areas. The alternate explanation, which is often referred to as the "social selection" or "drift" hypothesis, is that the general social incompetence of potential schizophrenics causes them gradually to drift down to the bottom socioeconomic stratum. Most of the evidence favors the latter interpretation. As early as 1953, Gerard and Houston noted that the inverse relationship of social class to schizophrenia did not hold for patients admitted directly to mental hospitals from their own family settings. The excess of schizophrenics with low socioeconomic backgrounds was due entirely to a disproportionate number of young schizophrenics who had left home to live in rented rooms and cheap lodging houses. Hare (1956) has reported similar findings in England. The downward drift of schizophrenics has been most clearly demonstrated in studies comparing the occupational levels of schizophrenic males with those of their fathers. In another study conducted in England, Goldberg and Morrison (1963) found that the occupational levels of the fathers of schizophrenics were on a par with those for the general population. However, the sons who developed schizophrenia showed a downward drift in occupational status as compared with their fathers. A similar decline in the occupational and social status of schizophrenic sons has been confirmed by studies in Norway (Grunfeld and Salvesen, 1968) and in Rochester, New York (Turner and Wagenfeld, 1967). Once the schizophrenic drops to the bottom of the heap, he stays there. In addition, a substantial proportion of his children who inherit a predisposition to schizophrenia fail to move up, so that they too eventually contribute to the heavy representation of schizophrenic patients at the lowest socioeconomic level in large industrialized urban areas.

ISOLATION AND ALIENATION

The underlying causes of the schizophrenic's estrangement from his social environment may be traced to an innate temperament that favors introvertive behavior and unfavorable parent-child experiences. Once started, however, the alienation process itself is an important factor in the development and sustaining of symptomatic behavior. The more the child avoids interaction and involvement with others, the less opportunity he has to acquire the skills necessary for harmonious interpersonal relationships. In addition, the isolated child has limited opportunity to acquire the beliefs, values, rules, and practices of his social group. His perceptions of himself, his peers, and the outer world are increasingly shaped by inner fantasies. The absence of friends and interpersonal communication deprives the potential schizophrenic of feedback information that might correct his distorted perceptions and idiosyncrasies.

The preschizophrenic is often keenly aware of his growing estrangement and may make vacillating efforts to relate to others, but his social incompetence, basic distrust, and lack of empathy make him open to rebuffs, which reinforce his tendency to withdraw. As Millon has noted (1969), the breach between the preschizophrenic and the larger community is progressively widened. The preschizophrenic eventually abandons whatever social amenities he may have acquired. He is increasingly mystified by the rules of interpersonal relations and experiences difficulty in making sense of the actions of others. Perplexed and bewildered, he feels doomed to wander alone in a strange and frightening world.

CULTURAL DIFFERENCES

The impact of the culture in shaping the overt symptoms of schizophrenia is generally accepted. Whether cultural factors affect the incidence rate is less certain. Murphy (1968) has questioned the validity of earlier reports of the low incidence of schizophrenia among the Hutterites. On the other hand, he has presented some evidence that the incidence of schizophrenia is excessively high among Irish Catholics, the people of northwest Croatia, and the Tamil-speaking people of south India and Ceylon. The most clear-cut data relate to the latter group. Several studies have reported a higher incidence of schizophrenia among Tamil university students in Singapore than among Chinese and Malay students. The rate of mental disorder in the Indian army has been found to be significantly higher among Tamil soldiers than among soldiers coming from other regions of the country. Murphy attributes the excessive rates in the three ethnic groups mentioned to cultural conflicts rather than to any specific social factor.

Summary: The Genain Quadruplets

Research data have clearly established that genetic factors are of key importance in predisposing an individual to the development of schizophrenic behavior. However, the phenotypic expression of the genetic predisposition is dependent on the interactive effect of other factors. In the absence of pertinent additional unfavorable agents, the genetic predisposition is not activated, but it is transmitted to offspring in full strength. The genetic component appears to consist in part of an introverted temperament. There is growing evidence that a contributory biological agent in some instances is mild brain damage resulting from complications during pregnancy and delivery. The confused status of findings with respect to the role of the family may reflect the significance of the dyadic or triadic interaction of the child and his parents. If the parents have psychological problems of their own, as they frequently do in schizophrenic families, their pathological interactions with one another and with the child may contribute to the development of schizophrenic or other abnormal reactions in their relatively more vulnerable children. Conversely, the defective functioning of the genetically predisposed, introverted, and mildly brain-damaged child may promote pathological emotional ties between the child and his biological or adoptive parents.

Our interpretation of the multiple interacting causes of schizophrenia may best be illustrated by a case study. This case is unusual in that it involves the occurrence of schizophrenia in all four members of a set of identical quadruplets. The study of the Genain quadruplets, reported by Rosenthal and his colleagues (1963), is a model of comprehensive coverage. For purposes of identification, the four girls were called Myra, Nora, Iris, and Hester. All four exhibited schizophrenic behavior by the age of twenty-four. Shared symptoms included catatonic posturing, hallucinations, panic reactions, social withdrawal, irritability, crying, screaming, vomiting, multiple aches and pains, confusion, blurred vision, and exhaustion. Each of the girls also exhibited certain distinctive reactions of her own, however, and they showed considerable variability in the severity of their psychoses and outcomes. Myra, the healthiest one, made a good recovery and married. At last report, when the quads were in their thirties, she was living in the community. The other three girls have shown a progressive downward pattern. All were in state hospitals at the time the study was concluded. Of the three, Nora had the most favorable prognosis and Hester the least favorable; Hester, in fact, was considered a hopeless chronic case.

On the basis of the wealth of data collected on the quads, confirmation could be found for practically all of the theories of schizophrenia. The father's family included several members with histories of psychosis. Atypical electroencephalographical records, suggestive of brain damage, were observed in the father and all of the girls. The turbulent home atmosphere and unwholesome interaction of the various members of the family provide support for social learning theories of schizophrenia. Parental quarrels were frequent and severe. The mother was domineering and overcontrolling. The father was a dependent, ineffectual person who periodically reacted against his inadequacy with violence, rage, and threats. Both parents were intrusive and denied the girls any privacy.

Both parents were unduly concerned with their health. The parental hypochondriacal model may have contributed to the host of somatic symptoms that the quads also manifested. For the mother, who was a frustrated nurse, the home was her hospital and later a private psychiatric ward. She was fearful of the health of the quads, constantly giving them medication and putting them to bed for long periods when they showed signs of the slightest fatigue. All the girls were periodically enuretic, even during adolescence.

From early childhood the quads exhibited traits identified with the premorbid personality of schizophrenics. They were described by their teachers as introverted, frail, anxious, reserved, stand-offish, precise, proper, and lacking in initiative, spontaneity, and drive. In part these characteristics might have reflected inborn temperament qualities, but the parents did everything possible to reinforce them. The quads were often literally fenced in, denied outside contacts, and made to keep to themselves as a self-contained impenetrable unit. They were deprived of opportunities to form associations and contacts outside the home, to learn what other people were like and how to behave with them. Even after they had grown up the girls were treated as children. All the members of the family were symbiotically involved with one another. Their attitude toward the outside world was one of apprehensive distrust. This attitude was particularly encouraged by the father, who saw threats everywhere. On occasions he patrolled the premises as an armed guard.

The secluded, socially isolated family unit provided abundant examples of irrational behavior to serve as models for the quads. The paternal grandmother, who lived with the family until the children were seven years old, was a highly unstable, irrational, suspicious, superstitious person. She literally drove the quads' mother almost to the point of suicide. The father was ill tempered, expressed homicidal threats, drank to excess, had black-out spells, and heard voices. At times he would attempt to gain the sympathy of the quads by feigning illness. More often he would express his inadequacy as a parent by violent shouting and fault-finding. As soon as one of the daughters became mentally disordered, he would concentrate his criticisms and verbal abuse on another, until all were disturbed.

As the strong member of the family, the mother used her position to keep the girls completely dependent on her. The mother's unresolved problems created difficulties for all the girls. Hester, the troublesome rebel, was crushed and rejected. The other three were prevented from developing personalities of their own and were assigned roles that represented some component of the mother's personality. Communication within the family was fuzzy, indirect, and often a classic example of the double bind. An unusual feature that illustrates both the poor communication and the symbiotic relationship was the phenomenon of echoing. When one of the girls was asked a question by an outsider in the presence of the mother, the mother would answer and the girl addressed would then echo her response. The isolated, restricted life of the quads prevented them from exploring, testing, and checking their perceptions and misconceptions of themselves and the outside world. In a way, irrational behavior was the standard within the family. Healthy members were resented and pressured until they too conformed.

The scapegoat theory of schizophrenia, which assumes that the family unconsciously selects and exploits one of its members as the victim for latent pathological components within the family, is supported by the life history of Hester. Why was Hester selected? As the last-born baby, the frailest, shortest, oddest, slowest to develop, and least intelligent of the quads, she was the natural victim. The selection appears to have been made mainly by the mother, who was critical of Hester from the first day because she cried all the time, was a feeding problem, and apparently was less docile then the other quads. According to the mother, Hester was always a problem to her. When she was young, it was cry, cry, cry. Later she was difficult to manage. If the mother tried to correct her, she became obstinate, fought back and broke things. Gradually the mother came to identify Hester's hostility and sexuality with her disliked husband. She described Hester as an extremely troublesome, unappreciative, deceiving, destructive child. Hester was also the chief target for the father's hostility. Her sisters accepted the designation of Hester as the "bad child" and the "baby," and were somewhat ashamed of her because of her masturbation and poor schoolwork. The onset of Hester's mental illness probably occurred before the age of fourteen, but her behavior was considered symptomatic of badness rather than of mental disorder. The early onset of her psychosis is suggested by the fact that by the age of fourteen her IQ test score had dropped from 105 to 77. Because of poor grades, she dropped out of school in her junior year of high school. All of her sisters graduated from high school and later obtained employment as secretaries. Hester was assigned the role of kitchen maid, the Cinderella who was picked on by everyone and expected to do all the dirty work. She accepted this negative image and acted accordingly. She was in fact bad tempered, destructive, and aggressive.

Hester was the personification of the mother's negative feelings toward belligerence and sexuality. But she was not the only one to be treated as an extension of some component of the mother's personality. Each daughter in turn internalized and attempted to live out her assigned role, and in so doing sacrificed her own personality. Iris represented the mother's repressed drives. She was assigned the role of the unappreciated, neglected child, whose demonstrated competence was never rewarded or even acknowledged. The mother's positive feelings were reserved for Nora and Myra. Nora, the firstborn and the healthiest during infancy, was expected to be the sweet, dependent child who was attached to the mother so completely that she could have no inner life of her own. Myra represented a projection of the mother's emotional needs for independence. In later years, Myra supplanted Nora as the mother's favorite.

Chaotic sexuality prevailed in the Genain home. The father, who became impotent by the time the girls were ten years old, frequently accused his wife of promiscuity. He refused to permit the girls to go out on dates, even when they were grown up and working, for fear they would become sexually involved. At the same time, he would pat their buttocks, feel their breasts, and enter their rooms to watch them dress and undress. The mother, who had had an illicit love affair when she was sixteen, was preoccupied with real or imagined sexual misconduct on the part of others. She was particularly concerned with the sexuality of Hester, who started masturbating at the age of three. The mother considered Hester a bad, oversexed girl. She attributed Hester's subsequent breakdown to an unsubstantiated confession she forced from her to the effect that Hester had on numerous occasions been sexually molested by the school janitor.

Despite severe punishment, Hester continued to masturbate, and was soon followed by Iris. When they were twelve, Hester and Iris were discovered by their mother engaging in mutual masturbation. A doctor was consulted about the problem, and he recommended that both girls be circumcised. The parents went along with his recommendation. The hospital records indicate that Iris and Hester were admitted for circumcision and the release of adhesions about the clitoris. The mother later reported that the doctor removed "all the mucous membrane to the uterus." Both girls resisted the operation and broke their stitches. Acting on the doctor's orders, the mother tied the girls' hands to the bed for thirty nights. This traumatic experience did not stop the masturbation, however.

According to the mother, three of the girls had a terrifying sexual experience shortly before the onset of psychosis. Within a span of two years, one after another of the girls allegedly found herself alone with a man (in an elevator, an office, a washroom). The man exposed himself, pushed the girl against the wall, and tried to undress her. In each instance the girl escaped being raped by fighting back and screaming. The exception was Hester. The mother was pretty sure that Hester had had a similar experience, but had not complained because she liked it, and had probably even encouraged the fellow.

In summary, the quads probably inherited a genetic predisposition to schizophrenia from their father. Under more favorable circumstances, one or all of the girls might have avoided becoming psychotic. The unwholesome home atmosphere and the personality defects of the parents did more than activate an inherent predisposition. From infancy onward, the quads were exposed to adverse environmental and learning experiences that reinforced and augmented their inherent vulnerability. The eventual schizophrenic outcome was the product of the complementary interaction of genetic and environmental factors. The variation in the severity of the quadruplets' psychoses may be attributed to variations in the prenatal as well as the postnatal environment. At birth Hester and Iris weighed much less than the other two girls.

References

ARIETI, S. "New View on the Psychodynamics of Schizophrenia." *American Journal of Psychiatry* 124, no. 4 (1967): 453–58.

BATESON, G.; JACKSON, D.; HALEY, J.; and WEAKLAND, J. "Toward a Theory of Schizophrenia." *Behavioral Science* 1 (1956): 251–64.

CAPUTO, D. V. "The Parents of the Schizophrenic." *Family Process* 2 (1963): 339–56.

DUNHAM, H. W. "Social Class and Schizophrenia." *American Journal of Orthopsychiatry* 34 (1964): 634–42.

ERLENMEYER-KIMLING, L. "Studies on the Offspring of Two Schizophrenic Parents." In *The Transmission of Schizophrenia,* ed. D. Rosenthal and S. S. Kety, pp. 65–83. New York: Pergamon Press, 1968.

FARIS, R., and DUNHAM, H. W. *Mental Disorders in Urban Areas.* Chicago: University of Chicago Press, 1939.

FLECK, S. "Comparison of Parent-Child Relationships of Male and Female Schizophrenics." *Archives of General Psychiatry* 8 (1963): 1–7.

FONTANA, A. "Familial Etiology of Schizophrenia: Is a Scientific Methodology Possible?" *Psychological Bulletin* 66 (1966): 214–27.

GERARD, D., and HOUSTON, L. G. "Family Setting and the Social Ecology of Schizophrenia." *Psychiatric Quarterly* 27 (1953): 90–101.

GOLDBERG, E. M., and MORRISON, S. L. "Schizophrenia and Social Class." *British Journal of Psychiatry* 109 (1963): 785–802.

GOTTESMAN, I. I., and SHIELDS, J. "Contributions of Twin Studies to Perspectives on Schizophrenia." In *Progress in Experimental Personality Research,* ed. B. A. Maher, vol. 3, pp. 1–84. New York: Academic Press, 1966.

GRUNFELD, B., and SALVESEN, C. "Functional Psychoses and Social Status." *British Journal of Psychiatry* 114 (1968): 733–37.

HALEY, J. "Direct Study of Child-Parent Interactions." *American Journal of Orthopsychiatry* 30 (1960): 460–67.

HARE, E. H. "Mental Illness and Social Conditions in Bristol." *Journal of Mental Science* 102 (1956): 349–57.

HESTON, L. L. "Psychiatric Disorders in Foster-Home-Reared Children of Schizophrenic Mothers." *British Journal of Psychiatry* 112 (1966): 819–25.

——— and DENNY, D. "Interactions Between Early Life Experience and Biological Factors in Schizophrenia." In *The Transmission of Schizophrenia,* ed. D. Rosenthal and S. S. Kety, pp. 363–76. New York: Pergamon Press, 1968.

KARLSON, J. *The Biological Basis of Schizophrenia.* Springfield, Ill.: Charles C. Thomas, 1966.

KOHN, M. L. "Social Class and Schizophrenia: A Critical Review." In *The Transmission of Schizophrenia,* ed. D. Rosenthal and S. S. Kety, pp. 155–73. New York: Pergamon Press, 1968.

KRINGLEN, E. "An Epidemiological-Clinical Twin Study on Schizophrenia." In *The Transmission of Schizophrenia,* ed D. Rosenthal and S. S. Kety, pp. 49–64. New York: Pergamon Press, 1968.

LAING, R. D. *The Divided Self: An Existential Study in Sanity and Madness.* Baltimore: Penguin Books, 1965.

LIDZ, T. "The Influence of Family Studies on the Treatment of Schizophrenia." *Psychiatry* 32 (1967): 235–51.

———, FLECK, S., and CORNELISON, A. R. *Schizophrenia and the Family.* New York: International Universities Press, 1965.

LU, Y. "Mother-Child Role Relationships in Schizophrenia: A Comparison of Schizophrenic Patients with Nonschizophrenic Siblings." *Psychiatry* 24 (1961): 133–42.

———. "Contradictory Parental Expectations in Schizophrenia." *Archives of General Psychiatry* 6 (1962): 219–34.

MEDNICK, S. A. "The Children of Schizophrenics." In *The Origins of Schizophrenia,* ed. J. Romano, pp. 179–200. New York: Excerpta Medica Foundation, 1967.

———. "Breakdown in Individuals at High Risk for Schizophrenia: Possible Predispositional Perinatal Factors." *Mental Hygiene* 54, no. 1 (1970): 50–61.

——— and SCHULSINGER, F. "Some Premorbid Characteristics Related to Breakdown in Children with Schizophrenic Mothers." In *The Transmission of Schizophrenia,* ed. D. Rosenthal and S. S. Kety. New York: Pergamon Press, 1968.

MEEHL, P. E. "Schizotaxia, Schizotypy, Schizophrenia." *American Psychologist* 17 (1962): 827–38.

MILLON, T. *Modern Psychopathology*. Philadelphia: Saunders, 1969.

MISHLER, E. G., and SCOTCH, N. A. "Sociocultural Factors in the Epidemiology of Schizophrenia: A Review." *Psychiatry* 26 (1963): 315–51.

MURPHY, H. B. M. "Cultural Factors in the Genesis of Schizophrenia." In *The Transmission of Schizophrenia*, ed. D. Rosenthal and S. S. Kety, pp. 137–55. New York: Pergamon Press, 1968.

POLLIN, W., and STABENAU, J. R. "Biological, Psychological, and Historical Differences in a Series of Monozygotic Twins Discordant for Schizophrenia." In *The Transmission of Schizophrenia*, ed. D. Rosenthal and S. S .Kety, pp. 317–32. New York: Pergamon Press, 1968.

PROUT, C. T., and WHITE, M. A. "The Schizophrenic's Sibling." *Journal of Nervous and Mental Disease* 123 (1956): 162–70.

ROSENTHAL, D. "An Historical and Methodological Review of Genetic Studies of Schizophrenia." In *The Origins of Schizophrenia*, ed. J. Romano, pp. 15–26. New York: Excerpta Medica Foundation, 1967.

———— et al. *The Genain Quadruplets*. New York: Basic Books, 1963.

————; WENDER, P. H.; KETY, S. S.; SCHULSINGER, F.; WELNER, J.; and OSTERGAARD, L. "Schizophrenics' Offspring Reared in Adoptive Homes." In *The Transmission of Schizophrenia*, ed. D. Rosenthal and S. S. Kety, pp. 377–91. New York: Pergamon Press, 1968.

SHIELDS, J. "Summary of the Genetic Evidence." In *The Transmission of Schizophrenia*, ed. D. Rosenthal and S. S. Kety, pp. 95–126. New York: Pergamon Press, 1968.

SLATER, E. "A Review of Earlier Evidence on Genetic Factors in Schizophrenia." In *The Transmission of Schizophrenia*, ed. D. Rosenthal and S. S. Kety, pp. 15–26. New York: Pergamon Press, 1968.

STABENAU, J., and POLLIN, W. "Comparative Life History Differences of Families of Schizophrenics, Delinquents, and 'Normals.' " *American Journal of Psychiatry* 124 (1968): 1526–34.

TIENARI, P. "Schizophrenia in Monozygotic Male Twins." In *The Transmission of Schizophrenia*, ed. D. Rosenthal and S. S. Kety, pp. 27–36. New York: Pergamon Press, 1968.

TURNER, R. J., and WAGENFELD, M. O. "Occupational Mobility and Schizophrenia: An Assessment of the Social Causal and Social Selection Hypotheses." *American Sociological Review* 32 (1967): 104–13.

WEAKLAND, J. H., and FRY, W. F. "Letters of Mothers of Schizophrenics." *American Journal of Orthopsychiatry* 32 (1962): 604–27.

WYNNE, L., and SINGER, M. "Thought Disorder and Family Relations of Schizophrenics: A Research Strategy." *Archives of General Psychiatry* 9 (1963): 191–98.

CHAPTER TEN

Affective Disorders
and Suicide

Affective psychoses are distinguished by extreme disturbances of mood, either elation or deep depression, which dominate mental life to such an extent that subjective feelings, ideas, and attitudes are relatively unaffected by rational considerations or factual data. The euphoric individual continues to express grandiose ideas and to proclaim his supreme happiness even after his uncontrolled expansive behavior has caused him to be hospitalized. The depressed patient is convinced of the seriousness of imaginary or trivial misdeeds and the hopelessness of his future. The pervasiveness of the distorted emotional perspective seriously interferes with the individual's capacity to cope with the ordinary demands of daily life in a reasonably effective and appropriate fashion. Affective psychoses account for approximately 6 percent of first admissions to public mental hospitals in the United States and 15 percent of first admissions to private hospitals. Some countries make more frequent use of this diagnostic category than we do. About 80 percent of patients hospitalized for affective disorders are depressed. The remaining 20 percent are characterized by alternating periods of elation and depression.

The three major types of affective psychoses listed in the 1968 *Diagnostic Manual* of the American Psychiatric Association are manic-depressive psychosis, involutional melancholia, and psychotic depressive reaction. The terms "mania" and "melancholia" have long histories. Both diagnoses were included in the ancient Hippocratic classification of mental disease. When Kraepelin developed his nomenclature system in 1896, he proposed that the diagnoses of manic-depressive psychosis and involutional melancholia be restricted to emotional disturbances without demonstrable brain pathology for which the prognosis was relatively favorable. Other "functional" psychotic reactions, marked mainly by disordered thinking, early onset of symptoms, and poor prognosis, were assigned to the new category of dementia praecox. Kraepelin's original description and differentiation of manic-depressive psychosis and involutional melancholia have been retained in the 1968 APA classification. Depressions that begin after the age of forty-five are classified as involutional melancholia. Agitation, feelings of guilt, and somatic complaints are commonly associated with the depression of involutional melancholia. The diagnosis of manic-depressive psychosis is applied to spontaneously occurring mood disturbances that begin during early adulthood and are marked by either elation and hyperactivity or depression and retardation of mental and motor activity. The concept of psychotic depressive reaction is of more recent origin. This diagnosis is favored when the individual has no prior history of affective disturbances and the depressive mood is attributable to some obvious loss or misfortune.

Manic-Depressive Reactions

The hypothesis that the symptoms of mental disorders represent extreme variations of normal personality traits is particularly applicable to manic-depressive reactions. Many normal individuals have periodic mood swings. For no apparent reason they are sometimes energetic, enthusiastic, optimistic, and highly confident. At other times they go to the opposite extreme and are mildly depressed, discouraged, relatively uncommunicative, self-deprecatory, and listless. When mood swings remain within acceptable limits, these individuals are referred to as cycloid or cyclothymic personalities. A manic attack is an extreme upswing, accompanied by excessive elation, hyperactivity, accelerated speech, and flight of ideas; a depressive attack is an extreme downswing, marked by a pervasive mood of sadness, motor retardation, poverty of ideas, and a slowing of mental activity. Manic attacks generally occur at an earlier age than depressive reactions, and they are usually of shorter duration. Prior to the discovery of effective remedies for relieving symptoms, the average duration of manic attacks was about three months and depressive reactions lasted about six to eight months. With modern drugs, overt manic symptoms can be brought under control in a week and depressive symptoms controlled in ten to fifteen days. Drug therapy is continued for several months. If medication is discontinued too soon there is a return of symptoms. Following the termination of the attack, the individual typically shows no aftereffects and becomes his old self again. Months or years later he may have one or more subsequent attacks. The disorder has been called an intermittent psychosis because of the frequent recurrence and disappearance of symptoms. Initial and later attacks may be either of the manic or depressive type. The frequently noted fact that a person may on one occasion exhibit a manic reaction and later on be depressed is the basis for considering manic-depressive psychosis a single clinical entity. Aretaeus, a famous physician of ancient Rome, is credited with first recognizing the dual nature of the disorder. In 1854 Falret suggested the name "circular madness." Occasionally patients show a mixture of symptoms; the prevailing mood may be one of dejection but the individual is hyperactive and talkative. In older patients, recurring attacks are usually of the depressive variety.

Reactions characterized by alternating manic and depressive phases are referred to as circular or bipolar. Usually there is an intervening normal period between attacks. The term "unipolar" is applied to cases in which recurring attacks are limited to periodic shifts from a normal to a manic state or from a normal to a depressive state. The latter sequence is more common. The frequency of recurring attacks varies considerably from patient to patient. In a follow-up study of 138 carefully selected manic-depressive patients, Rennie (1942) found that 22 percent had no subsequent attacks, 23 percent had two attacks, 25 percent had three attacks, 15 percent had four attacks, and another 15 percent had five or more. The overall figure of two or more attacks in 78 percent of the cases is somewhat higher than that reported in other studies. This finding may be due to the heavy preponderance of initial depressive reactions in the Rennie sample. The probability of recurrence is greater for depressive reactions than for manic reactions. Data reported by Perris (1968) indicate that the number of recurring episodes is significantly higher in bipolar than in unipolar cases. Perris noted no sex differences in the total number of episodes or the relative predominance of manic or depressive attacks. Most studies agree that the initial and subsequent attacks are more often depressive than manic.

INCIDENCE OF MANIC-DEPRESSIVE PSYCHOSIS

In 1933 manic-depressive psychosis was diagnosed in 13 percent of all first admissions to mental hospitals in the United States. By 1968 the figure had dropped to 2 percent. No comparable decline has been noted in other countries. In certain countries, such as England and Italy, the number of hospital first admissions classified as manic-depressive in recent years is about the same as for schizophrenia. There is a possibility that the decline in recorded cases of manic-depressive psychosis in the United States represents an actual decrease in the prevalence of this disorder, but it is more probable that the noted decrease is due to changing diagnostic practices and the trend toward treating manic-depressive patients in the community. Initial attacks may occur at any time between the ages of twenty and sixty. The peak age of first hospital admissions is forty to forty-five. Since many of these patients have histories of earlier mild attacks, the actual peak age of onset may be closer to thirty-five. Women are usually younger than men at the time of initial hospitalization. This represents a reversal of the sex pattern noted for schizophrenia (Landis and Page, 1938). In addition, manic-depressive psychosis is more prevalent in women than in men. About 65 percent of all manic-depressive patients admitted each year to private and public mental hospitals are women. Since men have a greater tendency than women to resort to alcohol when they feel depressed, the reason that the incidence rates for all affective psychoses are lower for men may be that many of them are classified as alcoholics instead. In a study of hospitalized alcoholics, Weingold and his associates (1968) noted that 70 percent of consecutively admitted patients reported mild to deep depression as measured by a standardized self-descriptive depression scale.

MANIC REACTIONS

The prevailing mood of the manic person is one of elation. He is expansive, humorous, optimistic, and carefree. He describes himself as being on top of the world and full of pep. He radiates exuberance and vitality. He reaches out for attention by attempting to be entertaining and friendly, sharing intimate confidences, making jokes, and so on. At times his striving for attention leads to braggadocio, profanity, and indecencies. The fact that he is usually not much disturbed by the discrepancy between his euphoric state and his awareness of being a patient in a mental hospital suggests that he vaguely realizes that his gaiety is a facade, a kind of desperate whistling in the dark. The surface thinness of the euphoria becomes apparent when the patient experiences some real or imagined slight or frustration. Then elation quickly gives way to irritability, arrogance, anger, and rage. The friendly manic may be temporarily transformed into a violent maniac.

The manic patient lives in the immediate present. Passing thoughts and urges are expressed instantly. In the middle of the night he may phone friends or public officials about trivial matters. He may impulsively engage in ruinous business undertakings. His lack of restraint may lead to sexual indiscretions or illegal acts. He is too busy rushing off in all directions to take time to eat and too excited to sleep. Loss of weight is common. The physical exhaustion of the manic, his impulsive actions, and his belligerent behavior when he is thwarted are largely responsible for his being referred for treatment. Hospitalization is a protective measure.

The manic's manner of speaking reflects his excited, pressured state. His speech is accelerated, and he shifts rapidly and unpredictably from one topic to another. It is possible to understand what he is saying, however, and to follow his erratic train of thought. In this respect the speech of the manic differs from the bizarre, idiosyncratic speech of the schizophrenic. When asked a question, the manic starts to give an appropriate answer, but his distractability soon leads to detours away from the original topic. Sentences are rarely completed. In the middle of a sentence he may go off on another thought, respond to some incidental external stimulus, play with the sound of words (puns, rhymes), or get lost in rambling details. The flight of ideas is suggestive of a camouflage or unconscious ruse designed to direct his own attention away from sensitive areas. The excited manic is apt to report perceptual errors that usually are more accurately described as illusions than as hallucinations. Impairment of attention and concentration may interfere with memory. Judgment is defective.

Depending on the relative intensity of symptoms, distinctions are made among hypomania, acute mania, and delirious mania. Patients may progress from one stage to the next or remain in a state of mild excitement. *Hypomania* is characterized by moderate elation, increased psychomotor activity, faulty judgment, and impulsiveness. Lack of restraint may lead to spending sprees, promiscuity, and annoying boisterous behavior. The circumstantial speech, impaired thinking, critical attitude, and superficial exalted ideas typical of hypomania can be seen in the following interview:

> *How are you today?*
> Oh, I'm superperfect. The state's only wasting their money keeping me here. How about a steak dinner tonight with peppermint ice cream? The service here is too slow. Why, there isn't a good nurse here. I could work circles around them.
> *Are you a nurse?*
> Well, I don't have my R.N. yet, but I have all of my requirements. You see, I'm too clever for you. Say, who's that nice young doctor you have here? Boy, I could go for him. I think I'll marry a doctor, a rich psychiatrist, and then open up four or five private hospitals so I could retire at thirty. I work fast. I could be the scrub nurse in the operating room and the superintendent of the joint. I want to be the big shot. My sister is a very brilliant girl. Her estimate is about ninety-five percent. She's a senior in college. She admires medical men, any man with a brain. My mother's father was a doctor, a horse doctor, so you see it all traces back.
> *Would you tell me something about yourself?*
> Have I got to dig that up again? I hope, I hope, I hope. Do I like men? Do I enjoy going to parties? I don't believe in falling for a guy. I think I'm better than any guy, anyway. I don't think much of myself, do I? I'm very conceited and very fussy and I don't eat things unless they're in courses, either.
> *What led to your being brought to the hospital?*

I'm trying to tell you. I went to interview Mrs. Johnson for a job. I was working at Dr. Smith's house just to get acquainted with things and get a line-up of positions. I thought I might work into a clue even though I'm not a graduate. So anyway, I got a job through a telephone call. She never saw me or anything. Her husband was a nice-looking guy. He had had some money but he lost it through drinking. I only drink to be sociable. Mrs. Johnson liked my appearance and personality and she said I would do, as I looked neat. I don't care if I go out with a medical man or a factory man. I can still adjust myself to the environment. She liked me so well she invited me to accept a date with her son, who is a licensed engineer. They have a beautiful house; you should see it. She got married a second time, to a Greek. She asked me to come down and take her daughter out horseback riding, because I go in for all kinds of sports. I have a regular outfit I wear. Of course, I said I would, but I was so busy I didn't get a chance to. I haven't a license but I do drive. I only know four policemen in town and if I got caught I probably would be in a jail instead of in this jail, but they couldn't catch me because I'm awfully smart.

How did you happen to come here?

I'm coming to that. I went over to the house to be interviewed for a job. I just walked in and observed the joint to see if I thought I'd like it. I saw a big fat bug last night. She took all my references and all that stuff. She almost took my prenatal record. I started to work and worked from one to six without stopping. She has a lot to learn. I left there that night and started out to see my friend. He's a six-footer. We make a nice couple. Last year we won a dance contest.

In *acute mania* behavior is less controlled. The following speech sample illustrates the extreme distractability, disorganized association of ideas, and increased inner pressure. The unchecked word deluge was released when the examiner asked the patient, "Why are you in this hospital?" The content is partly relevant. The patient was divorced and her former husband had recently remarried. She had two sons. A secretary was present to record the interview.

I came here to see the light. I want you to see with your eyes what you saw at night, by the light in the white night. How could you be a child and go into the wild? Kind sir, why are you so kind? Why did you drive a car to Buffalo on Route Twenty? You are twenty years old. Tell me, why did you send that card through the mail? Why do you look up? Why do gentlemen prefer blondes? Do you love your wife? You're beginning to get a little bald. You know babies are born without hair. Do you know why Leo the lion, l-i-o-n, was lionhearted? Do you have a heart? Do you know what you're doing? Doctor, listen, doctor, doctor, doctor, d-o-c-t-o-r. Don't make mothers go suffering on. Don't go near the fireplace over there. Listen. You heard it in West Bloomfield. You saw the bloom in the fields. Why was the light blooming in the fields at night? You have got to have tools to work.

Don't we need fish once in a while? Why do you write ABCs on the black-board? You can see white and black. Say, listen, listen, listen, l-i-s-t-e-n, I can see your tiepin. It isn't right. Listen, pins, pins, pins, p-i-n-s. Look at that girl write down.

A car just went by. There is a calendar. Time, time, time, t-i-m-e, give you all you want. Do you see the saw? Do you hear the buzz? The busy bee, the ABC. Say, listen, don't go away. I put Margie where she belonged. It was just like your hand. Is your hand still working? I was sitting' on that chair. Why did you just write the alphabet, daddy, because you are going to become a daddy and daddy knew that if he kept cleaning and cleaning and working and who was Jack? There are so many kinds of jack. Jack and the beanstalk, jack in your pants, jackpot, Jack and Jill. Daddy was kind to us, he was kind, he was kind. Weren't you kind? Weren't you good? You were working awfully hard. You understand you must look at a map. There was a girl and she was a bad girl and she had a bad map and this is what she did to me. She made me say something I wouldn't say and that's why I was still in school. Did you know they had stills in school? Just listen to the ABCs. Oh, the most beautiful thing, roses in bloom, roses in bloom. Is your name Rosenbloom?

I'll tell you a story and this is going to be a short-short story and that's just fiction. You must listen. They don't want you to get up until the sun gets up. What time do my sons get up? What time does my one son get up? What time do my two sons get up? What time do my three sons get up? Doctor, tell me when does the sun get up? I wish you were a nurse. I can see the sun coming through there. I tried to see a little better in the light because I don't want to go through those ABCs the hard way. I want to see it over for you and I want a new husband. People all over the whole universe do not understand the situation, and they don't want mothers all over the world to go on twisting that ring on their finger. Please listen carefully. You have to hear more than that, doctor. Why did you send on Christmas Day of all days in that old calendar? Why must you sit down and write? Why did you have to write so beautifully? Why didn't you do it, but why did you send it and when I said that you didn't, you said to me, "I am sending you a line, just a line to let you know that we are married."

No, this was the way it had to be. You understand why the school is set just a little back off the road. Do you understand why you have those children, my two boys? I don't see quite far enough and I started to look up but you see, there is a cage up there. You will see a cage now. Don't you see how wrong you are? Don't you see how you done, Mr. and Mrs., and used her name? Don't we need a plane? There is a drawer in there under that desk. Who is that woman just sitting there? Does she have a name? And is she on my plane?

Delirious mania is marked by a complete loss of control. The patient is wildly excited, disoriented, incoherent, and violent. Hallucinations and delusions are usually present. Sedation or physical restraint is required to avoid exhaustion and to prevent the patient from harming himself or others.

DEPRESSIVE REACTIONS

The core syndrome of the depressive phase of manic-depressive psychosis consists of (1) feelings of sadness, helplessness, despair, and hopelessness; (2) low self-esteem, pessimism, guilt feelings, and self-blame; and (3) behavior changes marked by disinterest, apathy, psychomotor retardation, and reduced mental activity. Concomitant physical symptoms include chronic fatigue, restless sleep, anorexia, weight loss, dry mouth, constipation, and reduced sex drive. Other common symptoms, which reflect individual personality variables, include anxiety, agitation, irritability, obsessive-compulsive tendencies, rigidity, immobility, demands for attention and love, impaired concentration, hypochondriacal complaints, and psychosomatic ailments. A large number of rating scales have been developed for obtaining quantitative measures of the intensity and frequency of depressive symptoms. Some of the scales (Hamilton, 1960; Cutler and Kurland, 1961) call for observer rating of depressed mood, guilt, suicidal tendencies, somatic symptoms, and so on. Others consist of similar items prepared in the form of a self-report questionnaire that is filled out by the patient. Self-rating scales have been devised by Zung (1965), Beck (1967), and Pilowsky and his associates (1969). The scales have been found to give highly consistent scores, and therefore are considered to have good reliability. However, there is considerable overlap in scores attained by depressed patients and patients assigned other diagnostic labels.

Factor analytic studies conducted by Grinker et al. (1961), Wittenborn (1962), Friedman et al. (1963), and Lorr et al. (1967) have identified five reaction patterns:

1. Depressive mood: dejection, despair, suicidal ideas, loss of interest in people and in usual activities.
2. Anxious self-blame: high anxiety level, self-castigation.
3. Retardation: slowing of action, thought, and speech.
4. Impaired functioning: loss of energy and drive; difficulty in making decisions; inability to get started, to concentrate, and to work.
5. Somatic symptoms: lack of appetitite, weight loss, disinterest in sexual activity, gastrointestinal symptoms.

These feelings, attitudes, and behavior changes are obviously not restricted to psychotic depressions. Normal individuals in mourning and depressed neurotics exhibit essentially similar reactions. The similarities in feelings and behavior of depressed normal, neurotic, and psychotic individuals illustrate again the artificiality of traditional psychiatric categories based on the medical model of separate and distinct disorders.

The Continuum Concept of Depressive Reactions

Normal, neurotic, and psychotic persons are all subject to periodic depressions. When they are depressed, persons in all three groups exhibit similar reactions. Differences consist largely of (1) the relative severity and duration of depressive behavior, (2) the relative appropriateness of the mood change to its known precipitating cause, (3) the degree of voluntary control of feelings and actions, and (4) the extent to which the depressive state interferes with general functioning. The continuity concept does not rule out differences in the etiology of normal, neurotic, and psychotic depressions. The greater severity and bizarreness of symptoms manifested by the psychotic (delusional ideas, preoccupation with suicide, strange somatic complaints, and gross impairment in functioning) suggest that his inherent adaptive resources are less effective than those of the normal or neurotic person. Family and twin studies indicate that genetic determinants are relatively more important in psychotic than in nonpsychotic depressive reactions.

NORMAL DEPRESSION

Many individuals, described as normal cyclothymes, are subject to periodic mood swings. Mild periods of depression, which may alternate with periods of increased energy and optimism, occur more or less spontaneously. During "letdown" periods, which may last for several days, the individual continues with his usual activities. His pace is slowed but his performance level is unaffected. He may be described by associates as unusually quiet, reserved, or moody. A more typical example of normal depression is the transient state of despondency and lethargy following some significant disappointment or misfortune. A period of mourning is an expected and normal reaction to the loss of a loved one.

Depressive reactions associated with bereavement may be as intense and prolonged as in neurotic and psychotic depressions. A person undergoing a normal depressive reaction retains considerable control of his feelings and actions. When the situation demands it, he can temporarily dry his tears and set aside his heavy burden of sorrow and despair so that his general behavior and functioning remain reasonably effective and appropriate. The expression of grief is largely personal and private. Interest in the outside world may be reduced, but the individual is aware of and responsive to his social environment. Guilt feelings and loss of self-esteem are minimal. The individual may be extremely unhappy and at times quite irritable, but he is not a threat to himself or a source of intolerable concern or annoyance to others. Relatives and friends understand and respect the sorrow of a person in mourning. Actually they would be more disturbed, and quite properly so, if he showed no grief following the death of a child or a spouse. The question of psychotherapy seldom arises. It is recognized that a person who has suffered a major loss needs and should be given time to work through his bereavement at his own pace. Acute grief reactions usually subside within a month or two, but ordinarily a period of a year or more is required to complete the mourning process in full.

Lindeman (1944) and Parkes (1965) have examined the relation of normal grief reactions to psychiatrically recognized depressive disorders. Both investigators concluded that despite the close similarity in symptoms, the two conditions are independent. A formal diagnosis of mental disorder was considered valid for very few bereaved persons seen in treatment. This finding casts doubt on the importance often attached to the death of a close member of the family as *the* cause for mental disorder.

Shakespeare has provided an insightful description of the depressive mood, self-devaluation, and envious thoughts often experienced by normal individuals when everything seems to be going wrong. He has also included an antidote or balancing factor. His well-known twenty-ninth sonnet is preceded by the lines: "But day doth daily draw my sorrows longer, and night doth nightly make grief's strength seem stronger."

> When, in disgrace with fortune and men's eyes,
> I all alone beweep my outcast state,
> And trouble deaf heaven with my bootless cries,
> And look upon myself, and curse my fate,
> Wishing me like to one more rich in hope,
> Featured like him, like him with friends possesst,
> Desiring this man's art, and that man's scope,
> With what I most enjoy contented least;
> Yet in these thoughts myself almost despising,
> Haply I think on thee,—and then my state,
> Like to the lark at break of day arising
> From sullen earth, sings hymns at heaven's gate;
> > For thy sweet love remember'd such wealth brings,
> > That then I scorn to change my state with kings.

NEUROTIC DEPRESSION

The onset of neurotic depressive symptoms is usually precipitated by some significant event. The neurotic has less control over his feelings and actions than the normal individual, but with effort he is capable of coping with his usual responsibilities. He lacks the fortitude and self-sufficiency of the depressed normal individual. He is more inclined to feel sorry for himself and to complain of his painful dejection, his loss of capacity for pleasure, his chronic fatigue and poor health. He is more demanding of love and attention and has a greater need for outside help. There is usually some impairment in work efficiency and productivity. Unlike the psychotic, the neurotic is free of delusions and does not make bizarre interpretations of his condition. He realizes that his depressive symptoms are part of his neurosis and that they will subside when he recovers. Hope is not lost; he tries to fight his depression. He looks forward to the time when he will be his normal self again. The neurotic may experience guilt, but he does not torture himself with remorse over imaginary misdeeds. He is not so likely to commit suicide as the depressed psychotic.

PSYCHOTIC DEPRESSION

When the psychotic person first experiences symptoms of depression, he typically does not know why he is depressed. If pressed for an explanation, he or his family can usually recall some adverse experience that he suffered in the recent or distant past, but the relevance of the offered explanation is often questionable. Financial worries and marital difficulties, which are frequently blamed, are fairly common human problems, and even genuinely traumatic experiences seldom wait for years to produce symptoms. Significantly, the depression is unrelated to external changes. The patient may attribute his despondency to the illness of some member of the family or to the loss of employment, but his symptoms continue unabated long after the relative makes a complete recovery or he is offered a good position. The patient may have had several previous attacks from which he recovered in a few months, but he is convinced that this time his condition is hopeless and incurable. The psychotic accepts his depression as an integral part of his being. He lives his depression. Feelings and behavior are controlled by delusions that cannot be altered by appeals to reason. Despite factual evidence to the contrary, he clings to sincerely held beliefs that he is guilty of unnameable sins, that he has ruined his family and violated the trust others placed in him, and that the world would be better off if he were dead.

In attempting to account for the loss of appetite and energy and the general sluggishness of bodily processes that are often associated with depressive feelings, the psychotic may introduce bizarre details: his blood has turned to water, his bones have decayed, his internal organs have disintegrated. His pervasive pessimistic outlook and morbid self-blame may make suicide an attractive solution. The profound inhibition of thought and action may lead to gross impairment in functioning, muteness, and immobility. The reduced mental productivity that is characteristic of psychotic depressions mainly reflects the patient's state of mind. The individual feels too exhausted, too incompetent, and too apathetic to do much of anything. If he is asked to perform some task, he may complain that he is too tired or that the task is beyond his capacity. There is usually no actual loss of mental abilities, however. When the patient's protests are casually ignored and the examiner treats him as if he were competent, most depressed patients show slight, if any, impairment in cognitive, perceptual, or psychomotor tests (Friedman, 1964).

Suicidal tendencies. The depressed psychotic places family and therapist in a difficult bind. If they are attentive to his complaints and respond sympathetically to his obvious suffering, they unwittingly reinforce "sick" behavior. If they refuse to listen to his endless woes or are critical of his behavior, he may be driven to develop symptoms so severe that his audience cannot ignore them. Suicidal thoughts afford a striking example of this dilemma. About 75 to 80 percent of depressed psychotic patients express suicidal ideas, 15 to 25 percent make actual attempts at suicide, and an estimated 5 percent eventually succed. The threat is too real to be ignored. The more concern and alarm the family shows in response to talk of suicide, the more the patient dwells on the subject, since it is guaranteed to elicit attention. If in desperation the family arranges for the compulsory hospitalization of the depressed person as a safety measure, he may interpret their action as proof of rejection or abandonment, and thus as justification for putting an end to his miserable, lonely existence. If comments about "ending it all" and "being better off dead" are not taken seriously, the depressed psychotic may feel compelled to try to kill himself to prove he was not simply seeking attention and sympathy. The depressed psychotic's preoccupation with suicide is genuine. He sincerely believes in the hopelessness of his condition. Life has no meaning or purpose for him. His present anguish is intolerable, the future is nonexistent or bleak, and the past is a painful reminder of his guilt, his unworthiness, and his failures (Arieti, 1959). A few patients carefully conceal their suicidal intent from their families so that they will not interfere. During the acute phase these patients may lack the energy to carry out their plans. Suicide frequently occurs when the patient appears to be on the road to recovery and family or hospital vigilence is relaxed. Usually the depressed patient takes only his own life, but occasionally a distraught father, worried about the fate of his wife and children after he is no longer there to look after them, will kill them too. Young depressed mothers may kill their children before killing themselves, but they are not so likely as men to consider their spouses incapable of getting along without them.

Types of psychotic depression. Two main approaches have been utilized in attempts to separate psychotic depressives into homogeneous subgroups. One is based on the relative predominance of certain symptom clusters as determined by clinical observations and factor analytic studies. The three principal syndromes thus delineated are (1) depressive mood with mental and psychomotor retardation; (2) depressive mood with agitation, guilt, and self-blame; and (3) depressive mood with self-pity, hypochondriacal complaints, and psychosomatic symptoms.

The second approach, which is favored in traditional diagnosis, is based on the relative severity of symptoms. The three levels generally recognized are simple depression, acute depression, and depressive stupor.

Simple depression consists of relatively mild reactions with no clear-cut delusions. A characteristic feature is a marked loss of feelings, interests, and drive. Inhibition or retardation of thought and action is common. The individual wakes up early and dull from a restless sleep. Ahead lies another gloomy, hopeless day. The mere thought of getting out of bed and dressing is exhausting. With effort he can care for his basic needs, but every movement is painfully slow. If someone asks him a question, he pauses for a long time before making a brief reply in a low, tired voice. Communication is clear, however, and he constructs his sentences in his usual fashion. Feelings and responses are inappropriate to the reality of the situation but consistent with the depressed mood. The occurrence of suicidal ideas is usually the main reason for hospitalization. The following excerpt from an interview with a middle-aged female patient illustrates many of the salient traits of simple depression (Page, 1947).

> *Have you been in a mental hospital before?*
> Yes.
> *How many times?*
> Twice.
> *How are you feeling now?*
> Well, sort of sad and low in spirits.
> *Can you compare your present feelings with how you feel when you are well?*
> When I was well, I woke up in the morning and was eager to get up and do my work. Now I find it very hard to do anything.
> *How do you feel when you awake in the morning?*
> Well, I want to stay in bed and have to force myself to get up and dress.
> *How do you feel after you are up and dressed?*
> Why, I just want to stay in one place and do nothing.
> *Do you sleep well?*
> Yes. It sometimes takes a little time to get to sleep, that's all.
> *Do you have a good appetite?*
> No, I'm not very interested in eating.
> *Why is that?*
> Well, the food has no taste, for one thing.
> *What ideas run through your head now?*

I just feel as if I didn't care about going on.
What do you mean?
Oh, I'd be better off dead.
Would you tell me more about that?
Oh, I never tried to do anything. I merely thought of it as an escape.
Escape from what?
I don't know. Just from myself, from the despondency.
What makes you despondent?
I don't know.
Did anything happen to upset you?
No.
Do you have many worries?
Oh, I worry some about myself, just trivial things.
What do you mean?
Oh, just about my appearance.
Is this a recent worry?
No, I've always worried about that.
What do you do all day?
Not very much.
Do you read?
No, I look at the headlines sometimes.
Did you read when you were at home?
Yes, I belong to the Book-of-the-Month.
Why don't you read here?
I try to, but I can't get interested in what I read.
Do you think you are as mentally alert as when you were well?
No. I can't retain what I read and I find it difficult to discuss anything with
other people.
Can you explain that a little more?
The words don't come as easily as they did before.
Anything else?
I don't grasp things like I did before.
Do you enjoy listening to music?
I used to.
And now?
I have no feeling for it.
Is your husband responsible for your being here?
No, I suggested that he bring me here.
Why?
I was despondent and felt I needed some protection.
Do you think you would have harmed yourself if you had stayed home?
I really don't know.
Do you want to get well?
Why, certainly!
How does the future look to you now?
Not very bright.

Acute depression may progress from simple depression, or the transition from normal behavior may be direct and abrupt. The chief characteristic is the presence of obvious psychotic features. The patient is completely absorped with his symptoms. Impairment of functioning is pronounced. Symptoms associated with simple depression may occur in more intense form. In addition, the patient may express deluded ideas of having inflicted ruin and disgrace on his family. Death is sought as a punishment for his misdeeds. There is a marked loss of appetite resulting in a considerable weight loss. Constipation is common. The patient may refuse food on the ground that he is not entitled to it or that his stomach has atrophied.

Depressive stupor is characterized by a massive paralysis of thought and action. The patient may be aware of what is going on about him but he does not respond to questions and is more or less immobilized. Severe cases may be confined to bed and may require spoon feeding.

Other Diagnoses of Severe Depressive Reactions

As we noted earlier, the 1968 APA classification lists involutional melancholia and psychotic depressive reaction as separate disorders, both of which are considered distinct from the depressive phase of manic-depressive psychosis. The seeming decline of manic-depressive psychosis in the United States is due in part to increasing use of the diagnoses of psychotic depressive reaction and involutional melancholia. Each accounts for a larger number of first admissions to mental hospitals than the category of manic-depressive psychosis. The principal designated feature that sets *involutional melancholia* apart from other depressions is the fact that the symptoms first occur during the climacteric period (ages forty-five to sixty-five), when significant biochemical and psychosocial changes typically take place in human beings. The menopause in women was once considered an important contributory factor. Other assumed identifying characteristics include a prepsychotic personality marked by rigidity, compulsive behavior, agitation, delusional ideas, feelings of guilt, severe insomnia, and somatic symptoms.

Psychotic depressive reaction, unlike the depressive phase of manic-depressive psychosis, is considered to be directly related to some significant loss or misfortune. By definition, then, the diagnosis of psychotic depressive reaction is applied only to persons who have no history of earlier depressions or of marked cyclothymic mood swings. If a subsequent attack occurs, the original diagnosis is changed to manic-depressive psychosis. Genetic factors are thought to be less pronounced in psychotic depressive reactions.

The validity of the assumption that involutional melancholia and psychotic depressive reaction constitute distinctive clinical entities has long been questioned by qualified experts. The symptom pattern, course, treatment, and prognosis of each of these disorders do not differ significantly from those of the depressive phase of manic-depressive psychosis. The latter, is turn, differs from depressive reactions noted in neurotic and normal persons mainly in severity of dysfunction. The criteria cited in defense of the use of separate diagnoses are artificial and arbitrary. Variations in age of onset, frequency of episodes, and type of personality before the occurrence of symptoms are more reasonably interpreted as manifestations of incidental individual differences than as diagnostic signs of separate disorders.

The relevance of the precipitating cause is a highly subjective matter. What others may regard as an insignificant event (the death of a pet, the loss of a job) may have critical symbolic significance to the patient. From my own point of view, too much emphasis has been placed on the importance of some loss as the key to depressive behavior. The explanation is too simple and too pat. If disappointments, failures, and the deaths of loved ones were the direct and only causes of psychotic depression, practically everyone would have recurring attacks. Depressive reactions, like other so-called mental disorders, are the end products of multiple interacting psychobiosocial factors. They represent characteristic ways in which certain types of individuals (mainly extraverted, cyclothymic, and compulsive personalities) usually respond when the cumulative stresses of life exceed innate and acquired adaptive resources. In order to justify the "loss" interpretation, it is frequently necessary to assume that a depression represents a delayed reaction to some disturbing event that occurred years ago. The "loss" explanation requires considerable twisting to account for the common observation that the onset of depression may follow a promotion, the birth of a wanted baby, or some outstanding success. The temporal sequence is less paradoxical when viewed from the broader perspective of the total life history of the individual. The final attainment of some objective that a person has been pursuing for most of his life may be a crushing disappointment if it falls short of his unrealistic aspirations or if it fails to offset the accumulated failures, mistakes, and deprivations of the past. Under such circumstances life may indeed appear hopeless.

Winokur and Clayton (1966) and Hopkinson and Ley (1969) have proposed a division of all affective disorders into two types. Distinguishing criteria are based on genetic and clinical differences noted in family histories. One type, which resembles manic-depressive psychosis of the bipolar variety, is characterized by early age of onset (twenty to forty), a tendency to recurrence, and a relatively high incidence of affective disorders among other members of the family. Attacks are often of the manic type. The second type usually occurs in families in which the incidence of affective disorders among first- and second-degree relatives is comparatively low. This second type has a late age of onset and is less likely to recur or to manifest itself in manic symptoms. Clinical impressions derived from other sources suggest that the first type is more often associated with a cyclothymic prepsychotic temperament, whereas compulsive features are more prevalent in the second type. More research is needed to confirm preliminary findings and to rule out the possibility that the noted differences between the two types are not artificial by-products of the inclusion of depressed, brain-damaged elderly persons in the late-onset group.

Etiological Factors in Affective Disorders

The occurrence of reaction patterns traditionally associated with affective disorders is an established fact. Whether the clinical syndromes represent one or more separate mental disorders and whether they are sharply differentiated from normal behavior are controversial issues. The meanings assigned to the labels of manic-depressive psychosis and involutional melancholia have important etiological implications. Acceptance of the concept of separate disorders includes a commitment to the premise that all persons diagnosed as suffering from one or another of these disorders are distinguished by certain pathogenic agents that are absent in normal individuals and in patients suffering from other disorders. If the diagnostic terms are interpreted as convenient labels that simply describe extreme variations in certain kinds of human behavior, the futile search for unique determinants is avoided. All that is necessary is to account for the greater than normal variation in mood, psychomotor activity level, and related reactions. This unfortunately is easier said than done.

The greater than usual variations in mood and behavior associated with affective psychosis are probably due to a combination of factors. From a genetic point of view, there is a good probability that manic depressive patients are distinguished by a greater instability of the biological mechanisms that regulate emotions and activity level. Under favorable conditions, this genetic predisposition is phenotypically expressed in mild mood swings and increased activity. Normal persons exhibiting these traits are often described as extraverts or cyclothymes. Some individuals who are genetically predisposed to mood swings impose rigid controls on their emotions. A more stable mood is thus achieved at the cost of compulsive defenses and inhibition of feelings. The risk of marked mood swings, and especially of severe depressive reactions, is increased when genetically predisposed individuals are taught at an early age to place great value on conformity or achievement. In order to earn the love of his parents, especially of his mother, during his formative years, the child must conform to her conventional standards of proper behavior and success. In later years, other authority figures and the impersonal "they" are substituted for the mother. The individual remains other-directed and dependent on external approval. Failure to live up to idealized and often unrealistic standards leads to periodic discouragement. The individual's acceptance of social values and his dependence on the goodwill and support of others preclude his blaming others too openly for his failures and shortcomings. His high aspirations, strong social needs, and basic temperament rule out schizophrenic resignation from human society. The remaining alternative is self-blame and oppressive gloom or a massive defense expressed in pseudoelation, expansiveness, and frenzied hyperactivity.

The onset of despair or compensatory overoptimism is usually delayed until adulthood, when the individual is confronted with the responsiblity of converting aspirations into realities and encounters disappointment. The pain of failure is aggravated by the fact that it is unexpected—and from his point of view undeserved. During childhood and early adolescence, his life experiences reinforce his favorable self-image. Parents and teachers are impressed by his high energy level, his buoyant spirits, his emotional expressiveness and sociability. His willingness to do what is expected of him leads to praise. He shows promise. The same qualities promote a surface popularity with his peers. As children, persons who later develop affective disorders appear to be well adjusted. They are rarely referred to child guidance clinics or juvenile courts. As adults they typically have good occupational records and are respected members of their communities. Having done all the "right" things, they feel entitled to appropriate rewards. The shattering threat of failure and loss of self-esteem, combined with their innate tendency toward lack of emotional control, leads to pervasive despair.

When such a person is young and still retains hope and vigor, he may put on a brave front. Mainly for his own benefit he attempts to conceal his desperate plight by erecting a facade of confidence and optimism. He is elated, boastful, and full of plans that must be executed immediately. The older person temporarily gives up the struggle and attempts to enlist the sympathy of others by making known his dejection and self-devaluation. The misfortunes and misdeeds he proclaims may be factual or imaginary. It doesn't really matter, since they are red herrings that he unconsciously drags across the path to divert attention from his real failure—the failure to live up to his personal expectations. This explains the inappropriateness of his reactions to his reported misfortunes and sins, and the fact that he makes no effort to remedy past misdeeds. His guilt and self-blame are genuine, but his denial of the real reasons and his exploitation of convenient substitutes make observers question his sincerity and regard his reported feelings and ideas as delusions.

THE IMPORTANCE OF HEREDITY

The significant role of genetic factors in severe mood disturbances has been repeatedly confirmed in family and twin studies of manic-depressive patients. Some studies have combined manic-depressive with other affective disorders. Rosenthal's (1970) comprehensive review of the extensive international literature on the subject indicates that the incidence of manic-depressive psychosis in the general population can be placed at approximately 0.7 percent. This chance morbidity risk represents the median figure of the incidence rates found in ten separate studies in various countries. Comparable expectancy rates for twins and relatives of manic-depressive patients (index cases) are shown in Table 10.1. These figures clearly indicate that manic-depressive and affective reactions occur much more frequently among first-degree relatives of index cases than among the general population. In general, the relative risk is directly related to closeness of genetic ties. If a monozygotic twin develops an affective disorder, the chance that his twin will develop a similar disorder (the concordance rate) is an impressive 70 percent. The concordance rate drops to 20 percent for dizygotic pairs. The risk of similar disorders in parents, siblings, and children of manic-depressives is more than ten times greater than for the general population. The expectancy rate found for siblings in some studies is as high as that noted for DZ twins in other studies. Most investigators have reported lower rates for siblings, however. In this respect the genetic data for manic-depressive psychosis differ from those for schizophrenia. The higher expectancy rates for DZ co-twins of manic-depressives than for their siblings suggest that environmental factors may be relatively more impor-

Table 10.1. Expectancy rates for affective disorders among relatives of index cases diagnosed as manic-depressives or affective psychotics

Kinship	Number of studies	Median expectancy rate	Percentage range
MZ twins	6	70%	50–93%
DZ twins	6	20	0–38
Parents	10	8	3–23
Siblings	9	9	3–23
Children	6	11	6–24
Uncles and aunts	2	3	1–4
Grandchildren	2	3	2–3

tant in the development of manic-depressive psychosis than of schizophrenia. Studies reviewed by Mendels (1970) indicate that siblings of index cases have a greater probability of developing manic-depressive psychoses if their early childhood environments are unfavorable. For more distant relatives—aunts, uncles, and grandchildren—the risk of developing affective disorders is about 3 percent. This figure, like all the others that have been cited, represents the median finding of several studies. The marked differences in rates reported in various studies (range figures in Table 10.1) are partly due to incidental factors. In a few of the twin studies, the number of cases was too small to permit us to consider the findings valid. Some investigators corrected for age in calculating expectancy rates for siblings and children; others did not. Some studies were more carefully controlled than others with respect to the selection of "pure" manic-depressive index cases, the diagnostic criteria applied to relatives, the elimination of doubtful cases, and so on.

Manic-depressive psychosis and schizophrenia. The available data, which are based on few cases, indicate that about a third of the children resulting from the mating of two manic-depressives develop the parental disorder. When one parent is a manic-depressive and the other is a schizophrenic, about a third of the children are psychotic. A slightly larger proportion are manic-depressive than schizophrenic. The relationship of manic-depressive psychosis to schizophrenia is complicated by the possible presence of both genotype defects in the same family. Most investigators have reported a few isolated cases of schizophrenia among the children, parents, and siblings of manic-depressive index cases. Rosenthal agrees with the majority opinion that manic-depressive psychosis and schizophrenia are genetically distinct and separate disorders. This conclusion leaves dangling the concept of schizo-affective psychosis. Although findings are inconsistent, there is some evidence that the genetic loading is greater in bipolar than in unipolar forms of manic-depressive reactions and more marked in manic-depressive psychosis than in involutional melancholia. Winokur and Clayton (1967) have suggested that the higher noted incidence of affective disorders in females may be due to modifying genes in the sex chromosomes. In their family studies they noted that when a mother had a history of an affective disorder, similar disorders were markedly more frequent in her daughters than in her sons. Affected fathers have an equal number of affected sons and daughters. The morbidity risk for sisters of female index cases is considerably greater than for brothers. Winokur and Clayton investigated but failed to confirm the hypothesis that the lower rate of affective disorders in males was due to a tendency to diagnose them as alcoholics.

Biological factors. The specific nature of the genetic component in manic-depressive psychosis is unknown. Biochemical changes involving the metabolism of norepinephrine, serotonin, sodium, and potassium have often been noted in mood-disordered patients. These findings are inconclusive, however, since it is difficult to decide whether the observed changes are the cause or the result of the emotional disturbance (Mendels, 1970). Electroencephalographic studies indicate that manic and depressed patients show no consistent abnormalities in the resting alpha rhythm. Kraines (1966) has advanced the theory that the manic-depressive syndrome is related to disturbances in hypothalamic functioning. This theory ties in neatly with the fact that the hypothalamus regulates mood, appetite, sleep, sexual activity, and drive. Manic reactions are presumed to be due to periodic hyperactivity of the hypothalamus, which leads to overresponsiveness of the emotional circuit, increase in energy level, and related changes. Depressive reactions are attributed to inhibition of hypothalamic function, which in turn limits sympathetic outflow and results in a general reduction of emotional responsiveness, drive, and activity. The hypothesis merits further research, but at present is highly speculative.

PSYCHOANALYTIC THEORY

Psychoanalysts view the "manic depressive character" as a particular style of relating to others and reacting to anxiety-arousing situations. They attribute the development of this behavioral pattern to the interaction of innate constitutional factors and certain parental ways of child rearing. The following account is a summary of observations and inferences made by Cohen et al. (1954) on the basis of their intensive study of a small group of manic-depressive patients.

Persons prone to manic-depressive psychosis are usually brought up in families that are set apart from the surrounding social environment. The isolation of the family may be due to membership in a minority group, recent loss of status due to reduced income, higher status than other families in the neighborhood enjoy, a broken home, or anything else that separates it socially from its neighbors. The family is distressed by this social difference, and an all-out attempt is made, particularly by the mother, to improve the family's acceptability in the community by fitting in with "what the neighbors think." In this attempt the children are used as instruments. They are inculcated with a strict and conventional concept of good behavior, and are taught that they have a family obligation to get good grades in school, to win prizes, and through their achievements to be considered by the community as credits to their parents. The child who later becomes a manic-depressive is often the one selected as the chief bearer of the burden of gaining acceptance for the family. The chosen one is usually the brightest, the best-looking, the most gifted, or in some other way outstanding.

The driving force behind the striving of the family is usually the mother. The child recognizes her as the authority in the family. She is feared and regarded as cold and unloving. At the same time, since she is the source of all rewards, her approval is desired and sought. The child sees the father as weak and unreliable, but lovable. The contemptuous attitude of the mother toward the father serves as an example to the child of what might happen to him if he should fail to achieve the goals she sets.

But this driving woman was not always cold and unloving, it seems. She was tender and affectionate while the child was a helpless, dependent baby. His early infancy was normal, and he developed an awareness of himself as a distinct person. (In this respect the prospective manic-depressive differs from the schizophrenic, who has a sketchy, blurred self-image.) By the end of the first year, however, the mother of the child destined to be a manic-depressive starts to take firm measures to check his growing independence and rebelliousness. Strong pressure is put on him to conform to her wishes and to abstain from "bad" behavior. The abrupt shift from a loving, all-gratifying mother to a tyrannical, punitive authority figure lays the groundwork for the manic-depressive's later ambivalent attitude toward authority figures.

The child's acceptance of the task of winning social acceptance for the family makes him feel responsible for whatever hardships or failures the family experiences. This feeling of responsibility and blame is carried over to his own family when he marries. As adults, persons susceptible to manic-depressive psychosis are conscientious, conventionally well behaved, hard-working, and often successful. They are outgoing and friendly, but their interpersonal relations lack depth. The cyclothyme's good humor, liveliness, and social facility gain him a wide circle of acquaintances but few intimate friends. In exchange for being pleasant, entertaining, and ingratiating, he expects that others will gratify his needs for love, attention, and success. The concept of reciprocity is missing. The person with a manic-depressive character structure has little to give. He is insensitive to the needs and feelings of others. His style is to establish dependent relationships with strong authority figures and thereby become the recipient of their assistance. Yet success and promotion may be perceived as threats if they involve the loss of a dependency relationship. The demandingness and exploitiveness of the potential manic-depressive eventually leads significant others to avoid or reject him. The harder he tries, the more annoyed they become and the less they give. When all hope is lost and he is faced with the crushing blow of abandonment, he enters into the psychotic state.

His symptoms represent an exaggeration of his characteristic behavior when he is in a healthy interval. While he is psychotic, his inner emptiness and dependence on others are openly expressed by a display of misery, appeals for attention and reassurance, ideas of personal bankruptcy, and so on. Difficulties with others are denied, so that he has no one to blame but himself.

Psychoanalysts interpret manic behavior as a defensive structure that the individual erects as a more tolerable substitute for feelings of despair and self-devaluation. It is better to pretend to be important than to admit to being nothing.

LEARNING THEORY

Reinforcement theory per se cannot account for the vulnerability of certain individuals to severe mood disturbances, but the choice and persistence of symptoms may in great measure be explained in terms of learning principles. The loss of interest, feelings of futility, and reduced activity level of the depressive may be attributed to a relative absence of positive reinforcements and/or a relative predominance of losses, frustrations, and other aversive stimuli. His unresponsiveness to his social environment leads to a decrease in external stimulation, which in turn confirms the dreary emptiness of his existence and sustains his low level of responsiveness. The sympathy and reassurance periodically elicited by a dejected appearance, self-accusations, and somatic complaints contribute to their recurrence and persistence. The elation of the manic is self-reinforcing. His uninhibited, jovial behavior is a source of welcome attention. As a result of successful past experiences, the manic-prone individual may have learned to rely on periodic spurts of hyperactivity to cope with his problems.

SOCIOCULTURAL FACTORS

Manic-depressive and related depressive reactions appear to be more or less randomly distributed at all socioeconomic levels. Where differences have been noted, incidence rates have been slightly higher among the upper classes. Affective psychoses constitute a larger proportion of first admissions to private than public mental hospitals. Cross-cultural studies (Murphy et al., 1967; Zung, 1969) indicate that the total prevalence of depressive reactions and the range of their symptoms are about the same throughout the world. However, the relative occurrence of specific symptoms is influenced by the particular culture, local religious beliefs, social class, and geography. Guilt feelings and self-accusation, for example, are strongly related to the Judeo-Christian tradition. Theatrical grief and self-neglect tend to be more characteristic of lower-class than upper-class populations.

Recent studies have refuted earlier claims that depressions are rare among primitive people (Prince, 1968). The discrepancy between earlier and later reports appears to be partly due to the failure of older studies to take account of cultural differences in ways of expressing depressive feelings. In African rural societies, depressive states are more often expressed in somatic complaints and ideas of persecution than in guilt and self-blame (Collomb, 1967). In former years, too, primitive people referred only troublesome persons for treatment at mission hospitals and clinics. Depressed persons, who were usually considered victims of bewitchment, were treated by native practitioners skilled in such matters.

Treatment of Affective Disorders

By definition, manic-depressive and other psychotic depressive reactions are characterized by spontaneous recovery. About 80 percent of attacks terminate well within nine months. As previously indicated, modern drugs can usually bring symptoms under control in a week or two. If symptoms persist over a year, the original diagnosis is often changed. In depressive cases, general psychomotor retardation is considered a favorable prognostic sign and somatic complaints are regarded as unfavorable signs (Kay et al., 1969). The main objectives of therapeutic intervention are to moderate the severity of symptoms, shorten the duration of attacks, and decrease the risk of exhaustion in manic patients and of suicide in depressed patients.

During the acute stages of manic reaction and psychotic depression most patients are not responsive to traditional forms of psychotherapy. The two most favored treatment procedures are electroconvulsive shock (ECT) and drug therapy. Comparative studies (Zung, 1968) suggest that ECT is slightly more effective than antidepressant drugs in the treatment of depressions. When the effects of ECT treatment are viewed in the light of learning theory, the method can be seen as a form of punishment training or negative reinforcement (Dies, 1968). Lithium carbonate has been found to be highly effective in the treatment of manic reactions but of doubtful value for depressed patients (Gattozzi, 1970; Baldessarini and Stephens, 1970). Imipramine and related tricyclic drugs are most widely used in the treatment of depressions.

Suicide

Suicide provides a good illustration of the common practice of utilizing mental illness as an "explanation" for inexplicable deviant behavior. It is true that the suicide rate among depressed and others types of mental patients is markedly higher than for the general population. On the other hand, a large proportion of persons who attempt or commit suicide are not mentally deranged. The independence of suicide and psychopathology is tacitly or explicitly acknowledged when suicide can be interpreted as a rational or altruistic act or when it is sanctioned or demanded by the culture. Thus a person with an incurable disease is usually not considered mentally unbalanced if he willfully shortens his life to put an end to excruciating pain. A person may be honored as a martyr if he sacrifices his life for a noble cause. When the custom of suttee prevailed in India, a high-caste widow was required to throw herself on the funeral pyre of her husband. In Japan, it was formerly considered obligatory for a person in disgrace to commit hara-kiri in the prescribed ceremonial manner.

The assumption of mental illness when acts of self-destruction cannot be explained on the basis of cultural sanctions is more humane than regarding them as crimes or shameful acts of cowardice, but calling suicide a manifestation of mental disorder does not make it so. In terms of the standard criteria of insanity applied in cases of homicide, the great majority of suicides would have to be adjudged sane, since they are capable of distinguishing right from wrong (M'Naghten rules) and the suicidal act is not the product of mental confusion or delusional ideas (Durham rule). At the most, about 25 percent of persons evaluated at community suicide prevention centers are so disturbed or disorganized that hospitalization is warranted. In the absence of suicidal tendencies, however, most of this group would not ordinarily be referred for psychiatric treatment. For a fuller understanding of suicide, its social, moral, and philosophical aspects should be considered along with its psychiatric implications.

EPIDEMIOLOGY

Statistical studies reviewed by Farberow and Shneidman (1961), Dublin (1963), and Hendin (1967) show that suicide is the tenth-ranking cause of death in the United States. It is virtually nonexistent before the age of ten but relatively common among adolescents; it is the fifth-ranking cause of death among persons from fifteen to twenty-four. The suicide rate is considerably higher among college students than among their nonacademic peers (Seiden, 1969). The annual suicide rate for all ages in the United States is about 11 per 100,000. The rate for white males increases directly with age and is highest for ages after seventy-five. For white females, the rate increases up to the age of fifty-five and then shows a gradual decrease. The suicide rates for nonwhite males and nonwhite females are lower than those for white males and white females respectively. Three times as many men commit suicide each year as women, but three times as many women make suicide attempts. Halfhearted suicidal gestures are particularly prevalent among adolescent girls.

Most persons who commit suicide communicate their intent beforehand, but most persons who express suicidal ideas do not follow through with successful attempts. The ratio of attempted to completed suicides is greater than 10 to 1. Of those who attempt suicide and fail, less than 10 percent complete the act on a later occasion. The lowest suicide rate is found among married people with children. The rate for married persons in general is only half as high as for single adults, and one-fourth to one-fifth the rate for the widowed and divorced. In the United States, Protestants have higher rates than Jews, and Jews have higher rates than Catholics. Suicide occurs with about equal frequency at all socioeconomic levels. The suicide rate is more directly related to change in status and group cohesion than to class level per se. The suicide rate increases in periods of economic depression and decreases during times of war. This finding may be due to the increased solidarity of the community when it feels itself threatened by a common enemy.

The suicide rate varies markedly from country to country. Hungary, Austria, Denmark, Japan, Sweden, and West Germany have unusually high rates; Italy, Ireland, Norway, Chile, Canada, Poland, and New Zealand have relatively low rates. Some primitive societies have comparatively low suicide rates while others have unusually high rates. Among the indigenous Kandrian of southwest New Britain the suicide rate is higher than that of most Western societies (Hoskin et al., 1969). Experiences involving shame or disaffiliation from the group appear to be the major contributory causes.

ETIOLOGICAL FACTORS

The tremendous effects of gender, religion, and cultural background on suicide rates emphasize the etiological importance of social factors. Twin data offer no support for the hypothesis of a genetic predisposition to suicide (Kallmann and Anastasio, 1946; Kallmann et al., 1949). The occasional occurrence of two or more suicides in the same family appears to be an example of copying behavior.

A major contribution to the sociological interpretation of suicide was made in 1897 by Emile Durkheim (1951). His main hypothesis was that suicide was associated with the individual's relationships and attachments within his social group. He distinguished among three types of suicides: altruistic, egoistic, and anomic. *Altruistic* suicide occurs when the individual is too closely integrated with his society. Close identification with family, friends, and associates may require that under certain circumstances the individual be prepared to sacrifice his life (the hara-kiri tradition, the disgraced officer in a highly tradition-bound culture who shoots himself to uphold the honor of his regiment). *Egoistic* suicide is self-destruction by a person who is rejected by his society or is unable to become integrated with it. *Anomic* suicide results from feelings of alienation from the society, and is especially characteristic of societies that lack cohesion.

This sort of social isolation is a common feature of suicide among adolescents. The high school or college student who exercises his death option is often literally "unknown" by peers and teachers. In these cases the existential transition from being to nonbeing is a small step. Some people who have felt dead for a long time view the terminal act as a kind of official technicality.

Cross-cultural studies indicate that the psychosocial correlates of suicide vary from country to country. The psychodynamics of suicide in Sweden, Denmark, and Norway are of particular interest on two counts: (1) the suicide rate is considerably lower in Norway than in other Scandinavian countries, and (2) both Denmark and Sweden have high suicide rates, but for different reasons. The main precipitating factor in Sweden is performance failure. Suicide among Swedish men is closely associated with failure in work. Among Swedish women, failure in heterosexual relationships is a common precipitating cause. In Denmark, performance suicide is rare. Here suicide is mainly associated with the frustration of dependency needs through separation, loss, or abandonment.

Hendin (1964) attributes this contrast in suicide patterns to national differences in child-rearing practices, social values, life styles, and methods of coping with psychosocial pressures. Swedish mothers tend to regard child-rearing as a chore rather than a pleasure. Their objective is to encourage independence, self-sufficiency, and separation in their children as early as possible. Children are evaluated by comparing their achievements with those of other children. Performance is also the yardstick by which husbands and wives are evaluated. Anger is handled through withdrawal and detachment. A popular Swedish expression is *tiga ihjäl,* meaning to kill with silence. Failure in performance leads to loss of self-esteem, to self-hatred, and frequently to suicide.

In Denmark, on the other hand, the emotional life of most mothers is centered on their children. Babies are cuddled, fondled, and encouraged to remain dependent. Danish mothers are more pleased with how well their children look and how much they weigh than the age at which they walk, talk, and do things for themselves. In exchange for unlimited gratification of dependency needs, the child is expected to curb his aggression. When a child misbehaves, he is confronted with the guilt-inducing reprimand "Look how much you have hurt Mamma!" Aggression is turned inward in the form of self-blame. Passivity and dependency are more valued than competition and outstanding success. The absence of heroic deeds is strikingly reflected in Hans Christian Andersen's fairy tales. The suicide of a Danish man is often precipitated by the loss of a dependency relationship to his mother or wife. Suicide among Danish women frequently follows childbirth, which represents a turning point in their own dependency needs.

In Norway, anger is handled more openly and aggression is directed outward. The repression of anger and internalization of aggression, which lead to guilt and self-hatred, are thereby avoided. The Norwegian solution to frustrations and disappointments is to see oneself as the injured party and to nurse one's anger. A paranoid life style of collecting injustices presumably provides a defense against self-blame and suicide. In their rearing of children Norwegian mothers strive for a balance between the clinging dependency of the Danes and the detached independence of the Swedes. They tend to be emotionally involved with their children and to enjoy them, but at the same time they encourage them to be independent and free. The Swedes' grim approach to work and success is rare in Norway, where the culturally shared fear of envy serves as a check on high aspirations. To be "good" is considered more desirable than to be successful. The deemphasis of performance reduces anxiety and self-blame for failure.

Suicide notes, explanations following unsuccessful attempts at suicide, and inferences derived from case histories all reflect the complexity and personal significance of the act (Hendin, 1967; Seiden, 1969). Some of the more frequently reported "reasons" are:

1. Chronic depression or loneliness. No purpose seen in continuing an empty, hopeless existence.
2. Guilt, remorse, self-punishment associated with wrongdoing.
3. Shame or fear of punishment for failure or acts of aggression.
4. Attempt to control, manipulate, or punish others.
5. Desire to escape from poor treatment at home, from the withholding of love, or some other unbearable situation.
6. Hope of entering a new life, being reunited with lost loved ones, or being reborn.
7. Impulsive reaction to the loss of a love object.

Some authorities have stressed the interpersonal nature of suicide. A suicidal attempt may be interpreted as a cry for help or a means of embarrassing or punishing others. Suicide may masquerade as homicide. Wolfgang (1959) concluded from a study of over five hundred criminal homicide cases that about one-fourth were actually perverse forms of suicide. The victim brought about his own death by persistently goading his selected executioner until he succeeded in provoking a murderous assault.

PREVENTION

The aura of taboo long associated with suicide is gradually being replaced by a scientific attitude. An important milestone was the opening in 1958 of the Los Angeles Suicide Prevention Center. Similar crisis centers have since been opened in major cities throughout the United States. Persons troubled by suicidal impulses may phone these centers day or night and arrange for short-term emergency treatment and/or referral to appropriate community agencies. The movement gained scientific respectability in 1966 with the establishment of the National Institute of Mental Health Center for Studies of Suicide Prevention. The new field developed professional status rapidly. It has its own journal, *Bulletin of Suicidology,* and its own professional association, the American Association of Suicidology. Members include physicians, psychiatrists, psychologists, social workers, clergyman, and other interested persons. Trained personnel have been assigned to medical examiners' and coroners' offices to conduct psychological autopsies. So far, the main dividend has been a sharp increase in research literature. Scales have been constructed to differentiate degrees of suicidal impulses, from threats made without serious intent to attempts that actually succeed (Darbonne, 1969; Wold, 1970). There is no evidence that the centers have had any appreciable effect in preventing suicides. Since only an estimated 2 percent of persons who contact suicide prevention centers would actually commit suicide if no one were waiting by a telephone for the sole purpose of talking them out of it, it is highly unlikely that the centers will result in any noticeable decrease in the national suicide rate. The best hope for a decrease in suicides lies in significant social change in attitudes and values.

Summary

Severe affective disturbances distinguished by extreme deviations in mood have traditionally been subdivided into the categories of manic-depressive psychosis, psychotic depressive reaction, and involutional melancholia. Further clinical subdivisions of manic-depressive reactions have been suggested on the basis of (1) bipolar and unipolar types, (2) severity of manic reactions (hypomanic, hypermanic, and delirious reactions), and (3) severity of depression (simple, acute, and stuporous depressions). It has recently been proposed that psychotic affective disturbances be divided into two separate disorders: bipolar and/or predominantly manic reactions characterized by early age of onset (twenty to forty), in which there is a strong genetic loading, and depressive reactions occurring relatively late in life, in which the genetic loading is less pronounced. An alternate approach is to disregard the historical concept of separate disorders and view affective psychoses as extreme variations of the mood swings characteristic of normal individuals described as cyclothymes. The continuum concept is particularly applicable to the similarities of behavior observed in normal mourning, neurotic depressions, and psychotic depressions. The continuum concept does not rule out the appropriateness of medical treatment.

Drugs and ECT have proved highly effective in shortening the duration of severe mood disturbances.

Depressive reactions and suicidal impulses are best considered as separate conditions. There is an increased risk of suicide during periods of depression, but many depressed persons are not suicidal, and most suicides do not suffer from any clearly defined psychiatric disorder. Suicide is basically a personal decision on the relative value of continued existence. The decision is influenced more by cultural and religious factors than by psychiatric considerations.

References

ARIETI, S. "Manic Depressive Psychosis." In *American Handbook of Psychiatry,* ed. S. Arieti, pp. 419–54. New York: Basic Books, 1959.

BALDESSARINI, R. J., and STEPHENS, J. H. "Lithium Carbonate for Affective Disorders." *Archives of General Psychiatry* 22 (1970): 72–77.

BECK, A. T. *Depression: Clinical, Experimental, and Theoretical Aspects.* New York: Harper & Row, 1967.

COHEN, M. B., et al. "An Intensive Study of Twelve Cases of Manic-Depressive Psychosis." *Psychiatry* 17 (1954): 103–37.

COLLOMB, H. "Methodological Problems in Cross-cultural Research." *International Journal of Psychiatry* 3 (1967): 17–19.

CUTLER, R. P., and KURLAND, H. D. "Clinical Quantification of Depressed Reactions." *Archives of General Psychiatry* 5 (1961): 280–85.

DARBONNE, A. R. "Study of Psychological Content in the Communications of Suicidal Individuals." *Journal of Consulting and Clinical Psychology* 5 (1969): 590–96.

DIES, R. R. "Electroconvulsive Therapy: A Social Learning Theory Interpretation." *Journal of Nervous and Mental Diseases* 146 (1968): 334–42.

DUBLIN, L. *Suicide: A Sociological and Statistical Study.* New York: Ronald Press, 1963.

DURKEIM, E. *Suicide.* New York: Macmillan, 1951.

FARBEROW, N. L., and SHNEIDMAN, E. S., eds. *The Cry for Help.* New York: McGraw-Hill, 1961.

FRIEDMAN, A. S.; COWITZ, B.; COHEN, H. W.; and GRANECK, S. "Syndromes and Themes of Psychotic Depression." *Archives of General Psychiatry* 9, (1963): 504–12.

———. "Minimal Effects of Severe Depression on Cognitive Functioning." *Journal of Abnormal and Social Psychology* 69 (1964): 237–43.

GATTOZZI, A. A. *Lithium in the Treatment of Mood Disorders.* National Clearinghouse for Mental Health Information publication no. 5033. Washington, D.C.: U.S. Government Printing Office, 1970.

GRINKER, R. R.; MILLER, J.; SOBSHIN, M.; NUNM, R.; and NUNNALLY, J. C. *The Phenomenon of Depressions.* New York: Harper & Row, 1961.

HAMILTON, M. A. "A Rating Scale for Depression." *Journal of Neurology, Neurosurgery, and Psychiatry* 23 (1960): 56–62.

HENDIN, H. *Suicide and Scandinavia.* New York: Grune & Stratton, 1964.

————. "Psychiatric Emergencies: Suicide." In *Comprehensive Textbook of Psychiatry*, ed. A. M. Freedman and H. I. Kaplan, pp. 1170–79. Baltimore: Williams & Wilkins, 1967.

HOPKINSON, G., and LEY, P. "A Genetic Study of Affective Disorder." *British Journal of Psychiatry* 115 (1969): 917–22.

HOSKIN, J. O.; FRIEDMAN, M. I.; and CAWTE, J. E. "A High Incidence of Suicide in a Preliterate-Primitive Society." *Psychiatry* 32 (1969): 200–10.

KALLMANN, F. J., and ANASTASIO, M. M. "Twin Studies on the Psychopathology of Suicide." *Journal of Heredity* 37 (1946): 171–80.

————; DEPORTE, J.; DEPORTE, E.; and FEINGOLD, L. "Suicide in Twins and Only Children." *American Journal of Human Genetics* 1 (1949): 113–26.

KAY, D. W. K.; GARSIDE, R. F.; ROY, J. R.; and BEAMISH, P. "Endogenous and Neurotic Syndromes of Depression: A Five- to Seven-Year Follow-up of 104 Cases." *British Journal of Psychiatry* 115 (1969): 389–99.

KRAINES, S. H. "Manic-Depressive Syndrome: A Psychologic Disease." *Diseases of the Nervous System* 27 (1966): 3–19.

LANDIS, C., and PAGE, J. D. *Modern Society and Mental Disease.* New York: Farrar & Rinehart, 1938.

LINDEMAN, E. "Symptomatology and Management of Acute Grief." *American Journal of Psychiatry* 101 (1944): 141–48.

LORR, M.; SONN, T. M.; and KATZ, M. M. "Toward a Definition of Depression." *Archives of General Psychiatry* 17 (1967): 183–86.

MENDELS, J. *Concepts of Depression.* New York: Wiley, 1970.

MURPHY, H. B. M.; WITTKOWER, E. D.; and CHANCE, N. A. "Cross-cultural Inquiry into the Symptomatology of Depression: A Preliminary Report." *International Journal of Psychiatry* 3 (1967): 6–15.

PAGE, J. D. *Abnormal Psychology.* New York: McGraw-Hill, 1947.

PARKES, C. B. "Bereavement and Mental Illness: Part I. A Clinical Study of the Grief of Bereaved Psychiatric Patients." *British Journal of Medical Psychology* 38 (1965): 1–12.

PERRIS, C. "The Course of Depressive Psychoses." *Acta Psychiatrica Scandinavia* 44 (1968): 238–48.

PILOWSKY, I.; LEVINE, S.; and BOULTON, D. M. "The Classification of Depression by Numerical Taxonomy." *British Journal of Psychiatry* 115 (1969): 937–45.

PRINCE, R. "The Changing Picture of Depressive Syndromes in Africa: Is It Fact or Diagnostic Fashion?" *Canadian Journal of African Studies* 1 (1968): 177–92.

RENNIE, T. A. C. "Prognosis in Manic-Depressive Psychoses." *American Journal of Psychiatry* 98 (1942): 801–14.

ROSENTHAL, D. *Genetic Theory and Abnormal Behavior.* New York: McGraw-Hill, 1970.

SEIDEN, R. H. *Suicide Among Youth, Bulletin of Suicidology* supplement. Washington, D.C.: U.S. Government Printing Office, 1969.

WEINGOLD, H. P.; LACHIN, A.; BELL, H.; and COXE, R. C. "Depression as a Symptom of Alcoholism: Search for a Phenomenon." *Journal of Abnormal Psychology* 73 (1968): 195–97.

WINOKUR, G., and CLAYTON, P. "Family History Studies: I. Two Types of Affective Disorders Separated According to Genetic and Clinical Factors." *Recent Advances in Biological Psychiatry* 9 (1966): 35–50.

————. "Family History Studies: II. Sex Differences and Alcoholism in Primary Affective Illness." *British Journal of Psychiatry* 113 (1967): 973–79.

WITTENBORN, J. R. "The Dimensions of Psychosis." *Journal of Nervous and Mental Disease* 134 (1962): 117–28.

WOLD, C. I. "Characteristics of 26,000 Suicide Prevention Center Patients." *Bulletin of Suicidology* 6 (1970): 24–28.

WOLFGANG, M. E. "Suicide by Means of Victim-Precipitated Homicide." *Journal of Clinical and Experimental Psychopathology* 20 (1959): 335–49.

ZUNG, W. K. "A Self-rating Depression Scale." *Archives of General Psychiatry* 12 (1965): 63–70.

————. "Evaluating Treatment Methods for Depressive Disorders." *American Journal of Psychiatry* 124 (1968): 40–48.

————. "A Cross-cultural Survey of Symptoms in Depression." *American Journal of Psychiatry* 126 (1969): 116–21.

CHAPTER ELEVEN

Neurotic Reactions

Symptom patterns associated with neurosis include acute anxiety, irrational fears, psychogenic blindness, amnesia, dual personality, obsessive thoughts, compulsive rituals, depressive mood, chronic exhaustion, feelings of unreality, and undue concern with the state of one's health. What do these varied reactions have in common to justify their being grouped together in the same category? One common characteristic that is particularly helpful in differentiating neurotic behavior from sociopathy is that in neurosis the main victim is the patient. The neurotic has been described as his own worst enemy. He is not a martyr or a masochist who enjoys suffering. He desperately wants to enjoy life and to be happy but his peace of mind is shattered by nameless fears, doubts, ideas of guilt, confused identity, frustrated aspirations, inferiority feelings, and somatic concerns.

A second common characteristic of neurotic reactions is the absence of delusions, hallucinations, and other bizarre behaviors associated with psychosis. Neurotics do not grossly misinterpret outer reality and they do not exhibit significant personality disorganization. The neurotic sees himself and is perceived by others as standing much closer to the normal than to the psychotic end of the mental health continuum. His symptoms may restrict his activity, reduce his efficiency, and cause him acute personal anguish, but he is aware of the way society expects him to behave, and by and large, his behavior remains within socially acceptable limits in work performance, interpersonal relations, and everyday activities. Basically, the neurotic's alignment with the normal is due to the fact that the neurotic recognizes his symptoms as symptoms. Unlike the psychotic, who accepts his delusions as real and lives them, the neurotic is capable of distinguishing his "sick" from his normal behavior. He is aware of the senselessness of

264

his anxiety and his self-defeating, defensive reactions. He would like nothing better than to be rid of his irrational fears, obsessions, compulsions, guilt feelings, and somatic ailments. But, try as he will, he is unable to do so. At best, he can with extreme effort moderate and regulate their expression so that his overt behavior does not appear to casual observers as irrational or obviously peculiar. His relative inability to control his symptoms adequately accentuates his anxiety by raising the haunting specter that he is losing his mind. The neurotic's awareness of the maladaptiveness of his reactions and the futility of his subterfuges is a major source of personal unhappiness. The unfavorable attitudes of close associates, who often regard the neurotic's behavior as attention-getting, foolish, or annoying, add to his problems.

With respect to the continuum concept of psychopathology, neurotic symptoms represent moderate deviations whereas psychotic symptoms represent extreme deviations from similar traits noted in normal individuals. Intergroup differences consist mainly of the degree to which specific behaviors are subject to voluntary control and rational interpretation, which in turn, influences the relative appropriateness and adequacy of psychosocial functioning. The contrasts noted in the previous chapters in ways in which normal, neurotic, and psychotic individuals manage depressive feelings also hold for other traits. Compulsive tendencies, for example, are present in all three groups. Many normal persons rigidly adhere to a fixed and highly predictable pattern of behavior. They resist changes in their scheduled life, but when circumstances demand it, they can and do alter their usual routines and customary ways of doing things. The neurotic is less flexible and adaptive. He may recognize the ridiculousness of his compulsive behavior but he experiences great difficulty in modifying established habits or in inhibiting impulses for prolonged periods. He retains sufficient control and judgment, however, to keep his behavior within reasonable bounds. Unlike the psychotic, he does not attribute his compulsive acts to a plot by enemies who are controlling his thoughts and impulses with the aid of some diabolic machine and forcing him to engage in repetitive rituals against his will. All human beings periodically experience vague aches and pains that are unrelated to specific or treatable illnesses. Normal individuals learn to ignore these incidental and transient symptoms; the neurotic may dwell upon them and exaggerate their significance; the psychotic may imagine that his body is undergoing some radical change or that certain organs are wasting away. Finally, neurotic behavior is more responsive than psychotic behavior to changes in the individual's life situation and more amenable to psychological forms of treatment since the neurotic maintains closer contact than the psychotic with his social environment.

The third rationale offered for considering the diverse forms of neurotic behavior as a single clinical entity is based on the anxiety theory of neurosis. A distinction is made between normal anxiety and neurotic anxiety. Both varieties consist of general unrest and vague feelings of apprehension. The normal individual is usually aware of the cause of his anxiety and is motivated by its presence to engage in some problem-solving activity that will eliminate the underlying cause. In neurosis, the individual is unaware of the cause of his dread and his anxiety level is considerably higher. For no apparent reason the neurotic is periodically overwhelmed by a massive, diffuse emotional reaction. Concomitant physiological sensations (palpitation, difficulty in breathing, cold sweat) intensify his state of alarm and apprehension. The next step in the anxiety theory of neurosis is more speculative. It is assumed that as a defense against the direct experiencing of terrifying anxiety attacks, the neurotic may unconsciously develop other "substitute" symptoms that serve to alleviate, displace, or otherwise regulate the intensity of anxiety. These defensive measures are more reflexive than reflective. To the extent that they succeed in warding off anxiety, they are self-reinforcing and in time become firmly established, stereotyped, habit responses that are not under the full control of the individual (Pfeiffer, 1968). The circumvented source of the anxiety, meanwhile, remains unresolved and unassimilated.

The American Psychiatric Association recognizes eight principal types of neurosis: anxiety neurosis, hysterical neurosis, phobic neurosis, obsessive-compulsive neurosis, depressive neurosis, neurasthenic neurosis, depersonalization neurosis, and hypochondriacal neurosis. It seems to many psychologists, however, that these are more appropriately regarded as descriptive names identifying certain kinds of reactions than as separate disorders.

ANXIETY NEUROSIS

Anxiety is the emotion of uncertainty. To a greater or lesser degree, it is present whenever a person is confronted with an unsolved problem or challenge that is vital to his well-being and for which he has no readily available solution. What makes neurotic anxiety an acutely frightening experience is that it is all-pervasive and yet objectless and nameless. The neurotic is sporadically seized with a feeling of impending but unidentifiable disaster. Since the neurotic is not clearly aware of the cause of his anxiety and is therefore uncertain as to what he should do, the anxiety remains free-floating and diffuse. He is apprehensive but is unable to account for his uneasiness. His state of alarm impairs concentration, reduces efficiency, increases irritability, and interferes with sleep. Physiological disturbances associated with emotional overreaction, which may include cardiac irregularities, breathing difficulties, excessive perspiration, tremors, and nausea, may be misinterpreted as signs of heart failure and impending death. Anxiety attacks occur unexpectedly, under any circumstances. During sleep, they may be expressed in nightmares. Between attacks the person is relatively free of symptoms.

One such neurotic, whom we shall call Mr. A., had achieved considerable success in college both as a student and as a campus personality. After graduation he married and accepted one of several attractive positions he had been offered. But he left his job after six weeks on the grounds that it was too nerve-racking, and he gave up his next position after two weeks because it was too dull and had no future. Shortly after starting on his third job, he began to complain that he was unhappy there too. He felt that his employer didn't like him and that his co-workers were unfriendly. On several occasions he asked his employer and fellow workers to tell him how he was doing on the job, but they never gave him a straight answer. Since he had already changed jobs twice within two months, his wife insisted that he stay with his present job. Shortly after that he began to develop acute anxiety symptoms. For no apparent reason, he would periodically feel dizzy, break out in a cold sweat, and tremble. At such times his stomach would churn, and it seemed that his heart was skipping beats. He went to see two physicians, both of whom assured him that he was in good physical condition. For a time he sought relief from his mounting tension through frequent intercourse. But by the time he made an appointment for a psychological examination, he had lost interest in sex. His wife stated that on two recent occasions he had been impotent. The wife was beginning to regret her marriage. She referred to her husband as a baby who needed a mother to take care of him, rather than a wife. Mr. A. had always been very strongly attached to his mother, and since his marriage he had gone to see her at least three times a week. The mother had high hopes for her son. She had objected to his marriage on the grounds that he was too young. She also objected to the girl her son married, because she was not a college graduate and had no money. After Mr. A. developed nervous symptoms, his mother blamed his wife for his condition. Therapy was discontinued after two visits because of a crisis precipitated by his wife. She gave him the choice of a divorce or moving to the West Coast, to get as far as possible from his mother. With great reluctance, Mr. A. agreed to move.

HYSTERICAL NEUROSIS

A distinction is made between hysterical conversion and hysterical dissociative reactions. Both types represent spontaneous, unplanned attempts to avoid anxiety by the exclusion of part of the self. Conversion reactions involve the exclusion of some bodily function, whereas dissociative reactions involve the exclusion of some components of the personality. In conversion reactions, it is assumed that the emotional energy associated with anxiety is transformed or "converted" into physical symptoms primarily involving the loss of sensory and motor functions. The disability is psychological; there is no relevant neurological or physical injury. Characteristic symptoms include paralysis, blindness, deafness, aphonia, and disturbances in sensations. The psychological nature of these somatic symptoms is particularly apparent in neurotic paralysis, anesthesia, and parasthesia, in which the area of the body affected conforms to popular conceptions rather than to neurological boundaries. For example, a hysterical paralysis of the arm typically stops abruptly at the shoulder, although any damage to the nerves of the arm would inevitably affect the shoulder area as well. An unusual feature of conversion reaction is the neurotic's apparent lack of concern over his symptoms. This attitude of *belle indifférence* was formerly considered to be an identifying characteristic. More recent studies suggest that only about one-third of hysterical patients are indifferent to the loss of sensory or motor function (Stephens and Kamp, 1962).

According to psychoanalytic theory, choice of symptom has a symbolic significance. The sacrificed function may represent a defense against a forbidden impulse or self-punishment for having such an impulse. Thus a paralysis of the hand may represent a defense against masturbation. In accord with the biblical injunction "If thine eye offend thee, pluck it out," blindness may constitute a self-imposed punishment for observing a forbidden scene.

Dissociative reactions represent unconscious attempts to escape from conflicts by isolating or separating inner sources of discord. Dissociative reactions include somnambulism, amnesia, fugue states, and dual personalities. In somnambulism, or sleepwalking, the major portion of the personality sleeps on while the dissociated segment reenacts some disturbing experience or attempts to reach some happier or safer place. In cases of amnesia, the patient retains most of his memory; he remembers practically all of his vocabulary, the social mores, the names of objects, and so on. Loss of memory is usually limited to personal identity and to specific life experiences of a traumatic nature. Fugue states are characterized by amnesia plus a flight from usual surroundings. A person with a fugue reaction literally runs away from personal problems by traveling to another town, taking on a different name, and starting a new life, oblivious of his former identity. Months or years later, he may suddenly recall his former identity and previous life and be at a loss to explain his present circumstances.

Dual personalities are rare. The few cases reported conform to the familiar Dr. Jekyll–Mr. Hyde model. The creation of two alternating personalities resolves conflicts between "good" and "bad" impulses. When the "good" person is in control, the "bad" person is absent, and vice versa. Usually there is a third personality who is in touch with and a blend of the other two. The "good" person is well behaved, restrained, somewhat depressed, conscientious, and highly moral. The "bad" person is naughty, fun-loving, uninhibited, and infantile. In Freudian terminology, the good personality is dominated by the superego, the bad personality is controlled by the pleasure-seeking id, and the third personality represents the coordinating, reality-oriented ego. Once established, each of the multiple personalities exhibits distinct and consistent characteristics. The spontaneous transition from one personality to another may occur at any time during sleep or when the person is awake. One personality recedes and is immediately replaced by another, whose actions, speech, values, and temperament are clearly different. The personality in charge at the moment may ridicule or offer apologies for the conduct of the other.

In contrast with fugue states, which are largely confined to men, nearly all of the few cases of multiple personality reported have been young women. The clinical picture is much the same in all cases. A classical study is that of Miss Beauchamp (Prince, 1908). The young lady exhibited three personalities, which were referred to as "The Saint," "The Devil," and "The Woman." The Saint was reserved, idealistic, conscientious, and sad. The Devil, also known as Sally, was a mischievous, fun-loving, troublesome imp. Sally liked to play tricks on the Saint—undoing her knitting, hiding her money, sending her boxes containing spiders. On occasion Sally would get drunk and leave the Saint with the hangover. The Woman personified the ambitions, self-interest, frailities of temper, and usual behavior of the average person. With the aid of hypnosis and suggestion, the real Miss Beauchamp was eventually put together by merging the Saint and the Woman and suppressing Sally.

Thigpen and Cleckley (1957) have described a similar dissociation of personality in their well-known case study of the *Three Faces of Eve*. Eve White was a demure, sad, conscientious, inhibited young lady who sought treatment for blinding headaches and periodic blackouts. Eve Black, who unexpectedly put in an appearance during one of the early therapy sessions, was gay, seductive, adventuresome, carefree, and uninhibited. Jane, the third personality, who later changed her name to Evelyn, represented a composite of Eve White and Eve Black.

PHOBIC NEUROSIS

Phobias consist of irrational, intense, persistent fears of specific objects or situations that are recognized by the individual, as well as by others, as inherently harmless. Some of the more common phobias have been assigned impressive Greek names:

acrophobia	fear of high places	nyctophobia	fear of darkness
agoraphobia	fear of open places	ochlophobia	fear of crowds
claustrophobia	fear of closed places	zoophobia	fear of animals or a particular animal

There are all kinds of fears, but only a few qualify as neuroses. To be afraid of dangerous animals and hazardous situations is normal and wise. Isolated specific fears that do not greatly inconvenience or disturb the individual—mild fear and avoidance of dogs, insects, escalators, public speaking, or air travel—are more appropriately referred to as idiosyncratic reactions than as neuroses. These nonneurotic fears, which may persist for long periods, are often the products of simple conditioning experiences during childhood. Neurotic phobias are more serious. A fear of crowds is indicative of a neurosis if the individual is so disturbed by the close presence of others that he is unable to use public transportation to travel to work, to shop in a crowded store, to attend parties, and so on. Characteristic reactions of phobic neuroses include feelings of apprehension, heart palpitations, nausea, fatigue, and faintness. If escape is not possible, panic may result. A widely accepted theory is that phobias represent the displacement of anxiety from its real source to some symbolic substitute object or situation. The advantage of this mechanism is that the person can now express his anxiety without being disturbed by awareness of its real cause. Thus anxiety associated with the repression of sexual temptation may be displaced to a fear of germs or dread of bodily contact. A conflict involving the acting out of hostile impulses may be expressed in a morbid fear of knives or guns. The specificity of the phobia permits the person to regulate somewhat his exposure to the externalized feared object. As long as he avoids the feared object, he can enjoy relative peace. However, the underlying anxiety remains and must be afforded periodic outlet. To be useful, the substitute object must be readily available. The popularity of phobias involving high places, open places, closed places, darkness, crowds, and germs is due to the fact that they ideally serve this purpose. With the passage of time, the underlying cause may fade and the phobia continue as a residual habit. Under these circumstances, the simple elimination of the surface phobic symptom is all that is required for a complete cure.

OBSESSIVE-COMPULSIVE NEUROSIS

Obsessions consist of spontaneously recurring words, thoughts, ideas, and impulses that a person is unable to exclude from his mind. He may be persistently plagued by unanswerable questions regarding the meaning of truth, repeatedly assailed by doubts regarding the correctness of past actions, or troubled by persistent impulses to shout obscenities or engage in some aggressive act. Compulsions overlap with obsessions, but they more specifically involve repetitive motor acts: compulsive hand-washing, complicated rituals of dressing and undressing, the repeated touching of parts of the body, and so on.

Like fears, not all obsessive-compulsive reactions are symptomatic of neurosis. Mild obsessive-compulsive tendencies may result in an orderly, efficient style of life. Persons obsessed with great ambitions may be highly productive and in the process find contentment and fulfillment. Neurotic obsessive-compulsive behavior serves no constructive purpose, is highly distressing to the individual, and often seriously impairs his functioning. The obsessive-compulsive neurotic realizes the senselessness of his behavior, but he has no choice. If he tries to suppress or resist unwanted thoughts or impulses, he experiences acute anxiety. His obsessive-compulsive reactions constitute a kind of magic that wards off inner tension. It is easier and more comforting to carry out the magic ritual than to face the underlying problem. The inconvenience of staying awake half the night counting one's pulse to prove that one is still alive is a small price to pay if this activity shuts off thinking about committing suicide. The mechanisms underlying obsessive-compulsive behavior include displacement, reaction formation, and undoing, as in Lady Macbeth's repeated washing of her hands to cleanse them of the blood of the murdered king.

DEPRESSIVE NEUROSIS

Neurotic depressive reactions are mood disorders in which anxiety is often mixed with guilt. Characteristic symptoms include feelings of dejection, helplessness, self-depreciation, hopelessness, restlessness, irritability, and insomnia. Unlike psychotic depressions, neurotic depressions are usually precipitated by some identifiable cause, such as the death of a loved person, the loss of some cherished possession, or personal failure; but they are less well controlled than normal sorrow or grief reactions following some personal loss, more prolonged, and more often complicated by feelings of self-reproach. Thus a wife who has frequently wished for her husband's death may be troubled by a mixture of neurotic depressive and guilt feelings when he actually does die. Secondary symptoms in the form of self-depreciation and feelings of remorse may represent ways of allaying guilt or inflicting self-punishment.

NEURASTHENIC NEUROSIS

The dominant feature of neurasthenia is chronic exhaustion. Beard (1880), the American psychiatrist who originally coined the term, attributed neurasthenia to a general weakening of the nerve cells produced by overwork. Though the term has been retained, Beard's definition of it has been discarded. Neurasthenia is now considered to result from persistent nonadjustive emotional reactions. Typical complaints include feelings of weakness, undue fatigability, loss of interest, vague aches and pains, and difficulty in thinking. Since the symptoms are related to underlying anxiety, they are not affected by rest or relaxation. There is also a tendency for the fatigue to be selective. The neurasthenic may be completely worn out by a few minutes of work, but he may experience no difficulty in dancing all night. Unlike hysterics, who tend to ignore their physical symptoms, neurasthenics are acutely aware of their ailments. They describe their symptoms in great detail to all who will listen, and are constantly seeking treatment. The neurasthenic often goes the rounds from clinic to clinic, from physician to faith healer to dispenser of patent medicines. Each new remedy brings about some temporary improvement; then there is a relapse, and off he goes in search of another cure. Since his physical health is usually good, the neurasthenic is frequently described as "enjoying poor health." The typical neurasthenic tends to be dependent. When he consults a physician, he expects him to assume responsibility for his health, happiness, and success. As Weiss and English (1943, p. 552) have noted, the message communicated by many neurasthenics is: "There's my story, Doctor. Now you pat me and rub me and feed me medicine and take my pains away and give me a good appetite and an easy bowel movement and a good night's sleep, and give me inspiration and happiness and tell me how to be successful. And while you are about it, get my mother-in-law out of the house and I'll pay you when I get a job."

DEPERSONALIZATION NEUROSIS

Depersonalization is a dreamlike state of haziness and estrangement. Everything seems unreal, different, and strange. The person may not be quite sure of the boundaries separating the self from the outside world. The self may be viewed with the detachment of an outside observer. A related phenomenon, called *déjà vu,* is the feeling that something seen for the first time has already been seen before.

HYPOCHONDRIACAL NEUROSIS

Hypochondria consists of exaggerated concern with one's physical or mental health when there is no detectable cause for worry. Despite repeated reassurance, the hypochondriac remains convinced that he has some disease. He is acutely sensitive to any irregularities in physical or mental functioning and may go to extreme measures to safeguard his health. The preoccupation is wholly mental; there is no loss or impairment in bodily functions. The concern with imaginary ailments may represent a displacement or substitution of anxiety related to some underlying emotional problem. Hypochondriasis appears to be more common among children and the aged than in other age groups (Kenyon, 1965). This age factor may be related to the typical occurrence of marked physical changes at the extremes of life. Care must be taken to differentiate hypochondriacal neurosis from somatic delusions, which are frequently present as secondary symptoms in psychoses.

OTHER FORMS OF NEUROSIS

The advantage and limitation of the APA classification system is that it is based on clinically observed symptom clusters. Specific diagnoses rest solely on descriptive differences. The issue of possible etiological differences is avoided. It is tacitly assumed that the causes for the varied reactions are much the same. Special diagnostic labels have been periodically introduced to identify and differentiate certain selected cases that seemingly have a particular etiology or explanation. An added implication in these special cases is that therapy, to be effective, should be tailored to fit the presumed underlying cause. Two of the older, more established special labels are war neurosis and occupational neurosis. A more recent addition is existential neurosis.

Existential neurosis. This disorder of contemporary life resembles neurasthenia and depression, but basically it consists of a state of alienation from self and society. Its key characteristics are a pervasive sense of the meaninglessness of one's life, loneliness, apathy, boredom, and aimlessness. Existential neurosis is associated with a premorbid personality devoid of psychological or humanistic identity (Maddi, 1967). The individual considers himself as nothing more than a player of social roles and an embodiment of biological needs. He accepts his social roles and biological needs as given, and may be quite successful in expressing them, but his development as a real person, with strong feelings, involvement, purpose, and direction, is stunted. An existential neurosis is precipitated when the individual is confronted with environmental or interpersonal stresses that interfere with the enactment of his social roles and the satisfaction of his biological needs, or which expose his inadequacy as a human being. Good examples of existential neuroses are found in the literary works of Albert Camus and Arthur Miller.

Occupational neurosis. Strictly defined, an occupational neurosis consists of some impairment in sensory and motor functions that are directly related to one's occupation—a singer's laryngitis, an athlete's sore back, especially when these ailments precede a scheduled performance rather than follow it. In most instances, the traditional diagnosis would be conversion hysteria. However, the designation of occupational neurosis may be extended to include a wider variety of neurotic reactions that follow industrial accidents or which are attributed to hazards associated with one's vocation. Presumed contributing factors include dissatisfaction with one's job, desire for disability compensation, hurt feelings, desire for attention and sympathy, and other assorted personal motives. Common complaints in accident compensation cases are anxiety, depression, headache, dizziness, poor memory, inability to concentrate, and conversion symptoms. Patients are often irritable, stubborn, and argumentative. They actually experience the symptoms they report, feel entitled to compensation, and resent any suggestion that they may be malingering. The granting of compensation or the termination of litigation usually results in some clinical improvement, but symptoms may persist long afterward.

A related rare disorder, one that is a product of confinement rather than occupation, is known as *Ganser's syndrome*. The condition is mainly noted in prisoners. The individual appears alert and normal but gives approximate, pseudo-stupid answers to questions. Thus he may say that two plus two equals five, call a hammer a saw, and so on. As a rule these people show spontaneous recovery within a few days or weeks. Ganser's syndrome may represent a mild dissociation state in which the prisoner unconsciously behaves as he thinks a mental patient would behave.

War neurosis. The causes of neurosis in combat troops are as varied and complex as the causes of neurosis in civilians during peacetime, but the immediate precipitating sources of stress are more obvious in war neurosis. The diagnostic labels of shellshock and combat fatigue, which were extensively used during the First and Second World Wars respectively, are self-explanatory. The real stress, of course, was not the sound of exploding shells or the fatigue of combat, but the threat to existence posed by the inescapable risks of battle. The range and variety of symptoms noted in war neurosis correspond to those of civilian life (Janis, 1951), but certain types of reaction are perhaps more prevalent in war neurosis, particularly during its early stages: recurring nightmares, startle reactions to loud noises, exhaustion, tremors, and a vacant, staring expression (Sargent and Slater, 1940). No simple relationship has been observed between a prior history of personality disturbance and vulnerability to war neurosis. In many instances, the stresses of combat apparently serve to reactivate past conflicts and lead to a recurrence of old symptoms. However, a large proportion of individuals with histories of prior neurosis show a high level of tolerance to war stresses, and many persons with records of good adjustment to civilian life develop symptoms, which often are transient (Raines and Kolb, 1943). The decisive factor may be the relative severity or duration of stress.

One important lesson learned during the Second World War was that when men exhibited signs of acute stress reaction, supportive therapy aimed at an early return to duty and administered in forward areas was far more effective than hospitalization. Hospitalization, which implied that the soldier was "sick," often led to chronic disability. A second lesson learned during the Korean and Vietnam wars was that setting time limits on tours of combat duty, so that the men could depend on being withdrawn from stress by some definite date, made the stress more tolerable and prevented many breakdowns (Brill, 1967). The favorable long-term outcome of most war neuroses has been shown in a study reported by Brill and Beebe

(1955). Five years later, only 14 percent of patients with histories of war neurosis reported that they were unable to work full-time because of continued symptoms. The great majority were either free of neurotic symptoms or had only mild complaints.

Choice of Neurosis

Attempts to account for the development of a particular type of neurosis have focused primarily on the preexisting personality of the neurotic. Symptoms are regarded as intensified manifestations of characteristic modes of reacting and adjusting to difficulties. As White has said (1964, p. 277), "Choice of symptom syndrome is by no means a 'decision' that is made at the last minute, when neurotic breakdown becomes unavoidable. There is an integral relationship between the symptoms finally produced and certain more general characteristics of the patient's personality which have been present for a long time." According to Eysenck (1961a), an inherited autonomic lability that is expressed in emotional overresponsiveness is the major etiological factor in all neuroses. The type of neurosis is related to the individual's relative position on the introversion-extraversion continuum. Persons high on neuroticism (emotional instability) and high on introversion are prone to develop anxiety, obsessive-compulsive, and depressive reactions. Hysterics are more extraverted than other types of neurotics, but they do not differ significantly from normal persons with respect to introversion-extraversion. It appears that the more extraverted hysterics acquire conditioned responses slowly, fail to learn social inhibitions, and are therefore impulsive and undersocialized. Introverts are quick to become conditioned and slow to build up reactive inhibition. They tend to become oversocialized and inhibited. Cameron (1963) differentiates between obsessive-compulsive and depressed patients on the basis of general orientation. The obsessive-compulsive patient is oriented toward gaining independence. He is obstinate, self-sufficient, and self-assertive. He is action-centered and tries to go it alone. The depressed patient, on the other hand, wants to be taken care of. He is oriented toward other people. He seeks reassurance, understanding, love, and help from others, but at the same time he resents his need of them.

Shapiro (1965) has related choice of neurosis to the individual's characteristic style of thinking, perceiving, feeling, and acting. The obsessive-compulsive style is distinguished by rigidity in thinking. Attention is narrowly focused, to the exclusion of new facts and different points of view. The dogmatic style serves as a way of overcoming doubt and uncertainty. For the obsessive-compulsive person, life is earnest. He is constantly under pressure to be engaged in some purposeful activity. He feels uncomfortable with any degree of freedom. Decisions are avoided, since the act of deciding carries with it a certain freedom of choice. When forced to choose, he is apt to invoke some rule or principle to provide the "right" or "proper" answer. His inability to relax restricts playfulness, spontaneous activity, and emotional expression.

The hysterical style presents a sharp contrast. Hysterical behavior is dramatic, theatrical, romantic, vivid, provocative, diffuse, and global. The hysteric's inability to maintain persistent concentration leads to distractability. Other investigators have reported similar observations. Female hysterics in particular have been described as egocentric, emotionally shallow, exhibitionistic, disorganized, immature, and sexually inhibited but flirtatious. Although partially valid, these and other observations on the relation of personality to type of neurosis are far from conclusive. Many kinds of personality are found in all forms of neurosis. Personality types associated with a particular neurosis also occur in other neuroses (Foulds and Caine, 1959; Stephens and Kamp, 1962; Rosenberg, 1967).

Choice of neurosis may be related to learning experiences associated with early home training. One possibility is that the child may imitate the parental model. There is no certainty that if the mother characteristically reacts to stress by developing nervous headaches, becoming depressed or fearful, or seeking escape in invalidism, the child will eventually do likewise; but the example is there and ready-made for adoption. A leaning toward hypochondriasis might be expected in a child reared in a health-conscious home where he is daily cross-examined on possible ailments, fed pills and health foods, routinely questioned on the regularity of his eliminative process, and required to have his temperature taken whenever he sneezes or looks listless. Cold, rigid, systematic, overconscientious parents who insist that their children assume responsibility for their actions at an early age and who set puritanical standards for them may foster obsessive-compulsive tendencies. Parents may contribute to a hysterical personality in a child by rewarding dependency, exhibitionism, coquetry, and histrionic behavior. All these examples are plausible; but as White (1964) has noted, the role of parental attitudes and training in symptom choice remains hypothetical. Carefully controlled longitudinal studies of children and their families are needed to provide more definite answers.

The Etiology of Neuroses

A neurosis is an integral part of the total personality. It consists essentially of the individual's more maladaptive attitudes, traits, and habit patterns. Along with the more adaptive attitudes, traits, and habit patterns, so-called neurotic symptoms are the products of the cumulative interaction of biological factors, environmental influences, and learning experiences. The content, severity, modification, and remission of neurotic behavior are therefore subject to maturation changes and new experiences. In other words, there are no specific, single causes. The particular combination of codeterminants may vary considerably from patient to patient.

AGE AND SEX

Neuroses occur at all ages, but the peak age for initial treatment is between twenty and forty. The total number of treated and untreated neurotics, regardless of age of onset, also is highest during the period between adolescence and early middle age (Shepherd and Gruenberg, 1957). Rates for women tend to be slightly higher in all age groups. This sex difference may be due to a tendency in our culture to view emotional symptoms as signs of weakness. We consider it "feminine" to express emotions openly, so girls are not taught to hide their feelings to anywhere near the extent that boys are. To be "manly" is to suppress most emotions and to be aggressive, so men are more likely than women to "act out" their personal difficulties and thus are more frequently classified as suffering from character or personality disorders.

GENETIC FACTORS

Most authorities who give full weight to the hereditary components of behavior consider that persons susceptible to neuroses inherit one or more polygenetically determined temperament traits associated with emotional instability. Whether behavior becomes sufficiently disordered to warrant a diagnosis of neurosis depends on the degree and nature of the stresses encountered by the individual. Since neurotic symptoms are exaggerations of preexisting traits and differ more in degree than in kind from similar traits common among normal persons, the diagnosis of neurosis is far from an exact science. In the few studies in which concordance rates of monozygotic (MZ) and dizygotic (DZ) twins have been compared, findings have been inconsistent. The overall findings, however, support the hypothesis of a hereditary determinant. When the findings of the five studies reviewed by Essen-Moller (1965) are combined, the concordance rate for neurosis is found to be 43 percent for forty-seven MZ pairs and 23 percent for fifty-six DZ pairs. Of more significance than the actual figures is the observation made by Shields and Slater (1961) that when both members of a pair were neurotic, there was much greater intrapair similarity in symptoms if the twins were monozygotic than if they were dizygotic.

The specificity of genetic predisposition is further suggested by family studies that have shown a tendency for the parents and siblings of neurotics to develop the same type of neurosis. The averaged findings of several studies indicated that 36 percent of the parents of anxiety patients and 17 percent of their siblings had histories of anxiety neuroses (Slater, 1964). Comparable figures for obsessive-compulsive patients were 18 percent for parents and 12 percent for siblings. The averaged findings of several studies of hysteria indicated that 10 percent of the parents of hysterics and 7 percent of their siblings had the same disorder. These results may, of course, also be interpreted as due to the common home environment of the patients, parents, and siblings. The possibility of assortative mating, which would have the effect of concentrating genes associated with neuroticism, has been raised by Slater and Woodside (1951). In comparing a series of normal and neurotic soldiers and their wives, these investigators found that the wives of neurotics were themselves more neurotic and came from more neurotic families than the wives of normal soldiers. Gottesman (1965) has also reported some evidence of assortative mating on the basis of correlations obtained between fathers and mothers on the Minnesota Multiphasic Personality Inventory (MMPI) scale. However, of the three scales that are considered to measure the traits that constitute the neurotic triad—hypochondriasis, hysteria, and depression—a statistically significant positive intraparent correlation was found only for hypochondriasis.

Data on the inheritance of neurotic tendencies, as measured by personality test scores on nonpatient populations, are more conclusive. The surprising 1937 findings of Newman, Freeman, and Holzinger, that separated MZ twin pairs were slightly more alike in emotional instability than MZ twins reared together, have been more recently confirmed by Shields (1962). In the earlier study, the intrapair correlations were .58 for the separated MZ pairs, .56 for the nonseparated MZ twins, and .37 for DZ twins. The corresponding figures reported by Shields were .53 for separated MZ twins, .38 for MZ twins reared together, and .11 for DZ pairs. These findings are difficult to interpret. One possibility is that when MZ twins are reared together one may bear the brunt of life experiences. When MZ twins are reared apart, the supportive influence of the co-twin is removed so that each manifests his genetic potentialities more fully. Significantly higher MZ than DZ intrapair correlations with respect to neuroticism have been reported by Carter (1933), Eysenck and Prell (1951), Vandenberg (1966), and others. Twin studies also provide some evidence of hereditary components associated with the relative responsiveness of the autonomic nervous system (Vandenberg, 1966).

DEVELOPMENTAL FACTORS

Most psychological theories of neurosis stress the importance of parent-child relationships and early life experiences as contributing influences in the development of personality flaws that predispose the child to neurotic behavior in later years. Supporting evidence consists mainly of retrospec- tive case-history data. The presumed pathogenic determinants cover a broad range:

1. Sex conflicts induced by early indoctrination in puritanical stan- dards or unresolved oedipal bonds. Parental exploitation of the child's love needs as a means of control or other disappointing earlier experiences may cause a child subsequently to avoid becom- ing emotionally involved with other persons.
2. Inferiority feelings resulting from unfavorable comparisons with siblings, belittlement, unrealistic expectations and goals set by par- ents, or past failures.
3. Conflicts regarding the expression of aggression related to strong parental disapproval and withdrawal of affection whenever the child attempted to assert himself, resist domination, or express hos- tile feelings.
4. Insecurity feelings resulting from overprotection, parental incon- sistencies, separations, or the expression of affection by the parents only when the child was "good."
5. Traumatic experiences during childhood that were either dismissed or ridiculed by parents or could not be discussed with parents. These unresolved fears form the nucleus for subsequent phobias.
6. Dependence and immaturity resulting from parental domination and indulgence; the sacrifice of autonomy and self-identity as the price paid for retaining parental affection and the security and safety thus provided.
7. Identification with and adoption of a parental model of neurotic behavior. For varied reasons, parents may actually encourage and reinforce hypochondriacal, compulsive, hysterical, and fearful be- havior in their children.

Clinical observations have repeatedly confirmed the occurrence of these and other developmental defects in neuroses. A plausible explanation of the patient's present symptoms can often be deduced from his earlier ad- verse learning experiences. However, the etiological significance of these developmental factors is challenged by the fact that many children who have histories of similar parent-child relationships or of similar early life experiences do not become neurotic. The great majority of the brothers and sisters of neurotics do not manifest overt signs of neurosis as adults. Since no two children have exactly the same relationships with their par- ents, the presence of subtle individual variations may account for the dif- ferential outcome of similar patterns of rearing and parent-child interac- tion. The more marked predisposition of certain persons to neurosis may also be due to the timing or particular combination of unfavorable experiences, the greater intensity or duration of conflicts, or the relative absence of favorable balancing factors within or outside the home. There is also the possibility that adverse environmental and learning experiences do not in themselves produce a neurosis. The interactive effect of an innate low threshold of anxiety and unfavorable life experiences may be required before neurosis can occur. And the inherent emotional instability of the potential neurotic not only may influence his reactions to situations, but may also affect the attitudes and behavior of his parents and the home atmosphere.

PSYCHOANALYTIC THEORY

Psychoanalytic theory considers that every neurosis results from a faulty resolution of the Oedipus complex, and hence is rooted in early childhood. The basic assumption is that anxiety originates from the inability or failure of the ego to control id impulses. Conflicts in later life reinstate this early anxiety. Symptoms represent defenses against a threatened breakdown of repression and the emergence of anxiety. In anxiety reactions, the underlying feelings of apprehension are overtly manifested. In phobias, the fears expressed represent an externalization and displacement of anxiety on specific objects. Obsessive-compulsive symptoms represent prohibitions against, atonements for, or disguised gratifications of repressed sexual or aggressive impulses. The primary purpose of compulsive ceremonials is to avoid awareness of the source of anxiety. The traumatic experience is presumably isolated from its affect and associated connections so that it is not readily accessible to recall. Depressive reactions are attributed to guilt feelings resulting from the superego's disapproval of the ego's failure to inhibit id impulses. Hysteria is interpreted as a denial of sexual conflict. It is assumed that the conversion of libidinal energy into physical symptoms provides an indirect expression of erotic impulses. In summary, neurotic symptoms constitute defenses designed to ward off anxiety resulting from intrapsychic unconscious conflicts, mainly sexual in nature, that are traced to repressed unfavorable parent-child relationships. The aim of therapy is to uncover the origin and resolve the underlying problem, and thereby remove the basic cause of symptoms.

The classical psychoanalytical explanation of phobias is seen in Freud's (1957) analysis of "Little Hans," a five-year-old boy who refused to go out into the street for fear a horse would bite him. With adult patients, the tracing of the childhood causes of neurosis rests on the recall of half-forgotten and often distorted remote events. In the case of Little Hans, the boy's father, who was a physician, contacted Freud soon after the appearance of the fear and treated his son under Freud's supervision. The problem was identified as an oedipal conflict. Hans was afraid that his unconscious feelings of hostility toward his father might lead to retaliatory punishment. More specifically, his fear of castration at the hands of the father was transformed into a fear of being bitten by a horse. This substitution and displacement maneuver solved the child's ambivalent love-hate feelings toward the father. At the same time, it provided a convenient and avoidable external target for the expression of repressed fear.

LEARNING THEORY

Dollard and Miller (1950) attempted to translate psychoanalytic concepts into the language of learning theory. They accepted the basic premise that inner conflicts constituted the main cause of neurosis, but for the traditional psychoanalytic concepts they substituted primary drives, acquired drives, reinforcement, stimulus generalization, and higher mediating mental processes. More recent advocates of the application of modern learning theory to neurosis have completely discarded psychoanalytic concepts.

Eysenck and Rachman (1965) describe three stages in the development of a neurosis. The first consists of a traumatic event or a series of traumatic events that produces strong unconditioned autonomic reactions. The immediate emotional reaction to traumatic events may be highly disruptive, but in normal individuals the effects are usually transitory. Because of innate autonomic instability, the potential neurotic's response to trauma tends to be stronger and more lasting. The second stage is reached if conditioning takes place, and previously neutral stimuli connected with the unconditioned stimuli now serve as signals that elicit the original maladaptive emotional behavior. As a rule, these conditioned reactions clear up spontaneously over a period of time. If the individual is repeatedly exposed to a conditioned stimulus that is not followed by the repetition of traumatic events, the absence of reinforcement leads to the gradual extinction of conditioned responses. Under certain circumstances, however, spontaneous remission or extinction does not occur. This brings us to the third stage, which is marked by an avoidance of the conditioned stimulus, which in turn prevents extinction. If a person who has been in a plane accident subsequently avoids air travel and hence is rewarded or effectively reinforced by having no further contact with the feared object, there is no opportunity for extinction to occur. The three-stage theory is particularly applicable to phobic reactions, anxiety states, and obsessive-compulsive disorders.

Learning theory agrees with psychoanalytic theory in stressing the importance of traumatic experiences or faulty learning in the etiology of neuroses. Beyond this point, however, they differ. Freud attributed the origin of all neuroses to fixation at the oedipal period of early childhood.

Learning theory sets no age limits; traumatic experiences following persistent conditioned responses may occur at any time. Freudian theory assumes the existence of some repressed intrapsychic conflict that is the source of surface symptoms. Until the underlying conflict is uncovered and resolved, symptoms will persist. The treatment of symptoms per se is considered futile, since other symptoms would soon be substituted. Learning theory attaches no importance to unconscious conflicts. There is no need to unravel the past. The symptom is the neurosis; get rid of the symptom, and there is no neurosis, no substitution of symptoms. Behavior therapy based on learning theory is concerned with present maladaptive habits. It focuses on the modification of behavior directly through learning and unlearning procedures, rather than insights gained by exploring and interpreting the unconscious.

STRESS AND CONFLICT

Studies of combat personnel exposed to the hazards of war provide a natural source of data for evaluating the role of stress in the etiology of neurosis. The overwhelming and inescapable strain imposed on airmen during World War II has been graphically described by Grinker and Spiegel (1945). In some overseas units it was a mathematical certainty that only a few men of each squadron would finish a tour of duty. In addition to the dangers of enemy activity, there was the ever-present risk of mechanical and structural failure of the planes on which the pilots' safety depended. Conflicts between the demands of duty and safety were augmented by identification with and loyalty to crew members. Many airmen stated that they suffered more when their crews were flying without them on combat missions than when they went along themselves. The spectre of death was pervasive. In the words of Grinker and Spiegel (1945, p. 35):

> The men suffer not only from the sense of bereavement, but from having seen the anguish of bloody and painful death. They cannot look away when the ship flying on their wing receives a direct flak hit and bursts into flame. The sight of their tentmates bailing out with burning parachutes, or exploded out of a disintegrating ship, becomes stamped on their memory. The empty beds in the tent at night reflect this memory, which does not disappear with the sending home of their buddy's clothes and personal effects. The grief persists and, though it is dulled by time, new losses may be added to it. In addition, the loss of friends stimulates increased anxiety. What happened to his buddy may well happen to himself, since they are so much alike,

The threat to life is not the only stress experienced by combat troops. Other associated pressures include lack of sleep, physical exhaustion, extremes of temperature, hunger, separation from families, injuries, illness, excessive responsibility, uncomfortable living conditions, and so on. What effect do these multiple stresses have on the incidence of neurosis? The main conclusion that may be drawn from the literature is that the impact of stress varies markedly with the individual. Some men break under mild stress, others tolerate prolonged, intense pressures without showing overt signs of emotional disturbances. Findings of some studies indicate that men with a prior psychiatric history are relatively more vulnerable to neurosis; other studies show that neurotic civilians often make excellent soldiers. With respect to more general findings there appears to be consensual agreement that the incidence of neurosis among combatants tends to be related to the casualty risk. One of the better controlled studies on this point is that reported by Tompkins (1959). As is apparent from the summary of his data reported in Table 11.1, the incidence of neurosis among flyers is directly related to the degree of danger as measured by casualty figures.

Table 11.1. Relation between actual danger and incidence of neurosis among combat fliers.

Duty	Relative incidence of neurosis	Flying hours per casualty
Night bombing	12.0%	160
Day fighting	6.0	188
Night fighting	3.4	231
Coastal reconnaissance	3.3	360
Training	1.1	1,960

Adapted from V. H. Tompkins, "Stress in Aviation," in *The Nature of Stress Disorder,* ed. J. Hambling (Springfield, Ill.: Charles C Thomas, 1959), pp. 73–80.

For civilian populations exposed to bombing, the psychological effects appear to be variable and transient. Janis (1951) has reported a comprehensive analysis of the psychological effects of air war on the civilian populations of Britain, Germany, and Japan during World War II. His main conclusions are:

1. The havoc produced by A-bomb attacks on Hiroshima and Nagasaki had no noticeable effect on the occurrence of psychosis, neurosis, and other severe disorders. The dominant reaction among the survivors was transient acute fear or anxiety. In some cases the emotional disturbance took the form of an acute depressive reaction.
2. Under conditions of severe and continued bombing, there was a marked incidence of temporary emotional shock, even among persons who were previously stable. Transient symptoms consisted

mainly of excess anxiety, mild depression, and apathy. These reactions were most likely to occur among those who had undergone near-miss experiences. Markedly predisposed persons with prior histories of neurosis often showed an exacerbation of their former symptoms. Some chronic neurotics improved. Most psychotic patients showed no essential change in their clinical condition.

3. Following heavy air attacks, there was a slight but definite increase in psychosomatic disorders. Peptic ulcers were most common. Other noted reactions were coronary insufficiency and menstrual difficulties.

4. Children exposed to the dangers and destruction of air raids were most apt to become emotionally disturbed if their parents or other adults exhibited overt signs of emotional upset in their presence. This observation supports Bandura and Walters' view (1963) of the importance of the influence of adult models on the behavior of children.

5. People exposed to a series of air raids tended to adapt and show increased capacity to withstand the stress of subsequent attacks. Spontaneous reactions, which probably contributed to emotional adjustment, included sightseeing in damaged areas, increased social interaction, and the development of fatalistic attitudes, rituals, and superstitions. The presence of other persons in communal shelters tended to lessen anxiety.

SOCIOCULTURAL FACTORS

The fact that neuroses occur in all cultures, including those in which the free expression of the sexual drive is limited only by the incest taboo, brings into question the importance attached by psychoanalysts to sexual conflicts. There is some evidence that hysterical-conversion reactions are relatively more common and obsessive-compulsive reactions less common in primitive than in more advanced cultures. In our own culture, field reports (Dohrenwend and Dohrenwend, 1967) indicate that the maximum prevalence rate for treated and untreated cases combined occurs about as often in the lowest social stratum as in other classes. At any one time, the number of neurotic patients in treatment is greatest in the highest socioeconomic class; but the incidence rate, or number of new cases that develop each year, is about the same at all social levels (Hollingshead and Redlich, 1958). The lower rate of neurotic patients in treatment in the lower classes may be due as much to a tendency of those with little education to view neurotic symptoms as manifestations of physical disease, for which medication and rest are required, as to their inability to afford psychotherapy. Symptoms appear to be somewhat related to social class. In general, higher socioeconomic groups more often manifest vague psychological symptoms, whereas the lower classes tend to show a predominance of physical and behavioral symptoms. As the psychiatrist sees it, "The Class V [lowest socioeconomic group] neurotic behaves badly, the Class IV aches physically, the Class III patient defends fearfully, and the Class I–II patient is dissatisfied with himself" (Hollingshead and Redlich, 1958, p. 240). More often than not, physicians go along with the bodily aches and complaints of the verbally inarticulate lower-class patient and prescribe medication, whereas the Class I patient is treated by subtle and prolonged psychotherapy.

Treatment of Neuroses

The method of choice in the treatment of neuroses is psychotherapy. All psychological forms of treatment start with an inquiry into the nature of the patient's problems and aim at producing some beneficial change in behavior or personality. The extent and nature of the inquiry, the processes or techniques used, and the kinds of changes sought vary markedly with the therapist's orientation and the patient's clinical condition and financial resources. The inquiry phase may range from one or two interviews devoted to a statement of the complaint and relevant case-history data to the hundreds of sessions required by psychoanalysis for the comprehensive unraveling and critical examination of the conscious and unconscious components of the personality. During the inquiry, as well as later on, the patient is encouraged by the understanding and nonjudgmental attitude of the therapist to speak freely and frankly on personal matters. The briefer the period of inquiry, the more use is made of a conversational, semistructured, question-and-answer type of interview, aimed at identifying the specific problem as quickly as possible so that the therapist can proceed to corrective measures. When the inquiry is intensive, extensive, and prolonged, the sessions are less structured. The patient is encouraged to tell his story in his own way and at his own pace, to report dreams, make free associations, and so on. The recognized purpose of the treatment sessions, reinforced by occasional comments by the therapist, serves to direct communication on more or less relevant topics.

Advocates of intensive inquiry maintain that the procedure itself has therapeutic value. It is commonly observed that patients experience a tremendous sense of relief at discussing honestly their fears, inadequacies, hates, and guilt feelings, or at revealing for the first time in their lives some secret shameful act or thought. This cathartic effect is usually transient and of limited therapeutic significance. Of greater importance is the fact that the repressed or hitherto avoided sources of anxiety are brought out in the open, where they can be dealt with objectively and rationally. Now that he can take a long look at his early experience with adult eyes, the patient may himself realize that he has been exaggerating the uniqueness and severity of his "sinful" or "depraved" behavior during childhood and adolescence. The seeming horrendousness and unpardonableness of one's misdeeds and faults may be further lessened by the therapist's lack of surprise or shock at the "awful" disclosures and his continued unconditional acceptance of the patient as a person of worth. The therapist does not condone, forgive, or minimize past mistakes. They did occur. Memory traces of the events along with associated affects are permanently imprinted on the patient's nervous system and subject to recall. What many therapists try to do is to help the patient distinguish between the unique self, worthy of esteem, and his actions, some of which may have been or still are undesirable and in need of correction.

COUNSELING PROCEDURES

Adler (1929), Rogers (1951), Kelly (1955), Phillips (1956), and others have noted that the rigid, maladaptive behavior of neurotics often appears to be causally related to faulty attitudes, unrealistic expectations and goals, and discrepancies between the individual's real and imagined ideal self. With some variations, these authors have recommended counseling to re-evaluate patients' personal constructs, aspirations, and value systems; to explore and try out alternate possibilities; and to trim expectations and goals to fit their capabilities and life circumstances. In principle, the counseling process involves an objective discussion and appraisal of possible alternatives, with the final decision left to the patient. In practice, the patient tends to follow the cues and adopt the value systems of the therapist. From Rogers' point of view, a criterion of successful therapy is increased agreement between the real and ideal selves.

One counseling procedure that borders on behavior therapy is rational-emotive psychotherapy, founded by Ellis (1967). One of his basic tenets is that neurotics needlessly create anxiety and anger by accepting uncritically certain irrational hypotheses: that it is essential to be loved or approved by virtually every significant person one meets; that to be considered a worthwhile person one should be competent in all respects; that it is catastrophic if one does not discover the solution to human problems. Ellis also holds that neurotics constantly, both consciously and unconsciously, tell themselves irrational, nonsensical things that keep them continually upset and impede their performance. Thus a person who is uneasy in social situations may constantly tell himself that people do not like him, that they speak disparagingly about him, that he is inferior to just about everyone he has ever met.

The therapist explains the general mechanisms of emotional disturbances and gives the patient some literature to read, and may direct him to engage in certain specific activities outside of therapy. Patients are seen once a week or less and encouraged to work out their own problems with significant people in their lives. The therapist repeatedly demonstrates that the maladaptiveness of the patient's behavior is not due to external events, but rather to his irrational interpretation of his experiences and his defeatist attitude that he is incapable of winning the acceptance of others because he doesn't measure up to them. The aims of therapy are to increase the patient's confidence and independence and to train him to react to life circumstances with a minimum of anxiety and hostility. The patient is taught that it is possible to accept himself as a worthwhile human being just because he exists. All that is expected of him is that he make some kind of interesting, satisfying life for himself and have some commitment to something outside of himself, whether to people, things, or ideas. His intrinsic value is not dependent on external criteria of popularity, achievement and the opinions of others. This down-to-earth approach works with some patients. Others prefer and respond better to therapies that encourage them to strive for maximum self-realization, to move toward people, to be less egocentric, and to establish genuine bonds of affection with others.

PSYCHOANALYTIC THERAPY

As we have seen, psychoanalytic therapy is aimed at strengthening the ego at the expense of the id by "lifting" repressed material from the unconscious to the conscious, where it can be interpreted and integrated with the rest of conscious content. With the aid of free association and dream analysis, the therapist facilitates the recall and assimilation of repressed material while maintaining a relatively objective, nonevaluative attitude. The interpretation and resolution of the transference phenomenon contributes to cognitive insight. Transference represents a repetition of the infantile neurosis, with the analyst serving as a convenient target for the expression of feelings and attitudes the child originally had for his parents. The fact that the analyst does not react to the projected feelings and attitudes as the parents did forces the patient to reexamine and correct his infantile reaction patterns.

Up to this point, most analysts are in accord. But many of them disagree on the necessary length of treatment, the desirability of countertransference, and the relative emphasis that should be placed on current rather than past difficulties. The traditional belief that the probability of recovery is directly related to length of treatment has been challenged by several analysts. Prolonged treatment over several years has not been found to be any more effective than shorter treatment. A more serious criticism is that prolonged therapy often leads to dependency and regressive attitudes. Alexander (1963) favors the periodic interruption of treatment to give the natural recuperative powers of the human personality a chance to function. During temporary interruptions, the patient often discovers he can take over his own management, an important step in gaining self-confidence. The orthodox view that the analyst should strive to remain a "blank screen" has been rejected by many analysts as unrealistic. Two-way interaction between therapist and patient is a more natural procedure, and many analysts have found it more effective. The classical Freudian emphasis on the reconstruction of the patient's childhood history is important in giving him an understanding of the source of his difficulties, but he is really more concerned with his present problems, and Alexander maintains that that's where the analyst's focus should be. The understanding of the past should be related to and subordinated to the patient's circumstances here and now. Finally, many analysts today are interested in combining the insights of psychoanalysis with the principles of learning theory. Analytic therapy may be regarded as an educational process aimed at the unlearning of the reactions of childhood and the acquisition of new, more effective, and more satisfying adult response patterns. The nonreinforced repetition of the infantile neurosis during transference may be interpreted as facilitating extinction. Countertransference, or an increase in the analyst's involvement with the patient, encourages and rewards the emergence of new, more adaptive responses.

BEHAVIOR THERAPY

The terms "behavior therapy" and "behavior modification" refer to a variety of techniques that utilize learning concepts to produce some desired change in behavior. Behavior therapy focuses on observable and measurable changes in specific responses. When the therapist seeks case-history information, his main concern is with the disturbing behavior or the specific symptom that is to be changed. Detailed information is obtained during the initial interviews on the types of stimuli or situations that elicit, aggravate, or ameliorate the symptom response, and the learning contingencies that have influenced and shaped the response and currently support it.

The early sessions may be devoted to a general discussion of the patient's problem, explanations, and reassurances. Patients under pressure to talk about their difficulties are permitted to do so, but this sort of traditional procedure is mainly used for purposes of clarification and the establishment of rapport. No attempt is made to identify the childhood determinants of neurosis or to help the patient gain insight and resolve intrapsychic conflicts. Since a basic premise of behavior theory is that neurotic symptoms represent persistent acquired habits that can be unlearned, the therapy proper starts with the application of some learning process. Certain techniques are favored for specific types of problems, but the general approach is one of experimentation. If one technique does not work, another is tried. The principal behavior modification procedures are counterconditioning, systematic desensitization, operant conditioning, and role rehearsal associated with assertive training (Wolpe and Lazarus, 1966; Ullmann and Krasner, 1965).

Counterconditioning. In 1924 M. C. Jones demonstrated the applicability of conditioning procedures in the treatment of a phobia. The subject in this now classic study was Peter, a three-year-old who had a great fear of furry objects. Treatment consisted of associating the sight of a rabbit with the pleasurable experience of eating. While Peter was happily eating, a rabbit in a cage was introduced at the far end of the room. On subsequent days the rabbit was brought closer and closer as Peter had his lunch. Care was taken to maintain a safe distance, so that the positive relaxed state associated with eating was stronger than the fear response. Under these conditions, Peter learned to accept and react favorably to the rabbit. By the end of the experiment he was able to stroke the rabbit without signs of fear. Moreover, the acquired positive response to the rabbit was generalized to other animals and furry objects.

Two other early proponents of counterconditioning in the elimination of fears were Burnham (1924) and Hollingworth (1930). Guthrie (1935) proposed that the basic rule for breaking a habit was to practice other responses to cues that initiated the habit. In 1958 Wolpe introduced his concept of reciprocal inhibition as the general principle underlying the counterconditioning of anxiety responses.

> The elimination of anxiety-response habits always seems to require the inhibition of anxiety by a competing response. The formal process is the establishment of conditioned inhibition through what has been called the "reciprocal inhibition principle": If a response inhibitory of anxiety can be made to occur in the presence of anxiety-evoking stimuli, it will weaken the bond between these stimuli and the anxiety [Wolpe and Lazarus, 1966, p. 12].

Systematic desensitization. There is a danger in the application of counterconditioning procedures: the anxiety response to a stimulus may be greater than the planned inhibitory response. The solution proposed by Wolpe and Lazarus is to break the anxiety-response pattern into small units that can be eliminated one by one. Using information obtained from the patient, the therapist establishes an anxiety hierarchy consisting of anxiety-evoking stimuli or situations arranged in descending order of intensity of reaction. An abbreviated hierarchy of stimuli related to a fear of flying, for example, might be:

1. Being airborne in a plane.
2. Sitting in a plane.
3. Going to an airport for the purpose of taking a trip by air.
4. Planning a trip by air.
5. Thinking about flying.
6. Watching an airplane in the sky.
7. Seeing a picture of an airplane.

The patient is given detailed instructions and practice in progressive relaxation. After he has attained the capacity to calm himself at will and is in a relaxed state, he is asked to imagine the scene or situation that is least anxiety-provoking. If this does not arouse any significant anxiety, the next scene in the hierarchy is presented. Usually three or four steps in the hierarchy are presented during an individual session, until the patient can imagine the most anxiety-provoking scene without becoming upset. When fear has been generalized to related stimuli, it may be necessary to work through several hierarchical sets. It is inferred that when desensitization is successful, the relaxation responses become connected to stimuli that formerly evoked anxiety. The goal, of course, is to generalize clinical improvements made in the therapeutic setting to real-life situations. Wolpe (1961) has reported complete or almost complete freedom from phobic reactions outside of the therapeutic setting in twenty-seven of thirty-nine randomly selected patients, or approximately seventy percent of the cases.

Operant conditioning. This procedure is based on the principle of reinforcement, which holds that behavior is largely controlled by its consequences and that it can be modified and maintained by manipulating the consequences. Bachrach, Erwin, and Mohr (1965) have reported an interesting example of control of eating behavior in an anorexic patient by operant conditioning techniques. Because of a pathological loss of appetite, the patient had lost 73 pounds over a number of years—and she had weighed only 120 to begin with. Now thirty-seven years old and weighing forty-seven pounds, she was in imminent danger of death by starvation if normal eating behavior were not quickly restored.

The first step in the treatment procedure was to establish a suitable environment. Before operant conditioning was begun, the patient was installed in an attractive hospital room with radio, television, books, records, and magazines readily available and with free access to visitors. Since she seemed to enjoy receiving visitors, playing records, and watching television, it was decided to use these as reinforcing contingents.

Without warning or explanation the patient was now transferred to a barren room overlooking the hospital courtyard and furnished only with a bed, night stand, and chair. Here she would stay, deprived of all pleasurable activities, unless she ate. Her family, the hospital administrators, and the nursing staff cooperated in this unusual procedure, but the patient herself was told nothing of the plan. Arrangements were made for a member of the training staff to eat each meal with her. The initial shaping schedule called for rewarding the patient for any activity associated with eating. If she lifted her fork toward the food, the experimenter would talk to her about something of interest. Step by step, the response required to attract the experimenter's attention and conversation was increased to lifting food toward her mouth, chewing, and so on. Other reinforcements were gradually introduced. At first the patient was permitted the use of a radio, television, or phonograph after a meal if she had eaten any part of it. If she ate nothing, nothing would be done in the way of reinforcement, and she would be left alone until the next meal. Gradually she was required to eat more and more of the meal in order to have access to the radio or television set. Meals were slowly increased in caloric value, and the patient was allowed her choice among alternative menus. As her weight began to rise, other reinforcements were added: the company of other patients in her room at mealtime, walks around the grounds, increased visits by members of her family, hair care, and so on. When it was discovered that although the patient was now eating, she was no longer gaining weight, the situation was changed to permit reinforcement only if there was a gain in weight, however slight.

After two months she had gained fourteen pounds. She was discharged from the hospital then, but continued to return at regular intervals for outpatient care. The assistance of the family was enlisted in carrying out a reinforcement program at home. She made a fairly good social adjustment in the community, but a year later she was readmitted to the hospital and the same reinforcement regimen was applied. When she was discharged a month later she had gained seven pounds, bringing her weight to eighty-eight pounds. She was offered a job as a general practical nurse in the hospital where she had been a patient, and she worked there for a year. When she quit her job—the hours were too demanding, she said—her weight had dropped to seventy-eight pounds.

Assertive training. Assertive training is recommended in the treatment of neurotics who have difficulty in expressing their feelings of anger and resentment when they are criticized or dominated by their parents, their employers, their husbands or wives, or other associates. The individual typically endures injustices and exploitation without standing up for his rights, and as a result, anxiety builds up and generalizes. The basic strategy, as proposed by Wolpe and Lazarus (1966), is to convince the patient

of the virtue of asserting his rights and to point out the emotional and social repercussions of inhibiting his anger. Citing some of the patient's own
interpersonal experiences, the therapist shows how the cumulative effects
of anxiety and tension can be avoided by dealing spontaneously with each
situation as it arises. Play-acting, or behavior rehearsal, as behaviorists prefer to call it, affords the patient an opportunity to learn and practice adaptive responses in "safe" situations. Incidents are reenacted, with the therapist and the patient frequently switching roles so that each plays the part
of the "other person." By playing the role of the patient, the therapist provides examples of assertive responses for the patient, who may need help
in defining the rights he may reasonably demand in a given situation and
in distinguishing between assertive and aggressive responses. The conquest
of anxiety depends on the consequences of the individual's attempts at self-
assertion. If his efforts result in punitive retaliation, he will be reluctant to
make further attempts. The therapist tries to avoid this by starting with a
mild counteraction to domination that has a high probability of successful
outcome. Each successful attempt reinforces the assertive role. As the patient gradually gains confidence and acquires a more favorable perception
of himself, the need for role-playing diminishes.

DRUG THERAPY

Tranquilizers and antidepressant drugs are extensively used in the treatment of neurosis. Their main advantage is that by relieving symptoms they
permit the patient, at slight cost in money and effort, to cope more effectively with his problems and responsibilities. On the other hand, the reduction in tension thus induced lowers motivation for seeking and continuing
with psychotherapy, which offers the possibility of a cure.

TREATMENT OUTCOME

Earlier reviews of studies of neurotic adults (Eysenck, 1961*b*) and children
(Levitt, 1957) showed that about two-thirds of treated patients recover or
show marked improvement within two years. The figure is quite stable regardless of the type of patient or the method of therapy. However, there is
some doubt whether this favorable finding can be credited to the effectiveness of psychotherapy. The spontaneous recovery rate of untreated patients
also runs about 65 to 70 percent. This finding does not necessarily rule out
the possibility of therapeutic effectiveness. Most of the earlier studies of
both treated and untreated populations were poorly controlled. A major
methodological difficulty is the problem of matching the relative severity
and kinds of problems presented by treated and untreated patients and by
patients given certain forms of therapy. The absence of valid, uniform criteria for evaluating improvement constitutes another major difficulty. Various criteria that have been used and suggested include the client's self-

evaluation, the therapist's subjective evaluation, and changes in the results obtained on objective and projective adjustment-measurement tests administered before and after therapy (Strupp and Bergen, 1969). Criteria of improvement in overt behavior include absence of symptoms formerly present, increased productiveness, more efficient use of potentialities, improved interpersonal relationships, and more positive, hopeful attitudes (Knight, 1941; Kennedy, 1960).

There is some evidence (Truax and Carkhuff, 1967; Bergen, 1966) that over a period of time most untreated patients show slight to moderate improvement, whereas the effects of therapy are more variable. Some patients get much better following therapy, and others become worse. The variable effects of treatment may be due to the application of the wrong procedures to specific patients or the ineptitude of the therapist. A recent rise in awareness that psychotherapy as currently practiced is not a unitary process applied to a unitary problem has led to a restatement of the problem. We need to ask not whether psychotherapy is effective, but rather which specific therapeutic interventions are effective in producing what specific changes in which specific patients under what specific conditions. Recent studies have indicated that behavior therapy may be more effective than other forms of therapy in the treatment of phobic reactions. More studies are required before a final evaluation can be made. It is characteristic of advocates of new approaches to report initial optimistic results. Experience may indicate that behavior therapy is particularly effective in treating certain types of neurosis but not necessarily the treatment of choice in all neuroses.

Experimental Neurosis in Animals

Some aspects of neurosis are restricted to man. Only human beings can describe the personal content of their neuroses and the subjective feelings associated with them. But the development of techniques for inducing neurotic disturbances of behavior in lower animals has afforded an opportunity for examining under controlled laboratory conditions the more overt or objectively observable components of neurosis. Animal research has been particularly helpful in evaluating the importance of constitutional factors, the role of stress, the nature of neurotic symptoms, and the relative effectiveness of certain forms of treatment. The significance of inherent constitutional factors in the relative vulnerability of individual animals to induced neurotic behavior has already been discussed in Chapter 6.

THE ROLE OF STRESS

The usual procedure for producing an experimental neurosis is to subject the animal to a conflict situation from which there is no excape. Restraint of activity and compulsory decision-making are essential. Exposing the animal to an unsolvable maze-learning problem that permits freedom of movement or avoidance of any response does not lead to neurosis. In the classical Pavlovian model, the animal is restrained by a harness and is required to discriminate between two conditioned stimuli that initially are readily differentiated but gradually become indistinguishable. A procedure utilized by Liddell (1944) begins by conditioning the animal to flex its foreleg when it hears a slow metronome beat. This is done by repeatedly pairing the sound of the beat with a mild shock to the foreleg. When the slow beat has become established as a dependable conditioned stimulus for eliciting the flexing of the leg, the metronome beat is speeded up. The quick beat is never accompanied by shock. Following repeated nonreinforced trials, the fast beat becomes a negative stimulus that serves as a cue for inhibition of the leg flection. After the animal has learned to make the correct discriminatory response, the two beats are gradually made more and more alike until the animal can no longer differentiate the positive or excitatory stimulus from the negative or inhibitory stimulus. At this point, disorganization occurs. The animal shows obvious signs of emotional distress, tears at the restraining apparatus, responds erratically to incidental stimuli, loses the capacity to make even simple discriminations, and may assume a rigid, cataleptic posture. This disorganization in behavior, with its accompanying autonomic disturbances, is persistent and resistant to treatment. Symptoms tend to be less pronounced outside the laboratory, but cues associated with the traumatic experience reinstate the emotional excitement and deviant behavior.

Neurotic sheep studied by Liddell were less gregarious than other sheep in the pasture. When startled, they would flee in the opposite direction from the rest of the flock. When dogs got into the pasture, it was invariably the neurotic sheep that were killed. The neurotic ewes had a higher abortion rate and often failed to establish adequate maternal-neote relations. Gantt (1944) has reported a detailed case history of a neurotic dog that manifested continued and varied symptoms over a twelve-year period, even though most of the years were spent on a farm. In short, exposure to stress produces enduring neurotic behavior in animals that previously were symptom-free.

Pavlov (1941) attributed the production of neurosis to a clash between cortical excitations and inhibitions or to an overstraining of the excitatory or inhibitory capacities of the animal. Masserman (1943) has demonstrated that it is possible to produce neurotic behavior in cats and other animals by creating a conflict of motives. As a first step, a cat is trained to respond to a signal of light by opening a food box to obtain a pellet of food. The animal is then trained to depress a switch that permits him to operate the feeding signal at will. After this self-feeding pattern has been established, a conflict is induced by subjecting the cat at irregular intervals to a mild shock or blast of air as he reaches for the food. Following several such experiences, the conflict resulting from the contraposing of the animal's needs and the unpredictability of results when he tries to satisfy them leads to a variety of maladaptive neurotic behavior patterns. Responses noted in a number of animals include trembling, rigid crouching, fast-pounding pulse, refusal of food leading to starvation, stereotyped or ritualistic movements, diarrhea, deviant sexual behavior, extreme timidity, and unpredictable aggression. As we noted in Chapter 6, genetic differences in temperament may account for some of the variations in the severity of behavior disorganization of animals under stress. But other factors are also important. Masserman (1961) found that cats that had been given free run of their quarters, permitted to mate at will, catch mice, and so on, were less adversely affected by exposure to stress than isolated cats confined to cages. And he goes on to draw a human parallel: people with multiple interests can better withstand frustration and conflict than those whose existence centers about a single vulnerable adaptation.

Studies conducted with rats and mice on the effects of infantile stimulation on adult emotionality point to a U-shaped relationship. Exposure to a moderate amount of stress during infancy (handling or shock) reduced adult emotionality, whereas animals that had never been handled and those that had been subjected to extreme infantile stimulation tended to show increased emotionality in adulthood (Myers, 1965; Adler, 1966).

The possibility that the prenatal emotional state of the mothers may influence the emotionality of their offspring has been investigated by Hockman (1961) and Thompson et al. (1962). Both researchers found that female rats subjected to stress experiences during pregnancy gave birth to offspring that were more emotional than control groups.

THE NATURE OF NEUROTIC SYMPTOMS

The similarity between neurosis in humans and neurotic reactions experimentally induced in animals provides further evidence that neuroses differ mainly in degree and duration from normal reactions to stress. No disease entity is involved. Neurotic reactions in animals, like those in humans, are involuntary, relatively uncontrollable, maladaptive, and obviously distressing to the organism. Two constant factors are diffuse emotional excitement or anxiety and rigid, inflexible, repetitive behavior (Wilson, 1963). Animal studies have helped clarify what Mowrer has referred to as the neurotic paradox: the fact that neurotic behavior seemingly defies common-sense pleasure-pain motivation theories and the laws of learning. The normal expectation is that actions that have favorable net effects are reinforced and repeated, whereas those that have unfavorable consequences are extinguished, inhibited, and abandoned. The neurotic persists in engaging in self-defeating, detrimental behavior month after month and year after year. Furthermore, as Freud has emphasized (1933), the neurotic will seek treatment at great sacrifice in time, money, and effort, but at the same time he will vigorously resist therapeutic efforts to free him of the symptoms that cause him and those about him so much suffering.

Alexander and French (1946) have suggested that the persistence of stereotyped neurotic behavior is related to the individual's avoidance of the problem. In normal development, new experiences modify past patterns. When the problem is too disturbing to face, no new learning occurs. An experimental confirmation of this possibility has been reported by Mowrer (1948). A rat is put at the left end of an alleyway about four feet long with high sides and ends. The floor of the alley consists of a grill that can be used for administering shock. Ten seconds after being placed at the left end of the alley, the rat is shocked by an electric charge that is run through the entire length of the grill. In the course of trial-and-error activity, the shocked rat discovers an opening at the extreme right end of the alley that leads into a small compartment where there is no shock. On subsequent trials the process is repeated. The rat is placed at the left end of the alley and shock is administered ten seconds later. After a few trials the rat learns to escape shock by running to the safe compartment within the ten-second period of grace. When this escape pattern has been well established, the procedure is revised by permanently charging the right half of the grill and leaving the grill at the left end uncharged. Upon being placed into the now "safe" left end, the rat promptly runs across the charged grill at the right to get to the compartment. This voluntary exposure to shock goes on for hundreds of trials. To cure the animal, the investigator blocks the entrance to the safety compartment. To escape from the charged right end of the alley, the rat retreats to the uncharged left end. Finding that this end is now free of shock, the rat discontinues his flight into shock.

A somewhat similar series of studies based on traumatic avoidance learning in dogs was conducted by Solomon and Wynne (1954). Their apparatus consisted of a shuttle box divided into two compartments by a barrier. A dog was placed in one compartment, which had a gridded floor. Ten seconds after the animal was placed in the compartment, a shock was administered through the grid. The animal soon learned to jump over the barrier, usually within two seconds after he had been placed in the compartment. This pattern continued through hundreds of extinction trials. If the barrier was raised so that it was not possible for the dog to jump over it, the animal exhibited signs of intense anxiety. Since the animal had not been remaining in the gridded portion of the box long enough to know that shock was no longer being administered, no new learning occurred, and the gridded compartment itself (the conditioned stimulus) continued to arouse anxiety, which was relieved by the instrumental response of jumping.

Unlike the dog, a human neurotic may realize that his symptoms are irrational and self-defeating, but as long as they are effective in relieving anxiety, they serve an important function, as the dog's do for him, and are self-perpetuating. Normal individuals avoid this dilemma by facing former areas of trauma and, in the light of more favorable or neutral subsequent experiences, learn new and more adaptive responses. Animal studies (Sandler, 1964) have shown that self-punishing or masochistic behavior can be explained on the basis of standard learning principles, without recourse to inferred concepts of guilt or superego conflicts. Through proper manipulation of stimuli and reinforcement agents, animals may be trained to tolerate severe electric shock with no overt signs of pain or distress, to administer self-punishment over long periods for meager and uncertain rewards, and even to work for punishment alone.

The initial adaptiveness of neurotic behavior is illustrated by Maier's (1949) experimental studies of frustration. He placed a rat on a jumping stand and confronted it with two cards placed side by side in the windows of a vertical screen. One card showed a black circle against a white background and the other a white circle against a black background. The cards could be latched in place or left free so that they could be easily knocked over. The rat was required to jump at the cards. If the "correct" response was made, the card fell over and the animal landed on a platform, where it found food. If the "incorrect" response was made, the animal hit the latched card with his nose and fell into a protective net. When the problem was solvable—when food was always obtained by jumping at the card with the white circle, for example, regardless of its position—the animal had no difficulty in learning the correct symbol. But when the problem was made unsolvable by latching the cards in random order, the animal soon refused to jump at all. If it was forced to do so by being shocked or exposed to a blast of air, the rat tended to settle eventually on a position stereotype. Most rats exposed to this situation consistently jumped at the card on the left or the card on the right, no matter which card it happened to be. Since this solution permitted a 50 percent chance of success, the stereotyped response actually assured maximum success. Also indicative of the adaptiveness of the response was the observation that once the fixated response had been acquired, the animal jumped more readily than he had before, appeared less nervous, and had fewer seizures.

As long as the problem remained unsolvable, the animal could not be faulted for its stereotyped response pattern, which in fact represented the best solution under the circumstances. But the persistence of the fixed-position response when the situation was altered so that a more effective solution was possible was suggestive of neurotic behavior. Animals that had acquired the habit of consistently jumping at the card on the right continued to do so even when the window to the left was kept open with food in plain sight. Like human neurotics, these animals apparently knew better, but persisted in their self-defeating behavior just the same. When placed on the jumping stand, they would appropriately turn and face the open window on the left, sniff the food, and then jump at the locked door on the right. This irrational response continued over numerous trials. Neither punishment nor extinction techniques were effective in eliminating the fixated response. When the fixated response was prevented, however, so that the animal had no alternative to the "correct" response, it was possible to train the animal to choose the reward card in five to ten trials.

Summary

Neurotic reactions are distinguished from psychosis by the absence of severe impairment in psychosocial functioning and of gross distortion of external reality. The neurotic experiences no delusions, hallucinations, or personality disorganization. He can usually carry on his work and meet his personal and social responsibilities with reasonable adequacy. The core problem is excessive anxiety, which may be expressed directly or in substitute reactions that are considered to be defenses against anxiety: hysterical conversion, hysterical dissociative, phobic, obsessive-compulsive, depressive, neurasthenic, depersonalization, and hypochondriacal reactions. The neurotic does not understand the nature or meaning of these reactions, but he does realize they are symptoms for which he should seek treatment. Neurotic reactions that appear to have some specific etiological background are sometimes assigned special labels: existential neurosis, occupational neurosis, war neurosis.

Proposed contributory causes include genetic endowment, autonomic instability, developmental flaws, unresolved intrapsychic conflicts associated with the Oedipus complex, unfavorable learning experiences, and exposure to overwhelming stress situations. The techniques of treatment tend to be related to the presumed dominant cause. About 65 to 70 percent of neurotic patients show good clinical improvement, whether or not they have received formal treatment. This somewhat surprising finding may be due to variations in the competence of therapists and the tendency of each therapist to have a favored approach that he uses with most of his patients. It is quite probable that highly qualified therapists who work only with certain kinds of problems or who adapt their methods to the patient obtain much better results than the statistical average.

References

ADLER, A. *The Practice and Theory of Individual Psychology.* New York: Harcourt, Brace, 1929.

ADLER, R. "Frequency of Stimulation During Early Life and Subsequent Emotionality in the Rat." *Psychological Reports* 18 (1966): 695–701.

ALEXANDER, F. "The Dynamics of Psychotherapy in the Light of Learning Theory." *American Journal of Psychiatry* 120 (1963): 440–48.

ALEXANDER, R., and FRENCH, T. M. *Psychoanalytic Therapy.* New York: Ronald Press, 1946.

BACHRACH, A. J.; ERWIN, W. J.; and MOHR, J. P. "The Control of Eating Behavior in an Anorexic by Operant Conditioning Techniques." In *Case Studies in Behavior Modification,* ed. L. P. Ullmann and L. Krasner, pp. 153–63. New York: Holt, Rinehart & Winston, 1965.

BANDURA, A., and WALTERS, R. H. *Social Learning and Personality Development.* New York: Holt, Rinehart & Winston, 1963.

BEARD, G. M. *A Practical Treatise on Nervous Exhaustion.* New York: Wood, 1880.

BERGEN, A. E. "Some Implications of Psychotherapy Research for Therapeutic Practice." *Journal of Abnormal Psychology* 71 (1961): 235–46.

BRILL, N. Q. "Gross Stress Reactions: Traumatic War Neurosis." In *Comprehensive Textbook of Psychiatry,* ed. A. M. Friedman, H. I. Kaplan, and H. S. Kaplan, pp. 1031–35. Baltimore: Williams & Wilkins, 1967.

——— and BEEBE, G. W. *A Follow-up Study of War Neuroses.* Veterans' Administration medical monograph. Washington, D.C.: U.S. Government Printing Office, 1955.

BURNHAM, W. H. *The Normal Mind.* New York: Appleton, 1924.

CAMERON, N. A. *Personality Development and Psychopathology.* Boston: Houghton Mifflin, 1963.

CARTER, H. D. "Twin Similarities in Personality Traits." *Journal of Genetic Psychology* 43 (1933): 312–21.

DOHRENWEND, B. S., and DOHRENWEND, P. F. "Field Studies of Social Factors in Relation to Three Types of Psychological Disorders." *Journal of Abnormal Psychology* 72 (1967): 369–78.

DOLLARD, J., and MILLER, N. E. *Personality and Psychotherapy.* New York: McGraw-Hill, 1950.

ELLIS, A. "Goals of Psychotherapy." In *The Goals of Psychotherapy,* ed. A. R. Mahrer. New York: Appleton-Century-Crofts, 1967.

ESSEN-MOLLER, E. "Twin Research and Psychiatry." *International Journal of Psychiatry* 1 (1965): 466–75. Originally published in *Acta Psychiatrica et Neurologica* 39 (1963): 65–77.

EYSENCK, H. J. "Classification and the Problems of Diagnosis." In *Handbook of Abnormal Psychology,* ed. H. J. Eysenck. New York: Basic Books, 1961 (*a*).

———. "The Effects of Psychotherapy." In *Handbook of Abnormal Psychology,* ed. H. J. Eysenck. New York: Basic Books, 1961(*b*).

——— and PRELL, D. B. "The Inheritance of Neuroticism: An Experimental Study." *Journal of Mental Sciences* 97 (1951): 441–65.

——— and RACHMAN, S. *The Causes and Cures of Neurosis.* San Diego, Calif.: Knapp, 1965.

FOULDS, G. A., and CAINE, T. M. "Symptom Clusters and Personality Types Among Psychoneurotic Men Compared with Women." *Journal of Mental Science* 105 (1959): 469–75.

FREUD, S. *New Introductory Lectures on Psychoanalysis,* trans. J. H. Sprott. New York: Norton, 1933.

————. "Analysis of a Phobia in a Five-Year-Old Boy." In *Collected Papers,* vol. 10, pp. 5–149. London: Hogarth Press, 1957.

GANTT, W. H. *Experimental Basis for Neurotic Behavior.* New York: Hoeber, 1944.

GOTTESMAN, I. "Personality and Natural Selection." In *Methods and Goals in Human Behavior Genetics,* ed. S. G. Vandenberg, pp. 63–80. New York: Academic Press, 1965.

GRINKER, R. R., and SPIEGEL, J. P. *Men Under Stress.* New York: McGraw-Hill, 1945.

GUTHRIE, E. R. *The Psychology of Learning.* New York: Harper, 1935.

HOCKMAN, C. H. "Prenatal Maternal Stress in the Rat: Its Effects on Emotional Behavior in the Offspring." *Journal of Comparative and Physiological Psychology* 54 (1961): 679–84.

HOLLINGSHEAD, A. B., and REDLICH, F. C. *Social Class and Mental Illness.* New York: Wiley, 1958.

HOLLINGWORTH, H. L. *Abnormal Psychology.* New York: Ronald Press, 1930.

JANIS, I. L. *Air War and Emotional Stress.* New York: McGraw-Hill, 1951.

JONES, M. C. "A Laboratory Study of Fear: The Case of Peter." *Journal of Genetic Psychology* 31 (1924): 308–15.

KELLY, G. A. *The Psychology of Personal Constructs.* New York: Norton, 1955.

KENNEDY, A. "Chance and Design in Psychotherapy." *Journal of Mental Science* 106 (1960): 3–10.

KENYON, F. E. "Hypochondriasis: A Survey of Some Historical, Clinical, and Social Aspects." *British Journal of Psychiatry* 38 (1965): 117–34.

KNIGHT, R. P. "Evaluation of the Results of Psychoanalytic Therapy." *American Journal of Psychiatry* 98 (1941): 434–44.

LEVITT, E. E. "The Results of Psychotherapy with Children: An Evaluation." *Journal of Consulting Psychology* 21 (1957): 189–96.

LIDDELL, H. S. "Conditioned Reflex Method and Experimental Neurosis." In *Personality and Behavior Disorders,* ed. J. McV. Hunt, vol. 1, pp. 389–412. New York: Ronald Press, 1944.

MADDI, S. R. "The Existential Neurosis." *Journal of Abnormal Psychology* 72 (1967). 311–25.

MAIER, N. R. F. *Frustration: The Study of Behavior Without a Goal.* New York: McGraw-Hill, 1949.

MASSERMAN, J. H. *Behavior and Neurosis.* Chicago: University of Chicago Press, 1943.

————. *Principles of Dynamic Psychiatry.* Philadelphia: Saunders, 1961.

MOWRER, O. H. "Learning Theory and the Neurotic Paradox." *American Journal of Orthopsychiatry* 18 (1948): 571–610.

MYERS, E. "Effects of Different Intensities of Postweaning Shock and Handling on the Albino Rat." *Journal of Genetic Psychology* 106 (1965): 51–58.

NEWMAN, H. H.; FREEMAN, N.; and HOLZINGER, K. J. *Twins: A Study of Heredity and Environment.* Chicago: University of Chicago Press, 1937.

PAVLOV, I. P. *Conditioned Reflexes and Psychiatry,* trans. W. H. Gantt. New York: International Publishers, 1941.

PFEIFFER, E. *Disordered Behavior.* London: Oxford University Press, 1968.

PHILLIPS, E. L. *Psychotherapy: A Modern Theory and Practice.* New York: Prentice-Hall, 1956.

PRINCE, M. *The Dissociation of a Personality.* New York: Longmans, 1908.

RAINES, G. N., and KOLB, L. C. "Combat Fatigue and War Neurosis." *Naval Medical Bulletin* 41 (1943): 923–36.

ROGERS, C. *Client-Centered Therapy.* Boston: Houghton Mifflin, 1951.

ROSENBERG, C. M. "Personality and Obsessional Neurosis." *British Journal of Psychiatry* 113 (1967): 471–77.

SANDLER, J. "Masochism: An Empirical Analysis." *Psychological Bulletin* 62 (1964): 197–204.

SARGENT, W., and SLATER, E. "Acute War Neuroses." *Lancet,* July 6, 1940, pp. 1–2.

SHAPIRO, D. *Neurotic Styles.* New York: Basic Books, 1965.

SHEPHERD, M., and GRUENBERG, E. M. "The Age for Neuroses." *Milbank Memorial Fund Quarterly* 3 (1957): 258–65.

SHIELDS, J. *Monozygotic Twins, Brought Up Apart and Brought Up Together.* London: Oxford University Press, 1962.

——— and SLATER, E. "Heredity and Psychological Abnormality." In *Handbook of Abnormal Psychology,* ed. H. J. Eysenck, pp. 298–343. New York: Basic Books, 1961.

SLATER, E. "Genetic Factors in Neurosis." *British Journal of Psychology* 55 (1964): 265–69.

——— and WOODSIDE, M. *Patterns of Marriage.* London: Cassell, 1951.

SOLOMON, R. L., and WYNNE, L. C. "Traumatic Avoidance Learning: The Principles of Anxiety Conservation and Irreversibility." *Psychological Review* 61 (1954): 353–84.

STEPHENS, J. H., and KAMP, M. "On Some Aspects of Hysteria: A Clinical Study." *Journal of Nervous and Mental Disease* 134 (1962): 305–15.

STRUPP, H. H., and BERGEN, A. E. "Some Empirical and Conceptual Bases for Coordinated Research in Psychotherapy: A Critical Review of Issues, Trends, and Evidence." *International Journal of Psychiatry* 7 (1969): 19–90.

THIGPEN, C. H., and CLECKLEY, H. M. *Three Faces of Eve.* New York: McGraw-Hill, 1957.

THOMPSON, W. R.; WATSON, J.; and CHARLESWORTH, W. R. "The Effects of Prenatal Maternal Stress on Offspring Behavior in Rats." *Psychological Monographs* 76, no. 38 (1962).

TOMPKINS, V. H. "Stress in Aviation." In *The Nature of Stress Disorder,* ed. J. Hambling, pp. 73–80. Springfield, Ill.: Charles C. Thomas, 1959.

TRUAX, C. B., and CARKHUFF, R. R. *Toward Effective Counseling and Psychotherapy: Training and Practice.* Chicago: Aldine, 1967.

ULLMANN, L. P., and KRASNER, L. *Case Studies in Behavior Modification.* New York: Holt, Rinehart & Winston, 1965.

VANDENBERG, S. G. "Contributions of Twin Research to Psychology." *Psylogical Bulletin* 66 (1966): 327–52.

WEISS, E., and ENGLISH, O. S. *Psychosomatic Medicine.* Philadelphia: Saunders, 1943.

WHITE, R. W. *The Abnormal Personality.* New York: Ronald Press, 1964.

WILSON, R. S. "On Behavior Pathology." *Psychological Bulletin* 60 (1963): 130–46.

WOLPE, J. *Psychotherapy by Reciprocal Inhibition.* Stanford, Calif.: Stanford University Press, 1958.

———. "The Systematic Desensitization Treatment of Neuroses." *Journal of Nervous and Mental Disease* 132 (1961): 189–203.

———. *The Practice of Behavior Therapy.* New York: Pergamon Press, 1969.

——— and LAZARUS, A. A. *Behavior Therapy Techniques.* New York: Pergamon Press, 1966.

CHAPTER TWELVE

Personality Disorders

The continuum concept of psychopathology assumes an intermediate or borderline state between normal and definitely abnormal behavior. The category of personality disorders bridges the gap between normal and neurotic or psychotic behavior. Personality disorders may be more accurately described as personality types marked by deeply ingrained maladaptive behavior patterns. The "disorder" consists essentially of flaws in the basic personality structure. More specifically, it involves defects in temperament, perception of self and others, general orientation to life, and characteristic mode of response. A diagnostic label of schizoid, compulsive, paranoid, hysterical, or antisocial personality indicates both the nature of the maladaptive behavior and its presumed relationship to more severe disorders. The concept of personality types is, of course, an artifact of convenience. Each individual is unique. For purposes of classification and clinical study, however, it is helpful to group together persons who share certain behavior characteristics in varying degrees. It is understood that the categories overlap and that persons placed in the same category show wide individual differences even in the traits they share. An analogous practice is the stratagem of arbitrarily differentiating among individuals, for rough descriptive purposes, on the basis of outstanding physical characteristics: tall and thin, short and stocky, tall and heavy, and so on.

The adult personality types described in the *Diagnostic and Statistical Manual* (DSM-11) of the American Psychiatric Association are listed in Table 12.1. The diagnostic terms proposed for use with children in the 1966 classification prepared by the Group for the Advancement of Psychiatry (GAP) are more general but cover essentially the same personality types. Millon (1969) has attempted to incorporate personality disorders within

303

Table 12.1. Three proposed lists of personality disorders
(*personality types*)

American Psychiatric Association	Group for the Advancement of Psychiatry	Millon
Paranoid	Mistrustful	Paranoid-inde-pendent-ambivalent
Cyclothymic		Cycloid-dependent-ambivalent
Schizoid	Isolated	Detached-active-avoidant
Explosive (aggressive)	Impulse-ridden	Ambivalent-active-negativistic
Obsessive-compulsive	Compulsive	Ambivalent-passive-conforming
Hysterical (histrionic)	Hysterical	Dependent-active-gregarious
Asthenic		Detached-passive-asocial
Antisocial (sociopathic)	Tension discharge	Independent-active-aggressive
Passive-aggressive	Oppositional	Ambivalent-active-negativistic
Inadequate		Dependent-passive-submissive
Passive-dependent	Overly dependent	
	Overly independent	Independent-passive-narcissistic

a broader theoretical framework. His main premise is that the traditionally recognized personality types may be interpreted as deviations from the norm in degree of detachment, dependence, independence, and ambivalence. Detachment and other key characteristics may be active or passive. For example, the hysterical personality is described as active-dependent and the inadequate personality as passive-dependent. All three classification systems recognize or imply that:

1. Personality disorders are distinguished by a restricted repertoire of behavior patterns. An individual diagnosed as having a personality disorder typically exhibits the same sort of behavior in all situations. He makes little or no attempt to vary his behavior to fit the circumstances. Thus he may be consistently aggressive, detached, suspicious, or dependent. The inappropriateness of such rigid response is self-defeating and leads to poor social adjustment.

2. The person who has a personality disorder accepts his behavior pattern as "normal" for him. He is not unduly disturbed either by the nature of his personality traits or by the frequent occurrence of interpersonal difficulties resulting from the inappropriateness of his stereotyped feelings, thoughts, and actions. He rarely seeks treatment on his own initiative. If his family or others insist on therapy, he is usually uncooperative. His unresponsiveness to therapy is understandable, since therapy poses a threat to his one and only way of behaving.

3. The personality type is fashioned through the complex and cumulative interaction of genetic, environmental, and experiential determinants. The biological endowment of the infant (activity level, responsiveness, adaptiveness, stability of affect) is often a critical influence on the direction of development. As Millon points out, the infant's distinctive reactivity pattern elicits distinctive counterreactions from his parents and others. Inherent constitutional tendencies thus shape the nature of the experiences to which the child is exposed. The circular interaction between the child's biological constitution and his restricted and repetitive environmental experiences leads to distinctive modes of perceiving, feeling, thinking, and behaving. Each year the pattern is more deeply etched. By adolescence or earlier it is firmly established and highly resistant to change.

4. Since cultural factors also influence personality development, certain types of pathological personalities may be more prevalent in some cultures or subgroups than in others, but all types occur in all cultures and socioeconomic groups.

5. The recognized personality types are neither pure nor homogeneous. Persons with the same diagnosis show wide individual differences. Mixed types are common. An individual may exhibit both schizoid and paranoid features, or hysterical and antisocial behavior.

6. As a rule the pathological process is arrested at the level of personality disorder. It does not automatically progress to a clearly defined neurosis or psychosis. The individual experiences varying degrees of difficulty in interpersonal adjustment, but competence of functioning in school and work is usually not significantly affected. There is one exception: the inadequate personality.

7. Although most persons with disordered personalities do not go on to develop a neurosis or psychosis, the rigidity and nonadaptiveness of their behavior makes them highly vulnerable to stress. If they do "break" and are forced to resort to more desperate coping devices, the choice of neurosis or psychosis is influenced by the premorbid personality. A schizoid personality is more apt to manifest a schizophrenic than a depressive syndrome. In the case of mixed personality types, the direction of further disorder is less predictable.

The reactions of mild pathological personalities tend to be more extreme than similar behavior patterns noted in normal individuals. Normal behavior is more diversified, more flexible, and hence more adaptive. Under appropriate circumstances it is normal to be aggressive, suspicious, dependent, detached, passive, and even antisocial.

The boundaries of personality disorders are vaguely defined. The diagnosis is often used as a catchall for personality, character, and behavior deviations that do not fit neatly into other recognized categories. With some justification the diagnosis may be extended to include antisocial personalities and mild or early stages of psychosis or borderline neurosis. Its application to sexual deviance, excessive drinking, and drug misuse is less defensible. When these behavior patterns are excluded, personality disorders account for about 10 percent of first admissions to public mental hospitals and 6 percent of admissions to private mental hospitals and general hospitals with separate inpatient psychiatric units. The peak age of first admissions is between fifteen and twenty-four. Males assigned this diagnosis outnumber females among admissions to public mental hospitals, but females outnumber males among admissions to private mental hospitals and general hospitals. The duration of hospital stay is brief. Personality disorders constitute a small fraction of 1 percent of the resident populations of public mental hospitals (*Patients in Mental Institutions, 1965*).

Paranoid Personality

Characteristic traits of the paranoid personality include unwarranted suspicion, jealousy, envy, general distrust of others, rigidity, hypersensitivity to slights, and exaggerated feelings of self-importance. Judging others by himself, the paranoid person takes it for granted that others feel hostile toward him. His readiness to perceive deceit and aggression lead to repeated social difficulties and counteraggression, which confirm and reinforce his distrust (Millon, 1969). Safety lies in independence and self-reliance. The resulting isolation and limited communication deprives the paranoid of reality checks that might modify his distorted views. As part of his defensive posture the paranoid projects blame for mistakes and shortcomings on others.

The disruptive effect of this orientation on interpersonal relations is clearly seen in the report of a middle-aged woman, recently married for the first time, who sought professional advice on how to cope with her extremely jealous husband. During the courtship period she had been unable to understand why he had had difficulty in his previous two marriages, both of which had ended in divorce. He was completely devoted to her. He was interested in everything she did, accompanied her everywhere, and gave the impression that he loved her so much that he couldn't let her out of his sight. His attentiveness and interest continued after they were married, but now his wife found them stifling. She had to account for everything she did while he was away at work. If he phoned during the day and she failed to answer, she had to face a cross-examination that night. If she casually looked at another man when they were out together, he would accuse her of flirting. If she received any mail, he would accuse her—all in fun, he would later claim—of having a lover, until in desperation she would permit him to read the letter. He was very critical of the way she dressed. If she ever made a disparaging remark about him, he would become angry and sulk for days. The only way she could get along with him was to humor him and flatter him. On occasions when her saturation point had been reached and she threatened to leave him, he would proclaim his need and love for her and plead for another chance. For a while he would improve, but soon he would revert to his old pattern of jealousy and suspicion.

PARANOID PERSONALITY AND PSYCHOSIS

When ideas of distrust and suspicion are so distorted and magnified that the individual is convinced he is being watched, followed, exploited, and persecuted by enemies, a diagnosis of psychosis takes precedence over paranoid personality. An obvious requirement is that the persecutory theme constitute a delusion with no factual basis or that it represents a gross and uncorrectable misinterpretation or exaggeration of some actual event or series of events. Diagnosis is frequently simplified by the added presence of delusions of grandeur, which may be incorporated into the persecutory theme. Thus the patient may attribute the enmity of his persecutors to their presumed resentment at his superior abilities or to attempts to discredit his rightful claim to some valuable property or invention.

Three types of paranoid psychosis have been differentiated. Patients characterized by bizarre, poorly organized delusions of persecution, hallucinations, disturbances in thinking, and significant impairment in general functioning are classified as *paranoid schizophrenics*. It is presumed that in these cases the underlying personality is more schizoid than paranoid.

When the delusional system is carefully elaborated, internally consistent, and more or less encapsulated, leaving the rest of the personality intact, a differentiation may be made between paranoia and paranoid state. *Paranoia* is extremely rare. It is characterized by the gradual development over many years of an elaborate paranoid system that is based on the misinterpretation or overextension of the implications of an actual event. If the fundamental premise is granted, the rest proceeds logically. In these cases it is often difficult to say how much of the patient's story of deception, intrigue, and exploitation is true and how much is elaboration.

Paranoid state is more common than paranoia but also comparatively rare. The delusional system is less well organized than in paranoia and more improbable. However, the ideas expressed are not too farfetched. The relative intactness of the rest of the personality enables the patient to carry on with his work and usual activities.

As long as the paranoid is guarded in the overt expression of his delusions or confides only in sympathetic listeners, his distorted perspective is discounted or tolerated. The social rule of reciprocity provides that everyone is entitled to a few harmless peculiarities or quirks. In the interest of peace, families may put up with obviously irrational behavior. Difficulties arise when the paranoid feels that he has suffered in silence long enough and starts to accuse or attack his persecutors. Psychiatric referral may follow direct threats, acts of aggression, appeals to authorities for help, the initiation of endless lawsuits, and so on. On occasion the paranoid person may become convinced that his enemies are closing in for the kill, and panic. Fortunately, such extreme reactions are rare. Most paranoid individuals quickly learn how far they can go without getting into trouble with society. The retention of control helps keep behavior within acceptable bounds.

Paranoia and paranoid state together account for less than 1 percent of first admissions to public and private mental hospitals. The prevalence rate is about the same for males and females. Paranoid patients tend to be brighter and better educated than most persons hospitalized with other diagnoses, but all socioeconomic levels are represented. The median age at time of hospital admission is about fifty.

The distinctive features of the paranoid state can be seen in the case of a man who initially requested a clinic appointment to discuss a marital problem. His wife refused to come with him but demanded a separate interview to check on her husband's story. She was granted her interview, but after hearing her husband's story and telling her own, she refused to return for treatment. Apart from variations in subjective interpretation, husband and wife agreed on the main facts. At the time of their interviews the husband was fifty-five years old and the wife was fifty. They had been married twenty-two years and had a daughter who had recently married. A current complaint of the wife was that the husband had given the daughter a generous check to help with the purchase of furniture. The wife did not object to the gift, but felt it should have been given jointly. She cited this incident as an example of her husband's sneaky behavior. The husband's story was that he couldn't very well discuss the gift with his wife, since they had more or less stopped talking to one another, even though they were living together and at his wife's insistence still shared the same bed. The wife saw no point in discussing her earlier history. Her sole concern was to expose her husband's inadequacies and infidelity.

Their marital history corresponded with that of similar cases described by Dupont and Grunebaum (1968). Both husband and wife were serious-minded and hard-working persons. During the period when she was manifesting paranoid symptoms, the wife continued with her routine shopping and domestic duties. Their social life since their marriage had been limited. Their home life, prior to recent events, was described as "normal," but "dull and empty" would be a more accurate description. The wife had insisted on discontinuing sexual intercourse following the onset of menopause when she was forty-two. The husband had passively given in to her wishes. In recent years he had spent as little time as possible in her company. On returning home from the office he occupied himself with gardening and refinishing furniture.

The wife had first accused him of infidelity five years prior to their clinic visits. The husband, who apparently was innocent, protested in vain. She could tell that he was seeing other women, she said, by the look in his eye, his general behavior, and his lack of sexual interest in her. Shortly after her accusation she hired a detective to collect evidence for a divorce. In his report the detective described several incidents that were essentially casual contacts the husband had with girls in his office, acquaintances in restaurants, and so on. Armed with this evidence, the wife started divorce proceedings. The husband contested the divorce to prove his innocence. The divorce petition was denied. The wife claimed that her lawyer had "sold her out" and the judge had been bribed.

Following the divorce failure, the wife became increasingly abusive and hostile. She spread stories about her husband's illicit affairs in the neighborhood. On several occasions she phoned her husband's employer to complain about his unfaithfulness. The husband sought revenge and refuge in silence. Next the wife took to cutting out articles in newspapers and magazines about wives who had murdered their husbands, and placed the clippings in his coat pockets. Finally she put a kitchen knife under her pillow, just in case her husband might attack her while she was asleep.

It was this episode that persuaded the husband that his wife was mentally ill, and he urged her to arrange for psychiatric treatment. To his surprise, she agreed. If he would fill out the necessary commitment papers, she would go along with "being framed" and go to a mental hospital. After a brief stay she would convince the hospital authorities that she had made a complete recovery and they would have to discharge her. (She had read an article on current policies of discharging patients as soon as possible.) Following her release from the hospital, she would kill her husband and get away with it on the grounds of a temporary recurrence of her psychosis. It was at this point that the husband arranged for a clinic appointment to discuss his marital problem.

PARANOID STATE AND PREJUDICE

In many ways a paranoid state is analogous to a firmly entrenched prejudice in which there is strong ego involvement. By carefully selecting supportive evidence and ignoring or distorting contradictory facts, an otherwise sensible person may be sincerely convinced of the validity of his prejudice. The presence of false beliefs and irrational attitudes need not interfere with judgment or competence with respect to other subjects.

As in the case of prejudices, a dominant person may impose his delusions on some submissive member of the family. The terms *folie à deux* and "psychosis of association" have been proposed to identify situations in which two people, usually but not necessarily members of the same family, concurrently share the same delusional system (Gralnick, 1942). This rare condition usually occurs in socially isolated families in which the submissive person (usually a wife or mother) has very limited contact with persons other than the paranoid. The submissive partner relies on the dominant one for reinforcement. Separation usually results in the gradual extinction of imposed delusional ideas in the dependent partner. The paranoid, like the prejudiced person, hangs on to his false beliefs. Treatment is usually ineffective. The general distrust of others includes the therapist.

CONTRIBUTORY FACTORS

Paranoid personality and paranoid state have traditionally been regarded as reaction patterns rather than as distinct disorders. No serious attempt has been made to relate paranoid behavior to some specific gene defect, biochemical defect, or brain pathology. Contributory factors are complex and may vary somewhat from patient to patient.

It is generally assumed that the process of acquiring a paranoid outlook starts early in life and develops gradually over thirty or more years. During infancy the potential paranoid fails to acquire what Erikson has referred to as a sense of basic trust in the goodwill of his social environment. Basic distrust of the intentions and motives of others may stem from parental rejection, undependability of parental response to early needs, the presence of a more favored sibling in the home, or some other situation that makes it impossible for the child to have confidence in others' intentions toward him. Inherent tendencies of temperament that make for independence and aggressiveness may contribute to unfavorable early social experiences in and outside the home and favor the emergence of a chip-on-the-shoulder attitude. Whatever the cause, from childhood the paranoid is committed to a pattern of self-reliance and distrust of others. The world is perceived as a cold, hostile place. The best course is to go it alone, confide in no one, and keep up one's guard. This approach leads to seclusiveness, a lack of understanding of others, and a defensive hypersensitivity to slights and humiliations.

The potential paranoid's perspective is narrow and egocentric. He has neither interest nor facility in putting himself in other people's shoes and seeing things from their point of view. Perhaps because of inherent aggressiveness, the paranoid-prone person reacts to failure and threats by attack rather than by schizophrenic retreat, depressive despair, or neurotic compromise. Favorable self-evaluation is protected by the projection of blame and fault on others. The individual's suspiciousness and aggressiveness tend to elicit rejection and counteraggression on the part of others, so that in effect he creates by his own actions a cold, hostile social environment.

The Freudian thesis that paranoia is associated with latent homosexuality offers an explanation for the clinical observation that the persecutor is usually a member of the paranoid's own sex. The assumption of a causal relationship between paranoid behavior and homosexuality has little foundation, however. There is no conclusive evidence that latent homosexuality (a slippery term to define) is more prevalent among paranoids than in the general population. Many paranoids show no homosexual tendencies, and most overt homosexuals never develop paranoid delusions. The paranoid's poor heterosexual adjustment is more probably due to suspicion and distrust than to sexual deviation.

According to Cameron (1959), psychotic delusions of persecution represent a desperate attempt to justify suspicions, to account for failure, and to explain the spying and persecution of others. All the pieces fall neatly into place with the invention of a *pseudocommunity*. The paranoid pseudocommunity, as Cameron defines it, is an imaginary organization of real or imagined persons who are united in some plot against the patient. An advantage of the pseudocommunity is that it brings the threat into focus. Instead of being confronted with a blurred, nameless "they," the patient with a clearly defined delusional system knows who the enemy is and can take appropriate defensive or offensive measures. His resistance to treatment is understandable, since a "cure" would require him to give up his all-purpose rationalization.

Cyclothymic Personality

Persons described as cyclothymic are characterized by recurring or alternating periods of mild depression and mild elation. Because of the mildness and short duration of their mood changes these individuals are considered to be basically normal persons. When in an elated state, the individual is energetic, enthusiastic, confident, and in good spirits. The world is his oyster. All things are possible. While in a depressed period, he is listless and pessimistic. His former good humor and optimism are replaced by worry, a sense of futility, and irritability. As in manic-depressive reactions, mood changes may be bipolar or unipolar. The onset of elation or depression may be independent of external circumstances.

The omission of a cyclothymic personality in the GAP classification of personality disorders in children is consistent with the psychodynamics of this personality type. Cycloid personalities tend to be dependent, pliant, submissive, and friendly. They strive to bolster basic feelings of insecurity by forming a strong attachment to one or two persons. In exchange for affection, loyalty, and subservience, they expect that the person with whom they have identified will take care of them. In order to gratify their strong needs for attention and approval, they conform to rules and social expectations and make themselves pleasant, cooperative, and amusing.

During childhood these attributes are assets. Difficulties arise during late adolescence and early adulthood, when the individual is expected to be independent and self-reliant. At this point he may resent his dependency but feel powerless to do anything about it. Doubts as to the dependability of the person who serves as his anchor line lead to anxiety and worry. The individual may sporadically lash out against the person who has failed him. More commonly, hostility is turned against the self and expressed in dejection and feelings of unworthiness. If the expected rewards of social conformity and compliance do not materialize, the individual feels betrayed and deserted, but usually he dares not openly vent his anger against those upon whom he is still dependent for attention and approval. Instead he attacks and blames himself. As a reaction against despondency or as a means of regaining favor, the individual may become more assertive, gregarious, and hyperactive. Artificial optimism may mask hopelessness, surface gaiety be substituted for despair, and boasts conceal feelings of inadequacy.

The potential adjustment difficulties of cyclothymes may be seen in the case of Dr. B., who married and opened an office in his home shortly after graduating from a school of optometry. To supplement his income while waiting for his practice to grow he obtained a position working two days a week for another optometrist. This still left him with some free time, so he opened a second office in a suburban town where he was the only optometrist. This venture worked out so well that he discontinued his part-time position and opened a third office in another suburb. He obtained a substantial bank loan to purchase equipment and a second car. By dividing his time between his three offices and working evenings, Dr. B. managed to earn an excellent income, but it brought small joy to his wife. She saw little of him, and that little was too much. He constantly found fault with her poor management, lack of ambition, and failure to give him 100 percent cooperation. On weekends he felt he should lead an active social life to compensate for his long working hours. His wife dreaded going out to parties with him, since he irritated friends with his boasts, arrogance, and practical jokes, which were often in poor taste. Then too there were periods when he was depressed and worried about his financial obligations and his unhappy marriage. But, as he constantly reminded everyone who would listen, he was a "success."

Schizoid Personality

Schizoid personality is differentiated from schizophrenia by the absence of delusions, hallucinations, and thought disorders. Persons with schizoid personalities are detached from reality but not out of touch with it. This critical distinction places them in the normal or borderline-normal category. They are typically described as shy, seclusive, emotionally cold, introverted, and reserved. They avoid situations in which they may be required to compete with others. The daydreams and inner emotional lives of schizoid personalities may be rich and intense, but their overt behavior is devoid of spontaneity and warmth.

Kretschmer (1936) has described several subtypes of schizoid personalities. Some are stiff, formal, and meticulously proper in social situations. Others give the impression of being fragile, delicate, and hypersensitive. Some are exclusively preoccupied with vague philosophical problems, impractical schemes, and futile missions. Some are recluses and eccentrics who from choice live alone and discourage visitors. Schizoid personalities may be highly creative and productive in occupations that permit them to work alone, but more often they are employed at simple jobs that are below their abilities.

In his description of the detached-avoidant personality, which corresponds to the schizoid personality, Millon notes that these individuals are not deficient in capacity for experiencing emotions, nor are they insensitive to the moods and feelings of others. Many are oversensitive to the actions of others and hyperalert to censure. Their detachment is a defensive reaction against unfavorable interpersonal experiences in the past: parental rejection, depreciation, belittlement.

The GAP classification favors the term "isolated personality" to describe children who tend "to exhibit distant, detached, cold, or withdrawn attitudes toward family and friends." The isolated child is typically unable to form warm and meaningful interpersonal attachments. His usual pattern of passivity and shyness may be periodically broken by unpredictable outbursts of rage, contrariness, or sadistic behavior. The surface behavior of overly inhibited children may superficially resemble that of schizoid personalities, but they may be distinguished by the fact that though they seem to wish for close interpersonal relationships, they are prevented from achieving them by their inhibitions, rather than by the schizoid's fear and ambivalence. In their own homes and with a few close friends they may be much less inhibited.

Explosive Personality

The explosive personality is also called an aggressive personality and emotionally unstable personality. As long as everything is going smoothly, the individual may appear well adjusted, but when he is frustrated or confronted with some minor stress, he loses control. Aggressive impulses are directly and forcefully expressed, either verbally or physically. Outbursts of rage are suggestive of infantile temper tantrums in their unpredictability and intensity. At the adult level, these uncontrolled and irrational attacks provoke anxiety and hostility in others and may have serious social repercussions. When calm is restored, the individual usually regrets his actions, but this does not prevent a repetition when he is frustrated again.

The negativistic-active-ambivalent personality described by Millon is more closely related to what the DSM refers to as the passive-aggressive personality. The GAP pattern that comes closest to the concept of the explosive personality is the neurotic personality, which is regarded as a subcategory of tension-discharge disorders. These children directly and immediately act out their aggressive feelings. Unlike the children described as impulse-ridden, they subsequently experience anxiety and guilt for their impulsive actions. At times they seem to invite punishment.

Obsessive-Compulsive Personality

Individuals with obsessive-compulsive personalities are characterized by rigid conformity, orderliness, strict conscience, and undue inhibition. Compulsive personalities tend to irritate associates with their attention to petty details, insistence on perfection, and inordinate scrupulousness. Their lack of tolerance, adaptability, and flexibility may cause them to be passed over for promotion to supervisory positions. Need for regularity may be expressed in preoccupation with bowel movements and a rigid sleep schedule. Many are obsessed with cleanliness, dental hygiene, special diets, and physical fitness. The compulsive pattern in children is similar to that of adults. The orderliness and conformity of children may be misinterpreted as a kind of (pseudomaturity) A distinction is made between transient periods of compulsive rituals engaged in by many children and a compulsive personality.

Millon describes ambivalent-passive-conforming personality as compulsive, rigid, overcontrolled, methodical, conscientious, self-righteous, disciplined, cheerless, and grim. These individuals tend to be industrious and efficient but they lack spontaneity, imagination, and creativeness. Conflicts are avoided by strict adherence to rules and conventions. Changes and deviations from accustomed routines are upsetting. Ambivalent-conforming personalities may be deferential and obsequious to superiors, but in their relations with subordinates they tend to be pompous, faultfinding and autocratic. According to Millon, the development of a compulsive personality appears to be related to parental overcontrol by contingent punishment. As long as the child operates within clearly defined but narrowly constricted boundaries, he is safe from parental criticism and condemnation. But if he goes beyond the stated limits or shows signs of initiative or independence, he encounters firm and harsh discipline. In addition, the parents are strong on moral training. Frivolous play and impulse gratification are frowned upon. The child is indoctrinated with a strong sense of responsibility for his actions. A tendency to guilt feelings is instilled by impressing the child with the terrible consequences of wrongdoing.

Hysterical Personality

The hysterical behavior pattern is mainly noted in adolescent girls and young women but may also be found in males. The adjective "histrionic" expresses the essence of the personality. The hysterical person is a self-dramatizing, self-centered, excitable, unstable, and often a player of roles. The artificiality of emotions is illustrated by the seductiveness often noted in hysterical women. When men respond to their provocative behavior, they are usually surprised and frightened. Experienced men are well aware of the underlying frigidity of coquettes. In defense of histrionic females, it must be said that their flirting is not a deliberate strategy to tease and frustrate. From their perspective, men misinterpret their signals. Their intent is simply to attract male interest and attention. The GAP description of the hysterical personality in children and adolescents is very similar to that for adults:

This group of children shows tendencies toward flamboyant, overdramatic, overaffective, oversuggestible, and coy behavior. They often appear to be overly dependent upon the environment for the establishment of their own independent identities. Despite their often misleading overt heterosexual behavior, they give evidence of unusual repression of sexual impulses and of difficulties in the establishment of their sexual identities and relationships. Masochistic needs for the experiencing of suffering or pain may be present unconsciously. Individuals in this category may be strongly manipulative or demanding in a passive-aggressive fashion.

Millon has emphasized the gregariousness and dependence of the hysterical personality. The two key traits are interlocked. Devoid of inner resources, the hysteric is heavily dependent on his social environment for stimulation, approval, and affection. In the pursuit of these objectives, he takes the initiative. He actively "courts" others by being vivacious, charming, agreeable, and seductive. He may develop an exquisite sensitivity to the moods and thoughts of others, but his own actions and feelings are shallow, simulated, and manipulative. He is a fraud, a player of games.

The hysteric's capacity for self-deception is strikingly illustrated in more severe hysterical neurotic reactions that include loss of memory, blindness, or paralysis. In his discussion of factors contributory to the development of the hysterical personality, Millon lists histrionic parental models, rivalry among siblings for parental attention, parental failure to provide a consistent and stabilizing set of values, reinforcement in the home of showoff behavior, and the presence during infancy of a variety of caretakers who supplied the child with intense, short-lived stimulus gratifications at irregular intervals.

Passive-Aggressive Personality

The passive-aggressive personality is also referred to as the oppositional syndrome and the negativistic personality. The passive-aggressive person is given to procrastination, stubbornness, refusal to talk, intentional inefficiency, contrariness, negativism, noncooperativeness, and general obstructionism. He may be chronically sullen and complaining, or he may disguise his negativism beneath a surface charm and agreeableness, so that it is only after a series of increasingly frustrating encounters that other people are able to recognize the hidden obstructionism of his behavior. These covert styles of expressing resentment and hostility are especially characteristic of insecure, dependent persons who dare not express their aggression openly. Reactions of this type can be more exasperating than direct attacks. A parent may feel justified in punishing a child who talks back or is destructive, but be at a loss as to how to discipline a child who refuses to eat, doesn't hear when called, "accidentally" breaks a prized cup when asked to help with the dishes, or sabotages parental aspirations by failing in school. The oppositional syndrome should not be confused with normal resistance to excessive demands or the child's healthy strivings toward self-direction and independence. Passive aggressiveness is the life style of the person, his typical way of behaving in most situations.

The frequent occurrence of passive-aggressive behavior in several members of the same family may be attributed to shared learning experiences or shared genes. Family discord, exploitation of children to gratify parental needs, and contradictory communications that make it impossible for any response to be "right" (the double bind) may all contribute to the development of passive-aggressive behavior. A follow-up study of a large group of passive-aggressive patients (Small et al., 1970) has indicated that when contrary interpersonal behavior is part of the character structure rather than merely a manipulative technique, it is resistant to change. With advancing age there is an increase in anxiety and manifestations of depression. Thought processes become more constricted and tangential, but these persons do not develop delusions or hallucinations. Over time, somatic complaints became more pronounced and persistent.

Antisocial or Sociopathic Personality

As a psychiatric concept the diagnosis of antisocial personality is loosely applied to a heterogeneous group of individuals whose life style is marked by the immediate gratification of impulses and egocentric desires without regard or concern for the feelings and welfare of others. In the pursuit of these objectives, sociopaths may engage in unethical, immoral, or criminal behavior. These are the people who in earlier times were referred to as rogues, ne'er-do-wells, black sheep, and scoundrels. They have no sense of loyalty or responsibility to family, friends, or society. Other people are regarded as dupes and suckers, to be used and exploited. Successful antisocial personalities or sociopaths may be quite charming, persuasive, and socially adroit. When caught in some misdeed, they may skillfully extricate themselves by lying, blaming others (including the victim), begging forgiveness, and making a show of remorse. The true sociopath, however, does not experience genuine anxiety, guilt, or remorse for the anguish and suffering he causes others. Punishment has no deterrent effect. All that is learned from past experience is to be more circumspect next time.

The impulsiveness, low frustration tolerance, and lack of empathy for the feelings of others are suggestive of inherent temperamental defects. The restless search for excitement and new experiences that characterizes many sociopaths (Quay, 1965) may also be related to inherent temperament. The sociopath's egocentricity makes him incapable of affection or love for others. On the other hand, the sociopath may be acutely sensitive to others' desire for a show of affection, which he can turn to his own profit. Cleckley has suggested that many sociopaths may actually be psychotic.

DEFINITIONS OF SOCIOPATHY

Prichard is credited with being one of the first to recognize sociopathy as a separate clinical entity. In 1837 he delineated a behavior pattern that be referred to as *moral insanity:*

> There is a form of mental derangement in which the intellectual faculties appear to have sustained little or no injury, while the disorder is manifested, principally or alone, in the state of the feelings, temper or habits. In cases of this nature, the moral and active principles of the mind are strongly perverted or depraved; the power of self-government is lost or incapable, not of talking or reasoning upon any subject proposed to him, for this he will often do with shrewdness and volubility, but of conducting himself with decency and propriety in the business of life.

Here is the DSM-11 definition of antisocial personality:

> This term is reserved for individuals who are basically unsocialized and whose behavior pattern brings them repeatedly into conflict with society. They are incapable of significant loyalty to individuals, groups, or social values. They are grossly selfish, callous, irresponsible, impulsive, and unable to feel guilt or to learn from experience and punishment. Frustration tolerance is low. They tend to blame others or offer plausible rationalizations for their behavior. A mere history of repeated legal or social offenses is not sufficient to justify this diagnosis.

The GAP classification includes antisocial personalities in the category of tension-release disorders. More specifically, the diagnosis is applied to children described as *impulse-ridden:*

> These children show shallow relationships with adults or other children, having very low frustration tolerance. They exhibit great difficulty in control of their impulses, both aggressive and sexual, which are discharged immediately and impulsively, without delay or inhibition and often without any regard for the consequences. Little anxiety, internalized conflict, or guilt is experienced by most of these children, as the conflict remains largely external, between society and their impulses. . . . The basic defect in impulse controls appears to be reinforced by a deficit in conscience or superego formation, with failure to develop the capacity for tension storage and for the postponement of gratifications. Such children ordinarily exhibit primitive defense mechanisms, with strong denial of dependent or other needs, projection of their hostile feelings onto adults or society, and rationalization of their own

behavior. . . . Stealing, fire-setting, vandalism, destruction, aggressive attack, and other antisocial acts may frequently occur, and behavior may shift at times from one form to another or several others; addiction is not infrequent in older children and adolescents. Although their judgment and time concepts are poor, they usually have adequate intelligence and their reality testing in certain areas is quite effective.

DIFFERENTIAL DIAGNOSIS

Although the distinctions are sometimes finely drawn, diagnostic differentiations are made among sociopathic personality, criminal behavior, and the antisocial reactions sometimes noted in neuroses and psychoses. One basic premise is that sociopathic behavior is related to some basic defect in the personality of the individual. This inference was explicitly indicated in the former diagnosis of *constitutional psychopathic personality*.

A large proportion of delinquents and criminals may be technically described as antisocial personalities, but many forms of criminal behavior represent chosen vocations. Particularly in the case of culturally disadvantaged individuals, certain types of criminal behavior may be regarded as desirable or acceptable ways of earning a livelihood. Within the social values of the subculture, the professional criminal may be regarded as loyal and dependable. Unlike the sociopath, the "normal" criminal is capable of establishing relationships of warmth and trust with others. His criminal antisocial behavior is frequently restricted to a particular type of activity. In other respects his behavior may conform to expected standards. A racketeer, for example, may be a good father and husband.

Neurotics who engage in antisocial behavior are differentiated by the fact that they typically exhibit anxiety and guilt for their actions. Neurotic antisocial behavior is not an expression of some basic personality defect, but represents the impulsive acting out of conflicts and tensions. A further distinguishing characteristic is that acting-out neurotics are capable of empathy and of forming meaningful affectional relationships with others.

Antisocial behavior in a psychotic is interpreted as an incidental symptomatic manifestation of his disorder. This interpretation is confirmed by the relative absence of overt antisocial behavior prior to and following the psychotic episode.

In brief, the diagnosis of adult offenders as antisocial personalities is based on (1) case-history data that indicate the repeated occurrence from early childhood of incorrigible, harmful, and authority-defying behavior in the home, in school, at work, and in the community; (2) the seeming absence of anxiety, guilt, or concern for the feelings of others; and (3) the absence of symptoms identified with other psychiatric disorders (delusions, mental retardation, and alcoholism). It is inferred from the persistence of wrongdoing (despite awareness of the rules, repeated warnings, and punishment) that these individuals are deficient in moral scruples and social feelings. The prevailing punitive attitude toward sociopaths of members of their own families as well as of society at large rests on the premise that these individuals knowingly, callously, and willfully violate established rules of social conduct because they are interested only in the immediate gratification of egocentric impulses and desires. An alternate, more objective viewpoint is that inherent and acquired personality defects are mainly responsible for the long-term persistence of antisocial behavior.

EPIDEMIOLOGY

The overlap with criminal behavior, alcoholism, and other diagnostic categories makes it difficult to estimate the prevalence of antisocial personalities. A conservative guess is that the label may be appropriately applied to about 1 percent of the total male population and about 0.50 percent of the female population. The reaction pattern is more frequently noted in lower socioeconomic groups but occurs at all class levels.

DEVELOPMENTAL HISTORY

Manifestations of sociopathy occur at an early age. These children are distinguished by impulsiveness, destructiveness, aggressiveness, and defiance of authority. Commonly noted antisocial activities include stealing, incorrigibility, truancy, lying, and running away from home. Sex experiences of a promiscuous and often deviant nature start early. The severity of antisocial behavior during childhood is the best predictor of adult sociopathy. Robins (1966) found that 43 percent of children referred to a psychiatric clinic who were found to have ten or more antisocial symptoms were diagnosed as antisocial personalities thirty years later. For clinic-referred children with fewer than three antisocial symptoms, the risk of adult sociopathy was only 4 percent. Practically all sociopaths have had several encounters with the police and courts by adulthood. Other typical findings among adult patients include excessive use of alcohol and drugs. wanderlust, frequent change of jobs, poor military records, many somatic complaints, and high incidence of divorce, separation, and marital conflict. After the age of thirty, about a third of these patients show a moderation of overt antisocial behavior, but interpersonal relations continue to be marked by irritability and hostility (Robins, 1966). The decline in antisocial behavior appears to be mainly a function of aging. Patients rarely attribute their improvement to help received from professional workers. Reasons most commonly offered for improvement are maturity, marriage, increased responsibilities, and fear of imprisonment.

TREATMENT

Hare (1970) has presented a cogent analysis of reasons for the failure of the traditional forms of therapy with sociopathic individuals. The effectiveness of psychotherapy is influenced by personal distress on the part of the patient, a strong desire to change, the establishment of a warm, trusting relationship with the therapist, and mutual expectation of beneficial results. Since the sociopath sees nothing wrong with his behavior, which he finds rewarding, at least in the short run, he has no incentive to change and no interest in establishing an emotional relationship with the therapist, of which he is incapable in any case. The therapist, for his part, has been conditioned by his training and experience to regard sociopathy as incurable.

RESEARCH DATA ON SOCIOPATHY

In contrast to the paucity of research data on other deviant personality types, the literature on antisocial personalities is extensive. The major conclusion that may be drawn is that the determinants of sociopathy are complex and interactive. The significance of specific variables is limited. A second general conclusion is that for meaningful results, the concept of antisocial personality must be sharply and clearly defined, with emphasis on objectively observable and measurable characteristics. The common practice of selecting subjects from reformatories and prisons is highly questionable, since these individuals constitute a restricted and biased sample.

Heredity. No genetic studies of persons clinically diagnosed as antisocial personalities have been reported. Composite figures of six twin studies conducted with institutionalized criminals and delinquents indicate a concordance rate for criminality of 66 percent for MZ twins and 32 percent for DZ twins (Table 6.2). To what extent these findings are applicable to antisocial personalities is unknown. The more recent finding that about 2 percent of incarcerated offenders have an extra Y chromosome is also based on a heterogeneous criminal population rather than a psychiatrically defined antisocial group. The XYY chromosome abnormality is most often noted in criminals over six feet tall who have been convicted of offenses involving violence (Montague, 1968). These "supermales" usually are of subnormal intelligence and have histories of severe acne during adolescence. The frequency of occurrence of the XYY chromosome pattern in the general male population has not been reliably determined, but it is assumed to be considerably below 2 percent.

Family setting. Data on the early childhood experiences of adults are subject to faulty recall of memories and retrospective distortion. Robins (1966) has avoided this pitfall by starting with a large group of 524 children seen in a child guidance clinic and then investigating their psychiatric status thirty years later. The median age of the children at referral was thirteen years. Since many of the children were initially referred for antisocial behavior, it was predicted that a substantial number would be diagnosed as sociopathic personalities as adults. In point of fact, ninety-four were so diagnosed on the basis of a standard set of criteria, independently of their early clinic records. After the diagnoses of adult sociopathic personality had been made, the child clinic records were examined to determine correlates and predictors of subsequent sociopathy. The psychiatric status of a control group of a hundred children was also investigated after thirty years had passed. The control group was matched for pertinent variables. Two main requirements for inclusion in the control group were that the child had not repeated a full grade and had no record of expulsion from school or transfer to a correctional institution.

The popular belief that low socioeconomic status contributes heavily to sociopathy was not confirmed. Both groups of children lived in the same lower-class neighborhood, but only 2 percent of the control children were diagnosed as sociopathic personalities as adults, as compared with 22 percent of the clinic-referred children. Careful study of the role of "bad companions" led to the conclusion that the excess availability of antisocial children in some neighborhoods was of minor importance. Antisocial children tend to seek each other out because of common interests and rejection by others. Antisocial boys who participated in gangs were neither more nor less likely to be sociopathic adults than were nonparticipant antisocial boys. Boys without severe antisocial behavior rarely grew up to be sociopaths, whether or not they had joined gangs.

The adjustment level of the mother was found to have no direct effect on the risk of adult sociopathy in the child. The presence of an antisocial father in the home, however, was a highly significant predictor of adult antisocial behavior in the child. The presence of an antisocial father was considered the chief underlying factor in the prevalence of family discord, inadequate supervision, and inconsistent discipline noted in the early histories of children who later were diagnosed as sociopathic personalities. Fathers who were cold, strict disciplinarians tended to have fewer sociopathic children. Broken homes, no matter what was responsible for the absence of the missing parent, did not differentiate children who became sociopaths from those who developed other disorders. The effect of parental rejection of a child was difficult to evaluate. Sometimes repudiation resulted from the parent's irresponsibility and at other times from the fact that the child's behavior was intolerable. Bell (1968) and Wiggins (1968) have called attention to the effect of the child's behavior on parental attitude and mode of disciplining. A problem child may cause his parents to shift back and forth between overindulgence and strictness, to be indifferent, or to reject the child. The interaction, of course, works both ways. Disturbed parents may elicit adverse reactions in their children.

Neurophysiological correlates. As Hare (1970) has noted in his comprehensive review, research findings in this area are more suggestive than conclusive. The hypothesis that sociopathy is associated with cortical immaturity is based on the frequent observation of a slow alpha EEG rhythm in adult sociopaths. A similar brain-wave pattern is characteristic of young children. There is some evidence that antisocial persons tend to show diminished autonomic activity, as measured by electrodermal and cardiac changes. Autonomic underactivity has been noted both in the resting state and in response to stress. The low cortical and autonomic arousal of sociopaths has been considered related to their apparent lack of anxiety and their hunger for stimulation and excitement, but physiological findings are inconsistent with these inferences and make their validity questionable.

Social learning deficit. The ineffectiveness of punishment as a deterrent plus the sociopath's apparent failure to acquire the social values of his culture have led to the hypothesis that antisocial behavior is related to an inherent inability to learn tasks that are dependent on fear for reinforcement. Some support for this theory has been demonstrated in experiments in which subjects were shocked for making wrong responses. Sociopaths tend to be less efficient than others in learning to avoid punishment, but they show no deficit in learning complex tasks under stressful conditions (Hare, 1970) or when monetary rewards are used as incentives (Schmauk, 1968). The poor learning of sociopaths in shock experiments may be due to an acquired adaptation or negative reaction to punishment.

Other Personality Types

ASTHENIC PERSONALITY

The asthenic behavior pattern corresponds to Millon's detached-passive-asocial personality. It is characterized by low energy level, easy fatigability, and absence of zest in living. These individuals tend to be complacent, apathetic, and distant.

INADEQUATE PERSONALITY

The inadequate individual is not mentally deficient, but he seemingly never does anything right. His behavior is characterized by ineptness, poor judgment, ineffectual responses to emotional and social demands, lack of stamina, and absence of drive. Like the diagnoses of other personality types, the label of inadequacy represents a social value judgment. The individual may have little interest in the achievement standards of his culture. In the context of his perspective and objectives, he may consider his behavior adequate and adaptive. The diagnosis is mainly applied to persons of low socioeconomic status. The general inadequacy is suggestive of the personality and behavior of simple schizophrenics.

PASSIVE-DEPENDENT PERSONALITY

The passive-dependent person is typically docile, plaintive, mildly dejected, clinging, and submissive. He tends to avoid voicing an opinion, since he can seldom be sure he will not offend someone. He resists the assumption of responsibilities that require independent judgment, since this too entails the risk of giving offense, and in any case he has little faith in his own judgment. He wants to be told what to do and how to do it. When his docility and "goodness" fail to bring him the rewards he expects, he experiences a sense of personal failure and simultaneous resentment at those who not only do not reward him, but themselves obtain rewards he feels they do not deserve. Not surprisingly, he is prey to a variety of physical ailments, which arise from or are exacerbated by the suppression of his conflicting emotions. Poor physical health serves to justify his failure to win the rewards he feels are otherwise due him.

NARCISSISTIC PERSONALITY

The narcissistic pattern corresponds to the spoiled-child reaction. The narcissistic person tends to be egocentric, disdainful, pretentious, boastful, and self-assured. He acts as if he is above the conventions and ethics of his cultural group and exempt from the responsibilities of reciprocity in social relations. His mere desire is justification for what he seeks. Others are expected to subordinate their wishes to his comfort (Millon, 1969).

Psychoanalytic Interpretation of Personality Disorders

The term "character disorders" is preferred to "personality disorders" in the psychoanalytic literature. The meaning is about the same. The term "character" refers to the basic personality structure of the individual and his customary mode of perceiving, reacting, and adapting. Maladaptive traits and behavior patterns that fall somewhere between normal functioning and neurosis on a morbidity scale are labeled character disorders.

Psychoanalysts recognize the contribution of genetic and environmental factors in shaping personality, but they maintain that character formation is closely related to psychosexual development. Fixation at a particular stage of early sexual development is thought to result in the relative predominance and persistence of personality and behavior traits associated with that stage (Fenichel, 1945; Blum, 1953). Thus fixation at the early oral stage leads to an *oral character,* marked by extreme dependence, which may be expressed in demanding behavior. Overcompensation may lead to an exaggerated independence. Overindulgence during infancy favors the development of such traits as optimism, self-assurance, and generosity. Early oral deprivation may lead to selfishness, pessimism, and a sadistic attitude toward others. Adult character traits that are presumed to be related to early anal fixation include frugality, obstinacy, and orderliness. The *anal character* is also associated with excessive cleanliness, compulsive behavior, and sadistic tendencies. Fixation at the oedipal level is associated with the *urethral character* and the *phallic character*. The urethral character, which is identified with an earlier age period than the phallic, is marked by ambition and competitiveness. The phallic character is characterized by recklessness, aggressiveness, and narcissism.

Summary

The concept of personality disorder fits in neatly with our basic premise that the behavior patterns associated with neurosis and psychosis represent extreme variations of reactions noted in normal individuals. These maladaptive personality patterns may be regarded as mild to moderate deviations from normal reactions. Deviations may be arrested at this level or proceed to more extreme and more disturbing reactions, identified as neuroses or psychoses. Many of these personality types correspond to the premorbid personalities of psychotic and neurotic patients. If a person develops a neurosis or psychosis, his symptoms will in all probability consist largely of an accentuation of preexisting faulty modes of perceiving, thinking, feeling, and reacting.

The principles and processes regulating the development of deviant and normal personalities are the same. From the moment of birth a continuing complex, reciprocal, and cumulative interaction occurs between the child and his social environment. The inherent and somewhat distinctive temperament of the infant influences the kinds of responses he elicits from his parents. In turn, the attitudes, feelings, temperaments, and behavior of the parents affect the infant's reactions. As the child's sphere of activity is enlarged, siblings, peers, and significant others become involved in the biosocial molding pattern. During the early formative years there may be considerable trial-and-error experimentation as child, parents, and others try out different roles and techniques for gaining their respective objectives. The fluidity of the interactive process and the unpredictable occurrence of fortuitous learning experiences permit considerable variability in personality outcome. In principle, a child may develop any one of a wide variety of behavior patterns. In actuality, the range of potential variations is limited. One limiting factor is the child's genetic endowment, which influences his activity level, the intensity of his feelings and reactions, his prevailing mood, general competence, and adaptability. The established personality characteristics of his parents, which influence parent-child relations, constitute a second major restriction. The available models and reinforcement contingencies in the home and community set further restrictions. Within the limits imposed by biosocial factors, the child endeavors to structure, interpret, and adapt to his environment. The behavior patterns acquired may not be ideal, but they may be the best available at the time. The tendency to react to new situations on the basis of previously acquired patterns leads to consistency of behavior and of response by others. Through frequent repetition, maladaptive as well as effective traits become deeply ingrained and relatively fixed. The rigidity of the behavior set interferes with the introduction of new responses, which, if favorably reinforced, would alter the pattern.

References

AMERICAN PSYCHIATRIC ASSOCIATION. *Diagnostic and Statistical Manual of Mental Disorders* (DSM-11). Washington, D.C., 1968.

BELL, R. A. "A Reinterpretation of the Direction of Effects in Studies of Socialization." *Psychological Review* 75 (1965): 81–95.

BLUM, G. S. *Psychoanalytic Theories of Personality.* New York: McGraw-Hill, 1953.

CAMERON, N. "The Paranoid Pseudocommunity Revisited." *American Journal of Sociology* 65 (1959): 52–58.

CLECKLEY, H. *The Mask of Sanity,* 4th ed. St. Louis: Mosby, 1964.

DUPONT, R. L., and GRUNEBAUM, H. "Willing Victims: The Husbands of Paranoid Women." *American Journal of Psychiatry* 125 (1968): 151–59.

FENICHEL, O. *Psychoanalytic Theory of Neurosis.* New York: Norton, 1945.

GRALNICK, A. "Folie à deux: The Psychosis of Association." *Psychiatric Quarterly* 16 (1942): 230–63.

GROUP FOR THE ADVANCEMENT OF PSYCHIATRY. *Psychopathological Disorders in Childhood: Theoretical Considerations and a Proposed Classification.* New York, 1966.

HARE, R. D. *Psychopathy: Theory and Research.* New York: Wiley, 1970.

KRETSCHMER, E. *Physique and Character.* London: Routledge & Kegan Paul, 1936.

MILLON, T. *Modern Psychopathology.* Philadelphia: Saunders, 1969.

MONTAGUE, A. "Chromosomes and Crime." *Psychology Today* 2 (1968): 42–49.

Patients in Mental Institutions, 1965. Public Health Service publication no. 1597. Washington, D.C.: U.S. Government Printing Office, 1968.

PRICHARD, J. C. *Treatise on Insanity.* Philadelphia: Haswell, Barrington, & Haswell, 1837.

QUAY, H. C. "Psychopathic Personality as Pathological Stimulation Seeking." *American Journal of Psychiatry* 122 (1965): 180–83.

ROBINS, L. N. *Deviant Children Grown Up.* Baltimore: Williams & Wilkins, 1966.

SCHMAUK, K. "A Study of the Relationship Between Kinds of Punishment, Autonomic Arousal, Subjective Anxiety, and Advoidance Learning in the Primary Sociopath." Unpublished Ph.D. dissertation, Temple University, 1968.

SMALL, I. F.; SMALL, J. G.; ALIG, V. B.; and MOORE, D. F. "Passive-Aggressive Personality Disorder: A Search for a Syndrome." *American Journal of Psychiatry* 126 (1970): 973–81.

WIGGINS, J. "Inconsistent Socialization." *Psychological Reports* 23 (1968): 303–36.

CHAPTER THIRTEEN

Alcoholism and Drug Use

Alcohol is the most extensively used of psychoactive drugs. The traditional practice of differentiating between alcohol and other drugs is in great measure due to the fact that most societies are more acceptive of alcohol than of opiates and other psychoactive drugs. Laws regulating the use of alcohol are much more tolerant than those for other drugs and the penalties are far milder. The common denominator in all psychoactive drugs is that they are toxic substances. Moderate doses produce a blurring of conscious awareness that serves as a satisfying "time out," during which anxieties and problems are temporarily set aside and the individual can relax, become "high," or experience what is euphemistically referred to as a transcendent state. Very large doses lead to a comatose condition and the possibility of a permanent escape from the pressures of life. Having acknowledged that alcohol and drug use are in the same general class, we can proceed to perpetuate the time-honored custom of considering alcoholism as a separate problem. The main justification for this procedure is that alcohol and other drugs are treated separately in the research literature. Little attention has been given to the fact that many chronic alcoholics also take other drugs.

Alcoholism

Figures on the extent and severity of alcohol use are very unreliable. A rough estimate is that about one-third of adult males in the United States are teetotalers. Another third are casual or social drinkers. Some of the members of this middle group drink only at parties and on special occasions. Others may take one to two drinks daily, usually at mealtime. The remaining third might be described as heavy drinkers. Some drink excessive amounts each day. Others restrict their consumption to sporadic overindulgence on weekends and on special occasions. Most of the men in this latter group do not consider themselves alcoholics, and this judgment is shared by their associates. From a psychiatric point of view, a diagnosis of alcoholism is restricted to those for whom drinking constitutes a relatively serious chronic problem in their personal, family, social, and occupational adjustment. A substantial proportion of heavy drinkers may drop to this state after years of drinking. At any one time, however, less than 5 percent of the total adult male population qualify as definite alcoholics. Of the known alcoholics in this country, there are about five men to every woman. But it is difficult to estimate how many women are secret alcoholics, since it is easier for women to confine their drinking to the privacy of their homes. If all female alcoholics were counted, a conservative guess is that the corrected sex ratio would be about 3 to 1. This is the ratio of men to women alcoholics who are admitted annually to general hospitals with psychiatric services in the United States. Women who become alcoholics generally begin serious drinking at a later age than men, but once started, they progress rapidly to a state of alcoholic addiction. The symptoms and drinking habits of alcoholic women differ somewhat from those of alcoholic men (Wanberg and Horn, 1970).

Alcoholics are found in all walks of life, without regard to intelligence, socioeconomic status, or occupational level. Alcoholism is a major cause of divorce, desertion, and family discord. It is also an important contributory factor in delinquency and crime. The cost to industry is estimated to be about $2 billion a year. About 15 percent of first admissions to mental hospitals are diagnosed as alcoholic. Alcoholism is also a symptom of many other forms of mental disorder.

DEFINITION OF ALCOHOLISM

Our general definition of psychopathology is also applicable to alcoholism. Like other forms of abnormal behavior, alcoholism is relatively independent of voluntary control, causes significant impairment in psychosocial functioning, and causes the individual to be a liability, threat, or source of distress to himself and others. As in other forms of psychopathology, impairment in voluntary control is the critical criterion of alcoholism. Some people are unable to abstain from drinking. Others are unable to control the amount they drink. Once started, drinking continues until the individual is intoxicated. Our definition is very similar to that proposed by the report of the Cooperative Commission on the Study of Alcoholism (Plaut, 1967, p. 39): "Alcoholism is defined as a condition in which an individual has lost control over his alcoholic intake in the sense that he is consistently unable to refrain from drinking or to stop drinking before getting intoxicated." Fox (1967) has defined alcoholism as a behavioral disturbance in which excessive intake of alcohol interferes with the physical or mental health of the individual and is usually accompanied by an impairment in interpersonal relationships. She also adds the important point that alcoholism is a form of addiction that is marked by an emotional and/or physiological dependence on alcohol.

INTOXICATING LIQUORS

Ethyl alcohol, the active ingredient in beer, wine, and whiskey, is a colorless, relatively odorless liquid. Alcohol breath is due to additives mixed with the alcohol. Ethyl alcohol is absorbed into the blood mainly from the small intestines. Some absorption also occurs from the stomach and lungs. The speed of absorption depends on the type and amount of food that the drinker has consumed and his emotional state. Carbon dioxide speeds up the absorption rate. This explains the quick high obtainable from drinking champagne. Alcohol is oxidized by the liver at a steady rate. It takes about an hour to oxidize an ounce of whiskey. A person may drink all day and remain sober if he limits his intake to an ounce of whiskey per hour. During the oxidation process, alcohol is converted into harmless acetic acid.

Methyl alcohol, also known as wood alcohol, has the same toxic effect as ethyl alcohol, but differs from it in two respects: (1) the rate of oxidation is much slower, which results in a much longer period of intoxication, and (2) the oxidation of methyl alcohol results in a highly toxic substance that damages the optic nerve and leads to blindness.

A third intoxicating agent, which shares with alcohol the essential characteristic of inducing anesthesia, is ethyl ether. Ether is obtained from the action of sulfuric acid on alcohol. Ether drinking was quite popular in Ireland, and to a lesser degree in England and Scotland, during the latter part of the nineteenth century. A fascinating account has been given by Kerr (1890). Half a wineglass of ether rapidly produces intoxication in the average person. As a substitute for alcohol, ether has the advantage of allowing a person to proceed from a sober state to marked inebriation and back to sobriety in a period of a couple hours. The rapidity of the effects of ether and the recovery from it permit a person to get drunk and become sober again six times a day. The physiological and psychological effects of ether are about the same as those of alcohol. A side effect of ether drinking consists of chronic and distressing inflammation of the stomach.

REASONS FOR DRINKING

The consumption of alcohol is a voluntary act engaged in for the explicit purpose of exchanging a state of sobriety for one of mild to severe intoxication. The general objective is a temporary change of consciousness and behavior. Mild inebriation is usually accompanied by a feeling of euphoria. More severe intoxication produces a hazy state that facilitates an escape from self and reality. The often-reported pleasant feeling while under the influence of alcohol consists essentially of an absence of negative feelings. Social drinking is usually characterized by a designated time limit during which the individual is expected to relax and have fun. By tacit agreement, participants at drinking parties are not only permitted but encouraged to be more outgoing than usual and to give freer expression to their impulses. The cocktail hour is often referred to as the happy hour, when individuals can say and do things without being held strictly accountable.

For the more habitual drinker, who often starts drinking in the morning, the hazy state induced by alcohol may serve a variety of purposes, depending on his particular needs. Thus alcohol may constitute a form of self-medication for moderating feelings of depression, reducing anxiety, and neutralizing resentment. Alcohol may provide an escape from the emptiness and futility of one's existence. It may serve as an unconscious means of expressing self-destructive tendencies. The individual persists in drinking because by and large alcohol fulfills whatever psychological function it is called upon to perform. It is also readily available. In the long run the results are harmful, but the immediate effects are satisfying. Once the habit is firmly established, it is self-perpetuating. The chronic alcoholic who says that he drinks because he is an alcoholic is not being evasive. Whatever reason he may have originally had for drinking may no longer be pertinent. The established habit is reason enough for drinking.

DEVELOPMENTAL STAGES OF ALCOHOLISM

The usual progression is from social drinking to a psychological dependence on alcohol to a physiological dependence. Physiological dependence is marked by a loss of control over drinking, a "craving" for alcohol, adaptive cell metabolism, and withdrawal symptoms. The sequence from psychological to physiological dependence may be rapid or may proceed slowly over a period of ten or more years.

Jellinek (1952) has outlined four stages of alcoholism. The first or *prealcoholic* phase is marked by an intensification of social drinking. The individual drinks to excess and begins to show signs of emotional or psychological dependence. The second or *prodromal* phase is marked by increased tolerance, surreptitious drinking, and preoccupation with alcohol. Periodic blackouts may occur. When he sobers up the following day, the individual may be unable to remember what he did while he was drunk. Guilt feelings are common, but the individual is unable to resist his compulsive desire for alcohol. The third or *crucial* phase marks the transition to a true state of alcoholism. Social drinking is largely replaced by solitary drinking. Behavior is alcohol-centered. The person starts drinking regularly in the morning and is unable to control his alcoholic intake. Alcohol takes precedence over friends, occupation, and family. Behavioral disturbances include persistent remorse, marked aggressive behavior, unfounded jealousy, and self-pity. During this phase the individual may lose his job, leave home, and experience his first hospitalization or imprisonment for alcoholism. Since his diet may consist largely of alcohol, he may suffer from nutritional deficiencies. Alcohol is now needed to counteract hangover symptoms: headache, diarrhea, and acute thirst. The final or *chronic* phase is marked by prolonged periods of intoxication that may last for several weeks. By this time most drinkers are homeless drunks.

The *Diagnostic and Statistical Manual* of the American Psychiatric Association recognizes three categories of alcoholism: episodic excessive drinking, habitual excessive drinking, and alcohol addiction. Persons who become intoxicated four to twelve times a year are described as episodic excessive drinkers. Those who are under the influence of alcohol more than once a week or who are intoxicated more than twelve times a year are classified as habitual excessive drinkers. The diagnosis of alcohol addiction is restricted to persons who are dependent on alcohol. Signs of dependence include an inability to go one day without drinking, the presence of withdrawal symptoms, or periods of heavy drinking that continue for three months or more.

For purposes of identification, the three principal patterns of drinking behavior have been labeled Alpha, Delta, and Gamma (Jellinek, 1960).

Alpha alcoholism is limited to psychological dependence. The individual drinks too much at the wrong time, but he does not progress to the point where he loses control of his drinking. He retains the ability to abstain from drinking and to regulate the amount he drinks. Drinking mainly serves as a means of reducing tension and bodily pain. Although relatively controlled, the persistent drinking leads to impairment in work efficiency and disturbed interpersonal relations.

Delta alcoholism is distinguished by an inability to abstain from drinking. The individual drinks practically every day, though he can regulate the amount and time of drinking. This pattern is frequently noted in beer- and wine-drinking countries such as Germany and France. The drinking pattern involves both psychological and physiological dependence. Withdrawal symptoms and craving occur if the person abstains from drinking.

Gamma alcoholism is mainly characteristic of Anglo-Saxon and Scandinavian countries, where whiskey is the favorite beverage. Gamma alcoholism is marked by a loss of control with respect to the amount of alcohol consumed. The Gamma drinker may go for weeks or months without touching a drop, but once he starts drinking he is unable to stop until he passes out. Gamma alcoholism also involves physiological dependence and withdrawal symptoms.

EFFECTS OF ALCOHOL

Intoxication. The behavioral signs of intoxication are due to the depressing effect alcohol has on the nervous system. Alcohol acts as a general anesthetic. As the concentration of blood alcohol increases, there is progressive impairment or reduction in normal brain functions. The stages of intoxication are described in Table 13.1. An important function of the cortex is to

Table 13.1. Effects of alcohol

Blood alcohol concentration	Behavioral effects
0.05%	Relaxation of restraints, talkativeness, informality, mild memory impairment.
0.10	Feeling of well-being, slurred speech, clumsiness, impulsiveness, poor coordination.
0.20	Unsteady gait, distortion of sensations (double vision), impaired speech, disjointed conversation, poor judgment, drowsiness. High accident risk if driving car.
0.40	Impaired perceptions, stuporous or comatose.
0.60	Loss of consciousness. High possibility of death due to cessation of breathing and heartbeat.

inhibit impulsive activity and emotional instability. The impairment of this cortical function accounts for the increase in excitement and the relative loss of restraint commonly noted in mild to moderate levels of intoxication. The disturbances in sensation, perception, speech, motor coordination, memory, and judgment more directly reflect the anesthetic effect of alcohol on the nervous system. When drinking is spaced out, the induced drowsiness tends to limit excessive intake. Large amounts consumed over a brief period may result in coma or death.

Loss of inhibitions. MacAndrew and Edgerton (1969) have criticized the popular view that alcohol, through its effects on the brain, temporarily breaks down the normally operative inhibitions in man with the consequent release of repressed sexual and aggressive impulses. They agree that alcohol, if taken in sufficient quantity, invariably results in impairment in sensory and motor functions; but they maintain that the behavioral effects of alcohol vary with the individual, with the occasion, and especially with the attitudes and traditions of the particular society. In societies in which drunkenness is accepted as a license or excuse for disorderly behavior and reduced responsibility, alcohol usage often leads to increased aggression, violence, sexual promiscuity, and other forms of misconduct. In other societies with different cultural rules and customs, members may consume prodigious amounts of alcohol without engaging in unruly, belligerent, or immoral behavior. A wealth of anthropological observations indicates that in certain societies drunkenness is characterized by increased self-preoccupation, social detachment, joviality, or friendliness.

Delirium tremens. Delirium tremens is the most dramatic of withdrawal reactions. It usually occurs only in habitual drinkers, either after sustained intoxication or following a period of relative abstinence. Early symptoms include restlessness, irritability, and disturbed sleep accompanied by terrifying dreams. The delirious phase is marked by profound confusion, tremor, illusions, and visual hallucinations. The patient "sees" insects, bugs, and small animals crawling over him. The usual reaction is one of acute fear. Other symptoms include tremors, rapid irregular pulse, excessive perspiration, indistinct speech, disorientation, and heightened distractability. Convulsive seizures occasionally occur. The reaction usually lasts from three to five days. Good nursing care is required to cope with the patient's extreme psychological and physiological disturbance. Sedation and restraints are contraindicated. Paraldehyde and tranquilizers are usually administered to quiet the patient. Nutritional deficiencies are treated by vitamins and a diet high in carbohydrates.

Acute alcoholic hallucinosis. Acute hallucinosis occurs primarily in individuals with schizoid traits. Apparently prolonged use of alcohol serves to release latent schizophrenic tendencies. The key symptom consists of auditory hallucinations. Frequently the voices accuse the person of sexual misconduct: males tend to be accused of homosexuality and females of promiscuity. Victims may angrily protest their innocence or be too terrified to answer at all. Depressive feelings are common. In addition to the fact that hallucinations are auditory rather than visual, acute alcoholic hallucinosis differs from delirium tremens in several respects. Persons with delirium tremens tend to be confused, disoriented, and out of touch with their environment; those with acute hallucinosis are usually well oriented and experience no distortion of perception. Some persons with acute hallucinosis respond favorably to tranquilizers, antidepressants, and vitamins; others go on to manifest typical schizophrenic reactions that may persist for several months.

Korsakoff-Wernicke syndrome. The vitamin deficiency that frequently accompanies prolonged alcoholism may result in degeneration of the nerves. The condition is called Korsakoff's syndrome if the degeneration is largely confined to the cerebrum and peripheral nerves, and Wernicke disease if the brain stem is the site of the degenerative process. Psychiatric symptoms include amnesia, falsification of memory, and disorientation in time and place. To fill in memory gaps, the individual may report fictitious but plausible memories. The person is seemingly unaware of his fabrication. In most instances he is quite jovial. Since the condition is caused by nutritional deficiencies, many cases respond well to a vitamin-enriched diet and clear up in a month or two. In other cases there is a more or less permanent impairment in psychological functioning (Noyes and Kolb, 1963).

Somatic symptoms. Prolonged use of alcohol may lead to cirrhosis of the liver, peripheral neuritis, endocrine disturbances, and other physical symptoms. Most of these organic disorders are due to nutritional deficiencies.

Direct observations. Tamerin and Mendelson (1969) have reported the results of an interesting study in which four male alcoholics were directly observed over a sustained period of experimental intoxication. The subjects, who ranged in age from thirty-seven to forty-six, all had long histories of chronic alcoholism. During the ten weeks of the experiment the men were restricted to a closed research unit. The schedule consisted of a two-week observation period, three weeks during which the men were periodically provided with liquor, a ten-day withdrawal period, a three-week period of free access to liquor, and a final ten-day withdrawal period.

During the observation period the men reported that they expected to be more relaxed, more comfortable, and less depressed once they started drinking. And so, in fact, they were—at least in the beginning. But after a brief period of pleasure, continued drinking had the opposite effect. Even though the experiment sanctioned drinking, the men experienced more distress when they were drunk than when they were sober. They felt remorseful and guilty and worthless, they cried, they thought of suicide. These adverse reactions were intensified during the free-access period, when the men drank more over a shorter period and hence were more intoxicated. The total amount consumed during the free-access period was about the same as during the more spaced-out programmed drinking period.

When sober, the men were polite to each other but distant, inhibited, and bored. Left to themselves, they kept busy with aimless repetitive activities. Their behavior was described as rigid and restrictive. Intoxication stimulated group interaction. When they were drunk they became increasingly aggressive and open, freely expressed disapproval and hostility, and engaged in heated discussions. They were more interested in one another, and more interesting. There was a great deal of mutual support. At the same time they were more irritable and exhibited a childish demandingness. Incoherent, rambling speech and social regression set in as intoxication increased. By the end of each drinking period the men were uniformly unshaven, unkempt, and sloppy. With the return to sobriety, they resumed their formal, distant relationships.

Observations with respect to the popular hypothesis that alcoholics have strong latent homosexual tendencies were inconclusive—as usual. While they were drunk the men were more affectionate and engaged in closer physical interactions, but homosexuality was never directly expressed, and in fact the men manifested greater heterosexual interest. When they were sober they treated the female nurses with the same distant politeness they showed toward each other; when they were drunk they sought greater physical contact with them. This could be interpreted as a general reaching out for human contact, male or female, in men who when sober led lonely, isolated lives.

AUTOBIOGRAPHY OF AN ALCOHOLIC

I took my first drink during my freshman year at college, the night I was initiated into my fraternity. One of the boys sold me on the idea that it was the thing to do in order to show I was a good sport. That first drink wasn't especially memorable. After all, one doesn't become a drunk overnight. I was a social drinker all during my college days. I've had many good times and suffered to some extent on the mornings after. In those days it never occurred to me to drink in the morning. I couldn't bear the sight of the stuff. I don't think it affected my scholarship much. In any event, I graduated— not brilliantly, but I did get my degree.

After college I began to drink more seriously. It was about two years after my school days that I took my first drink in the morning. I can see now that that morning was the beginning of the end. By then I was married and the father of a young son, but this added responsibility didn't seem to make any difference. Drinking was no longer a minor sport for me—I was becoming a pro. Now I drank every morning if I had had anything the night before—and I usually had.

Mysteriously enough, I managed to hold my first job for eleven years, but finally my boss reached the end of his endurance, and at almost the same time, so did my wife. Why go into all the details? Happy moments, yes, but terrible hours, too. Unbearable embarrassments, loss of friends, even jail. By this time, of course, I was really trying my damnedest to quit drinking. I spent hundreds of dollars on psychiatrists, and when I lost my job I went away to a private sanitarium for a month. This was an impressive experience, but it did me no good. I had the idea that this was a chance to build myself up physically, and when I got out I'd be able to start all over again—and this time I could handle it. I would never under any circumstances get drunk again.

From there I went to New York City and got a new job without much trouble. I started drinking again, but not the same way I had before. I'd have a couple of drinks, and then the next day it would be three, and the next day maybe four. This would go on for four or five weeks, and all this time I'd be going to work every day and managing not to make too many mistakes. Then the morning would come when I just couldn't make it to the office. For three or four days I'd stay in my apartment and drink. I wouldn't go out at all except to lay in another supply of the sauce. Eventually the time would come when I'd be so weak and jittery that I knew I'd have to quit or I'd die—so I'd quit. Because when I was drinking I wasn't eating, I knew I ought to eat at least a little during these jags, and I'd fix a sandwich or something, but then I'd look at it and the thought of actually eating it was enough to make me sick. I was living alone and I didn't know anyone in New York well enough to ask for help, so the upshot was that I generally went to a hospital for a few days. Then I'd come out sober and repentant, and I'd be all right for a month or so, and then I'd start the whole thing over again.

Finally, after losing my job again, I decided that the first thing I had to do was go somewhere where I wouldn't be able to get a drink for a long time. And I did. The particular details aren't important, but what I've discovered about this whole business is: first, we problem drinkers must realize that we can never become moderate drinkers. The "reformed drunk" who becomes a moderate drinker never was a drunk in the true sense of the word. The real reformed alcoholic becomes a teetotaler. Second, and most important of all, we must decide that we don't *want* to become moderate drinkers. So long as the alcoholic persists in admiring the moderate drinker, so long as he wants to be a moderate drinker himself, sooner or later he's going to try it, and the only possible result is disaster. [Adapted from "Can the Alcoholic Become a Moderate Drinker?"]

DETERMINANTS OF ALCOHOLISM

The magical, all-purpose placebo effect of alcohol offers a more adequate explanation for its use than for its abuse. Most people who drink stop short of incapacitating intoxication. The great majority of excessive drinkers somehow manage to regulate and control both their drinking patterns and their behavior while under the influence of alcohol so that their functioning is not grossly impaired. What differentiates the chronic alcoholic, whose life is dominated and wrecked by alcohol? There is no simple explanation on which everyone can agree. The following summary of contributory factors represents the general trends of thought to be found in the extensive literature on the subject, but the formulation is more theoretical than factual.

Tension reduction. Alcohol is one of many instrumental aids invented and exploited by man to alter self-perception and behavior and to help him cope with life problems. A major attraction of alcohol is that it quickly produces a hazy, relaxed state that is usually highly effective in temporarily reducing conscious awareness of anxiety, discontent, depression, and other negative feelings. This "therapeutic" function has been confirmed by animal studies. In their pioneer investigation of the effects of alcohol on emotionally disturbed animals, Masserman and Yum (1946) first induced neurotic reactions in cats by exposing them to an unsolvable approach-avoidance conflict. Whenever the hungry cat approached the food box, he received an electric shock. Given a choice of fluids, neurotic cats showed a greater preference for alcohol than did normal cats. While they were under the influence of alcohol, their neurotic symptoms diminished. Conger (1951) has demonstrated that alcohol resolves experimentally induced conflicts in animals by decreasing the intensity of fear-motivated avoidance responses.

Sociocultural factors. Social and cultural factors influence the extent of alcohol consumption, patterns of drinking, and the incidence of alcoholism (Bates, 1946; Jellinek, 1960). Where the use of alcohol is prohibited, as among the Moslems and Mormons, the incidence rates of drinking and of alcoholism are very low. During the early years of national prohibition in the United States, the incidence of alcoholic first admissions to mental hospitals dropped sharply. The use of alcohol need not be related to alcoholism, however. The attitudes and customs of a culture may favor the use of alcoholic beverages but be strongly opposed to drunkenness. Among orthodox Jews, for example, the drinking of wine is an integral part of religious observances but excessive drinking is considered a desecration, a diverting of a sacred function to a profane purpose. The more secular use of alcohol by the Irish as a lubricant for all social occasions may contribute to the high incidence of alcoholism among them.

Italy has one of the highest rates of alcohol consumption in the world, and one of the lowest rates of alcoholism. Italians regard wine as a mealtime beverage. The pattern is established early in life. During dinner, the young child may be served a glass of very diluted wine. The concentration is gradually increased as he gets older. Excessive drinking or the use of alcohol except as an accompaniment of food or on special occasions is frowned upon. A person who drinks for the sake of drinking or who is frequently intoxicated is regarded as "vulgar," a low order of glutton.

France shares with Italy a high rate of alcohol consumption, with wine constituting the main beverage. In contrast to Italy, however, France has a much higher rate of alcoholism. A contributory factor is the more permissive and indulgent attitude of the French toward drinking. Particularly among the working class, a man may start drinking a little at breakfast and continue with an occasional drink throughout the day and evening. In Italy, drinking is a respected personal option. A Frenchman runs the risk of giving offense if he declines a drink.

In countries where drinking is accepted, wide variations in the use of alcohol may be noted with respect to geographical area, religious affiliation, and socioeconomic status. Data based on surveys in the United States indicate higher rates of drinking in northern and coastal states than in south-central states. Members of liberal Protestant denominations drink more than those affiliated with evangelical and nontraditional churches (Christian Scientists, Jehovah's Witnesses, and so on). In large cities, drinking is more prevalent among higher socioeconomic groups.

Family influences. The old belief that alcoholism runs in certain families is true, though the inference that heredity is responsible is at best only partly true. The "like father, like son" pattern of alcoholism may be partly due to genetic factors, but imitative learning and shared environmental experiences play larger roles in the making of an alcoholic family. An unduly large proportion of the children of alcoholics who remain at home follow in their parents' footsteps, but children of alcoholics reared in foster homes run no greater risk of becoming alcoholics than the children of nonalcoholics (Roe et al., 1945).

Individual factors. The innate and acquired characteristics of the individual constitute a critical determining factor in the etiology of alcoholism. The social environment may exert great pressure on a person to drink or abstain, but the final decision rests with the individual. If a person is persuaded or wants to try alcohol, in itself a selective factor, his next step depends on the effect alcohol or the total drinking experience has on him. Reactions to the use and the effects of alcohol vary considerably from person to person. Some people take to alcohol immediately: it's just what they were looking for. Others gradually learn to enjoy drinking, or turn to it in a crisis. Still others, in part because of biological factors, may find that alcohol does nothing for them. Drinking only makes them dizzy, sick, or unable to stay awake. Some of these people do experience the usual "release" effects of alcohol, but discontinue drinking because it makes them behave in ways they later regret—or because they're afraid it might.

If a person does continue drinking, individual factors influence the amount he will drink and the frequency with which he will drink. Drinkers with emotional problems and those handicapped by feelings of inadequacy may reasonably be expected to make more extensive use of alcohol and to become more dependent on it than others. Psychiatric studies of chronic alcoholics usually reveal the coexistence of other personality problems (De Vito et al., 1970). Frequently recorded diagnoses include passive-aggressive personality, explosive personality, schizoid personality, and antisocial personality. Depressive reactions are common. A small number of alcoholics are classified as neurotic or psychotic. Alcohol appears to facilitate and increase the "acting out" of aggressive tendencies, especially in deviant personalities.

Personality test data confirm the wide diversity of personality character-istics noted among alcoholics in clinical studies. Alcoholics tend to attain higher scores for anxiety and sociopathy and lower scores for frustra-tion tolerance than normal controls (MacAndrew and Geertsma, 1964; Meneker, 1967). However, there is no evidence of a distinctive alcoholic personality. The main difference between normal persons and alcoholics is that alcoholics report more traits indicative of general maladjustment (Goss and Morosko, 1969). Even this general finding may more accurately describe the alcoholic's personality when high than when sober. Partington (1970) has demonstrated that alcoholics tend to think of themselves in dualistic ("Dr. Jekyll–Mr. High") terms. Their own evaluation of the sober self is much more favorable than their description of the high self. Many of the unfavorable psychological traits observed in alcoholics disappear when they become consistently abstinent (Fox, 1965).

One way to eliminate the contaminating effect of alcoholism on person-ality measurement is to obtain personality measures on a large sample of boys and subsequently to compare the early personality traits exhibited by those who later became alcoholics with the early traits of those who did not. Two such longitudinal studies have been reported by McCord and McCord (1960) and by Jones (1968). The population in the McCords' study consisted of lower-class Boston youths. Jones's population was com-posed largely of middle-class boys in California. The findings in both studies were the same. At the time of initial study, boys who in later years became alcoholics were characterized by inadequate control of impulses, underlying dependency, and compensatory overemphasis on masculinity. The consistency of results obtained with the two diverse groups of boys strongly indicates that these traits may serve as predisposing factors. Yet not all boys who have these traits grow up to become alcoholics. Some de-velop other types of problems. Others are indistinguishable from the gen-eral population. The actual final outcome depends on the cumulative inter-action of multiple biological, social, and psychological variables.

The determinants of alcoholism, then, are complex and varying. Sanford (1968) has suggested that the personality correlates of alcoholism may vary with the motives for and patterns of drinking. The person who uses alcohol as self-indulgence or to obtain relief from personal problems may have little in common with the man whose heavy drinking is a continuation of a long established family custom and who derives a great deal of satis-faction from the feeling of group solidarity associated with drinking.

TREATMENT OF ALCOHOLISM

Practically every conceivable medical, punitive, and psychotherapeutic technique has been tried in the treatment of alcoholism. Multidisciplinary and comprehensive approaches have been recommended to deal with the medical, social, family, personal, and legal problems associated with alcoholism (Fox, 1967; Catanzaro, 1968). The shotgun approach makes it difficult to isolate the effectiveness of specific techniques, but this is a minor point. No single method can claim much success. Often the difference between failure and success depends on the chance establishment of a satisfying relationship between the alcoholic and another person, a new position, or a serious illness.

Detoxification. Following a prolonged period of intoxication, many patients show symptoms of alcohol poisoning (Salzberger, 1967): restlessness, confusion, irritability, belligerence, fright, tremors, nausea. About half of hospitalized alcoholics have hallucinations, delusions, and memory loss. About 15 percent have delirium tremens. Treatment includes withdrawal of alcohol, vitamins, and a diet high in carbohydrates. Drugs commonly used to quiet the patient and provide relief from distress include paraldehyde, tranquilizers, and antidepressants. Toxic symptoms generally subside within two or three days.

Drug therapy. Alcoholics who remain in treatment beyond the acute stages of intoxication usually continue to receive tranquilizers or antidepressants. Antabuse (disulfriam) is sometimes used to help motivated, cooperative patients resist the temptation to drink. Persons who tend to commit crimes when intoxicated may be placed on probation rather than sent to jail if they agree to take antabuse. The offender is required to swallow a pill each day in the presence of his probation officer as a condition for continued probation. In all cases the alcoholic must be fully informed beforehand of the disastrous consequence of drinking while on antabuse. The deterrent effect of antabuse is due to the fact that its presence in the body interferes with the usual metabolism of alcohol (Billet, 1968). If an alcoholic drink is taken within four days after an antabuse pill has been swallowed, a toxic substance called acetaldehyde is formed. Acetaldehyde induces a throbbing headache, flushing of the face, spasms of coughing, vomiting, heart palpitation, labored breathing, and blurred vision. One such experience suffices. The limitation of the method is that the person can resume drinking whenever he wishes by simply discontinuing the antabuse.

Some experimental studies have been reported on the use of LSD (lysergic acid diethylamide) in the treatment of alcoholics. Generally LSD has been used to facilitate recall and self-awareness as an adjunct to a psychodynamically oriented therapy (Ditman, 1967). Most experts object to the procedure on the grounds that the potential harm of LSD outweighs whatever utility it may have as a therapeutic aid.

Behavior modification. Aversive conditioning and other techniques based on learning principles have been employed since 1930 in the treatment of alcoholics (Frank, 1967). Earlier studies utilized a nausea-inducing emetic as the aversive unconditioned stimulus. The alcoholic was injected with a quick-acting emetic. A minute or two before the onset of nausea he was asked to drink one of a variety of alcoholic beverages, which he promptly vomited. The experience was repeated several times over a period of a week or more to establish a conditioned association between the sight, taste, and smell of alcohol and vomiting. More recent studies have used electric shock as the aversive stimulus. The alcoholic is instructed to sip or sniff alcohol. As he does so, he receives a shock of controlled intensity. Periodically a glass of orange juice or some other non-alcoholic drink is substituted for alcohol, with no accompanying shock. Avoidance conditioning is thus restricted to alcoholic beverages. Aversive conditioning may be augmented by the addition of other behavior modification techniques. McBrearty et al. (1968) have described a broad-spectrum approach that includes didactic training, relaxation, and desensitization.

Individual therapy. Traditional forms of individual psychotherapy that involve the talking out of problems, the search for underlying causes, and patient self-understanding have not fared well in the treatment of alcoholism. Alcoholism interferes with the establishment of an effective patient-therapist relationship. For psychotherapy to succeed, the therapist and patient must work together in an atmosphere of mutual trust, confidence, and positive regard; alcohol dissolves interpersonal relationships far more readily than it cements them. Most therapists, for their part, find it difficult to establish and maintain a feeling of empathy with the alcoholic. They weary of his denials, become discouraged with his relapses, and end up questioning the sincerity of his motivation. The alcoholic then feels more misunderstood and rejected than ever. The failure of insights gained through therapy to prevent his drinking convinces him of the hopelessness of his condition. In any case, alcoholism is as much a family problem as an individual problem.

Family therapy. When the family is still interested in the alcoholic, family therapy is often effective in moderating drinking, reducing home friction, and alleviating the burden of guilt and remorse carried by the alcoholic. Though women are often blamed for driving men to drink, the wife of the alcoholic is not responsible for his alcoholism. This is his doing. Often she is an innocent victim. It sometimes happens, however, that a woman originally selects her husband because his drinking satisfies her own neurotic needs. After marriage her need to dominate, control, punish, or be the long-suffering martyr may nudge him deeper into alcoholism. In these cases, family therapy may provide the assistance she needs in resolving her own problems. When the wife is an innocent victim, family therapy may be helpful in improving the discordant relationship created by the recurring family crises resulting from excessive drinking.

Group therapy. Group therapy is considered to be one of the more effective approaches to alcoholism (Thomas, 1968). Usually the group consists of about ten alcoholics who meet once or twice weekly. The structure and direction of sessions vary with the leader. The alcoholic who has long experienced isolation and rejection finds acceptance and identification in the company of others who share a common problem. The supportive atmosphere facilitates candid discussion of personal experiences, failures, and resentments. Since all the members are experts in the use of denial, rationalization, and projection, they are quick to expose these defensive maneuvers. The individual is forced to face the truth about his drinking. The success of any member in abstaining offers encouragement to the others.

Alcoholics Anonymous. Alcoholics Anonymous is an informal organization of men and women run by alcoholics for alcoholics. The only requirement for membership is an honest desire to stop drinking. There are no dues or fees. Local groups in cities and towns throughout the country meet regularly to share their experiences in order to gain strength to resolve their common problem and to help others. Instead of depending on alcohol, members are encouraged to depend on each other. Although the movement is nonsectarian, great stress is placed on spiritual values and reliance on God for guidance and assistance. At meetings each member publicly confesses that he was and is an alcoholic. One of the twelve steps that constitute the guiding principles of A.A. calls for the individual to admit to God, to himself, and to another human being the exact nature of his wrongdoings. Each member is urged to make a list of all persons he has harmed and to try to make amends whenever possible. A.A. offers the alcoholic fellowship and direction. Through helping others he reinforces his own sobriety and builds up his self-esteem. A.A. has sponsored an auxiliary organization, called Al-Anon, for members of alcoholics' families. There are no valid statistics on the effectiveness of A.A., but the viability and growth of the organization suggest that it serves a useful function for some alcoholics. Its emphasis on a higher power makes it relatively ineffective for those who do not respond to this approach.

Outcome and aims. The extreme heterogeneity of the alcoholic population makes it very difficult to evaluate the outcome of alcoholism. Prognosis tends to be favorable for alcoholics who have not progressed beyond the stage of psychological dependence and who are still employed and living in a family setting. Prognosis is very poor for homeless Skid Row derelicts. When alcoholism is associated with severe personality disorganization, outcome is less favorable than when the personality is relatively intact. A second complicating variable is the strictness of the criteria employed in evaluating outcome. From 40 to 60 percent of treated alcoholics have sober periods lasting six months or longer. The number of "cured" alcoholics who maintain total and complete sobriety for life is quite small. Most authorities agree that few alcoholics succeed in going back to moderate social drinking.

Chafetz (1967), however, has questioned the desirability of insisting on permanent abstinence as the only criterion of successful treatment. As he sees it, adherence to this strict goal hinders therapy. When relapses occur, as they almost invariably do, the therapist is disappointed, the patient is disturbed by feelings of guilt and failure, and his family loses hope. A more rational approach is to aim for a reduction of alcoholic behavior by concentrating on family adjustment, occupational effectiveness, and social adequacy. In the evaluation of treatment effectiveness, as Chafetz points out, account must be taken of the possible development of substitute symptoms during periods of abstinence.

PREVENTION OF ALCOHOLISM

The Cooperative Commission on the Study of Alcoholism has outlined a comprehensive program for the prevention of alcoholism (Plaut, 1967). One broad approach aims at improving the general mental health of the population. Sources of environmental stress would be reduced if we improved the quality of family life and created a more humane society that afforded ample room for diversity and for individual self-realization. The use of alcohol as a self-prescribed remedy for problems in living might be lessened through the development of programs designed to help people acquire better ways of coping with difficulties and through the availability of community facilities and crisis centers for the prompt treatment of disturbed individuals and families.

A second broad approach aims at changing attitudes toward drinking and drinking patterns through large-scale educational endeavors and concurrent changes in laws and rules. With the cooperation of government agencies, the schools might contribute to this endeavor by providing students with factual information on the roles and effects of alcohol. In a predominantly drinking society it is futile to aim for the abolition of alcohol. This was demonstrated by the failure of the 1920–1933 prohibition experiment. The objective of the educational program should be to correct current misconceptions regarding drinking and to substitute a rational attitude for the current widespread emotionalism. Drinking is neither a sign of moral weakness nor a test of manliness or sophistication. Excessive drinking is harmful, but mild to moderate drinkers derive pleasure and comfort from the relaxing effects of alcohol. There should be no pressure to drink, and abstinence should be respected, but neither should there be any pressure to make beer and wine unavailable. A repressive attitude toward drinking tends to encourage its use by adolescents as a form of rebellion. Drinking for its own sake should be discouraged. When drinking is acceptable to the persons concerned, it should be integrated with other activities, such as family dinners and social functions. The serving of beer and wine in college cafeterias and at college social functions might tend to discourage excessive drinking off campus. The rules of hospitality need revision. Both host and guests should share the responsibility of seeing to it that no one drinks so much that his behavior becomes objectionable or dangerous to others. The dangers of driving while under the influence of alcohol must be stressed in driver education courses.

Other Mind-Altering Drugs

Drugs other than alcohol that are sought for the pleasure they may give are usually classified in four main categories.

1. *Opiates*. Also referred to as narcotics, these drugs relieve physical and psychic pain, induce a state of euphoria in some individuals, and lead to drowsiness and sleep. The primary drug is opium; morphine, heroin, and codeine are derived from it.

2. *Hallucinogens*. Here is included a variety of drugs that produce perceptual alterations, illusions, visual hallucinations, euphoria, and mood changes. The best known are marijuana, hashish, and lysergic acid diethylamide (LSD). Others are mescaline, which is obtained from the dried buttons of the peyote cactus, and psilocybin, which is the active ingredient of a vivid red-capped mushroom. Peyote is used in religious rites among the American Indians of the Southwest, and the "sacred mushroom" serves a similar function among certain Indian groups in Mexico.

3. *Stimulants*. The more technical name is analeptics. With the exception of cocaine, which is obtained from the coca leaf, these stimulants are synthetic chemicals. Collectively known as amphetamines, they include Benzedrine, Dexedrine, and Methedrine. Amphetamines increase energy level and have an exhilarating effect. Prior to the discovery of their mind-altering function, amphetamines were extensively used as medical aids in weight reduction, to diminish fatigue, and repel sleep.

4. *Sedatives*. Here are included the habit-forming barbiturates, which in mild doses have a relaxing effect and in moderate doses induce sleep. Large doses are lethal.

DRUG EFFECTS

The effects of drugs vary with their purity, the dosage, the method of administration, personality variables, the setting, and the expectations of the user. Mild doses may have no harmful effects, but massive doses lead to delirium, confusion, or death. Amphetamine pills taken orally produce a mild to moderate exhilaration. When injected intravenously, the same drug may precipitate psychotic-like reactions. Drugs that have little or no effect on normal individuals may lead to panic or acute psychotic episodes in more unstable individuals. Users who anticipate behavior changes or who take drugs for the specific purpose of becoming high usually report more marked reactions than skeptical persons who question the ability of drugs to dominate them. On different occasions the same person may show considerable variation in behavior following the use of the same drug. Good trips on LSD may be interspersed with bad trips. The effects of most drugs are enhanced when they are taken in group situations, in which participants provide mutual stimulation and reinforcement. The solitary marijuana smoker does not experience the same feeling of warmth and friendliness toward his fellow man as group users who sit in a circle and pass a cigarette or pipe from person to person.

The effects of drugs are greatly influenced by the mental set and the psychological expectations of the user. Cues and suggestions offered by experienced users influence the anticipated reactions of beginners and thereby structure and perpetuate certain patterns of reactions to specific drugs. Thus drug behavior may to a considerable degree be interpreted as the acting out of expected roles with variations introduced by the particular needs and characteristics of the individual (Coe and Sarbin, 1966). The effects of mental set and expectation on drug behavior are not isolated phenomena. Laboratory experiments have repeatedly demonstrated that set and expectation may lead to unusual reactions in normal persons. Barber and Calverley (1964) found that task-motivating instructions are as effective as hypnotic induction in producing auditory and visual hallucinations. Orne and Scheibe (1964) compared the reactions of experimental and control groups to sensory deprivation. Both groups spent an equal amount of time in an isolation chamber. The experimental group was asked to report any visual imagery, unusual feelings, difficulties in concentration, hallucination, or the like. Subjects were told that such experiences were not unusual in the conditions to which they were to be subjected. Experimental subjects were also informed that by pressing a red button, labeled "Emergency Alarm," they could obtain immediate release from the experiment. The control subjects were given no instructions that might lead them to expect unusual reactions. Under these conditions, the experimental group more frequently reported perceptual distortions, restlessness, spatial disorientation, anxiety, and unpleasant emotions. Some of their reactions were similar to those commonly experienced by drug users: visions of multicolored spots, wavering walls, and the spontaneous movement of inanimate objects. Some thought that they had been left behind or trapped in a burning building. One experimental subject pressed the panic button and gave "disorganization of senses" as a reason for ending the experiment. One of the control subjects also became upset and signalled to be let out of the room.

The complexities of drug behavior may be simplified by distinguishing between the physiological changes induced by drugs and the user's interpretation of and reactions to these changes. The direct effects of drugs are essentially restricted to changes in conscious awareness and in sensory, motor, and autonomic functions. Some drugs are stimulants that lead to increased activity and alertness. Others are depressants that result in a relaxed or drowsy state—a feeling of floating. Some drugs act on the visual system and produce hallucinatory sensations consisting mainly of changing colors and forms. When this happens, the individual in characteristic human fashion tries to make sense of these strange experiences or to structure them in some meaningful way. The basic process is no different than "seeing" specific objects or scenes in cloud formations or in ink blots. Since the stimuli are internal, their interpretation is generally based on personal feelings, thoughts, impulses, and fantasies. The setting and expected effects contribute to the imposed perception and reaction. In brief, drugs are not directly responsible for the visions of celestial beauty, the paranoid reactions, the oceanic tranquility, the horrors, the rapturous colored music, the fears, or the illuminating insights reported by drug users. These psychological side effects are contributed by the individual.

MOTIVES FOR DRUG USE

There are as many reasons for using drugs as for using alcohol, and most of them are the same. The preference for drugs among young people today is partly due to the fact that they are able to persuade themselves that drugs are their own thing, whereas alcohol belongs to the rejected parental generation. The fact that drugs are considered illegal and are disapproved of by the establishment makes their use all the more attractive as symbols of rebellion. Other advantages that young people find in the new drugs are that they are faster acting and far more potent than alcohol. Many young people initially try drugs out of curiosity. The more adventuresome may be challenged by the dramatic experiences promised by LSD and the dangers of heroin and Methedrine. To the usual motives of alleviation of tension and escape from problems are added the thrill of adventure, risk-taking, and the heady experience of jousting with death. Particularly among young users the tremendous pressure of the peer group may lead to the periodic use of drugs as a passport to social acceptance through conformity. For alienated persons the camaraderie and feeling of togetherness of the drug subculture may satisfy social needs.

THE EXTENT OF THE PROBLEM

In recent years there has been a tremendous increase in the use of drugs of all types. Data reported on arrests for drug offenses in England are representative of similar increases in other countries. The number of marijuana offenses in the United Kingdom increased from 235 in 1960 to 3,071 in 1968. During the same period, drug offenses involving the use of heroin and other potent drugs jumped from 28 to 1,099 (see Table 13.2). These fig-

Table 13.2. Recent increases in drug offenses in the United Kingdom

Year	Number of drug offenses		
	Opium	Marijuana	Heroin and related drugs
1960	15	235	28
1961	15	288	61
1962	16	588	71
1963	20	663	63
1964	14	544	101
1965	13	626	128
1966	36	1,119	242
1967	58	2,393	573
1968	73	3,071	1,099

Adapted from H. B. Spear, "The Growth of Heroin Addiction in the United Kingdom," *British Journal of Addiction,* 64 (1969): 245–55.

ures do not include the much larger number of unrecorded offenses. In the United States the explosion in the use of drugs first started on college campuses during the early 1960s. More recently drug use has become prevalent in high schools and even in the lower grades. There has also been increased drug use among adults in the more liberal sectors of the middle and upper classes.

Although multiple drug use is common, choice of drugs is related to age and socioeconomic class. Among college students marijuana is by far the most popular, followed by the amphetamines. Heroin use continues to be most prevalent in lower socioeconomic groups and particularly among minority groups. In some cities many young children have taken to sniffing glue and drinking cough medicines for kicks. Barbiturates have traditionally been associated with middle-class adults, but their use is spreading to younger age groups. At one time drug use was largely restricted to cities, but it has spread to small towns and rural areas. One indication of the extent of the problem is that most preadolescents and adolescents are quite familiar with the argot of drug users.

Glossary of Slang Terms Relating to Drug Abuse

Acid: LSD, LSD-25 (lysergic acid diethylamide)

Bang: Injection of drugs

Barbs: Barbiturates

Bennies: Benzedrine, an amphetamine

Blank: Extremely low-grade narcotic

Blast: Strong effect from a drug

Blue angels: Amytal, a barbiturate

Bombita: Amphetamine injection, sometimes taken with heroin

Bum trip: Bad experience with psychedelic drugs

Busted: Arrested

Chipping: Taking narcotics occasionally

Cokie: Cocaine addict

Cold turkey: Sudden withdrawal of narcotics

Cop out: Quit, take off, confess, defect, inform

Cut: Dilute drugs by adding milk, sugar, or another inert substance

Dexies: Dexedrine, an amphetamine

Downers: Sedatives, alcohol, tranquilizers, narcotics

Dynamite: High-grade heroin

Fix: Injection of narcotics

Floating: Under the influence of drugs

Freakout: Bad experience with psychedelics; also, a chemical high

Good trip: Happy experience with psychedelics

Goofballs: Sleeping pills

Grass: Marijuana

Hash: Hashish, the resin of cannabis

Hearts: Dexedrine tablets (shape)

Hooked: Addicted

Horse: Heroin

Joint: Marijuana cigarette

Jolly beans: Pep pills

Kick the habit: Stop using narcotics

Lemonade: Poor heroin

Mainline: Inject drugs into a vein

Meth: Methamphetamine (also known as Methedrine, Desoxyn)

Pot: Marijuana

Reefer: Marijuana cigarette

Roach: Marijuana butt

Run: An amphetamine binge

Scag: Heroin

Snow: Cocaine

Speed: Methedrine, an amphetamine

Stick: Marijuana cigarette

Strung out: Addicted

Uppers: Stimulants, cocaine, psychedelics

Weed: Marijuana

Yellowjacket: Nembutal, a barbiturate

THE LABELS OF ADDICTION

The pejorative attitude of society toward those who use drugs for pleasure is reflected in the immoral and illegal connotations of the term "drug addict." In the argot of users, drugs are occasionally assigned favorable labels (jolly beans, blue angels), but heavy users are unfavorably described as "hooked," "potheads," "acid heads," and "speed freaks." The indiscriminate application of the label of drug addict to all users has led to confusion and controversy. At the present time, an otherwise normally functioning student who takes a few puffs of pot once or twice a month at parties is technically a drug user. If apprehended and found to be in possession of a fraction of an ounce of marijuana, he is subject to arrest. Yet he is obviously not in the same class as the drug addict whose whole life revolves about the obtaining and use of heroin.

More precise terms are needed to differentiate harmless from harmful use of drugs. The usefulness of such a change of labels may be seen in the recent substitution of the terms "psychological dependence" and "physiological dependence" for the unsatisfactory concept of drug addiction. The substituted terms are not perfect, since "dependence" may be easily misconstrued as implying some defect in character. But when "psychological dependence" is used as it is intended, it indicates a learned reaction pattern acquired and sustained through reinforcement, and thus falls in the same category as other habits and acquired tastes and is subject to the usual learning principles involved in habit-breaking. Physiological dependence is more complicated. It is signaled by physical withdrawal symptoms when the user stops taking the drug to which he is addicted. The source of the problem is a change in cell metabolism, which necessitates a period of time for metabolic readjustment. Tolerance is also a physiological matter. The body quickly adapts to the presence of certain drugs, so that increasing amounts are required to produce reactions formerly produced by small doses.

CONSEQUENCES OF DRUG USE

As with alcohol, the harmful effects, if any, of drug use vary with the product used, the amount consumed, the individual characteristics of the user, and other factors. The abuse of drugs by young people has a long list of consequences, none of them favorable: early dropping out of school; inability to obtain or hold a job; disruption or severing of family ties; conflict with the law; malnutrition; high risk of infectious disorders through use of unsterile preparations, syringes, and needles; increased exposure to venereal diseases; precipitation of psychotic episodes; and shortening of life through physical neglect, accidental overdose, or suicide. In contrast with alcoholics, who often have records of twenty years or more of heavy drinking, most addicts have relatively short histories of drug abuse. They either stop or die. Although findings are inconclusive, there is some evidence that LSD produces chromosomal changes that may lead to genetic defects in the infants of parents who have taken the drug at any time prior to the pregnancy of the mother. It is an established fact that when a woman takes heroin during pregnancy, the child is born with a physiological dependence on the drug and at birth exhibits typical withdrawal symptoms:

excessive yawning, tremors, diarrhea, hyperactivity, excess mucus, and sneezing.

OPIATES

Opium. Opium is the name of the juice obtained from the flower pod of a particular type of poppy. On exposure to the air, the juice coagulates to form a gum. The pain-killing and soporific effects of opium have been known for centuries. Since ancient times it has been smoked or eaten in the Near and Far East to induce a tranquil, relaxed state of mind conducive to pleasant dreams while awake. In comparison with its chemical derivatives, opium is a relatively mild drug, but it is no less habit-forming. Increasing amounts are required to compensate for the tolerance that is built up and to prevent withdrawal symptoms. Gradually the chronic user drifts into an idle life of indifference in which his sole concern is opium.

Morphine. A German druggist isolated the active chemical ingredient in opium in 1803. Appropriately, he named his discovery morphine, after Morpheus, the Greek god of sleep and dreams. The invention in 1855 of the hypodermic syringe provided the means of maximizing the effects of morphine through intravenous injection. The extensive use of morphine as a pain reliever during the Civil War resulted in the addiction of many soldiers. The continued medical use of the drug during the early decades of the twentieth century caused many treated patients unwittingly to acquire the morphine habit. The availability of morphine contributes to its excessive use by physicians. About 1 percent of physicians become addicted to opiates at some time during their professional lives.

Heroin. Heroin is a derivative of morphine. For many years after its discovery in 1898 heroin was considered a safe substitute for morphine for medical purposes. Unfortunately, it has turned out to be far more potent and much more harmful. Heroin is the drug of choice for 90 percent of narcotics users. Most of the recent additions to the narcotics-using population are adolescents who started on milder drugs in their early teens and soon progressed to heroin. Most have dropped out of school and are unemployed. Their full-time occupation is drugs. They have to hustle to make contact with sellers, stay ahead of police, and obtain money to purchase drugs. Money presents a big problem, since few heroin users are capable of earning enough money in legitimate jobs to support their habits, which average about $20 a day but may run much higher. Sooner or later most male addicts turn to theft, females to prostitution.

The high induced by heroin consists of a pleasant, drowsy state that lasts about four hours. When an addict is in this state he is said to be "nodding," because a characteristic reaction is a sleepy nodding of the head. When junkies get together there are no outbursts of hilarity or aggression and no sexual activity. The frequently heard stories of orgies and sexual attacks by addicts are myths. The use of heroin blocks the sex impulse. Users tend to be inadequate, passive-dependent persons. Their one topic of conversation is drugs. They exchange experiences, compare notes on the relative merits of combining heroin with other drugs, and discuss sources of supply. The future is limited to the next fix. This is serious, since the dreaded withdrawal symptoms set in twelve to sixteen hours after the last shot.

Once a heroin user becomes thoroughly hooked, he no longer experiences the euphoria he enjoyed in the beginning. Now he needs the drug simply to function normally and avoid withdrawal symptoms. These symptoms tend to be quite uniform. Early reactions include frequent yawning, dilation of the pupils, profuse sweating, restlessness, and a watery flow from eyes and nose. The hair on the skin stands erect. If heroin is taken then, the symptoms subside; if not, the addict goes on to suffer violent cramps, frequent vomiting, diarrhea, chills, aches, agitation, and insomnia. The skin characteristically resembles that of a plucked chicken; hence the expression "cold turkey" for sudden withdrawal of drugs. The expression "kick the habit" also is related to withdrawal symptoms. The later stages of withdrawal include muscular twitches and spasmodic kicking of the feet. The withdrawal period usually lasts a week. The severity of symptoms is greatest between the second and third days. Symptoms may be moderated by a gradual reduction in the intake of drugs rather than sharp withdrawal. This procedure extends the withdrawal period over two or more weeks (Maurer and Vogel, 1967).

Hospitalization is sometimes recommended for the treatment of withdrawal symptoms, particularly if the addict is among the 20 to 30 percent of heroin users who are also addicted to barbiturates. Sudden withdrawal of barbiturates usually results in severe convulsions. Practically all patients can be cured of physiological dependence in a matter of weeks. The elimination of psychological dependence is more difficult. About 90 percent of users discharged as "clean" following hospital treatment become readdicted within six months of their return to home territory (Hunt and Odoroff, 1963). Several methods have been proposed for preventing readdiction and furthering rehabilitation:

1. *Substitution of methadone or cyclazocine for heroin.* Both methadone and cyclazocine are synthetic pain-killers and both provide cross-tolerance to heroin. The patient receives a daily oral dose that is gradually increased until full tolerance is reached. Once he is able to tolerate a full dose of the substitute without experiencing any effect from it, continued daily doses block the action of heroin. The patient feels no need for heroin as

long as he keeps taking the substitute, and if he nevertheless does take heroin or some other opiate, it has no effect on him. Thus no purpose is served by the continued use of narcotics. The addict is able to function normally without them.

The patient who has built up a tolerance to methadone or cyclazocine experiences no sedative or euphoric effect from it. However, either drug leads to physiological dependence and to withdrawal symptoms if its use is discontinued. The substitution of one addictive drug for another raises a serious ethical issue. The pragmatic justification is that by eliminating the stranglehold of narcotics and freeing the addict of the ever-pressing need to obtain funds, by whatever means, these substitute drugs help the addict to resume a productive role in society if this is what he really wants. The daily doses of the substitutes cost only a few cents each. Favorable results in selected cases have been reported by Dole and Nyswander (1968) with the use of methadone, and by Resnick et al. (1970) with cyclazocine.

2. *Total and continued treatment.* Brill and his associates (1963) have described a comprehensive community-centered program for the rehabilitation of the addict following his withdrawal from physiological dependence on drugs. During the course of a five-year experiment, a number of social agencies cooperated in providing former addicts with vocational training, aid in finding jobs and housing, financial assistance, family counseling, casework, psychiatric therapy, and other services. One general conclusion was that addiction should be regarded as a chronic disorder. Permanent abstinence is too much to expect, at least right away. A more feasible goal is to help the addict hold a job and abstain from drug use as long as he can. A second general conclusion was that the usual methods of social work are not applicable to the drug addict. The caseworker must reach out to help the addict and be highly flexible in his approach. He can't sit in his middle-class office and wait for the addict to come in to discuss his problems. It is not enough to make community facilities available to the addict. He requires a great deal of help to make use of the services offered. The long-term results of such a community-centered program have not yet been reported.

3. *Treatment by former addicts.* Considerable interest has recently been expressed in the treatment of addicts by former addicts. Charles E. Dederich, a former alcoholic, started the movement known as Synanon in 1958 on the West Coast (Yablonsky, 1965). Not all people who seek help at Synanon in building meaningful lives are drug addicts, but most of them are. A similar East Coast program was established at Daytop Lodge in 1963. Since then, other centers have been opened in several cities. All of these centers provide live-in therapeutic communities, staffed by former addicts or others who have emerged from the social underworld.

The program at Daytop Lodge has been described by Shelly and Bassin (1965). Shortly after a newcomer's arrival at the center he is interviewed by a team of clean-cut, conventionally dressed young men who start questioning him in a kindly, sympathetic manner. After he has fed them the usual line given to professional workers in the mental health field, the interviewers cut him short. In blunt, four-letter words they tell him that he is talking sheer drivel. On this and subsequent interviews the message is forcefully conveyed that the addict alone is responsible for his addiction. The only valid explanation is that he is stupid. He is not sick. He simply has no more sense or responsibility than a three-year-old. If he wants to grow up and become a man, he can stay. Otherwise, the door is open and he can get lost. If he decides to stay, he must do as he is told. Certain primary rules are strictly enforced: no use of drugs or alcohol, no physical violence, no shirking of responsibility. There can be no more lying or cheating. Watchwords are honesty and reliability. Treatment consists largely of group therapy. The usual explanations based on intellectual theories, childhood deprivations, and so on are hooted down. The focus is kept on present behavior. Members of the group interact at gut level. They critically examine each other and take each other apart. At marathon encounters that may last twenty-four hours, the search for the naked truth about oneself is relentlessly pursued. Supplementary programs, including weekly parties with invited outside guests, are aimed at resocialization. The length of treatment is usually a year or more, but members may leave whenever they wish, and some stay on indefinitely, eventually assuming staff responsibilities and making a career of the movement. Many addicts have been helped by this approach but no reliable figures on the results of treatment are available.

Characteristics of narcotics users. Willis (1969) has reported a comparative study of young narcotics users in the United States and the United Kingdom. The social class backgrounds of the English subjects were more varied and generally higher than the class backgrounds of the American subjects, most of whom came from underprivileged socioeconomic environments. The English group also had a better work history. In other respects, however, the two groups were essentially similar. When compared with a control group of nonaddicts, the American and English narcotics users were found to have higher incidences of parental loss through death or separation, family psychiatric disturbances, persistent truancy during childhood, impotence, delinquency, and criminal behavior.

Willis' overall impression that the drug users in both national groups were highly disturbed individuals is consistent with other findings. Gilbert and Lombardi (1967) compared test scores on the Minnesota Multiphasic Personality Inventory (MMPI) of a group of young male narcotics addicts with scores of a nonaddicted group of similar socioeconomic status. Psychopathy indicators were found to be more widespread among addicts. Traits noted more frequently in the addicted group included depression, tension, insecurity, feelings of inadequacy, and difficulty in forming lasting and warm interpersonal relationships. Hill and his associates (1960) noted that adolescent and adult hospitalized addicts exhibited similar deviant personality characteristics. On the MMPI scale both age groups showed high Pd (psychopathy) scores.

HALLUCINOGENS

Marijuana, hashish, LSD, mescaline, and psilocybin are more accurately described as phantasmagorogenic than hallucinogenic drugs. The perceptual experiences of colors and designs induced by these drugs are similar to hallucinations in the fact that they originate within the person rather than in external reality; but they differ from true hallucinations, as experienced by psychotics, in the fact that the drug user realizes that they are not real experiences, but special effects produced by the drug. He knows that when the action of the drug wears off, the show will be over. The dictionary definition of "phantasmagoria" neatly fits the drug experience: "a shifting series of illusions or deceptive appearances, as in a dream, in which figures increase or diminish in size, dissolve, pass into each other, etc." The recently coined term "psychedelic" may serve as well as any to identify and distinguish these drugs and their effects.

The intended objective in taking LSD and related drugs is not to blank out the mind, but to open it to new inner experiences. The illusion of being more alert and creative accentuates the desired effect. Mood changes are incidental: the psychic event is the goal. Psychedelic drugs may be considered introvertive drugs. The high consists of an intensification of subjective experiences, of increased self-absorption and detachment, of passive euphoria. The "hashish laughter" occasionally noted in extravertive persons is a personal rather than a social reaction. Psychedelic drugs are often taken in group settings, but boisterous gregariousness is not part of the scene. Continued use of any of the hallucinogenic drugs studied so far leads to psychological dependence, but there is no increase in tolerance and no evidence of withdrawal symptoms following discontinuance of drug use.

Marijuana. Of all drugs taken for their pleasurable effects, marijuana is the most widely used in the United States today. Fortunately, it is also the mildest. A conservative estimate is that about 50 percent of college students have smoked marijuana at least once and that about 25 percent do so at least once a month. A slight impairment in psychological functioning may occur while it is being smoked, but periodic use has no known harmful effects. The major objection is that its frequent use by young people may lead to loss of interest in schoolwork and early dropping out of school. Heavy use leads to psychological dependence. A small percentage of marijuana users go on to stronger drugs. It has been speculated that they would probably have done so even if they had not started with pot; there is no way of reaching a final judgment on this.

Marijuana consists of a crude mixture of the flowery tops, leaves, seeds, and stems of female plants of Indian hemp. The taller male plant contains very little of the active ingredient and is used mainly in making rope. The sticky resin exuded by the tops of the female plants is known as hashish. Hashish is much more potent than marijuana. The active ingredient in the resin has been synthesized. It is known as trans-tetrahydrocannabinol (THC). Marijuana is usually smoked; hashish is smoked or eaten.

Persons who have smoked marijuana characteristically report a feeling of mental relaxation accompanied by physical languor. Mental alertness is retained but there is a diminution of interest in mental and physical activity. The "cool" of the marijuana smoker is a quiet, passive state. Time seems to pass slowly. Some users experience an intensification of sensory impressions. Perceptual distortions are more characteristic of hashish than of marijuana. Weil, Zinberg, and Nelson (1968) have reported a carefully controlled experimental study on the clinical and psychological effects of marijuana. Comparisons were made of reactions by regular and naïve users—persons who had had no prior experience with marijuana—who smoked marijuana or placebo cigarettes in a neutral laboratory situation. Placebo cigarettes were made from the chopped stalks of male hemp plants, which contain no active ingredient. They made a number of interesting findings:

1. The intoxicating properties of marijuana varied with the mental set or the psychological expectation of the subject. All chronic users who knew that they were smoking high-grade marijuana became high. The naïve subjects showed no definite intoxication from smoking marijuana cigarettes, with one exception: a naïve subject who had previously expressed a desire to get high became markedly euphoric. He laughed continuously while taking his first battery of tests.

2. Naïve subjects showed impaired performance on simple intellectual and psychomotor tests after smoking marijuana. Regular users showed either mild impairment or some slight improvement in performance.

3. Marijuana smoking resulted in a moderate increase in heart rate and caused a reddening of the conjunctivae of the eyes. No changes were noted in pupil size or blood sugar level.

4. The psychological and physiological effects of marijuana approach a

maximum intensity within a half hour of inhalation. The effects were diminished after one hour and completely dissipated by the end of three hours.

An interesting account of the marketing of marijuana has been contributed by Goode (1969). The wholesale importing is usually arranged by semi-independent entrepreneurs with criminal backgrounds. Shipments are divided and passed on to big dealers. The big dealers sell to small dealers, who in turn break up their purchases into pound packages that are sold to user-sellers. The user-sellers usually sell one-ounce packages (enough to make about 40 joints) to regular users. The buyer of a one-ounce package may sell some of his supply to more moderate users. The quantity involved is so small, however, that the profit motive at this level is incidental. Sales of less than an ounce are largely accommodations or favors to friends. Marijuana is often shared with friends in much the same way as a bottle of liquor. More is given away, especially to female friends, than is sold. Periodic users rarely purchase the drug. They depend on being offered some at parties or when they visit regular users. The average user smokes about two joints a day, which brings the cost to less than a dollar a day. The monetary aspect is too small to encourage stealing to support the habit. In contrast to the heroin addict, who typically consumes all he can purchase within twenty-four hours or less, the marijuana user spaces out the consumption of his supply over several days or weeks. He usually keeps some on hand as a reserve.

LSD. The natural source of lysergic acid diethylamide is a purple fungus (ergot) that infects rye plants. Some of the incidents of mass hysteria of former times may have occurred when members of a community ate baked goods prepared with infested grain. In its synthetic form LSD is an odorless, colorless liquid of tremendous potency. A gram supplies thousands of doses. All that is required to launch a person on a fantastic eight-hour trip into inner space is a sugar cube or a piece of paper containing a tiny amount of the drug. LSD reached its peak of popularity about 1965. Since then its use among college students has declined sharply, largely because of increased awareness of the frequency of bad trips and of the spontaneous recurrence (flashback) of hallucinatory and related experiences months after the last dose, the occasional onset of a schizophrenic-like psychosis following an LSD experience, and fear of chromosomal defects or brain damage (Smart and Bateman, 1967). Experimental data on chromosome and brain damage are inconclusive. A difficulty in assessing the specific effects of LSD on organic brain impairment is that most acid heads also take a variety of other drugs. Cohen and Edwards (1969) have concluded that there is no evidence that heavy use of LSD results in a generalized psychoneurological dysfunction. The only difference they found between the performance of LSD users and a matched control group on a wide variety of psychological tests was that the LSD users showed impairment in spatial visual orientation. Each of the LSD users had a history of having used LSD on more than fifty occasions, and most had also used other drugs, but none of them was on drugs at the time of testing. An inverse relationship was noted between general intelligence and frequency of LSD use. This finding is subject to two interpretations. Excessive use may have caused intellectual impairment, or low intelligence may have led to frequent use of LSD.

Although specific reactions to LSD are greatly influenced by personal factors and the setting in which it is taken, the drug itself appears to have certain specific effects. Most users report unusual and constantly changing distortions in perception and apperception. A second common reaction is a feeling of detachment. It is as though the individual were watching a show in which everything was somewhat unreal and the improbable was ordinary. The individual is overwhelmed with the spontaneous spectacle of brilliant colors and intricate designs. In kaleidoscopic fashion, real and imagined objects and persons change, flow, and merge together. Synesthesia, or the mixing of sensory modalities, often occurs: a color may be not only seen, but heard and tasted and felt. People commonly feel a surge of creativity while on LSD, but their actual performances show no increase in creative ability, and often show a distortion of the creative process (Cohen, 1964). Katz, Waskow, and Olsson (1969) noted the presence of intense but contradictory emotions in their subjects. Characteristic physiological reactions include pupillary dilation, excessive perspiration, tremors, alternating hot and cold flashes, increased heart rate, and a rise in blood pressure.

Other hallucinogens. Mescaline, the active ingredient of peyote cactus buttons, and psyilocybin, the active ingredient of the "divine mushroom," have the same general effects as LSD. The hallucinogenic mushrooms of Mexico and their religious significance for native users have been discussed by Wasson (1959). An early account of the effects of mescaline, reported by S. Weir Mitchell in 1896, is of interest for the light it casts on the constancy of reactions and the importance of individual factors. Mitchell was one of the first to test the validity of the feeling of increased mental ability associated with hallucinogenic drugs. He found that mescaline improved neither his mental competence nor his creativity. His visions were described in dramatic terms. He reported seeing "a tall, richly finished Gothic tower," "an abrupt rush of countless points of white light, as if the unseen millions of stars in the Milky Way were to flow in a sparkling river before the eye," "rippled purples, half transparent, and of ineffable beauty," and "huge precious stones, but uncut, some being more like masses of transparent fruit." The visions of his less imaginative medical colleague Dr. Eshner consisted of stars, crescents, points of light, and mosaics.

STIMULANTS

Cocaine. The early Incas of Peru chewed coca leaves for their invigorating effect, and their descendants still do. The active ingredient, cocaine, was isolated in 1855. Applied externally, cocaine is a local anesthetic. When it is swallowed, sniffed, or injected, it has a stimulating effect. As the exhilarating effects wear off, there is a counterreaction of depression and irritability. Large doses of cocaine sometimes result in a characteristic hallucinatory experience: the user sees and feels minute bugs crawling under the skin. Tolerance for cocaine increases, but there are no withdrawal effects.

Amphetamines. During the Second World War, both sides made extensive use of the stimulant action of amphetamines to counteract fatigue and exhaustion. After the war, the drugs were used in nasal inhalants for the relief of cold symptoms. The public soon discovered that amphetamines were effective pep-up and stay-awake pills. This discovery led to their popularity among students preparing for examinations and long-distance truck drivers. Drug users found other applications for them.

The three most widely used amphetamines are Benzedrine (bennies), Dexedrine (dexies), and Methedrine (speed). Amphetamine use quickly leads to psychological dependence. When taken orally and in moderate doses, these drugs increase activity level and have an exhilarating, mildly euphoric effect. When they are injected intravenously, these reactions are sharply accentuated. The effects of mainlining Methedrine in a group setting have been described by Carey and Mandell (1968). The drug lives up to its slang name. Almost before the needle is withdrawn, the user experiences a rush or flash of sensation. This initial reaction has been compared to an electric shock, a multiple orgasm, and being splashed suddenly by cold water. Afterward the individual feels extremely alert and full of energy. A person on a long run may stay awake two or more days. During this period he feels heightened restlessness, engages in compulsive aimless activity, experiences rapid mood changes, and reacts to quite ordinary situations with unexpected aggressiveness. For some the racing world produced by speed gets out of control and may lead to a freakout or temporary psychosis marked by panic, delusions, and hallucinations. Chronic excessive users gradually develop a paranoid outlook. When high they report hearing police running down the hall to arrest them or see little men with machine guns moving in for the kill. During such episodes as these the person high on speed can be very dangerous. Believing himself about to be attacked, he may decide to attack first. But what goes up must come down, and the speed freak comes down with a crash. Following an interval of sleep the individual is highly irritable, belligerent, and impulsive. The aftereffects are so unpleasant that the individual either gives up Methedrine or quickly turns to it again to regain the feeling of being high. The chronic Methedrine mainliner is unemployed, has no friends except other users, and is dependent on theft for money to purchase his supply. Only the young use Methedrine in this way; older persons can't stand the pace. Neither can the young, but many of them don't live long enough to find it out.

SEDATIVES

Sedatives and tranquilizing drugs of various types are extensively used as medicines. When taken in the small doses prescribed by physicians, these drugs are useful in relieving tension and inducing sleep. High doses produce toxic effects, physiological dependence, and withdrawal reactions. A major group of sedatives, often misused by drug addicts, are those derived from barbituric acid.

Barbiturates. Among the commonly used barbiturates are Amytal (called blue heavens), Luminal (purple hearts), Nembutal (yellow-jackets), and Seconal (red devils).

There are two distinct groups of chronic users. One is composed of middle- and upper-class persons, often unhappy housewives, who usually start taking a barbiturate for insomnia. The mind-dulling effect of the drug is gradually exploited as a universal remedy for emotional problems. The second group consists of drug addicts who use barbiturates as supplements to other drugs or as more readily available substitutes. Barbiturates are commonly used to accentuate the effects of heroin and to moderate the stimulating actions of amphetamines. Barbiturates act as central nervous system depressants. General reactions include drowsiness, mental confusion, and impaired motor coordination. The associated loss of control may lead to overt belligerence in passive-aggressive users. Barbiturates are dangerous in two ways: an overdose results in death, and withdrawal symptoms are severe. Withdrawal symptoms, which last about a week, may include delirium, delusions, hallucinations, and convulsions.

DRUGS AND THE LAW

The rationale for drug laws is that it is the responsibility of society to prohibit the import, manufacture, sale, and use of objects that endanger the health, safety, and welfare of its members. The principle behind the laws is clear and universally recognized. The interpretation and implementation of the laws raise a number of questions. How harmful must a drug be before its prohibition is warranted? If an individual has been informed of the risk involved in taking a dangerous drug and still desires to use it, should he be permitted to do so if his use of it does no harm to others? Should a person who persists in taking a prohibited drug be treated as a criminal or as a sick person? Most societies have preferred to play it safe and prohibit the use of drugs that may have harmful effects, even if, as in the case of marijuana, their harmfulness has not been established beyond all possibility of dispute. Past experiences support this decision. Time and again drugs considered relatively innocuous or even beneficial have later turned out to be harmful. Once the use of a drug is widely accepted, it is extremely difficult to enforce its prohibition. When potentially harmful drugs have beneficial medical values, it must be determined whether they do more good than harm, and this is not always easy to do. A case in point is the use of methadone, which currently may be legally obtained on a medical prescription, as a substitute for heroin in the treatment of addicts. This is a medical and social problem, and a serious one; but to make it a moral issue is to add to the problem, not to solve it.

Most countries have adopted sterner measures against the importers, distributors, and sellers of illicit drugs than against users. When a user of drugs also sells them, he is more likely to be arrested for selling than for possession. The legal distinction between a punishable and nonpunishable offense is sometimes a fine one. The fact that a person is known to be an addict is not legal grounds for arrest. If an addict voluntarily applies for treatment or is hospitalized because of physical or psychological reactions following drug use, no criminal charges are pressed against him. But possession of even a small amount of an illicit drug is legal grounds for arrest. In England, physicians may prescribe narcotics for registered addicts but not for nonregistered addicts. If a registered addict is found to be in possession of an illicit drug other than the one for which he is registered, he is subject to arrest and punishment. Recently England has sharply curtailed the right of physicians to prescribe drugs for registered addicts because of abuses of the system. Too many registered addicts applied for and received excessive amounts of drugs, which they then sold on the black market or shared with friends, who in turn became addicted. The failure of the English plan is not an isolated case. A similar program for providing addicts with drugs under medical supervision was tried in the United States during the early 1920s. It was a total disaster.

The current policy in the United States, as defined by federal, state, and local laws, is that possession or sale of illicit drugs constitutes a criminal offense. In the case of first or mild offenders, however, the present trend in most jurisdictions is for judges to impose a fine or to place the offender on probation rather than to impose a jail sentence. The emphasis is on treatment rather than punishment. This attitude is reflected in the Narcotic Addict Rehabilitation Act, which was passed by Congress in 1966. An important provision of the act is that certain persons charged with a violation of federal law who are determined to be addicted to narcotic drugs "should, in lieu of prosecution or sentencing, be civilly committed for confinement and treatment designed to effect their restoration to health and return to society as useful members." Under the terms of the act, certain criminal charges against an addict are dismissed if he completes a comprehensive treatment program that may last three years. During most of this time the addict lives and works in the community but is required to participate in an intensive rehabilitation program tailored to his needs. His urine is tested at frequent but unpredictable intervals so that any use of drugs may be quickly detected.

Summary

From prehistoric times man has sought magic substances that, in Shakespeare's words, would "pluck from the memory a rooted sorrow, raze out the written troubles of the brain, and with some sweet oblivious antidote cleanse the stuff'd bosom of that perilous stuff which weighs upon the heart." The search has been highly productive. Starting with alcohol and opium, a wide variety of sweet oblivious antidotes has been found. The value of these discoveries, most of which were accidental, is another matter. The drugs have proved highly effective in temporarily easing the mind, shutting off the demands and pressures of reality, alleviating pain and anxiety, increasing energy, lifting the spirits, and opening the door to strange new experiences. These mind-altering and mood-changing functions, when appropriately used, could be considered positive values. On the negative side, excessive chronic use of drugs has resulted in great harm to the individual, his family, and society.

Both the persistence of drug abuse and the relative ineffectiveness of conventional treatment procedures are due to the tremendous reinforcing effect of drugs. Alcohol and other drugs deliver what is expected of them immediately and with a high degree of dependability. The transitory nature of their effects is easily corrected by a repeat dose. As an extra dividend, today's high helps the individual to forget his regrets for the past and the bleakness of his future. Therapeutic hope lies in a comprehensive, long-term program, preferably staffed by former drug users, which offers unqualified acceptance, medical assistance to combat the craving for drugs, job training and placement, and social rehabilitation.

The prevention of addiction to drugs and alcohol is a goal still to be sought. Before we can reach it we must have more solid facts on its many causes than are available to us now. Legal measures are expediencies born of desperation. Attempts to curtail the availability of drugs and to discourage their use by arresting offenders have been ineffective. Better results may be obtained by educational procedures aimed at changing cultural attitudes and practices with respect to drinking and drug use. Another promising lead is to be found in comprehensive community mental health programs. Research data indicate that chronic alcoholics and drug users are characterized by unstable family backgrounds, unresolved dependency conflicts, and poor social adjustment during the formative years. The high incidence of heroin use among underprivileged minority groups in this country and the rejection of contemporary values by alienated young middle- and upper-class drug users seem to place our whole society in a double bind. The equalization of socioeconomic opportunities might reduce the motivation of underprivileged youths to turn to narcotics and would presumably help to lift them into the middle class, whose values are seen as so distasteful by many of its young members that they turn to drugs to escape them. Yet the broadening of socioeconomic opportunities need not be incompatible with the development of more humanistic and humane values. Perhaps the problem is not so much that one group has too little and the other too much, but that both face too many obstacles in achieving a sense of purpose and self-esteem.

References

BARBER, T. X., and CALVERLEY, D. S. "An Experimental Study of 'Hypnotic' (Auditory and Visual) Hallucinations." *Journal of Abnormal and Social Psychology* 68 (1964): 13–20.

BATES, R. F. "Cultural Differences in Rates of Alcoholism." *Quarterly Journal of Studies on Alcohol* 6 (1946): 480–99.

BILLET, S. L. "Antabuse Therapy." In *Alcoholism: The Total Treatment Approach,* ed. R. J. Catanzaro, pp. 90–104. Springfield, Ill.: Charles C Thomas, 1968.

BRILL, L., et al. *Rehabilitation in Drug Addiction.* U.S. Department of Health, Education, and Welfare mental health monograph no. 3. Washington, D.C.: U.S. Government Printing Office, 1963.

"Can the Alcoholic Become a Moderate Drinker?" *Mental Hygiene* 23 (1939): 80–86.

CAREY, J. T., and MANDELL, J. "A San Francisco Bay Area 'Speed Scene.'" *Journal of Health and Social Behavior* 9 (1968): 164–74.

CATANZARO, R. J., ed. *Alcoholism: The Total Treatment Approach.* Springfield, Ill.: Charles C Thomas, 1968.

CHAFETZ, M. E. "Alcoholism." In *Comprehensive Textbook of Psychiatry,* ed. A. M. Freedman and H. I. Kaplan, pp. 1011–26. Baltimore: Williams & Wilkins, 1967.

COE, W. C., and SARBIN, T. R. "An Experimental Demonstration of Hypnosis as Role Enactment." *Journal of Abnormal Psychology* 71 (1966): 400–6.

COHEN, S. *The Beyond Within: The LSD Story.* New York: Atheneum, 1964.

——— and EDWARDS, A. E. "LSD and Organic Brain Impairment." In National Institute of Mental Health, *Drug Dependence,* pp. 1–4. Washington, D.C.: U.S. Government Printing Office, December 1969.

CONGER, J. J. "The Effects of Alcohol on Conflict Behavior in the Albino Rat." *Quarterly Journal of Studies on Alcohol* 12 (1951): 1–29.

DE VITO, R. A.; FLAHERTY, L. A.; and MOZDZIERZ, G. T. "Toward a Psychodynamic Theory of Alcoholism." *Diseases of the Nervous System* 31 (1970): 43–49.

DITMAN, K. S. "The Use of LSD in the Treatment of the Alcoholic." In *Alcoholism: Behavioral Research,* ed. R. Fox, pp. 256–71. New York: Springer, 1967.

DOLE, V. P., and NYSWANDER, M. E. "The Use of Methadone for Narcotic Blockade." *British Journal of Addiction* 63 (1968): 55–57.

FOX, R. "Psychiatric Aspects of Alcoholism." *American Journal of Psychotherapy* 19 (1965): 408–16.

———. "A Multidisciplinary Approach to the Treatment of Alcoholism." *American Journal of Psychiatry* 123 (1967): 769–78.

FRANK, C. M. "Behavior Modification and the Treatment of the Alcoholic." In *Alcoholism: Behavioral Research,* ed. R. Fox, pp. 186–203. New York: Springer, 1967.

GILBERT, J. G., and LOMBARDI, D. N. "Personality Characteristics of Young Male Narcotic Addicts." *Journal of Consulting Psychology* 31 (1967): 536–38.

GOODE, E. "The Marijuana Market." *Columbia Forum* 12 (1969): 4–8.

GOSS, A., and MOROSKO, T. E. "Alcoholism and Clinical Symptoms." *Journal of Abnormal Psychology* 74 (1969): 682–84.

HILL, H. E.; HAERTGEN, C. A.; and GLASER, R. "Personality Characteristics of Narcotics Addicts as indicated by the MMPI." *Journal of Genetic Psychology* 62 (1960): 127–39.

HUNT, G. H., and ODOROFF, M. E. *Follow-Up Study of Narcotic Drug Addicts After Hospitalization.* U.S. Public Health Service report no. 77. Washington, D.C.: U.S. Government Printing Office, 1963.

JELLINEK, E. M. "Phases of Alcohol Addiction." *Quarterly Journal of Studies on Alcohol* 13 (1952): 673–78.

———. *The Disease Concept of Alcoholism.* New Haven, Conn.: Hillhouse Press, 1960.

JONES, M. C. "Personality Correlates and Antecedents of Drinking Patterns in Adult Males." *Journal of Consulting and Clinical Psychology* 32 (1968): 2–12.

KATZ, M. M.; WASKOW, I. E.; and OLSSON, J. "Characterizing the Psychological State Produced by LSD." *Journal of Abnormal Psychology* 73 (1969): 1–14.

KERR, N. "Ether Drinking." *New Review* 3 (1890): 536–46. Also reprinted in National Institute of Mental Health, *Drug Dependence,* pp. 15–19. Washington, D.C.: U.S. Government Printing Office, 1969.

MACANDREW, C., and EDGERTON, R. B. *Drunken Comportment: A Social Exploration.* Chicago: Aldine, 1969.

────── and GEERTSMA, R. "A Critique of Alcoholism Scales Derived from the MMPI." *Quarterly Journal of Studies on Alcohol* 25 (1964): 68–76.

McBREARTY, J. F.; GARFIELD, Z.; DICHTER, M.; and HEATH, G. "A Behaviorally Oriented Treatment Program for Alcoholism." *Psychological Reports* 22 (1968): 287–98.

McCORD, W., and McCORD, J. *Origins of Alcoholism.* Stanford, Calif.: Stanford University Press, 1960.

MASSERMAN, J. H., and YUM, K. S. "An Analysis of the Influence of Alcohol on Experimental Neuroses in Cats." *Psychosomatic Medicine* 8 (1946): 36–52.

MAURER, D. W., and VOGEL, V. H. *Narcotics and Narcotic Addiction.* Springfield, Ill.: Charles C Thomas, 1967.

MENEKER, T. "Anxiety About Drinking in Alcoholics." *Journal of Abnormal Psychology* 72 (1967): 43–49.

MITCHELL, S. W. "Remarks on the Effects of *Anhelonium lewinii* (The Mescal Button)." *British Medical Journal* 2 (1896): 1625–28. Also reprinted in National Institute of Mental Health, *Drug Dependence,* pp. 12–19. Washington, D.C.: U.S. Government Printing Office, 1969.

NOYES, A. P., and KOLB, L. C. *Modern Clinical Psychiatry.* Philadelphia: Saunders, 1963.

ORNE, M. T., and SCHEIBE, K. E. "The Contribution of Nondeprivation Factors in the Production of Sensory Deprivation Effects." *Journal of Abnormal and Social Psychology* 68 (1964): 3–12.

PARTINGTON, J. T. "Dr. Jekyll and Mr. High: Multidimentional Scaling of Alcoholics' Self-evaluation." *Journal of Abnormal Psychology* 75 (1970): 131–38.

PLAUT, T. F. A. *Alcohol Problems: A Report to the Nation by the Cooperative Commission on the Study of Alcoholism.* New York: Oxford University Press, 1967.

RESNICK, R. B.; FINK, M.; and FREEDMAN, A. M. "A Cyclazocine Typology in Opiate Dependence." *American Journal of Psychiatry* 126 (1970): 1256–60.

ROE, A.; BURKS, B.; and MITTLEMAN, B. "Adult Adjustment of Foster Children of Alcoholic and Psychotic Parentage and the Influence of the Foster Home." *Memoirs of the Section on Alcohol,* Yale University, 1945.

SALZBERGER, G. J. "The Acute Alcoholic Debauch." *Diseases of the Nervous System* 28 (1967): 387–89.

SANFORD, N. "Personality and Patterns of Alcohol Consumption." *Journal of Consulting and Clinical Psychology* 32 (1968): 13–17.

SHELLY, J. A., and BASSIN, A. "Daytop Lodge: A New Treatment Approach for Drug Addicts." *Corrective Psychiatry and Journal of Social Therapy* 11 (1965): 186–95. Also reprinted in *Behavior Disorders,* ed. O. Milton and R. G. Wahler, pp. 289–97. Philadelphia: Lippincott, 1969.

SMART, R. G., and BATEMAN, K. "Unfavorable Reactions to LSD." *Canadian Medical Association Journal* 97 (1967): 1214–21.

SPEAR, H. B. "The Growth of Heroin Addiction in the United Kingdom." *British Journal of Addiction* 64 (1969): 245–55.

TAMERIN, J. S., and MENDELSON, J. H. "The Psychodynamics of Chronic Inebriation: Observations of Alcoholics During the Process of Drinking in an Experimental Group Setting." *American Journal of Psychiatry* 125 (1969): 886–99.

THOMAS, M. "The Group Therapies." In *Alcoholism: The Total Treatment*

Approach, ed. R. J. Catanzaro, pp. 127–45. Springfield, Ill.: Charles C Thomas, 1968.

WANBERG, K. W., and HORN, J. L. "Alcoholism Symptom Patterns of Men and Women: A Comparative Study." *Quarterly Journal of Studies on Alcohol* 31 (1970): 40–61.

WASSON, R. G. "The Hallucinogenic Mushrooms of Mexico." *Transactions of the New York Academy of Sciences* 21 (1959).

WEIL, A. T.; ZINBERG, N. E.; and NELSON, J. M. "Clinical and Psychological Effects of Marijuana in Man." *Science* 162 (December 13, 1968): 1234–42.

WILLIS, J. H. "Drug Dependence: Some Demographic and Psychiatric Aspects in United Kingdom and United States Subjects." *British Journal of Addiction* 64 (1969): 135–46.

YABLONSKY, L. *The Tunnel Back: Synanon.* New York: Macmillan, 1965.

CHAPTER FOURTEEN

Sex Deviance

Normal sexual behavior consists of voluntary genital intercourse between a physiologically mature male and female who are not closely related. The qualifying term "voluntary" serves the dual purpose of excluding rape and of implying discrimination and control with respect to choice of partner and time and place of sexual expression. The presence of love and affection between partners is a desirable and often critical condition for optimal enjoyment, but this is an ideal rather than essential element. The other qualifying phrases in the definition eliminate pedophilia and incest. The term "genital intercourse" refers specifically to the biological criteria that associates sex behavior with procreation. It also identifies the mode of adult heterosexual activity that is most approved by society. Normal human sex behavior, however, also includes foreplay and variations in technique engaged in by consenting partners for purposes of added stimulation or pleasure. Variations accepted by many people include fellatio (mouth-penis), cunnilingus (tongue-clitoris), and anal intercourse. Masturbation is regarded as normal behavior when it serves as a substitute of expediency or of necessity for heterosexual activity. The assumption, of course, is that the act will be performed in such a manner as to not to offend the rules of decency. Masturbation, in moderation, is the least harmful means of release of sexual tensions in children and adolescents, and in adults who through choice, circumstances, religious commitment, or social rules are deprived of heterosexual opportunities.

The concept of sexual deviation is restricted to (1) conditions in which erotic activities are preferred with or restricted to members of one's own sex or (2) rituals in which heterosexual participation is involuntary or incidental. Sex deviants have no erotic interest in members of the opposite sex and derive little or no stimulation or gratification from normal heterosexual activities. The normal sex act may be feared or regarded with disgust. These distinguishing features differentiate sexual deviations from nymphomania, satyriasis, promiscuity, prostitution, and related forms of heterosexual behavior in which the intensity of the heterosexual drive, its frequency of expression, the number of partners, and the underlying motivation differ from the cultural norms. Impotence in males and frigidity in females are regarded as psychosomatic disorders rather than sex deviations. Impotent men and nonorgasmic women retain their heterosexual identity and may make repeated desperate efforts to satisfy their sexual feelings in conventional ways. They are prevented from doing so by emotional blocks that interfere with adequate performance and gratification.

General Characteristics of Sexual Deviation

It is not uncommon for individuals to exhibit two or more forms of deviant behavior. For classification purposes, however, most of the recognized sexual deviations may be grouped into three categories:

1. Deviation in sex identity: homosexuality, lesbianism, transsexuality.
2. Deviation in sexual mode: transvestism, masochism, sadism, exhibitionism, voyeurism.
3. Deviation in sexual object: bestiality, fetishism, pedophilia.

The term "deviation" is favored to "disorder," since most sex deviants do not manifest significant disturbances in personality organization or functioning. This does not mean that sexual deviations do not occur among mental patients. Because of their poor premorbid social adjustment, psychotic persons run a high risk of resorting to deviant and at times bizarre forms of sexual gratification. But there is no justification for considering sexual deviations per se as manifestations of mental disorder. Persons diagnosed as sex deviants comprise a small fraction of 1 percent of all persons admitted to mental hospitals. The sexual deviations of persons living in the community rarely qualify as disordered behavior, since (1) the degree of control exercised by the individual over his total behavior (including deviant impulses) is comparable to that of normal heterosexuals, and (2) there is no serious impairment in higher order psychosocial functioning. Apart from their preference for nonconventional sex objects and unusual modes of sex behavior, most deviants are indistinguishable from the general population in educational level, occupational competence, social status, and moral-ethical standards. Many hold responsible positions and are recognized leaders in their communities. Quite a few known homosexuals have attained fame and fortune, particularly in the literary and other creative fields. The term "lesbianism" is derived from the homosexual practices of the Greek poetess Sappho and her coterie of young women on the island of Lesbos.

Some deviants are disturbed by their impulses, and attempt to deny or repress them. Most learn to accept and live with the fact that they are "different." Inner adjustment is often facilitated by rationalizations to the effect that they were born that way or are innocent victims of childhood conditioning experiences that have distorted their feelings and behavior patterns. A few overcompensate and persuade themselves that their gray world is a gay one. The main area of maladjustment lies in the deviant's relationship with society. Degrees of tolerance vary with place and time, but by and large most societies are vigorously opposed to "unnatural" sexual activities. A deaf ear is usually turned to the deviant who protests his right to individual self-expression as long as he does not seduce minors or harm others. Even if he confines his idiosyncratic behavior to the privacy of his home or practices it discreetly with a few like-minded friends, public sentiment forces him to live in fear of detection and exposure. The instability and transiency of most homosexual liaisons often lead to jealousy, recriminations, and betrayal. More open expression of deviant behavior with strangers leaves the individual exposed to blackmail, arrest, and imprisonment. When deviants voluntarily seek treatment—which they rarely do—fear of exposure or arrest is usually an important incentive. Convicted sex offenders are often given the option of treatment or jail.

Homosexuality

Homosexuality is the most prevelant form of sexual deviation. Broadly defined, the term refers to an erotic interest in members of one's own sex. The vagueness of this definition may be sharpened by restricting its application to physical sexual acts between members of the same sex that lead to orgasm. This affords a more precise description of homosexual *behavior* but is of little value in differentiating homosexual *persons* from heterosexual persons. Only a small percentage of individuals who have had one or more homosexual experiences think of themselves as homosexuals or are considered homosexuals by others. The Group for the Advancement of Psychiatry (1955) has clarified the issue by differentiating between homosexual behavior and the homosexual individual. The homosexual person has little or no sexual interest in members of the opposite sex. Heterosexual activities either are distasteful to him or fail to evoke a response. Homosexual contacts, on the other hand, are accompanied by strong erotic arousal, pleasure, and satisfaction. As a result of this differential reinforcement, the homosexual usually confines his interpersonal sexual activities to members of his own sex. Sexual fantasies and dreams are limited to homosexual experiences.

Persons who engage in homosexual behavior but who think of themselves as heterosexual are not homosexual. Given a choice, they prefer partners of the opposite sex. Homosexual experiences during childhood that terminate with the passage from adolescence to adulthood fall into this category. Transient boyhood experiences may range from mutual masturbation to the practice of permitting adults to perform homosexual acts on them for money. In the latter case, the act usually consists of fellatio (Reiss, 1964).

Persons who are basically heterosexual may occasionally engage in homosexual behavior out of curiosity, in search of thrills, while under the influence of alcohol, or when isolated for a long time from members of the opposite sex. Most of the homosexual behavior that goes on in prisons is of this variety. Both male and female prisoners turn to members of their own sex because partners of the opposite sex are not available. On release from prison they usually return promptly to heterosexual activities.

The differentiation between heterosexuality and homosexuality is further complicated by the fact that some individuals seek and enjoy erotic relations with members of both sexes. A substantial number of homosexuals marry and raise families while engaging in extramarital homosexual affairs. The wives of such men are frequently extremely bitter about this form of infidelity. ("I could compete with another woman, but how can I compete with a man?")

PREVALENCE OF HOMOSEXUALITY

In view of the haziness of criteria, estimates of the prevalence of homosexuality have to be qualified. Although controversial and dated, the Kinsey findings are still the best available. Kinsey and his associates (1948) found that 37 percent of all males interviewed had had homosexual experiences to the point of orgasm after the onset of adolescence. Eight percent engaged exclusively in homosexual activities for three or more years between the ages of sixteen and fifty-five. Four percent of males reported that they were exclusively homosexual from adolescence on. The corresponding Kinsey figures for females (1953) were substantially lower. Only 13 percent of females had had sexual contact with other females to the point of orgasm.

MISCONCEPTIONS ABOUT HOMOSEXUALITY

Contrary to popular belief, it is impossible to differentiate homosexuals on the basis of their appearance, style of dress, or mannerisms. Some male homosexuals, referred to as "queens," are effeminate in manner and may on occasion wear female attire. Others are conventionally masculine in appearance and behavior. Many male homosexuals prefer masculine types as partners. Some lesbians, referred to as "butches," adopt masculine styles of behavior; others, known as "femmes," are conventionally feminine in appearance and personality. Butches prefer femmes as partners; femmes may or may not prefer butches.

A second common misconception is that the individual homosexual consistently plays either an active or a passive role. He may, but by no means necessarily. It is more usual for the homosexual to play alternating roles, sometimes being the active partner, at other times or with other persons assuming the passive role.

A third common misconception is that homosexual behavior is always a matter of choice: the homosexual simply prefers partners of his own sex. This seems to be true of some homosexuals, but not of all. The individual who turns to members of his own sex for sexual and emotional satisfaction because he is unable to respond to members of the opposite sex, for whatever reason, cannot be said to have a choice.

FEMALE HOMOSEXUALS

Kenyon (1966*a*, 1966*b*) and Saghir and Robins (1969) have conducted comprehensive studies of female homosexuals living in the community. Subjects were selected on the basis of membership in homophile organizations. Women who join such organizations are not necessarily representative of the total lesbian population, and may differ in significant ways from lesbians who prefer anonymity; but with this caveat we can gain useful insights from these investigators' findings:

1. Homosexual emotional attachments and cognitive rehearsals typically occurred before adolescence. The pattern of orientation was well established by the end of adolescence.

2. About two-thirds had had sexual intercourse with men. Most gave it up as unsatisfactory after a few tries.

3. About 25 percent had been married, but with rare exceptions these marriages soon terminated in divorce.

4. About one-half engaged in masturbation when they were not involved in homosexual affairs.

5. The most common homosexual practice was mutual manual stimulation of the genitals. Cunnilingus ranked second. Other practices, which were infrequent, included insertion of some object into the partner's vagina, full body contact, and the kissing and caressing that are common among heterosexual couples.

6. Homosexual women tended to be more successful than homosexual

men in establishing relationships that lasted a year or more—frequently much more. As long as the affairs lasted, the overwhelming majority were faithful to each other.

7. Lesbians reported poor relationships with their parents more often than control groups of "straight" women, and a higher proportion of lesbians reported unhappy childhoods.

8. Histories of psychopathology and of homosexuality were more frequent in the families of lesbians than in those of control subjects. A substantial number of lesbians reported periodic depressive moods.

9. Twenty percent of the lesbians reported that they believed they had not been brought up and treated as girls by their parents. None of the control subjects made such a report.

10. Seduction during early childhood appeared to be unrelated to subsequent homosexuality.

MALE HOMOSEXUALS

The composite clinical portrait that emerges from studies of male homosexuals is similar in some respects to that of lesbians, but there are several differences. Research studies reported by Bieber (1967), Apperson and McAdoo (1968), and Saghir and his associates (1969, 1970) indicate that:

1. Homosexual self-identity and orientation start before adolescence and are well established by the end of adolescence. About two-thirds never experience heterosexual fantasies.

2. Homosexual men report extremely active sex lives. The usual pattern is four or more sexual encounters with other males each week, supplemented by masturbation four or more times a week.

3. Homosexuals are promiscuous and unfaithful. Affairs are largely casual and impersonal—pickup contacts that end when the sex act is completed. Relationships lasting more than a year do occur, but they are usually characterized by much casual infidelity.

4. Before the age of fifteen, mutual masturbation is the most common practice. After fifteen, fellatio occurs most frequently. Next in order of frequency at the adult level is anal intercourse.

5. A considerably smaller percentage of homosexual men than homosexual women have had heterosexual experiences or have tried marriage. Fear of impotence in heterosexual relationships or complete lack of sexual response to women may account for this difference.

6. About an equal number of male and female homosexuals have received therapy (roughly 20 percent), generally without success. Depressive reactions and excessive drinking tend to be more characteristic of homosexual than control subjects.

7. Childhood seduction by adult males does not appear to be an important contributory factor in most instances.

8. The majority of mothers of male homosexuals are described as overly possessive, overly controlling, seductive, and emasculating. Although not all studies agree on these maternal characteristics, there is general agreement among investigators that fathers of homosexuals are distant, cold, and often hostile. As children, homosexual men tend to be submissive and closely involved emotionally with their mothers. Fathers are usually feared and disliked.

HEREDITARY FACTORS

No consistent hormonal, chromosomal, or other physical abnormalities have been found in homosexuals. Twin studies have usually been limited to a small number of cases, which introduces the problem of sampling errors. The literature includes six separate studies, all conducted with males. A grand total of fifty-five MZ twins and thirty-nine DZ twins have been examined (Rosenthal, 1970). For the six studies the median concordance rate is 50 percent for MZ twins and 14 percent for DZ twins. These figures are difficult to interpret, since most studies did not indicate whether the homosexuality was exclusive, chronic, or limited to a few experiences. A further complicating factor is that a wide range of psychopathology has been observed in the families of most homosexuals. Especially in the case of hospitalized or imprisoned homosexuals, homosexual behavior may be a secondary reaction to some more fundamental psychopathology. The most that can be claimed from a genetic point of view is that innate factors may exert some predisposing influence. But sexual attraction to members of one's own sex is undoubtedly strongly shaped by faulty psychosexual development during childhood and subsequent learning experiences. Clinical evidence suggests that the influence of predisposing genetic factors in males is cancelled if the son has a strong identification with a loving father.

PSYCHOANALYTIC VIEWS

Freud assumed that homosexuality had a biological basis, but that life experiences were decisive in determining the effect, if any, that biological factors would have on actual behavior. Other psychoanalysts have attributed homosexuality to a variety of factors, such as strong identification of the son with the mother to the point of imitating her sex-object choice; unconscious fear of castration by females; and absence of a favorable male model in the home with whom the boy can identify. The fathers of homosexual sons are thought to be either weak and ineffective or hostile and feared. Followers of Sullivan interpret homosexuality as a difficulty in interpersonal relations with either sex (Bieber, 1967).

Psychoanalytic explanations for female homosexuality stress castration fears and unresolved mother attachment. Other suggested explanations for lesbianism include fear and distrust of the opposite sex, defiance of social rules, expression of sexual independence, and a learned rejection of the traditional feminine roles (Thompson, 1964).

Transsexuality

Transsexualism is the misidentification of one's own gender. The male has the standard anatomical and biological equipment of his sex, but from early childhood thinks of himself as a female. He feels that nature has made a terrible mistake by giving him a female personality in a male body. Conversely, the female transsexual thinks of herself as a male. Clinical studies of this condition have been reported by Pauly (1968), Money and Primrose (1968), and Baker (1969). In contrast to the homosexual male, who is interested in his male sex organ and derives pleasure from its use and admiration by other males, the transsexual is ashamed of his male organ. He wants to be a female, and believes that in all essential respects, except for a few unfortunate anatomical details, he *is* a female. In sexual relations with males, the transsexual male always assumes the receptor role. Anal intercourse is regarded as a substitute for vaginal intercourse. The transsexual male prefers to have sexual relations with nonhomosexual men. In his erotic fantasies he may visualize himself with large breasts, a vagina, long hair, and feminine body contours. Since the male organ is denied, transsexual males rarely masturbate, and may not have erections while having sexual relations with males. Stimulation of the penis by sex partners is unpleasant and undesired. During sex play the transsexual male attempts to minimize any attention his partner may focus on the rejected organ. The personality profiles of male transsexuals are more typical of women than of men. They have interests that the culture identifies as feminine, and describe themselves as submissive rather than aggressive.

Transsexualism is rare in either sex, but appears to be less common in females than in males. The incidence of transsexualism has been estimated at 1 per 100,000 of the general male population, 1 per 400,000 of the female population. Female transsexuals show "masculine" profiles on personality tests. As children they were tomboys, enjoyed fighting, and preferred boys' games and activities. They are sexually attracted to women, and in their love-making take the male role. They are ashamed of their breasts and try to minimize their size. In her sex fantasies the female transsexual sees herself as a male, flat-chested, broad-shouldered, and complete with penis (Money and Brennan, 1968).

Interpretation. The simplist explanation for transsexualism is biological variation. Studies of sex differences in temperament and interests have demonstrated that males show wide individual differences in traits defined as masculine and that women differ markedly in the degree to which they exhibit traits defined as feminine. A percentage of men are more "feminine" than most women and vice versa. Transsexual individuals may thus be understood as persons in the middle of the male-female continuum who are highly motivated to do something about their condition. In these cases parental reinforcement of cross-sexual identity and role-playing may be a contributory factor.

Treatment. Psychotherapy and drug therapy are of little value. What these individuals want and seek is a physical change consonant with their cross-sexual identity. Surgical operations have recently been developed for removing the male sex organs and creating artificial vaginas. Female patients undergo operations for removal of the breasts and uterus and creation of artificial penises, which function normally in the process of urination but are not capable of erection. Practically all transsexuals who have had conversion operations are pleased with the results. Except for the ability to bear children, an artificial vagina effects a complete functional transformation from male to female. Some states permit males who have had the operation to adopt women's names, to receive amended birth certificates stating their sex as female, and to marry. Many of these converted females have adopted children to complete their roles as women, and there is no evidence that they are necessarily inadequate as wives or as mothers.

Transvestism

Transvestism is the practice of wearing the clothing of the opposite sex. Since the label is rarely applied to females, we shall limit our discussion to males who dress in female attire. A distinction must be made between the transvestite and the homosexual or transsexual, who may also cross-dress. The homosexual disguises himself in female clothing in order to be more attractive to the minority of homosexuals who are interested in men who appear feminine. The transsexual male dresses as a female because he feels more comfortable and natural wearing apparel consistent with his psychological sex identity; he is not sexually excited by dressing as a woman. The true transvestite is usually masculine in appearance and behavior and heterosexual in his sex identity and orientation. He cross-dresses because the feel and touch of intimate feminine clothing is sexually stimulating to him. This behavioral peculiarity is usually isolated, so that it does not interfere with the individual's functioning, efficiency, or overall adjustment. The transvestite typically wears female attire only in private. Often cross-dressing is part of a masturbation ritual. The transvestite puts on his feminine clothes and then masturbates while looking at himself in a mirror. In effect, he has sexual intercourse with himself. He is male and female, a completely self-sufficient heterosexual unit. After the sex act, he changes back to his usual male clothing and goes about his regular affairs.

About two-thirds of transvestites are married, and most of these have children (Buckner, 1970). Cross-dressing is concealed from the children, but the wife is usually in on the secret. Some transvestites have sex relations with their wives while wearing female clothing. Cross-dressing often starts as a fetish. In his teens, the individual may use articles of female clothing to provide friction while masturbating. Most boys who experiment with this technique later replace female clothes with females. The adult transvestite incorporates or identifies with the female symbols. While dressed as a female, he plays the role of a woman who gratifies his male sex needs. His penis assures him of his maleness.

Studies of personal characteristics of transvestites indicate that they are less aggressive than normal controls, are more restrained, prefer passive activities to excitement and change, and are relatively withdrawn from social involvement. They describe themselves as self-reliant and independent (Bentler and Prince, 1969).

Marks and Gelder (1967) have reported successful treatment of transvestites by aversion training. Shock was administered to the forearm or leg of the patient while he was in the process of dressing or imagining scenes involving women's clothing. The criterion for treatment effectiveness consisted of diminished erection responses to actual or imagined cross-dressing.

Other Forms of Sex Deviance

SADISM AND MASOCHISM

The sadist attains sexual stimulation and pleasure by inflicting pain on another person. The masochist derives erotic stimulation and gratification from the experiencing of pain. Often the two go together. Minor bites, scratches, and bruises inflicted or received in the heat of heterosexual passion don't count. The sadist and the masochist are not stimulated by the normal sexual act. Erotic arousal and gratification are obtained from whipping or being whipped, burning or being burned by a lighted cigarette, trampling or being trampled, or otherwise torturing or being tortured. Humiliating and degrading acts may be substituted for physical pain. Cooperative partners are usually sought in "full service" houses of prostitution, which include specialists in such activities. A do-it-yourself variation consists of masturbating while simultaneously inflicting pain on oneself or conjuring up torture fantasies.

The fusion of aggression and sexuality is an unsolved enigma, but the relationship between them has long been recognized by students of animal as well as human behavior. Especially among birds, courting rituals often bear such a striking resemblance to aggressive behavior that the courting male must add special signals to reassure the female that his intent is not really aggressive. Normal heterosexual behavior between human beings also resembles aggressive behavior to the untutored eye. It is common for children who inadvertently witness intercourse between their parents to interpret it as a physical attack by the father on the mother. Thus, although the etiology of sadism and masochism is difficult to unravel, they appear to be two more examples of normal reactions carried to deviant extremes.

EXHIBITIONISM AND VOYEURISM

Exhibitionism and voyeurism, which involve sexual arousal through visual stimulation, are almost exclusively associated with males. Male and female interest in nudity is normal; exhibitionism and voyeurism are considered deviant reactions when they are substitutes for more mature heterosexual expression and when the behavior is regarded as offensive or indecent by the victim (usually a female), who is an involuntary participant. The voyeurs and exhibitionists get their kicks from peeking and exposing. In most instances they would panic and run away if a female showed positive interest in having them proceed beyond the visual stage.

Exhibitionism, technically defined, is the act of exhibiting an erect penis to a female who is a total stranger. Usually the exposure occurs on the street or in some other public place. The purpose is self-stimulation. No attempt is made to detain or molest the involuntary viewer. The voyeur, or Peeping Tom, reverses the situation. He surreptitiously peeks into windows to spy on women while they are undressing. When the show is over, he silently steals away. Voyeurs and exhibitionists are usually lonely, insecure men who either have no interest in the sex act or are too fearful of rejection or impotence to approach women. Their tendency to return repeatedly to the scene of their "crimes" until they are apprehended by the police is suggestive of guilt feelings and need for punishment.

BESTIALITY

Bestiality is sexual intercourse between a human being and an animal of another species. The practice is a pathological form of behavior when the animal is preferred as a sex object although a human partner is available (or could with a little effort be found). The misuse of animals for sexual purposes by farm boys or isolated shepherds is thus not, strictly speaking, pathological, nor is the use of animals as sex objects in religious rituals among primitive people. As a habit pattern of choice, bestiality is usually symptomatic of a serious personality problem.

FETISHISM

A fetish is an inanimate object that serves as a substitute for a human love object. Fetishism is limited to males. The fetish is usually some article of female attire, such as a shoe or an undergarment. The fetishist is typically unable to complete a sexual act except while holding the object that has become his fetish. He makes love to a shoe, if that is his fetish, not to a woman. Unlike a child with his security blanket, however, he does not require some particular shoe; almost any woman's shoe will do. Most psychoanalysts interpret fetishism as a defense against castration anxiety (Lorand and Balint, 1956). Other investigators have found that an object can become a fetish when it is associated in a man's mind with his first orgasm in response to a girl or woman, if the orgasm occurred suddenly and was totally unanticipated.

PEDOPHILIA

Pedophilia is the practice of using children as sex objects. The typical pedophiliac is a sexually inadequate and often impotent male who molests children. As a rule, his behavior consists of self-exposure and stroking the body or sex organ of the child. In some cases insertion may be attempted.

Treatment of Sexual Deviants

Psychotherapeutic and psychoanalytic methods of treating sexual deviants have had poor records of success. Early reports on the use of aversive conditioning procedures have been more encouraging (Feldman, 1966). This form of behavior modification has been applied with some indications of success in all types of sex deviancy with the exception of transsexualism. A few investigators have used Pavlovian conditioning, pairing noxious scenes with scenes involving the undesired behavior (Barlow, Leitenberg, and Agras, 1969). The more common procedure has been to use operant conditioning methods. The first step is to elicit a sexual response by having the individual view, imagine, or engage in some activity directly related to his particular form of deviant behavior. If he is a homosexual, he may be shown pictures of attractive nude men. As soon as he shows signs of arousal, he is given a mild shock that serves as an aversive stimulus. The shock is terminated when the picture of a nude male is replaced by a picture of a nude female (Rachman and Teasdale, 1969).

Behavior therapists have been concerned with the use of electric shock on ethical and practical grounds. There are limits to the amount of shock that can ethically be administered in the guise of therapy; yet if the shock is too mild, it may lose its aversive significance. Mandel (1970) has suggested an alternative aversive stimulus for use with male homosexuals. The subject is first shown a color slide of a very attractive nude male. As soon as he indicates that he feels some sexual arousal, the behavior therapist superimposes another image on the first from a second projector. The second slide covers the naked male with running sores. The patient is asked to focus his attention on those regions of the body that are now covered with sores, and to signal when the picture has aroused a feeling of digust. At his signal the juxtaposed images are removed from the screen and replaced by a color slide showing an attractive nude woman. The patient is asked to relax and concentrate on the "relief" stimulus. If the patient shows no erotic feelings within a minute, the picture of the woman is removed. If arousal occurs, the heterosexual stimulus is removed after a few seconds. The technique appears promising, but it is too new to permit any conclusive evaluation of its possibilities.

Summary

The major recognized forms of sexual deviation are homosexuality, transsexuality, transvestism, sadism, masochism, exhibitionism, voyeurism, fetishism, and pedophilia. These conditions are characterized by unconventional and socially disapproved methods of erotic arousal and gratification. Sexual deviations should not be considered forms of mental disorder. Most sex deviants do not manifest significant disturbances in personality organization or in functioning. Deviant orientations and forms of behavior usually start during childhood. Constitutional and experiential factors appear to be involved in their etiology and development. The preliminary results of recent studies indicate that aversive therapy may be more effective in treating sexual deviants than the traditional forms of psychotherapy—which are not successful at all. A sincere desire on the part of the patient to alter his behavior is a necessary but seldom a sufficient condition for change. Sexual deviations are notoriously resistant to attempts to eliminate them. They appear to have many possible causes, but there is little general agreement on any specific cause. It is therefore probably asking too much of any form of treatment that it have uniformly successful long-term results on all forms of sexual deviance, or even on all cases of any particular form of abnormal sexual behavior.

References

APPERSON, L. B., and McADOO, W. G., JR. "Parental Factors in the Childhood of Homosexuals." *Journal of Abnormal Psychology* 73 (1968): 201–6.

BAKER, H. T. "Transsexualism: Problems in Treatment." *American Journal of Psychiatry* 125 (1969): 1412–18.

BARLOW, D. H.; LEITENBERG, H.; and AGRAS, W. S. "Experimental Control of Sexual Deviation Through Manipulation of the Noxious Scene in Overt Sensitization." *Journal of Abnormal Psychology* 74 (1969): 596–601.

BENTLER, P. M., and PRINCE, C. "Personality Characteristics of Male Transvestites," pt. 3. *Journal of Abnormal Psychology* 74, no. 2 (1969): 140–43.

BIEBER, I. "Homosexuality." In *Comprehensive Textbook of Psychiatry,* ed. A. M. Friedman, H. I. Kaplan, and H. S. Kaplan, pp. 963–76. Baltimore: Williams & Wilkins, 1967.

BUCKNER, H. T. "The Transvestite Career Path." *Psychiatry* 33 (1970): 381–89.

FELDMAN, M. P. "Aversion Therapy for Sexual Deviations: A Critical Review." *Psychological Bulletin* 65 (1966): 65–79.

GROUP FOR THE ADVANCEMENT OF PSYCHIATRY. *Report on Homosexuality with Particular Emphasis on This Problem in Government Agencies.* Report no. 30. New York, 1955.

KENYON, F. E. "Studies in Female Homosexuality: Social and Psychiatric Aspects." *British Journal of Psychiatry* 114 (1968a): 1337–43.

———. "Studies in Female Homosexuality: Sexual Development, Attitudes, and Experience." *British Journal of Psychiatry* 114 (1968b): 1343–50.

KINSEY, A. C.; POMEROY, W. B.; and MARTIN, C. E. *Sexual Behavior in the Human Male.* Philadelphia: Saunders, 1948.

——— and GEBHARD, P. H. *Sexual Behavior in the Human Female.* Philadelphia: Saunders, 1953.

LORAND, S., and BALINT, M., eds. *Perversions: Psychodynamics and Therapy.* New York: Random House, 1956.

MANDEL, K. L. "Preliminary Report on a New Aversive Therapy for Male Homosexuals." *Behavior Research and Therapy* 8 (1970): 93–95.

MARKS, I. M., and GELDER, M. G. "Transvestism and Fetishism: Clinical and Psychological Changes During Faradic Aversion." *British Journal of Psychiatry* 113 (1967): 711–29.

MONEY, J., and BRENNAN, J. G. "Sexual Dimorphism in the Psychology of Female Transsexuals." *Journal of Nervous Mental Disease* 147 (1968): 487–99.

——— and PRIMROSE, C. "Sexual Dimorphism and Dissociation in the Psychology of Male Transsexuals." *Journal of Nervous Mental Disease* 147 (1968): 472–86.

PAULY, I. B. "The Current Status of the Change of Sex Operation." *Journal of Nervous Mental Disease* 147 (1968): 460–71.

RACHMAN, S., and TEASDALE, J. *Aversion Therapy and Behavior Disorders: An Analysis.* Coral Gables, Fla.: University of Miami Press, 1969.

REISS, A. J. "The Social Integration of Queers and Peers." In *The Other Side: Perspectives on Deviance,* ed. H. S. Becker, pp. 181–210. New York: Free Press, Macmillan, 1964.

ROSENTHAL, D. *Genetic Theory and Abnormal Behavior.* New York: McGraw-Hill, 1970.

SAGHIR, M. T., and ROBINS, E. "Homosexuality: Sexual Behavior of the Female Homosexual." *Archives of General Psychiatry* 20 (1969): 192–201.

———— and WALBRAN, B. "Homosexuality: Sexual Behavior of the Male Homosexual." *Archives of General Psychiatry* 21 (1969): 219–29.

———— and GENTRY, K. A. "Homosexuality: Psychiatric Disorders and Disability in the Male Homosexual." *American Journal of Psychiatry* 126 (1970): 1079–86.

THOMPSON, C. M. *Interpersonal Psychoanalysis.* New York: Basic Books, 1964.

CHAPTER FIFTEEN

Physical Disorders with
Associated Psychosocial Disturbances

In previous chapters we have repeatedly emphasized the interaction of biological and psychosocial factors in the shaping of personality and behavior. A second recurring theme, which has been less explicitly stressed, is the concurrent presence of physiological disturbances in behavior disorders. Depressive states, for example, are marked by loss of appetite, chronic fatigue, menstrual irregularities, somatic complaints, and reduced energy level. Anxiety is as much a physiological disturbance as it is a psychological reaction. Alcoholism is a problem of physical health as well as of mental health. This interaction of physical, psychological, and social factors is equally evident in physical disorders. Psychosocial factors are often important contributing agents in the development, precipitation, and persistence of bodily diseases. The feelings, attitudes, and ideas of a person suffering from tuberculosis, cancer, or a broken leg are integral parts of his total illness. Psychological and social factors are of particular importance in three types of physical disorders:

1. Physical conditions of which the causes and cures are mainly psychological. Outstanding examples are impotence, orgasmic inadequacy, and related forms of sexual dysfunctions.

2. Physical disorders marked by structural changes or impaired bodily functioning in which emotional and social factors are often involved in the production and maintenance of symptoms. This category may be broadly

defined to include practically all medical diseases, but we shall be mainly concerned with those disorders in which emotional factors frequently have major etiological significance. Bronchial asthma, essential hypertension, and peptic ulcer are representative of this group of disorders. When these disorders have principally physical causes, patient response to medical treatment is usually consistent with the known effectiveness of available remedies. In selected cases in which psychological variables are of major importance, the elimination of symptoms may depend more on the resolution of underlying personality problems than on the effectiveness of medication. Physical disorders in which emotions and attitudes are of critical importance are popularly referred to as *psychosomatic reactions*.

3. Organic brain disorders involving brain tissue damage which are marked by impairment in cerebral functions. This category includes physical and psychosocial disturbances associated with senile brain disease, cerebral arteriosclerosis, and convulsive disorders.

Sexual Dysfunctions

Impotence, premature ejaculation, orgasmic inadequacy, and vaginismus are classic examples of physical conditions in which emotions, attitudes, and mental set are key factors in the impairment of normal physiological functioning. The interaction is circular. Psychological blocks interfere with the adequacy of sexual performance, and the inadequacy of performance reinforces the intensity and persistence of psychological barriers. The wide prevalence of impaired sexual functioning in both males and females was initially documented in studies conducted by Kinsey and his associates (1948, 1953). In 1966 Masters and Johnson reported the results of their innovative research studies on the psychophysiology of human sexual response. More recently (1970) they have made a major contribution to the understanding and treatment of human sexual inadequacy. Their study is a model of effective scientific research in a significant area of human maladjustment. Comprehensive and relevant data were obtained through intensive individual study of nearly eight hundred persons with serious sexual problems. In a field where previous therapeutic efforts have been dismal failures, the Masters and Johnson approach has been proved effective in eliminating symptoms in 80 percent of all treated individuals within two weeks. More significantly, the cures appear to be permanent. Follow-up data indicate that less than 3 percent of all successfully treated patients suffered a return of symptoms in a period of more than five years. Masters and Johnson currently are continuing the treatment program described in their report.

NATURE OF SYMPTOMS

Impotence is the inability of a mature male to achieve and maintain an erection of sufficient rigidity to permit successful sexual intercourse. A distinction is sometimes made between primary and secondary impotence. Masters and Johnson apply the designation of primary impotence to men who have never been capable of successful coital insertion. If a man has had one or more successful experiences of either a heterosexual or homosexual nature, his present inability to achieve and maintain an erection adequate for intercourse is classified as secondary impotence. Fifteen percent of the impotent males treated by Masters and Johnson suffered from the primary variety. In these cases contributory etiological factors included undue maternal influence, psychological restrictions originating with strict religious training, homosexual activities, and personal devaluation from traumatic experiences with prostitutes or other partners. Secondary impotence was mainly related to fear of inadequate performance resulting from past failures. Experiences commonly associated with the acquisition of a fear response were premature ejaculation on earlier occasions and isolated incidents of performance failure while under the influence of alcohol. Especially in insecure males, one humiliating failure, particularly if it brings taunts from a frustrated sex partner, is sufficient to arouse intense anxiety that may lead to impotence on subsequent occasions.

The second most common male complaint in the Masters and Johnson study was premature ejaculation. Usually this condition is defined as quickness of response. A person is considered a premature ejaculator if he cannot control his discharge for at least thirty seconds after penetration. Masters and Johnson prefer a more functional definition. They define a man as a premature ejaculator if more often than not he cannot delay the ejaculatory process after intravaginal containment for a sufficient length of time to satisfy his partner. The major factor in the development of chronic premature ejaculation appears to be initial introduction to sexual activity in circumstances that required quick completion of the act: lack of privacy, the possibility of interruption or discovery, or a partner who for one reason or another insisted on "getting it over with" as soon as possible.

Another form of male inadequacy, which is relatively rare, is called ejaculatory incompetence. The male with this condition is capable of maintaining an erection during intercourse for an hour or longer but is unable or unwilling to proceed to ejaculation. The advantage of prolonged intercourse is outweighed by the frustration that may be experienced by the woman as well as the man at the incompleteness of the act, or by such a superabundance of orgasms in the woman that she is totally exhausted while her partner is still unsatisfied. Fear of pregnancy has been suggested, along with disinterest in the female partner, suspicion that the woman has been unfaithful, fear of contaminating the woman or of being contaminated by her, strict religious training, and emotional conflicts of various sorts. The condition may occur only occasionally, in reaction to specific stress situations, or may be a more generalized response.

Masters and Johnson found orgasmic dysfunction to be the main complaint among the women they studied. Slightly more than half of all the women treated had never experienced an orgasm or climax. Their condition was described as primary orgasmic deficiency. The remainder, who were classified as manifesting situational orgasmic deficiency, rarely achieved orgasm, but they had done so on one or more occasions. Some of these women expressed little or no interest in or need for sexual expression. They would be described by laymen as frigid. Eight percent of all women treated suffered from vaginismus, an involuntary muscular spasm that constricts the vaginal opening. The reflex contraction is stimulated by imagined, anticipated, or real attempts at vaginal penetration. Severe vaginismus makes normal intercourse extremely painful or impossible. Masters and Johnson attribute female sexual dysfunction primarily to sociocultural conditioning that has taught women to inhibit, reject, or distort their natural sex feelings. Inadequate and biased information about female sexuality, when reinforced by traumatic experiences during adolescence, either correctly or incorrectly interpreted by the inexperienced girl, create a built-in signal system that automatically cuts in and inhibits normal response to sexual stimuli.

TREATMENT OF SEXUAL DYSFUNCTIONS

Participants in the Masters and Johnson treatment program come from all over the country. Most are referred by physicians, psychologists, and clergymen. Those accepted for treatment are required to live for two weeks in special quarters set up at the treatment center in St. Louis. Patients are regarded and treated as guests. Provisions are made to ensure their enjoyment of a "vacation" during the time spent in the city, but the real purpose of the residential requirement is to isolate the guests from home and business cares and to create a sex-focused environment for intensive therapy. If a patient is married, both husband and wife must agree to participate in the treatment. This requirement is based on the key premise that there is no such thing as an uninvolved partner in any marriage in which there is any form of sexual inadequacy. Since sexual behavior represents an interaction between two persons, the partner ultimately is the critical factor. The marital unit is the patient. An unmarried man may bring a girl friend, or be provided with a female partner from a list of carefully selected volunteers. As a matter of policy women are not provided with male volunteer partners.

The first step in treatment consists of a detailed case history. Information is obtained on etiological factors, the onset and severity of symptoms, and the psychosocial effect of the sexual dysfunction. The history-taking interview also provides information on the basic personalities of the partners and the results they expect from therapy. Regardless of the specific problem, the first three days are spent in becoming oriented to the situation, indoctrination, and exchange of information. The balance of the two weeks is focused on the specific complaint.

In general, the treatment program is educational in nature. Patients are given every opportunity to ask questions and to discuss problems. Misconceptions and errors are corrected. Technical information is supplied. Specific suggestions are made, but decisions and the details of implementing them are left to the individuals. There is no observation of the patients during intimate moments. The general aim of therapy is to provide a relaxed, nondemanding setting in which patients may give free rein to sexual thoughts and feelings. Great emphasis is placed on nonverbal communication through touching and feeling. An often repeated precept is that neither an erection nor an orgasm can be willed or wished into being. The more one deliberately strives to obtain either an erection or an orgasm, the more one is doomed to failure. The best procedure is to relax, adopt a "give to get" attitude, and let the natural processes of the body take over. The two-week duration of treatment imposes a time limit, but within this period there is no rush, no feeling that "tonight is the night." Progress from A to B is considered more desirable than an attempt to jump abruptly from A to Z, which is unlikely to be successful.

Treatment is structured as an interactive process between the partners in which successful outcome depends on mutual understanding and cooperation. It is apparent from the authors' descriptions, however, that their therapeutic program places major responsibility on the woman, whether the dysfunction is in her or in her partner. The special techniques devised for eliminating premature ejaculation require the female partner to stimulate the male organ manually and periodically to apply a carefully described manual "squeeze" procedure to regulate the intensity of male arousal. The woman is in control of the insertive process and of the pacing of pelvic thrusts, whether the problem to be eliminated is male impotence or female orgasmic deficiency. In the early stages of symptom treatment, Masters and Johnson consider it essential that the woman assume the superior position, while the man lies beneath her. Later on, the lateral position, which also gives the female considerable control and freedom of action, is recommended. Masters and Johnson consider that from a treatment point of view, the conventional position, with the man above the woman, is not beneficial. They have developed a number of specific techniques for the elimination of particular symptoms, which are described and illustrated in their report.

It is not to be supposed from all this that women alone are responsible for all sexual problems, and that it is therefore up to them to eliminate them. Masters and Johnson emphasize the fact that both partners are involved in the problems of either, and that both must cooperate in eliminating them. Their reversal of the traditional roles in the sex act is a therapeutic technique, not a social judgment or a procedure recommended for all persons at all times.

Treatment results. Masters and Johnson have reported their results in terms of failure rates. Failure rates have the advantage of being more precise than success rates: the patient's condition remained unchanged or worsened. Success rates are more ambiguous; they may refer to mild improvement or complete recovery. However, no great harm is done in converting the Masters and Johnson figures into success rates, since the criterion was specific: the continued presence or absence of the original symptom for which the patient sought treatment. By the end of the two-week period of intensive treatment, 83 percent of the male and 81 percent of the female subjects reported symptom elimination. Follow-up data covering a five-year period for some subjects and a shorter period for others indicated no return of symptoms in 80 percent of the persons treated. The long-term success rate was the same for males and females. Best results were obtained with vaginismus, which was eliminated in 100 percent of the cases treated. Premature ejaculation was successfully eliminated in 97 percent of cases. A favorable outcome of 70 percent was reported for secondary impotence and of 60 percent for primary impotence. Success rates for primary and situational orgasmic dysfunction were 82 percent and 75 percent respectively. The overall success rate for the treatment of persons over fifty years of age was 70 percent. The authors conclude that normal sex behavior can be continued beyond the age of eighty if the person is in good physical health and has an interesting and cooperative partner. The persons treated had a much lower divorce rate than the general population. Several couples who had been in the process of separation or divorce prior to treatment were reunited following treatment. The one major limitation of the Masters and Johnson study is that most of the patients were from the upper class. Professional acceptance of the therapeutic approach is indicated by the fact that physicians and their spouses composed 10 percent of all married couples treated. The majority of the physicians treated were psychiatrists.

Psychosomatic Reactions

The official APA designation for psychosomatic reactions is *psychophysiological disorders*.

> This group of disorders is characterized by physical symptoms that are caused by emotional factors and involve a single organ system, usually under autonomic nervous system innervation. The physiological changes involved are those that normally accompany certain emotional states, but in these disorders the changes are more intense and sustained. The individual may not be consciously aware of his emotional state [*Diagnostic and Statistical Manual*, 1968].

Reactions are classified in accordance with the organ system involved:

1. Skin disorders.
    (*a*) Neurodermatitis: chronic reddening and thickening of the skin with intense itching.
    (*b*) Psoraisis: scaly patches of skin.
    (*c*) Eczema: itchy skin with exudation of liquid.
    (*d*) Hives: itching and swelling of the skin.
2. Musculoskeletal disorders.
    (*a*) Rheumatoid arthritis: stiffening of joints.
    (*b*) Low backache.
    (*c*) Muscle cramps.
3. Respiratory disorders.
    (*a*) Bronchial asthma: shortness of breath, wheezing, gasping for air, sensation of choking.
    (*b*) Hyperventilation: sighs, difficulty in breathing, tingling of extremities, fainting.
    (*c*) Persistent hiccups.
4. Gastrointestinal disorders.
    (*a*) Peptic ulcer: localized gastric pain due to inflammation or lesions of the stomach wall.
    (*b*) Duodenal ulcer: pain associated with inflammation or lesions of the first portion of the small intestines.
    (*c*) Colitis: inflammation or spasms of the colon.
    (*d*) Anorexia nervosa: lack of appetite.
    (*e*) Diarrhea.
    (*f*) Constipation.
5. Cardiovascular disorders.
    (*a*) Essential hypertension: high blood pressure.
    (*b*) Raynaud's disease: poor circulation resulting in cold hands and feet.

The presence of some actual somatic pathology is an essential characteristic of psychosomatic disorders. The physical pathology may consist of a structural change, a disturbance in functioning, or both. The asthmatic child's wheezing, choking, and gasping for air are due to bronchial obstructions. An excessive secretion of acid is responsible for the inflammation and lesions of the lining of the stomach of the ulcer patient. His subjective feelings of pain and distress are genuine. He may die if internal bleeding occurs. A tension headache hurts just as much as a headache produced by a blow on the head. There is no malingering or faking of symptoms. The patient has a physical illness, is worried about his condition, seeks medical treatment, and follows medical advice. Only 1 percent of patients seen in psychiatric clinics and by psychiatrists in private practice are diagnosed as suffering from psychosomatic disorders. Psychotherapy is usually a last resort when continued medical treatment proves ineffective.

The psychological component of many psychosomatic disorders is indicated by the effectiveness of placebos in alleviating or curing many physical symptoms. The minor pains and aches of infants are usually promptly cured by the mother's cuddling and stroking of the baby. The mother's kiss has the magical power to make a child's pain go away. Experimental studies have repeatedly demonstrated the extreme sensitivity of gastrointestinal, cardiac, and electrodermal responses to interpersonal stimulation. Animal studies have shown that the entrance of a person into an experimental room often elicits a marked increase in a dog's heart rate (Lynch, 1969). Petting a dog while he is being shocked not only decreases cardiac indicators of fear and pain but also may reduce motor responses. When shock is accompanied by petting, the dog may show no overt signs of being shocked.

THEORIES OF PSYCHOSOMATIC DISORDERS

Psychosomatic disorders may be interpreted as unsuccessful bodily reactions to stress situations. In these cases the sequence of alarm, resistance, and adaptation that occurs in response to stress (Selye, 1956) has an unfavorable outcome; the individual is left with distressing symptoms. Stress theory, however, fails to answer three questions: Why do some individuals successfully adapt to the stress of life and others fail to do so? Why are certain failures of adaptation manifested in symptoms identified with psychosomatic disorders? Why do some persons who manifest psychosomatic symptoms develop asthma while others develop ulcers, essential hypertension, hives, or some other specific condition?

The usual answer to the first question is that some individuals, because of less favorable genetic endowment and life experiences than others, have lower thresholds of stress tolerance. The standard answer to the second question is equally vague. It is assumed that certain combinations of innate or acquired defects result in psychosomatic symptoms, whereas other combinations lead to neurotic or psychotic behavior patterns. More specific theories have been proposed to account for the occurrence of specific psychosomatic disorders. One of the older but still active theories postulates that specificity of symptoms is determined by the relative weakness of a particular organ system. Thus a weakness in the respiratory system favors the development of asthma and a weakness of the gastrointestinal system leads to a selective vulnerability to ulcers. The organ weakness may have multiple causes. The clinical observation that members of certain families often share a susceptibility to gastric, cardiovascular, or skin disorders has been interpreted as the result of some genetically transmitted weakness of a particular organ system (Wolf, 1953). But the tendency of certain symptom patterns to run in families may also be explained as a result of learning and imitation. A mother who always develops headaches in stress situations may serve as a model for her children. Intrafamilial concern with special diets, the regularity of elimination, and the state of one's stomach may favor gastric symptoms. There is also the possibility that some prior illness may have focused attention on or weakened a particular organ system. In examining the medical histories of asthmatic patients, Rees (1964) found that a large proportion had records of previous respiratory infections. This finding does not rule out the possible significance of heredity, since predisposing genetic factors may have contributed to the individual's relative vulnerability to respiratory infections. Individual differences in genetic susceptibility offer the simplest explanaton for the repeatedly noted fact that some monkeys develop ulcers when subjected to stress situations that call for "executive" decisions, while others exposed to the same experiences do not (Brady, 1958).

A second theory related to the stress theory is that an inherited specificity of response pattern influences symptoms. Studies conducted with college students by Lacey and his associates (1958) indicate that the autonomic response patterns of particular individuals tend to be highly stable and consistent. Some persons characteristically react to all stress situations by a marked rise in blood pressure; others show a greater change in heart rate or galvanic skin response. Malmo and Shagass (1949) noted that patients suffering from headaches tend to react to experimentally induced stress with an increase in muscle tension, whereas heart patients show a greater cardiovascular response. Supportive evidence for the theory of autonomic specificity has also been reported by Wenger and his associates (1961).

Attempts to relate selectivity of psychosomatic symptoms to personality variables have been unsuccessful. In comparison with the general population, persons with psychosomatic disorders may show greater dependence-independence conflicts, greater repressed hostility, and higher levels of anxiety, but experimental findings do not support the hypothesis that certain personality characteristics are directly correlated with particular psychosomatic disorders (Buss, 1966). A more promising lead that warrants further research is the hypothesis suggested by Graham and his associates (1962), that the attitude of the individual influences the psychosomatic reactions he experiences. Some examples are given in Table 15.1. Little is known of the relation of socioeconomic status to psychosomatic ailments. In one of the few studies in this area, Rennie and Srole (1956) noted that arthritis and hypertension are most prevalent in the lower class, colitis and hives in the upper class, and heart symptoms in the middle class.

Table 15.1. Relation of patient attitude to psychosomatic reactions

Disorder	Patient attitude
Ulcers	Feels deprived of what is due him and wants to get even.
Hypertension	Feels threatened with harm and has to be ready for anything.
Asthma	Feels left out in the cold and wants to shut the person or situation out.
Colitis	Feels he is being injured or degraded and wishes he could get rid of the responsible agent.
Eczema	Feels he is being frustrated and can do nothing about it except take it out on himself.
Acne	Feels he is being picked on and wants to be left alone.
Psoriasis	Feels there is a constant gnawing at him and that he has to put up with it.
Rheumatoid arthritis	Feels tied down and wants to get free.
Low backache	Wants to run away.
Raynaud's disease	Wants to take hostile physical action.

In summary, the causes of psychosomatic disorders are multiple and interactive. Predisposing genetic factors may influence tolerance to stress and specificity of response. The release or activation of genetic vulnerabilities is dependent on the occurrence of significant stress. Life experiences that focus attention on or weaken a particular organ system or which lead to the development of certain attitudes may be influential in the development of particular symptoms.

PSYCHOSOMATIC DISORDERS AND NEUROSIS

At one time psychosomatic disorders were interpreted as "organ neuroses." More recently a differentiation has been made on the basis of the observation that psychosomatic reactions, unlike neurotic symptoms, have no symbolic significance and do not serve as defenses against anxiety. Two further reasons have been given for differentiating psychosomatic disorders from conversion hysteria: (1) psychosomatic disorders typically involve changes in the structure or functioning of internal organs (stomach, heart, respiratory system), whereas conversion symptoms are characterized by a loss of peripheral sensory and motor functions (blindness, paralysis, deafness); and (2)—a controversial distinction—psychosomatic reactions are innervated and controlled by the autonomic nervous system, whereas conversion symptoms are innervated and controlled by the central nervous system.

THE ROLE OF THE AUTONOMIC NERVOUS SYSTEM

The autonomic nervous system is directly involved in the stimulation and regulation of physiological responses associated with psychosomatic symptoms. On this point there is no controversy. Serious objections, however, have been raised with regard to the exclusive role of the autonomic nervous system in the mediation of visceral responses. This issue has significant implications for therapy. If psychosomatic symptoms were entirely regulated by the autonomic nervous system, and hence involuntary, learning procedures that involve the participation of the central nervous system would presumably have limited therapeutic effectiveness. More specifically, operant conditioning procedures would be relatively ineffective in modifying psychosomatic responses. Miller (1969) and DiCara (1970) have challenged the exclusive role of the autonomic nervous system in the control of visceral reactions. In a series of ingenious animal experiments they have demonstrated the effectiveness of operant conditioning procedures in modifying visceral and glandular responses. They controlled for the possibility that operant conditioning might result in the learning of skeletal responses, which in turn would cause visceral changes, by immobilizing the animals. Rats were injected with curare, a drug that selectively blocks the motor end plates of skeletal muscles without eliminating neural control of visceral responses. The subjects had to be maintained on artificial respiration, since curare also paralyzes muscles involved in breathing. Two types of reinforcing agents were used. In some studies rats were rewarded by stimulation of the pleasure centers of the brain whenever they spontaneously made a visceral response in the direction predetermined by the design of the experiment. For example, if the objective of the study was to decrease heart rate, the animal was rewarded only when the heart rate showed a slight spontaneous decrease. The second incentive consisted of termination of electric shock to the tail when the animal spontaneously showed a predecided increase or decrease in a particular autonomic response. The results obtained clearly demonstrated that rats could learn to increase or decrease the heart rate, the frequency of intestinal or stomach contractions, the rate of urine formation, the relative flow of blood in the stomach wall, the amount of blood in the tail or the right ear, the systolic blood pressure, and the brain wave pattern. The control of muscle movements in the Miller study discounts the possibility that changes in autonomic responses produced by operant procedures in human subjects are artifacts of voluntary movements.

Successful application of operant conditioning in increasing or decreasing heartbeat in human subjects has been reported by Engel and Chism (1967), Lang, Stroufe, and Hastings (1967), Ascough and Sipprelle (1968), and others. Kimmel and Kimmel (1963) and Greene (1966) have demonstrated successful operant conditioning of galvanic skin responses in human subjects. These studies, along with the Miller-DiCara experiments, provide a scientific basis for increased use of operant conditioning procedures in the treatment of psychosomatic disorders. The Miller-DiCara studies also lend strong support to the argument that learning and conditioning may contribute to the acquisition of psychosomatic disorders.

TREATMENT OF PSYCHOSOMATIC DISORDERS

Persons suffering from psychosomatic disorders typically seek and prefer medical forms of treatment to psychotherapy. This orientation is consistent with the physical nature of their overt symptoms. The greater "respectability" of physical illness in comparison with emotional disorders is also an important consideration. Psychotherapists also favor initial referral to physicians for laboratory tests, diagnosis, and medication. To deny a patient any relief of symptoms he might obtain from drugs, diet, and other available medical aids is unethical. Medical examination is also essential to rule out the possibility that the patient's symptoms may be due to an infection or some other organic pathogenic agent for which a specific type of medication or surgery is the only effective remedy. When it is apparent that emotional factors play an important role in the manifestation of symptoms, psychotherapists may be helpful as consultants. A team approach may be used, physician and psychotherapist sharing treatment responsibility. In the team approach either participant may assume the major role in accordance with the needs of the patient. As in the treatment of other problems in living, the choice of psychotherapeutic method may range from psychoanalysis to behavior modification. Treatment may focus on the individual alone or may involve other family members. Psychotherapeutic procedures that work well with some patients are ineffective with others.

The periodic recurrence of symptoms makes it difficult to assess the relative effectiveness of various forms of medical or psychotherapeutic treatment. Symptoms tend to come and go, with their intensity more directly related to the changing tides of personal stress than to therapeutic intervention. The recurring idea that a psychosomatic disorder offers a protective defense against the development of a more serious disorder may be partly a rationalization dreamed up by frustrated therapists.

Organic Brain Disorders Accompanied by Psychosocial Disturbances

The human brain has multiple functions. Besides serving as the coordinating and controlling center for physiological processes associated with sensation, emotion, and motor response, it is the key organ in perception, attention, comprehension, learning, memory, thinking, and intelligence. Other important brain functions include conscious awareness and the orderly integration of diverse cerebral activities. Extensive brain damage usually leads to some impairment in all functions. Frequently noted psychological defects include mental confusion, disorientation as to time, place, and person, poor recall of recent events, memory loss, faulty judgment, and impaired intelligence.

The most common cause of brain damage is aging. There are marked individual differences with respect to age of onset of significant cortical degeneration, but if a person lives long enough, his brain will eventually succumb to the ravages of time. Significant decline in brain functioning usually does not begin before the age of sixty-five, though in rare cases the disintegration process starts as early as forty. These atypical presenile conditions, sometimes referred to as Pick's disease, are thought to be due to an inherited neurological defect. Pick's disease is often noted in several members of a family. It is distinguished by characteristic brain pathology.

Other causes of transient or permanent brain damage include head injuries, intoxicating drugs, infections, and metabolic disturbances. Cerebral metabolic insufficiency associated with brain damage from various causes may lead to delirium. Delirium is frequently noted in persons approaching or recovering from a coma, in intoxicated individuals, and in persons with high fevers. The reaction is transient and consists largely of extremely defective brain functioning. The delirious patient is typically confused, disoriented, incoherent, and out of touch with reality. Perceptual disturbances include misidentification of persons, misinterpretation of stimuli, and hallucinations. The bewildered patients may show signs of extreme apprehension or panic.

The psychological disturbances described so far represent direct expressions of brain malfunctioning. In addition, brain-damaged persons may exhibit a variety of secondary reactions that are more closely related to preexisting personality defects than to brain damage. Secondary reactions may range from an exaggeration of lifelong maladaptive traits (suspiciousness, querulousness, passive dependence, egocentricity, rigidity, irritability) to full-blown neurotic or psychotic reactions. These secondary reactions may be provoked, released, or accentuated by the added strain placed on the individual by brain malfunction, but they are not caused by the brain disorder. There is no relation between the severity of secondary psychogenic symptoms and the extent of brain damage. In cases of acute or transient brain disorders, secondary symptoms may persist long after the direct effects of brain damage have disappeared. Secondary symptoms may be alleviated or eliminated by psychotherapy or medication without affecting impairment in functioning directly due to brain damage.

ACUTE AND CHRONIC BRAIN DISORDERS

Acute brain disorders are differentiated from chronic brain disorders on the basis of the reversibility of the organic brain damage. The clinical symptoms are the same in both forms of brain disorder: both are characterized by the usual syndrome of direct psychological defects, and secondary reactions may or may not be present in either. Acute brain disorders are marked by temporary impairment in brain tissue function. The organic pathology is reversible and the patient returns to his usual level and mode of functioning in a few days or weeks. The main causes of acute brain disorder are alcohol or drug intoxication, head injuries, and systemic infections. In chronic brain disorders, the brain damage is irreversible and permanent. Over time the patient may show some improvement in psychological functioning, but the more typical pattern is a gradual and progressive decline. The two most prevalent types of chronic brain disorder are senile brain change and cerebral arteriosclerosis. Other chronic conditions include brain tissue damage associated with alcoholism and convulsive disorders. Deterioration of the central nervous system due to syphilitic infection (general paresis) was formerly a widespread chronic brain disorder. The discovery of antibiotic drugs that provide effective treatment for syphilis has virtually eliminated this condition as a psychiatric disorder. The handbooks of psychiatry edited by Arieti (1959) and Freedman and Kaplan (1967) include comprehensive reviews of the neurological, medical, and psychiatric aspects of organic brain disorders.

Cerebral arteriosclerosis and senile brain disorders are both disorders of old age. The direct and secondary psychosocial symptoms of the two disorders are the same. The diagnostic differentiation is made on the basis of etiological factors and neuroanatomical pathology. It is presumed that predisposing genetic factors influence age of onset and severity of brain disintegration in senile brain disease. Postmortem studies indicate that senile brain disease is marked by a generalized atrophy of the brain (especially of the frontal lobe), shrinkage of the cerebral cortex, and the presence of a large number of rounded granular masses that are referred to as senile plaques. A diagnosis of arteriosclerosis implies the presence of some pathology of the cerebral arteries which blocks the flow of nutrient blood to cortical cells. A cerebral hemorrhage, popularly called a stroke, is considered indicative of some pathology of the cerebral arteries. The term arteriosclerosis, which refers specifically to a hardening of the cerebral arteries, is technically a misnomer. The fault usually is due to occlusion of the arteries by fatty deposits. The medical term for this condition is atherosclerosis. Both disorders usually occur after the age of sixty-five. The median age for cerebral arteriosclerosis is between seventy and seventy-five and for senile brain disease about eighty. Brain syndromes associated with cerebral arteriosclerosis account for 12 percent of first admissions to public hospitals, as compared with 4 percent for senile brain disease. A substantial number of elderly patients exhibit both types of brain pathology.

PSYCHOSOCIAL ASPECTS OF AGING

With or without the added strain of brain pathology, the biological process of aging constitutes a significant source of frustration and stress. Some of the problems directly related to the aging process are poor physical health, impairment in vision and hearing, loss of vigor, reduction in psychological competence, and loss of youthful physical attractiveness. Concomitant problems that are indirectly associated with biological decline include occupational retirement, reduced income, loss of spouse and old friends, reduction in social status, and the increased risk of death. The problems are real and usually inescapable. Preventive measures and direct solutions are usually not available. From a psychological point of view, however, the most critical issue is not the presence of problems but the individual's reactions to them. The great majority of aged persons manage somehow to cope with the problems of aging. Insofar as possible, they try to plan ahead so that old age will not become an agonizing period of pain, disability, want, and loneliness. Most men probably realize the desirability of facing the reality of retirement before it is actually upon them and of preparing for the inevitable reduction in income, social status, and feelings of personal worth, though actually making these adjustments may be difficult. A feeling of purpose and meaningfulness in living may be retained through launching a new career, part-time work, or the cultivation of avocational interests. Other constructive adaptive approaches used by both men and women include the correction of treatable physical disabilities, the maintenance and replacement of friends, continued participation in varied activities, and the preservation of independence and self-reliance. The less fortunate evade or deny the realities of biological decline, turn to others for support with mixed feelings of dependence and resentment, or find refuge in preexisting neurotic or psychotic patterns of escape or defense. Those who in the past have succeeded in maintaining a marginal adjustment may manifest more marked overt symptoms in later years.

Minor forms of maladjustment commonly noted during old age include increased social withdrawal, irritability, egocentricity, suspiciousness, compulsive behavior, resistance to change, preoccupation with physical health, increased anxiety, agitation, and periodic outbursts of helpless rage. The two major maladaptive reactions are depression and paranoid trends. The theoretical premise that depressive behavior represents a reaction to some significant loss has considerable face validity in the case of retired persons who have experienced the loss of health, income, children, friends, and loved ones. Depressions in elderly persons are characterized by the usual symptom patterns: dejection, pessimism, loss of self-esteem, guilt, self-condemnation, sleep irregularities, and somatic complaints. The high suicide rate of aged men may be partly attributed to self-blame and self-attack for a sense of failure in life. Paranoid reactions in the aged often represent an externalization of blame. Rather than accept responsibility for failure to provide for the future, the individual attacks the social system. The ill will and hostility of neighbors and the duplicity of former friends serve as convenient explanations for the individual's lack of friends and loneliness. The parent who was preoccupied with his own concerns when his children were young accuses them of neglect and ingratitude when the tables are turned.

The multiple needs and deficiences of the aged require a broad-spectrum treatment program. Their pressing financial needs have been alleviated to some extent by social security and medicare programs, but without independent means or the personal assistance of people who care for them, old age can still be a disaster. The longevity and general adjustment of the aged can be greatly improved by adequate diet and treatment of infections. When elderly persons are emotionally disturbed, tranquilizing and antidepressant drugs are effective in relieving tension and bringing disruptive behavior under control. Short-term psychotherapy or counseling is often extremely helpful in eliminating specific maladaptive habits, improving outlook on life, and restoring social involvement. There are advantages and disadvantages to living with one's children. The gains of being cared for within the family have to be balanced against the loss of independence and the amount of inconvenience or discomfort an elderly parent's presence creates for other family members. As a rule it is best for the elderly to remain in familiar surroundings, but placement in a nursing home or a geriatric hospital may be required if the old person is physically or mentally disabled and needs close supervision and protective care.

CONVULSIVE DISORDERS

The term "convulsive disorder" is a generic label applied to a pattern of periodic loss of consciousness, motor disturbances, or epileptic seizures. Attacks are spontaneous and unpredictable. They may occur once or twice in a lifetime, or several hundred times a year. The main diagnostic criterion is the presence of abnormal electroencephalographic (EEG) brain wave patterns. EEG irregularities may be present during normal sleep as well as while an attack is in progress. The consistent finding of EEG abnormality in convulsive disorders has led to the suggestion that these conditions might be more precisely defined as cerebral dysrhythmia.

Historically, a distinction has been made between idiopathic epilepsy and symptomatic epilepsy. There is good evidence that susceptibility to idiopathic epilepsy is genetically determined. The concordance rate for idiopathic epilepsy is significantly greater among MZ twins than among DZ twins. Seizures occur five times more frequently among members of the families of affected persons than among the general population (Page, 1947; Lennox and Lennox, 1960). The role of heredity is less pronounced in symptomatic epilepsy. These seizures are attributed to some incidental brain pathology or toxic condition. In symptomatic epilepsy, the occurrence of abnormal EEG patterns tends to be restricted to a focal area. The abnormality in brain waves is more generalized in cases of idiopathic epilepsy.

A clinical differentiation is made between *grand mal, petit mal,* Jacksonian, and psychomotor attacks. The *grand mal* attack is the most dramatic. About 50 percent of victims report an "aura" that precedes a seizure and signals its onset. The aura may consist of a mood change, a dreamy state, muscular twitchings, or sensory disturbances. The onset of the convulsion is marked by a characteristic epileptic cry and sudden loss of consciousness. The person falls to the floor as if struck by an unseen blow. The fall is so sudden that it may result in injuries. The first stage of the convulsion consists of a tonic phase, in which the entire musculature is in extreme tonic spasm. This is followed by a clonic phase, which consists of alternating flexing and stretching of the muscles. The victim may slam his head against the floor, bite his tongue, and wet and soil himself. The attack usually lasts about two minutes and is followed by deep, noisy breathing. Frothy saliva, sometimes tinged with blood, often appears at the mouth. In a short time the person spontaneously comes out of the coma. Some complain of headache and tiredness; others feel relieved and refreshed.

Petit mal is characterized by recurring periods of loss of consciousness that usually last about twenty seconds. The person suddenly interrupts whatever he is doing at the time, but he does not fall. External signs may be limited to a turning up of the eyes, a nodding of the head, or a slight jerking movement of the body. The attack may pass unnoticed by others and by the epileptic himself unless it causes an obvious halt in conversation, a suspension of walking movements, or the dropping of an object the person was holding. Some individuals have numerous attacks during the day. It is not uncommon for epileptics to have both *petit mal* and *grand mal* seizures.

Jacksonian epilepsy originates in a focal point of cerebral excitation. The attack usually starts with twitching movements of the fingers or a corner of the mouth. The twitching spreads gradually until it becomes a generalized *grand mal* seizure. Consciousness is usually retained as long as the jerking movements are confined to the extremities.

Psychomotor attacks are also referred to as temporal lobe epilepsy. The condition is marked by lapses of consciousness, irregular muscular movements, disturbances in thought or affect, stereotyped behavior, and *grand mal* seizures.

Convulsive disorders are present in about one in every three hundred persons in the general population. Drugs are available for the control of attacks, so that most epileptics today lead normal lives relatively free of attacks. Since the drugs have toxic effects, medical supervision is necessary. When an identifiable area of the brain is the source of focal seizures, surgical intervention may correct the condition.

On the basis of chance alone, all types of character disorder, neurosis, and psychosis may be expected to occur among persons with convulsive disorders. In view of the frequency of convulsive disorders in the general population, it would be surprising if this were not so. The question is whether the incidence of psychopathology in general or of some particular psychological disorder is more prevalent among epileptics than in the general population. Factual data on this point are inconclusive. Extensive research studies have failed to confirm the once popular notion that epileptics as a group were characterized by distinctive personality traits (Tizard, 1962). When the underlying brain damage is extensive or involves critical areas, the epileptic may show impairment in cognitive functioning. Secondary reactions may include resentment at social or occupational discrimination because of the disability, fear of humiliation if seizures should occur in public, reduced self-confidence, and general discontent.

Summary

Sexual dysfunctions provide a good example of the reciprocal interaction of psychobiosocial variables in the etiology and correction of behavior disturbances. Impotence and orgasmic deficiency may be defined as physical symptoms originating and expressed in interpersonal situations for which educational retraining and learning constitute the most effective treatment.

Genetic and biological factors influence relative vulnerability to psychosomatic and organic brain disorders, but the phenotypic expression and the treatment of these disorders are dependent on psychosocial factors. Experimental studies, which have demonstrated the successful application of operant conditioning procedures in regulating visceral and glandular changes, provide a scientific basis for the application of learning principles to the acquisition and treatment of physical symptoms associated with psychosomatic disorders.

A person's reactions to impairments in functioning caused by brain disorders often have greater psychopathological significance than the actual destruction of brain tissue. The fusion of genetic, medical, socioeconomic, personality, and interpersonal variables is particularly evident in the complexity and diversity of the adjustment problems of the aged.

References

AMERICAN PSYCHIATRIC ASSOCIATION. *Diagnostic and Statistical Manual of Mental Disorders* (DSM-11). Washington, D.C., 1968.

ARIETI, S., ed. *American Handbook of Psychiatry,* vol. 2. New York: Basic Books, 1959.

ASCOUGH, J. C., and SIPPRELLE, C. N. "Operant Verbal Conditioning of Autonomic Responses." *Behavior Research and Therapy* 6 (1968): 363–70.

BRADY, J. V. "Ulcers in 'Executive' Monkeys." *Scientific American* 199 (1958): 95–100.

BUSS, A. H. *Psychopathology.* New York: Wiley, 1966.

ENGEL, B. T., and CHISM, R. A. "Operant Conditioning of Heart Rate Speeding." *Psychophysiology* 3 (1967): 418–26.

DICARA, L. V. "Learning in the Autonomic Nervous System." *Scientific American* 222 (January 1970): 30–39.

Specific Attitudes in Initial Interviews with Patients Having Different 'Psychiatry.* Baltimore: Williams & Wilkins, 1967.

GRAHAM, D. T.; LUNDY, R. M.; BENJAMIN, L. S.; and KABLER, F. K. "Some Specific Attitudes in Initial Interviews with Patients Having Different "Psychosomatic' Diseases." *Psychosomatic Medicine* 24 (1962): 257–66.

GREENE, W. A. "Operant Conditioning of the GSR Using Partial Reinforcement." *Psychological Reports* 19 (1966): 571–78.

KIMMEL, E., and KIMMEL, H. D. "A Replication of Operant Conditioning of the GSR." *Journal of Experimental Psychology* 65 (1963): 212–13.

KINSEY, A. C.; POMEROY, W. B.; and MARTIN, C. E. *Sexual Behavior in the Human Male.* Philadelphia: Saunders, 1948.

——— and GEBHARD, P. H. *Sexual Behavior in the Human Female.* Philadelphia: Saunders, 1953.

LACEY, J. I., and LACEY, B. C. "Verification and Extension of the Principle of Autonomic Response Stereotype." *American Journal of Psychology* 71 (1958): 50–73.

LANG, P. J.; STROUFE, L. A.; and HASTINGS, J. E. "Effects of Feedback and Instructional Set on the Control of Cardiac-Rate Variability." *Journal of Experimental Psychology* 75 (1967): 425–31.

LENNOX, W. J., and LENNOX, M. A. *Epilepsy and Related Disorders.* Boston: Little, Brown, 1960.

LYNCH, J. J. "Social Responding in Dogs: Heart Rate Changes to a Person." *Society for Psychophysiological Research* 5 (1969): 389–93.

MALMO, R. B., and SHAGASS, C. "Physiologic Study of Symptom Mechanisms in Psychiatric Patients under Stress." *Psychosomatic Medicine* 11 (1949): 25–29.

MASTERS, W. H., and JOHNSON, V. E. *Human Sexual Response.* Boston: Little, Brown, 1966.

———. *Human Sexual Inadequacy.* Boston: Little, Brown, 1970.

MILLER, N. E. "Learning of Visceral and Glandular Responses." *Science* 163 (January 31, 1969): 434–45.

PAGE, J. D. *Abnormal Psychology: A Clinical Approach to Psychological Deviants.* New York: McGraw-Hill, 1947.

REES, L. "The Importance of Psychological, Allergic, and Infective Factors in Childhood Asthma." *Journal of Psychosomatic Research* 7 (1964): 253–62.

RENNIE, T., and STROLE, L. "Social Class Prevalence and Distribution of Psychosomatic Conditions in an Urban Population." *Psychosomatic Medicine* 18 (1956): 449–57.

SELYE, H. *The Stress of Life.* New York: McGraw-Hill, 1956.

TIZARD, B. "The Personality of Epileptics: A Discussion of the Evidence." *Psychological Bulletin* 59 (1962): 196–210.

WENGER, M. A.; CLEMENS, T. L.; COLEMAN, D. R.; CULLEN, T. D.; and ENGEL, B. T. "Autonomic Response Specificity." *Psychosomatic Medicine* 23 (1961): 185–93.

WOLF, H. G. *Stress and Disease.* Springfield, Ill.: Charles C Thomas, 1953.

CHAPTER SIXTEEN

Disordered Behavior
in Children

The criteria for disordered behavior in children are more loosely interpreted than the criteria for adult disorders, but the key features are the same. Initial diagnosis is usually made by parents or teachers. The behavior deviations considered indicative of psychopathology consist mainly of uncontrolled or uncontrollable defects in psychosocial functions. In evaluating the significance or severity of deviant behavior in children, psychologists focus attention on (1) the relative inadequacy or inappropriateness of the behavior to the age of the child and attending circumstances, and (2) the extent to which the behavior is detrimental, disruptive, maladaptive, or a source of undue distress, concern, or threat to the child, his family, or society. A child's behavior problems are more directly related to developmental defects than an adult's, and more emphasis is placed on a child's failure to attain age-appropriate levels of psychosocial adequacy than on loss or impairment of functioning. As with adults, the presence of uncontrolled or uncontrollable behavior (with allowance made for age) is usually the critical factor in referring a child for diagnosis and treatment. Defects in a child's psychosocial behavior are considered indicative of psychopathology when neither parents nor teachers are able to cope effectively with his personal, social, or educational problems. When the behavior is antisocial, referral may be initiated by court officials.

Difficulties in Classification

Children may exhibit any of the symptom patterns noted in adults plus certain reactions that are more or less restricted to children. The concept of discrete disorders, each of which is distinguished by a specific cause and marked by a specific set of symptoms, is even less applicable to disorders of childhood than to those of adults. A reaction that is accepted as normal behavior at a certain age may in an older child be considered a sign of delayed development or a symptomatic manifestation of an emotional problem. Enuresis, or bedwetting, for example, is normal in infants, but a sign of delayed development in a five-year-old and a regressive reaction in a ten-year-old who has been free of this condition for over seven years.

The problem of classification of adult behavior symptoms is somewhat simplified by the fact that symptoms tend to reflect the characteristic habit patterns of the individual and are relatively stable. There is usually a cohesiveness and consistency in symptom clusters. Children's personalities are less structured; individual styles of reacting are still in the process of development. Behavior is more fluid, changeable, transient, and unpredictable. Temporary compulsive bedtime ceremonies may occur in children otherwise free of obsessive-compulsive traits. Within the space of a moment or two a child may be happy and miserable, submissive and assertive, friendly and aggressive. A child may be well behaved at home and a discipline problem at school, or vice versa. His behavior is controlled by external events to a greater degree than an adult's. In the absence of firmly established habit patterns designed to cope with difficulties, children rely on trial-and-error improvisation. If a reaction (symptom) works, in the sense that it relieves tension, elicits a favorable response from the environment, or is otherwise reinforced, it will probably be repeated. The response may be generalized to other, similar situations, and if it is repeatedly reinforced, it may become a characteristic style or mode of reacting. If it does not work, it is usually discarded and another is tried. This changeableness of response, which is related to the issue of choice of symptoms, represents a flexible approach to difficulties. It is not necessary to invoke the more hypothetical principle of symptom substitution, which assumes that new symptoms are the surface manifestations of inner conflicts, and that until the underlying conflict is resolved, new symptoms will replace discarded ones. If a "good" response emerges or can be acquired through therapy, there is no need to uncover and liquidate the presumed repressed conflict.

An interesting description of a child's trial-and-error experimentation in symptom formation and the manner by which it was skillfully extinguished has been reported by Ullmann and Krasner (1969, p. 158). The child was at a summer camp for handicapped children.

At first the child was self-punishing—hitting, slapping and biting himself. When this did not cause the counselors concern, he threw tantrums in which he beat his head against the ground or trees. He gave this up and next took his clothes off in public, but this led to no other counselor behavior than his being put to bed (taking off clothes meant preparation for bed). The child gave up the undressing behavior and proceeded to steal food from other children's plates even though his own was heaped high. To keep other children from imitating the stealing, counselors placed the child in a room to eat by himself. In this situation the child began defecating and smearing feces over himself, the walls, floors, and his belongings. When this behavior did not elicit special concern on the part of the counselors, it ceased after five days. Next, the child piled all the children's shoes together early in the morning. Sorting shoes before breakfast became a morning game for the group, and after a week, this behavior also stopped. The "shoe game" was the last of a spectacular series of antisocial behaviors, none of which were reinforced with attention, concern, or giving the child his way. If any of these behaviors had been reinforced, the pattern of maladaptive behavior might well have continued for a longer period of time.

GAP Classification System

Since the maladaptive reactions of disturbed children do not fall into neat, clearly defined diagnostic categories, the classification system described in the 1966 report of the Committee on Child Psychiatry of the Group for the Advancement of Psychiatry is admittedly arbitrary and artificial; but it is as useful as any other for organizing in some semblance of order the bewildering variety of symptoms noted in children. The GAP classification recognizes ten major categories:

Healthy responses	Psychotic disorders
Reactive disorders	Psychophysiological disorders
Developmental deviations	Brain syndromes
Psychoneurotic disorders	Mental retardation
Personality disorders	Other disorders

The nature and kinds of behavior deficits commonly observed in children are listed below. The above "disorders" consist of different combinations of the following disturbances in functioning.

ABBREVIATED GAP LIST OF CHILDREN'S BEHAVIOR SYMPTOMS

   I. Disturbances related to bodily functions.
      A. Eating: anorexia, food rituals, regurgitation.
      B. Sleeping: bedtime rituals, nightmares, somnambulism.
      C. Bowel function: constipation, anal masturbation, smearing.
      D. Bladder function: enuresis, resistance to training, retention.
      E. Speech: aphonia, stuttering, elective mutism.

    F. Motor patterns: apraxia, catalepsy, tics, mannerisms.

    G. Rhythmic patterns: head banging, body rocking, whirling.

    H. Habit patterns: nose picking, thumb-sucking.

    I. Sensory disturbances: anesthesia, hallucinations, paresthesia.

    J. Other disturbances: headaches, acne, asthma, hypertension.

II. Disturbances related to cognitive functions.

    A. Learning failure: underachievement, reading disability.

    B. Disturbances in thinking: impaired reality testing, associative disorders.

    C. Disturbances in memory: amnesia, memory impairment.

    D. Disturbances in awareness: confusion, delirium, dissociation.

III. Disturbances in affective behavior.

    A. Fearful behavior: multiple or specific fears.

    B. Manifest anxiety: separation anxiety, apprehension, panic states.

    C. Depressive symptoms: dejection, agitation, retardation of response.

    D. Euphoric behavior: elation, manic behavior, giggling.

    E. Hypochondriacal behavior: preoccupation with disease.

    F. Other affective states: rage, guilt, shame, inferiority.

IV. Disturbances related to development.

    A. Physical growth: accelerated, retarded, or uneven growth.

    B. Maturational patterns: regressive, retarded, or uneven maturation.

V. Disturbances in social behavior.

    A. Aggressive behavior.

        1. Externally directed: destructive behavior, fighting.

        2. Internally directed: self-injury, suicidal attempts.

    B. Antisocial behavior: cheating, fire setting, vandalism.

    C. Oppositional behavior: disobedience, passive-aggressive behavior.

    D. Isolating behavior: autism, excessive shyness, paranoid tendencies.

    E. Dominance-submission: boastfulness, rebelliousness, manipulation of others.

    F. Dependence-interdependence: clinging, whining, excessive independence.

    G. Sexual adjustment: exhibitionism, homosexuality, promiscuity.

VI. Disturbances in integrative behavior.

    A. Impulsive behavior.

    B. Incapacity to play.

    C. Low anxiety tolerance.

D. Low frustration tolerance.
E. Overuse of adaptive mechanisms.
F. Disorganized behavior.
G. *Folie à deux*.
VII. Other behavior disturbances.
A. Stereotyped behavior: perfectionism, compulsive behavior.
B. Temper tantrums.
C. Hallucinations: auditory, visual, olfactory.
D. Delusions: ideas of reference, somatic symptoms, persecutory ideas.
E. Malingering.
F. Addictive behavior: alcoholism, drug use, glue-sniffing.

HEALTHY RESPONSES

The main function of the category of "healthy responses" is to direct attention to the normality and appropriateness at certain ages or in some circumstances of reactions that may be misperceived as symptoms of pathology by overconcerned parents: thumb-sucking in infants, mild separation anxiety frequently exhibited by preschool children, the frequent confusion of adolescents concerning identity and dependence-independence, and so on. The category may also be used to indicate areas of strengths that may serve to offset and thereby modify the significance of deviations.

REACTIVE DISORDERS

Reactive disorders are transient situational reactions and other conditions that are considered to represent reactions to particular events or series of events. The diagnosis of reactive disorder is restricted to cases in which the situation does in fact represent an emotional trauma to the particular child; the reaction is causally related to the specific event and not simply coincident with it. Typical situations that precipitate reactive disturbances are illness, hospitalization, loss of a parent, school pressures, and the attitudes and behavior of peers. The reaction may take the form of arrest in development or may be expressed in a variety of other symptoms. Symptoms may be influenced by the nature of the stress; the age, development level, and personality makeup of the child; and past experiences. Most neurotic traits, habit disturbances, mild conduct disorders, and depressive reactions exhibited by infants deprived of adequate mothering would be included in this category. Specific symptoms include lack of appetite, apathy, withdrawal, overt aggressive acts, passive-aggressive behavior, regressive enuresis, preoccupation with fantasy, and overt panic. As a rule, reactive disorders are transient and temporary, but they can lead to chronic disabilities. An additional diagnosis is usually indicated if the reaction persists or is superimposed upon one of the other disorders.

DEVELOPMENTAL DEVIATIONS

Development is a function of the interaction of maturational patterns and of experience or learning. Maturation is largely dependent on a biologically determined sequential series of specific steps. Maturation level influences both the child's potentialities for development and his responsiveness. To a considerable degree, some type of innate filter system minimizes the effect of stimulation on a child before he has reached a maturational stage that permits him to cope with the particular stimuli.

Technically, developmental deviations include precocious as well as retarded or distorted development of personality, although most examples of precocious development are more reasonably considered healthy responses. The category thus serves mainly to identify negative or undesirable deviations that exceed the range of normal variability. The deviation may occur at a time, in a sequence, or to a degree not expected for a given age level. The deviation may apply to a restricted range of functions or may involve almost the total maturational timetable. Typical deviations in early development include delayed speech, delayed toilet training, and poor coordination.

During infancy and early childhood, responses tend to be uncontrolled, generalized, and diffuse. An important aspect of development is the increasing differentiation, integration, and control of behavior. Difficulties in the monitoring and integration of input stimuli may lead to hyperactivity, underactivity, impulsiveness, or apathy. Defects in speech development include disorders in articulation, rhythm, phonation, and speech comprehension. More extreme deviations, such as the relative mutism of autistic children, would be classified as symptoms of psychotic behavior. The most prevalent of the deviations in cognitive functions is reading disability. Other learning problems include delayed or impaired proficiency in spelling, writing, and arithmetic. Examples of deviations in social development include shyness, lack of social skills, emotional immaturity, aggressive behavior, and inability to relate effectively to peers. A common concern of parents is the presence of characteristics culturally defined as masculine in girls and characteristics considered feminine in boys. (Often this sort of concern indicates a greater problem in the parents than in the child, though the child is certain to suffer from it.) Markedly precocious or delayed heterosexual interests may also be perceived as problems. Less controversial areas of developmental deviation include marked overcontrol or undercontrol of emotions and impulses, failure to develop frustration tolerances consistent with one's age, and the overuse of defense mechanisms.

PSYCHONEUROTIC DISORDERS

The symptomatic manifestations of neuroses in children parallel those in adults. The main difference is that the traditional symptom patterns associated with obsessive-compulsive, hysterical, neurasthenic, and other neurotic reactions are less clearly defined in children. Anna Freud (1965) distinguishes between archaic fears often expressed by children and regular phobias. Phobias can usually be traced to some frightening experience or are based on regression and conflict. Archaic fears—fear of darkness, loneliness, strangers, thunder and lightning—appear to be innate. As a rule, archaic fears disappear spontaneously with increased maturity. The preoccupation with physical symptoms that is frequently noted in children is often dismissed as "growing pains." According to psychoanalytic theory, these symptoms may represent hypochrondriacal tendencies in children who feel neglected or rejected by their mothers.

PERSONALITY DISORDERS

The emergence of deeply ingrained maladaptive personality patterns starts in childhood. During the early years personality traits are more flexible than they become later. The names assigned to personality types in children d ffer somewhat from those used for adults. The GAP lists these childhood personality types:

Compulsive	Impulse-ridden
Hysterical	Neurotic
Anxious	Overly inhibited
Overly dependent	Overly independent
Oppositional	Sociosyntonic
Isolated	Sexual deviant
Distrustful	Other types

With the exception of the overly independent and sociosyntonic personality, these have already been described in Chapter 12. The concept of the sexual deviant personality in children requires some further explanation.

The *overly independent personality* is characterized by premature strivings for independence, which may bring the child into conflict with limits set by adults. As a rule these children are not destructive or antisocial, but their insistence on self-direction and autonomy may result in their refusal of needed help and guidance. The overly responsible grownup behavior may represent a reaction against feelings of dependence.

The child with a *sociosyntonic personality* would be considered antisocial if it were not for the fact that his reactions are consonant with those of the neighborhood group, the gang, or even the family. These children are sometimes described as socialized delinquents.

The label of *sexual deviant personality* is applied to children who persistently engage in homosexual behavior or other forms of sexual offense, when the deviation is regarded as the major personality disturbance that pervades and dominates the child's personality functioning and orientation. Transient sexual deviations are usually classified as developmental disorders.

A more general personality type that is not specifically included in the GAP classification is the aggressive-delinquent child. A good description has been provided by Rexford (1959).

> These children have long been unmanageable at home, in school, and the neighborhood. They may even be well known to the police, who have preferred no charges because of their youth. They may be bright but rarely have they performed well in school and have marked learning blocks. They tend to be hostile, resentful, over-active individuals, often extremely skilled in their performance of antisocial acts, confident that all people lie, steal, and cheat whenever it is to their advantage. They may never have learned to delay or otherwise manage their instinctual wishes except by doing, taking, or saying what they wished. They have a short attention span and find it hard to tolerate frustration of any kind. The parents usually report that they were difficult babies in relation to feeding, sleeping, and toilet training. They were never successfully disciplined; the parents usually tell of many punitive attempts to curb the child's behavior. These children's life experiences have been so unrewarding and their primitive feelings and fantasies so little transformed and sublimated that they view the outside world as a hostile place, other people as their enemies, and themselves in the position of having to strike out before they are struck down.

PSYCHOTIC DISORDERS

Psychoses are rare in young children. Less than 5 percent of all children under fifteen referred for psychiatric or psychological examination are diagnosed as psychotic. In practically all cases, the symptom pattern is suggestive of schizophrenia. True affective psychoses are almost never seen prior to adolescence. Depending in part on the age of the child, a distinction is made between infantile autism, symbiotic or interactional psychosis (second to fifth years), schizophreniform psychosis (sixth to thirteenth years), and psychosis of adolescence. The clinical picture varies somewhat with the age of the child. Professional opinion varies as to whether the variations in symptoms noted among infants, preschool children, and older children constitute distinct disease entities or represent different age forms of the same disorder. Regardless of age of onset, the prognosis is poor and in most cases similar. With the exception of those few who recover or are reclassified as mentally defective, psychotic children are diagnosed as schizophrenics in adulthood. The Committee on Child Psychiatry (1966) lists the following general criteria for the diagnosis of childhood psychosis:

1. Severe and continued impairment of emotional relations with other persons.
2. Aloofness and a tendency toward preoccupation with inanimate objects.
3. Absence of speech or poor development of speech.
4. Disturbances in sensory perception.
5. Bizarre or stereotyped behavior and motility patterns.
6. Marked resistance to change in environment or routine.
7. Outbursts of intense and unpredictable panic.
8. Absence of a sense of personal identity.
9. Blunted, uneven, or fragmented intellectual development.

Infantile autism. The syndrome of infantile autism, originally described by Kanner in 1943, has been confirmed by Rieser (1963), Rimland (1964), O'Gorman (1967), and other investigators. The disorder is differentiated from other forms of childhood psychosis by its early age of onset (during the first year of life) and certain more or less distinctive behavioral features. Unlike mental retardates, autistic infants appear alert, exhibit good motor development, and show fragmentary evidence of normal functioning at their age level. The assumption of normal latent intelligence is borne out in some cases by their adequate performance in later years. However, many infants who are initially diagnosed as autistic turn out to be indistinguishable from mental defectives.

The most outstanding characteristic of early autism is the infant's failure to develop and manifest normal awareness of and responsiveness to the mother and other human beings. People are treated as objects. The child's deficiency in relating to others is indicated by the absence of anticipatory responses to being lifted by the parents, absence of the plastic molding displayed by normal children when cradled in their parents' arms, failure to react to the presence or absence of the mother, avoidance of eye contact, absence of crying, and the lack of or delay of the typical infant smiling response. The infant shows no interest in playing peek-a-boo or pat-a-cake and is devoid of affection or emotional involvement with others. Speech is either absent or markedly delayed. If the child does speak, his utterances are often restricted to a poorly modulated, parrot-like repetition of sounds without affective or communicative content. No attempt is made to converse or answer questions. That the problem is one of communication rather than speech per se is indicated by the absence of attempts at non-verbal communication.

A heightened sensitivity to stimulus change is often apparent. This is expressed in an obsessive insistence on sameness. Changes in the social environment or alterations in routine are met with outbursts of temper or acute anxiety. Some autistic children exhibit a marked aversion to granular foods, sniff at their food, and show bizarre food preferences. Some stimuli may evoke extreme irritability while others bring no response at all. These children appear to be more responsive to self-produced than external stimulation. There is no evidence of hallucinations. Discontinuities in development may occur. The child may start crawling at the usual age and then stop for several months. Words spoken at ten months may not be repeated again for a year or more. Motor disturbances include whirling of the body or objects, flapping of the hands, darting and lunging, bizarre stereotyped reactions, posturing, toe walking, teeth grinding, and head banging. Autistic children have difficulty distinguishing the self from the nonself. It is not uncommon for an autistic child to regard himself as a kind of mechanical object or machine. The communication barrier makes it difficult to administer intelligence tests and to evaluate responses. Answers, when scorable, are uneven in quality. Yet the potentiality for normal or above-average mental ability is inferred from their alert expressions and the sporadically high levels of their motor performance.

Many of the features of infantile autism may be seen in the case study of a five-year-old boy reported by Ornitz and Ritvo (1968). The boy had been an inpatient in a psychiatric hospital for a year. Pregnancy and delivery had apparently been normal. The parents, of working-class background, had noted that the child showed atypical behavior and development from infancy as compared with his older sibling. Initial psychiatric referral had been made when the child was three years old. According to information supplied by the parents, the boy was irritable and oversensitive as an infant. He was unusually sensitive to visual detail and spent considerable time regarding the movements of his fingers. He completely ignored auditory stimulation. At an age when children are normally interested in toys, he rejected toys and other objects presented to him. If they were placed in his hands, he would let them fall or flick them away.

When he was four months old he began to make repetitive movements, from which he could be distracted only with difficulty. He rolled his head from side to side, over and over; he twirled beads and other objects for long periods. He failed to show any anticipatory response to being picked up till after he was a year old. He never made eye contact with his parents or responded to their attempts to play games with him. He used others as an extension of himself. As his parents said, "He pushes us to his needs."

He sat up without support at seven months but did not walk alone until sixteen months. He started to make spontaneous sounds by six months and syllables by twelve months, but he made little attempt to imitate sounds or words spoken by his parents. By the time he was three he had developed a ten-word vocabulary, but after that he stopped using words altogether. He never combined words into phrases. Between eighteen and twenty-four months he occasionally waved bye-bye in imitation of his father, but then abandoned this activity. From the time he was two years old he whirled himself as if he were a toy and exhibited repetitive, rapid oscillation of the hands. He refused to chew food and remained on baby foods until he was three. While he was in the hospital, he was never observed to use toys or other objects in any appropriate way. He merely kept on spinning objects and himself and flapping his hands as his parents reported he had done at home.

The case of Joey, the nine year old "mechanical boy" described by Bettelheim (1959), is somewhat extreme but it serves to illustrate the lack of human attributes associated with autistic children. The explanation given by Bettelheim is that Joey had converted himself into a machine because he did not dare to be human. Joey not only believed that he was a machine but his mechanical behavior created the impression in others that he was a machine. His pantomime of being controlled by wires was so convincing that observers tended to look twice to make sure he was not actually plugged in to an outlet somewhere. When the "machinery" was idle and Joey was still the staff had to concentrate to be aware of his presence. Case history data indicated that the boy had been strong and healthy at birth. By the time he was a year old, he had become remote and inaccessible. His mother, who was a socially detached person herself, had ignored his existence. His preoccupation with mechanical things started early. One of his ideas was that liquids had to be pumped into him through an elaborate system built of straws. He put together pieces of apparatus to create a machine to "live him" while he slept. Other pieces of machinery controlled his eating and elimination.

Practically every conceivable technique has been used in the treatment of autistic children. Usually residential placement is the first step. Bettelheim (1950) places great stress on providing a permissive environment in which children are indulged and given immediate gratification of their wishes. Operant behavior modification procedures have been successfully used with autistic children in helping them to acquire speech and other socially desirable behaviors (Metz, 1965; Ferster and Simmons, 1966; and Lovaas et al., 1967).

Outcome in autism is about the same as in other forms of childhood schizophrenia (Eisenberg and Kanner, 1956). About 25 percent "recover," and the number can be stretched to a maximum of 35 percent if all children who achieve a minimal social adjustment in school and community are included. Another 25 percent show some clinical improvement. Even children considered to have made successful recoveries, however, continue to show serious impairment in human relationships, marked egocentrism, lack of social skills, and apparent inability to identify and empathize with others. Most children who learn to speak by the age of five succeed in making some sort of social adjustment. Those who have no useful language function by that time usually exhibit other signs of severe mental retardation, and end up being reclassified as feebleminded. Since the development of speech is highly correlated with innate intelligence, it may be the underlying prognostic indicator (Rutter et al., 1967).

The specific determinants of infantile autism are unknown. A combination of genetic, organic, and psychological factors is probably involved. One or another of these etiological agents may be relatively more important in specific cases. Twin studies strongly favor a genetic interpretation. With one exception, both co-twins of monozygotic pairs have been found to be concordant for infantile autism in all reported cases (Ornitz and Ritvo, 1968). Concordance for the disorder is rare among dizygotic twins.

Eisenberg and Kanner (1956) noted that about 8 percent of the known siblings of one hundred autistic children studied could be regarded as probably autistic or emotionally disturbed. The nature of the genetic defect is still unknown. The results of most electroencephalographic studies of autistic infants have been negative, but positive findings increase with the age of the children tested. Sorosky and his associates (1968) have suggested that autistic children suffer from an imbalance of the excitatory and inhibitory mechanisms of the central nervous system, with primary involvement of the central vestibular mechanism. The failure of the normal inhibitory process to check excitation would account for the sustained overreactivity, whirling, hand flapping, and repetitive speech sounds. Excessive neural inhibition would account for the autistic child's unresponsiveness to sensory stimuli, prolonged immobility, and posturing. A major limitation of this neurological explanation is that it does not apply to the cardinal symptom, which is the child's lack of human feelings. The same limitation holds for Rimland's (1964) suggestion that the symptoms of autism may be due to some defect in the reticular system of the brain.

Early reports that the parents of autistic children tend to be cold, isolated, and obsessive have recently been questioned (Ornitz and Ritvo, 1968). Many of the parents of autistic children are warm and loving and provide a normal emotional climate. Most of those parents of autistic children who are in fact emotionally cold have nevertheless managed to raise one or more other children who are not autistic. The coldness and detachment noted in some of these parents may be at least in part reactions to the unresponsiveness of their autistic children. Early studies suggested that an unusually high proportion of the parents of autistic children were college graduates or professional people, but this appears to have been a sampling error. More recent reports indicate that these children come from every socioeconomic class (Levine and Olson, 1968). Infantile autism appears to be far more prevalent in boys than in girls.

Interactional psychotic disorder. Some children who develop normally during the first year or two begin to show psychotic reactions between the ages of two and five. In contrast to autistic infants, who are unable to relate to and identify with the mother, these children show what Mahler (1952) has designated a symbiotic mother-child relationship. The symbiotic child cannot bear to be separated from his mother. At an age when the normal child begins to take steps toward individuation and separation, the symbiotic child clings to his mother, becomes progressively more dependent on her, and shows acute separation anxiety. This reaction is regarded as a symbiotic psychosis if in addition to the intense mother attachment the child shows a distorted perception of reality, gives up previously acquired communicative speech, has frequent temper tantrums, or shows signs of panic, loss of identity, a regressive retreat into autism, and other related symptoms. The psychotic reaction is often triggered by a separation from the mother associated with enrollment in nursery school, hospitalization, or the birth of a sibling.

Other psychoses of infancy and early childhood. This is a catchall category that includes children with atypical development who may exhibit a mixture of autistic or symbiotic reactions, emotional aloofness, and distortion of reality. Here also may be included what Spitz (1945, 1946) has called "hospitalism" and "anaclitic depression." Hospitalism designates the lack of development and progressive mental deterioration of infants reared in foundling homes and institutions that provide no mothering and inadequate stimulation. These infants have a high death rate. Anaclitic depression is a state of depressive withdrawal and debilitation occurring in children who are separated from their mothers between six and eight months of age and for whom substitute mothers are not available. Symptoms include dejection, excessive crying, screaming or not responding at all when adults touch them or pick them up, and a frozen expression. Complete recovery usually occurs if the mother resumes care of the child. If the mother does not return and the child continues to live in an institutional setting under conditions of emotional deprivation, deterioration frequently progresses until it ends in an early death. Spitz's conclusions have been criticized by Pinneau (1955) as oversimplified, overgeneralized, and lacking in scientific rigor.

A more modest evaluation of the effects of maternal deprivation has been reported by Beres and Obers (1950). They noted that many children separated from their mothers in infancy and institutionalized for up to four years were socially deficient, immature, and intolerant of frustration, but the effects of maternal deprivation were neither consistent nor permanent. The group showed a remarkable degree of improvement with increasing age. About half were judged to have made a satisfactory social adjustment by adolescence.

Schizophreniform psychosis. Psychotic reactions occurring in children between the ages of six and thirteen and paralleling the symptoms of adult schizophrenia are called schizophreniform psychosis rather than schizophrenia because there are developmental differences between them and because this disorder does not necessarily lead to schizophrenia in adulthood. Symptoms include looseness of association in thought processes, intense temper outbursts, hypochondriacal tendencies, marked withdrawal, preoccupation with fantasies, and a breakdown in reality testing. Other commonly observed reactions are magical thinking, stereotyped motor patterns, inappropriate mood swings, ideas of reference, aggressive outbursts, self-mutilating behavior, and attempts at suicide. Lauretta Bender (1961) concluded from her extensive study of child schizophrenics that these children suffer from some form of brain pathology, as evidenced by abnormal EEG patterns, which interferes with normal biological development. She attributed the lag in development, which presumably starts in the embryonic stage, to genetic factors. The genetic aspects of schizophreniform psychosis have been investigated by Kailmann and Roth (1956). Their findings indicate concordance rates of 71 percent for MZ twins, 17 percent for DZ twins, 13 percent for parents, and 12 percent for siblings.

Psychoses of adolescence. The usual forms of adult schizophrenic reactions may occur during adolescence. In addition, some adolescents exhibit what is described as an acute confusional state. This disorder has an abrupt onset and is usually transient, with good recovery. Symptoms include identity confusion, intense anxiety, depressive trends, and impairment in thinking. The disorder is distinguished from schizophrenia by an absence of a true thought disorder or a marked breakdown in reality testing and the relative retention of capacity for adaptive behavior and meaningful emotional relationships.

Periods of excitement and depression are common during adolescence, but the manic and depressive psychotic episodes that occur in adults are seemingly rare. The relatively high suicide rate among adolescents seems to indicate that some type of severe depressive reaction is quite common during the late teens. The symptomatic expression of depression in adolescents consists of boredom, unusual fatigue, inability to concentrate, and feelings of being unloved and unwanted (Toolan, 1962). This syndrome falls short of the traditional criteria of psychosis.

PSYCHOPHYSIOLOGICAL DISORDERS

The interaction of psyche and soma may produce symptoms in either system: psychological and emotional factors may contribute to the production and maintenance of physical ailments, and physical illness may contribute to personality and emotional disturbances.

With the exception of genital disorders, which usually occur after puberty, all of the psychosomatic disorders noted in adults (see Chapter 15) also occur in children. One of the more intensively studied psychosomatic disorders in children is bronchial asthma (Schneer, 1963). As with other psychosomatic disorders, authorities differ on its determinants and associated characteristics. The following account is mainly a summary of the views expressed by Finch (1967). Bronchial asthma is marked by wheezing, labored breathing. Attacks occur sporadically and last from a few minutes to several days. The life-threatening impairment in breathing is a terrifying experience for the child and his parents. The disorder is presumed to be caused by a combination of emotional factors and sensitivity to certain allergens. It is not uncommon for asthmatic children also to have eczema, migraine, rheumatoid arthritis, and other psychosomatic difficulties. Because excitement or exertion may precipitate attacks, these youngsters tend to lead restricted, isolated, quiet lives. Children who have frequent and severe attacks may be placed in special residential centers for asthmatic children for long periods. Asthmatic attacks have been interpreted as reactions to threats of being separated from the mother or as means of controlling the mother. Since many asthmatic children improve when they are hospitalized and suffer relapses when they return home, the theory of separation anxiety requires some modification. One suggested explanation is that the child has ambivalent feelings toward the mother; he both desires and objects to a close dependency relationship. The attack may be interpreted as both a cry for help and a procedure for alarming and thus punishing the mother. Favored treatment consists of medical care for allergies combined with psychotherapy for the child and his parents.

The psychological reaction of children to physical illness represents the other side of the psychophysiological coin. Young children take health for granted. They do not understand sickness and are frightened by it. Preschool children often misinterpret illness as punishment for misdeeds— an idea not altogether unknown among adults. This animistic belief is reinforced by seeing the distraught expressions of the parents, feeling pain, being jabbed with a huge needle, being subjected to the indignity of an enema, and finally being deserted and banished to a hospital. For the older child, surgery may be a nameless terror. To the threat of loss of control and possible death through drugs and anesthesia is added the fear of body mutilation and change. Acutely ill children tend to be irritable, restless, or listless, to refuse food, and to be troubled by nightmares. Some form of regression is usually noted, particularly if the illness persists for several days or weeks. In young children this may be expressed in clinging behavior, the reappearance of thumb-sucking, and the transient loss of speech, walking ability, and bowel control. Older children may show increased dependency, egocentricity, and critical demanding behavior. Parents tend to encourage regression by babying sick children. The relation of psychosomatic concepts to illness in children has been examined in greater detail by Prugh (1963).

BRAIN SYNDROMES

A distinction is made between symptoms directly related to brain function and associated behavior disturbances. The former, which tend to be related to degree of organic damage, include instability of affect and impairment of perceptual-motor learning, memory, and related cognitive functions (Grassi, 1968; Hall and La Driere, 1969). Associated behavior dysfunctions are independent of degree of actual brain damage. Severe personality and conduct disturbances may be exhibited by children with relatively minor brain damage. Conversely, children with gross brain damage may show surprisingly little behavior disturbance other than impairments directly related to damaged brain tissue. Associated behavior disturbances, which may consist of any of the symptoms included in the GAP list, are precipitated by brain disorders or are by-products of brain damage, but are not direct and inevitable results of brain disorder. Choice of symptoms is primarily determined by predisposing personality patterns, the nature of current conflicts, the child's level of development, and interactions within the family. The main conclusion that can be drawn from experimental studies of brain-damaged children is that symptoms and test findings are inconsistent and vary markedly from child to child (Kessler, 1966). The concept of brain disorders is not a distinct, clearly defined clinical entity.

Acute brain syndromes are differentiated from chronic brain syndromes in children, as they are in adults. Reactions associated with acute brain disorders are transient and recovery is generally good. The symptoms, which commonly include delirium, wild agitation, confusion, and hallucinatory experiences, are caused by infections, metabolic disturbances, and intoxication due to alcohol, drugs, or poison. Chronic brain syndromes are relatively permanent and irreversible. The usual symptoms are those previously described as directly related to brain dysfunction. Some major

Psychopathology

causes are birth injury, cerebral palsy, and intracranial tumor. Diffuse cortical damage resulting from birth injuries frequently results in hyperactivity, distractability, impulsiveness, and learning difficulties. After the acute phase of encephalitis, more commonly known as sleeping sickness, children often show marked personality changes. Some encephalitic children exhibit sociopathological behavior, such as lying, stealing, running away, sexual offenses, and cruelty. Unlike autistic children, most brain-damaged children relate adequately to other people. They may actually be too friendly and uninhibited, so that they ask personal questions of strangers and tell family secrets. By and large most brain-damaged children conform to social norms.

In recent years increased attention has been given to behavioral disturbances and disabilities that appear to be related to minimal or barely detectable deviations in structure or function of the central nervous system. The term "minimal brain syndrome" is generally applied to a wide variety of symptoms in children whose intelligence is about average or above average. The ten characteristics most often cited, as reported by Clements (1966), are listed below in order of frequency. These characteristics are most common in brain-injured children but may also occur as isolated symptoms in otherwise normal children and in disturbed children free of brain damage.

1. Hyperactivity.
2. Perceptual-motor impairment.
3. Emotional lability.
4. General coordination impairment.
5. Disorders of attention (short attention span, distractability, perseveration).
6. Impulsivity.
7. Disorders of memory and thinking.
8. Specific learning disabilities.
   (a) Reading.
   (b) Arithmetic.
   (c) Spelling.
9. Disorders of speech and hearing.
10. Equivocal neurological signs and electroencephalographic irregularities.

MENTAL RETARDATION

In 1961 the American Association on Mental Deficiency adopted the following operational definition: "Mental retardation refers to sub-average general intellectual functioning which originates in the developmental period and is associated with impairment in adaptive behavior." More specifically, mental retardation usually originates in infancy and early childhood. Equal emphasis is attached to "sub-average intellectual functioning" and "impairment in adaptive behavior." Mental retardates show a *general* deficiency in mental abilities, learning aptitude, sensory and motor development, capacity for self-care, social skills, and potential for earning their livings as adults. The justification for the traditional use of an IQ score below 70 as the main criterion of mental retardation is that intelligence is more or less correlated with other significant characteristics and is much the easiest to measure and express in quantitative terms. However, the AAMD recommends that both the quantitative measure (IQ score) and the social-adaptive behavior must be impaired before a diagnosis of mental retardation is made. The degrees of retardation recognized by the AAMD and their general characteristics are shown in Table 16.1.

Table 16.1   Levels of mental retardation

Degree of retardation	Characteristics
Mild	IQ: 55–69 Maximum educational potential: about sixth grade With training and supervision, capable of marginal self-support as adults Distribution: about 85% of total mental retardate population; about 2% of general population
Moderate	IQ: 40–54 Maximum educational potential: about second grade Can be trained in self-care and to do simple work in sheltered environment Distribution: about 10% of total mental retardate population
Severe	IQ: 25–39 Maximum educational, training, and self-care capability: roughly that of average 6-year-old Need close supervision Distribution: about 5% of total mental retardate population
Profound	IQ: 0–24 Maximum educational, training, and self-care capability: little or none Require custodial or nursing care Distribution: less than 1% of total mental retardate population

The Interpretation of Symptoms

The directness of disordered behavior in children simplifies the interpretation of their symptoms. Sensitive mothers realize that crying in healthy children, regressive behavior, and vague somatic aches and pains are signals for attention and loving care; that temper tantrums are precipitated by frustrations; and that defiance, elimination problems, and running away often represent protest. Parents are also aware that their anxieties, fears, and depressive moods create insecurities and affective disturbances in their children. Good parents endeavor to be calm, relaxed, united, and congenial when their children are present. Quarrels between husband and wife and discussion of serious problems are postponed until the children are asleep or absent. Complete harmony at all times, however, is an ideal that is seldom, if ever, attainable in reality, and attempts to pretend that it is are not likely to be successful. It is more helpful for a child to learn that love and mutual esteem can survive occasional discord than to be taught that perfect harmony is to be expected.

Psychoanalytic insights are frequently helpful in explaining the normality of age-pertinent traits and in accounting for developmental deviations (A. Freud, 1965). Fixation at or difficulties associated with the oral phase are often involved when children are demanding, clinging, or devouring in their relationships with others, are greedy and insatiable, or have unusual attitudes toward food and eating. Food refusal may be associated with distorted ideas of becoming pregnant. Obstinacy, indecisiveness, stinginess, rigidity, and destructiveness may be associated with anal trends. Reaction formation against former exhibitionistic tendencies associated with the phallic phase may account for extreme shyness and modesty. Underlying oedipal castration fears may lead to overcompensation expressed in exaggerated assertiveness and aggression. Undue concern for the health and safety of parents may indicate repressed death wishes. Resistance to going to bed at night in older children may be related to inner struggles against masturbation. In her balanced account of homosexuality, transvestism, and fetishism in children, Anna Freud (1965) stresses two main points: (1) these acts, when performed by preadolescents, do not have the same significance as they do in later years and should not be considered perversions; (2) the occurrence of these developmental deviations during childhood is not a reliable prognostic sign of future choice of sex object. In most instances the tendency toward maturity and "biological reasonableness" favors normal heterosexuality in adulthood. Favorable heterosexual experiences during adolescence or adulthood outweigh childhood conditionings and fixations. However, predisposed individuals may regress to earlier forms of erotic satisfaction if frustrations are encountered in heterosexual development during adolescence.

Family Interaction

The mothers of disturbed children have been traditionally described as overanxious, domineering, lacking in emotional warmth, controlling, covertly rejecting, and oversolicitous. The fathers have been described as either extremely overbearing and aggressive or impersonal, passive, and submissive. It is now realized that these stereotypes represent a gross over-simplification. The attitudes of parents toward their children are constantly changing (Brody, 1956). Of greater significance than the specific attitudes of parents is the interaction between the parents and the general atmo-sphere of the home. The same conclusion applies to the significance of specific child-training practices (Sewell et al., 1955). The greater the mal-adjustment of the parents, the greater the possibility that they may displace on their children their anxieties and hostilities (Mitchell, 1969).

Ackerman (1968) has presented a comprehensive account of the role of the family as a whole in the development and emergence of disordered behavior in children. His main conclusion is that behavior disturbances in children are expressions of the emotional warp of the entire family. Chil-dren absorb and reflect the "sick" qualities of their parents. The child is often the pawn of unresolved conflicts between the parents. The occur-rence of overt symptoms in the child is regularly preceded by family con-flicts. The entire family, then, should be treated as a unit. If only the child is treated, the continued presence of family problems will block his prog-ress. If the treated child should improve, a sibling may be substituted as the family problem. Ackerman has differentiated a variety of healthy and pathological family types, which are described in Table 16.2.

Two basic explanations have been suggested to account for the fact that one or more children reared by disturbed parents may be relatively unaf-fected: (1) the affected child may be more vulnerable because of genetic handicaps; (2) the unaffected child may refuse to become involved in con-flicts between his parents or may be rescued by favorable relationships with grandparents, relatives, or friends outside the family (Spiegel, 1957).

It is also possible that the attitude of parents toward a child may be a reaction to the child's personality and behavior; the differential responses of parents to their children may be due as much to individual differences in the children as to differential attitudes in the parents. Several investi-gators (Donnelly, 1960; Klebanoff, 1959) have noted that mothers are much more upset by and rejecting of their disturbed children than they are of their normal children. Practically all studies concerned with parent-child interactions as possible determinants of psychopathology have focused on parents whose children already manifest severe behavior disorders, and thus throw no light on the parents' attitudes before they recog-nized their need for help in coping with their disturbed children. It is quite possible that a mother may have been warm, loving, and accepting toward her child in the beginning, but after years of unsatisfactory expe-riences with a contrary, unresponsive, or otherwise difficult child may in

Table 16.2   Family Types

Family type	Characteristics
Healthy	Parents compatible, share realistic goals, cooperate in search for compromises to conflicts; show tolerance of differences based on mutual understanding and respect. Pleasure, responsibility, and authority are shared. Each shows appropriate concern for development and welfare of other family members as well as for self.
Immature-protective	Parents show need to relate to and depend on others.
Competitive	Intrafamilial relationships motivated by envy, jealousy, and competition.
Neurotic-complementary	Weaker partner depends on stronger partner for support. Children are expected to sacrifice specific parts of their identities in exchange for protection and acceptance.
Complementary-acting out	Unconscious complicity in family pattern of acting out of impulses and antisocial tendencies.
Detached and emotionally isolated	Family equilibrium dependent on members' maintaining required degree of emotional distance and isolation.
Master-slave	Husband or wife seeks omnipotent control of the other. Symbiotic relationship: master needs slave, slave needs master. Perversion of goals of love and sharing. Objective of master is to dominate, degrade, and ultimately destroy the partner.
Regressive	Negative orientation to life; shared expectation of imminent catastrophe that can be averted only by total sacrifice. Individual members must surrender rights to live and grow in order to assure survival of other members. This type of family frequently produces psychotic children.

Adapted from N. W. Ackerman, "The Role of the Family in the Emergence of Child Disorders," in *Foundations of Child Psychiatry,* ed. E. Miller (New York: Pergamon Press, 1968), pp. 509–33.

self-defense have become more impersonal in her reactions. Children can contribute to the maladjustment of their parents as well as the reverse. When the harassed mother complains that her child "drives her nuts," she may be speaking literally.

Outcome of Therapy

In a review of studies published up to 1957 on the efficacy of psychotherapy with children, Levitt reported an overall improvement of 67 percent at close of therapy and 78 percent following an average follow-up interval of five years. Approximately the same percentage of improvement was found in groups of untreated children. The results of a more recent survey (Levitt, 1963), in which an attempt was made to report outcome for specific types of disorders, are given in Table 16.3. The overall findings were similar to those in earlier reports: 65 percent of the total group showed improvement. Children classified as presenting special symptoms showed the most favorable outcome, acting-out children the poorest. Interestingly, the outcome for psychosis was slightly more favorable than for neurosis. Once again the figures showed no more favorable outcome for treated than for nontreated children. Types of treatment given the children covered a broad range: behavior modification techniques, environmental manipulation, nondirective counseling of children, counseling of parents, and the use of adjunctive drugs.

Table 16.3   Summary of data from 24 studies on efficacy of therapy in childhood behavior disorders

Type of disorder	Number of studies	Number of cases	Total % improved
Neurosis	3	230	61%
Acting-out behavior	5	349	55
Special symptoms	5	213	77
Psychosis	5	252	65
Mixed	6	697	68
TOTAL	24	1,741	65

Adapted from E. E. Levitt, "Psychotherapy with Children: A Further Evaluation," *Behavior Research and Therapy,* 1 (1963): 45–51.

Discouraging results have also been reported in three studies of treatment programs aimed at the prevention or curtailment of delinquency in high-risk children in adolescence (Powers and Witmer, 1951; Tait and Hodges, 1962; Meyer, Borgatta, and Jones, 1965). In all three studies no significant differences were noted in the subsequent delinquent behavior of treated adolescents and nontreated control groups.

More favorable results have been obtained in the treatment of isolated symptoms. High success rates have been consistently found in the treatment of enuresis by the use of conditioning procedures (De Leon and Mandell, 1966; Baker, 1969). The single-signal system, originally developed by Mowrer and Mowrer (1938), consists of placing an electric pad under the bed sheet so that a bell rings at the first sign of bed-wetting. This serves to wake the child in time to go to the bathroom. A more elaborate double-signal system has been developed by Lovibond (1963). Apart from waking the child, the conditioning procedure is helpful in establishing sphincter control so that the child can sleep through the night without wetting. If relapses occur, they are readily corrected by resuming treatment.

Good results have also been reported in the treatment of school phobias with a variety of techniques (Kennedy, 1965; Berecz, 1968). The secret is apparently to restore school attendance promptly. Lovaas and his associates (1967) have shown that imitative procedures, when combined with the use of food as a reinforcing agent for "correct" response, are effective in the development of complex and socially useful behaviors in schizophrenic children.

A thirty-year follow-up study of children seen in a child guidance clinic found that antisocial behavior in childhood is not predictive of any specific kind of deviance in later years; antisocial children grow up to exhibit all kinds of deviant behavior (Robins, 1966). Compared with the normal control group, the antisocial children had more marital difficulties in later years, were more often imprisoned, had poorer occupational histories, and showed a higher degree of economic and social impoverishment. Former patients of the child guidance clinic were diagnosed as sociopathic personalities significantly more often than control subjects, and more frequently required treatment for alcoholism, schizophrenia, hysteria, and chronic brain syndrome. No differences were noted between the two groups in the frequency of manic-depressive psychosis or of anxiety neurosis. Fifty-two percent of the control subjects were free of psychiatric illness throughout their adult lives, as compared with only 20 percent of the clinic-referred children. Children referred to the clinic with few symptoms fared no worse than the control subjects, but there was a positive correlation between the severity of antisocial behavior during childhood and the severity of adult maladjustment.

Summary

The criteria of psychopathology in children are the same as for adults. Behavior is considered indicative of abnormality to the extent that it constitutes a source of undue liability, disturbance, or threat to the individual, his family, or society. Abnormal behavior in adults is characterized by loss of self-control and by psychosocial functioning that is sufficiently impaired to be considered inadequate, inappropriate, and maladaptive. In the case of children, greater emphasis is placed on failure to attain age-appropriate levels of adequate psychosocial functioning. In other words, the stress is on developmental defects rather than on the impairment of previously acquired proficiency. Further, the inability of parents or teachers to control the child's behavior is given greater weight than the child's loss of voluntary control.

The kinds of disorders observed in children parallel those noted in adults. They include the familiar categories: transient situational reactions, neuroses, psychoses, maladaptive personality types, psychosomatic reactions, organic brain disorders, and mental retardation. The clinical manifestations of these disorders are different in children than in adults, however. In general, children's symptoms tend to be more fluid and changeable than adults'. Infantile autism appears to be a unique disorder limited to children. The causes of childhood psychopathology, like those of behavior disorders in adults, are multiple, cumulative, and interactive.

References

ACKERMAN, N. W. "The Role of the Family in the Emergence of Child Disorders." In *Foundations of Child Psychiatry,* ed. E. Miller, pp. 509–33. New York: Pergamon Press, 1968.

AMERICAN ASSOCIATION ON MENTAL DEFICIENCY. *A Manual on Terminology and Classification.* Willimantic, Conn., 1961.

BAKER, B. L. "Symptom Treatment and Symptom Substitution in Enuresis." *Journal of Abnormal Psychology* 74 (1969): 42–49.

BENDER, L. "The Brain and Child Behavior." *Archives of General Psychiatry* 4 (1961): pp. 531–48.

BERECZ, J. M. "Phobias of Childhood: Etiology and Treatment." *Psychological Bulletin* 70 (1968): 694–720.

BERES, D., and OBERS, S. J. "The Effects of Extreme Deprivation in Infancy on Psychic Structure in Adolescence." In *Psychoanalytic Study of the Child,* vol. 5, pp. 212–35. New York: International Universities Press, 1950.

BETTELHEIM, B. *Love Is Not Enough.* New York: Free Press, 1950.

———. "Joey: A Mechanical Boy." *Scientific American,* March, 1959, pp. 3–9.

BRODY, S. *Patterns of Mothering.* New York: International Universities Press, 1956.

CLEMENTS, S. E. *Minimal Brain Dysfunction in Children.* Public Health Service publication no. 1415. Washington, D.C.: U.S. Government Printing Office, 1966.

COMMITTEE ON CHILD PSYCHIATRY. *Psychopathological Disorders in Childhood: Theoretical Considerations and a Proposed Classification.* Report no. 62, vol. 6. New York: Group for the Advancement of Psychiatry, 1966.

DE LEON, G., and MANDELL, W. "A Comparison of Conditioning and Psychotherapy in the Treatment of Functional Enuresis." *Journal of Clinical Psychology* 22 (1966): 326–30.

DONNELLY, E. M. "The Quantitative Analysis of Parental Behavior Toward Psychotic Children and Their Siblings." *Genetic Psychological Monographs* 62 (1960): 331–76.

EISENBERG, L., and KANNER, L. "Early Infantile Autism, 1943–55." *American Journal of Orthopsychiatry* 26 (1956): 556–66.

FERSTER, C. B., and SIMMONS, J. "Behavior Therapy with Children." *Psychological Record* 16 (1966): 65–71.

FINCH, S. M. "Psychophysiological Disorders." In *Comprehensive Textbook of Psychiatry,* ed. A. M. Freedman, H. I. Kaplan, and H. S. Kaplan, pp. 1409–10. Baltimore: Williams & Wilkins, 1967.

FREUD, A. *Normality and Pathology in Childhood.* New York: International Universities Press, 1965.

GRASSI, J. R. "Performance and Reminiscence of Brain-Damaged, Behavior-Disordered, and Normal Children on Four Psychomotor and Perceptual Tests." *Journal of Abnormal Psychology* 73 (1968): 492–99.

HALL, L. P., and LA DRIERE, L. "Patterns of Performance on WISC Similarities in Emotionally Disturbed and Brain-Damaged Children." *Journal of Consulting and Clinical Psychology* 33 (1969): 357–64.

KALLMANN, F. J., and ROTH, B. "Genetic Aspects of Pre-adolescent Schizophrenia." *American Journal of Psychiatry* 112 (1956): 599–606.

KANNER, L. "Autistic Disturbances of Affective Contact." *Nervous Children* 2 (1943): 217–50.

KENNEDY, W. A. "School Phobia: Rapid Treatment of 50 Cases." *Journal of Abnormal Psychology* 70 (1965): 285–89.

KESSLER, J. W. *Psychopathology of Childhood.* Englewood Cliffs, N.J.: Prentice-Hall, 1966.

KLEBANOFF, L. B. "Parental Attitudes of Mothers of Schizophrenic, Brain-Injured, and Retarded and Normal Children." *American Journal of Orthopsychiatry* 29 (1959): 445–54.

LEVINE, M., and OLSON, R. P. "Intelligence of Parents of Autistic Children." *Journal of Abnormal Psychology* 73 (1968): 215–17.

LEVITT, E. E. "The Results of Psychotherapy with Children: An Evaluation." *Journal of Consulting Psychology* 21 (1957): 189–96.

———. "Psychotherapy with Children: A Further Evaluation." *Behavior Research and Therapy* 1 (1963): 45–51.

LOVAAS, O. I.; FREITAS, L.; NELSON, K.; and WHALEN, C. "The Establishment of Imitation and Its Use for the Development of Complex Behavior in Schizophrenic Children." *Behavior Research and Therapy* 5 (1967): 171–81.

LOVIBOND, S. H. "Intermittent Reinforcement in Behavior Therapy." *Behavior Research and Therapy* 1 (1963): 127–32.

MAHLER, M. S. "On Child Psychosis and Schizophrenia." In *The Psychoanalytic Study of the Child,* vol. 7, pp. 286–305. New York: International Universities Press, 1952.

METZ, J. R. "Conditioning Generalized Imitation in Autistic Children." *Journal of Experimental Child Psychology* 2 (1965): 389–99.

MEYER, H. J.; BORGATTA, E. F.; and JONES, W. C. *Girls at Vocational High: An Experiment in Social Work Intervention.* New York: Russell Sage Foundation, 1965.

MITCHELL, K. M. "Concept of 'Pathogenesis' in Parents of Schizophrenic and Normal Children." *Journal of Abnormal Psychology* 74 (1969): 423–24.

MOWRER, O. H., and MOWRER, W. M. "Enuresis: A Method for Its Study and Treatment." *American Journal of Orthopsychiatry* 8 (1938): 436–59.

O'GORMAN, G. *The Nature of Childhood Autism.* London: Butterworth, 1967.

ORNITZ, E., and RITVO, E. R. "Perceptual Inconstancy in Early Infantile Autism." *Archives of General Psychiatry* 18 (1968): 76–98.

PINNEAU, S. R. "The Infantile Disorders of Hospitalism and Anaclitic Depression." *Psychological Bulletin* 52 (1955): 429–52.

POWERS, E., and WITMER, H. *An Experiment in the Prevention of Delinquency: The Cambridge-Somerville Youth Study.* New York: Columbia University Press, 1951.

PRUGH, D. G. "Toward an Understanding of Psychosomatic Concepts in Relation to Illness in Children." In *Modern Perspectives in Child Development,* ed. A. J. Solnit and S. A. Provence. New York: International Universities Press, 1963.

REXFORD, E. N. "Some Meanings of Aggressive Behavior in Children." *Annals of the American Academy of Political and Social Science,* March 1959, pp. 10–18.

RIESER, D. E. "Psychosis of Infancy and Early Childhood as Manifested by Children with Atypical Development." *New England Journal of Medicine,* 1963, pp. 790–98.

RIMLAND, B. *Infantile Autism.* New York: Appleton-Century-Crofts, 1964.

ROBINS, L. N. *Deviant Children Grown Up.* Baltimore: Williams & Wilkins, 1966.

RUTTER, M.; GREENFELD, D.; and LOCKYER, L. "A Five- to Fifteen-Year Follow-up of Infantile Psychosis: II. Social and Behavioural Outcome." *British Journal of Psychiatry* 113 (1967): 1183–99.

SCHNEER, H., ed. *The Asthmatic Child.* New York: Harper & Row, 1963.

SEWELL, W. H.; MUSSEN, P. H.; and HARRIS, C. W. "Relationships Among Child-Training Practices." *American Sociological Review* 20 (1955): 137–48.

SOROSKY, A. D.; ORNITZ, E. M.; BROWN, M. B.; and RITVO, E. R. "Systematic Observations of Autistic Behavior." *Archives of General Psychiatry* 18 (1968): 439–49.

SPIEGEL, J. P. "The Resolution of Role Conflict Within the Family." *Psychiatry* 20 (1957): 1–16.

SPITZ, R. A. "Hospitalism." In *The Psychoanalytic Study of the Child,* vol. 1, pp. 53–74. New York: International Universities Press, 1945.

———. "Anaclitic Depression." In *The Psychoanalytic Study of the Child,* vol. 2, pp. 313–42. New York: International Universities Press, 1946.

TAIT, C. W., and HODGES, E. F. *Delinquents, Their Families, and the Community.* Springfield, Ill.: Charles C Thomas, 1962.

TOOLAN, W. M. "Depression in Children and Adolescents." *American Journal of Orthopsychiatry* 32 (1962): 404–15.

ULLMANN, L. P., and KRASNER, L. *A Psychological Approach to Abnormal Behavior.* Englewood Cliffs, N.J.: Prentice-Hall, 1969.

CHAPTER SEVENTEEN

Social Deviance and Community Mental Health

The recent acceleration of social and political change has been accompanied by a sharp increase in deviant behavior. In the United States, as in other countries, established authority and the status quo are being challenged not only by underprivileged minority groups but also by middle-class youth and college students. Increased delinquency and crime, protest marches, the hippie movement, draft evasion, the widespread use of drugs, riots, burnings, bombings, the killing of police and public officials, kidnapping, the hijacking of planes—all these acts of passive and active aggression have been interpreted as symptoms of a "sick" society. Some of the more extreme rebels believe that the "sickness" is so pervasive and hopeless that the only recourse is to destroy the present society and build a new one according to a different plan or no plan at all, trusting to the old myth that man is inherently "good" and only institutions are evil. In today's theology the devil has been replaced by another fallen angel, the Establishment.

What is the relationship of the social deviance of protest to psychopathology? The majority opinion of psychopathologists is that mental disorders are restricted to individuals; it is meaningless to refer to a total society as neurotic, psychotic, or sociopathic. Furthermore, there is no conclusive evidence that the total incidence of psychopathology varies significantly from one society to the next. Permissive and repressive, benevolent and tyrannical, simple and complex cultures may favor the development of certain types of symptomatic reactions; but in all societies the proportion of individuals who are unable to cope effectively and appropriately with the inevitable problems of human existence will be about the same. Effective adaptation is essentially a function of individual mental set. In general, the least adaptive 10 percent of the population are assigned some label equivalent to the concept of mental disorder in our society.

This does not mean that the society has no effect on human adjustment. The amount of stress, frustration, deprivation, insecurity, and conflict generated by a society may very well influence the relative severity and duration of disordered functioning as well as the relative predominance of certain types of symptoms. During the past fifty years there has been a marked moderation of symptomatology among mental patients in the United States. Persons admitted to mental hospitals are increasingly being diagnosed as neurotic or victims of some mild personality disorder rather than psychotic. The extreme disorganization of personality and the bizarre reactions formerly prevalent among psychotic patients are rarely seen today. The present more hopeful outlook for the rehabilitation of psychologically disturbed persons is partly due to improvements in therapeutic techniques, but the reduction in the severity of disturbances may also be a major factor.

Most psychopathologists do not consider that the acts of terrorism and violence of some social rebels are in themselves indicative of psychopathology. Acts of social protest are quite different from the behavior of the mentally disturbed in a number of significant ways. One important distinction is the matter of purpose or goal. The antisocial or aggressive behavior of the mentally disturbed is usually an expression of some personal grievance or the acting out of a delusion or hallucination; the acts of violence of social rebels represent attempts to speed up or control the direction of some "corrective" social change. The goal is usually stated in altruistic terms. Nearly always there is some factual basis for the protest, which is recognized by the larger society. Frequently the public is in general agreement that some social change is desirable and supports the movement toward the correction of inequities so long as it proceeds in an orderly fashion within legally recognized boundaries. As a rule, the deviance lies in the method rather than the goal. Pathological behavior is not motivated by any laudable end. No society or minority subgroup advocates social changes that they recognize would result in an increase in the prevalence or political power of neurotics, psychotics, sociopaths, mental defectives, chronic alcoholics, or users of harmful drugs.

Acts of violence committed by social rebels fail to meet either the legal rules of insanity or the recognized criteria of psychopathology. Social activists know the nature and quality of their destructive, hostile actions and are capable of distinguishing right from wrong. They show neither impairment of psychosocial abilities nor loss of voluntary control. Their offenses are premeditated, deliberate, and executed according to plan. Time, place, and target are carefully selected for maximum results. No guilt is experienced because the individual is convinced of the righteousness of his cause. The destruction of property and life, along with the risk to self, are rationalized and discounted as sacrifices that must be made to produce a "better" society.

The reaction of society to social and political nonconformists depends on the evaluation made of the deviant behavior by the great majority of the population or the governing body. More often than not, any change in the status quo is resisted on the principle that the familiar is preferable to the unknown. As a rule, harmless forms of deviance are ridiculed but tolerated. When deviants engage in overt acts that violate established mores or which pose real or imagined threats to the safety and welfare of the group, the usual societal reaction is to remove the deviants. Formerly they were exiled or executed. Today they are imprisoned. There are two recognized legal grounds for the compulsory incarceration of "troublesome" and "dangerous" persons: mental illness and criminal behavior. Neither is directly applicable to acts of protest committed by social activists, but since their imprisonment rests on court action by which they have been found guilty of the actual violation of existing laws, their behavior may at least technically be considered criminal. The morality of treating social dissidents as ordinary criminals is another matter. Yet the alternative of committing them to institutions for the mentally ill is the greater of the two evils. To be labeled and treated indefinitely as a mental patient is far worse than to be temporarily imprisoned as a martyr or hero for fighting for one's ideals.

As a behavior science, psychopathology is not directly concerned with the values and ethics of social change except insofar as changes may improve the mental health of the total population. The present state of knowledge does not permit confident prediction. There is, however, a good probability that the severity and possibly the prevalence of human anguish might be materially reduced by the following measures:

1. *The recognition that no single human problem takes precedence over the creation of a more humane society in which every person is accepted as a fellow human being and treated with respect.* Not only should allowances be made for individual differences, but diversity should be regarded as an asset contributing to the enrichment of the group rather than a liability to be abolished. Practices that systematically lead to mistrust, disparagement, brutal competition, loss of self-esteem, social alienation, and loneliness must not be tolerated. The human need for close interpersonal relatedness is reflected in the growing interest in communes—a movement

to be followed with interest, although it must be acknowledged that historically the only communes that have achieved noted success have been based on strong ideologies that effectively separate the in-group from the out-group, thus defeating the purpose of brotherhood in the society at large. There are no easy answers, and there are no answers at all unless we ask the right questions.

2. *The reduction of stresses associated with war, economic depression, mass relocation of populations, and political unrest.* The actual or threatened loss of life, identity, income, family, and security brought about by these social ills are major sources of needless suffering and mental torment.

3. *Improvement of medical and physical care.* The sector of the population in greatest need of medical services is the poor, but all classes would benefit from improved prenatal care, avoidance of birth injuries, adequate diet, prompt and effective treatment of disabling diseases, improved housing, and all the other factors that increase physical and mental well-being.

4. *The elimination of discriminatory practices that deny equal social and economic opportunity to women and to members of minority groups.* Depriving individuals of opportunity for maximum personal growth and self-actualization leads to frustration, resentment, hostility, apathy, despair, and feelings of unworthiness.

5. *The improvement of the family unit.* In one way or another, the family is the major factor in mental health. Genetic data make clear the importance of discretion in the selection of a mate if one wishes to decrease the risk of psychopathology in the family. When both husband and wife have family histories of psychosis, they would be well advised to refrain from having children. Most couples who want children should experience little difficulty in adopting some whose biological parents and grandparents are known to have been free of severe mental disorders. Too many individuals who have little interest in marriage or aptitude for child rearing nevertheless marry and have children in response to social pressure. The frequent results are divorce and psychologically scarred children. The present concern with the population explosion may serve to deglamorize large families, but some specific program will be required to discourage high-risk persons from having any children at all.

6. *The establishment of comprehensive mental health services in the community.* Some progress in this area has already been made, as we shall see in a moment. There are two main advantages in locating mental health centers in the community. One is the increased accessibility of services to those who need them. Particularly in disadvantaged communities composed largely of minority groups, residents are more willing to attend neighborhood centers than to visit distant, strange facilities. The proximity factor also facilitates prompt intervention in crises. A second major ad-

vantage is that each community can tailor its services to particular local needs. The recently established community centers differ from the traditional outpatient clinics in that they offer services for a wide variety of problems, many of which are only remotely related to the traditional concepts of mental disorder.

Community Mental Health

The idea of providing comprehensive mental health services in the community is an outgrowth of recommendations made by the Joint Commission on Mental Illness and Mental Health. The commission was authorized by Congress in 1955 to conduct a study of the mental health of the nation and to present its recommendations to federal and state officials. One of the recommendations of the commission's 1961 report, *Action for Mental Health,* was the establishment of community mental health centers to serve both children and adults as part of state or regional systems for the care of mental patients in the community. New York State was the first to enact legislation providing for the creation of community centers, with its Community Mental Health Services Act of 1954. In 1963 Congress passed the Community Mental Health Centers Act. This and subsequent supporting legislation have provided financial aid to states, on a participation basis, for the building and staffing of community centers serving designated catchment areas. A similar program was established in Great Britain by Parliament's passage of the Mental Health Act of 1959.

Federal funding has facilitated the rapid growth of the community mental health movement. By 1968 more than three hundred centers had been established in the United States. Most are attached to established general or psychiatric hospitals and serve the surrounding community. In large cities geographical boundaries have been drawn demarcating the catchment areas or populations served by specific centers. The general objective is to mobilize and utilize the resources of the community for the treatment and prevention of mental disorders and other forms of deviance and impairment in psychosocial functioning. Toward this end, the active participation of local residents and organizations is sought in establishing policies and in developing services desired or needed to meet the particular mental health needs of the local community. Attention is given to strengthening positive factors as well as eliminating sources of stress in the social environment. Community involvement represents a significant change from the authoritative doctor-patient relationship; members of the professional staff are agents of or advisers to the local residents, who are perceived as clients. The historical background of the recurring interest in the community approach to psychopathology has been reviewed by Ewalt and Ewalt (1969) and R. B. Caplan (1969). Its general objectives and principles have been outlined by Smith and Hobbs (1966), Roberts et al. (1966), and Klein (1968). Susser (1968) has reviewed and analyzed community mental health care in Britain.

COMMUNITY SERVICES AND PROGRAMS

By law, centers receiving federal assistance in the United States are required to provide inpatient and outpatient services, partial hospitalization services (day care, night care, or weekend care), emergency services, and consultation services to the community. In addition, community centers have experimented with a wide variety of other approaches: home visits, family therapy, special education programs for young children, delinquency prevention, work with drug users, vocational and social rehabilitation of patients discharged from mental hospitals, walk-in clinics, and training programs in leadership and self-government for residents of catchment areas. Staff personnel may serve as consultants to schools, church groups, police, and other social agencies. Shore and Mannino (1969) have described a variety of strategies designed to translate community mental health ideas into action programs. Recent issues of the *Community Mental Health Journal* and *Mental Hygiene* contain a number of articles giving detailed accounts of new programs.

Services for children. Innovative procedures for the treatment and prevention of emotional problems in children have been described by several investigators. Hobbs (1968) has reported a program for the reeducation of emotionally disturbed children in residential schools located in the community. The schools, staffed entirely by teacher-counselors who are backed by consultants in the fields of pediatrics, psychiatry, psychology, and education, provide intensive short-term treatment that permit the child to be separated from his family and regular community for as brief a time as possible. The central aim is to help children acquire competence in coping with relevant day-to-day problems. Insofar as possible, practical improvements are also made in the child's home, school, and neighborhood. In effect, the goal is to modify the child's behavior so that his family, school, and community will tolerate his presence. Cure is considered a meaningless concept. One finding of this study is that human behavior is remarkably responsive to expectations. Goals and procedures are couched in the idiom of competence and self-fulfillment.

Hunt (1968) has substituted the concept of incompetence for mental disease. The objective of therapy is thus to increase the child's competence level. This can best be done by providing a stimulating problem-solving environment during infancy and early childhood. Research studies suggest that children of parents from lower-class backgrounds receive inadequate training in the motivation habits, symbolic skills, and social standards that underlie competence. Lower-class parents tend to be relatively uncommunicative with their children, do not encourage them to be curious about the world about them, and do not give reasons for their actions. A good child in the lower-class family is a quiet, passive child who shows little initiative and curiosity and does not disturb the activities of adults. Motivation is modeled on immediate gratification rather than acceptance of relative privation now for the sake of more substantial rewards later. Hunt mentions the familiar projects of Head Start and Get Set, but is more interested in the establishment of nursery centers for children and parents in which the mothers can observe what teachers are doing and can apply the same procedures in the home to stimulate the child's learning and to extend his competence.

Cowen and Zax (1968) have described a variety of programs concerned with the early detection and prevention of emotional disturbances in schoolchildren. They have been interested in assessing the effectiveness of mothers, retired persons, and college students as teaching assistants in schools, so that children may have more individual attention. Persons such as these who are oriented toward the emotional and educational needs of disturbed children appear to be effective in improving the subsequent adjustment and achievement of children who in earlier grades were tagged as potential problems.

Aftercare of hospitalized patients. Mental hospitals in this country are currently making a concerted effort to decrease the number of chronic resident patients. From 1965 to 1969 the resident population of mental hospitals decreased 23 percent. Nine states have reported a decrease of 40 percent or more (Mental Health Statistics, 1970). The large number of patients annually discharged back to the community has necessitated the expansion of local facilities and programs for the care and rehabilitation of patients with residual defects. The availability of drugs for moderating overt symptoms has made community care feasible, but supplementary programs are needed to enable former resident patients to continue to live outside of the hospital setting. Community aftercare facilities include day-care centers, day or night hospitals, halfway houses, foster homes, social clubs for formerly hospitalized patients, and sheltered workshops. These aftercare facilities serve three main functions:

1. They relieve families of the continuous burden of caring for patients by providing places where they may spend several hours each day.

2. By providing guided social experiences, they help patients to learn or relearn social skills (Weinman et al., 1970).

3. They offer assistance in vocational counseling and training and job

placement (Koltuv and Neff, 1968). For patients with irreversible residual defects, sheltered workshops offer the possibility of partial self-support in surroundings adapted to their needs.

Services for Skid Row residents. Many large cities have areas where social derelicts gather. Many of these homeless men are alcoholics, but 15 to 20 percent of them are nondrinkers who have sought refuge from joblessness and social pressures in the impersonal environment of Skid Row. Surveys conducted by Bloomberg et al. (1966), Plaut (1967), and others reveal that most Skid Row residents are middle-aged or elderly men without effective family or friendship ties. A large number of them have never married. Well-educated and married men who go on occasional benders can be found there, but the vast majority of these are transients who sooner or later return to their jobs and families. Most long-term residents are unskilled. For these men, many of whom are chronic alcoholics or former schizophrenics, Skid Row provides a community where living costs are low and missions make up the difference between the cost of bare survival and a minimal income. Skid Row serves as a labor market where employers seek day laborers. Many of the men living in these areas have never been arrested for public drunkenness. Some are regularly employed. Skid Row men are usually not found in alcoholic wards or in mental hospitals. Attempts to abolish Skid Row communities by relocating the residents has proved to be a difficult task. Most of the men are opposed to relocation. Many of them suffer from chronic physical illnesses as well as psychosocial problems. These homeless men need a wide variety of services, especially medical care, vocational training or placement, psychological or social assistance, and inexpensive lodgings. For some a protective facility of some type, such as a halfway house or a domiciliary institution, is necessary. Skid Row serves as a good illustration of the reinforcing interaction between the individual and his social environment. Each needs and sustains the other. Intervention is required to break up the dyadic relationship.

ORIENTATION AND MODELS

The traditional medical model of disease is deemphasized in community mental health work. Little attention is paid to intrapsychic or childhood causes of problems. The focus is on the difficulties confronting the individual here and now, and the ways in which he may best be helped to cope with his difficulties so that functioning competence may be quickly restored. Rehabilitation rather than cure is the goal. Prevention is given higher priority than treatment. No satisfactory substitute for the disease model has yet been developed. Community mental health work has a mainly educational orientation: it is directed toward the acquisition of skills and attitudes that contribute to increased self-direction, competence, and self-confidence. It is more concerned with solving problems than with gaining insights.

Kelly (1968) has noted some analogies between community mental health programs and the biological concept of ecology, which is concerned with the relationship of organisms or groups of organisms with their environment. One of the basic principles of ecology is that intervention anywhere in a biological system alters the total organization. Social systems too are affected by changes in any of their parts, and the ultimate effects of intervention are difficult to predict. Social environments, like biological environments, also affect styles of adaptation. Certain types of environment may require particular kinds of changes in adaptative behavior.

A third model, which has greater potential application, is the public health movement. The main thrust of public health is toward prevention (Bloom, 1965). The great success of public health measures in improving physical health has little to do with the traditional medical approach of early detection and prompt treatment. Early identification and treatment may shorten the duration of illness and thereby reduce the prevalence rate, but this approach has no effect on the number of new cases or the incidence rate. The efforts of public health officials have been more profitably focused on the elimination of the causes of disease. Impressive victories have been won against disease through improvement in sanitation, the purification of water, mass inoculations, the destruction of disease-spreading insects, and educational programs.

The application of the public health model of prevention to community mental health has been discussed by G. Caplan (1964) and others. *Primary prevention* consists of corrective measures that prevent the occurrence of a disorder or decrease a person's risk of developing it. Community mental health organizations emphasize primary prevention in prenatal programs aimed at the avoidance of premature birth and prenatal disturbances that may lead to brain damage, well-baby clinics, preschool programs, and local facilities to handle social crises. Prompt, effective counseling of persons in stress situations often makes the difference between personal growth and prolonged maladjustment. Marriage counseling, family services, legal aid societies, suicide-prevention centers—all these serve to aid persons in moments of crisis.

Secondary prevention is aimed at reducing the prevalence rate of psychosocial disorders by shortening the duration of disability. The realization of this objective depends on early detection and prompt, effective treatment. Early signs of impending disturbances usually are noted by teachers, policemen, clergymen, or physicians. Community centers may utilize these sources of referral by working closely with the schools, churches, police departments, and family agencies. Many agencies offer basic courses for neighborhood groups on the means of detecting mental disturbances and the procedures to follow in dealing with them and obtaining professional help for people who may need it. The facilities of the centers may be used for treatment, or patients may be referred to other agencies. Walk-in clinics and store-front facilities that offer immediate consultation may be helpful in shortening the duration of disorders.

Tertiary prevention is the reduction of residual defects that often persist long after a mental disorder has ended. The goal is the effective rehabilitation of the mentally disordered person and his return to maximum productivity as quickly as possible. Ideally, plans for rehabilitation should start with the onset of the disorder. Mental health workers should try to anticipate the effect of the disorder on the patient's subsequent productivity, the possible need for a new job, the extent to which the disorder may result in a disruption of functioning, and the reactions of others. Every effort should be made to avoid committing a patient to a mental hospital in order to avert the risks of desocialization and the difficulties that confront the patient when he returns to the community. A common problem of discharged mental patients is that there is no place for them to go. Their families may not be willing or able to accept them, and the stigma of having been committed to a mental hospital may interfere with their gaining employment. When hospitalization cannot be avoided, the availability of aftercare facilities often makes the difference between rehospitalization and successful readjustment to life in the community.

MENTAL HEALTH PERSONNEL

The professional staff of community centers consists largely of psychiatrists, psychologists, and social workers. Since the traditional professional training of these specialists is not particularly relevant to the types of services provided in community centers, the usual barriers between professions tend to break down and staff members work together on a more equal footing than they do in more traditional institutions. Much of the work with clients is actually done by people recruited from the community who have received on-the-job training. In addition to relieving the manpower shortage (Albee, 1959), community co-workers have proved highly effective in relating to clients (Reiff and Reissman, 1964). Clients tend to accept them more readily than they do the professionals, since they share many of the clients' own attitudes and expectations. Nonprofessionals engage in all forms of therapy, and their success rate is comparable to that of professionals. It is worth noting that a survey of a representative sample of the American population conducted by Gurin et al. (1960) indicated that only 18 percent of troubled persons consulted psychiatrists or psychologists;

the remainder sought the help of community advisers and agencies. More people in the latter group reported they were helped than those who visited professionally trained specialists.

MIDDLE-CLASS VERSUS LOWER-CLASS VALUES

The entry of mental health specialists into ghettos and slums has helped to bridge the communication gap between the middle and lower class. One interesting observation has been that the standard theories of psychopathology and psychotherapy, which have been mainly derived from the study of middle-class patients, have limited applicability to the poor. Middle-class patients tend to attribute their problems to some personal difficulty, for which psychotherapy provides a relevant approach. Lower-class patients are more inclined to attribute their problems to external hardships and defects in society. They therefore look for help in coping with environmental problems rather than in resolving inner conflicts. As Reiff has noted (1966), middle-class persons see themselves moving toward self-actualization. If they encounter difficulties, they seek help in removing personal obstacles that stand in the way of attaining a full, rich life. Low-income people, on the other hand, have little expectation that the future will be much better than the present. They live in a world of limited opportunities that afford little role flexibility. They are primarily concerned with the here and now. They have specific immediate objectives, and they seek concrete help in attaining them. For this group, self-determination is a more realistic and more meaningful goal than self-actualization.

A second interesting point has been the reappraisal of the tendency (often unconscious) of professionally trained persons to try to impose their standards and values on lower-class clients. If the poor were to accept the middle-class virtues of maximum education, planning for the future, postponement of gratification, and self-actualization, their economic status might be improved; but the assumption that the acceptance of these middle-class values would automatically improve the mental health of the poor is a myth. The middle class has its own hangups and mental disorders. It is significant that the revolution against contemporary society is spearheaded by middle-class youth. From the point of view of mental health, it is questionable whether the middle class's tendency to blame itself for failure is an improvement over the lower class's strategem of projecting blame onto society. If the poor produce more paranoids and sociopaths, the middle class has higher rates of neurosis and depression. In many ways the personal interdependence and sharing of the lower class represents a better solution to the vicissitudes of life than the independence, self-sufficiency, and loneliness of suburbia. The preference of the lower class for direct, immediate "remedies" to problems (a better job, a bigger apartment, a stronger pill) offers greater possibilities of shortening the duration of psychiatric disabilities than prolonged verbal therapies aimed at self-understanding. Psychotherapy has a poor record of success. The faulting of the poor for their greater concern with the immediate present than with the future reflects a lack of understanding of their pressing current needs and the bleakness of their future. Day-to-day survival takes precedence over long-term planning for self-actualization. Unless there is some assurance that the sacrifices of today will pay off in greater satisfactions tomorrow, there is little purpose in postponing pleasure. The middle class has tended to exaggerate the "sinfulness" of immediate gratification. There is nothing wrong with immediate gratification so long as it does not actually entail future penalties, and this is a matter more difficult to predict than many people like to think. Each age has its particular sources of pleasure, which can be fully appreciated only at that time. Old age is not the time to enjoy the postponed pleasures of youth.

EVALUATION

It is still too early to evaluate the significance of the community mental health movement. So far the main emphasis has been on exploring new avenues of approach. Research interests have tended to be subordinated to the immediate pressures of providing needed services. On the credit side, the movement represents a continuation of the humanistic approach initiated by Pinel. The focus on the prompt restoration of functioning in disturbed persons is in line with the premise that behavior disorders represent problems in living; there is no disease to cure. Another positive feature is the participation of representatives of various disciplines and of nonprofessionals as partners in the search for increasingly effective ways of preventing and treating psychosocial disabilities.

Summary

Acts of passive or active aggression committed by dissenters as means of speeding up or effecting social change represent a special form of social deviance that is independent of psychopathology and only technically related to criminal behavior. Social rebels are not mentally disturbed in terms of the legal rules of insanity or of the key criteria of psychopathology. The notion of a sick society is more a journalistic than a scientific concept. The available evidence indicates that the total incidence of psychopathology is about the same in all societies. However, the particular type of psychosocial disturbance and the relative severity of personality disorganization are probably related to the level of stress and the kinds of frustration encountered in a particular society. The major advantage of the current interest in community mental health is that it provides needed services for the poor, who have long been a neglected sector of the population. Acceptance of middle-class standards by the poor might improve their economic status, but whether it would improve their mental health is debatable. Psychosocial problems are not limited to the poor. By adopting the middle-class values, the poor would become susceptible to middle-class problems. "I've been rich and I've been poor," the old joke goes, "and believe me, rich is better." That may be, though the proposition is being questioned by an increasing number of people; but if it is, it does not necessarily follow that neurosis and depression are better than paranoid tendencies and sociopathy. (Nor, of course, are paranoid tendencies and sociopathy to be accepted and justified as "part of the system.") Direct attack on immediate problems, which is characteristic of the community mental health approach, offers the poor greater promise of therapeutic effectiveness than the traditional preoccupation with insight and the reconstruction of the personality. The value of the community mental health movement as a means of primary prevention remains a moot issue, but it is reasonable to take an optimistic view of its effectiveness in secondary and tertiary prevention.

References

ALBEE, G. W. *Mental Health Manpower Trends.* New York: Basic Books, 1959.

BLOOM, B. L. "The 'Medical Model' Miasma Theory and Community Mental Health." *Community Mental Health Journal* 1 (1965): 333–38.

BLOOMBERG, L.; SHIPLEY, T. E.; SHANDLER, I. W.; and NIEBUHR, H. "The Development, Major Goals, and Strategies of a Skid Row Program: Philadelphia." *Quarterly Journal of Studies on Alcohol* 27, no. 2 (1966): 242–58.

CAPLAN, G. *Principles of Preventive Psychiatry.* New York: Basic Books, 1964.

CAPLAN, R. B. *Psychiatry and the Community in Nineteenth-Century America.* New York: Basic Books, 1969.

COWEN, E. L., and ZAX, M. "Early Detection and Prevention of Emotional Disorder: Conceptualizations and Programming." In *Research Contributions from Psychology to Community Mental Health,* ed. J. W. Carter, pp. 46–59. New York: Behavioral Publications, 1968.

EWALT, J. R., and EWALT, P. L. "History of the Community Psychiatry Movement." *American Journal of Psychiatry* 126 (1969): 43–52.

GURIN, G. G.; VEROFF, J.; and FELD, S. *Americans View Their Mental Health.* New York: Basic Books, 1960.

HOBBS, N. "Reeducation, Reality, and Community Responsibility." In *Research Contributions from Psychology to Community Mental Health,* ed. J. W. Carter, pp. 7–18. New York: Behavioral Publications, 1968.

HUNT, J. McV. "Toward the Prevention of Incompetence." In ibid., pp. 19–45.

JOINT COMMISSION ON MENTAL ILLNESS AND MENTAL HEALTH. *Action for Mental Health.* New York: Basic Books, 1961.

KELLY, J. G. "Toward an Ecological Conception of Prevention Interchanges." In *Research Contributions from Psychology to Community Mental Health,* ed. J. W. Carter. New York: Behavioral Publications, 1968.

KLEIN, D. C. *Community Dynamics and Mental Health.* New York: Wiley, 1968.

KOLTUV, M., and NEFF, W. L. "The Comprehensive Rehabilitation Center: Its Role and Realm in Psychiatric Rehabilitation." *Community Mental Health Journal* 4 (1968): 251–59.

MENTAL HEALTH STATISTICS. *Provisional Patient Movement and Administration Data, State and County Mental Hospitals, United States, 1968–69.* Chevy Chase, Md.: National Institute of Mental Health, 1970.

PLAUT, T. F. A. *Alcohol Problems: A Report to the Nation by the Cooperative Commission on the Study of Alcoholism.* New York: Oxford University Press, 1967.

REIFF, R. "The Etiological and Technological Implications of Clinical Psychology." In *Community Psychology: A Report of the Boston Conference on the Education of Psychologists for Community Mental Health,* ed. C. C. Bennet et al., pp. 51–64. Boston: Boston University, 1966.

——— and REISSMAN, F. *The Indigenous Nonprofessional: A Strategy of Change in Community Action and Community Mental Health Programs.* National Institute of Labor Education report no. 3, November 1964.

ROBERTS, L. M.; HALLECK, S. L.; and LOEB, M. B. *Community Psychiatry.* Madison, Wis.: University of Wisconsin Press, 1966.

SHORE, M. F., and MANNINO, F. V., eds. *Mental Health and the Community: Problems, Programs, and Strategies.* New York: Behavioral Publications, 1969.

SMITH, M. B., and HOBBS, N. "The Community and the Community Mental Health Center." *American Psychologist* 21 (1966): 499–509.

SUSSER, M. *Community Psychiatry: Epidemiologic and Social Themes.* New York: Random House, 1968.

WEINMAN, B.; SANDERS, R.; KLEINER, R.; and STEPHEN, W. "Community-Based Treatment of the Chronic Psychotic." *Community Mental Health Journal* 6 (1970): 13–22.

Glossary

Abreaction. The release and venting of repressed emotions.

Acrophobia. Morbid fear of high places.

Acute alcoholic hallucinosis. A mental disorder of heavy drinkers, principally of those with schizoid traits, characterized by auditory hallucinations.

Acute brain disorders. Disturbances in psychosocial behavior caused by temporary and reversible impairment in brain tissue functioning. The patient returns to his usual level and mode of functioning in a few days or weeks.

Acute depression. A psychotic disorder marked by dejection so profound that the individual is completely absorbed and incapacitated by it.

Acute mania. A psychosis marked by extreme distractability, disorganized association of ideas, and increased inner pressure.

Acute schizophrenic episode. A psychotic reaction that is often associated with confusion, perplexity, ideas of reference, emotional turmoil, dream-like dissociation, and general excitement.

Affect. Emotion or feeling.

Affective psychosis. A psychosis characterized by extreme depression or elation that dominates the mental life of the individual and is responsible for whatever loss of contact he has with his environment.

Agoraphobia. Morbid fear of open spaces.

Alarm reaction. The first stage of Selye's general-adaptation syndrome, characterized by the mobilization of defenses to cope with stress.

Alcoholics Anonymous. An organization composed of alcoholics who have stopped drinking and have joined together to support each other's resolve and to treat alcoholism by means of personal, religious, and social rehabilitation.

Alcoholism. A condition characterized by loss of control over the intake of alcohol. The alcoholic is consistently unable to refrain from drinking or, once started, to stop before becoming intoxicated.

Alienation. A feeling of the lack or loss of relationships to others.

Altruistic suicide. A form of suicide that occurs among persons so closely integrated with their societies that their own survival takes second place to the presumed needs of the group, especially in certain socially defined circumstances.

Alzheimer's disease. Slow, progressive presenile mental deterioration resulting from generalized atrophy of the brain.

Ambivalence. Concurrent opposing emotions, attitudes, or desires toward an object.

Ambulatory schizophrenic. A person manifesting a mild schizophrenic reaction who functions well enough to live in the community, without requiring hospitalization.

Amnesia. Total or partial loss of memory.

Amok. A culture-bound type of rage reaction among Malays, in which the disturbed individual would suddenly grasp a dagger and run wildly about, slashing at anyone in his way.

Anaclitic depression. A state of depressive withdrawal and debilitation occurring in children who are separated from their mothers between the ages of six and eight months, and for whom substitute mothers are not available.

Anal character. A personality type marked by excessive cleanliness, compulsive behavior, and sadistic tendencies. Freudian theory assumes that the anal character is a result of fixation at or regression to the phase of development during which the child's chief source of pleasure sensations is the anus.

Analgesia. Loss or impairment of sensitivity to pain.

Anhedonia. Impaired ability to experience or integrate feelings of pleasure.

Anomic suicide. The taking of one's own life because of a feeling of social separation or isolation; a form of suicide that is especially characteristic of societies that lack cohesion.

Anomie. A lack of the feeling of belonging, of social norms or values.

Anorexia nervosa. Serious loss of weight and malnutrition resulting from self-imposed dietary limitations.

Anoxia. A physiological condition arising from lack of sufficient oxygen.

Anxiety. A state of emotional tension characterized by apprehension, diffuse fearfulness, and somatic disturbances associated with emotional overreaction.

Anxiety reaction. A neurotic disorder characterized by persistent morbid anxiety with frequent acute anxiety attacks.

Aphasia. Impaired ability to speak, comprehend, or communicate orally, usually attributable to brain defects.

Aphonia. Loss or marked impairment of voice without associated organic pathology.

Apoplexy (stroke). Sudden diminution or loss of consciousness with possible paralysis due to brain hemorrhage.

Archetype. An inherited universal thought form that predisposes man to experience critical events common to the human race. A concept of Carl Jung.

Arteriosclerosis. Degenerative thickening and hardening of the walls of the arteries, occurring usually in old age.

Assertive training. A form of behavior therapy for neurotics who have difficulty in expressing their anger and resentment when they are unjustly criticized or dominated by others. The basic strategy is to convince the patient of the virtue of asserting his rights and to point out the emotional and social repercussions of inhibiting his anger.

Asthenic personality. A personality type characterized by low energy level, easy fatigue, and a loss of zest. Asthenic persons tend to be complacent, apathetic, and distant.

Asthma. A psychophysiological disorder characterized by labored breathing, wheezing, a sense of constriction in the chest, coughing, and gasping for air.

Ataractics. See *Neuroleptic drugs.*

Atrophy. Wasting away or shrinking of a bodily organ.

Aura. Sensations signaling the onset of a convulsive seizure.

Autistic thinking. Gratification of desires in fantasy rather than practical attempts to gratify them in reality.

Autonomic nervous system. That part of the nervous system that regulates the activity of glands, viscera, heart, and smooth muscles. The autonomic system is less subject to voluntary control than the cerebrospinal or central nervous system.

Autonomy. Self-reliance, independence; the sense of being an individual in one's own right.

Autosome. Any chromosome other than those determining sex.

Avoidance conditioning. A form of conditioning in which the organism learns to behave in a certain way in order to avoid an unpleasant stimulus.

Behavior therapy. Treatment procedures based on conditioning or learning principles, a form of therapy that singles out some specific target behavior and undertakes to change it rather than attempting to uncover the underlying cause.

Behaviorism. A school of thought that considers the data of psychology to consist solely of objective, observable organismic activity, especially physical actions in response to stimuli.

Belle indifférence. An apparent lack of concern by hysterical neurotics about their loss of sensory and motor functions.

Catatonia. A subtype of schizophrenia characterized by stupor or excitement, negativism, stereotyped movements, mutism, muscular rigidity, and waxy flexibility.

Catharsis. The discharge of emotional tension associated with repressed traumatic material by "talking it out."

Cathexis. The investment of an object, idea, or action with special significance of affect for the individual.

Character disorder. Any personality disorder other than neurosis or psychosis, usually of a mild nature and consisting essentially of lifelong, deeply ingrained maladaptive traits.

Chemotherapy. Treatment of behavior disorders by means of psychoactive drugs that reduce emotional tensions. Particularly useful in decreasing bizarre psychotic behavior and aiding psychotic patients in maintaining contact with the social environment.

Childhood symbiosis. Moderate to marked dependence in early childhood, characterized by gross immaturity and a pathological attachment to the mother.

Chlorpromazine. The first widely used tranquilizing drug; effective in reducing hyperactivity, impulsiveness, and aggressiveness and helpful in controlling hallucinations, delusions, and destructive behavior.

Chromosomes. Separable rodlike bodies in the nuclei of cells that contain the genes.

Chronic brain disorders. Disturbances in psychosocial functioning caused by brain damage that is irreversible and permanent. Over time the patient may show improvement in functioning, but the more typical pattern is a gradual and progressive decline.

Client-centered therapy. A form of therapy developed by Carl Rogers, characterized by unconditional acceptance of the patient by the therapist, a high degree of permissiveness (nondirectiveness), and the reflection of the client's feelings by the therapist.

Colitis. A psychophysiological disorder characterized by inflammation or spasm of the colon.

Coma. A state of profound stupor or unconsciousness with complete insensibility from which the individual cannot be aroused.

Combat fatigue. See *War neurosis.*

Compensation. A common defense against feelings of inadequacy, failure, or personal defects, consisting of exaggerated efforts aimed at attaining success or distinction either in one's area of inferiority or in some other field.

Compulsion. An involuntary, irresistible impulse to do or say something against one's will or better judgment.

Concordance rate. A term used in genetic studies to indicate the extent to which some specific disorder occurs in both of two persons more or less closely related—twins, other siblings, parent and child, and so on. A concordance rate of 68 percent for schizophrenia in monozygotic twins indicates that among all pairs of identical twins studied of whom one was schizophrenic, 68 percent of their co-twins were also schizophrenic. The concordance rate thus is an indication of probability: if one monozygotic twin becomes schizophrenic, the probability that his co-twin will eventually develop the same disorder can be reckoned at 68 percent.

Confabulation. The spontaneous invention of imaginary experiences to fill memory gaps, without conscious intent to deceive.

Congenital. Existing at birth or before birth, but not necessarily hereditary.

Contingent. Dependent on special associated circumstances.

Conversion reaction. An hysterical reaction in which repressed material finds an outlet in physical symptoms.

Convulsive disorder. A psychophysiological disorder characterized by periodic loss of consciousness, motor disturbances, or epileptic seizures of short duration.

Crime. The violation, by an intentional act of commission or omission, of the recognized laws of society for which punishment is prescribed by law.

Critical period. A period during maturation when the organism is physiologically "prepared" to learn in response to a given type of stimulus. Alternatively, a period of acute stress.

Cultural relativism. The idea that behavior regarded as pathological in one society may be normal in another.

Culture-bound. Occurring in and limited to a particular society or culture.

Cunnilingus. Use of the tongue or mouth in erotic play with female genitals, especially stimulation of the clitoris.

Cyclothymic personality. A personality characterized by mild, frequently alternating elation and sadness, apparently stimulated by internal rather than external events.

Decompensation. Progressive personality disintegration evidenced in loss of control of behavior and decreased awareness of reality.

Delirious mania. A psychotic reaction marked by wild, uncontrolled excitement and disorientation. May be accompanied by hallucinations and delusions.

Delirium. A transient reaction in which the individual is typically confused, disoriented, incoherent, and out of touch with reality. Frequently noted in persons approaching or recovering from comas, in persons under the influence of alcohol or other drugs, and in persons with high fevers.

Delirium tremens (DTs). Delirium occurring in alcoholics following a prolonged period of drinking.

Delusion. A fixed, obviously false belief that is not in keeping with the individual's cultural training and which cannot be corrected by argument or presentation of reliable evidence.

Dementia praecox. Obsolete term for schizophrenia.

Denial. A defense mechanism that consists of an unconscious, selective perceptual "blindness" that protects the individual from facing intolerable thoughts, wishes, deeds, and situations.

Deoxyribonucleic acid (DNA). The principal component of the genes.

Depersonalization. A feeling of estrangement from oneself; a feeling of strangeness or unreality.

Depression. An emotional state of dejection, gloom, and feelings of worthlessness and guilt.

Depressive stupor. A psychotic reaction characterized by a massive paralysis of thought and action.

Derealization. A subjective feeling that one's environment has significantly changed and is no longer what it used to be.

Dermatitis. Inflammation of the skin, frequently of psychogenic origin.

Deterioration. Progressive impairment of mental functions and feelings.

Detoxication effects. Physical symptoms occurring in some alcoholics following the abrupt cessation of alcoholic intake after a prolonged period of intoxication: restlessness, confusion, irritability, belligerent attitude, fright, tremors, nausea.

Disorientation. Mental confusion resulting in the inability to orient or locate oneself correctly with respect to time, place, or person.

Displacement. A defense mechanism consisting of the transference to some neutral and inappropriate idea or object of an emotion originally associated with another idea or object.

Dissociative reaction. A neurotic reaction characterized by the temporary dissociation of certain segments of memory, thought, or personality from the total personality. See *Amnesia; Dual personality; Fugue; Somnambulism.*

Dizygotic (DZ) twins. Twins produced by the fertilization of two ova; siblings conceived and born at about the same time. Also known as fraternal twins.

Double bind. Direct communications accompanied by indirect and intrinsically contradictory messages, so that no matter which message the individual responds to, he is bound to be "wrong."

Down's syndrome. A well-known type of mental deficiency associated with the presence of an extra chromosome. Formerly called mongolism because of accompanying physical characteristics that give the victim of the disorder a superficially oriental appearance.

Drift hypothesis. The idea that the general social incompetence of potential schizophrenics causes them gradually to drift down to the lowest socioeconomic level.

Dual personality. A rare form of hysteria consisting of the creation of two alternating personalities to resolve conflicts between "good" and "bad" impulses.

Duodenal ulcer. Inflammation or lesions of the upper portion of the small intestines, caused by physiological reaction to emotional stress.

Durham rule. A test of insanity that is accepted in the District of Columbia, according to which an accused person cannot be held criminally responsible if his unlawful act was the product of a mental disease or mental defect. Similar to New Hampshire rule.

Dysmenorrhea. Painful menstruation.

Dyspareunia. Painful or difficult sexual intercourse.

DZ twins. See *Dizygotic twins.*

Echolalia. Involuntary automatic repetition of words spoken by another person.

Echopraxia. Involuntary automatic imitation of gestures or movements made by another person.

Eczema. An inflammation of the skin accompanied by itching and oozing lesions that become scaly and crusted. A psychophysiological disorder.

Ego. The conscious part of the personality structure that mediates and resolves conflicts between the id, the superego, and environmental conditions. A psychoanalytic concept.

Ego ideal. The person or "self" the individual thinks he could and should be.

Electra complex. In psychoanalytic theory, an excessive emotional attachment (love) of daughter for father, usually associated with a negative feeling toward the mother.

Electroencephalogram (EEG). A record obtained by amplifying and recording the electrical activity of brain cells.

Empathy. The ability to understand and to some extent share the feelings of another person.

Encephalitis lethargica. Sleeping sickness; an epidemic form of inflammation of the brain, usually signaled by high fever and drowsiness. Residual psychological and physical symptoms are often noted.

Endogenous. Pertaining to causal influences that originate in sources within the individual.

Enuresis. Bed-wetting; involuntary passing of urine by older children or adults.

Epidemiology. The study of the incidence, distribution, and control of physical or mental disorders; the sum of the factors involved in these disorders.

Epilepsy. A neurological disorder characterized by short periods of partial or complete loss of consciousness, occurring suddenly and sometimes accompanied by convulsions and other psychomotor disturbances.

Eros. The life forces, particularly the libido or sex drive. A psychoanalytic concept.

Etiology. The causes of a disease or abnormal condition; the study of causes.

Euphoria. An exaggerated feeling of well-being.

Exhibitionism. Self-display; as a form of sex deviance, the exposure by a man of his sex organ to a female who is a stranger and an involuntary observer.

Existentialism. A school of thought that emphasizes the uniqueness and freedom of the individual and the critical significance of meaning, purpose, and value.

Existential neurosis. A state of alienation from self and society, characterized by loneliness, apathy, boredom, aimless activities, and a pervasive sense of the meaninglessness of life.

Exogenous. Pertaining to causal influences that originate in sources outside the individual.

Experimental neurosis. Abnormal behavior experimentally induced in animals or human beings; usually induced by difficult problems of discrimination.

Explosive personality. A personality type characterized by loss of control under minor stress and direct expression of aggressive impulses either verbally, physically, or both.

Externalization. The experiencing of internal processes and emotions as occurring outside the self.

Extinction. The elimination of an acquired response through lack of reinforcement.

Extravert. A person who directs his energies and interests outside himself, enjoys social activities, and expresses himself in action. A personality type delineated by Jung.

Factor trait. A relatively independent trait cluster derived from commonalities exhibited in behavior or test performance.

Fantasy. Daydream; also, an ego defense mechanism by means of which the individual escapes from the world of reality and gratifies his desires in fantasy achievements.

Fellatio. Insertion of the penis into the mouth of another person for purposes of sexual gratification.

Fetishism. The substitution of an inanimate object, such as a shoe or glove, for a human love object as a source of sexual arousal and release.

Fixation. The arrest of psychosexual development at some childhood level. A psychonanalytic concept.

Flight of ideas. Fragmentary skipping from one verbalized but unfinished idea to another, with no logical progression.

Folie à deux. A delusional system shared by two persons closely associated with each other.

Folie en famille. The illusion fostered within the family that abnormality is normal.

Fraternal twins. See *Dizygotic twins.*

Free association. The process of making and reporting mental connections among ideas, memories, emotions, and sensations, no matter how trivial or "improper" they seem. A basic psychoanalytic technique regarded as a means of access to the unconscious.

Frigidity. The inability on the part of a woman to experience sexual pleasure or gratification; technically, the inability to experience orgasm.

Frustration. The thwarting of a need or desire.

Fugue. A psychological and geographical flight from one's usual environment, during which the individual forgets who he is and assumes a new personality. Following recovery, he has no recollection of his experiences during the fugue period.

Ganser's syndrome. Speech and behavior that are nonsensial but not irrelevant to the situation or the subject being discussed. Differentiated from malingering.

Gene. A submicroscopic unit of inheritance arranged within the chromosomes; a segment of DNA.

General-adaptation syndrome. A set of symptoms, described by Selye, that occur in response to excessive stress, consisting of alarm reaction, resistance, and exhaustion.

Generalization. The transference of learning acquired in one situation to another situation that is somewhat similar to the first.

General paresis. A psychosis resulting from progressive brain pathology produced by syphilis and characterized by a variety of mental and neurological symptoms.

Genotype. The particular combination of genes possessed by the individual.

Gerontology. The study of old age, with particular attention to disorders and their treatment.

Gonads. Testes or ovaries.

Grand mal. A form of epilepsy characterized by sudden loss of consciousness and convulsions.

Halfway houses. Houses in the community where patients live and work together in a controlled environment.

Hallucination. A sensory perception experienced in the waking state in the absence of any corresponding external stimuli; for example, hearing a nonexistent voice.

Hallucinogen. A chemical agent, usually derived from a plant, that produces hallucinations; also known as psychotomimetic drug.

Hawthorne effect. Improvement in behavior or increased output resulting from expression of interest in the individual's welfare by significant others.

Hebephrenia. A clinical subtype of schizophrenia characterized by peculiar mannerisms, silliness, bizarre behavior, and hallucinations.

Hedonism. The doctrine that pleasure is the primary good or value in life.

Heterosexuality. Sexual orientation toward persons of the opposite sex; the mature stage of psychosexual development.

Homeostasis. Tendencies of organisms to maintain a stable state of equilibrium.

Homosexuality. Erotic interest in members of one's own sex; more specifically, preference or exclusive capacity for sexual acts leading to orgasm with members of the same sex.

Hospitalism. A lack of development and progressive mental deterioration in infants reared in foundling homes and institutions that fail to provide adequate stimulation and mothering.

Huntington's chorea. A hereditary neurological condition characterized by involuntary jerky movements and gradual mental deterioration. Onset of symptoms occurs in middle life.

Hypertension. High blood pressure.

Hypnoanalysis. Hypnosis used as an aid in psychoanalytic treatment.

Hypnosis. An induced trance state marked by heightened suggestibility and automatic compliance, within limits imposed by the individual's values and conscience, with the instructions of the hypnotist. Also regarded as a form of role playing.

Hypochondriasis. A neurotic syndrome characterized by a persistent and exaggerated concern about diminished health and energy in the absence of demonstrable organic pathology.

Hypomania. A form of affective psychosis characterized by moderate elation, increased psychomotor activity, faulty judgment, and impulsivity.

Hypothalamus. Key structure at the base of the brain; important in temperature regulation, emotion, and motivation.

Hysteria. A neurotic condition characterized by conversion and dissociative reactions.

Id. In psychoanalytic theory, the personification of the unconscious. The id is concerned with the immediate gratification of primitive impulses, especially sexual and aggressive drives.

Ideas of reference. A delusion characterized by the perception of meaning, usually unfavorable to the self, in the casual remarks or acts of others.

Identical twins. See Monozygotic twins.

Identification. A defense mechanism through which an individual, without conscious awareness, satisfies frustrated desires by psychologically assuming the role or some of the traits of another person.

Identity crisis. Mental disturbances occurring mainly in youth, associated with difficulty in recognizing or establishing a unified personality that persists without regard to time, circumstance, or role.

Idiopathic. Of unknown causation; something presumed to be inherent in the individual's constitutional makeup.

Idiot. Obsolete term referring to a person with severe mental retardation, requiring complete custodial care.

Illusion. A false perception of a real sensory impression; e.g., seeing a twisted branch as a snake.

Imbecile. Obsolete term referring to a person with moderate to severe mental deficiency, requiring supervision in simple tasks of self-care.

Implosive therapy. A treatment procedure that requires the patient to imagine and/or speak about objects or situations that cause him intense anxiety.

Impotence. The inability of a mature male to achieve and maintain an erection of sufficient rigidity to permit successful coitus. Not necessarily associated with sterility.

Imprinting. A form of learning in very young animals which determines the course an instinctive behavior pattern will take; e.g., a duckling learns to follow the first moving object it sees, and is thus said to be *imprinted* on that particular object (usually the mother).

Inadequate personality. A personality pattern characterized by ineptness, poor judgment, ineffectual responses to emotional and social demands, low stamina, and absence of drive.

Incidence rate. The number of new cases of a disorder per unit of population developing in a specific population during a designated period of time.

Incompetence. Inability to manage one's personal affairs and property with ordinary prudence. A legal concept.

Index cases. A term used in genetic studies to identify those members of a population of related persons whose clinical behavior pattern meets predetermined criteria. The prevalence of the same behavior pattern in other members of the family is determined by comparing their behavior traits with those of the index cases. Also called proband cases.

Infantile autism. Severe impairment of development beginning during the first year of life and characterized by failure to develop or manifest normal awareness and responsiveness to other human beings, mutism, and repetitive meaningless acts. It is assumed the child is not mentally defective.

Insanity. Any mental disorder that permits a person accused of a criminal act to be adjudged not responsible for that act. A legal concept that has no medical or psychological significance.

Instrumental conditioning. A type of conditioning by which the subject learns to make a predetermined response, such as pressing a lever, in order to obtain a reward.

Interactional psychotic disorder. A psychotic reaction occurring in children between the ages of two and five who have shown normal prior development, characterized by an abnormal symbiotic relationship between child and mother. The child cannot bear to be separated from the mother.

Introjection. A defense mechanism characterized by the internalization of the attitudes, values, and behavior of another person, so that feelings associated with this other person may be directed toward the self.

Introvert. A personality type formulated by Jung and characterized by social awkwardness, emotional reserve, and self-absorption.

Involutional melancholia. A psychosis of undetermined origin with initial onset between the ages of forty and sixty-five, characterized by severe depression, agitation, ideas of guilt, depreciation, and suicidal tendencies.

Irresistible impulse rule. A test of insanity that is usually used as a supplement to the M'Naghten rules. Where the rule is accepted, an offender is not considered criminally responsible if his criminal act was the result of an irresistible impulse stemming from impaired mental functioning.

Isolation. A defense mechanism by which a thought is dissociated from an emotion otherwise connected with it.

454   *Psychopathology*

Jacksonian epilepsy. A convulsive disorder originating in cerebral excitation, characterized by local twitching that gradually spreads until it terminates in a *grand mal* seizure.

Kleptomania. A recurring neurotic compulsion to steal objects, especially without economic motive. As a rule no use is made of the stolen objects.
Koro. A form of sexual anxiety formerly occurring among Chinese men, characterized by fear that the sex organ was shrinking and disappearing into the abdomen, and that when this occurred the victim would die. A culture-bound form of the male dread of impotence.
Korsakoff's syndrome. A memory disorder of toxic-organic origin that sometimes follows the delirium or stupor of chronic alcoholism and other toxic states, marked by memory loss and invention of "fill-in" material.

Labile. Characterized by instability or changeability.
Latah. An intense fear reaction among Malays, marked by shuddering and the involuntary imitation of the actions and words of others.
Lesbian. A female homosexual.
Libido. A Latin word that originally signified sexual passion; now a psychoanalytic term indicating the aim and energy strength of the sex drive.
Life style. An individual's basic personality pattern, including goals. See also *Style of life.*
Lithium carbonate. A drug used in the treatment of manic attacks.
Lobotomy. The removal of or severing of nerve fibers in a lobe of the brain; an operation previously performed to relieve some mental disorders, now discredited.
Logorrhea. Excessive and often incoherent speech.
LSD. See *Lysergic acid diethylamide.*
Lunacy. Mental derangement. The term is a legacy of the superstitious belief that the stars and especially the moon were somehow associated with madness.
Lysergic acid diethylamide (LSD). A very potent synthetic hallucinogen.

M'Naghten rules. The most widely used legal test of insanity in the United States, according to which a person accused of a criminal offense must be found not guilty by reason of insanity if at the time he committed the offense, in the judgment of the jury, he "was laboring under such a defect of reason, from disease of the mind, as not to know the nature and quality of the act he was doing or . . . did not know he was doing what was wrong."
Malingerer. One who deliberately pretends to have some illness or disability, for motives of personal gain.

Manic-depressive reaction. A set of psychotic reactions characterized by prolonged periods of excitement and overactivity, or by periods of depression and underactivity, or by alternation or mixture of the two.

Mannerism. A stereotyped, recurring gesture, posture, or movement that has no apparent purpose.

Marital schism. A form of marital discord in which husband and wife compete in attempting to enlist the sympathies of their children, each undercutting the other. Thought to be characteristic of some schizophrenic families.

Marital skew. A marital pattern in which the psychopathology of the dominant spouse is accepted and treated as normal by the other marital partner. Thought to be characteristic of some schizophrenic families.

Masochism. A form of sexual deviation in which an individual obtains sexual satisfaction from being subjected to physical pain or otherwise mistreated.

Mental retardation. Subnormal intellectual functioning that originates at birth or during early childhood. It is associated with impairment of either maturation or learning and social adjustment, or both.

Metrazol therapy. An obsolete form of shock treatment for mental disorders, consisting of injections of the drug metrazol for the purpose of inducing convulsions.

Migraine. A severe form of headache, often accompanied by nausea and vomiting.

Milieu therapy. A form of therapy characterized by intensified social interaction and informal communication between staff and patients, and by group activities directed toward "normal" functioning.

Mongolism. See *Down's syndrome.*

Monoamine oxidase inhibitors. Drugs used in the treatment of depression.

Monozygotic twins. Identical twins who are the products of a single fertilized ovum.

Moron. Obsolete term denoting a person with a mild degree of mental retardation.

Multiple personality. A type of hysterical dissociative reaction characterized by the development of two or more relatively independent and alternating personality systems in the same individual.

Mutism. Inability or refusal to speak.

MZ twins. See *Monozygotic twins.*

Narcissism. In Freudian usage, an early stage of psychosexual development characterized by marked love of self.

Narcissistic personality. A personality type marked by egocentrism, disdain, pretentiousness, boastfulness, and exaggerated self-assurance.

Narcolepsy. A psychophysiological condition marked by brief periods of deep sleep in inappropriate situations.

Narcosynthesis. A therapeutic technique based on the use of certain drugs, such as sodium amytal, to facilitate the recall and expression of repressed emotions and memories.

Narcotic drugs. Drugs that lead to physiological dependence and increased tolerance, such as morphine and heroin. See also *Opiates.*

Negative practice. A therapeutic technique that requires the deliberate repetition of some undesirable motor habit as a means of eliminating the habit.

Negative reinforcement. The administration of an aversive stimulus following the occurrence of some particular behavior, for the purpose of decreasing the frequency of occurrence of the behavior.

Negativism. Impulsive contrary behavior; the tendency to do the opposite of what is requested.

Neologism. The coining of new words, usually by condensing and combining two or more words; a common occurrence among schizophrenics. Schizophrenic neologisms are meaningful to those who coin them but not to others.

Neurasthenia. A neurotic condition marked by chronic weakness, easy fatigability, and sometimes exhaustion.

Neurodermatitis. Chronic psychogenic reddening and thickening of the skin, with intense itching.

Neuroleptic drugs. Drugs that diminish agitation, anxiety, and aggression without inducing sleep or impairment of intelligence. More commonly referred to as tranquilizers; also known as ataractics.

Neuroses. Emotional disorders characterized primarily by anxiety and manifested in either behavioral or physical symptoms, unaccompanied by either gross distortion or misinterpretation of external reality or by gross personality disorganization.

New Hampshire rule. A legal test of insanity accepted in New Hampshire, according to which an accused person is not considered criminally responsible if his unlawful act was the product of a mental disorder.

Nyctophobia. Morbid fear of the dark or night.

Obsession. A spontaneously recurring thought or impulse that persistently intrudes itself into a person's mind, even against his wishes. The individual usually realizes the irrationality of his obsession but cannot dismiss it from his mind.

Obsessive-compulsion reaction. A neurotic reaction characterized by persistent irrational thoughts, impulses, and actions.

Occupational neurosis. A neurosis characterized by the functional impairment of some occupational skill; for example, writer's cramp.

Oedipus complex. The libidinal response of a boy to his mother. According to Freud, boys between the ages of four and six feel sexual desire for their mothers and see their fathers as hated rivals. An unresolved oedipal attachment is thought by Freudian psychoanalysts to be the major cause of neurosis in adult males.

Operant conditioning. A learning technique based on the principle of reinforcement, which holds that behavior is largely controlled by its consequences and thus can be modified or maintained by manipulating the consequences of particular forms of behavior.

Opiates. Opium, an addictive drug consisting of the dried juice of the opium poppy, and its derivatives (morphine, heroin, codeine), which relieve physical and psychic pain, induce euphoria in some persons, and lead to drowsiness and sleep. See also *Narcotic drugs.*

Oral character. A personality type assumed by Freudian psychoanalysts to result from fixation at or regression to the phase of development during which the mouth is the child's chief source of pleasurable sensations. The early oral phase is associated with dependence, the late oral phase with aggressive tendencies.

Organic brain syndrome. Instability and shallowness of affect accompanied by impairment of orientation, memory, judgment, and learning ability, resulting from impairment of brain tissue function.

Orientation. The act or process of locating the self in the environment with respect to time, place, and person; psychological bearings.

Overinclusiveness. A form of thought disorder associated with schizophrenia and marked by the intrusion of irrelevant or inappropriate associations into the stream of thought.

Paranoia. A rare psychosis characterized by the gradual development of logical, well-systematized delusions of persecution and/or grandeur based on the misinterpretation of or generalization of reactions to an actual event or series of events.

Paranoid personality. A mildly deviant personality type marked by suspiciousness, envy, jealousy, and stubbornness.

Paranoid reaction. A psychotic disorder marked by delusions of persecution and/or grandeur. When delusions are fragmented, bizarre, and accompanied by hallucinations, the disorder is classified as a subtype of schizophrenia; when delusions are well systematized, the condition is considered a variation of paranoia.

Passive-aggressive personality. A mildly deviant personality type marked by oppositional tendencies, negativism, obstructionism, contrariness, and uncooperativeness.

Passive-dependent personality. A mildly deviant personality type characterized by submissiveness, clinging behavior, and the making of covert demands.

Pedophilia. A form of sexual deviation in which an adult (usually a male) uses a child as a sex object.

Pellagra. A vitamin-deficiency disease characterized by disturbances of the alimentary tract, patchy skin pigmentation, and a variety of neurological and mental symptoms.

Peptic ulcer. A psychophysiological disorder characterized by inflammation or lesions of the stomach wall.

Perseveration. Involuntary continuation and repetition of a behavioral response.

Petit mal. A mild form of epilepsy characterized by momentary loss of consciousness unaccompanied by convulsive seizures.

Phallic character. A personality type assumed by Freudian analysts to result from fixation at or regression to the late oedipal stage of development and marked by recklessness, aggressive tendencies and narcissim.

Phenomenology. A personality theory that stresses the critical importance of the individual's subjective perception of himself and the outer world in the determination of behavior.

Phenotype. Actual or observable physical and behavioral traits that are determined by the interaction of an individual's genotype and the environment.

Phenylketonuria (PKU). An inherited defect in protein metabolism that results in profound mental retardation unless treatment is initiated very soon after birth.

Phobic reaction. A form of neurosis marked by irrational and intense fear of something that is normally not a real source of danger. The feared object presumably has symbolic significance.

Piblokto. A fearlike reaction among Arctic Eskimos, in some respects resembling *latah* among the Malays. The crazed Eskimo runs outdoors naked in winter weather and mimics the sounds of Arctic birds and animals. The condition may be indirectly related to a calcium deficiency.

PKU. See *Phenylketonuria.*

Placebo. An inactive substance that may have some therapeutic effect when administered to a person who believes it to be an active drug.

Pleasure principle. A tendency to direct behavior toward the immediate gratification of drives and desires and the avoidance of pain and dissatisfaction, regardless of future consequences. Considered by Freudian psychoanalysts to be the underlying motivation of the behavior of children and some neurotics.

Positive reinforcement. A learning procedure characterized by attempts to increase the frequency of occurrence of a particular response by rewarding its occurrence in some relevant way.

Posturing. The maintenance of unusual positions for long periods.

Potlatch. A ceremonial feast of the Kwakiutl Indians at which a chief gains prestige for his tribe and humiliates visiting chiefs by ostentatiously burning and giving away valuable goods that have been accumulated for the occasion, requiring elaborate reciprocation; a culturally regulated substitute for war. Also, similar activities carried on within a local group for the purpose of gaining or maintaining personal prestige.

Preconscious. The storehouse of surface memories that are readily subject to recall.

Premature ejaculation. The inability on the part of a man to delay the ejaculatory process during sexual intercourse for a sufficient length of time to satisfy his partner. The condition may be chronic or may occur only occasionally.

Premorbid. Existing prior to manifest pathology.

Prevalence. The total number of cases of a particular disorder currently existing in a given population at any particular time. The prevalence rate is determined by dividing the number of cases by the total population.

Primary gain. The reduction of anxiety as the principal advantage accruing from a neurotic symptom.

Primary prevention. The institution of procedures that will prevent the occurrence of a disorder or decrease the risk that a person will develop it.

Proband cases. See *Index cases.*

Process schizophrenia. Schizophrenic reactions characterized by early onset of symptoms, which include poor interpersonal adjustment, progressive social withdrawal, and inadequate functioning, with unfavorable prognosis. Contrasted to reactive schizophrenia.

Prognosis. Prediction as to the probable course and outcome of a disorder.

Projection. A defense mechanism characterized by the placing of blame for one's faults, mistakes, and misdeeds on others as a means of safeguarding self-esteem and avoiding self-censure.

Psoriasis. A chronic skin condition marked by itchy red patches covered with white scales.

Psychiatry. The medical specialty that is concerned with the study and treatment of mental disorders.

Psychoanalytic theory. A system of theories developed by Freud and his followers to explain normal and abnormal behavior, with emphasis on psychosexual development, the importance of early childhood experiences and repressions in the determination of adult behavior, and the role of the unconscious in the development of intrapsychic conflicts and processes.

Psychoanalytic therapy. A highly structured form of psychotherapy developed by Freud to uncover and resolve repressed intrapsychic conflicts dating from early childhood. Among its special techniques are free association, dream analysis, and the concept of transference.

Psychodrama. A form of group therapy in which the patient's problems are acted out.

Psychogenic. Originating in emotional conflict or mental disorder.

Psychomotor attacks. Seizures marked by lapses of consciousness, irregular muscular movements, disturbances in thought or affect, and convulsions. Also referred to as temporal lobe epilepsy.

Psychopathology. A behavior science concerned with the study of maladaptive behavior, its etiology, development, diagnosis, and therapy.

Psychophysiological reactions. Physical disorders in which symptoms are precipitated and maintained by emotional factors. Symptoms vary widely but invariably involve a single organ system that is largely controlled by the autonomic nervous system. Popularly referred to as psychosomatic disorders.

Psychosis. A severe mental disorder that significantly interferes with the individual's capacity for adequate self-support and appropriate interpersonal behavior, characterized by gross personality disorganization, distortion of reality evidenced by delusions and hallucinations, and marked impairment in voluntary control of thoughts, emotions, and actions.

Psychosomatic reactions. See *Psychophysiological reactions.*

Psychotherapy. A general term for treatment of mental disorders by psychological procedures. Most psychotherapies involve the talking out of problems.

Psychotic depressive reaction. Depression that appears directly related to some recent loss suffered by a person with no prior history of any affective disturbance.

Rational-emotive therapy. A directive form of psychotherapy developed by Albert Ellis, based on the premise that disturbed persons needlessly create anxiety and anger in themselves by accepting uncritically certain irrational hypotheses.

Rationalization. A defense mechanism characterized by the minimization of failure and justification of socially disapproved behavior by invented excuses and "reasonable" explanations; the unwitting substitution of "good" for real reasons.

Raynaud's disease. A psychophysiological reaction marked by poor circulation resulting in cold hands and feet.

Reaction formation. A defense mechanism characterized by the concealment of an unaccepted trait or impulse by behavior expressive of a directly opposite characteristic, which enables the individual to deny to himself the existence of the trait or impulse he cannot accept.

Reactive schizophrenia. Schizophrenic reactions apparently causally related to some current stress experienced by a person whose prepsychotic psychosocial development has been seemingly normal, and characterized by less severe deficits and better prognosis than process schizophrenia.

Reality principle. A tendency to defer the gratification of drives and desires in the interests of long-range goals or in response to pressures from the physical and social environments.

Reciprocal inhibition. A therapeutic technique based on the principle that the ability of a stimulus to evoke anxiety may be diminished if a response inhibitory of anxiety can be made to occur in the presence of the anxiety-evoking stimulus.

Regression. A defense mechanism characterized by a reversion to earlier modes of gratification as a means of escape from current difficulties.

Reliability. The extent of agreement among independent examiners regarding the diagnosis of a patient's disorder.

Remission. Significant improvement following a period of pathology.

Repression. The spontaneous or nondeliberate exclusion from the field of conscious awareness of memories, impulses, and ideas whose presence, if recognized, would constitute a source of anxiety, guilt, or humiliation.

Residual deviance. The concept, advanced by Scheff, that mental disorders consist of the forms of rule breaking that remain after all other explicitly recognized forms of deviance have been excluded.

Resistance. Opposition to therapeutic efforts, especially a defensive reluctance to explore repressed material.

Rheumatoid arthritis. A psychophysiological disorder characterized by a painful stiffening of the joints.

Sadism. A form of sexual deviation marked by the infliction of pain on another person as a means of achieving sexual arousal and release.

Schizo-affective reaction. A condition in which the emotional disturbances of manic-depressive psychosis are combined with the disordered thought and behavior patterns associated with schizophrenia.

Schizoid personality. A mildly deviant personality type characterized by social withdrawal, introvertive tendencies, and extreme shyness.

Schizophrenia. A psychosis that usually has its onset in early adulthood and is characterized by disordered thinking, delusions, hallucinations, social withdrawal, and bizarre behavior.

Schizophreniform reaction. A psychotic reaction characterized by acute onset of schizophrenic symptoms and clear-cut precipitating factors, with a relatively good prognosis. Similar to reactive schizophrenia.

Schizotaxia. The inherited neural defect that is the essential prerequisite for or predisposing factor in schizophrenia.

Schizotypic personality. A personality type delineated by Meehl and characterized by disturbances in thinking, interpersonal aversiveness, anhedonia, and ambivalence, limited to persons genetically predisposed to schizophrenia but not necessarily destined to become psychotic.

Secondary gain. Advantages other than the reduction of anxiety gained through a neurotic symptom.

Secondary prevention. The reduction of the prevalence rate of a disorder by effective treatment that shortens the duration of disability.

Self-actualization. The drive to realize one's inherent potentials.

Senile dementia. A psychosis of old age characterized by brain atrophy and progressive mental deterioration.

Sexual deviant. A person who prefers or requires some form of sexual activity other than heterosexual coitus for erotic stimulation and gratification. See *Exhibitionism; Fetishism; Homosexuality; Masochism; Pedophilia; Sadism; Transsexuality; Transvestism; Voyeurism.*

Shaping. The process of gradually leading a subject to give a particular response by selective reinforcement of a series of other responses that come progressively closer to the response desired.

Shellshock. See *War neurosis.*

Shock therapy. The induction of coma or convulsion by the use of drugs or electricity as a means of treating mental disorders.

Social breakdown syndrome. A set of symptoms consisting of dependency, apathy, withdrawal, lack of responsibility, and general deterioration of behavior, resulting from prolonged confinement in a mental hospital.

Sociopath. An individual who exhibits antisocial behavior that may or may not be criminal. Sociopathy represents a borderline category between criminal behavior and psychopathology.

Somnambulism. Sleepwalking; a trancelike state in which a person, while asleep, walks about and engages in complex activities that he does not remember on awakening. A form of dissociative reaction.

Stereotypy. The persistent repetition of apparently senseless words, acts, or gestures.

Stimulant drugs. Drugs that increase energy level and diminish fatigue, such as cocaine and the amphetamines.

Stimulus generalization. The process whereby a conditioned response is elicited by stimuli other than but similar to the conditioned stimulus.

Stress. Any condition, biological or psychological, that taxes the coping capacities of an individual.

Stupor. A condition of partial or complete unconsciousness marked by unresponsiveness and lethargy.

Style of life. A relatively enduring pattern of behavior that is tailored to overcome inferiority complexes. A concept of Adler.

Sublimation. A defense mechanism whereby unacceptable or thwarted impulses are channeled or transformed into socially approved substitute activities.

Superego. The division of the personality structure that enforces the morals and ethics instilled by the parents and the society. A Freudian concept.

Suppression. The deliberate exclusion from consciousness of thoughts or feelings.

Symptomatic epilepsy. A convulsive condition resulting from some acquired brain pathology or toxic condition rather than genetic defect.

Syndrome. A group of symptoms that occur together and which are more or less distinctive of a particular pathological condition.

Temperament. Inherent emotional style reflected in susceptibility and responsiveness to emotional stimulation, prevailing mood, and intensity of feelings.

Tertiary prevention. The prevention of permanent disability through the reduction of residual secondary defects that often persist long after the actual disorder has ended.

Tic. A recurring involuntary muscular twitch.

Token economy system. The use of tokens that can be exchanged for rewards as a means of reinforcing desired behavior, particularly among hospitalized mental patients.

Tranquilizers. See *Neuroleptic drugs.*

Transference. The tendency on the part of patients undergoing psychotherapy to express toward the therapist attitudes and feelings they had and may still have toward their parents and significant others. The working through of these transferred attitudes and feelings is an important feature of psychoanalytic treatment.

Transsexuality. A form of sex deviance distinguished by gender misidentification: the transsexual has the sex organs of one sex but thinks of himself or herself as being in all other respects a member of the opposite sex.

Transvestism. A form of sex deviation in which the individual, invariably a male, is sexually stimulated by wearing the clothes of the opposite sex. The typical transvestite is heterosexual; most are married.

Tremor. A series of rapid, involuntary spasms involving a small group of muscles.

Unconscious. The reservoir of man's inherited primitive impulses and acquired repressions that are not readily accessible to awareness but which have an important effect on behavior. A psychoanalytic concept.

Undoing. A defense mechanism whereby guilt for past misdeeds is expiated through symbolic acts.

Vaginismus. A female psychosomatic disorder marked by an involuntary muscular spasm that constricts the vaginal opening, making sexual intercourse painful or impossible.

Validity. The extent to which a measuring instrument actually measures what it is supposed to measure.

Verbigeration. Continual repetition of words or sentences. A feature of schizophrenia.

Voyeurism. The derivation of sexual arousal and release from the sight of sexual organs or sexual acts.

War neurosis. A neurotic condition resulting from prolonged exposure to the stress of combat in wartime. Called shellshock during World War I and combat fatigue during World War II.

Windigo. A culture-bound form of mental disorder among the Ojibwa Indians of Canada, characterized by an obsession with the desire to eat human flesh and the misperception of friends and neighbors as edible animals; a syndrome related to periodic famine but attributed by the society to possession by a man-eating evil spirit, which can be routed by feeding the victim meat and fat.

Zoophobia. Irrational fear of animals usually harmless to man.

Index

Ackerman, N., 123, 421
Ackerman, P. T., 148
Acute alcoholic hallucinosis. *See* Alcoholic psychosis
Acute mania, 237–38
See also Manic-depressive psychosis
Acute schizophrenic episode, 183
See also Schizophrenia
Adler, A., 56, 116–17, 131, 286
Adler, R., 295
Adolescence, psychoses of, 409, 415–16
See also Childhood and adolescence, disorders of
Adoption studies, 195, 219–20
Affective psychoses, 32, 232–55, 409
etiological factors in, 248–55
modal age for, 168
treatment of, 255
use of label of, U.S. vs. U.K., 21
See also Depression; Manic behavior; Manic-depressive psychosis; Psychoses; Schizo-affective reaction
Aftercare facilities, community, 434–35
Age:
and mental disorders, 167–69
and neuroses, 277
and personality disorders, 306
and sociopathy, 320
See also Aging, disorders of
Aggressive-delinquent personality, 409
Aging, disorders of, 394–97
Agras, W. S., 378
Albee, G. W., 14–15, 186, 437
Alcoholic psychosis, 30, 334
Alcoholics Anonymous, 343
Alcoholism, 34, 328–45
classification of, 26
definition of, 329–30
determinants of, 337–40
effects of, 333–36
and intoxicating liquors, 330
patterns of, 332–33
prevention of, 344–45

reasons for, 330–31
sociocultural factors in, 338–39
stages of, 331–32
treatment of, 341–44
Alexander, F., 288
Alexander, R., 296
Alienation, 224
Allport, G., 124, 137
American Association on Mental Deficiency, 418
American Association of Suicidology, 260
American Psychiatric Association. *See* APA classification
Amnesia, 268
Amok, 162
Amphetamines, 345–46, 359–60
Anal character, 325
Analeptics. *See* Stimulant drugs
Anal stage of development, 112
Anastasio, M. M., 257
Ancient societies, 82–83
Anhedonia, 192
Animal magnetism, 87–88
Animal studies:
on genetics of behavior, 147–51
on neuroses, 293–98, 338
on visceral and glandular responses, 392–93
Anomie, 166–67
Anorexia nervosa, 34
treatment of, by operant conditioning, 290–91
Anthropologists in mental health field, 16
Antisocial behavior:
in adults. *See* Sociopathy
in children, 318–20, 424
Anxiety, 33, 118–19
neurotic, 266–67, 278, 280, 281
in schizophrenia, 192–93
APA classification, 22–29, 222–23, 266
of alcoholism, 332
of adult personality types (table), 304
advantages of, 28–29, 273